THE PAPERS OF

James Madison

SPONSORED BY
THE UNIVERSITY OF VIRGINIA

THE PAPERS OF

James Madison

VOLUME 15

24 MARCH 1793–20 APRIL 1795

EDITED BY

THOMAS A. MASON   ROBERT A. RUTLAND

JEANNE K. SISSON

UNIVERSITY PRESS OF VIRGINIA

CHARLOTTESVILLE

The Papers of James Madison have been edited with financial aid from the Ford, Mellon, and Rockefeller Foundations, the National Historical Publications and Records Commission, and the Commonwealth of Virginia. The Virginia Historical Society has provided aid-in-kind. From 1956 to 1970 the editorial staff was maintained jointly by the University of Chicago and the University of Virginia. The University of Chicago Press published volumes 1 through 10 (1962–1977).

First published 1985

Library of Congress Cataloging in Publication Data (Revised)
Madison, James, Pres. U.S., 1751–1836.
    Papers.
    Vol. 8–   edited by R. A. Rutland and others.
    Vols. 11–   published by the University Press of
Virginia.
    Bibliographical footnotes.
    CONTENTS: v. 1. 16 Mar. 1751–16 Dec. 1779.–
v. 2. 20 Mar. 1780–23 Feb. 1781.–v. 3. 3 Mar.–31 Dec.
1781. [etc.]
    1. Virginia–Politics and government–Revolution,
1775–1783–Collected works. 2. United States–Politics
and government–Revolution, 1775–1783–Collected works.
3. United States–Politics and government–1783–1865–
Collected works. I. Hutchinson, William Thomas,
1895–1976, ed. II. Rachal, William M. E., 1910–1980, ed.
III. Rutland, Robert Allen, 1922– ed. IV. Charles F.
Hobson, 1943– ed. V. Thomas A. Mason, 1944– ed.
E302.M19   973.5′1′0924   62–9114
ISBN 0–8139–1059–5

Printed in the United States of America

To

FRANCIS L. BERKELEY, JR.

Contents

CONTENTS

CONTENTS

CONTENTS

CONTENTS

1795

CONTENTS

Preface

The pace of Madison's life, first set during 1780 and usually involving long round trips between Virginia and the national capital, moved to a different tempo by 1793. The routes of travel remained the same, but Madison was now a national figure coming from a safe congressional district. Freed from worries concerning reelection, Madison developed a partnership with Thomas Jefferson involving nothing less dramatic than the formation of a political party. Determined to maintain the integrity of the Constitution he had been so instrumental in framing, Madison perceived an ominous threat to constitutional republicanism in the Federalist policies of Alexander Hamilton. Around Hamilton rallied the political elements that, Madison was convinced, sought to turn the work of the Federal Convention of 1787 into a pallid imitation of the British Constitution, complete with everything the British admired—ministerial government, public debt, a central bank, a large navy—except a king.

In this volume Madison is recognized as the opposition leader of the House of Representatives, but the lack of party discipline prevented a repetition of the legislative successes he achieved in the First Congress. In the Third Congress, debate and persuasion counted for little as the divisions gradually hardened between Federalists and Republicans. Consistently, Madison's side was the losing one. On issues involving tariff schedules, excises, and a naval buildup, Madison was among the nays when the ayes had it. Only when British seizures of American vessels in the West Indies alarmed the Federalists did Madison find himself voting with the majority on a nonintercourse bill and embargo resolutions.

Sometimes personal matters and politics were mixed. Madison's friend and political ally Thomas Jefferson became thoroughly tired of serving in Washington's cabinet, resigned, and went into semiretirement. Both men had been embarrassed by the turnaround of public opinion forced by the behavior of the French minister to the United States, Citizen Genet, who quickly dissipated the goodwill Americans felt for the French revolutionary movement by his incredibly tactless conduct. One political or social blunder followed another, until Madison and Jefferson realized the Federalists were making great capital of the Frenchman's diplomatic ineptitude. In August 1793 Madison and Monroe marshaled public opinion by drafting resolutions on Franco-American relations and organizing public meetings in several Virginia communities where Republicans were dominant. As adopted by those meetings, the resolutions not only endorsed the French alliance but also dissociated the Republican cause from

Genet. The French minister was recalled, but the domestic political crisis he fomented challenged Republicans to develop their policies and organization.

Jefferson's departure for Monticello placed a heavier burden on Madison, who became the central figure in the emerging Republican party. He accepted honorary French citizenship as a gesture identifying himself with the transatlantic movement for liberty and equality. With Jefferson gone, there was little fraternity in the capital at Philadelphia as Hamilton's influence on Washington grew apace. The president's Neutrality Proclamation, by reducing the wartime alliance with France almost to a nullity, was Hamilton's trump card in a game designed to discredit the pro-French Republicans. As the proclamation's polarizing effects spread, Madison's relations cooled with some of his erstwhile political colleagues such as Edward Carrington, Daniel Carroll of Rock Creek, Francis Corbin, and Henry Lee.

The strains and suspicions generated in the process of creating an opposition party can be seen in the correspondence between Madison and Jefferson. From April 1793 onward, most of their letters to each other that went by public post were unsigned. Beginning in August, they even encoded some sensitive passages. They probably took these precautions because Federalists controlled the post office. Significantly, signed correspondence—such as Jefferson's second letter of 11 August 1793 to Madison—was sent by private bearer.

This turn of events bewildered Madison, for he identified the anti-French Federalists as a group hostile to republican ideas on taxes, the public debt, and the size of the American army and navy. The price paid for British trade was too high, Madison believed, and he was armed with statistics to prove that France was in fact America's best customer. Thus he continued his earlier effort to enact legislation that would penalize the British if they continued their discrimination against Yankee goods and ships. Madison sought a commercial discrimination that would promote trade with countries granting America a most-favored-nation status and penalize Great Britain for its rigid anti-American trade policies. Yet the Federalists in the Third Congress managed to prevent Madison's proposals from coming to a vote. His resolutions calling for reciprocity won applause from a far-flung constituency: a New York town meeting, a Virginia militia regiment in Richmond, and a committee of American captains languishing in Jamaica as a result of the British seizure of their ships. Federalist efforts in Congress were bolstered by the administration's diplomatic initiative in sending Chief Justice John Jay to England to negotiate the problems of enforcing the 1783 Treaty of Paris. Suspicious of Federalist motives, Madison feared that Jay would concede vital American commercial interests to Great Britain.

As in 1792, Madison took the defender's role against Hamilton's newspaper attacks on republican men and principles. Jefferson wanted to avoid personal involvement but urged Madison to reply to Hamilton's "Pacificus" essays that defended the Neutrality Proclamation while attacking France and its American friends. Madison reluctantly counterattacked with the "Helvidius" articles pointing to Hamilton's errors and setting forth the essence of republicanism. In the aftermath of the Whiskey Insurrection, President Washington disparaged the "self-created societies" of Republicans that formed the backbone of the new party. Madison came as close as he ever came to being furious. Foreign threats, such as the Algerine captures of American ships and sailors, were bad enough; but Madison saw in the domestic attacks an even greater threat to American liberty. For if only the forms of a republic existed while the Constitution was manhandled by Anglophile Federalists, then the struggle of the past twenty years had been unavailing.

Appropriately, this volume concludes on a note of disappointment. In his pamphlet *Political Observations*, Madison expressed his frustration as he catalogued the legislative successes that the Federalists had achieved in the first session of the Third Congress. Historians and political scientists who have argued that the nationalist Madison of 1787 was not the Madison who spoke of states' rights in 1798 will find this little-known pamphlet instructive. Madison clearly considered himself an exponent of constitutional government and neither a nationalist nor a states' righter. The liberal constructionism of Federalists was a bitter draught for Madison to swallow in 1794.

Madison still found a few rays of sunshine during the two years covered by the documents in this volume. Jefferson had escaped the deadly yellow fever epidemic of 1793 in Philadelphia, as had his friend Dr. Benjamin Rush; and the pretty young widow Dolley Payne Todd also survived. Her husband and baby son both died during the scourge, leaving her with a two-year-old son, a modest estate, and a need for the security Madison could provide. All the circumstances of the courtship are not known, but Aaron Burr arranged a formal introduction for Madison, and in short order he became first suitor and then bridegroom. Thus Madison acquired a domestic partner while his political ties with Jefferson were strengthened by the contest waged in legislative halls and newspaper columns on behalf of republican principles.

Acknowledgments

The editors are grateful for the valuable contributions of the research assistants of *The Papers of James Madison*: Janet K. Miller and Ann L. Goedde. The following persons provided helpful advice and assistance:

William Beiswinger and Lucinda Goodwin of the Thomas Jefferson Memorial Foundation; Wayne W. Dobson of the Tusculum College Library, Greeneville, Tennessee; David M. Ellis of Hamilton College, Clinton, New York; James Gilreath of the Rare Book and Special Collections Division, Library of Congress; Mary Giunta and Sara Dunlap Jackson of the National Historical Publications and Records Commission research staff; Gregg L. Lint and Celeste Walker of the Adams Family Papers; Ann Miller of the Orange County Historical Society, Orange, Virginia; Noreen O'Gara of the Boston Public Library; Robert E. Shalhope of the University of Oklahoma; Arthur F. Stocker of the University of Virginia; Paulette S. Watson and Rosalie M. Sullivan of the James Monroe Law Office-Museum and Memorial Library, Fredericksburg, Virginia; and James E. Wootton of Ash Lawn, home of James Monroe, Charlottesville.

Editorial Method

The editorial guidelines set forth in *The Papers of James Madison*, 1:xxxiii–xxxix and 8:xxiii, have been followed in this volume, with this exception: missing or illegible words (or portions of words), usually in a damaged or torn manuscript, are restored within angle brackets. Words either consistently or occasionally spelled incorrectly, as well as variant or antiquated spellings, are left as written without editorial notice. Words misspelled so as to appear to be a printer's error are corrected through additions in brackets or followed by the device [*sic*]. The brackets used by JM and other correspondents have been rendered as parentheses. Slips of the pen have been silently corrected, while substantial errors or discrepancies have been annotated. The speeches made by JM in the House of Representatives and essays printed in newspapers have been edited only by the silent correction of obvious typographical errors. Otherwise, the original punctuation and spelling have been retained. Notations and dockets made by various editors and collectors through the years have not been recognized in the provenance unless germane to an understanding of the document. The same rule has been applied to routine endorsements and slight textual changes JM made on documents that he retrieved late in his lifetime. When the only enclosures mentioned are newspapers or similar ephemeral publications that would have been immediately separated from the document, the absence of these items has not been noted in the provenance.

When standing alone the symbol DLC is employed to cite the Madison Papers in the Library of Congress. In most other cases, symbols from the Library of Congress's *Symbols of American Libraries* (11th ed.; Washington, 1976) have been used to designate the libraries and other archival depositories holding the original copies of the cited documents. The location symbols for depositories used in this volume are:

DLC	Library of Congress, Washington, D.C.
DNA	National Archives, Washington, D.C.
CSmH	Henry E. Huntington Library, San Marino, California
KyU	University of Kentucky, Lexington
MB	Boston Public Library
MdAN	United States Naval Academy, Annapolis, Maryland
MeHi	Maine Historical Society, Portland
MHi	Massachusetts Historical Society, Boston
NAlI	Albany Institute of History and Art, New York

NcD   Duke University, Durham, North Carolina
NHi   New-York Historical Society, New York City
NjP   Princeton University, Princeton, New Jersey
NjR   Rutgers—The State University, New Brunswick, New Jersey
NN   New York Public Library, New York City
OFH   Rutherford B. Hayes Library, Fremont, Ohio
PHi   Historical Society of Pennsylvania, Philadelphia
PPAmP   American Philosophical Society, Philadelphia
PPIn   Independence Hall National Park, Philadelphia
ScU   University of South Carolina, Columbia
Vi   Virginia State Library, Richmond
ViHi   Virginia Historical Society, Richmond
ViU   University of Virginia, Charlottesville

Abbreviations

FC   File copy. Any version of a letter or other document retained by the sender for his own files and differing little if at all from the completed version. A draft, on the other hand, is a preliminary sketch, often incomplete and varying frequently in expression from the finished version. Unless otherwise noted, both are in the sender's hand. A letterbook copy is a retained duplicate, often bound in a chronological file, and usually in a clerk's hand.

JM   James Madison.

Ms   Manuscript. A catchall term describing numerous reports and other papers written by JM, as well as items sent to him which were not letters.

RC   Recipient's copy. The copy of a letter intended to be read by the addressee, in the sender's hand unless otherwise noted.

Tr   Transcript. A copy of a manuscript, or a copy of a copy, customarily handwritten and ordinarily not by its author or by the person to whom the original was addressed.

Abstracts and Missing Letters. In most cases a document is presented in abstract form because of its trivial nature, its great length, or a combination of both. Abstracted letters are noted by the symbol §.

The symbol ¶ indicates a "letter not found" entry, with the name of the writer or intended recipient, the date, and such other information as can be surmised from the surviving evidence. If nothing other than the date of the missing item is known, however, it is mentioned only in the notes to a related document.

Short Titles for Books and Other Frequently Cited Materials

In addition to these short titles, bibliographical entries are abbreviated if a work has been cited in the previous volumes.

Annals of Congress.   *Debates and Proceedings in the Congress of the United States* ... (42 vols.; Washington, 1834–56).

ASP.   *American State Papers: Documents, Legislative and Executive, of the Congress of the United States* ... (38 vols.; Washington, 1832–61).

BDC.   *Biographical Directory of the American Congress, 1774–1971* (Washington, 1971).

Boyd, *Papers of Jefferson.*   Julian P. Boyd et al., eds., *The Papers of Thomas Jefferson* (21 vols. to date; Princeton, N.J., 1950–).

CVSP.   William P. Palmer et al., eds., *Calendar of Virginia State Papers and Other Manuscripts* (11 vols.; Richmond, 1875–93).

Dallas.   A. J. Dallas, *Reports of Cases Ruled and Adjudged in the Several Courts of the United States, and of Pennsylvania* ... (4 vols.; Philadelphia, 1790–1807).

DAR Patriot Index.   National Society of the Daughters of the American Revolution, *DAR Patriot Index* (Washington, 1966).

Evans, and Evans supp.   Charles Evans, ed., *American Bibliography ... 1639 ... 1820* (12 vols.; Chicago, 1903–34). Roger P. Bristol, ed., *Supplement to Charles Evans' American Bibliography* (Charlottesville, Va., 1970).

Fitzpatrick, *Writings of Washington.*   John C. Fitzpatrick, ed., *The Writings of George Washington, from the Original Manuscript Sources, 1745–1799* (39 vols.; Washington, 1931–44).

Ford, *Writings of Jefferson.*   Paul Leicester Ford, ed., *The Writings of Thomas Jefferson* (10 vols.; New York, 1892–99).

Heitman, *Historical Register Continental.*   F. B. Heitman, *Historical Register of Officers of the Continental Army during the War of the Revolution* (Washington, 1914).

Heitman, *Historical Register U.S. Army.*   Francis B. Heitman, *Historical Register and Dictionary of the United States Army, from Its*

Organization, September 29, 1789, to March 2, 1903 (2 vols.; Washington, 1903).

Hening, *Statutes.*   William Waller Hening, ed., *The Statutes at Large; Being a Collection of All the Laws of Virginia, from the First Session of the Legislature, in the Year 1619* (13 vols.; Richmond and Philadelphia, 1819–23).

JCC.   Worthington C. Ford et al., eds., *Journals of the Continental Congress, 1774–1789* (34 vols.; Washington, 1904–37).

JHDV.   *Journal of the House of Delegates of the Commonwealth of Virginia, Begun and Held at the Capitol, in the City of Richmond.* Volumes in this series are designated by the month in which the session began.

Madison, *Letters* (Cong. ed.).   [William C. Rives and Philip R. Fendall, eds.], *Letters and Other Writings of James Madison* (published by order of Congress; 4 vols.; Philadelphia, 1865).

Madison, *Writings* (Hunt ed.).   Gaillard Hunt, ed., *The Writings of James Madison* (9 vols.; New York, 1900–1910).

OED.   *Oxford English Dictionary.*

PJM.   William T. Hutchinson et al., eds., *The Papers of James Madison* (1st ser., vols. 1–10, Chicago, 1962–77; vols. 11–, Charlottesville, Va., 1977–).

PJM-PS.   Robert A. Rutland et al., eds., *The Papers of James Madison: Presidential Series* (1 vol. to date; Charlottesville, Va., 1984–).

Senate Exec. Proceedings.   *Journal of the Executive Proceedings of the Senate of the United States of America* (3 vols.; Washington, 1828).

Shepherd, *Statutes.*   Samuel Shepherd, ed., *The Statutes at Large of Virginia, from October Session 1792, to December Session 1806 . . .* (new ser.; 3 vols.; Richmond, 1835–36).

Swem and Williams, *Register.*   Earl G. Swem and John W. Williams, eds., *A Register of the General Assembly of Virginia, 1776–1918, and of the Constitutional Conventions* (Richmond, 1918).

Syrett and Cooke, *Papers of Hamilton.*   Harold C. Syrett and Jacob E. Cooke, eds., *The Papers of Alexander Hamilton* (26 vols.; New York, 1961–79).

Tyler's Quarterly.   *Tyler's Quarterly Historical and Genealogical Magazine.*

U.S. *Statutes at Large.*   *The Public Statutes at Large of the United States of America . . .* (17 vols.; Boston, 1848–73).

VMHB.   *Virginia Magazine of History and Biography.*

WMQ.   *William and Mary Quarterly.*

Madison Chronology

ca. 17 March	JM departs with Monroe from Philadelphia, bound for Virginia.
18 March	Reelected to House of Representatives.
April	Accepts honorary French citizenship.
22 April	Washington signs Neutrality Proclamation.
16 May	Citizen Genet arrives in Philadelphia.
20 June	John Taylor of Caroline sends JM a draft of his *Enquiry into the Principles and Tendency of Certain Public Measures*; JM later consults Monroe and Jefferson about its publication.
ca. 22 July–ca. 20 August	JM writes the five "Helvidius" essays.
20 August–1 September	Visits Monroe's home near Charlottesville; with Monroe's aid, JM edits Taylor's *Enquiry into the Principles*.
24 August–18 September	Philadelphia *Gazette of the U.S.* publishes "Helvidius" essays.
ca. 24–27 August	With Monroe as coauthor, JM drafts resolutions on Franco-American relations.
3 September	Staunton public meeting approves resolutions paraphrasing those drafted by JM and Monroe.
10 September	Caroline County public meeting passes resolutions based on the JM-Monroe draft.
25 September	Jefferson, en route from Philadelphia, visits JM at Montpelier.
3 October	Ambrose Madison, JM's younger brother, dies.
10 October	Charlottesville public meeting approves resolutions on Franco-American relations paraphrasing the JM-Monroe draft.
14 October	Yellow fever in Philadelphia concerns Washington, who seeks JM's advice on an alternative meeting place for next session of Congress.
16 October	JM visits Jefferson at Monticello, accompanied by Monroe.
ca. 25–26 October	Jefferson visits JM at Montpelier.

22 November	Traveling from Montpelier, JM arrives in Fredericksburg; arranges northward journey with Monroe.
24 November–ca. 1 December	JM and Monroe travel from Fredericksburg to Philadelphia.
2 December 1793–9 June 1794	JM attends first session of Third Congress, lodging with Monroe at 4 North Eighth Street.
27 December	Speaks on behalf of open galleries in House.

1794

3 January	JM offers seven resolutions to implement Jefferson's report on foreign commerce, including higher duties on British ships and goods.
10 January	Opposes relief appropriation for Santo Domingan refugees.
14, 30, and 31 January	Makes extended speeches in support of his resolutions on commercial discrimination.
6, 7, and 11 February	Opposes naval armament for confrontation with Algerine corsairs; argues that sum appropriated is too small to be effective.
12 March	Republican Society of South Carolina at Charleston commends JM's proposals regarding trade with Great Britain.
21 March	House defeats proposed embargo, 48 to 46.
25 March	In a reversal of form, House passes thirty-day embargo on foreign trade.
26 March	House appoints JM to select committee on ways and means.
18 April	JM supports nonintercourse bill suspending commerce with Great Britain, owing to violations of American neutrality.
19 April	Senate confirms John Jay's appointment as envoy extraordinary to Great Britain.
1–2 May	JM opposes excise on tobacco unsuccessfully.
12 May	Votes with majority to discontinue embargo.
ca. 25 May	Declines post as U.S. minister to France.
30 May	Opposes Federalist attempt to increase size of army to 10,000 men.
ca. 1 June	JM courts Dolly Payne Todd in Philadelphia.
9 June	Congress adjourns.

ca. 11–13 June	JM departs from Philadelphia with Monroe; reaches Baltimore.
17–ca. 20 June	Travels to Fredericksburg with Joseph Jones.
ca. 22–ca. 24 June	Finishes final leg of journey from Philadelphia; arrives at Montpelier.
ca. 20–ca. 25 August	Visits Jefferson at Monticello.
15 September	Marries Dolley Payne Todd at Harewood in Jefferson County.
15–19 September	Remains with bride at Harewood.
20 September– 3 October	JM and bride visit Nelly Madison Hite and her husband in Frederick County.
ca. 10–ca. 15 October	Newlyweds travel to Philadelphia; take lodgings at 4 North Eighth Street.
3–17 November	Second session of Third Congress convenes but cannot proceed until Senate achieves quorum.
4 November 1794– 3 March 1795	JM attends second session.
19 November	John Jay signs treaty between U.S. and Great Britain.
24–28 November	Argument over "self-created" Democratic-Republican societies erupts in House.
15 December	JM reports a naturalization bill from committee.
17 December	Opposes reimbursing citizens who lost property in Whiskey Rebellion.

1795

1–2 January	JM supports amendment to naturalization bill requiring prospective citizens to forsake titles of nobility.
3 March	Third Congress adjourns.
16 March	JM reelected to House of Representatives.
ca. 6 April	Departs from Philadelphia for Virginia, accompanied by his wife, stepson, and sister-in-law Anna Payne.
20 April	JM's pamphlet *Political Observations* published in Philadelphia.

THE PAPERS OF
James Madison

To Thomas Jefferson

DEAR SIR   ALEXANDA. Mar: 24: 93
I wrote at Baltimore, but the letter being too late for the mail, I have
suppressed it. It contained nothing of consequence. We[1] arrived here to
day (2 OC) and shall proceed to Colchester tonight. Our journey has
been successful; tho' laborious for the horses. The roads bad generally
from Head of Elk; on the North of Baltimore, and thence to George
Town, excessively so. I am just told by Mr. R. B. Lee here, that Rutherford is elected, so is Griffin, Nicholas,[2] & New.[3] The other elections are
unknown here.[4] Yrs. always & affey.

JS. MADISON JR

RC (DLC). Docketed by Jefferson, "recd. Mar. 30."

1. James Monroe was JM's traveling companion.
2. John Nicholas (ca. 1764–1819), brother of George and Wilson Cary Nicholas,
served as a Republican congressman, 1793–1801, from the district composed of
Culpeper, Fauquier, and Stafford counties. He became JM's political ally in the
Third and Fourth Congresses (Manning J. Dauer, "The Two John Nicholases,"
American Historical Review, 45 [1939–40]: 340–41).
3. Anthony New (1747–1833) was a Republican congressman from the district
including King and Queen, King William, Essex, Middlesex, and Caroline counties,
1793–1805 (*BDC*, p. 1466; Hening, *Statutes*, 13:332).
4. On the Virginia congressional elections held on 18 Mar., see Madison in the
Third Congress, 2 Dec. 1793–3 Mar. 1795.

From Thomas Jefferson

TH: JEFFERSON TO J. MADISON.   [25 March 1793]
The idea seems to gain credit that the naval powers combining against
France will prohibit supplies even of provisions to that country. Should
this be formally notified I should suppose Congress would be called, because it is a justifiable cause of war, & as the Executive cannot decide the
question of war on the affirmative side, neither ought it to do so on the
negative side, by preventing the competent body from deliberating on
the question. But I should hope that war would not be their choice. I
think it will furnish us a happy opportunity of setting another precious
example to the world, by shewing that nations may be brought to do
justice by appeals to their interests as well as by appeals to arms. I should
hope that Congress instead of a denunciation of war, would instantly
exclude from our ports all the manufactures, produce, vessels & subjects
of the nations committing this aggression, during the continuance of the
aggression & till full satisfaction [be] made for it. This would work well

in many ways, safely in all, & introduce between nations another umpire than arms. It would relieve us too from the risks & the horrors of cutting throats. The death of the king of France[1] has not produced as open condemnations from the Monocrats as I expected. I dined the other day in a company where the subject was discussed. I will name the company in the order in which they manifested their partialities, beginning with the warmest Jacobinism & proceeding by shades to the most heartfelt aristocracy. Smith (N. Y.) Coxe. Stewart. T. Shippen. Bingham. Peters. Breck.[2] Meredith. Wolcott. It is certain that the ladies of this city, of the first circle are all open-mouthed against the murderers of a sovereign, and they generally speak those sentiments which the more cautious husband smothers. I believe it is pretty certain that Smith (S. C.) and miss A. are not to come together. Ternant[3] has at length openly hoisted the flag of monarchy by going into deep mourning for his prince. I suspect he thinks a cessation of his visits to me a necessary accompaniment to this pious duty. A connection between him & Hamilton seems to be springing up. On observing that Duer was secretary to the old board of treasury, I suspect him to have been the person who suggested to Hamilton the letter of mine to that board which he so tortured in his Catullus.[4] Dunlap has refused to print the peice which we had heard of before your departure,[5] and it has been several days in Bache's hands, without any notice of it. The President will leave this about the 27th. inst. & return about the 20th. of April. Adieu.

RC (DLC: Rives Collection, Madison Papers); FC, Tr (DLC: Jefferson Papers). RC franked and addressed by Jefferson to JM at Orange, "to the care of mr. James Blair / Fredericksburg." Postmarked "25 MR."

1. News of the execution of Louis XVI on 21 Jan. became known in Philadelphia by 15 Mar. (Parsons, *Diary of Jacob Hiltzheimer*, p. 190).

2. A native of Boston, the merchant Samuel Breck moved to Philadelphia in 1792.

3. Jean Baptiste de Ternant, the French minister accredited in August 1791, was succeeded by Edmond Charles Genet in May 1793.

4. In "An American" No. 1 of 4 Aug. 1792, Hamilton had drawn unfavorable inferences from Jefferson's 26 Sept. 1786 letter to John Jay, conveying proposals that the American debt owed to France be transferred to a consortium of Dutch bankers. He expanded his charges in "Catullus," nos. 2, 5, and 6, of 19 Sept., 24 Nov., and 22 Dec. 1792 (Syrett and Cooke, *Papers of Hamilton*, 12:162, 399–401, 13:229–31, 348–54).

5. Jefferson may have alluded to John Beckley's essay, which by 9 Apr. was anonymously published as a pamphlet: *An Examination of the Late Proceedings in Congress, Respecting the Official Conduct of the Secretary of the Treasury* (Richmond, 1793, Evans 26245). Evans erroneously attributed this pamphlet to John Taylor of Caroline (Ammon, *James Monroe*, p. 596 n. 69).

§ Notes on Accounts with James Monroe. *Ca. 29 March 1793.* JM itemized sums paid to or for Monroe, and payments received from him, from 1786 to March 1793, producing a balance in JM's favor. On the verso JM summarized joint expenses incurred with Monroe on their journeys to and from Philadelphia to attend the Second Congress.

Ms (NN). 2 pp. In JM's hand. Conjectural date based on JM's departure from Alexandria for Orange ca. 24 Mar.

From Thomas Jefferson

TH: J. TO J. MADISON.   PHILADA. Mar. 31. 1793.

Nothing remarkeable this week. What was mentioned in my last respecting Bache's paper was on misinformation, there having been no proposition there. Yours of the 24th. from Alexandria is received. I inclose you the rough draught of a letter I wrote on a particular subject on which the person to whom it is addressed desired me to make a statement according to my view of it.[1] He told me his object was perhaps to shew it to some friends whom he wished to satisfy as to the original destination of the 3. mill. of florins, and that he meant to revive this subject. I presume however he will not find my letter to answer his purpose. The President set out on the 24th. I have got off about one half my superfluous furniture already and shall get off the other half within two or three days to be shipped to Virginia: & shall in the course of the week get on the banks of the Schuylkill.[2] Ham. has given up his house in Market Street & taken a large one in Arch. Street near 6th.

RC and enclosure (DLC); FC, FC of enclosure, Tr, and Tr of enclosure (DLC: Jefferson Papers). The two-page enclosure includes interlineations and marginalia not in the FC of enclosure.

1. Jefferson enclosed a draft of his letter to Hamilton of 27 Mar. 1793 (DLC: Hamilton Papers). Printed in Syrett and Cooke, *Papers of Hamilton*, 14:255–56, the letter explained "the view I had of the destination of the loan of three millions of florins obtained by our bankers in Amsterdam previous to the acts of the 4th. & 12th. of Aug. 1790. when it was proposed to adopt it under those acts." The administration of that loan was the subject of Giles's third resolution of 27 Feb. 1793, censuring Hamilton's official conduct (*Annals of Congress*, 2d Cong., 2d sess., 900).

2. Jefferson was planning to resign as secretary of state and rented for the summer a house near Gray's Ferry from Moses Cox (Malone, *Jefferson and His Time*, 3:57–58).

¶ To Thomas Jefferson. Letter not found. *31 March 1793, Orange.* In his list of letters to Jefferson (DLC: Rives Collection, Madison Papers), JM noted that this letter, like that of 24 Mar., concerned "Elections in Virga." Received by Jefferson 9 Apr. (Jefferson's Epistolary Record [DLC: Jefferson Papers]).

To the Minister of the Interior
of the French Republic

Sir   Virginia. April 1793

I have recd. your letter of the 10th. of Octr.[1] accompanying the decree of the National assembly of the 26. of Augst. last; which confers the title of French Citizen on several foreigners among whom I have the honor to be named.

In the catalogue of sublime truths and precious sentiments recorded in the revolution of France, none is more to be admired, than the renunciation of those prejudices which have perverted the artificial boundaries of nations into exclusions of the philanthropy which ought to cement the whole into one great family. The recitals of the Act which you communicate, contain the best comment on this great principle of humanity: and in proportion, as they speak the magnanimity of the French Nation, must claim the gratitude & affection of the Individuals so honorably adopted into her citizenship. For myself I feel these sentiments with all the force which that reflection can inspire; and I present them with peculiar satisfaction as a Citizen of the U. S. which have borne so signal a part towards banishing prejudices from the World & reclaiming the lost rights of Mankind; & whose public connection with France is endeared by the affinities of their mutual liberty, and the sensibility testified by the Citizens of each Country to every event interesting to the fortunes of the other.

To this tribute of respectful affection, I beg leave to add my anxious wishes for all the prosperity & glory to the French Nation which can accrue from an example corresponding with the dignified maxims they have established, and compleating the triumphs of Liberty, by a victory over the minds of all its adversaries.

Be pleased, Sir, to accept acknowledgts. due to the sentiments you have personally expressed in transmittg. the public act with which you were charged.

J. M.

Draft (DLC). In the upper left margin JM wrote "(Copy)." The RC (not found) was enclosed in JM to Jefferson, 29 May 1793. Jefferson then delivered it to Edmond Charles Genet, the French minister to the U.S., since the addressee, Jean Marie Roland, had resigned as minister of the interior in France (Jefferson to JM, 9 June 1793).

1. *PJM*, 14:381.

¶ From Ambrose Madison. Letter not found. *4 April 1793*. Described as a one-page letter in the lists probably made by Peter Force (DLC, series 7, container 2).

From Thomas Jefferson

TH: J. TO J. MADISON.   PHILADELPHIA Apr. 7. 93.

We may now I believe give full credit to the accounts that war is declared between France & England. The latter having ordered Chauvelin to retire within eight days, the former seemed to consider it as too unquestionable an evidence of an intention to go to war, to let the advantage slip of her own readiness, & the unreadiness of England. Hence I presume the first declaration from France.[1] A British packet is arrived. But as yet we learn nothing more than that she confirms the accounts of war being declared. Genest not yet arrived. An impeachment is ordered here against Nicholson their Comptroller general, by a vote almost unanimous of the house of Representatives.[2] There is little doubt I am told but that much mala fides will appear: but E. R. thinks he has barricaded himself within the fences of the law.[3] There is a good deal of connection between his manœuvres & the *accomodating* spirit of the Treasury deptmt. of the US. so as to interest the impeachors not to spare the latter. Duer now threatens that, if he is not relieved by certain persons, he will lay open to the world such a scene of villainy as will strike it with astonishment.[4] The papers I *occasionally* inclose you, be so good as to return, as they belong to my office. I move into the country tomorrow or next day. Adieu your's affectionately.

RC (DLC); FC (DLC: Jefferson Papers).

1. France declared war on Great Britain and the Dutch Republic on 1 Feb.

2. John Nicholson, comptroller general of Pennsylvania, had weathered an attempt to remove him from office in 1790. Early in 1793 the Pennsylvania House of Representatives appointed a committee to investigate his accounts. On that committee's recommendation—presented by Albert Gallatin—the House impeached Nicholson on 5 Apr. for redeeming his own state loan certificates instead of exchanging them for federal certificates. A year later the state Senate acquitted Nicholson, but he resigned as comptroller general (Arbuckle, *John Nicholson*, pp. 47–48, 52–59).

3. U.S. attorney general Edmund Randolph was a debtor to Nicholson and in private practice represented him in a case which was separate from but related to the impeachment (ibid., pp. 57–58).

4. William Duer, former assistant secretary of the treasury, had speculated in ventures that collapsed in March 1792, precipitating a financial panic in New York. Since that time he had been in debtors' prison.

From James Maury

MY DEAR SIR   LIVERPOOL 9 Apl 1793

I have sometimes been drawn into Letters of Recommendation to you, not with my own intire aprobation, for which I beg your pardon. 'Tis tho' by no means so on this Occasion. The Bearer the Revd Mr Toulmin[1] goes to our Country on an Errand wherein we are so much interested, that I come forward with all my Heart & intirely of my own accord to request you particularly to favor him with your good offices in a Tour he makes thro' the United States with the View of fixing on an abiding place for himself & some friends here, who are to become our fellow Citizens & will be valuable acquisitions as well for their Virtue & Knowlege as their property—among them is the virtuous Eddows of Chester.[2] I am with particular Esteem & Regard your friend

JAMES MAURY

RC (DLC). Docketed by JM, with the notation: "recommending Mr. Toulmin."

1. The Reverend Harry Toulmin, an English Unitarian minister, emigrated to the U.S. to escape the political and religious reaction of the 1790s. En route to America his ship was stopped by a French privateer who allowed him to proceed when shown Toulmin's letters of introduction (probably including this one). He presented the letter to JM at Montpelier and visited Jefferson and Monroe in early August 1793. He also gave JM a description of an English threshing machine, an invention that was currently of interest to Jefferson and to JM, whose family was planning to build a gristmill in Madison County. Toulmin settled in Kentucky, where he became president of Transylvania Seminary. As secretary of the Commonwealth of Kentucky, 1796–1804, and judge of the superior court for the eastern district of the Mississippi Territory, 1804–19, he corresponded frequently with JM (Marion Tinling and Godfrey Davies, eds., *The Western Country in 1793: Reports on Kentucky and Virginia by Harry Toulmin* [San Marino, Calif., 1948], pp. vii, xv, 3; "Comments on America and Kentucky, 1793–1802," *Register of the Kentucky Historical Society*, 47 [1949]: 9; Toulmin, "Some account of a threshing machine at Charles Mordaunt's Esqr, Halsal, near Omskirk, Lancashire," n.d. [DLC]).

2. Ralph Eddowes was a student of Joseph Priestley's. Like his mentor, he emigrated in 1794 and became a founding member of the First Unitarian Society of Philadelphia (Sowerby, *Catalogue of Jefferson's Library*, 2:185; Scharf and Westcott, *History of Philadelphia*, 2:1405).

To Thomas Jefferson

DEAR SIR   ORANGE April 12. 1793

Your favor of the 31. Ult: and the preceding one without date have been received. The refusal of Dunlap in the case you mention confirms the idea of a combined influence against the freedom of the Press. If symtoms of a dangerous success in the experiment should shew themselves, it will be necessary before it be too late to convey to the public through the channels that remain open, an explicit statement of the fact and a proper warning of its tendency. In the mean time it is perhaps best to avoid any premature denunciations that might fix wavering or timid presses on the wrong side. You say that the subject of the 3 Mil. flos. is to be revived. Have you discovered in what mode; whether through the next Congs. or thro' the press; and if the latter, whether avowedly or anonymously. I suspect that the P. may not be satisfied with the aspect under which that and other parts of the fiscal administration have been left.[1]

As far as I can learn, the people of this country continue to be united & firm in the political sentiments enpressed [*sic*] by their Reps. The re-election of all who were most decided in those sentiments is among the proofs of the fact. The only individual discontinued, is the one who dissented most from his colleagues. The vote at the election stood thus —for R. 886—S. 403—W. 276.[2] *It is said* that the singular vote on assuming the balances, gave the coup de grace to his popularity. We were told at Alexa. that if the member for that district had been opposed, his election wd. have failed;[3] and at Fredg. that a notice of G's vote on the resolutions of censure had nearly turned the scale agst. him.[4] I have seen & conversed with Mr. F. Walker.[5] I think it impossible he can go otherwise than right. He tells me that I. Cole, and not Clay as in the Newspaper is elected for the Halifax District.[6] Hancock,[7] is the new member from the district adjoining Moore;[8] & Preston for that beyond him.[9] I fell in with Mr. Brackenridge on his way to Kentucky. He had adverted to Greenup's late vote[10] with indignation and dropped threats of its effect on his future pretensions.

The sympathy with the fate of Louis has found its way pretty generally into the mass of our Citizens; but relating merely to the man & not to the Monarch, and being derived from the spurious accts. in the papers of his innocence and the bloodthirstyness of his enemies, I have not found a single instance in which a fair statement of the case, has not new modelled the sentiment. "If he was a Traytor, he ought to be punished as well as another man." This has been the language of so many plain men to me, that I am persuaded it will be found to express the universal sentiment whenever the truth shall be made known.

Our fields continue to anticipate a luxuriant harvest. The greatest danger is apprehended from too rapid a vegetation under the present warm & moist weather. The night before last it received a small check from a smart frost. The thermometer was down at 37° and we were alarmed for the fruit. It appears however that no harm was done. We have at present the most plentiful prospect of every kind of it.

Will you be so good, in case an oppy. shd. offer to enquire of Docr. Logan[11] as to the plows he was to have made & sent to Mrs. House's; and to repay there what may have been advanced for those & two or three other articles that were to be forwarded to Fredg. by water. I forgot to make the proper arrangements before I left Philada. Adieu Yrs. Affy.

RC (DLC). Unsigned. Docketed by Jefferson, "recd. Apr. 22."

1. JM later repeated his suspicions in his account of how Washington was embarrassed by Hamilton's defense against the Giles resolutions (Fleet, "Madison's 'Detatched Memoranda,'" *WMQ*, 3d ser., 3 [1946]: 545-48).

2. Robert Rutherford, John Smith, and Alexander White were the candidates in the congressional election of 18 Mar. in the district composed of Frederick and Berkeley counties (Hening, *Statutes*, 13:331-32).

3. Richard Bland Lee was reelected in the district that included Alexandria. He and Alexander White—both Federalists—were the only Virginians who voted for assumption of state debts on 26 July 1790. According to one of Jefferson's accounts of the "Compromise of 1790," JM persuaded White and Lee to support assumption in return for locating the permanent capital on the Potomac, which bordered their constituencies (*Annals of Congress*, 1st Cong., 2d sess., 1755; *PJM*, 13:243-46; Boyd, *Papers of Jefferson*, 17:207, 208 n. 4).

4. Samuel Griffin (a Federalist who represented the district that included Henrico, Hanover, New Kent, Charles City, and James City counties) voted against two, favored one, and abstained on three of Giles's resolutions (Hening, *Statutes*, 13:332; *Annals of Congress*, 2d Cong., 2d sess., 955-56, 959-60, 963).

5. Francis Walker (1764-1806) of Castle Hill, Albemarle County, was the brother of John Walker. He represented his county in the House of Delegates, 1788-91 and 1797-1801, and the congressional district composed of Albemarle, Amherst, Fluvanna, and Goochland counties, 1793-95. Before the Virginia redistricting act of 1792, those counties had been part of JM's constituency (*BDC*, p. 1869; Swem and Williams, *Register*, p. 441; Hening, *Statutes*, 12:654, 13:332).

6. Isaac Coles defeated Matthew Clay (1754-1815) in the congressional election in the district including Halifax, Pittsylvania, and Campbell counties. Clay was a delegate from Halifax County, 1790-94, and a Republican congressman, 1797-1813 and 1815 (*BDC*, pp. 767, 749; Hening, *Statutes*, 13:331; Swem and Williams, *Register*, p. 360).

7. George Hancock was elected from the congressional district including Franklin, Bedford, Botetourt, Henry, and Patrick counties (Hening, *Statutes*, 13:331).

8. Andrew Moore was reelected in the congressional district composed of Augusta, Rockingham, Shenandoah, Rockbridge, and Bath counties (ibid.).

9. Francis Preston (1765-1836) represented Montgomery County in the House of Delegates, 1788-89, and the congressional district composed of Wythe, Greenbrier, Kanawha, Lee, Russell, Montgomery, Grayson, and Washington counties, 1793-97. In the Third Congress he survived an attempt by his opponent, Abram Trigg, to contest his election. Moving to Abingdon, he served in the House of Delegates from Washington County, 1812-14, and in the state Senate, 1816-20 (*BDC*, pp. 1567, 56 n. 26; Swem and Williams, *Register*, p. 419; Hening, *Statutes*, 13:331).

10. Congressman Christopher Greenup of Kentucky voted against two and abstained on four of Giles's resolutions (*Annals of Congress*, 2d Cong., 2d sess., 955-56, 959-60, 963).

11. The Quaker physician George Logan helped to found the Philadelphia Society for Promoting Agriculture in 1785 and designed a plow which Jefferson arranged to have made for JM. He served as a Republican in the state House of

Representatives, 1796–97 and 1798–1801, and in the U.S. Senate, 1801–7. His un-
official peace mission to France during the Quasi-War resulted in the "Logan Act"
of 1799, which prohibited private negotiations with foreign governments. None-
theless, during JM's presidency Logan went on another private peace mission, in
1810 (Frederick B. Tolles, *George Logan of Philadelphia* [New York, 1953], pp.
55–294 passim).

To James Monroe

DEAR SIR   Apl. 14. 93.
    I understand by the waggoner charged with bringing up our several
articles from Fredericksburg and who returned on friday that the Vessel
had not sailed from Philada. when last heard of; but was expected at
Fredg. by the time of his getting down again. As he set out with another
load immediately, he is probably there by this time, and may be looked
for here about wednesday or thursday. It will be best however for you
to wait for more certain information before you send your waggon off.
In order to accelerate the business, I have given weekly instructions to
the driver charged with it to apply for your Box &c which was to be
removed from Mr. Jones's to Mr. Anderson's and wrote him on the
subject. The answer given to the first application was that no articles
whatever had come to Mr. A. The waggoner at the next trip was told by
Mr. A. whom I had then desired to make enquiry at Mr. Jones, that
application had been made there, but Mr. Jones being absent & no white
person in the House, no account of the things was obtained. I have now
directed a third application to be made & have referred to Mr. Lewis
as the proper quarter. It would seem that Pembroke either misunderstood
his orders, or has been less attentive to his trust than he promised. To
guard more effectually agst. delay, I think you wd. do well in dropping
a line to Mr. Lewis if an immediate oppy. should offer. My last letter
from Mr. J–f–n is of the 31st. Ult. It decides nothing as to peace or
war; and contains nothing worth repeating but an inclosure which will
be most properly communicated when I can shew you the letter itself.
A preceding letter says that the idea gains ground of a probable combination for preventing all commerce with France in the article of provisions; and that Ternant had hoisted the flag of Monarchy by going into
full mourning for the fate of his Prince. I believe it will not be in my
power to see you in Albemarle during the Court: but count with assurance on the pleasure of seeing both Mrs. M. & yourself here as soon as the
Court is over. Present her with my best respects. Adieu. Yrs. Affey.
                                                      Js. MADISON JR.

RC (DLC). Addressed by JM.

9

To James Monroe

Dr Sir Apl. 15. 93

Since sealing the inclosed[1] I have a letter from Mr. Jef—son of Aprl. 7. He says war is certainly declared between Engd. & F. & inclosed a newspaper which gives the acct. The decln. commenced on the part of the latter, and seems to be grounded on its alledged actual existance on the part of the former. "An impeachment (says Mr. J.) is ordered here agst. Nicholson the Comptroller, by a vote almost unanimous of the H. of Reps. There is little doubt, I am told but that much mala fides will appear: but E. R. thinks he has barricaded himself within the fences of the law. There is a good deal of connection between his manœuvres & the *accomodating* spirit of the Treasy. Dept. of the U. S. so as to interest the Impeachors not to spare the latter. Duer now threatens that if he is not relieved by certain persons; he will lay open to the world such a scene of villainy as will strike it with astonishment." I give you Mr. J.s own words that you may judge in what degree any part of them are confidential. Adieu

J. M. Jr

RC (DLC). Addressed by JM to Monroe, "Hond by Mr. Nicholas."

1. JM to Monroe, 14 Apr. 1793.

From Thomas Jefferson

Dear Sir PHILADELPHIA Apr. 28. 1793.

Yours of the 12th. inst. is received, and I will duly attend to your commission relative to the ploughs. We have had such constant deluges of rain & bad weather for some time past that I have not yet been able to go to Dr. Logan's to make the enquiries you desire, but I will do it soon. We expect mr. Genest here within a few days.[1] It seems as if his arrival would furnish occasion for the *people* to testify their affections without respect to the cold caution of their government. Would you suppose it possible that it should have been seriously proposed to declare our treaties with France void on the authority of an ill-understood scrap in Vattel 2.§.197. ('toutefois si ce changement &c—gouvernement')[2] and that it should be necessary to discuss it? Cases are now arising which will embarras us a little till the line of neutrality be fairly understood by ourselves, & the belligerant parties. A French frigate is now bringing here, as we are told, prizes which left this but 2. or 3. days before. Shall we permit her to sell them? The treaty does not say we shall, and it says we shall not permit the like to England? Shall we permit France to fit out privateers here? The treaty does not stipulate that we shall, tho' it says we shall not permit the English to do it. I fear that a fair neutrality will prove a disagreeable pill to our friends, tho' necessary to keep us out of the calamities of a war. Adieu, my dear Sir. Your's affectionately

Th: Jefferson

RC (DLC); FC, Tr (DLC: Jefferson Papers).

1. Edmond Charles Genet, French minister to the U.S., landed at Charleston on 8 Apr. and arrived in Philadelphia on 16 May.

2. In a meeting on 19 Apr., the cabinet discussed whether or not the 1778 treaty with France was still valid, since the French government had changed from a monarchy to a republic. According to Jefferson's "Anas," Edmund Randolph said that the treaty remained valid, but on Hamilton's "undertaking to present to him the authority in Vattel (which we had not present) and to prove to him that, if the authority was admitted, the treaty might be declared void, E. R. agreed to take further time to consider." In the section from which Jefferson here quotes, Vattel observed: "However, if these changes [which have taken place within a state] are such as to render the alliance useless, dangerous, or unsatisfactory to him [the sovereign], he is at liberty to disclaim it; for he can say with good reason that he would not have entered into an alliance with that Nation if it had been under its present form of government." On 22 Apr. Washington issued the Neutrality Proclamation, and on 28 Apr. Jefferson submitted to him a report on the French treaty which rebutted Hamilton's arguments and the reference from Vattel (Ford, *Writings of Jefferson*, 1:227, 6:217, 218–31; Vattel, *Law of Nations* [1916 ed.], 3:175; Fitzpatrick, *Writings of Washington*, 32:430–31).

¶ To Thomas Jefferson. Letter not found. *29 April 1793, Orange.* Acknowledged in Jefferson to JM, 13 May 1793. In his list of letters to Jefferson (DLC: Rives Collection, Madison Papers), JM noted that this letter concerned "political sentiments of Va." Received by Jefferson 8 May (Jefferson's Epistolary Record [DLC: Jefferson Papers]).

From Thomas Jefferson

Th: J. to J. Madison.   May. 5. 93.

No letter from you since that of Apr. 12. I received one from mr. Pinckney[1] yesterday informing me he expected to send me by the next ship a model of the threshing mill. He had been to see one work, which with 2. horses got out 8. bushels of *wheat* an hour. But he was assured that the mill from which my model was taken get outs [*sic*] 8 quarters (i.e 64 bushels) of *oats* an hour with 4. horses. I have seen Dr. Logan.

Your ploughs will be done in a week & shall be attended to. Seal & forward Monroe's letter[2] after reading it. Adieu. Your's affectly.

P. S. I inclose a Boston paper[3] as a proof of what I mention to Monroe of the spirit which is rising.[4] The old tories have their names now raked up again; & I believe if the author of 'Plain truth'[5] was now to be charged with that pamphlet, this put along side of his present Anglomany would decide the voice of the yeomanry of the country on his subject.

RC (DLC); FC, Tr (DLC: Jefferson Papers). RC addressed by Jefferson.

1. Thomas Pinckney to Jefferson, private letter of 13 Mar. 1793 (DNA: RG 59, Diplomatic Despatches, Great Britain).

2. Jefferson to Monroe, 5 May 1793 (Ford, *Writings of Jefferson*, 6:238–40).

3. Jefferson may have enclosed an article written over the pseudonym "Freeman" which denounced as "tories" the American opponents of the French Revolution (Boston *Columbian Centinel*, 20 Apr. 1793).

4. In his letter to Monroe of 5 May 1793, Jefferson wrote: "The war between France & England seems to be producing an effect not contemplated. All the old spirit of 1776. is rekindling. The newspapers from Boston to Charleston prove this; & even the Monocrat papers are obliged to publish the most furious Philippics against England" (Ford, *Writings of Jefferson*, 6:238).

5. [James Chalmers], *Plain Truth, Addressed to the Inhabitants of America* (Philadelphia, 1776; Evans 15088). This pamphlet was written against Thomas Paine's *Common Sense*. Jefferson erroneously attributed it to Hamilton (Thomas R. Adams, "The Authorship and Printing of *Plain Truth* by 'Candidus,'" *Papers of the Bibliographical Society of America*, 49 [1955]: 231 and n. 4).

To Thomas Jefferson

DEAR SIR   ORANGE May 8th. 1793.

Your last recd. was of the 28 Apl. The rect. of all the preceeding is verified by the uninterrupted dates of the Gazettes inclosed. I anxiously wish that the reception of Genest may testify what I believe to be the real affections of the people. It is the more desireable as a seasonable plum after the bitter pills which it seems must be administered. Having neither the Treaty nor Law of Nations at hand I form no opinion as to the stipulations of the former, or the precise neutrality defined by the latter. I had always supposed that the terms of the Treaty made some sort of difference, at least as far as would consist with the Law of Nations, between France & Nations not in Treaty, particularly G. Britain. I should still doubt whether the term *impartial* in the Proclamation is not stronger than was necessary, if not than was proper. Peace is no doubt to be preserved at any price that honor and good faith will permit. But it is no less to be considered that the least departure from these will not only be most likely to end in the loss of peace, but is pregnant with every other evil that could happen to us. In explaining our engagements under the Treaty with France, it would be honorable as well as just to adhere to the sense that would at the time have been put on them. The attempt to shuffle off the Treaty altogether by quibbling on Vattel is equally contemptible for the meanness & folly of it. If a change of Govt. is an absolution from public engagements, why not from those of a domestic as well as of a foreign nature; and what then becomes of public debts &c &c. In fact, the doctrine would perpetuate every existing Despotism, by involving in a reform of the Govt. a destruction of the Social pact, an annihilation of property, and a compleat establishment of the State of Nature. What most surprizes me is that such a proposition *shd. have been discussed*.

Our weather has not been favorable of late, owing more to want of sun, than excess of rain. Vegetation of all sorts even the wheat, nevertheless continues to flourish; and the fruit having no longer any thing to fear from frost, we are sure of good crops of that agreeable article. Yrs. Always & Affy.

Js. MADISON JR.

Will you send me a copy of the little pamphlet advertised under the title of an Examination of the proceedings in the case of the Secy. of the Treasy?

RC (DLC). Docketed by Jefferson, "recd. May 16." JM apparently enclosed a "plan of a house" which has not been found (Jefferson to JM, 19 May 1793, and n. 1).

From John Taylor

DR. SIR   CAROLINE May 11. 1793

By Colo. Monroe an opportunity occuring, I take it to inform you, that I have not been idle since my return. Upon reflection, it seemed to me, that at the next Session of Congress, and at its very commencement, a direct, firm and resolute attack should be made upon the bank law. The news papers are improper channels through which to make a considerable impression on the public mind, because they are a species of ephemeræ, and because the printers are not orthodox in general as to politicks. Hence a pamphlet appeared most advisable, and I have written, in length sufficient for a pamphlet.[1] If its merit is counted by its pages, it is not deficient, but whether it possesses any other species of worth, myself, you know cannot judge. So soon then as I could transcribe it, I purposed to forward it to you, that a determination might be had whether it ought to be commited to the flames or the press. Having no motive but the public good, there is not that kind of paternal sensibility about me, which sometimes attaches us even to deformity. Therefore when you see the work, freely correct, censure or condemn, without supposing it possible that the burning a few sheets of paper will affect me.

Could you not spare time to see us in this neighbourhood. Mr: Pendleton was but two days ago expressing his wish, with anxiety, that your father, old Mr: Taylor and yourself would come and take pot luck with us this spring?

But this work. If it is worth any thing, I have shot my bolt, and therefore I may now justly, and beneficially give place to some other person, who is full charged. If it is worth nothing, then it proves that I ought to make room for another, who may do some good, in the good cause. Either way, the public will be served by my withdrawing from its service.

Hawkins was here a day or two, with Macon and Giles. He appeared to strive to arrange himself right. A gentleman who knew him better than I do, informed me, that the most likely thing to fix him, would be a letter from you. Some thing in a kind of friendly stile. And having three or four pointed sentences against the bank law, and expressing a necessity for its repeal. His situation in his state is a little awkward, & he will probably strive to put it to rights. To help him along, he would shew your letter, and if you made a Carthago est deleta[2] business of the bank Law, he would get so far inlisted in the idea, among his own countrymen, that he could not retract. When your letter was seen, the reader would take up the idea, and gore Hawkins upon the subject. I cannot say more here, and perhaps I ought to apologise for having said so much on such a subject. I am Sir Yr: mo: obt: Sert.

JOHN TAYLOR

RC (DLC). Addressed by Taylor to JM at Orange. Docketed by JM.

1. [John Taylor], *An Enquiry into the Principles and Tendency of Certain Public Measures* (Philadelphia, 1794; Evans 27782). The publishing history of this pamphlet is discussed in Robert E. Shalhope, *John Taylor of Caroline: Pastoral Republican* (Columbia, S.C., 1980), pp. 219, 275-76 nn. 7-10.

2. Cato the Elder, a model of republican virtue, concluded all his speeches in the Roman Senate with the phrase: "In my opinion, Carthage must be destroyed." By this tactic he incited the Third Punic War, which accomplished the result he desired (Plutarch, *Marcus Cato*, ch. 27, *Plutarch's Lives*, Loeb Classical Library [11 vols.; London, 1914-26], 2:383).

From John Dawson

Dear Sir!   May 13. 1793.

Our correspondence has been discont[in]ued for some time, much against my wish.

On Friday last Citizen Gennet passd this place on his way to Philadelphia. He appears to me to be a man possessd of much information, added to the most engageing & agreeable manners that I ever saw. He is very easy, communicative & dignified & will precisely suit the taste of our countrymen. All who have seen him are delighted, & if I mistake not he will do much honour to the republic he represents, & will soon throw Hammond, Vanberkle[1] & Co far behind him.

We have an account this Morning from Norfolk, which is said to come by an American ship from London—which I most sincerely hope is not true, tho I fear much—"that there has been a violent mob in Paris, & have put to death Petion, Condorset, Monvel & several others."[2] With much esteem Yr. friend & Sert

J Dawson

RC (DLC).

1. Pieter Franco van Berckel succeeded his father as Dutch minister to the U.S. in 1787 (Abraham Jacob van der Aa et al., eds., *Biographisch Woordenboek der Nederlanden* [1852–78; 7 vols.; Amsterdam, 1969 reprint], 1:108).

2. This report was erroneous. Jérôme Pétion de Villeneuve committed suicide in June 1794; the marquis de Condorcet died in prison in April 1794; and dramatist Jacques-Marie Boutet de Monvel survived until 1811 (Ludovic Lalanne, *Dictionnaire historique de la France* [2d ed.; Paris, 1877], pp. 1447–48, 575–76, 1318).

From Thomas Jefferson

Th: J. to J. Mad.   [13 May 1793]

I wrote you on the 5th. covering an open letter to Colo. Monroe. Since that I have received yours of Apr. 29. We are going on here in the same spirit still. The Anglophobia has seised violently on three members of our council. This sets almost every day on questions of neutrality. H. produced the other day the draught of a letter from himself to the Collectors of the customs,[1] giving them in charge to watch over all proceedings in their districts contrary to the laws of neutrality or tending to infract our peace with the belligerent powers, and particularly to observe if vessels pierced for guns should be built, and to inform *him* of it. This was objected to 1. as setting up a system of espionage, destructive of the

peace of society. 2. transferring to the Treasury departmt. the conservation of the laws of neutrality & our peace with foreign nations. 3. it was rather proposed to intimate to the judges that the laws respecting neutrality being now come into activity, they should charge the grand juries with the observance of them; these being constitutional & public informers, & the persons accused *knowing* of what they should do, & having an opportunity of justifying themselves. E. R. found out a hair to split, which, as always happens, became the decision. H. is to write to the collectors of the customs,[2] who are to convey their information to the Attornies of the districts, to whom E. R. is to write to receive their information & proceed by indictment. The clause respecting the building vessels pierced for guns was omitted. For tho' 3. against 1. thought it would be a breach of neutrality, yet they thought we might defer giving a public opinion on it as yet. Every thing my dear Sir, now hangs on the opinion of a single person, & that the most indecisive one I ever had to do business with. He always contrives to agree in principle with one, but in conclusion with the other. Anglophobia, secret Antigallomany, a federalisme outrée, and a present ease in his circumstances not natural, have decided the complexion of our dispositions, and our proceedings towards the Conspirators against human liberty & the Assertors of it, which is unjustifiable in principle, in interest, and in respect to the wishes of our constituents. A manly neutrality, claiming the liberal rights ascribed to that condition by the very powers at war, was the part we should have taken, & would I believe have given satisfaction to our allies. If any thing prevents it's being a mere English neutrality, it will be that the penchant of the P. is not that way, and above all, the ardent spirit of our constituents. The line is now drawing so clearly as to shew, on one side, 1. the fashionable circles of Phila., N. York, Boston & Charleston (natural aristocrats), 2. merchants trading on British capitals. 3. paper men, (all the old tories are found in some one of these three descriptions) on the other side are 1. merchants trading on their own capitals. 2. Irish merchants. 3. tradesmen, mechanics, farmers & every other possible description of our citizens. Genest is not yet arrived tho' hourly expected. I have just heard that the workmen I had desired from Europe were engaged & about to embark. Another strong motive for making me uneasy here.[3] Adieu my dear Sir.

RC (DLC); FC, Tr (DLC: Jefferson Papers). RC addressed by Jefferson and docketed, probably by JM, "—1793." Date assigned by comparison with Jefferson to JM, 19 May 1793.

1. This draft has not been found, but for evidence of its contents from the correspondence of Jefferson and Randolph, see Syrett and Cooke, *Papers of Hamilton*, 14:412–14 n. 1.

2. The Treasury Department Circular to the Collectors of the Customs, 4 Aug. 1793 (ibid., 15:178–81), instructed the collectors to inform not only the U.S. attorneys but also the state governors of violations of the Neutrality Proclamation in their districts. After JM retired from the presidency, Charles Jared Ingersoll (the 1812 Federalist vice-presidential candidate) asked him "upon what principle this was done, particularly the using of Governors of States in aid of federal exigencies." JM replied: "It wd. seem, that the Exercise of Executive power in the cases referred to without the intervention of the Judiciary, was regarded as warranted by the L. of N. ["law of nations" interlined by JM] as part of the Local Law, and that the State Executive became the Fedl. instruments, by virtue of their authority over the Militia. If the term 'instructed' was used in the call on them, it is one that wd. not be relished now by some of them at least" (Ingersoll to JM, 26 Dec. 1829 [DLC: Rives Collection, Madison Papers]; JM to Ingersoll, 8 Jan. 1830 [draft, DLC]).

3. Jefferson had been planning a major addition to Monticello. Construction was to begin after his impending resignation as secretary of state (Malone, *Jefferson and His Time*, 3:232–33).

From James Monroe

DEAR SIR   ALBEMARLE May 18. 1793.

I have just returned home from an attendance on the courts at Fredbg & Richmond & promise myself repose at least for a short time. I called on Colo. Taylor from whom I enclose you a letter.[1] I found he had been very busily employed upon some subjects of an interesting nature since he reached home. He has written near 60. (56. I believe) folio pages upon the subject of the bank and the funds in which I found many useful & judicious observations addressed in his humorous style concluding in the sentimt. that the bank shod. be demolished & proprietors of the latter excluded from the publick councils.[2] His idea is that it be published in a pamphlet & abt. the commencement of the next session. I think it may be much curtailed & in some instances strengthen'd—he proposes to forward it to you as soon as transcribed for that purpose. It has been revised by Mr. Pendleton & approved. He says that altho' the old gentn. was right in the outline of his politicks yet he had no idea of the extent to which things had been hurried, or of the turpitude which had obtained in the publick councils.

I saw Giles and Parker in Richmond. They were in spirits & inculcating doctrines to wh. that loyal city seemed a stranger. Mr Dawson I think their only associate in sentiment.

I have heard nothing from Phila. except a line from Mr. Beck[le]y, nor have I seen the piece left behind.[3] I cod. wish Taylor had, or might yet be possessed, of a copy, before his escapes him, as it is precisely on the same subject & terminating in the same result—only his more copious & comprehensive. Mr. Beckley says he has sent a packet for you covering some of the copies for us both.

I found Mrs. M. & child well. We are preparing our lower office, plaistering &ca for our accomodation that the upper may be appropriated to our friends. In a few days we hope to have this accomplished. We hope soon for the pleasure of yr. company. We shall be quite in retirement, unvisited I believe by any one unless Mr. Jones shod. call on his return, so that we hope you will come up shortly.

Peter will bring the articles at yr. house; and likewise some [of?] Wilsons if arrived. Our best respects to the fam⟨il⟩y. Sincerely I am yr. friend & s⟨ervt.⟩

JAS. MONROE

RC (DLC). Addressed by Monroe to JM at Orange.

1. John Taylor to JM, 11 May 1793.
2. JM and his Republican colleagues had recently proposed excluding from Congress the directors and stockholders of the Bank of the United States. John Beckley had sent Jefferson a list of such congressmen (Notes on Proposed Constitutional Amendments, ca. 3 Mar. 1793, *PJM*, 14:490 and nn.; Jefferson, "Anas," 23 Mar. 1793, Ford, *Writings of Jefferson*, 1:223).
3. Beckley's pamphlet, *Examination of the Late Proceedings*.

From Thomas Jefferson

TH: J. TO J. MAD.   PHILA. May 19. 1793.

I wrote you last on the 13th. Since that I have received yours of the 8th. I have scribbled on a separate paper some general notes on the plan of a house[1] you inclosed. I have done more. I have endeavored to throw the same area, the same extent of walls, the same number of rooms, & of the same sizes, into another form so as to offer a choice to the builder. Indeed I varied my plan by shewing what it would be with alcove bedrooms, to which I am much attached. I dare say you will have judged from the pusillanimity of the proclamation, from whose pen it came.[2] A fear lest any affection should be discovered is distinguishable enough. This base fear will produce the very evil they wish to avoid: for our constituents seeing that the government does not express their mind, perhaps rather leans the other way, are coming forward to express it themselves. It was suspected that there was not a clear mind in the P's consellors to receive Genet. The citizens however determined to recieve him. Arrangements were taken for meeting him at Gray's ferry in a great body. He escaped that by arriving in town with the letters which brought information that he was on the road. The merchants i.e. Fitzsimmons & co. were to present an address to *the P.* on the neutrality proclaimed. It contained much wisdom but no affection. You will see it in the papers inclosed.³ The citizens determined to address *Genet.* Rittenhouse, Hutcheson,⁴ Dallas,⁵ Sargeant &c were at the head of it. Tho a select body of only 30. was appointed to present it, yet a vast concourse of the people attended them. I have not seen it: but it is understood to be the counteraddress.⁶ Ternant's hopes of employment in the French army turn out to be without grounds. He is told by the minister of war expressly that the places of Marechal de camp are all full. He thinks it more prudent therefore to remain in America. He delivered yesterday his letters of recall, & mr. Genet presented his of credence. It is impossible for any thing to be more affectionate, more magnanimous than the purport of his mission. 'We know that under present circumstances we have a right to call upon your [*sic*] for the guarantee of our islands. But we do not desire it. We wish you to do nothing but what is for your own good, and we will do all in our power to promote it. Cherish your own peace & prosperity. You have expressed a willingness to enter into a more liberal treaty of commerce with us; I bring full powers (& he produced them) to form such a treaty, and a preliminary decree of the National convention to lay open our country & it's colonies to you for every purpose of utility, without your participating the burthens of maintaining & defending them. We see in you the only persons on earth who can love us sincerely & merit to be so loved.' In short he offers every thing & asks nothing. Yet I know the offers will be opposed, & suspect they will not be accepted. In short, my dear Sir, it is impossible for you to concieve what is passing in our conclave: and it is evident that one or two at least, under pretence of avoiding war on the one side have no great antipathy to run foul of it on the other, and to make a part in the confederacy of princes against human liberty. The people in the Western parts of this state have been to the excise officer & threatened to burn his house &c. They were blacked & otherwise disguised so as to be unknown. He has resigned, & H. says there is no possibility of getting the law executed there, & that probably the evil will spread. A proclamation is to be issued, and another instance of my being forced to appear to approve what I have condemned uniformly from it's first conception. I expect every day to receive from mr. Pinckney the model of the Scotch threshing machine. It was to have come in a ship which arrived 3. weeks ago, but the workman had not quite finished it. Mr. P. writes me word that the machine from which my model is taken threshes 8. quarters (64. bushels) of oats *an hour*, with 4. horses & 4. men. I hope to get it in time to have one erected at Monticello to clean out the present crop. I inclose you the pamphlet you desired. Adieu.

RC (DLC); FC (DLC: Jefferson Papers). Enclosure not found, but see n. 1.

1. JM was helping with the design of his brother William's house, Woodberry Forest, in Madison County (Hunt-Jones, *Dolley and the "Great Little Madison,"* p. 63; Elizabeth Copeland Norfleet, *Woodberry Forest: The Extended View* [Orange, Va., 1979], pp. 179–83).

2. Washington's Neutrality Proclamation of 22 Apr. was based on a draft by Edmund Randolph (Reardon, *Edmund Randolph*, p. 223).

3. On 17 May the *Federal Gazette* published the address of "the Merchants and Traders of Philadelphia" and Washington's reply.

4. The physician James Hutchinson, professor of chemistry at the University of Pennsylvania since 1791, was a leader in organizing the Republican party during the election of 1792. He died in the Philadelphia yellow fever epidemic on 5 Sept. 1793 (Raymond Walters, Jr., "The Origins of the Jeffersonian Party in Pennsylvania," *Pa. Mag. Hist. and Biog.*, 66 [1942]: 443, 445–48, 451–53).

5. Alexander James Dallas was a Republican lawyer. His law reports, first published in 1790, later included U.S. Supreme Court cases. Secretary of the Commonwealth of Pennsylvania from 1791, he worked closely with Hutchinson during the election of 1792 and in founding the Democratic Society of Pennsylvania in 1793. In 1814 he became secretary of the treasury in JM's cabinet (Raymond Walters, Jr., *Alexander James Dallas: Lawyer-Politician-Financier, 1759–1817* [Philadelphia, 1943], pp. 24–25, 32–45, 187).

6. On 18 May the *Federal Gazette* published the address of "the Citizens of Philadelphia" with Genet's reply.

From Hubbard Taylor

DEAR SIR   CLARKE COUNTY 23d May 1793

Your last of the 16th. March[1] was handed me by Colo. Orr. I am much obliged to you for the papers inclosed. I am sorry to find the necessaty of calling the conduct of so high an officer as the Secretary of the Treasury into question: but at the same time am very happy to find such strict enquiry and examination of Matters so important to the publick good.

Indian Affairs are in my opinion in a very bad way, little benifit will result either from the treaty or Army this year.[2] I am well pursuaded that but a small proportion of the Indian tribes will attend the treaty, and while we are feasting a few at the expence of the U. States they will have parties commiting the most barbarous massacres on our defenceless inhabitants. God only knows when we are to be free'd from them by the present mode of Conducting Military matters.

I long much to hear some thing respecting the trade of the Mississippi the time draws on that great quanti[ti]es of Tobo., Flour, Beef, pork, Hemp, &c will be for market. Improvements in this Country is almost beyond conception, both as to society and agriculture as well as an increase of Inhabitants the latter of which has been considerable the fall & Spring past—which has occationed the Lands in the interior parts of the Country to sell high unimproved Lands frequently from £75 to £100 ℔ 100 Acres, those improved from 25/ to 40/- ℔ acre. You may Judge from this what our Country would soon be if the Indians was at peace, the Mississippi open, & the titles to our Lands adjusted; if I live to see all those take place, I shall behold the happiest & richest Country in the world: But the want of either of these three obje[c]ts will operate greatly to lessen the advantages dependant on the other two.

Our Court of appeals[3] has now begun to do business—and I beleave from what I can learn will give pretty general Satisfaction. I have not a copy of the Rules by me or wd. inclose them, if I should procure them before the bear[e]r of this Letter sets out will send them. Our papers generally contain nothing of consequence but what comes through the Atlantic States—and being too often filled with personal abuse renders them not worth sending a distance. Our relations both in Jefferson and this quarter are all well, and are geting themselves well fixed with good little farms Comfortable Houses & plentifull Stocks, which are necessary appendages for an agreable life.

You will be pleased to remember me to all yr Fathers & brothers Famil[i]es in which Clary[4] beg leave to Join. And beleave me to be at all times Dr. Sir Yr sincere & Affe: hble sert:

H. Taylor

RC (DLC). Docketed by JM.

1. Letter not found.

2. In late April three commissioners—Timothy Pickering, Benjamin Lincoln, and former Virginia governor Beverley Randolph—set out for Lower Sandusky to negotiate with the Indians of the Northwest. At the same time, Maj. Gen. Anthony Wayne was preparing a punitive expedition. The Indians' aims were equally contradictory, and negotiations were broken off in August. Disease among Wayne's troops brought an inconclusive end to the campaign of 1793. "Eventually, the administration's dual policy of negotiation and escalation caused the first crisis in civil-military relations between the new army and its civilian superiors in American history" (Richard H. Kohn, *Eagle and Sword: The Federalists and the Creation of the Military Establishment in America, 1783-1802* [New York, 1975], pp. 151-55).

3. Disputed land claims in Kentucky were the major source of litigation. Framers of the Kentucky 1792 constitution hoped to resolve this grievance by providing for a court of appeals with original jurisdiction over land cases (Coward, *Kentucky in the New Republic*, p. 34).

4. Clarissa Minor Taylor (d. 1842) of Spotsylvania County married Hubbard Taylor in 1782 (*VMHB*, 29 [1921]: 372).

To Thomas Jefferson

Dear Sir   May 27. 1793

I have recd. your letter with the unsealed one for Monroe & have for-warded the latter. Your subsequent one, which I calculate to have been written on the 12th. inst:[1] came to hand two days ago. I feel for your situation but you must bear it. Every consideration private as well as public require a further sacrifice of your longings for the repose of Monticello. You must not make your final exit from public life till it will be marked with justifying circumstances which all good citizens will respect, & to which your friends can appeal. At the present crisis, what would the former think, what could the latter say? The real motives, whatever they might be would either not be admitted or could not be explained; and if they should be viewed as satisfactory at a future day, the intermediate effects would not be lessened & could not be compen-sated. I am anxious to see what reception Genest will find in Philada. I hear that the fiscal party in Alexa. was an overmatch for those who wished to testify the American sentiment. George Town it is said re-paired the omission. A public dinner was intended for him at Fredericks-burg, but he passed with such rapidity that the compliment miscarried. It would not be amiss, if a knowledge of this could be in a proper mode get to him. I think it certain that he will be misled if he takes either the fashionable cant of the Cities or the cold caution of the Govt. for the sense of the public;[2] and I am equally persuaded that nothing but the habit of implicit respect will save the Executive from blame if thro' the mask of Neutrality, a secret Anglomany should betray itself. I forgot when I requested your attention to my plows to ask the favor of you to pay for them, & to let me know the amount of your several advances. Yours always & affy.

Js. Madison Jr

The plows are to be consigned to the care of Mr. Jno. Anderson Mercht: Fredg. Billy at Mrs. Houses was charged to look out for the first Vessel that offers. If the Newspapers shd. present one to your eye be so good as to let him have notice that he put them on board.

RC (DLC). Docketed by Jefferson, "recd. June 4."

1. Jefferson to JM, 13 May 1793.

2. For a Federalist perspective on Genet's reception in America, see John Steele to Alexander Hamilton, 30 Apr. 1793 (Syrett and Cooke, *Papers of Hamilton*, 14:358–60).

From Thomas Jefferson

May 27. 1793.

I wrote you last on the 19th. The doubts I then entertained that the offers from the Fr. rep. would be declined, will pretty certainly be realized. One person represents them as a snare into which he hopes we shall not fall. His second of the same sentiment of course. He whose vote for the most part, or say always, is casting, has by two or three private conversations or rather disputes with me, shewn his opinion to be against doing what would be a mark of predilection to one of the parties, tho not a breach of neutrality in form. And an opinion of still more importance is still in the same way. I do not know what line will be adopted: but probably a procrastination, which will be immediately seen through. You will see in the papers two blind stories, the one that DuMourier is gone over to the Austrians; the other that he has cut to peices 10,000 Prussians, & among them the K. of Prussia & D. of Brunswick. The latter has come through another channel, placing Custiné instead of Du-Mourier, & sayg nothing of the K. & Duke. But no attention is paid to either story. We want an intelligent prudent native, who will go to reside at N. Orleans as a secret correspondent, for 1000. D. a year. He might do a little business, merely to cover his real office. Do point out such a one. Virginia ought to offer more loungers equal to this & ready for it, than any other state. Adieu. Yours affectionately.

RC (DLC); FC, Tr (DLC: Jefferson Papers). Unsigned.

To Thomas Jefferson

DEAR SIR   ORANGE May 29. 93.

I wrote you two or three days ago with an inclosure of Newspapers &c since which I have been favored with yours of the 19th. I thank you for the plans & observations which far exceeded the trouble I meant to give you. The sentiments expressed by Genest would be of infinite service at this crisis. As a regular publication of them cannot be expected till the meeting of Congress, if then, it were to be wished they could in some other mode make their way to the press. If he expressed the substance of them in his verbal answer to the address, or announces them in open conversation, the Printers might surely hand them to the public. The affection to France in h⟨er st⟩ruggles for liberty would not only be increased by a knowledge that she does not wish us to go to war; but prudence would give its sanction to a bolder enunciation of the popular sentiment. I inclose a letter to the French Minister of the Interior which has been written some time. I pray you to look it over with an eye to every proper consideration, and if you find a particle in it wrong or doubtful not to seal & forward it, till I have an opportunity of makg. the requisite variations. I hope your model of the Threshing Machine is by this time arrived & answerable to expectation. You will have much use for it if your harvest should turn out according to the promises of our fields in this quarter. Wheat was never known to be more uniformly excellent. Adieu. Yrs. always & affy.

Js. MADISON JR

RC (DLC). Damaged by removal of seal. Docketed by Jefferson, "recd. June 6." Enclosure not found, but see JM to the minister of the interior of the French republic, April 1793, and n.

From Thomas Jefferson

June 2. 1793.

I wrote you on the 27th. Ult. You have seen in the papers that some privateers have been fitted out in Charleston by French citizens, with their own money, manned by themselves, & regularly commissioned by their nation. They have taken several prizes & brought them into our ports. Some native citizens had joined them. These are arrested & under prosecution, & orders are sent to all the ports to prevent the equipping privateers by any persons foreign or native. So far is right. But the vessels so equipped at Charleston are ordered to leave the ports of the US. This I think was not right. Hammond demanded further a surrender of the prizes they had taken. This is refused, on the principle that by the laws of war the property is transferred to the captors. You will see, in a paper I inclose, DuMourier's address to his nation, & also Saxe Cobourg's. I am glad to see a probability that the constitution of 1791. would be the term at which the combined powers would stop.[1] Consequently that the reestablishment of that is the worst the French have to fear. I am also glad to see that the combiners adopt the slow process of nibbling at the strong posts on the frontiers. This will give to France a great deal of time. The thing which gives me uneasiness is their internal combustion. This may by famine be rendered extreme. E. R. sets out, the day after tomorrow, for Virginia. I have no doubt he is charged to bring back a faithful statement of the dispositions of that state. I wish therefore he may fall into hands which will not deceive him. Have you time & the means of impressing Wilson Nicholas, (who will be much with E. R.) with the necessity of giving him a strong & perfect understanding of the public mind?[2] Considering that this journey may strengthen his nerves, and dispose him more favorably to the proposition of a treaty between the two republics, knowing that in this moment the division on that question is 4. to 1. & that the last news has no tendency to proselyte any of the majority, I have myself proposed to refer taking up the question till his return. There is too at this time a lowering disposition perceivable both in England & Spain. The former keeps herself aloof & in a state of incommunication with us, except in the way of demand. The latter has not begun auspiciously with C. & S. at Madrid,[3] and has lately sent 1500. men to N. Orleans, and greatly strengthened her upper posts on the Missisipi. I think it more probable than otherwise that Congress will be convened before the constitutional day. About the last of July this may be known. I should myself wish to keep their meeting off to the beginng of October, if affairs will permit it. The invasion of the Creeks is what will most likely occasion it's convocation. You will see mrs. House's death mentioned in the papers.[4] She extinguished almost like a candle. I have not seen mrs. Trist since, but I am told she means to give up the house immediately, & that she has suffered great loss in her own fortune by exertions hitherto to support it. Browse is not returned, nor has been heard of for some time. Bartram[5] is extremely anxious to get a large supply of seeds of the Kentucky coffee tree. I told him I would use all my interest with you to obtain it, as I think I heard you say that some neighbor of yours had a large number of the trees. Be so good as to take measures for bringing a good quantity if possible to Bartram when you come to Congress. Adieu. Yours affectionately.

RC (DLC); FC (DLC: Jefferson Papers). Unsigned. RC addressed by Jefferson.

1. Charles François Dumouriez's letter of 2 Apr. "to the French Nation" and the duke of Saxe-Coburg's proclamation of 5 Apr. (*Federal Gazette*, 1 June 1793). Dumouriez, commander of the French army in the Austrian Netherlands, was defeated by Saxe-Coburg at Neerwinden and defected to the Austrians. Dumouriez's letter and Saxe-Coburg's proclamation pledged to restore the French Constitution of 1791.

2. Edmund Randolph married Wilson Cary Nicholas's sister Elizabeth in 1776. On 24 June 1793 he reported to Washington his impressions of Virginians' opinions on the Neutrality Proclamation (Conway, *Edmund Randolph*, pp. 36, 151–53).

3. William Carmichael and William Short were in Madrid as commissioners negotiating a treaty with Spain.

4. Mrs. Mary House died on 28 May. Her boardinghouse at Fifth and Market streets had been JM's lodging in Philadelphia (*Federal Gazette*, 29 May 1793).

5. The naturalist William Bartram and his brother, John, Jr., were partners in a botanical garden at Kingsessing, across the Schuylkill River from the house Jefferson was renting at Gray's Ferry (Jefferson to Martha Jefferson Randolph, 26 May 1793, Ford, *Writings of Jefferson*, 6:267).

From Thomas Jefferson

June 9. 1793.

I have to acknolege the receipt of your two favors of May 27. & 29. since the date of my last which was of the 2d. inst. In that of the 27th. you say 'you must not make your final exit from public life till it will be marked with justifying circumstances which all good citizens will respect, & to which your friends can appeal.' To my fellow-citizens the debt of service has been fully & faithfully paid. I acknolege that such a debt exists: that a tour of duty, in whatever line he can be most useful to his country, is due from every individual. It is not easy perhaps to say of what length exactly this tour should be. But we may safely say of what length it should not be. Not of our whole life, for instance, for that would be to be born a slave. Not even of a very large portion of it. I have now been in the public service four & twenty years; one half of which has been spent in total occupation with their affairs, & absence from my own. I have served my tour then. No positive engagement, by word or deed, binds me to their further service. No commitment of their interests in any enterprize by me requires that I should see them through it. I am pledged by no act which gives any tribunal a call upon me before I withdraw. Even my enemies do not pretend this. I stand clear then of public right in all points. My friends I have not committed. No circumstances have attended my passage from office to office, which could lead them, & others through them, into deception as to the time I might remain; & particularly they & all have known with what reluctance I engaged & have continued in the present one, & of my uniform determination to retire from it at an early day. If the public then has no claim on me, & my friends nothing to justify, the decision will rest on my own feelings alone. There has been a time when these were very different from what they are now: when perhaps the esteem of the world was of higher value in my eye than every thing in it. But age, experience & reflection, preserving to that only it's due value, have set a higher on tranquility. The motion of my blood no longer keeps time with the tumult of the world. It leads me to seek for happiness in the lap and love of my family, in the society of my neighbors & my books, in the wholesome occupations of my farm & my affairs, in an interest or affection in every bud that opens, in every breath that blows around me, in an entire freedom of rest or motion, of thought or incogitancy, owing account to myself alone of my hours & actions. What must be the principle of that calculation which should balance against these the circumstances of my present existence! Worn down with labours from morning till night, & day to day; knowing them as fruitless to others as they are vexatious to myself, committed singly in desperate & eternal contest against a host who are systematically undermining the public liberty & prosperity, even the rare hours of relaxation sacrificed to the society of persons in the same intentions, of whose hatred I am conscious even in those moments of conviviality when the heart wishes most to open itself to the effusions of friendship & confidence, cut off from my family & friends, my affairs abandoned to chaos & derangement, in short giving every thing I love, in exchange for every thing I hate, and all this without a single gratification in possession or prospect, in present enjoyment or future wish. Indeed my dear friend, duty being out of the question, inclination cuts of[f] all argument, & so never let there be more between you & me, on this subject.

I inclose you some papers which have passed on the subject of a new loan. You will see by them that the paper-Coryphæus is either undaunted, or desperate. I believe that the statement inclosed has secured a decision against his proposition.[1] I dined yesterday in a company where Morris & Bingham were, & happened to set between them. In the course of a conversation after a dinner Morris made one of his warm declarations that, after the expiration of his present Senatorial term, nothing on earth should ever engage him to serve again in any public capacity. He did this with such solemnity as renders it impossible he should not be in earnest. The President is not well. Little lingering fevers have been hanging about him for a week or ten days, and have affected his looks most remarkeably. He is also extremely affected by the attacks made & kept up on him in the public papers. I think he feels those things more than any person I ever yet met with. I am sincerely sorry to see them. I remember an observation of yours, made when I first went to New York, that the satellites & sycophants which surrounded him had wound up the ceremonials of the government to a pitch of stateliness which nothing but his personal character could have supported, & which no character after him could ever maintain. It appears now that even his will be insufficient to justify them in the appeal of the times to common sense as the arbiter of every thing. Naked he would have been sanctimoniously reverenced. But inveloped in the rags of royalty, they can hardly be torn off without laceration. It is the more unfortunate that this attack is planted on popular ground, on the love of the people to France & it's cause, which is universal. Genet mentions freely enough in conversation that France does not wish to involve us in the war by our guarantee. The information from St. Domingo & Martinique is that those two islands are disposed & able to resist any attack which Great Britain can make on them by land. A blockade would be dangerous, could it be maintained in that climate for any length of time. I delivered to Genet your letter to Roland. As the latter is out of office, he will direct it to the Minister of the Interior. I found every syllable of it strictly proper. Your ploughs shall be duly attended to. Have you ever taken notice of Tull's horse-houghing plough?[2] I am persuaded that that, where you wish your work to be very exact, & our great plough where a less degree will suffice, leave us nothing to wish for from other countries as to ploughs, under our circumstances. I have not yet received my threshing machine. I fear the late long & heavy rains must have extended to us, & affected our wheat. Adieu. Your's affectionately.

RC (DLC); FC (DLC: Jefferson Papers). Unsigned. Enclosures not found, but see n. 1.

1. Presumably Jefferson meant Hamilton was the "paper-Coryphæus." Jefferson probably enclosed a copy of his 5 June opinion (Ford, *Writings of Jefferson*, 6:283–85) on Hamilton's proposal for a new Dutch loan of three million florins to be applied toward the refinancing of the U.S. public debt (Hamilton to Washington, 3 June 1793, Washington to Hamilton, 6 June 1793, Syrett and Cooke, *Papers of Hamilton*, 14:516, 521–22).

2. English agricultural reformer Jethro Tull described the "Four-coulter Plough" in his *Horse-Hoeing Husbandry* (4th ed.; London, 1762), pp. 285–307 and plate 1.

To Thomas Jefferson

MY DEAR SIR   ORANGE June 13. 93.

My last was of the 27 May.[1] It inclosed among other things a letter to the French Ministre de l'Interieur, in answer to one inclosing a Decree of the Nat: Assemb. On the propriety of the answer I wished your freest judgment; and as the sending one at all may be rendered by events improper, I must request the favor of you not to forward the letter, if intelligence should confirm such to be the State of things that it would be totally mal-apropos *there*. Provided it be proper there, and consequently proper in itself, I shall not trouble myself about any comments which the publication attending all such things, may produce here. The letter preceding my last as well as the last, contained some other papers which I wish to know have been reced.

Your two last favors were of May 27. & June 2. The latter confirms the apostacy of Dumourier, but relieves us from the more alarming account of his being supported in it by the army. Still however much is to be dreaded from the general posture of things. Should they take a turn decidedly wrong, I fear little regard will be paid to the limited object avowed by the Austrian General in his first proclamation. In fact if the plan of Dumourier had succeeded, it is probable that under the clause of the Proclamation relating to an amendment of imperfections in the Constitution of 1791 the form of the national sanction would have been obtained, as in the Restoration of Charles II, to whatever establishment military despotism might please to dictate. The only hope of France, next to the success of her own efforts, seems to lie in the number of discordant views of her combined enemies.

I observe that the Newspapers continue to criticise the President's proclamation; and I find that some of the criticisms excite the attention of dispassionate & judicious individuals here. I have heard it remarked by such with some surprise that the P. should have declared the U. S. to be neutral in the unqualified terms used, when we were so notoriously & unequivocally under *eventual engagements* to defend the American possessions of F. I have heard it remarked also that the impartiality enjoined on the people was as little reconciliable with their moral obligations, as the unconditional neutrality proclaimed by the Government is with the express articles of the Treaty. It has been asked also whether the Authority of the Executive extended by any part of the Constitution to a declaration of the *Disposition* of the U. S. on the subject of war & peace? I have been mortified that on these points I could offer no bona fide explanations that ought to be satisfactory. On the last point I must own my surprise that such a prerogative should have been exercised. Perhaps I may have not attended to some part of the Constitution with sufficient care, or may have misapprehended its meaning: But, as I have always supposed & still conceive, a proclamation on the subject could not properly go beyond a declaration of the fact that the U. S. were at war or peace, and an enjunction of a suitable conduct on the Citizens. The right to decide the question whether the duty & interest of the U. S. require war or peace under any given circumstances, and whether their disposition be towards the one or the other seems to be essentially & exclusively involved in the right vested in the Legislature, of declaring war in time of peace; and in the P. & S. of making peace in time of war. Did no such view of the subject present itself in the discussions of the Cabinet? I am extremely afraid that the P. may not be sufficiently aware of the snares that may be laid for his good intentions by men whose politics at bottom are very different from his own. An assumption of prerogatives not clearly found in the Constitution & having the appearance of being copied from a Monarchical model, will beget animadversion equally mortifying to him, & disadvantageous to the Government. Whilst animadversions of this sort can be plausibly ascribed to the spirit of party, the force of them may not be felt. But all his real friends will be anxious that his public conduct may bear the strictest scrutiny of future times as well as of the present day: and all such friends of the Constitution will be doubly pained at infractions of it under auspices that may consecrate the evil till it be incurable.

It will not be in my power to take the step with the Friend of our Friend, which you recommend.[2] It is probable too that it would be either unnecessary or without effect. If the complexion of the former be such as is presumed, he will fairly state the truth & that alone is wanted. If, as I deem not impossible, his complexion be a little different from the general belief, there would be more harm than good in the attempt. The great danger of misconstruing the sentiment of Virginia with regard to Liberty & France is from the heretical tone of conversation in the Towns on the post-road. The voice of the Country is universally and warmly right. If the popular disposition could be collected & carried into effect, a most important use might be made of it in obtaining contributions of the necessaries called for by the danger of famine in France. Unfortunately the disaffection of the Towns which alone could give effect to a plan for the purpose, locks up the public gratitude & beneficence.

Our fine prospects in the wheat fields have been severely injured by the weather for some time past. A warm & moist spring had pushed the wheat into rather a luxuriant state. It had got safe into the head however, and with tolerable weather would have ripened into a most exuberant crop. Just as the grain was in a milky state, the weather became wetter than ever, and has continued raining or cloudy almost constantly since. This has brought on a little of the rust, and pretty universally in this quarter a decay of the ear called the Rot. Should the weather be ever so favorable henceforward, a considerable proportion will be lost: And if unfavorable, the loss may be almost entire. We are at this moment both excessively wet & hot. The forwardest wheat is turning fast & may be nearly safe. The generality is not sufficiently advanced to be out of danger of future or beyond the effect of past causes.

The (Kentucky) Coffee Trees in this Neighbourhood are all too young to bear for some years. I will do all I can to get the seed for Bartram from Kentucky as soon as possible. Adieu.

RC (DLC). Unsigned. Docketed by Jefferson, "recd. June 22."

1. JM meant his letter to Jefferson of 29 May.
2. JM alluded to Jefferson's expressed hope that Wilson Cary Nicholas might exert his influence on Edmund Randolph (Jefferson to JM, 2 June 1793).

¶ From John Hatley Norton. Letter not found. *15 June 1793*. Acknowledged in JM to Norton, 12 Sept. 1793, which also mentions another letter (not found) from Norton. Both letters inquire about the possibility of presenting a claim to Congress for damages inflicted by Continental troops on houses in York County during the Revolution.

To Thomas Jefferson

Your favor of the 9th. I recd. late last night by a messenger from the neighbourhood of Fredg. who returns early this morning. I have therefore not had time to read the papers inclosed in it and even the letter itself but hastily. Its silence as to France is a cordial to the fears we have been kept in by the newspapers & reports here, of hearing every moment of her final catastrophe. If the army had stood by Dumourier's treason, as was the uncontradicted idea for a time, scarce a possibility seemed to remain of any other result. I fell in two days ago with French Strother who was returning circuitously from Richmond. He had seen W.[1] Nicholas on his way, & spoke of him as among the decided friends of the French cause. In general I discovered that his testimony and conviction corroborated the fact that the people of this country, where you can not trace the causes of particular exceptions, are unanimous & explicit in their sympathy with the Revolution. He was in Richmond during the session of the Court of the U. S. & heard the opinions of the Judges on the subject of the British debts. Jay's he says was that the depreciated paymts. into the Treasury discharged the debtor, but leave the State liable to the Creditor.[2] It would be a hard tax on those who have suffered themselves by the depreciation to bear such a burden. It would be severely felt by those who put money into the Treasury on loan & have received certificates by the scale, & those again further reduced by the modifications of the assumption. I asked S. who told me he was under the same roof with Jay & a good deal in his Society, what language he held on French topics. He never opened his lips, was the answer. In Fredg. on his way to Richmond, he was less reserved. I understood that in a conversation there with M. Page who was full of zeal, on the side of France, his enmity broke out in a very decided tone.

We have had no rain since my last which was of the 13th. The wheat however has continued to suffer, partly by the rust, but cheifly by the rot. In the lower country the damage is said to be very great. In this quarter I think very saving crops will be made; perhaps as much as would be called a good crop in ordinary years. Several fields I examined yesterday, will I am confident not lose as much by the late bad weather, as they had gained beyond the medium fecundity by the previous influence of the season. I have not heard from Albemarle, but have no reason to doubt that it has as good fare as its neighbour county. The harvest will commence in two or three days here.

My imagination has hunted thro' the whole State without being able to find a single character fitted for the mission to N. O. Young Marshal seems to possess some of the qualifications, but there would be objections of several sorts to him. In general the men of understanding in this Country are either preoccupied or too little acquainted with the world in the sense necessary for such functions. As a mercantile mask would be politic, the difficulty of providing a man here is the greater.

My plows I find have been finished & forwarded. They are not meant so much as innovations here, as models of a proper execution. One of them is the common barr share, the other a plow preferred in the practice of Dr. Logan. I have Tull & have noticed superficially that you allude to. We are not yet ripe for such nice work. In a former letter I asked the favor of you to see to the re-payment of the price, and must still rely on your goodness for that purpose. The price will be made known by Billey.[3] Yrs. always & affy.

J. M. JR.

RC (DLC). Addressed and marked *"private"* by JM. Docketed by Jefferson, "recd. June 27."

1. At a later time JM interlined "C" here.

2. Pre-Revolutionary debts owed to British creditors remained an unresolved issue after the U.S. circuit court at Richmond failed to reach a decision in *Jones* v. *Walker* in December 1791. Although the plaintiff (a British creditor) died, his executor continued the suit as *Ware* v. *Hylton* (3 Dallas 199). In 1779 the defendant had paid part of his debt into the Virginia loan office in accordance with a 1777 state law sequestering British debts and submitted in evidence a receipt signed by Jefferson as governor. On 7 June 1793 the circuit court upheld the validity of the debt except for that portion paid to the state. Chief Justice John Jay argued in a dissenting opinion that the debt-collecting provision in the Treaty of Paris of 1783 took precedence over the state law. In 1796 the Supreme Court overturned the circuit court ruling, on the same grounds Jay had argued in his dissent (Richard B. Morris, *John Jay: The Nation and the Court* [Boston, 1967], pp. 83–91; Charles F. Hobson, "The Recovery of British Debts in the Federal Circuit Court of Virginia, 1790 to 1797," *VMHB*, 92 [1984]: 187–92).

3. Jefferson paid William Gardner $34 for delivering the plow that George Logan had designed for JM. Gardner was the former slave Billey whom JM had manumitted. He had become a merchant's agent in Philadelphia (Ketcham, *James Madison*, p. 374; Brant, *Madison*, 3:380).

¶ From Thomas Jefferson. Letter not found. *17 June 1793.* Mentioned in Jefferson to JM, 23 June: "My last was of the 17th. if I may reckon a single line any thing." Acknowledged in JM to Jefferson, 29 June: "Your last was of the 17th. inst: & covered *one* paper of the 12th."

To Thomas Jefferson

DEAR SIR   ORANGE June 19. 1793.

The date of my last was the 17th. It acknowledged yours of the 9th.
instant. Our harvest commenced today. It will turn out I think far beyond expectation. On one of two little farms I own, which I have just
surveyed, the crop is not sensibly injured by either the rot or the rust,
and will yield 30 or 40 perCt. more than would be a good crop in ordinary years. This farm is on the Mountain Soil. The other is on a vein of
limestone and will be less productive, having suffered a little both from
the rot & the rust. My father's & brother's crops will not be inferior to
mine. From these samples, and those of the neighbourhood generally as
far as I am informed, the alarm which has of late prevailed is greater than
the calamity. I have not heard from the neighbourhood of Monticello,
but can not doubt that its situation ensures it an equal fortune with the
similar one here. The weather at present is extremely favorable for the
harvest, being dry. It is the reverse however for the laborers, being excessively hot. The Thermometer at this moment (4 OC. P. M.) is up
at 96°.

Every Gazette I see (excerpt [sic] that of the U. S.) exhibits a spirit
of criticism on the anglified complexion charged on the Executive politics. I regret extremely the position into which the P. has been thrown.
The unpopular cause of Anglomany is openly laying claim to him. His
enemies masking themselves under the popular cause of France are playing off the most tremendous batteries on him. The proclamation was in
truth a most unfortunate error. It wounds the National honor, by seeming to disregard the stipulated duties to France. It wounds the popular
feelings by a seeming indifference to the cause of liberty. And it seems
to violate the forms & spirit of the Constitution, by making the executive
Magistrate the organ of the disposition the duty & the interest of the
Nation in relation to war & peace, subjects appropriated to other departments of the Government. It is mortifying to the real friends of the P.
that his fame & his influence should have been unnecessarily made to
depend in any degree on political events in a foreign quarter of the
Globe: and particularly so that he should have any thing to apprehend
from the success of liberty in another country, since he owes his pre-
eminence to the success of it in his own. If France triumphs the ill-fated
proclamation will be a mill-stone, which would sink any other character,
and will force a struggle even on his.

Your plan is much approved & will be adopted by my brother. I find
I was misunderstood in my enquiry as to the proper width of the Portico: I did not mean the proportion it ought to bear to the side of the

House to which it is attached: but the interval between the columns & the side of the House; or the distance which the Pediment ought to project. If there be any fixt rule on this subject, I will thank you to intimate it in your next. Yrs. always & affey.

RC (DLC). Unsigned. Docketed by Jefferson, "recd. June 29."

From John Taylor

DEAR SIR   CAROLINE June 20. 1793

In coming from Philadelphia, alone, and meditative, after Congress had risen, the occurrences which had trodden on each others heels, in too rapid succession for much reflection during the session, began to pass muster in my mind, and to peice themselves together, so as to exhibit an unity of design. Connecting these with several important laws of the union, a variety of fantasies were engendered between them, some of which, like youthful dreams, made such an impression [on] me, that I have employed the few intervals of leisure which have occured, in writing them down. And they are now presented to you.

Several ideas and arguments, which I thought it adviseable to impress, are repeated. The impropriety of repetitions was not forgotten, but it was remembered that the performance was pro tempora—Oh tempora! The plagiarisms are few, and chiefly from myself. There is neither title or dedication. When the work was finished, I felt myself ready to exclaim, as Quin did on seeing a person ridiculously attired—

> "Angels & ministers of grace defend us!
> Be thou a spirit of grace or goblin damned,
> Bring with the[e] airs from heaven or blasts from hell,
> Be thy intents wicked or charitable,
> Thou comest in such a questionable shape,
> That I will speak to thee. I'll call thee—
> By G—d I don't know what to call thee." [1]

Some of my friends must therefore stand godfather to the brat, and baptize it, either with the holy ghost—or with fire.

And if Brutus could surmount a natural affection for his offspring of flesh and blood, so as calmly to behold the axe do its office, when the good of the commonwealth required it;[2] doubt not but that my amor patriæ, can in humble imitation of his Example, attain apathy enough towards mine of ink and paper, to bear with great composure its contorsions in the flames.

Having no private object in view, and knowing how much better you can judge of the publick good—besides you are impartial—I pray you to arrest without reserve this mischief—if it be a mischief. In this event, the only reprieve I will ask for it, is, that you will return it to me, to undergo perpetual imprisonment, by way of refining upon its punishment.

And if it is reclaimable by correction—correct it.

Should you approve of the production, ought it to appear in a pamp[h]let or in the newspapers. The latter are meer ephemere, and tho' containing merit, read & forgotten. The best political essays being often supposed to proceed from the printers in a course of trade. Besides the sphere of their circulation is circumscribed.

Or would it be proper to print it in phila., to be distributed either among the state assemblies at their fall meeting, or at the opening of the next Congress. In the latter case, to make a direct impression on the members of Congress; in the first, to subjoin the influence of their constituents.

The repeal of the bank law, and some emendations of the constitution, are the only fruits, to be expected from any such impression, and therefore it seems to me, that on the very meeting of the next Congress, a firm and bold attempt should be made to gather them.

Even a disapointment will not frustrate every use of such an attempt. It will operate as a check—gain time for new elections—and alarm the publick mind into a discussion of principles.

If the performance is adjudged worthy of being printed in a pamp[h]let, I submit it to you, whether it ought not to be done in the cheapest stile, for the sake of circulation, for it will hardly have merit enough to circulate itself.

But how is it to get printed? I would expend fifty dollars for my share, in that way, or more, if I ought.

I have not written to Mr: Jefferson, because a justification for wasting any portion of his time did not present itself. But if you have an opportunity, the production may be laid before him, and I hereby invest him with a power over it, coextensive with your own.

I would also wish Colo. Monroe to see it. And altho' it has been out of my power to prevent its being known here, that I have been writing something, it is my wish that no one else should be told what that something is.

If you could have been a week here, and the work is capable of being turned to any use, how useful might it have been made? Indeed you may yet give it great value, if you please. It begins and ends with a blank sheet.

Mr: Pendleton approves of its doctrines, and recommends its publication.

Through Randolph, whom I have not seen, I learn that the President believes, that the Virga. interest as it is called, designs to attack him, and that it gives him great unneasiness. Of what individuals he supposes the interest to be compounded, I know not. However this idea, with the comments on his conduct in the papers—the addressing arts—and the cunning insinuation, that the republicans mean to intimidate him, correspond to inlist him in a party. I am not so conversant in cabinet affairs, as to form even a conjecture, touching his reclaimability from this error, or whether a well manufactured dedication to him, would operate towards that object?

I am convinced from the same source, that no impression unfavourable to the se——y of the treasury, was made last winter, on the president's mind. R informed Mr: Pendleton, that the President thought him an honest man, and he brought & presented to him all Hamilton's reports, bound up in one book.

Besides, in the case touching the suability of a state, page 20. the attorney concludes his argument with these very extraordinary, and *unnecessary* expressions. "The states need not fear an assault from *bold ambition*, or any *approaches* of *covered stratagem*."[3] I consider him as the best thermometer by which to measure the president's opinions at present.

But to return to this same production. Let me ask, whether political rectitude will not suffer me to with:draw from the political world? If I can earn my wages, they are earned. My bolt is shot. If the publick good should be advanced by it, my discharge is demandable on the score of Service—if not, it will be due on the score of insufficiency. Cannot you think of some other as sharp set as I have been, to substitute in the place of one, gorged as I am, with publick service?

Besides, since I have been beating my brains for the good of the nation, two white hairs have appeared on the top of my head, and have caused me to think very gravely.

I give up the idea as to H.[4] It would probably succeed, but it might do mischief.

A man who has "given pledges to fortune," is confined within a magical circle, and can therefore promise nothing. Had my inclinations only governed my conduct, I should have accepted of your invitation without hesitation; but there are duties to be discharged.

And yet a trip to the mountains would probably help me, for I feel as if my malady last fall had regenerated me for the worse. Such a gratification of my wishes, would be a considerable consolation for a suspension of health. I am with great respect & esteem Yr: mo: obt: Sert.

JOHN TAYLOR

RC (DLC). Addressed by Taylor to JM at Orange. Docketed by JM. Taylor enclosed a draft (not found) of his pamphlet, *Enquiry into the Principles*. Portions of it were first printed in a Philadelphia newspaper (JM to Taylor, 20 Sept. 1793; Taylor to JM, 25 Sept. 1793).

1. James Quin, a famous Shakespearean actor on the English stage, parodied *Hamlet*, act 1, sc. 4, lines 39–44.

2. Lucius Junius Brutus was the founder of the Roman republic. When two of his sons were exposed in a conspiracy to restore the former king, Brutus as consul passed judgment on them and watched their execution (Plutarch, *Publicola*, ch. 6, *Plutarch's Lives* [1914–26 ed.], 1:515).

3. *A Case Decided in the Supreme Court of the United States, in February, 1793. In Which Is Discussed the Question—"Whether a State Be Liable to Be Sued by a Private Citizen of Another State?"* (Philadelphia, 1793; Evans 25370). JM's copy of this pamphlet is in the Madison Collection, Rare Book Department, University of Virginia Library. Attorney General Edmund Randolph was plaintiff's counsel in *Chisholm* v. *Georgia* (2 Dallas 429).

4. Benjamin Hawkins (see Taylor to JM, 11 May 1793).

From Thomas Jefferson

DEAR SIR   June 23. 1793.

My last was of the 17th. if I may reckon a single line any thing. Yours of the 13th. came to hand yesterday. The proclmn. as first proposed was to have been a declaration of neutrality. It was opposed on these grounds 1. that a declaration of neutrality was a declaration there should be no war, to which the Executive was not competent. 2. that it would be better to hold back the declaration of neutrality, as a thing worth something to the powers at war, that they would bid for it, & we might reasonably ask as a price, the *broadest privileges* of neutral nations. The 1st. objection was so far respected as to avoid inserting the term *neutrality*, & the drawing the instrument was left to E. R. That there should be a proclamn. was passed unanimously with the approbation or the acquiescence of all parties. Indeed it was not expedient to oppose it altogether, lest it should prejudice what was the next question, the boldest & greatest that ever was hazarded, and which would have called for extremities, had it prevailed. Spain is unquestionably picking a quarrel with us. A series of letters from her commissioners here prove it. We are sending a courier to Madrid. The inevitableness of war with the Creeks, and the probability, I might say the certainty of it with Spain (for there is not one of us who doubts it,) will certainly occasion your convocation. At what time I cannot exactly say. But you should be prepared for this important change in the state of things. The President is got pretty well again. He sets off this day to Mount Vernon, & will be absent a fortnight. The death of his manager, hourly expected, of a consumption, is the call.[1] He will consequently be absent on the 4th. of July. He travels in a Phaeton & pair. Doctr. Logan sends you the inclosed pamphlet.[2] Adieu. Your's affectionately.

RC (DLC); FC (DLC: Jefferson Papers). Unsigned. RC addressed by Jefferson. For enclosure, see n. 2.

1. Anthony Whitting died on 21 June (Freeman, *Washington*, 7:96).

2. Jefferson probably enclosed [George Logan], *Letters, Addressed to the Yeomanry of the United States: Shewing the Necessity of Confining the Public Revenue to a Fixed Proportion of the Net Produce of the Land; . . . By a Farmer* (Philadelphia, 1791; Evans 23507). JM's copy of this pamphlet is in the Madison Collection, Rare Book Department, University of Virginia Library.

To Thomas Jefferson

MY DEAR SIR   June 29. 93.

Your last was of the 17th. inst: & covered *one* paper of the 12th. The weather has been very unfavorable for saving our crops of wheat. It has been from the commencement of the harvest either rainy, cloudy, or hot & damp. I still hope however our crops will be respectable. I have not been able to learn how Albemarle has fared. I have no reason to apprehend that you have more to complain of than we have. The present appearance of the weather is rather favorable. A few days more will put the wheat out of its reach.

My last was of the 19th. I have since seen several of the Natl. Gazettes which continue to teem with animadversions on the Proclamn. My opinion of it was expressed in my last. I foresee that a communication of it will make a part of the Speech to the next Congs. & that it will bring on some embarrassments. Much will depend on events in Europe; and it is to be regretted that the popularity of the President, or the policy of our Government should ever be staked on such contingencies. I observe that our vessels are frequently & insolently seized & searched for French goods. Is not this complained of by our own people as a breach of the *Modern* law of nations; and whilst British goods are protected by the Neutrality of our bottoms, will not remonstrances come from France on the subject? The present conveyance to Fredg. being made known at this instant only, I am obliged to conclude in haste with assurances of the affection with which I remain Dear Sir Yrs. sincerely

J. M. JR

RC (DLC). Docketed by Jefferson, "recd. July 8."

From Thomas Jefferson

June 29. 1793.

I wrote you on the 23d. and yesterday I received yours of the 17th. which was the more welcome as it acknoleged mine of the 9th. about the safety of which I was anxious. I now risk some other papers, the sequel of those conveyed in that. The result I know not. We are sending a courier to Madrid to make a last effort for the preservation of honorable peace. The affairs of France are recovering their solidity: and from the steadiness of the people on the defection of so popular & capital a commander as Dumourier, we have a proof that nothing can shake their republicanism. Hunger is to be excepted; but the silence of the late papers on that head & the near approach of harvest makes us hope they will weather that rock. I do not find that there has been serious insurrection but in Brittany, and there, the noblesse having been as numerous as the people, & indeed being almost the people, the counterrevolutionary spirit has been known always to have existed since the night in which titles were suppressed. The English are trying to stop the torrent of bankruptcies by an emission of 5. millions of Exchequer bills, to be loaned on the pawn-broking plan: consequently much inferior to the assignats of France. But that paper will sink to an immediate level with their other public paper, & consequently can only complete the ruin of those who take it from government at par, & on a pledge of pins, buckles &c of double value, which will not sell so as to pay storage in a country where there is no specie, and now we may say no paper of confidence. Every letter which comes expresses a firm belief that the whole paper system will now vanish into that nothing on which it is bottomed. For even the public faith is nothing, as the mass of paper bottomed on it is known to be beyond it's possible redemption. I hope this will be a wholsome lesson to our future legislature. The war between France and England has brought forward the Republicans & Monocrats in every state so openly, that their relative numbers are perfectly visible. It appears that the latter are as nothing. H. is endeavoring to engage a house in town for the next year. He is in the country for the summer.

As I must ere long put my general plan of farming into the hands of my Elkton manager,[1] I have lately endeavored to establish a proper succession of crops for a farm of red highland of about 500. acres of open land fit for culture. In all successions of crops, the feilds must be supposed equal, each feild to go through the same succession, and each year's crop be the same. On these data, the laws of combination pronounce that the number of feilds & number of years constituting a compleat rotation, must be always equal. If you cultivate three equal feilds only, your rotation will be of 3. years, 5. feilds, 5 years &c. I propose 8. feilds of 60. acres

each, & of course an 8. years rotation, in the following succession. 1st.
year, wheat & fall fallow. 2d peas with Indn. corn thinly planted. 3d.
wheat & fall fallow. 4th. potatoes with Indn. corn thinly planted. 5th.
rye or barley & fall fallow. 6th. 7th. & 8th. red clover. The following
diagram will shew the system better; the initials of every article only
being written in each square or feild, to wit   cl. for clover

				co.	corn
f.	fallow
pe.	peas
po.	potatoes
r.	rye
w.	wheat.

	1st year	2d	3d	4th	5th	6th	7th	8th
A	wf	pe. co.	wf	po. co.	rf	cl.	cl.	cl.
B	pe. co.	wf.	po. co.	rf.	cl.	cl.	cl.	wf.
C	wf	po. co.	rf.	cl.	cl.	cl.	wf.	pe. co.
D	po. co.	rf.	cl.	cl.	cl.	wf.	pe. co.	wf.
E.	rf.	cl.	cl.	cl.	wf.	pe. co.	wf.	po. co.
F	cl.	cl.	cl.	wf.	pe. co.	wf.	po. co.	rf.
G	cl.	cl.	wf.	pe. co.	wf.	po. co.	rf.	cl.
H.	cl.	wf	pe. co.	wf	po. co.	rf.	cl.	cl.

This gives 2. feilds of wheat   120. acres
   1.   of rye or barly   60
   1.   of peas & corn   60
   1.   of potatoes & corn   60.
   1. of the 1st. year's clover   60
   1. 2d.   do   60
   1. 3d.   do.   60
                  480.

Also 2. eighths of your farm are cleansing ⎫
  3. eighths   fallowing ⎬ every year.
  3. eighths   resting ⎭
  8.

Bye articles as follow.
Oats & flax, a few acres only wanting. To be with the new sown clover.
Hemp, turneps, pumpkins, in the new clearings.
Artichokes in a perpetual feild.
Orchard grass in the hill sides too steep for the plough. Qu?
Lucerne, St. foin, cotton, in appropriate feilds.
Buckwheat to be ploughed into the washed lands.
When a 9th. feild shall be added by new clearings, add it to the rotation
as a feild at absolute rest or spring fallowed.
So of a 10th. &c.
As you are now immersed in farming & among farming people, pray
consider this plan for me, well, and give me your observations fully &
freely as soon as you can. I mean to ask the same from the President, and
also from my son in law. Cattle to be raised in proportion to the provision
made for them. Also what number of labourers & horses will be necessary? Errors are so much more easy to avoid than to correct afterwards,
that I am anxious to be well advised before I begin. Adieu, Yours affectionately.

P. S. June 30. Since writing the above yours of June 19. is received. A
Portico may be from 5. to 10. diameters of the column deep, or projected
from the building. If of more than 5. diameters there must be a column in
the middle of each flank, since it must never be more than 5. diameters
from center to center of column. The portico of the Maison quarrée[2] is
3 intercolonnations deep. I never saw as much to a private house. The
Commissioners (Irvine &c) yesterday delivered in their books & accounts,[3] so that that business is closed. The result not yet known. In
Fenno's paper of yesterday you will see a peice signed pacificus[4] in defence of the proclmn. You will readily know the pen. I know it the more
readily because it is an amplification only of the topics urged in discussing the question when first proposed. The right of the *Executive* to

declare that we are *not bound to execute the guarantee* was then advanced by him & denied by me. No other opinion expressed on it. In this paper he repeats it, & even considers the proclamation as such a declaration. But if any body intended it as such (except himself) they did not then say so. The passage beginning with the words 'the answer to this is &c['] is precisely the answer he gave at the time to my objection that the Executive had no authority to issue a declaration of neutrality, nor to do more than declare the actual state of things to be that of peace. 'For until the new government is acknoleged the treaties &c are of course suspended.' This also is the sum of his arguments the same day on the great question which followed that of the Proclamn., to wit Whether the Executive might not, & ought not to declare the treaties suspended? The real—milk and water—views of the Proclamn. appeared to me to have been truly given in a piece[5] published in the papers soon after, & which I knew to be E. R's from it's exact coincidence with what he had expressed. Upon the whole, my objections to the competence of the Executive to declare neutrality (that being understood to respect the future) were supposed to be got over by avoiding the use of that term. The declaration of the *disposition* of the US. can hardly be called illegal, tho' it was certainly officious & improper. The truth of the fact lent it some cover. My objections to the impolicy of a premature declaration were answered by such arguments as timidity would readily suggest. I now think it extremely possible that Hammond might have been instructed to have asked it, & to offer *the broadest neutral privileges*, as the price, which was exactly the price I wanted that we should contend for. But is it not a miserable thing that the three heresies I have above quoted from this paper, should pass unnoticed & unanswered, as they certainly will? For none but mere bunglers & brawlers have for some time past taken the trouble to answer any thing. The Probationary odes (written by S. G. T. in Virga.) are saddled on poor Freneau,[6] who is bloodily attacked about them.

RC (DLC); FC, partial Tr (DLC: Jefferson Papers). Unsigned. Jefferson made several minor additions to the RC that do not appear on the FC or partial Tr. Enclosures not found.

1. Late in 1792 Jefferson hired Samuel Biddle of Elkton, Maryland, as overseer of Monticello. He took up his duties in October 1793 (Betts, *Jefferson's Garden Book*, pp. 182–84).
2. During his term as U.S. minister to France, Jefferson admired the Maison Carrée, the first century B.C. Roman temple at Nîmes. He used it as the model of his design for the Virginia Capitol at Richmond (Jefferson to JM, 20 Sept. 1785, *PJM*, 8:367, 369 n. 1).
3. "Report of the Commissioners of Accounts of the balances due to and from the several States" (*ASP, Miscellaneous*, 1:ix, 69).

4. Printed in Syrett and Cooke, *Papers of Hamilton*, 15:33–43.

5. On 29 Apr. *Dunlap's Am. Daily Advertiser* published an unsigned and un-titled article that defended the administration's neutrality policy by arguing that France had not requested American military support in the present war under the terms of the 1778 treaty. No evidence has been found to substantiate Jefferson's attribution of this article to Edmund Randolph, although that newspaper later published his "Germanicus" essays (see Monroe to JM, 18 Feb. 1795, n. 1).

6. Philip Freneau's Philadelphia *National Gazette* anonymously published St. George Tucker's "Probationary Odes of Jonathan Pindar" in thirteen installments from June through September 1793. The series was reprinted as a pamphlet in 1796 (Evans 31320).

From Thomas Jefferson

DEAR SIR   July 7. 1793.

I wrote you on the 30th. ult. and shall be uneasy till I have heard you have received it. I have no letter from you this week. You will perceive by the inclosed papers that they are to be discontinued in their present form & a daily paper published in their stead, *if subscribers enough can be obtained*. I fear they cannot, for nobody here scarcely has ever taken his paper. You will see in these Colo. H's 2d. & 3d. pacificus.[1] Nobody answers him, & his doctrine will therefore be taken for confessed. For god's sake, my dear Sir, take up your pen, select the most striking heresies, and cut him to peices in the face of the public. There is nobody else who can & will enter the lists with him. Never in my opinion, was so calami-tous an appointment made, as that of the present minister of F. here. Hotheaded, all imagination, no judgment, passionate, disrespectful & even indecent towards the P. in his written as well as verbal communica-tions, talking of appeals from him to Congress, from them to the people, urging the most unreasonable & groundless propositions, & in the most dictatorial style &c. &c. &c. If ever it should be necessary to lay his com-munications before Congress or the public, they will excite universal indignation. He renders my position immensely difficult. He does me justice personally, and, giving him time to vent himself & then cool, I am on a footing to advise him freely, & he respects it. But he breaks out again on the very first occasion, so as to shew that he is incapable of correcting himself. To complete our misfortune we have no channel of our own through which we can correct the irritating representations he may make. Adieu. Yours affectionately.

RC (DLC); FC (DLC: Jefferson Papers); Tr (MHi). Unsigned.

1. Philadelphia *Gazette of the U.S.*, 3 and 6 July 1793; reprinted in Syrett and Cooke, *Papers of Hamilton*, 15:55–63, 65–69.

From Thomas Jefferson

July 14. 93.

I wrote you on the 7th. since which yours of the 29th. of June is received acknoledging mine to the 17th. of June. I am anxious to know as early as possible the *safe* delivery of my letters to you. I am not able to say any thing more about the convening of Congress at an earlier day than the regular one. I have lately suspected some disinclination to it. But the grounds are slight. I must see you & be with you some days before it meets. Whether here or at Monticello must depend on the time of it's meeting. But we shall have warning enough to arrange the particulars. I am excessively afraid that an open rupture will take place between the Fr. min. & us. I think there has been something to blame on both sides, but much more on his. He is so evidently in the wrong that those are pressing for an appeal to the people, who never looked towards that tribunal before. They know too well that the whole game is played into their hands, & that there is right enough on both sides to marshal each nation with it's own agents, and consequently against one another, & consequently also us with England. I have written a long letter to-day to Munroe, & must therefore be shorter with you. Adieu. Your's affectionately.

RC (DLC); FC (DLC: Jefferson Papers). Unsigned. In the place of the salutation, Jefferson wrote and apparently tried to erase "Dear."

To Thomas Jefferson

DEAR SIR   July 18. 1793

The season of harvest havg. suspended all intercourse with Fredg. your favor of the 7th. inst: has but just been recd. That of the 29th. Ult: came to hand at the same time. The preceding one of the 23d. would have been acknowledged before but for the cause above mentioned. The present is the first opportunity and like several others leaves me but a moment to prepare for it.

I have read over the subject which you recommend to my attention. It excites equally surprise & indignation, and ought certainly to be taken notice of by some one who can do it justice. In my present disposition which is perfectly alienated from such things, and in my present situation which deprives me of some material facts and many important lights, the task would be in bad hands if I were otherwise better qualified for it. I am in hopes of finding that some one else has undertaken it. In the mean time I will feel my own pulse, and if nothing appears, may possibly try to supply the omission. Return my thanks to Docr. Logan for the pamphlet & also for the plows arrived at Fredg, tho' by a singular succession of errors & accidents lie still on the road between this and that. Your acct. of G——[1] is dreadful. He must be brought right if possible. His folly will otherwise do mischief which no wisdom can repair. Is there no one thro' whom he can be *effectually* counselled. D. L. F:[2] is said to be able, and if himself rightly disposed as I have understood him to be, might perhaps be of great use. The result of the Harvest is perhaps less favorable than I once supposed. I hope however the crop of wheat as to quantity at least will be tolerable. Of the quality I have great apprehensions. The season for getting it in was as bad as was possible. Every other article of our cultivation is prosperous, and will help to make amends, if the rest of the year be favorable. The corn is particularly luxurient in all quarters. Yrs. always & affy

RC (DLC). Unsigned. Docketed by Jefferson, "recd July 29."

1. At a later time JM added the remaining letters of "Genet."
2. At a later time JM added the remaining letters of "De La Forest." The comte de La Forest, who had held French diplomatic posts in America since 1783, became consul general for New York, Pennsylvania, New Jersey, and Delaware in October 1792 (Abraham P. Nasatir and Gary Elwyn Monell, *French Consuls in the United States: A Calendar of Their Correspondence in the Archives Nationales* [Washington, 1967], pp. 560–61).

From Thomas Jefferson

July 21. 93.

I wrote you on the 14th. since which I have no letter from you. It appears that two considerable engagements took place between France & the combined armies on the 1st. & 8th. of May. In the former the French have had rather the worst of it, as may be concluded by their loss of cannon & loss of ground. In the latter they have had rather the best: as is proved by their remaining on the ground, & their throwing relief into Condé which had been the object of both battles. The French attacked in both. They have sent commissioners to England to sound for peace. Genl. Felix Wimpfen is one. There is a strong belief that the bankruptcies & demolition of manufactures through the three kingdoms, will induce the English to accede to peace. E. R. is returned. The affair of the loan has been kept suspended, & is now submitted to him.[1] He brings very flattering information of the loyalty of the people of Virginia to the general government, & thinks the whole indisposition there is directed against the Secretary of the Treasury *personally*, not against his measures. On the whole he has quieted uneasiness here. I have never been able to get a sight of Billy till yesterday. He has promised to bring me the bill of your ploughs which shall be paid. Adieu. Your's affectionately.

RC (DLC); FC (DLC: Jefferson Papers). Unsigned.

1. Washington wanted more time to consider Hamilton's proposal for a new Dutch loan and solicited further information and opinions from cabinet members (Hamilton to Washington, 15 and 24 June 1793, Washington to Hamilton, 20 June 1793, Syrett and Cooke, *Papers of Hamilton*, 14:550–54, 15:9–10, 21–24; Jefferson, "Second Opinion on New Loan," 17 June 1793, Ford, *Writings of Jefferson*, 6:303–6).

To Thomas Jefferson

DEAR SIR   July 22. 1793

My last was on the 18th. and acknowledged yours of the 30th. ult:[1] & 7th. inst. I had not then time to mention that W. N.[2] passd. an evening with me on his way home from his brother's where he had met E. R.[3] on his return to Pha. From his conversation, his sentiments are right & firm on the French Revoln. and in other respects I discovered no symptoms of heresy. He spoke particularly & emphatically of the unquestionable unanimity of the Country in favor of the cause of F. I have no doubt that he held this language to every one, and consequently that the impressions depending on him have been rightly made. I could not but infer from all that he said with regard to E. R. that he considered the sentiments of him on French affairs as similar to his own, and to such as were expressed by myself. Some allowance however in all such conversations must be made for the politeness or policy of respecting the known sentiments of the party to which they are addressed or communicated. He had seen the first part of H's publication[4] and spoke of it as from that quarter. He expressed some surprise at the doctrines & cabinet efforts of the Author as he had learnt them from E. R. and seemed unable to account for some things without suspecting H. of a secret design to commit and sacrifice the Pt. His ideas on this subject must have grown out of the language of E. R. if not actually copied from it. I have read over with some attention the *printed* papers you inclosed, and have made notes towards a discussion of the subject.[5] I find myself however under some difficulties first from my not knowing how far concessions have been made on particular points behind the curtain, 2dly. from my not knowing how far the P. considers himself as actually committed with respect to some doctrines, 3dly. from the want of some lights from the Law of Nations as applicable to the construction of the Treaty, 4th. from my ignorance of some material facts—such as whether any call was made by G. B, or any other Belligerent power for the intentions of the U. S. prior to the Proclamation—whether F. was heard on the subject of her constructions & pretensions under the Treaty—whether the Ex. had before them any authentic documents or entered into any discussions, on the question whether the war between F. & G. B is offensive or defensive &c: I do not mean that all such information ought to be brought into the controversy, tho' some of it is necessary & some more might be used to advantage. But all or most of it seems proper in order to avoid vulnerable assertions or suppositions which might give occasion to tr[i]umphant replies. If an answer to the publication be undertaken, it ought to be both a solid, and a prudent one. None but intelligent readers will enter into such a controversy, and to their minds it ought principally to be accomodated. If you can lay your hands on the Explanatory publication of the real object of the Proclamn.[6] referred to in your last, or the preceding one, send it to me. The one I had is no longer in my hands. I expect to day to receive your letter next in date to the 7th.

RC (DLC). Unsigned. Docketed by Jefferson, "recd. Aug. 1."

1. JM referred to Jefferson's letter of 29 June, which had a postscript of 30 June.

2. At a later time JM here interlined "W. C. Nicholas."

3. At a later time JM here interlined "Ed: Randolph."

4. "Pacificus" No. 1.

5. JM's "notes" were drafts of the "Helvidius" essays.

6. On the newspaper essay, which Jefferson attributed to Edmund Randolph, concerning the Neutrality Proclamation, see Jefferson to JM, 29 June 1793, and n. 5.

From Thomas Jefferson

July 28. 93.

Your last was of June 29. acknoledging mine of the 17th. Since that I wrote you June 23. 29. July 1.[1] 7. 14 & 22.[2] I have only time to mention the death of Roger Sherman.[3] Adieu.

July 28. 93.

Your last received was of June 29. which acknoleged a scrip of mine of June 17. Consequently my subsequent letters of June. 23. 29. July 1. 7. 14. & 22. are unacknoleged, and give me so much anxiety lest some infidelity should be practised on the road, that I am afraid to do any thing more than warn you of it, if it should be so. I will send this through mr. Maury, and the newspaper as usual through mr. Blair. If there is any thing wrong this may get to you. Roger Sherman is dead. Adieu.

FC (DLC: Jefferson Papers); Tr (ViU). Unsigned. Jefferson probably cut the RC (not found) in two and enclosed the briefer message with newspapers sent via James Blair in Fredericksburg.

1. Letter not found (also listed in Jefferson's Epistolary Record [DLC: Jefferson Papers]).

2. Jefferson no doubt meant his letter of 21 July.

3. Sherman, who served with JM in the Continental Congress, Federal Convention, and House of Representatives, died on 23 July.

To Thomas Jefferson

DEAR SIR   July 30. 1793

My last was of the 22d inst. I have since red. yours covering the paper now returned, that covering the report of the Commsrs of Accts between the U. S. & the particular States, and that of the 21st. inst. The intermediate one of the 14th. was left by mistake in a secure place by the person who was to bring it up from Fredg., and is not yet arrived. The delay has been inconvenient as it deprives me of part of the publication which I wish to see in all its parts before I formed a regular view of any. As I intimated in my last I have forced myself into the task of a reply. I can truly say I find it the most grating one I ever experienced; and the more so as I feel at every step I take the want of counsel on some points of delicacy as well as of information as to sundry matters of fact. I shall be still more sensible of the latter want when I get to the attack on French proceedings, & perhaps to the last topic proposed by the writer, if I ever do get to it. As yet I have but roughly and partially gone over the first; & being obliged to proceed in scraps of time, with a distaste to the subject, and a distressing lassitude from the excessive and continued heat of the season, I can not say when I shall finish even that. One thing that particularly vexes me is that I foreknow from the prolixity & pertinacity of the writer, that the business will not be terminated by a single fire, and of course that I must return to the charge in order to prevent a triumph without a victory.

Do you know what is the idea of France with regard to the defensive quality of the Guarantee;[1] and of the criterion between offensive & defensive war which I find differently defined by different jurists; also what are the ideas of the P. on these points. I could lay my course with more advantage thro' some other parts of the subject if I could also know how far he considers the Procln. as expressing a neutrality in the sense given to that term, or how far he approves the vindication of it on that ground.

I am sorry to find the journey to Virga. from which useful lessons were hoped, ending in a confirmation of errors.[2] I can only account for it by supposing the public sentiment to have been collected from tainted sources wch. ought to have suggested to a cautious & unbiassed mind the danger of confiding in them. The body of the people are unquestionably attached to the Union, and friendly to the Constitution: but that they have no dissatisfaction at the measures & spirit of the Government, I consider as notoriously untrue. I am the more surprised at the misconception of our Friend as the two latest sources consulted, the two brothers[3] I mean, are understood to be both of them, right[l]y disposed as well as correctly informed.

I have got my plows at last. They are fine ones & much admired. Repeat my thanks to Dr. Logan if you have an oppy. & think of it. The *patent plow* is worth your looking at if you should visit his farm. You will see your theory of a mouldboard[4] more nearly realised than in any other instance, and with the advantage of having the iron wing, which in common bar shares or in great lies useless under the wood, turned up into the sweep of the Board & relieving it from the brunt of the friction. By fixing the Colter, which is detached, to the point of the share, it will I think be nearly compleat. I propose to have one so constructed. The detached form may answer best in old clean ground; but will not stand the shocks of our rough & rooty land, especially in the hands of our ploughmen.

Little wheat having been yet tried in bread I can not say how the quality will turn out. The more I see & hear of it, the more I fear it will be worse than was at first supposed. The Corn suffers now for want of rain, but appearances as to that article are on the whole very flattering. The worst effect of the dry weather, at present felt, is the extreme hardness of the earth which makes plowing, particularly in fallow land, but barely possible. So many heavy rains on ground wet for six months, succeeded by the present hot spell, has almost beat it & baked it into Brick.

RC (DLC). Unsigned. Docketed by Jefferson, "recd. Aug. 9."

1. By article 11 of the Franco-American alliance treaty of 1778, the U.S. undertook to defend the French West Indies (Miller, *Treaties and Other International Acts*, 2:39).

2. JM alluded to Edmund Randolph's recent sounding of political opinion in Virginia.

3. John and Wilson Cary Nicholas.

4. For documents relating to Jefferson's experiments with the "mouldboard of least resistance," see Betts, *Jefferson's Farm Book*, pp. 47-50.

From Thomas Jefferson

Aug. 3. 93.

Yours of July 18. & 22. are received & have relieved my anxi[e]ties about mine of June 27.[1] 30. & July 7. Those of July 14. 21. & 28. I hope soon to have acknoleged. We have decided unanimously to *require*[2] the *recall of Genet. He will sink the republican* interest if they do not *abandon him. Hamilton pressed eagerly an appeal* to the *people*. It's consequences you will readily seize, but *I hope we shall prevent it* tho the *president is inclined* to it. The *loan* is agreed to to the full extent on *E. R.'s advice*[3] splitting off a *few dollars* to give himself the airs of *independence.*

I will send you the little peice written by him on *the proclamation* if I can find it. I will here note your several requisitions in your letter of July 22. 1. What concessions have been made on particular points behind the curtain. I think it is better you should not know them. 2. How far *the president* considers himself as committed with respect to some doctrines. He is certainly uneasy at those grasped at by *Pacificus* and as *the author* is universally known & I believe indeed denied not even by himself, it is foreseen that the vulnerable points, well struck, stab the party vitally. 3. Lights from the law of nations on the constructions of treaties. Vattel has been most generally the guide. Bynkershoeck often quoted, Wolf sometimes. 4. No call was made by any *power* previous to the *proclamation. Genet* has been fully heard on his most unfounded pretensions under *the treaty*. His ignorance of every thing written on the subject is astonishing. I think he has never read a book of any sort in that branch of science. The question whether the war between France & Gr. Br. is offensive or defensive *has not been particularly discussed. Hamilton* has insisted it was offensive by the former. I will send you the French collection of papers on that subject. A paper inclosed will lead you to inform yourself on questions which may come into discussion perhaps at the next session of Congress. They were prepared *for the judges who however will not agree* I believe *to give opinions*.[4] *I informed the president by letter three* days ago that *I should resign* the last day of *September*. Consequently *I shall see you* the middle of *October*. Adieu.

RC (DLC); FC (DLC: Jefferson Papers); Tr (MHi). Unsigned. Italicized words are those encoded by Jefferson using the code he sent JM on 11 May 1785. FC decoded interlinearly by Jefferson. The cipher key that Jefferson enclosed in his letter to JM of 18 Aug. 1793 is filed with this letter in the Madison Papers (DLC). Enclosure not found, but see n. 4.

1. Jefferson probably meant his letter of 23 June, which is acknowledged in JM to Jefferson, 18 July 1793.
2. Jefferson's interlinear decoding on the FC reads "request."

3. Jefferson's interlinear decoding on the FC reads "opinion." After further consideration, Washington approved Hamilton's proposal for a new Dutch loan (Washington to Hamilton, 27 July 1793 [two letters], Syrett and Cooke, *Papers of Hamilton*, 15:136–37, 137). Randolph's opinion has not been found.

4. Jefferson evidently enclosed a copy of twenty-nine questions submitted to the Supreme Court concerning American neutrality and obligations under the treaties with France. The cabinet had discussed those questions on 12 and 18 July, but on 8 Aug. the justices declined to answer them, arguing that to do so would violate the constitutional provision of separation of powers (Dorothy Twohig, ed., *The Journal of the Proceedings of the President, 1793–1797* [Charlottesville, Va., 1981], pp. 195 n. 1, 203 and n. 1; Jefferson to the justices of the Supreme Court, 18 July 1793, Ford, *Writings of Jefferson*, 6:351–52, 352 n. 1).

To Thomas Jefferson

Augst. 5 93

At the date of my last which was on thursday last,[1] yours of the 14. had not arrived. I have since recd. it. That of the 28th. is also just handed me. A review of mine will shew you that all yours from June 23 forward have now been acknowledged. Your acct. of the ticklish situation with respect to Genet in the 14th. is truly distressing. His folly would almost beget suspicions of the worst sort. The consequences you point out in case matters come to an extremity are so certain & obvious that it is hardly conceivable he can be blind to them. Something must be done if possible to get him into a better train. I find by the paper of the 27. that P. has entered & I suppose closed his last topic.[2] I think it a feeble defence of one important point I am striking at: viz. the making a declaration *in his sense of it*, before the arrival of Genet. I argue that the Act does not import a decision agst. the Cas: fed:[3] from the manifest impropriety of doing so on the ground that F was the aggressor in *every* war, without at least waiting for evidence as to the question of fact who made the first attack admitting for the sake of argt. that to be the criterion. A difficulty has occurred which will retard my remarks more than I expected. They must be prepared for the *same Gazette*, consequently copied into another hand. I am laying a plan for havg it done here, but it cannot be done as quickly as I wish. The drouth begins to be severe & alarming for the corn. In a hurry yrs. always

RC (DLC). Unsigned. Docketed by Jefferson, "recd. Aug. 13."

1. Since the previous Thursday was 1 Aug., JM probably meant his letter of 30 July.

2. On 27 July the Philadelphia *Gazette of the U.S.* published the seventh and final installment of Hamilton's "Pacificus" series (Syrett and Cooke, *Papers of Hamilton*, 15:130–35).

3. Casus fœderis: the case of the treaty; i.e., the condition (war between France and Britain) under which the U.S. would be obliged to provide military support to France as stipulated in the 1778 Franco-American treaty.

From John Taylor

DR. SIR   CAROLINE August 5th. 1793

I have this moment parted with Giles & Venable, who have been two days at my house; the contents of the packet I sent you by Mr: Maury were stated to them, and they request me to convey their respects, and their decided opinions to you. They think the production[1] ought to be printed and dispersed as soon as possible. It may produce in the virga. Assembly a repeal of the bank laws,[2] and an expulsion of bank paper, on Mr: Jefferson's idea—and this will operate against the banking system in Congress—1st. As it removes the argument of the state approbation of the banking system. 2ly. As it will tend to draw specie from the other states to Virga, which effect will be foreseen. 3ly. As it will leave the other states exclusively subject to the bank tax. These gentlemen have promised to see me again in October. Permit me to ask the favour of hearing from you. Mr: Pendleton purposes shortly to visit his son in law Mr: R. Taylor,[3] which will afford a good opportunity. Having but a moment, I will employ it in an Ejaculation—BE HAPPY! With great respect I am Sir Yr: mo: obt: st.

                                                                     JOHN TAYLOR

RC (DLC). Addressed by Taylor to JM at Orange. Docketed by JM.

1. Taylor's pamphlet, *Enquiry into the Principles.*
2. During its 1792 session, the Virginia General Assembly passed acts establishing state banks at Alexandria and Richmond (Hening, *Statutes,* 13:592–607).
3. Robert Taylor (1763–1845) of Orange County was married in 1784 to Frances Pendleton (1767–1831), daughter of Edmund Pendleton, Jr., nephew and namesake of the judge (*VMHB,* 41 [1933]: 85–86).

To Thomas Jefferson

DEAR SIR   Augst. 11. 93

Yrs. of Aug: 3. has just come to hand. All the precedg. have been ackd. I am extremely mortified in looking for the Key to the Cypher, to find that I left it in Philada. You must therefore repeat any thing that may be of use still to be known, particularly any thing that may relate to the time of your leavg. Phila. which I wish to know as long as possible before it takes place. The task on which you have put me, must be abridged so as not to go beyond that period. You will see that the first topic is not yet compleated.[1] I hope the 2d. & 3. to wit the meang. of the Treaty & the obligations of gratitude will be less essential. The former is particularly delicate; and tho' I think it may be put in a light that wd. reflect ignominy on the author[2] of P. yet I had rather not meddle with the subject if it cd. be avoided. I can not say when I shall be able to take up those two parts of the job. Just as I was embarking in the general subject I recd. from the reputed Author of Franklyn[3] a large pamphlet written by him agst. the fiscal system, particularly the Bank; which I could not but attend to. It is put on a footing that requires me to communicate personally with Monroe, whom I ought to have seen before this, as the publication of the work is to be contrived for the Author. It really has merit; always for its ingenuity, generally for its solidity, and is enriched with many fine strokes of imagination, and a continued vein of pleasantry & keen satire, that will sting deeply. I have recd. a letter from the Author wishing to hear from me. I must therefore take a ride as far as Charlottesville as soon as I make out the next packet for you, and suspend the residue of the business till I return. I shall endeavor in my absence to fulfil a promise to Wilson Nicholas which will lengthen the suspension. I forwd. to F——[4] a copy of the little thing of Ld. Ch:[5] the last sentence is struck out as not necessary, and which may perhaps wound too indiscriminately certain characters, not at present interested in supporting public corruptions.[6] The drouth has done irreparable injury to the Corn in many parts of the Country. It has been interrupted within a few days past, by a pretty extensive rain. We shared in it here but scantily. I understand that at Charlottesville which had been favd. with several preceding ones, it was plentiful. Be good eno' to contrive an excuse to Mr. R. at Monto: for my not forwding. the Gazettes latterly:[7] if you have not already thought of it. I know not how to apologize myself—and shall feel some awkwardness, as I shall not carry them when I go into his neighbourhood.

RC and enclosure (DLC). RC unsigned; docketed by Jefferson, "recd. Aug. 17." For enclosure, see n. 5.

1. JM was drafting his "Helvidius" essays, the first two of which he probably sent to Jefferson on 12 Aug.

2. Hamilton was author of the "Pacificus" essays.

3. The Philadelphia *National Gazette* published John Taylor's six essays on 16, 20, 23, and 27 Feb. and 2 and 20 Mar. 1793, all bearing the pseudonym "Franklin."

4. Probably Philip Freneau, editor of the *National Gazette*.

5. JM enclosed an "Extract from Ld. Chatham's Speech in the debate on the Falkland's Islands" of 2 Nov. 1770. The one-page extract, in an unknown hand, denounced the "monied interest" as "that *bloodsucker*, that *muckworm*, which

calls itself *the friend of government,* . . . under this description I include the whole race of commissaries, jobbers, contractors, clothiers and remitters." This portion of Chatham's speech, printed in *Hansard's Parliamentary Debates,* 16:1106–7, was well known in JM's circle (Thomas Pleasants, Jr., to JM, 4 Mar. 1791, *PJM,* 13:403, 404 n. 4). Jefferson made a press copy (n.d. [DLC: Jefferson Papers]) and returned the extract in his 18 Aug. 1793 letter to JM, with which it is filed in the Madison Papers (DLC).

6. At a later time an editor, probably John C. Payne (Dolley Payne Todd's brother), placed a bracket and asterisk here. For paragraph inserted in printed texts (Madison, *Letters* [Cong. ed.], 1:592; Madison, *Writings* [Hunt ed.], 6:141 n.), see JM to Jefferson, 12 Aug. 1793, and n.

7. In his 19 Aug. 1793 letter to Thomas Mann Randolph, Jr., Jefferson wrote, "Mr. Randolph must not think amiss of mr. Madison's not forwarding Fenno's papers for a while. It is my fault" (DLC: Jefferson Papers).

From Thomas Jefferson

DEAR SIR   Aug. 11. 1793.

I wrote you last on the 3d. inst. Your's of July 30. came to hand yesterday. Besides the present which goes by post, I write you another today to go by mr. D. Randolph who sets out the day after tomorrow for Monticello, but whether by the direct route or viâ Richmond is not yet decided. I shall desire that letter to be sent to you by express from Monticello. I have not been able to lay my hands on the newspaper which gave a short but true view of the intention of the proclamation. However having occasion to state it in a paper which I am preparing,[1] I have done it in the following terms, and I give you the very words from the paper, because just as I had finished so far, *the president* called on me, I read it to him, he said it presented fairly his view of the matter, he recalled to my mind that I had, at the time, opposed it's being made a declaration of neutrality on the ground that the Executive was not the competent authority for that, & therefore that it was agreed the instrument should be drawn with great care. My statement is in these words. 'On the declaration of war between France & England, the US. being at peace with both, their situation was so new & unexperienced by themselves that their citizens were not, in the first instant, sensible of the new duties resulting therefrom, & of the laws it would impose *even on their dispositions*[2] towards the belligerent powers. Some of them imagined (and chiefly their transient sea-faring citizens) that they were free to indulge those dispositions, to take side with either party, & enrich themselves by depredations on the commerce of the other, & were meditating enterprizes of this nature, as was said. In this state of the public mind, and before it should take an erroneous direction difficult to be set right, & dangerous to themselves & their country, the President thought it expedient, by way of Proclamation, to remind our fellow citizens that we were in a state of peace with all the belligerent powers, that in that state it was our duty neither to aid nor injure any, to exhort & warn them against acts which might contravene this duty, & particularly those of positive hostility, for the punishment of which the laws would be appealed to, and to put them on their guard also as to the risks they would run if they should attempt to carry articles of contraband to any.' —— 'Very soon afterwards we learnt that he[3] was undertaking to authorize the fitting & arming vessels in that port, enlisting men, foreigners & citizens, & giving them commissions to cruize and commit hostilities against nations at peace with us, that these vessels were taking & bringing prizes into our ports, that the Consuls of France were assuming to hold courts of Admiralty on them, to try, condemn & authorize their sale as legal prize, & all this before mr. —— had presented himself or his credentials to the President, before he was received by him, without his consent or consultation, & directly in contravention of the state of peace existing & declared to exist in the Pres's proclmn., & which it was incumbent on him to preserve till the constitutional authority should otherwise declare. These proceedings became immediately, as was naturally to be expected, the subject of complaint by the representative here of that power against whom they would chiefly operate &c.' This was the true sense of the proclamn. in the view of the draughtsman & of the two signers, but H. had other views. The instrument was badly drawn, and made the P. go out of his line to declare things which, tho' true, it was not exactly his province to declare. The instrument was communicated to me after it was drawn, but I was busy, and only run an eye over it to see that it was not made a declaration of neutrality, & gave it back again, without, I believe, changing a tittle.

Pacificus has now changed his signature to 'No Jacobin.' Three papers under this signature have been publd. in Dunlap.[4] I suppose they will get into Fenno. They are commentaries on the laws of nations, & on the different parts of our treaty with France. As yet they have presented no very important heresy. Congress will not meet till the legal day. It was referred to a meeting at my office to consider & advise on it. I was for calling them. Kn. against it. H said his judgment was against it, but he would join any two who should concur so as to make a majority either way. R was pointedly against it. We agreed to give our opinions separately, & tho' the P. was in his own judgment for calling them, he acquiesced in the majority. I pass on to the other letter: so Adieu. Your's affectionately.

RC and enclosure (DLC); FC (DLC: Jefferson Papers). RC unsigned. Unless otherwise noted, italicized words are those encoded by Jefferson using the code he sent JM on 11 May 1785. Jefferson enclosed a newspaper article which he marked "by E. R." Published in the Philadelphia *Federal Gazette* on 30 July, the article argued that the U.S. circuit court acquittal of Gideon Henfield (an American citizen who was charged with violating treaty terms) "does not by any means amount to a decision, that it is not unlawful to enlist on board French privateers."

    1. Jefferson was preparing his official letter to the U.S. minister to France (Gouverneur Morris) of 16 Aug. In that letter he used the passages within quotation marks that follow in this letter to JM (Ford, *Writings of Jefferson*, 6:376–77).

    2. Underlined by Jefferson.

    3. Edmond Charles Genet.

    4. *Dunlap's Am. Daily Advertiser* published the first four of Hamilton's ninepart "No Jacobin" series on 31 July and 5, 8, and 10 Aug. (Syrett and Cooke, *Papers of Hamilton*, 15:145–51, 184–91, 203–7, 224–28).

From Thomas Jefferson

DEAR SIR   PHILADELPHIA Aug. 11. 1793.

    I write a second letter to-day, because going by a private conveyance[1] I can venture in it a paper which never could have been hazarded by the post. Timely information of it's contents (which must be sacredly kept to yourself unless you have an opportunity of communicating them to Monroe) may enable you to shape your plan for the state of things which is actually to take place.[2] It would be the moment for dividing the Treasury between two equal chiefs of the Customs, and Internal taxes, if the Senate were not so unsound. A declaration of the true sense of the Constn. on the question of the bank, will suffice to divorce that from the government, tho' made by a single house. Censures on censurable things clearly confessed in the report &c. With respect to the Proclamation, as the facts it declared were true, and the desire of neutrality is universal, it would place the republicans in a very unfavble. point of view with the people to be cavilling about small points of propriety; & would betray a wish to find fault with the President in an instance where he will be approved by the great body of the people who consider the substance of the measure only, & not the smaller criticisms to which it is liable. The conduct of Genet too is transpiring & exciting the indignation it is calculated to excite. The towns are beginning generally to make known their disapprobation of any such opposition to their govmt. by a foreigner, are declaring their firm adherence to their President, & the Proclamation is made the groundwork of these declarations. In N. York, while Genet was there, the vote of a full meeting of all classes was 9. out of 10. against him, i.e. for the Proclamation. We are told that the cortege which was collected to recieve him (except the committee) consisted only of boys & negroes. All the towns Northwardly are about to express their adherence to the proclamation & chiefly with a view to manifest their disapprobation of G's conduct. Philadelphia, so enthusiastic for him, before his proceedings were known, is going over from him entirely, and if it's popular leaders have not the good sense to go over with them, they will go without them, & be thus transferred to the other party. So in Congress, I believe that it will be true wisdom in the Republican party to approve unequivocally of a state of neutrality, to avoid little cavils about who should declare it, to abandon G. entirely, with expressions of strong friendship & adherence to his nation & confidence that he has acted against their sense. In this way we shall keep the people on our side by keeping ourselves in the right. I have been myself under a cruel dilemma with him. I adhered to him as long as I could have a hope of getting him right, because I knew what weight we should derive to our scale by keeping in it the love of the people for the French cause & nation, and how important it was to ward off from that cause & nation any just grounds of alienation. Finding at length that the man was absolutely incorrigible, I saw the necessity of quitting a wreck which could not but sink all who should cling to it. It is determined to insist on his recall, and I am preparing a statement of his conduct to be laid before the Executive council. Hamilton & Knox have pressed an appeal to the people with an eagerness I never before saw in them. They made the establishment of the democratic society here the ground for sounding an alarm that this society (which they considered as the *antifederal & discontented faction*) was put into motion by mr. G. and would by their corresponding societies in all the state draw the mass of the people, by dint of misinformation, into their vortex & overset the governmt. The Pres. was strongly impressed by this picture, drawn by H. in three speeches of ¾ of an hour length each. I opposed it totally, told the President plainly in their presence, that the intention was to dismount him from being the head of the nation, & make him the head of a party: that this would be the effect of making him in an appeal to the people declare war against the Republican party. R. according to his half-way system between wrong & right urged the *putting off* the appeal. The Pr. came into his idea; or rather concluded that the question on it might be put off indefinitely to be governed by events. If the demonstrations of popular adherence to him become as general & warm as I believe they will, I think he will never again bring on the question: if there is any appearance of their supporting Genet, he will probably make the appeal. I can by this confidential conveyance speak more freely of R. He is the poorest Cameleon I ever saw having no colour of his own, & reflecting that nearest him. When he is with me he is a whig, when with H. he is a tory, when with the P. he is what he thinks will please him. The last is his strongest hue, tho' the *2d. tinges him very strongly. The first is what I think he would prefer in his heart if he were in the woods where he could see nobody, or in a society of *all whigs*. You will remark an expression in the inclosed paper with respect to him.[3] It has in some degree lessened my apprehensions of the estimation in which the Pr. held him. Still it is not the less true that his opinion always makes the majority, & that the President acquiesces *always* in the majority; consequently that the government is now solely directed by him. As he is not yet openly thrown off by the whig party, it gives to the public a false security that fair play is given to the whiggism of the Pr. by an equal division of whig & tory among his counsellors. I have kept on terms of strict friendship with him hitherto, that I might make some good out of him, & because he has really some good private qualities. But he is in a station infinitely too important for his understanding, his firmness, or his circumstances. I mentioned to you that we had convened the judges to consult them on the questions which have arisen on the law of nations. They declined being consulted. In England you know such questions are referred regularly to the judge of Admiralty. I asked E. R. if we could not prepare a bill for Congress to appoint a board or some other body of advice for the Executive on such questions. He said he should propose to annex it to his office. In plain language this would be to make him the sole arbiter of the line of conduct for the US. towards foreign nations. You ask the sense of France with regard to the defensive quality of the guarantee. I know it no otherwise than from Genet. His doctrine is that without waiting to be called on, without waiting till the islands were attacked the moment France was engaged in war, it was our duty to fly to arms as a nation, & the duty of everyone to do it as an individual. He insisted much on Henfeild's counsel[4] (who were engaged & paid by him) defending Henfeild on this ground. But they had more sense. Adieu. Your's affectionately

TH: JEFFERSON

P. S. The Pres. is extremely anxious to know your sentiments on the Proclamation. He has asked me several times. I tell him you are so absorbed in farming that you write to me always about ploughs, rotations &c.

* When he is with people whom he thinks he can guide, he says without reserve that the party in opposition to the fiscal system, are antifederal, and endeavoring to overturn the constitution. These people name you as having apostatised from your antient federalism, & myself as having never been of that sentiment. I say *they* name us, because my information is not expressly that R. named us so to them.

RC and enclosure (DLC); FC, Tr (DLC: Jefferson Papers). Jefferson enclosed a press copy of his notes (3 pp.; original in DLC: Jefferson Papers) on a conversation with Washington, dated 6 Aug. 1793. These notes became part of Jefferson's "Anas" (Ford, *Writings of Jefferson*, 1:256-59).

1. The RC was enclosed in Jefferson to Thomas Mann Randolph, Jr., 11 Aug. 1793 (DLC: Jefferson Papers [docketed as received 30 Aug.]), which was carried by David Meade Randolph.

2. According to the enclosed notes on the conversation with the president of 6 Aug., Jefferson discussed his proposal to resign on 31 Sept. as secretary of state. Washington told Jefferson "that Colo. Hamilton had 3. or 4. weeks ago written to him, informg him that private as well as public reasons had brought him to the determination to retire, & that he should do it towards the close of the next session . . . that he supposed he had fixed on the latter part of the next session to give an opportunity to Congress to examine into his conduct." In his 11 Aug. 1793 letter to Washington (press copy, DLC: Madison Papers; Ford, *Writings of Jefferson*, 6:367), Jefferson agreed to stay on as secretary of state until 31 Dec. "if his continuance in office . . . would, by bringing the two appointments nearer together, enable him to marshal them more beneficially to the public." Hamilton's resignation did not take effect until 31 Jan. 1795.

3. In the enclosure, Jefferson recorded that he suggested Edmund Randolph as a temporary successor until a permanent secretary of state could be found. Washington reportedly replied: "I do not know that he is fit for it nor what is thought of mr. Randolph."

4. Three Philadelphia Republican lawyers defended Gideon Henfield: Peter S. Duponceau, Jared Ingersoll, and Jonathan Dickinson Sergeant (Malone, *Jefferson and His Time*, 3:120).

To Thomas Jefferson

[12 August 1793]

The paper for J. F.[1] could not otherwise get to him than with your aid. You must therefore take the trouble of having it handed into the post office whence the penny post will take it, unless you can do it at some shorter hand. I wish you to look over what is sd. critically, and if you think there be any thing of importance wrong, or that may do more harm than good, that you will either erase it, where that will not break the sense, or arrest the whole till I can make the correction. Delay I know is bad; but vulnerable parts that wd. be siezed for victories & triumphs would be worse. I beg you also to attend particularly to three passages slightly marked with a pencil, the first, the declaration of the principles & sentiments of the author—2d. beginning with "Writers such as Locke & Montesqeue &c["]—to the pencil mark in the ¶. 3 the quotation from the Federalist. If you think the first had better be omitted it can come out without leavg. the least gap. So can the 2d. My doubts as to that proceed from the danger of turning the controversy too much into the wilderness of Books: I use Montesqeue also from memory, tho I believe witht. inaccuracy. The 3d. can also come out witht. affecting the piece, and I wish you to erase it if you think the most scrupulous delicacy, conjecturing the author, cd. disapprove it. One No. more or 2 short Nos. will close the first topic & supersede the last. They will be sent as soon as finished & copied. These wd. have been sent somewhat sooner, but for the delay caused by the last circumstance.

RC (DLC). Attached to JM to Jefferson, 11 Aug. 1793 in the Madison Papers (DLC). Probably a wrapper for "Helvidius," nos. 1 and 2. The verso of the sheet was first docketed, in an unknown hand, 30 July 1793, then that date was crossed through and 11 Aug. 1793 written above. An early editor, probably John C. Payne, headed this sheet: "*to follow as a closing paragraph after the bracket in the letter of 11th. Aug. '93" (see JM to Jefferson, 11 Aug. 1793, n. 6). Conjectural date here assigned by comparison with JM to Jefferson, 20 Aug. 1793.

1. John Fenno was editor of the Philadelphia *Gazette of the U.S.* (see Madison's "Helvidius" Essays, 24 Aug.–18 Sept. 1793).

From Thomas Jefferson

DEAR SIR   Aug. 18. 93.

My last was of the 11th. since which yours of the 5th. & 11th. are received. I am mortified at your not having your cypher. I now send the key of the numbers in mine of the 3d. This with my letter of the 11th. by post & another of the same date by Davy Randolph who will be at Monticello the last week of this month will put you in possession of the state of things to that date. The paper I now inclose will fill up chinks & needs not a word of explanation. To these I must add that orders are given to drive out of our ports the privateers which have been armed in them before the 5th. of June, by gentler means if it can be done, & if not, by the ultima ratio: and we are seising the prizes brought in since Aug. 7. to restore them to their owners. For those between June 5. & Aug. 7. we engage restitution or compensation. The inclosed paper will explain these distinctions of date, & justify the proceedings.[1] I return you the little thing of Ld. Chath's[2] because, for particular reasons, were it now to appear it would be imputed to me, & because it will have more effect if publd. after the meeting of Congress. I rejoice at the resurrection of Franklin. There was a charming thing from the same pen (I conjecture) on the subject of instrumentality lately publd. by Freneau from the Virga. papers.[3] The addresses in support of the proclmn. are becoming universal, and as universal a rising in support of the President against Genet. Observe that the inclosed paper[4] has been only read in cabinet for the 1st. time as yet. On that reading H. objected to expressions implying a censure on other nations ('the war of liberty on herself &c').[5] He thought expressions of frdship to France suited the occasion. But R. protested against every expression of friendship to that nation lest they should offend the other party, and intimated that he should move to eradicate them all. It will pretty effectually tear up the instrument if he succeeds. Nous verrons. Adieu.

P. S. You are free to shew the inclosed to Colo. Monroe. If the appeal which I have mentioned to you, should be pushed, I think that by way of compromise, I shall propose that instead of that, the whole correspondence be laid before Congress, merely as a matter of information. What would you think of this?

RC and enclosed key (DLC); FC and FC of enclosed key (DLC: Jefferson Papers); Tr and Tr of enclosed key (MHi). RC unsigned. The enclosed cipher key is filed with Jefferson to JM, 3 Aug. 1793, in the Madison Papers (DLC). Between the two columns of the key Jefferson wrote: "many numbers are inserted which were not in the letter, merely to baffle all attempts to make out what was in it." For other enclosures, see nn. 1, 2, and 4.

1. Jefferson probably enclosed a copy of his 7 Aug. letter to Genet (Ford, *Writings of Jefferson*, 6:365–66).

2. Jefferson enclosed the extract of Lord Chatham's speech that JM had previously sent to him (see JM to Jefferson, 11 Aug. 1793, n. 5).

3. On 3 Aug. the Philadelphia *National Gazette* reprinted from the *Va. Gazette, and Richmond and Manchester Advertiser* of 22 July an essay, over the pseudonym "Turn-Coat," which attacked Hamilton's funding system. No evidence has been found to substantiate Jefferson's attribution of this essay to John Taylor, author of the "Franklin" essays.

4. Jefferson must have enclosed a draft of his official letter to Gouverneur Morris —antedated 16 Aug. 1793—which was discussed in cabinet meetings on 15, 20, and 23 Aug. (Ford, *Writings of Jefferson*, 6:371–93, 397). A press copy of this letter is in the Madison Papers (DLC).

5. This phrase, characterizing the possibility of conflict between France and the U.S., was deleted from the letter to Morris. According to Jefferson's notes on the cabinet meeting of 20 Aug., "H. moved to strike out these words 'that of liberty warring on herself.' He urged generally that it would give offence to the combined powers, that it amounted to a declaration that they were warring on liberty, that we were not called on to declare that the cause of France was that of liberty" (Ford, *Writings of Jefferson*, 1:259). A press copy of these notes is in the Madison Papers (DLC).

¶ From James Monroe. Letter not found. *Ca. 19 August 1793.* Mentioned in JM to Jefferson, 20 Aug. 1793. Seeks consultation with JM before Monroe departs for a court session (of the state district court that convened at Staunton on 1 Sept.).

To Thomas Jefferson

Your favor of the 11th. came to hand the day before yesterday. I am just setting off to Monroe's and hope to prevent the trouble of an express from Monticello with the letter referred to in it. I have already acquainted you with the immediate object of this visit. I have just recd. a line from him expressing a particular desire to communicate with me, and reminding me that he sets off the last of this month for the Courts, and of course will be occupied for some days before with preparations. This hurries me: and has forced me to hurry what will be inclosed herewith, particularly the last No. V which required particular care in the execution.[1] I shall be obliged to leave that & the greater part of the other Nos. to be transcd. sealed up & forwarded in my absence. It is certain therefore that many little errors will take place. As I can not let them be detained till I return, I must pray you to make such corrections as will not betray your hand. In pointing & *erasures* not breaking the sense, there will be no difficulty. I have already requested you to make free with the latter. You will find more quotations from the Fedt. Dark them out if you think the most squeamish Critic could object to them. In No. 5. I suggest to your attention a long preliminary remark into which I suffered myself to be led before I was aware of the prolixity. As the piece is full long without it, it had probably better be lopped off. The propriety of the two last paragraphs claims your particular criticism. I wd. not have hazarded them without the prospect of your revisal, & if proper, your erasure. That which regards Spain &c. may contain unsound reasoning, or be too delicate to be touched in a Newspaper. The propriety of the last, as to the President's answers to addresses, depends on the truth of the fact, of which you can judge. I am not sure that I have seen all the answers. My last was of the 12th. & covered the 2 first Nos. of H——s.[2] I am assured that it was put into the post office on tuesday evening. It ought therefore to have reached you on Saturday last. As an oppy. to Fredg may happen before more than the 3d. No. may be transcribed, it is possible, that this may be accompanied by that alone.

The drouth has been dreadful to the Corn. There has been no rain making any sensible impression for seven weeks, of the hottest weather of the hottest year rem[em]bered: and at the very period critical to that crop. Yesterday afternoon we had a small shower—and more seemed to be passing around us. No weather however can now possibly add 5 perCt. to the prospect. There can not be more than half crops made generally & much less in many places. Yrs. affy

RC (DLC). Unsigned. Addressed and marked *"private"* by JM. Docketed by Jefferson, "recd Aug. 30." JM probably enclosed drafts of "Helvidius," nos. 3 and 4.

1. JM apparently waited until September to send "Helvidius" No. 5 to Jefferson (Jefferson to JM, 8 Sept. 1793).

2. At a later time JM here interlined "Helvidius."

To Thomas Jefferson

DEAR SIR   AT COL. M——[1] [ca. 22 August 1793]

I left home the day before yesterday which was the date of my last. It was to be accompanied by 2. & perhaps tho' not probably 3 additional Nos. of H–l–vd–s. The last towit No. 5. contained two paragraphs the one relating to the accession of S. & P. to the war against F. the other to the answer's of the P. to the addresses on his proclamation, which I particularly requested you to revise, and if improper, to erase. The whole piece was more hurried than it ought to have been, and these paragraphs penned in the instant of my setting out which had been delayed as late as would leave eno' of the day for the journey. I mention this as the only apology for the gross error of fact committed with respect to the term neutrality, which it is asserted the P. has not used in any of his answers. I find on looking into them here, that he used it in the first of all to the Merchts. of Philada.[2] and in one other out of three which I have examined. I must make my conditional request therefore an absolute one as to that passage. If he should forbear the use of the term in all his answers subsequent to the perversion of it by Pacificus, it will strengthen the argument used; but that must be a future & contingent consideration. Mr. D. R.[3] was not arrived yesterday. The family here well–so also at M. as you will no doubt learn from the Spot itself. Adieu. Yrs. Affy

RC (DLC). Unsigned. Docketed by Jefferson, "abt Aug. 22. 93. / recd. Sep. 2."

1. JM wrote from James Monroe's home near Charlottesville.

2. In his letter of 17 May 1793 "To the Merchants and Traders of the City of Philadelphia," Washington asserted that "the happiness and best interests of the people of the United States, will be promoted by observing a strict neutrality" (Fitzpatrick, *Writings of Washington*, 32:460).

3. David Meade Randolph.

Madison's "Helvidius" Essays
24 August–18 September 1793

A mixture of morality and political expediency was brewing on the American political scene during the summer of 1793. A full-strength potion known as the two-party system was about to emerge, giving form and content to the contests first fought in the ratification struggle of 1787–88. The catalytic agent was the French Revolution and its aftermath, for President Washington's Neutrality Proclamation posed a dilemma to JM and his political colleagues who were sympathetic to French republicanism. To them, the 1778 alliance with France was still in force and obligated the United States to defend the French West Indies. They welcomed the abolition of the monarchy and felt little remorse at the execution of their erstwhile benefactor, Louis XVI. JM himself accepted honorary French citizenship from the revolutionary regime. American Republicans viewed neutrality as dishonorable: an abandonment of political principles and treaty obligations, dictated by the Federalists' desire to maintain profitable trade with the belligerent European powers, particularly Great Britain. Yet they were bound by personal loyalty and political expediency to avoid a direct attack on Washington.

Domestic politics polarized as the new French minister to the United States, Edmond Charles Genet, indiscreetly mocked the president's proclamation by passing out military commissions and letters of marque to American citizens. Hamilton entered the fray with his "Pacificus" essays, charging Republicans with subordinating American foreign policy to French interests. Washington's proclamation had scrupulously avoided the term "neutrality," but the treasury secretary defended the document by giving it a Federalist interpretation and arguing for a suspension of the French treaty. Jefferson was alarmed, not least because Hamilton—safely disguised under a pseudonym—was publicly airing confidential cabinet discussions.

American military and naval strength was no match for that of the European belligerents, and Republicans opposed a naval armament and a standing army. The president's foreign policy, moreover, enjoyed wide political support. In these circumstances, the secretary of state accepted the necessity of a de facto neutrality. To Jefferson, however, the administration's headlong announcement of neutrality threw away a trump card in negotiations with the British for the commercial treaty that the American government had so long desired: "I now think it extremely possible that Hammond [the British minister to the United States] might have been instructed to have asked it, & to offer *the broadest possible neutral privileges*, as the price, which was exactly the price I wanted that we should contend for." Jefferson lamented that "none but mere bunglers & brawlers have for some time past taken the trouble to answer any thing." Without an authoritative reply to Hamilton, Jefferson insisted, "his doctrine will therefore be taken for confessed. For god's sake, my dear Sir, take up your pen, select the most striking heresies, and cut him to peices in the face of the public. There is nobody else who can & will enter the lists with him" (Jefferson to JM, 29 June 1793 [postscript of 30 June] and 7 July 1793).

Even as Jefferson was prevailing upon JM to defend the French alliance, he had come to recognize the necessity of dissociating Franco-American relations from Genet. The French minister had become a political liability. "Never in my opinion, was so calamitous an appointment made," Jefferson wrote. "He will sink the republican interest if they do not abandon him" (Jefferson to JM, 7 July and 3 Aug. 1793 [partly in code]). Thus the challenge to JM was delicate and unenviable: affirm loyalty to Washington and avoid discussing the merits of neutrality, but question the constitutionality of declaring neutrality by executive proclamation; distance the Republicans from Genet, yet advocate American support for the French Revolution. He wrote with other disadvantages as well; while he could draw on his general knowledge of international law and his library at Montpelier, many source materials were unavailable in rural Virginia.

JM took up the task reluctantly: "I can truly say I find it the most grating one I ever experienced" (JM to Jefferson, 30 July 1793). He began work on the "Helvidius" essays by 22 July and completed them by 20 August. He was distracted by other literary duties; he consulted Monroe on drafting the Resolutions on Franco-American Relations of circa 27 August and editing John Taylor of Caroline's *Enquiry into the Principles and Tendency of Certain Public Measures*. As a result of these limitations, JM was dissatisfied with his performance as "Helvidius." He had his drafts copied by a friend or relative at Montpelier to preserve anonymity, then sent them to Jefferson in Philadelphia. He authorized his friend to do considerable editing, but the secretary of state was pleased with the work and made only minor changes. Jefferson arranged for their delivery to Federalist John Fenno's *Gazette of the United States*. JM wanted his reply to appear in the same newspaper that had published "Pacificus."

Though he was writing for the popular press, JM primarily aimed the "Helvidius" series to persuade an audience with an intellectual interest in politics, as he had done in *The Federalist*. "None but intelligent readers will enter into such a controversy," he believed, "and to their minds it ought principally to be accomodated" (JM to Jefferson, 22 July 1793). For his pseudonym he chose the name of Helvidius Priscus, the first-century Roman leader who, as described by Tacitus, resisted the imperial regime. Because of the political constraints on his argument, JM focused on the issue of executive versus legislative control of foreign policy. In his treatment of war powers, he advocated legislative supremacy and strict construction of executive powers, doctrines which became hallmarks of Republican constitutional theory. To Federalists, JM seemed to have departed from the principles of strong central government that he had advocated only five years before. Yet he quoted "Publius" of 1788 to rebut "Pacificus" of 1793, implying that Hamilton himself had abandoned the constraints on executive power that had reassured readers of *The Federalist*. Thus the "Helvidius" essays revealed how much the issues and alignments of American politics had changed since the contest over the ratification of the Constitution. (For a recent discussion of the "Helvidius" essays in the context of political theory, see Richard Loss, introduction to Alexander Hamilton and James Madison, *The Letters of Pacificus and Helvidius* [1845; Delmar, N.Y., 1976 reprint], pp. ix–xv.)

"Helvidius" Number 1

[24 August 1793]

SEVERAL pieces with the signature of PACIFICUS were lately published, which have been read with singular pleasure and applause, by the foreigners and degenerate citizens among us, who hate our republican government, and the French revolution; whilst the publication seems to have been too little regarded, or too much despised by the steady friends to both.

Had the doctrines inculcated by the writer, with the natural consequences from them, been nakedly presented to the public, this treatment might have been proper. Their true character would then have struck every eye, and been rejected by the feelings of every heart. But they offer themselves to the reader in the dress of an elaborate dissertation; they are mingled with a few truths that may serve them as a passport to credulity; and they are introduced with professions of anxiety for the preservation of peace, for the welfare of the government, and for the respect due to the present head of the executive, that may prove a snare to patriotism.

In these disguises they have appeared to claim the attention I propose to bestow on them; with a view to shew, from the publication itself, that under colour of vindicating an important public act, of a chief magistrate, who enjoys the confidence and love of his country, principles are advanced which strike at the vitals of its constitution, as well as at its honor and true interest.

As it is not improbable that attempts may be made to apply insinuations which are seldom spared when particular purposes are to be answered, to the author of the ensuing observations, it may not be improper to premise, that he is a friend to the constitution, that he wishes for the preservation of peace, and that the present chief magistrate has not a fellow-citizen, who is penetrated with deeper respect for his merits, or feels a purer solicitude for his glory.

This declaration is made with no view of courting a more favorable ear to what may be said than it deserves. The sole purpose of it is, to obviate imputations which might weaken the impressions of truth; and which are the more likely to be resorted to, in proportion as solid and fair arguments may be wanting.

The substance of the first piece, sifted from its inconsistencies and its vague expressions, may be thrown into the following propositions:

That the powers of declaring war and making treaties are, in their nature, executive powers:

That being particularly vested by the constitution in other departments, they are to be considered as exceptions out of the general grant to the executive department:

That being, as exceptions, to be construed strictly, the powers not strictly within them, remain with the executive:

That the executive consequently, as the organ of intercourse with foreign nations, and the interpreter and executor of treaties, and the law of nations, is authorised, to expound all articles of treaties, those involving questions of war and peace, as well as others; to judge of the obligations of the United States to make war or not, under any casus federis or eventual operation of the contract, relating to war; and, to pronounce the state of things resulting from the obligations of the United States, as understood by the executive:

That in particular the executive had authority to judge whether in the case of the mutual guaranty between the United States and France, the former were bound by it to engage in the war:

That the executive has, in pursuance of that authority, decided that the United States are not bound: And,

That its proclamation of the 22d of April last, is to be taken as the effect and expression of that decision.

The basis of the reasoning is, we perceive, the extraordinary doctrine, that the powers of making war and treaties, are in their nature executive; and therefore comprehended in the general grant of executive power, where not specially and strictly excepted out of the grant.

Let us examine this doctrine; and that we may avoid the possibility of mistating the writer, it shall be laid down in his own words: a precaution the more necessary, as scarce any thing else could outweigh the improbability, that so extravagant a tenet should be hazarded, at so early a day, in the face of the public.

His words are—"Two of these (exceptions and qualifications to the executive powers) have been already noticed—the participation of the Senate in the *appointment of officers*, and the *making of treaties*. A *third* remains to be mentioned—the right of the legislature to *declare war, and grant letters of marque and reprisal*."[1]

Again—"It deserves to be remarked, that as the participation of the Senate in the *making treaties*, and the power of the legislature to *declare war*, are *exceptions* out of the general *executive power*, vested in the President, they are to be construed *strictly*, and ought to be extended no farther than is essential to their execution."[2]

If there be any countenance to these positions, it must be found either 1st, in the writers, of authority, on public law; or 2d, in the quality and operation of the powers to make war and treaties; or 3d, in the constitution of the United States.

It would be of little use to enter far into the first source of information, not only because our own reason and our own constitution, are the best guides; but because a just analysis and discrimination of the powers of government, according to their executive, legislative and judiciary qualities are not to be expected in the works of the most received jurists, who wrote before a critical attention was paid to those objects, and with their eyes too much on monarchical governments, where all powers are confounded in the sovereignty of the prince. It will be found however, I believe, that all of them, particularly Wolfius, Burlamaqui and Vattel,[3] speak of the powers to declare war, to conclude peace, and to form alliances, as among the highest acts of the sovereignty; of which the legislative power must at least be an integral and preeminent part.

Writers, such as Locke and Montesquieu, who have discussed more particularly the principles of liberty and the structure of government, lie under the same disadvantage, of having written before these subjects were illuminated by the events and discussions which distinguish a very recent period. Both of them too are evidently warped by a regard to the particular government of England, to which one of them owed allegiance;* and the other professed an admiration bordering on idolatry. Montesquieu, however, has rather distinguished himself by enforcing the reasons and the importance of avoiding a confusion of the several powers of government, than by enumerating and defining the powers which belong to each particular class. And Locke, notwithstanding the early date of his work on civil government, and the example of his own government before his eyes, admits that the particular powers in question, which, after some of the writers on public law he calls *federative*, are really *distinct* from the *executive*, though almost always united with it, and *hardly to be separated into distinct hands.*[4] Had he not lived under a monarchy, in which these powers were united; or had he written by the lamp which truth now presents to lawgivers, the last observation would probably never have dropt from his pen. But let us quit a field of research which is more likely to perplex than to decide, and bring the question to other tests of which it will be more easy to judge.

2. If we consult for a moment, the nature and operation of the two

* *The chapter on prerogative,*[5] *shews how much the reason of the philosopher was clouded by the royalism of the Englishman.*

powers to declare war and make treaties, it will be impossible not to see that they can never fall within a proper definition of executive powers. The natural province of the executive magistrate is to execute laws, as that of the legislature is to make laws. All his acts therefore, properly executive, must pre-suppose the existence of the laws to be executed. A treaty is not an execution of laws: it does not pre-suppose the existence of laws. It is, on the contrary, to have itself the force of a *law*, and to be carried into *execution*, like all *other laws*, by the *executive magistrate*. To say then that the power of making treaties which are confessedly laws, belongs naturally to the department which is to execute laws, is to say, that the executive department naturally includes a legislative power. In theory, this is an absurdity—in practice a tyranny.

The power to declare war is subject to similar reasoning. A declaration that there shall be war, is not an execution of laws: it does not suppose pre-existing laws to be executed: it is not in any respect, an act merely executive. It is, on the contrary, one of the most deliberative acts that can be performed; and when performed, has the effect of *repealing* all the *laws* operating in a state of peace, so far as they are inconsistent with a state of war: and of *enacting* as *a rule for the executive*, a *new code* adapted to the relation between the society and its foreign enemy. In like manner a conclusion of peace *annuls* all the *laws* peculiar to a state of war, and *revives* the general *laws* incident to a state of peace.

These remarks will be strengthened by adding that treaties, particularly treaties of peace, have sometimes the effect of changing not only the external laws of the society, but operate also on the internal code, which is purely municipal, and to which the legislative authority of the country is of itself competent and compleat.

From this view of the subject it must be evident, that although the executive may be a convenient organ of preliminary communications with foreign governments, on the subjects of treaty or war; and the proper agent for carrying into execution the final determinations of the competent authority; yet it can have no pretensions from the nature of the powers in question compared with the nature of the executive trust, to that essential agency which gives validity to such determinations.

It must be further evident that, if these powers be not in their nature purely legislative, they partake so much more of that, than of any other quality, that under a constitution leaving them to result to their most natural department, the legislature would be without a rival in its claim.[6]

Another important inference to be noted is, that the powers of making war and treaty being substantially of a legislative, not an executive nature, the rule of interpreting exceptions strictly, must narrow instead of enlarging executive pretensions on those subjects.

3. It remains to be enquired whether there be any thing in the consti-

tution itself which shews that the powers of making war and peace are considered as of an executive nature, and as comprehended within a general grant of executive power.

It will not be pretended that this appears from any *direct* position to be found in the instrument.

If it were *deducible* from any particular expressions it may be presumed that the publication would have saved us the trouble of the research.

Does the doctrine then result from the actual distribution of powers among the several branches of the government? Or from any fair analogy between the powers of war and treaty and the enumerated powers vested in the executive alone?

Let us examine.

In the general distribution of powers, we find that of declaring war expressly vested in the Congress, where every other legislative power is declared to be vested, and without any other qualification than what is common to every other legislative act. The constitutional idea of this power would seem then clearly to be, that it is of a legislative and not an executive nature.

This conclusion becomes irresistible, when it is recollected, that the constitution cannot be supposed to have placed either any power legislative in its nature, entirely among executive powers, or any power executive in its nature, entirely among legislative powers, without charging the constitution, with that kind of intermixture and consolidation of different powers, which would violate a fundamental principle in the organization of free governments. If it were not unnecessary to enlarge on this topic here, it could be shewn, that the constitution was originally vindicated, and has been constantly expounded, with a disavowal of any such intermixture.

The power of treaties is vested jointly in the President and in the Senate, which is a branch of the legislature. From this arrangement merely, there can be no inference that would necessarily exclude the power from the executive class: since the senate is joined with the President in another power, that of appointing to offices, which as far as relate to executive offices at least, is considered as of an executive nature. Yet on the other hand, there are sufficient indications that the power of treaties is regarded by the constitution as materially different from mere executive power, and as having more affinity to the legislative than to the executive character.

One circumstance indicating this, is the constitutional regulation under which the senate give their consent in the case of treaties. In all other cases the consent of the body is expressed by a majority of voices. In this particular case, a concurrence of two thirds at least is made necessary, as a substitute or compensation for the other branch of the legislature, which on certain occasions, could not be conveniently a party to the transaction.

But the conclusive circumstance is, that treaties when formed according to the constitutional mode, are confessedly to have the force and operation of *laws*, and are to be a rule for the courts in controversies between man and man, as much as any *other laws*. They are even emphatically declared by the constitution to be "the supreme law of the land."

So far the argument from the constitution is precisely in opposition to the doctrine. As little will be gained in its favour from a comparison of the two powers, with those particularly vested in the President alone.

As there are but few it will be most satisfactory to review them one by one.

"The President shall be commander in chief of the army and navy of the United States, and of the militia when called into the actual service of the United States."

There can be no relation worth examining between this power and the general power of making treaties. And instead of being analogous to the power of declaring war, it affords a striking illustration of the incompatibility of the two powers in the same hands. Those who are to *conduct a war* cannot in the nature of things, be proper or safe judges, whether *a war ought* to be *commenced, continued*, or *concluded*. They are barred from the latter functions by a great principle in free government, analogous to that which separates the sword from the purse, or the power of executing from the power of enacting laws.

"He may require the opinion in writing of the principal officers in each of the executive departments upon any subject relating to the duties of their respective offices; and he shall have power to grant reprieves and pardons for offences against the United States, except in case of impeachment." These powers can have nothing to do with the subject.

"The President shall have power to fill up vacancies that may happen during the recess of the senate, by granting commissions which shall expire at the end of the next session." The same remark is applicable to this power, as also to that of "receiving ambassadors, other public ministers and consuls." The particular use attempted to be made of this last power will be considered in another place.

"He shall take care that the laws shall be faithfully executed and shall commission all officers of the United States." To see the laws faithfully executed constitutes the essence of the executive authority. But what relation has it to the power of making treaties and war, that is, of determining what the *laws shall be* with regard to other nations? No other certainly than what subsists between the powers of executing and enacting laws; no other consequently, than what forbids a coalition of the powers in the same department.

I pass over the few other specified functions assigned to the President, such as that of convening of the legislature, &c. &c. which cannot be drawn into the present question.

It may be proper however to take notice of the power of removal from office, which appears to have been adjudged to the President by the laws establishing the executive departments; and which the writer has endeavoured to press into his service. To justify any favourable inference from this case, it must be shewn, that the powers of war and treaties are of a kindred nature to the power of removal, or at least are equally within a grant of executive power. Nothing of this sort has been attempted, nor probably will be attempted. Nothing can in truth be clearer, than that no analogy, or shade of analogy, can be traced between a power in the supreme officer responsible for the faithful execution of the laws, to displace a subaltern officer employed in the execution of the laws; and a power to make treaties, and to declare war, such as these have been found to be in their nature, their operation, and their consequences.

Thus it appears that by whatever standard we try this doctrine, it must be condemned as no less vicious in theory than it would be dangerous in practice. It is countenanced neither by the writers on law; nor by the nature of the powers themselves; nor by any general arrangements or particular expressions, or plausible analogies, to be found in the constitution.

Whence then can the writer have borrowed it?

There is but one answer to this question.

The power of making treaties and the power of declaring war, are *royal prerogatives* in the *British government*, and are accordingly treated as Executive prerogatives by *British commentators*.

We shall be the more confirmed in the necessity of this solution of the problem, by looking back to the æra of the constitution, and satisfying ourselves that the writer could not have been misled by the doctrines maintained by our own commentators on our own government. That I may not ramble beyond prescribed limits, I shall content myself with an extract from a work which entered into a systematic explanation and defence of the constitution, and to which there has frequently been ascribed some influence in conciliating the public assent to the government in the form proposed. Three circumstances conspire in giving weight to this cotemporary exposition. It was made at a time when no application to *persons* or *measures* could bias: The opinion given was not transiently mentioned, but formally and critically elucidated: It related to a point in the constitution which must consequently have been viewed as of importance in the public mind. The passage relates to the power of making treaties; that of declaring war, being arranged with such obvious propriety among the legislative powers, as to be passed over without particular discussion.

"Tho' several writers on the subject of government place that power *(of making treaties)* in the class of *Executive authorities,* yet this is *evidently* an *arbitrary disposition.* For if we attend *carefully,* to its operation, it will be found to partake *more* of the *legislative* than of the *executive* character, though it does not seem strictly to fall within the definition of either of them. The essence of the legislative authority, is to enact laws; or in other words, to prescribe rules for the regulation of the society. While the execution of the laws and the employment of the common strength, either for this purpose, or for the common defence, seem to comprize *all* the functions of the *Executive magistrate.* The power of making treaties is *plainly* neither the one nor the other. It relates neither to the execution of the subsisting laws, nor to the enaction of new ones, and still less to an exertion of the common strength. Its objects are contracts with foreign nations, which have the *force of law,* but derive it from the obligations of good faith. They are not rules prescribed by the sovereign to the subject, but agreements between sovereign and sovereign. The power in question seems therefore to form a distinct department, and to belong properly neither to the legislative nor to the executive. The qualities elsewhere detailed as indispensable in the management of foreign *negociations,* point out the executive as the most fit agent in those transactions: whilst the vast importance of the trust, and the operation of treaties *as Laws,* plead strongly for the participation of the whole or a part of the *legislative body* in the office of making them." Federalist vol. 2. p. 273.[7]

It will not fail to be remarked on this commentary, that whatever doubts may be started as to the correctness of its reasoning against the legislative nature of the power to make treaties: it is *clear, consistent* and *confident,* in deciding that the power is *plainly* and *evidently* not an *executive power.*

HELVIDIUS.

Printed copy (Philadelphia *Gazette of the U.S.,* 24 and 28 Aug. 1793). The essay is prefaced with the following letter: "Mr. Fenno, Please to give a place in your Gazette to the following observations. The Printers who may have re-published the pieces, signed Pacificus, are also requested to re-publish these, and will no doubt be candid enough to do so." Reprinted in [James Madison], *Letters of Helvidius: Written in Reply to Pacificus, on the President's Proclamation of Neutrality. Published Originally in the Year 1793* (Philadelphia, 1796; Evans 30734), pp. 3–13. Samuel Harrison Smith published this pamphlet.

1. "Pacificus" No. 1 (Syrett and Cooke, *Papers of Hamilton,* 15:39).
2. Ibid., 15:42.

3. JM referred to the authors of three works on international law: Christian Wolff, *Institutions du droit de la nature et des gens*, trans. Elie Luzac (6 vols.; Leiden, 1772), Jean Jacques Burlamaqui, *Principes du droit politique* (Amsterdam, 1751), and Emmerich de Vattel, *The Law of Nations*, first published in French in 1758. By 1790 JM owned an English translation of Vattel, first published in 1760. Jefferson purchased copies of Wolff and Burlamaqui in France for JM (Memorandum of Books, August 1790, *PJM*, 13:288; Jefferson to JM, 1 Sept. 1785, enclosure, Boyd, *Papers of Jefferson*, 8:462, 464).

4. John Locke defined the federative power as "the Power of War and Peace, Leagues and Alliances, and all the Transactions, with all Persons and Communities without the Commonwealth" (*Two Treatises of Government*, ed. Peter Laslett [Cambridge, 1960], p. 383). JM here summarized the *Second Treatise*, chap. 12.

5. Locke, *Second Treatise*, chap. 14.

6. The text printed on 24 Aug. ends here.

7. *The Federalist* No. 75 (Syrett and Cooke, *Papers of Hamilton*, 4:629). JM cited M'Lean 1788 edition (Evans 21127). Because JM (unlike most of his audience) knew that Hamilton was the author of both that essay and "Pacificus" No. 1, he here used his opponent's earlier words to rebut "Pacificus."

From Thomas Jefferson

Aug. 25. 93.

You will percieve by the inclosed papers that Genet has thrown down the gauntlet to the President by the publication of his letter & my answer,[1] and is himself forcing that appeal to the people, and risking that disgust, which I had so much wished should have been avoided. The indications from different parts of the continent are already sufficient to shew that the mass of the republican interest has no hesitation to disapprove of this intermeddling by a foreigner, and the more readily as his object was evidently, contrary to his professions, to force us into the war. I am not certain whether some of the more furious republicans may not schismatise with him.

The following arrangements are established.

Sep. 10. the Pr. sets out for Mt. Vernon, & will be here again the 30th.

Oct. 5th. or a little sooner I set out to be absent 6. weeks, by agreement. Consequently I shall be here again about Nov. 17. to remain to Dec. 31. I break up my house the last of Septemb. Shall leave my carriage & horses in Virginia & return in the stage, not to have the embarrasment of ploughing them through the mud in January. I shall take private lodgings on my return. Billy who is just going on a nautical expedition to Charleston, called on me yesterday to desire I would send you the inclosed account which he said was necessary for you to debit those for whom the articles were. Adieu.

RC (DLC); FC, partial Tr (DLC: Jefferson Papers). Unsigned. Enclosures not found.

1. On 13 Aug. the N.Y. *Diary* published an announcement by John Jay and Rufus King that Genet had threatened to "appeal to the people from certain decisions of the President." Genet denied the charge and wrote Washington on the same day asking the president to confirm this denial. Jefferson replied on 16 Aug. that the French minister should direct all communications to the president through the secretary of state and that the president "declines interfering in the case." Genet gave the two letters to the N.Y. *Diary*, which published them on 21 Aug. (Malone, *Jefferson and His Time*, 3:135–36 and nn. 8–11). The letters were reprinted in Philadelphia in *Dunlap's Am. Daily Advertiser*, 24 Aug. 1793.

To Thomas Jefferson

DEAR SIR   Aug: 27. 1793

I wrote you a few lines by the last post from this place just to apprize you of my movement to it. I have since seen the Richmond & the Philada. papers containing, the latter the certificate of Jay & King[1] & the publications relating to the subject of it, the former the proceedings at Richmond[2] dictated no doubt by the Cabal at Philada. It is painful to observe the success of the management for putting Wythe at the head of them. I understand however that a considerable revolution has taken place in his political sentiments under the influence of some disgusts he has recd. from the State Legislature.[3] By what has appeared I discover that a determination has been formed to drag before the public the indiscretions of Genèt; and turn them & the popularity of the P. to the purposes driven at. Some impression will be made here of course. A plan is evidently laid in Richd. to render it extensive. If an early & well digested effort for calling out the real sense of the people be not made, there is room to apprehend they may in many places be misled. This has employed the conversation of —— & myself. We shall endeavor at some means of repelling the danger; particularly by setting on foot expressions of the public mind in important Counties, and under the auspices of respectable names. I have written with this view to Caroline, and have suggested a proper train of ideas, and a wish that Mr. P. would patronise the measure.[4] Such an example would have great effect. Even if it shd. not be followed it would be considered as an authentic specimen of the *Country* temper; and would put other places on their guard agst. the snares that may be laid for them. The want of opportunities, and our ignorance of trust worthy characters will circumscribe our efforts in this way to a very narrow compass. The rains for several days have delayed my trip to the Gentleman[5] named in my last. Unless tomorrow shd. be a favorable day, I shall be obliged to decline it altogether. In two or three days I shall be in a situation to receive & answer your letters as usual. That by Mr. DR.[6] has not yet reached me.

RC (DLC). Unsigned. Docketed by Jefferson, "recd. Sep. 9."

1. Reprinted in the Philadelphia *National Gazette* on 17 Aug.
2. On 21 Aug. the Richmond *Va. Gazette, and General Advertiser* published the resolutions adopted by a Richmond public meeting on 17 Aug. See Resolutions on Franco-American Relations, ca. 27 Aug. 1793, Editorial Note.
3. Wythe was probably offended by "An act reducing into one, the several acts concerning the High Court of Chancery," passed by the General Assembly on 29 Nov. 1792, that extended the time limit within which appeals could be made from chancery to the Virginia Supreme Court of Appeals. Under the presidency of Edmund Pendleton, the Court of Appeals overturned most of Wythe's chancery decisions favoring British creditors, notably *Page* v. *Pendleton and Lyons* of 3 May 1793 (Hening, *Statutes*, 13:411, 421; Imogene M. Brown, *American Aristides: A Biography of George Wythe* [Rutherford, N.J., 1981], pp. 258–59, 261).
4. At JM's request, John Taylor organized a public meeting in Caroline County. On 10 Sept. Taylor's cousin Edmund Pendleton presided at the meeting, which adopted resolutions paraphrasing those drafted by JM and Monroe. See Resolutions on Franco-American Relations, ca. 27 Aug. 1793, Editorial Note.
5. Wilson Cary Nicholas (see JM to Jefferson, 11 Aug. and second letter of 2 Sept. 1793).
6. David Meade Randolph.

Resolutions on Franco-American Relations

EDITORIAL NOTE

In August 1793 relations dramatically deteriorated between the Washington administration and the French minister to the United States, Edmond Charles Genet. Federalists circulated a report that he had threatened to appeal to the American people against Washington's neutrality policy. His denial of this report only made matters worse since Genet wrote directly to Washington, thereby drawing a sharp rebuke from the secretary of state. Federalists were first off the mark in organizing public meetings—a characteristic of American politics ever since the Stamp Act crisis—as vehicles for marshaling public opinion. In Virginia and many other states, these Federalist-sponsored meetings passed resolutions denouncing Genet and supporting the president's Neutrality Proclamation. Hamilton probably urged John Marshall and excise supervisor Edward Carrington to hold such a meeting in Richmond. Under the chairmanship of Jefferson's former law tutor, George Wythe, the 17 August meeting passed resolutions that in effect hurled a gauntlet into the heartland of republicanism (Jefferson to JM, second letter of 11 Aug., 25 Aug. 1793, and n. 1; JM to Jefferson, 27 Aug. 1793; Wythe to Jefferson and Edmund Randolph, 17 Aug. 1793, Jefferson to Wythe, 1 Sept. 1793 [DLC: Jefferson Papers]).

JM quickly took up the challenge. From 20 August to 1 September he visited at Monroe's house near Charlottesville, where the two Republicans planned "an early & well digested effort for calling out the real sense of the people . . . particularly by setting on foot expressions of the public mind in important Counties, and under the auspices of respectable names." JM was trying to educate the public and influence opinion in favor of Republican principles: "The Country is too much uninformed, and too inert to speak for itself; and the language of the towns which are generally directed by an adverse interest will insidiously inflame the evil" (JM to Jefferson, 27 Aug. and second letter of 2 Sept. 1793). He and Monroe drafted resolutions with an eye toward the same political constraints that had governed the arguments of the "Helvidius" essays. They advocated solidarity with republicanism and revolution in France, while affirming loyalty to Washington and avoiding a discussion of neutrality's merits.

Monroe attended the district court at Staunton and carried a draft of the resolutions to Archibald Stuart. As secretary of the 3 September public meeting, Stuart presented the resolutions. John Marshall had encouraged Federalist Gabriel Jones to bring forward resolutions similar to those passed at Richmond. The Staunton meeting, however, paraphrased resolutions from the draft by JM and Monroe. The draft avoided any mention of Genet, but the Staunton meeting added a resolution that dissociated Republicans from the French minister: "We most sincerely desire that the imprudence and indiscretion of a servant of France on the one hand, or of the ill judged interference of our own citizens (not in the executive department) on the other, may not disunite two nations, who have embraced the same principles of freedom, and who we believe esteem each other most ardently" (Richmond *Va. Gazette, and General Advertiser*, 2 Oct. 1793; the Staunton resolutions were also published as a broadside [Evans 26204]; see also JM to Stuart, 1 Sept. 1793). The reference to "the ill judged interference of our own citizens (not in the executive department)" struck at Chief Justice John Jay and Senator Rufus King, New York Federalists who had published the report of Genet's threat to appeal to the people against the president.

JM also urged John Taylor to organize a public meeting in Caroline County. On 10 September Taylor's cousin Edmund Pendleton presided at the meeting, which adopted resolutions that followed closely those drafted by JM and Monroe. As had happened at Staunton, the Caroline County meeting added a resolution obliquely criticizing Genet, Jay, and King: "That . . . all Applications of a Minister . . . to the people . . . are highly improper, & tend to create parties & dissensions amongst Us. . . . We therefore declare our disapprobation of certain Attempts in late News-paper publications, to make some alledged behaviour of that kind in the Minister of the French Nation, if any such really existed, the means of withdrawing our affection, either from the beloved President, or our Respectable Allies." Pendleton then sent a copy of the resolutions to Washington, and Jefferson drafted the president's reply to Pendleton (DLC: Washington Papers; printed in Richmond *Va. Gazette, and General Advertiser*, 25 Sept. 1793; see also JM to Jefferson, 27 Aug. 1793; Pendleton to Washington, 11 Sept. 1793, Mays, *Papers of Edmund Pendleton*, 2:613–15; Jefferson, "Heads of answer to the Caroline resolns.," 22 Sept. 1793 [DLC: Jefferson Papers]; Washington to Pendleton, public letter of 23 Sept. 1793, Fitzpatrick, *Writings of Washington*, 33:91–92; Taylor to JM, 25 Sept. 1793).

When the district court met at Charlottesville on 15 September, the opposition of John Nicholas, Jr. (Federalist clerk of Albemarle County), was sufficient to thwart the disorganized Republicans. At the next meeting of the county court, however, Albemarle citizens approved resolutions that generally paraphrased those drafted by JM and Monroe (Monroe to JM, 25 Sept. 1793, and n. 5; Nicholas Lewis to Washington, 24 Oct. 1793 [DLC: Washington Papers]).

Elsewhere in Virginia, the resolutions drafted by JM and Monroe met with less success. After the district court at Fredericksburg adjourned, Republicans convened a 7 October meeting of citizens from the several counties in the judicial district. With James Mercer in the chair, the meeting deliberated resolutions similar to those drafted by JM and Monroe. Unexpectedly, Federalists invaded the meeting, referred the resolutions to a committee charged with expressing the sense of the meeting, and obtained a postponement until the following day. When the meeting reconvened, Federalist excise inspector Edward Stevens maneuvered the proceedings into a bland session where the committee, fearful that any resolutions might be "overexpressive of their own sentiments," merely urged citizens to hold other meetings in their own counties and act independently. According to Monroe's account of the incident, the Republicans "awed the sects, tories, & their assistants into silence" so the meeting could pass no resolutions. Thus the Fredericksburg Republicans were stalemated but obtained a victory of sorts when their resolutions were printed in a Richmond newspaper (*Va. Herald, and Fredericksburg Advertiser*, 3 Oct. 1793; Richmond *Va. Gazette, and General Advertiser*, 16 and 23 Oct. 1793; Monroe to Jefferson, 14 Oct. 1793, Hamilton, *Writings of Monroe*, 1:278–79).

Stevens convened a meeting at Culpeper Court House on 21 October. Despite Federalist influence, the meeting endorsed the French alliance. While JM was satisfied with the Culpeper resolutions, he considered those approved by another Federalist-sponsored meeting in Fauquier County "to be a servile eccho of those in Richmond." Thus, as a vehicle for mobilizing public opinion, the model resolutions that he and Monroe drafted were a qualified success. Their approval in Caroline County, Staunton, and Charlottesville and their mixed reception elsewhere reflected the strengths and weaknesses of the fledgling Republican political organization in Virginia (*Va. Herald, and Fredericksburg Advertiser*, 3 Oct. and 14 Nov. 1793; Stevens to Washington, 25 Oct. 1793 [DLC: Washington Papers]; JM to

Monroe, 29 Oct. 1793; see also Harry Ammon, "The Genet Mission and the Development of American Political Parties," *Journal of American History*, 52 [1965–66]: 730–37).

[ca. 27 August 1793]

It being considd. that 'tis at all times the right & at certain periods the duty of the people to declare their principles & opinions on subjts. wch. concern the Natl. interst.; that at prest. conjuncture this duty is rendered the more indispensable by the prevailing practice of decly. resolns. in places where the inhabts can more easily assemble & consult than in the Country at large, and where interests views & politl. opinions different from those of the great body of the people, may happen to predominate, whence there may be danger of unfair & delusive inferences concerng. the true & generl sense of the people; It being also considd. that under the disadvantage a great proportion of the people labr. in their distant & dispersed situation from the want of timely & correct knowledge of particular incidents & the condt. of particular persons connected with public transactions, it is most prudent & safe, to wait with a decent reserve for full & satisfactory information in relation thereto, & in public declarations to abide by those great principles, just sentiments & estabd. Truths wch. can be little affected by personal or transitory occurrenc[e]s.

Therefore as the sense of the prest. Meeting

Resd. That the Constin. of the U. S. ought to be firmly & vigilantly supported agst. all direct or indirect attempts that may be made to subvert or violate the same.

That as it is the interest of U. S. to cultivate the preservation of peace by all just & honble. means, the Ex. Authy. ought to be supported in the exercise of its constil. powers & functions for enforcing the laws existg. for the purpose.

That the eminent virtues & services of our illustrious fellow Citizen G. W. P. of U. S. entitle him to the highest respect & lastg. gratitude of his Country, whose peace liby. & safety must ever remind it of his distingd. agency in promoting the same.

That the eminent & generous aids rendd. to the U S. in their arduous struggle for liberty, by the Fr. Nation, ought ever to be remd. & ackd. with gratitud⟨e⟩ & that the spectacle exhd. by the severe & glorious Contest in which it is now engaged for its own liberty, ought & must be peculiarly interesting to the wishes, the friendship & the sympathy of the people of America.

That all attempts which may be made in whatever form or disguise to alienate the good will of the people of Amera. from the cause of liberty & Repubn. Govt. in F. have a tendency to weaken their affection to the free principles of their own Govts. and manifest designs wch. ought to be narrowly watched & seasonably counteracted.

That such attempts to disunite nations mutually attachd. to the cause of liberty, & viewd. with unfriendly eyes by all who hate it, ought more particularly to be reprobated at the present crisis, when such vast efforts are making by a combination of Princes & nobles to crush an example that may open the eyes of all mankind to their natl. & pol: rights.

That a dissolution of the honble. & beneficial connection between the U. S. & F wd. obviously tend to forward a plan of connecting them with G. B. as one great leadg step towds. assimilating our Govt. to the form & spirit of the British Monarchy; and that this apprehension is greatly strenghd. by the active zeal displayed by persons disaffected to the Amn. Revn. & by others of known Monarchl. princ[i]ples, in propagating prejudices agst. the French Nation & Revolution.

Ms (DLC). In JM's hand; drafted with the assistance of Monroe. Headed in an unknown hand: "Sketch of Resolutions referred to in Letter of 2nd. Sept. 1793." Enclosed in JM's second letter to Jefferson of that date. Conjectural date assigned on the basis of evidence in JM to Jefferson, 27 Aug. 1793.

¶ To John Taylor. Letter not found. *Ca. 27 August 1793.* Mentioned in JM to Jefferson, 27 Aug. 1793, and JM to Taylor, 20 Sept. 1793. Acknowledged in Taylor to JM, 25 Sept. 1793. Written from Monroe's home near Charlottesville, the letter urges Taylor to organize a public meeting in Caroline County, suggests resolutions supporting the French alliance, and proposes that Edmund Pendleton patronize the measure. Informs Taylor that his draft of *Enquiry into the Principles* has been sent to Jefferson in Philadelphia.

"Helvidius" Number 2

[31 August 1793]

THE doctrine which has been examined, is pregnant with inferences and consequences against which no ramparts in the constitution could defend the public liberty, or scarcely the forms of Republican government. Were it once established that the powers of war and treaty are in their nature executive; that so far as they are not by strict construction transferred to the legislature, they actually belong to the executive; that of course all powers not less executive in their nature than those powers, if not granted to the legislature may be claimed by the executive: if granted, are to be taken *strictly*, with a residuary right in the executive; or, as will hereafter appear, perhaps claimed as a concurrent right by the executive; and no citizen could any longer guess at the character of the government under which he lives; the most penetrating jurist would be unable to scan the extent of constructive prerogative.

Leaving however to the leisure of the reader deductions which the author having omitted might not chuse to own, I proceed to the examination of one, with which that liberty cannot be taken.

"However true it may be (says he) that the right of the legislature to declare war *includes the right of judging* whether the legislature be under obligations to make war or not, it will not follow that the executive is *in any case* excluded from a *similar right* of judging in the execution of its own functions."[1]

A material error of the writer in this application of his doctrine lies in his shrinking from its regular consequences. Had he stuck to his principle in its full extent, and reasoned from it without restraint, he would only have had to defend himself against his opponents. By yielding the great point, that the right to declare war, *tho' to be taken strictly*, includes the right to judge whether the nation be under obligation to make war or not, he is compelled to defend his argument not only against others but against himself also. Observe how he struggles in his own toils.

He had before admitted that the right to declare war is vested in the legislature. He here admits that the right to declare war includes the right to judge whether the United States be obliged to declare war or not. Can the inference be avoided, that the executive instead of having a similar right to judge, is as much excluded from the right to judge as from the right to declare?

If the right to declare war be an exception out of the general grant to the executive power; every thing included in the right must be included in the exception; and being included in the exception, is excluded from the grant.

He cannot disentangle himself by considering the right of the executive to judge as *concurrent* with that of the legislature. For if the executive have a concurrent right to judge, and the right to judge be included in (it is in fact the very essence of) the right to declare, he must go on and say that the executive has a concurrent right also to declare. And then what will he do with his other admission, that the power to declare is an exception out of the executive power.

Perhaps an attempt may be made to creep out of the difficulty through the words "in the execution of its functions." Here again he must equally fail.

Whatever difficulties may arise in defining the executive authority in particular cases, there can be none in deciding on an authority clearly placed by the constitution in another department. In this case the constitution has decided what shall not be deemed an executive authority; tho' it may not have clearly decided in every case what shall be so deemed. The declaring of war is expressly made a legislative function. The judging of the obligations to make war, is admitted to be included as a legislative function. Whenever then a question occurs whether war shall be declared, or whether public stipulations require it, the question necessarily belongs to the department to which these functions belong— And no other department can be *in the execution of its proper functions*, if it should undertake to decide such a question.

There can be no refuge against this conclusion, but in the pretext of a *concurrent* right in both departments to judge of the obligations to declare war, and this must be intended by the writer when he says, "it will not follow that the executive is excluded *in any case* from a *similar right* of judging &c."

As this is the ground on which the ultimate defence is to be made, and which must either be maintained, or the works erected on it, demolished; it will be proper to give its strength a fair trial.

It has been seen that the idea of a *concurrent* right is at variance with other ideas advanced or admitted by the writer. Laying aside for the present that consideration, it seems impossible to avoid concluding that if the executive[2] has a concurrent right with the legislature to judge of obligations to declare war, and the right to judge be essentially included in the right to declare, it must have the same[3] right to declare as it has to judge; & by another analogy, the same right to judge of other causes of war, as of the particular cause found in a public stipulation. So that whenever the executive *in the course of its functions* shall meet with these cases, it must either infer an equal authority in all, or acknowledge its want of authority in any.

If any doubt can remain, or rather if any doubt could ever have arisen, which side of the alternative ought to be embraced, it can be with those only who overlook or reject some of the most obvious and essential truths in political science.

The power to judge of the causes of war as involved in the power to declare war, is expressly vested where all other legislative powers are vested, that is, in the Congress of the United States. It is consequently determined by the constitution to be a *Legislative power*. Now omitting the enquiry here in what respects a compound power may be partly legislative, and partly executive, and accordingly vested *partly* in the one, and *partly* in the other department, or *jointly* in both; a remark used on another occasion is equally conclusive on this, that the same power, cannot belong *in the whole*, to *both* departments, or be properly so vested as to operate *separately* in *each*. Still more evident is it, that the same *specific function or act*, cannot possibly belong to the *two* departments and be *separately* exerciseable by *each*.

Legislative power may be *concurrently* vested in different legislative bodies. Executive powers may be concurrently vested in different executive magistrates. In legislative acts the executive may have a participation, as in the qualified negative on the laws. In executive acts, the legislature, or at least a branch of it, may participate, as in the appointment to offices. Arrangements of this sort are familiar in theory, as well as in practice. But an independent exercise of an *executive act*, by the legislature *alone*, or of a *legislative act* by the executive *alone*, one or other of which must happen in every case where the same act is exerciseable by each, and the latter of which would happen in the case urged by the writer, is contrary to one of the first and best maxims of a well organized government, and ought never to be founded in a forced construction, much less in opposition to a fair one. Instances, it is true, may be discovered among ourselves where this maxim, has not been faithfully pursued; but being generally acknowledged to be errors, they confirm, rather than impeach the truth and value of the maxim.

It may happen also that different independent departments, the legislative and executive, for example, may in the exercise of their functions, interpret the constitution differently, and thence lay claim each to the same power. This difference of opinion is an inconvenience not entirely to be avoided. It results from what may be called, if it be thought fit, a *concurrent* right to expound the constitution. But *this species* of concurrence is obviously and radically different from that in question. The former supposes the constitution to have given the power to one department only; and the doubt to be to which it has been given. The latter supposes it to belong to both; and that it may be exercised by either or both, according to the course of exigencies.

A concurrent authority in two independent departments to perform the same function with respect to the same thing, would be as awkward in practice, as it is unnatural in theory.

If the legislature and executive have both a right to judge of the obligations to make war or not, it must sometimes happen, though not at present, that they will judge differently. The executive may proceed to consider the question to-day, may determine that the United States are not bound to take part in a war, and *in the execution of its functions* proclaim that determination to all the world. To-morrow, the legislature may follow in the consideration of the same subject, may determine that the obligations impose war on the United States, and *in the execution of its functions*, enter into a *constitutional declaration*, expressly contradicting the *constitutional proclamation*.

In what light does this present the constitution to the people who established it? In what light would it present to the world, a nation, thus speaking, thro' two different organs, equally constitutional and authentic, two opposite languages, on the same subject and under the same existing circumstances?

But it is not with the legislative rights alone that this doctrine interferes. The rights of the judiciary may be equally invaded. For it is clear that if a right declared by the constitution to be legislative, and actually vested by it in the legislature, leaves, notwithstanding, a similar right in the executive whenever a case for exercising it occurs, *in the course of its functions:* a right declared to be judiciary and vested in that department may, on the same principle, be assumed and exercised by the executive *in the course of its functions:* and it is evident that occasions and pretexts for the latter interference may be as frequent as for the former. So again the judiciary department may find equal occasions in the execution of *its* functions, for usurping the authorities of the executive: and the legislature for stepping into the jurisdiction of both. And thus all the powers of government, of which a partition is so carefully made among the several branches, would be thrown into absolute hotchpot, and exposed to a general scramble.

It is time however for the writer himself to be heard, in defence of his text. His comment is in the words following:

"If the legislature have a right to make war on the one hand, it is on the other the duty of the executive to preserve peace, till war is declared; and in fulfilling that duty, it must necessarily possess a right of judging what is the nature of the obligations which the treaties of the country impose on the government; and when in pursuance of this right it has concluded that there is nothing inconsistent with a state of neutrality, it becomes both its province and its duty to enforce the laws incident to that state of the nation. The executive is charged with the execution of all laws, the laws of nations, as well as the municipal law which recognizes, and adopts those laws. It is consequently bound, by faithfully executing the laws of neutrality, when that is the state of the nation, to avoid giving a cause of war to foreign powers."

To do full justice to this master piece of logic, the reader must have the patience to follow it step by step.

If the legislature have a right to make war on the one hand, it is on the other, the duty of the executive to preserve peace till war is declared.

It will be observed that here is an explicit and peremptory assertion, that it is the *duty* of the executive *to preserve peace*, till *war is declared*.

And in fulfilling that duty it must necessarily possess a right of judging what is the nature of the obligations which the treaties of the country impose on the government: That is to say, in fulfilling *the duty to preserve peace*, it must necessarily possess the right to judge whether *peace ought to be preserved;* in other words *whether its duty should be per-*

formed. Can words express a flatter contradiction? It is self evident that the *duty* in this case is so far from *necessarily implying the right*, that it *necessarily excludes it.*

And when in pursuance of this right it has concluded that there is nothing in them (obligations) inconsistent with a state of neutrality, IT BECOMES *both its province and its duty to enforce the laws incident to that state of the nation.*

And what if it should conclude that there is something inconsistent? Is it or is it not the province and duty of the executive to enforce the same laws? Say it is, you destroy the right to judge. Say it is not, you cancel the duty to[4] obey.

Take this sentence in connection with the preceeding and the contradictions are multiplied. Take it by itself, and it makes the right to judge and conclude whether war be obligatory, absolute, and operative; and the duty to preserve peace, subordinate and conditional.

It will have been remarked by the attentive reader that the term *peace* in the first clause has been silently exchanged in the present one, for the term *neutrality*. Nothing however is gained by shifting the terms. Neutrality means peace; with an allusion to the circumstance of other nations being at war. The term has no reference to the existence or non-existence of treaties or alliances between the nation at peace and the nations at war. The laws incident to a state of neutrality, are the laws incident to a state of peace, with such circumstantial modifications only as are required by the new relation of the nations at war: Until war therefore be duly authorised by the United States they are as *actually* neutral when other nations are at war, as they are at peace, (if such a distinction in the terms is to be kept up) when other nations are not at war. The existence of *eventual* engagements which can only take effect on the declaration of the legislature, cannot, without that declaration, change the *actual* state of the country, any more in the eye of the executive than in the eye of the judiciary department. The laws to be the guide of both, remain the same to each, and the same to both.

Nor would more be gained by allowing the writer to define than to shift the term neutrality. For suppose, if you please, the existence of obligations to join in war to be inconsistent with neutrality, the question returns upon him, what laws are to be inforced by the executive until effect shall be given to those obligations by the declaration of the legislature? Are they to be the laws incident to those obligations, that is incident to war? However strongly the doctrines or deductions of the writer may tend to this point, it will not be avowed. Are the laws to be enforced by the executive, then, in such a state of things, to be the *same* as if no such obligations existed? Admit this, which you must admit if you reject the other alternative, and the argument lands precisely where it embarked—in the position, that it is the absolute duty of the executive in all cases to preserve peace till war is declared, not that it is "*to become the province and duty of the executive*" after it has concluded that there is nothing in those obligations inconsistent with a state of peace and neutrality. The right to judge and conclude therefore so solemnly maintained in the text is lost in the comment.

We shall see whether it can be reinstated by what follows—

The executive is charged with the execution of all laws, the laws of nations as well as the municipal law which recognizes and adopts those laws. It is consequently bound, by faithfully executing the laws of neutrality when that is the state of the nation, to avoid giving cause of war to foreign powers.

The first sentence is a truth, but nothing to the point in question. The last is *partly true* in its proper meaning, but *totally untrue* in the meaning of the writer. That the executive is bound faithfully to execute the laws of neutrality, whilst those laws continue unaltered by the competent authority, is true; but not for the reason here given, to wit, to avoid giving cause of war to foreign powers. It is bound to the faithful execution of these as of all other laws internal and external, by the nature of its trust and the sanction of its oath, even if turbulent citizens should consider its so doing as a cause of war at home, or unfriendly nations should consider its so doing, as a cause of war abroad. The duty of the executive to preserve external peace, can no more suspend the force of external laws, than its duty to preserve internal peace can suspend the force of municipal laws.

It is certain that a faithful execution of the laws of neutrality may tend as much in some cases, to incur war from one quarter, as in others to avoid war from other quarters. The executive must nevertheless execute the laws of neutrality whilst in force, and leave it to the legislature to decide whether they ought to be altered or not. The executive has no other discretion than to convene and give information to the legislature on occasions that may demand it; and whilst this discretion is duly exercised the trust of the executive is satisfied, and that department is not responsible for the consequences. It could not be made responsible for them without vesting it with the legislative as well as with the executive trust.

These remarks are obvious and conclusive, on the supposition that the expression "laws of neutrality" means simply what the words import, and what alone they can mean, to give force or colour to the inference of the writer from his own premises. As the inference itself however in its proper meaning, does not approach towards his avowed object, which is to work out a prerogative for the executive to judge, in common with the legislature, whether there be cause of war or not in a public obligation, it is to be presumed that "in faithfully executing the laws of neutrality" an exercise of that prerogative was meant to be included. On this supposition the inference, as will have been seen, does not result from his own premises, and has been already so amply discussed, and, it is conceived, so clearly disproved, that not a word more can be necessary on this branch of his argument.

HELVIDIUS.

Printed copy (Philadelphia *Gazette of the U.S.*, 31 Aug. 1793). Reprinted in [Madison], *Letters of Helvidius*, pp. 14-22. For JM's later revisions, see nn. 2-4.

1. This argument in "Pacificus" No. 1 and other quotations from that essay used by JM in "Helvidius" No. 2 are found in Syrett and Cooke, *Papers of Hamilton*, 15:40.

2. In retirement, JM corrected the "Helvidius" essays for a new edition, published by Jacob Gideon, Jr., in which is here added "as such" (*The Federalist, on the New Constitution, Written in the Year 1788, by Mr. Hamilton, Mr. Madison, and Mr. Jay; with an Appendix, Containing the Letters of Pacificus and Helvidius, on the Proclamation of Neutrality of 1793; . . . A New Edition. The Numbers Written by Mr. Madison Corrected by Himself* [Washington, 1818], p. 606). JM noted that "I have limited the corrections to errors of the press and of the transcriber, and a few cases in which the addition of a word or two seemed to render the meaning more explicit" (JM to Richard Cutts, 14 Mar. 1818, Madison, *Letters* [Cong. ed.], 3:60).

3. In later edition, "concurrent" is here added (*The Federalist with Helvidius* [1818 ed.], p. 606).

4. In later edition, this sentence concludes "preserve peace, till war is declared" (ibid., p. 610).

To Archibald Stuart

DEAR SIR   Sepr 1. 1793

Being well persuaded of your attachment to the public good, I make no apology for mentioning to you a few circumstances which I conceive to be deeply connected with it. It appears by accounts recd. by Col: Monroe & myself from Mr Jefferson, as well as by the face of the late Newspapers that a variance of a very serious nature has taken place between the federal Executive and Mr. Genet the French Minister. From whatever causes it may have particularly resulted, and whatever blame may belong to the latter, the event will give great pain to all the enlightened friends of those principles of liberty on which the American & French Revolutions are founded, & of that sound policy which ought to maintain the connection between the two countries. Unfortunately this character is not due to every description of persons among us. There are some who dislike republican Government. There are others who dislike the connection with France. And there are others misled by the influence of both. From those quarters attempts are already issuing to make the worst instead of the best of the event, to turn the public sensation with respect to Genet against the French Nation, to give the same turn to the public veneration for the President to produce by these means an animosity between America & France, as the hopeful source of a dissolution of their political & commercial union, of a consequent connection with G. B. and under her auspices, of a gradual approximation towards her Form of Government. In this state of things Is it not the duty of all good citizens to deliberate on the best steps that can be taken for defeating the mischief? And can there be any doubt that a true and authentic expression of the sense of the people will be the most effectual as well as the most proper antidote that can be applied? It is as little doubtful in my opinion what the sense of the people is. They are attached to the Constitution. They are attached to the President. They are attached to the French Nation and Revolution. They are attached to peace as long as it can be honorably preserved. They are averse to Monarchy. And to a political connection with that of Great Britain, and will readily protest against any known or supposed designs that may have this change in their situation for their object. Why then can not the sense of the people be collected on these points, by the agency of temperate & respectable men who have the opportunity of meeting them. This is the more requisite in the Country at large at present, as the voice of particular places distinguished by particular interests & opinion may otherwise, be mistaken for that of the nation, and every hope be thence cut off, of preserving the esteem & affection as yet existing between the French & the American people. A great deal might be said on this subject. To you a very little will suffice: and the less as you will learn from Col: Monroe all the particulars which may explain the ground of what I have taken the liberty of suggesting. I shall only therefore add my request that you will consider this letter as entirely *Confidential*, and as a proof of the esteem & regard with which I am Dear [Sir] Your sincere friend & Hble servt.

Js. MADISON JR

RC (ViHi). Addressed by JM to Stuart at Staunton, "Hond. by Col Monroe." For the context of this letter, see Resolutions on Franco-American Relations, ca. 27 Aug. 1793, Editorial Note.

From Thomas Jefferson

Sep. 1. 93.

My last was of the 25th. Since that I have received yours of the 20th. and Colo. M's of the 21st.[1] Nothing further has passed with mr. Genet, but one of his Consuls[2] has committed a pretty serious deed at Boston, by going with an armed force taken from a French frigate in the harbour, and rescuing a vessel out of the hands of the marshal who had arrested her by process from a court of justice. In another instance he kept off the Marshal by an armed force from serving a precept on a vessel. He is ordered consequently to be arrested himself prosecuted & punished for the rescue, and his Exequatur will be revoked. You will see in the newspapers the attack made on our commerce by the British king in his *additional instructions* of June 8.[3] Tho' we have only newspaper information of it, *provisional* instructions are going to mr. Pinckney to require a revocation of them and indemnification for all losses which individuals may sustain by them in the mean time. Of the revocation I have not the least expectation. I shall therefore be for laying the whole business (respecting both nations) before Congress. While I think it impossible they should not approve of what has been done disagreeable to the friendly nation, it will be in their power to soothe them by strong commercial retaliations against the hostile one. Pinching their commerce will be just against themselves, advantageous to us, and conciliatory towards our friends of the hard necessities into which their agent has driven us. His conduct has given room for the enemies of liberty & of France to come forward in a stile of acrimony against that nation which they never would have dared to have done. The disapprobation of the agent mingles with the reprehension of his nation & gives a toleration to that which it never had before. He has still some defenders in Freneau's & Greenleaf's papers. Who they are I know not: for even Hutcheson & Dallas give him up. I inclose you a Boston paper which will give you a specimen of what all the papers are now filled with. You will recognise mr. A—— under the signature of Camillus.[4] He writes in every week's paper now, & generally under different signatures. This is the first paper in which he has omitted some furious incartade against me. Hutcheson says that Genet has totally overturned the Republican interest in Philadelphia. However, the people going right themselves, if they always see their republican advocates with them, an accidental meeting with the Monocrats will not be a coalescence. You will see much said & gainsaid about G's threat to appeal to the people. I can assure you it is a fact. I received yesterday the M. S. you mentioned to me from F——n.[5] I have only got a dozen pages into it, and never was more charmed with any thing. Profound arguments presented in the simplest point of view entitle him really to his antient signature. In the papers received from you[6] I have seen nothing which ought to be changed, except a part of one sentence, not necessary for it's object, & running foul of something of which you were not apprised.

A malignant fever has been generated in the filth of Water street which gives great alarm.[7] About 70. people had died of it two days ago, & as many more were ill of it. It has now got into most parts of the city & is considerably infectious. At first 3. out of 4. died. Now about 1. out of 3. It comes on with a pain in the head, sick stomach, then a little chill, fever, black vomiting & stools, & death from the 2d. to the 8th. day. Every body, who can, is flying from the city, and the panic of the country people is likely to add famine to disease. Tho becoming less mortal, it is still spreading, and the heat of the weather is very unpropitious. I have withdrawn my daughter from the city, but am obliged to go to it every day myself. My threshing machine is arrived at New York. Mr. Pinckney writes me word that the original from which this model is copied threshes 150 bushels of wheat in 8. hours with 6. horses and 5. men. It may be moved either by water or horses. Fortunately the workman who made it (a millwright) is come in the same vessel to settle in America. I have written to persuade him to go on immediately to Richmd. offering him the use of my model to exhibit, and to give him letters to get him into immediate employ in making them.[8] I expect an answer before I write to you again. I understand that the model is made mostly in brass, & in the simple form in which it was first ordered, to be worked by horses, it was to have cost 5. guineas, but mr. Pinckney having afterwards directed it to be accomodated to a water movement also, it has made it more complicated, and costs 13. guineas. It will thresh any grain from the Windsor bean down to the smallest. Adieu.

P. S. The market, was the last winter from 25. to 50 percent higher than it was in the winter preceding. It is now got to from 50. to 100. percent higher. I think by the winter it will be generally 100 percent on the prices of 1790. European goods are also much risen. Of course you must expect a rise in the boarding houses compounded of these two. In the mean time the produce of the farmer, say wheat, rice, tobacco has not risen a copper. The redundancy of paper then in the cities is palpably a tax on the distant farmer.

P. S. Sep. 2. I have made great progress into the M. S. and still with the same pleasure. I have no doubt it must produce great effect. But that this may be the greatest possible, it's coming out should be timed to the best advantage. It should come out just so many days before the meeting of Congress as will prevent suspicions of it's coming with them, yet so as to be a new thing when they arrive, ready to get into their hands while yet unoccupied, before the panic of the culprits shall be over, or any measures for defeating it's first effect may be taken. I will direct it to appear a fortnight before their meeting unless you order otherwise. It might as well be thrown into a church yard, as come out now.

RC (DLC); FC, partial Tr (DLC: Jefferson Papers). Unsigned. RC docketed by JM.

1. Hamilton, *Writings of Monroe*, 1:270–72.

2. Antoine Charbonnet Duplaine became French vice-consul for New Hampshire,. Massachusetts, and Rhode Island on 5 June (Nasatir and Monell, *French Consuls*, p. 549). For details of the incident which Jefferson here describes, see Charles Marion Thomas, *American Neutrality in 1793: A Study in Cabinet Government* (New York, 1931), pp. 212–19.

3. On 28 Aug. the Philadelphia *Federal Gazette* published the British order in council of 8 June (reprinted in *ASP, Foreign Relations*, 1:240), which expanded the definition of contraband to include "corn, flour, and meal" and authorized the seizure of any ships "attempting to enter any blockaded port." In his 7 Sept. letter to Thomas Pinckney (press copy, DLC: Madison Papers), Jefferson directed the U.S. minister to Great Britain to protest the order (Ford, *Writings of Jefferson*, 6:412–16). JM's copy of *Congress of the United States. In Senate, May 12th, 1794. On Motion, Ordered, That the Memorial of Mr. Pinckney, the Answer of Mr. Hammond, and the Letter of the Secretary of State of the 1st of May to Mr. Hammond Relative to the British Instructions of the 8th of June Last, Be Printed . . .* (Philadelphia, 1794; Evans 27892) is in the Madison Collection, Rare Book Department, University of Virginia Library. This pamphlet includes the later diplomatic correspondence relating to the order in council (reprinted in *ASP, Foreign Relations*, 1:448–54).

4. On 17 and 24 Aug. Federalist Benjamin Russell's Boston *Columbian Centinel* published essays by "Camillus" attacking the Republican party and Genet and defending Hamilton. No evidence has been found that either John Adams or John Quincy Adams wrote those essays. A more likely candidate is Fisher Ames, who had used the pseudonym "Camillus" in 1787 and was drafting newspaper essays in 1793 (Winfred E. A. Bernhard, *Fisher Ames: Federalist and Statesman, 1758–1808* [Chapel Hill, N.C., 1965], pp. 50, 218–19).

5. JM and Monroe sent Jefferson, circa 22 Aug., the draft of *Enquiry into the Principles* by John Taylor, who had previously written the "Franklin" essays.

6. In his 20 Aug. letter to Jefferson, JM had enclosed drafts of "Helvidius," most likely numbers 3 and 4.

7. In early August infected persons among approximately two thousand Santo Domingan refugees introduced yellow fever into Philadelphia (J. H. Powell, *Bring Out Your Dead: The Great Plague of Yellow Fever in Philadelphia in 1793* [Philadelphia, 1949], pp. vii–viii, 5, 16, 293).

8. James Makittrick Adair informed Jefferson that he had arrived in New York from London bearing letters from Pinckney and "a box . . . containing the model of a threshing mill." Jefferson replied that if William Hutton, who had made the model, "will go immediately to Virginia, he may quickly make a fortune by building threshing machines," since farmers there could avoid destruction of wheat crops by insects if they threshed soon after harvest. Adair arranged to have the model sent to Philadelphia but reported that Hutton was already committed "to superintend the erection of a Cotton Mill at Newhaven in Connecticut" (Adair to Jefferson, n.d. [docketed as received 30 Aug. 1793], Jefferson to Adair, 1 Sept. 1793, Adair to Jefferson, 9 Sept. 1793 [DLC: Jefferson Papers]).

To Thomas Jefferson

DEAR SIR   Sepr. 2. 93

I write this by your servant on his way to George Town with a Horse. He applies to me for his best route. I advise the circuitous one by Fredg. in preference to the shorter one, in which he would probably lose more by mistakes than would be equal to the difference between the two in point of distance. I left Monroe's yesterday. My stay was spun out by waiting for Mr. D. R. who did not arrive at Monto: till Friday evening. Your letter by him was duly recd. On getting home last night I found your subsequent one of the 18th. inst.[1] I have not yet read the paper inclosed in it. I shall write you in the course of the day by another opportunity for the post which will afford me time to say what I could not say now without detaining the Servant.

RC (DLC). The lower portion of the page, probably containing JM's signature, has been clipped. Docketed by Jefferson, "recd. Sep. 8."

1. JM should have written "ultimo," referring to Jefferson's letter of 18 Aug. 1793.

To Thomas Jefferson

DEAR SIR   Sepr. 2d. 1793

I dropped you a few lines this morning by the servant going to George Town with your horse. I had not time, without detaining him to say more than that I had your two favors of the 11th. Ult: by Mr. D. R.[1] and of the 18th. by post. The former was communicated to Monroe, as shall be the latter in case of opportunity. The conduct of Genèt as developed in these, and in his proceedings as exhibited in the newspapers, is as unaccountable as it is distressing. The effect is beginning to be strongly felt here in the surprize and disgust of those who are attached to the French cause, and viewed this minister as the instrument for cementing instead of alienating the two Republics. These sensations are powerfully reinforced by the general and habitual veneration for the President. The Anglican party is busy as you may suppose in making the worst of every thing, and in turning the public feelings against France, and thence, in favor of England. The only antidote for their poison, is to distinguish between the nation & its Agent, between principles and events; and to impress the well mea[n]ing with the fact that the enemies of France & of Liberty are at work to lead them from their honorable connection with these, into the arms and ultimately into the Government of G. B. If the genuine sense of the people could be collected on the several points comprehended in the occasion, the calamity would be greatly alleviated if not absolutely controuled. But this is scarcely possible. The Country is too much uninformed, and too inert to speak for itself; and the language of the towns which are generally directed by an adverse interest will insidiously inflame the evil. It is however of such infinite importance to our own Government as well as to that of France, that the real sentiments of the people here should be understood, that something ought to be attempted on that head. I inclose a copy of a train of ideas sketched on the first rumour of the war between the Ex. & Genet, and particularly suggested by the Richmond Resolutions, as a groundwork for those who might take the lead in county meetings. It was intended that they should be modified in every particular according to the state of information and the particular temper of the place. A copy has been sent to Caroline with a hope that Mr. P. might find it not improper to step forward. Another is gone to the District Court at Staunton in the hands of Monroe, who carried a letter from me on the subject to A. Stuart; and a third will be for consideration at the District Ct. at Charlottesville. If these examples should be set, there may be a chance of like proceedings elsewhere: and in themselves they will be respectable specimens of the principles and sensations of the Agricultural, which is the commanding part of the Society. I am not sanguine however that the effort will succeed. If it does not, the State Legislatures, and the federal also if possible, must be induced to take up the matter in its true point of view. Monroe & myself read with attention your despatch by D. R. and had much conversation on what passed between you & the P. It appd. to both of us that a real anxiety was marked to retain you in office, that over & above other motives, it was felt that your presence and implied sanction might be a necessary shield against certain criticisms from certain quarters; that the departure of the only counsellor possessing the confidence of the Republicans would be a signal for new & perhaps very disagreeable attacks; that in this point of view, the respectful & conciliatory language of the P. is worthy of particular attention; and that it affords a better hope than has existed of your being able to command attention, and to moderate the predominant tone. We agreed in opinion also that whilst this end is pursued, it would be wise to make as few concessions as possible that might embarrass the free pursuit of measures which may be dictated by Repubn. principles & required by the public good. In a word we think you ought to make the most of the value we perceive to be placed on your participation in the Ex: Counsels. I am extremely glad to find that you are to remain another quarter. The season will be more apropos in several respects; and it will prevent any co-operation which a successor might be disposed to make towards a final breach with France. I have little hope that you will have one whose policy will have the same healing tendency with yours. I foresee, I think, that it will be either King, if Johnson is put at the Treasy: or E. Rutlege, if Walcot should be put there. I am glad the President rightly infers my determination from antecedent circumstances, so as to free me from imputations in his mind connected with the present state of things.[2] Monroe is particularly solicitous that you should take the view of your present position & opportunities above suggested. He sees so forcibly the difficulty of keeping the feelings of the people as to Genèt distinct from those due to his Constituents, that he can hardly prevail on himself absolutely, and *openly*, to abandon him. I concur with him that it ought to be done no further than is forced upon us, that in general silence is better than open denunciation and crimination; and that it is not unfair to admit the apologetic influence of the errors in our own Government which may have inflamed the passions which now discolor every object to his eye: such as the refusal in the outset of the Government to favor the commerce of F. more than that of G. B—the unfortunate appt. of G. M.[3] to the former: the language of the proclamation—the attempts of Pacificus to explain away & dissolve the Treaty, the notoriety of the Author, and the appearance of its being an informal manifestation of the views of the Ex. &c.

I paid a short visit to Mr. W. N.[4] as I proposed. He talks like a sound Republican, and sincere friend to the French cause in every respect. I collected from him that E. R. had admitted to him that he drew the Procln., that he had been attacked on it at Chatham by Mr. Jos: Jones, that he reprobated the comment of Pac–f–s[5]–&c. W. N observed that H.[6] had taken the Ex. in by gaining phrases of which he could make the use he has done. The circumstances which derogate from full confidence in W. N. are 1st. his being embarked in a variety of projects which call for money, and keep him in intercourse with the merchts. of Richd. 2d. his communication & intimacy with Marshal of whose *disinterestedness* as well as understanding he has the highest opinion. It is said, that Marshal who is at the head of the great purchase from Fairfax, has lately obtained pecuniary aids from the Bank or people connected with it.[7] I think it certain that he must have felt, in the moment of the purchase an absolute dependence on the monied interest, which will explain him to every one that reflects, in the active character he is assuming. I have been obliged to write this in great haste, the bearer impatiently waiting the whole time.

I hope you have rcd. the five Nos. of Hel–v–d–s. I must resume the task I suppose, in relation to the *Treaty*—& *Gratitude*. I feel however so much awkwardness under the new posture of things, that I shall deliberate whether a considerable postponement at least may not be adviseable. I found also on my return a House full of particular friends who will stay some weeks and receive & return visits from which I can not decently exclude myself. If I sd. perceive it impossible or improper to continue the publication so as to avail myself the channel used to the press, I shall suspend it till I see & talk with you on the whole matter. Adieu.

RC (DLC). Unsigned. Docketed by Jefferson, "recd. Sep. 14." Enclosed Resolutions on Franco-American Relations, ca. 27 Aug. 1793. This is the last 1793 letter JM listed in his 1783–1818 calendar of letters to Jefferson. The calendar resumes with the 1798 entries (DLC: Rives Collection, Madison Papers).

1. David Meade Randolph.

2. According to the notes on his conversation with Washington that Jefferson enclosed in his second letter to JM of 11 Aug., the president "returned to the difficulty of naming my successor, he said mr. Madison would be his first choice, but he had always expressed to him such a decision against public office that he could not expect he would undertake it." Late in life, JM sought to dispel derogatory inferences that were drawn from his willingness to serve as secretary of state under Jefferson but not under Washington: "The part I had borne, in the origin and adoption of the Constitution, determined me at the outset of the Govt. to prefer a seat in the House of Representatives; as least exposing me to the imputation of selfish views. . . . Having commenced my Legislative career as I did, I thought it most becoming to proceed under the original impulse to the end of it" (JM to Henry Lee, 3 Mar. 1834, Madison, *Writings* [Hunt ed.], 9:532–33).

3. At a later time JM filled in the remaining letters of "Gour Morris."

4. At a later time JM filled in the remaining letters of "W. C Nicholas."

5. Hamilton's "Pacificus" essays.

6. At a later time JM filled in the remaining letters of "Hamilton."

7. Through his position as counsel for the Fairfax estate in several cases since 1786, John Marshall learned of the desire of Lord Fairfax's heir, Denny Martin Fairfax, to sell the Northern Neck lands remaining in his personal inheritance. Marshall assembled a partnership including his brother James Markham Marshall, his brothers-in-law John Ambler and Rawleigh Colston, and Henry Lee. James Markham Marshall went to London and there contracted for the land purchase in February 1793. A year later he returned to Europe to borrow on the security of lands owned by his father-in-law, Robert Morris. The deal was not concluded until 1806. Albert Beveridge insisted that John Marshall "received no money from the Bank for the Fairfax purchase" (Johnson, *Papers of John Marshall*, 2:140–49; Beveridge, *Life of John Marshall*, 2:203–11, 101; see also Note on Fairfax Lands by John Taylor of Caroline, n.d. [DLC]).

"Helvidius" Number 3

[7 September 1793]

IN order to give color to a right in the Executive to exercise the Legislative power of judging whether there be a cause of war in a public stipulation—two other arguments are subjoined by the writer to that last examined.

The first is simply this, "It is the right and duty of the Executive to judge of and interpret those articles of our treaties which give to France particular privileges, *in order to the enforcement of those privileges*,"[1] from which it is stated as a necessary consequence, that the Executive has certain other rights, among which is the right in question.

This argument is answered by a very obvious distinction. The first right is essential to the execution of the treaty *as a law in operation*, and interferes with no right invested[2] in another Department. The second[3] is not essential to the execution of the treaty or any other law; on the contrary the article to which the right is applied, cannot as has been shewn, from the very nature of it be *in operation* as a law without a previous declaration of the Legislature; and all the laws to be enforced by the Executive remain in the mean time precisely the same, whatever be the disposition or judgment of the Executive. This second right would also interfere with a right acknowledged to be in the Legislative Department.

If nothing else could suggest this distinction to the writer, he ought to have been reminded of it by his own words "in order to the enforcement of those privileges"—was it in order to *the enforcement* of the article of guaranty, that the right is ascribed to the Executive?

The other of the two arguments reduces itself into the following form: The Executive has the right to receive public Ministers; this right includes the right of deciding, in the case of a revolution, whether the new government sending the Minister, ought to be recognized or not; and this again, the right to give or refuse operation to pre-existing treaties.

The power of the Legislature to declare war and judge of the causes for declaring it, is one of the most express and explicit parts of the Constitution. To endeavor to abridge or *effect*[4] it by strained inferences, and by hypothetical or singular occurrences, naturally warns the reader of some lurking fallacy.

The words of the Constitution are "he (the President) shall receive Ambassadors, other public Ministers and Consuls." I shall not undertake to examine what would be the precise extent and effect of this function in various cases which fancy may suggest, or which time may produce. It will be more proper to observe in general, and every candid reader will second the observation, that little if any thing more was intended by the clause, than to provide for a particular mode of communication, *almost* grown into a right among modern nations; by pointing out the department of the government, most proper for the ceremony of admitting public Ministers, of examining their credentials, and of authenticating their title to the privileges annexed to their character by the law of nations. This being the apparent design of the Constitution, it would be highly improper to magnify the function into an important prerogative, even where no rights of other departments could be affected by it.

To shew that the view here given of the clause is not a new construction, invented or strained for a particular occasion—I will take the liberty of recurring to the cotemporary work already quoted, which contains the obvious and original gloss put on this part of the Constitution by its friends and advocates.

"The President is also to be authorised to receive Ambassadors and other public Ministers. This, though it has been a rich theme of declamation, is more a matter of *dignity* than of *authority*. It is a circumstance, that will be *without consequence* in the administration of the government, and it is far more convenient that it should be arranged in this manner, than that there should be a necessity for convening the Legislature or one of its branches upon every arrival of a foreign Minister, though it were merely to take the place of a departed predecessor." Fed. vol. II. p. 237.[5]

Had it been foretold in the year 1788 when this work was published, that before the end of the year 1793, a writer, assuming the merit of being a friend to the Constitution, would appear, and gravely maintain, that this function, which was to be *without consequence* in the administration of the government, might have the consequence of deciding on the validity of revolutions in favor of liberty, "of putting the United States in a condition to become an associate in war," nay "of laying the *Legislature* under an *obligation* of *declaring* war," what would have been thought and said of so visionary a prophet?

The moderate opponents of the Constitution would probably have disowned his extravagance. By the advocates of the Constitution, his prediction must have been treated as "an experiment on public credulity, dictated either by a deliberate intention to deceive, or by the overflowings of a zeal too intemperate to be ingenuous."[6]

But how does it follow from the function to receive Ambassadors and other public Ministers that so consequential a prerogative may be exercised by the Executive? When a foreign Minister presents himself, two questions immediately arise: Are his credentials from the existing and acting government of his country? Are they properly authenticated? These questions belong of necessity to the Executive; but they involve no cognizance of the question, whether those exercising the government have the right along with the possession. This belongs to the nation, and to the nation alone, on whom the government operates. The questions before the Executive are merely questions of fact; and the Executive would have precisely the same right, or rather be under the same necessity of deciding them, if its function was simply to receive *without any discretion to reject* public Ministers. It is evident, therefore, that if the Executive has a right to reject a public Minister it must be founded on some other consideration than a change in the government or the newness of the government; and consequently a right to refuse to acknowledge a new government cannot be implied by the right to refuse a public Minister.

It is not denied that there may be cases in which a respect to the general principles of liberty, the essential rights of the people, or the overruling sentiments of humanity, might require a government, whether new or old, to be treated as an illegitimate despotism. Such are in fact discussed and admitted by the most approved authorities. But they are great and extraordinary cases, by no means submitted to so limited an organ of the national will as the Executive of the United States; and certainly not to be brought, by any torture of words, within the right to receive Ambassadors.

That the authority of the Executive does not extend to[7] question, whether an existing government ought to be recognized or not, will still more clearly appear from an examination of the next inference of the writer, to wit, that the Executive has a right to give or refuse activity and operation to pre-existing treaties.

If there be a principle that ought not to be questioned within the United States, it is, that every nation has a right to abolish an old government and establish a new one. This principle is not only recorded in every public archive, written in every American heart, and sealed with the blood of a host of American martyrs; but is the only lawful tenure by which the United States hold their existence as a nation.

It is a principle incorporated with the above, that governments are established for the national good and are organs of the national will.

From these two principles results a third, that treaties formed by the government, are treaties of the nation, unless otherwise expressed in the treaties.

Another consequence is that a nation, by exercising the right of changing the organ of its will, can neither disengage itself from the obligations, nor forfeit the benefits of its treaties. This is a truth of vast importance, and happily rests with sufficient firmness on its own authority. To silence or prevent cavil, I insert however, the following extracts:

"Since then such a treaty (a treaty not *personal* to the sovereign) directly relates to the body of the State, it subsists though the form of the republic happens to be changed, and though it should be even transformed into a monarchy—For the State and the nation are always the same whatever changes are made in the form of the government—and the treaty concluded with the nation, remains in force as long as the nation exists." Vattel, B. II. § 185.[8]

"It follows that as a treaty, notwithstanding the change of a democratic government into a monarchy, continues in force with the new King, in like manner; if a *monarchy* becomes a *republic*, the treaty made with the King does not expire on that account, unless it was manifestly personal." Burlam. part IV, c. IX, § 16. ¶ 6.[9]

As a change of government then makes no change in the obligations or rights of the party to a treaty, it is clear that the Executive can have no more right to suspend or prevent the operation of a treaty, on account of the change, than to suspend or prevent the operation, where no such change has happened. Nor can it have any more right to suspend the operation of a treaty in force as a law, than to suspend the operation of any other law.[10]

The logic employed by the writer on this occasion, will be best understood by accommodating to it the language of a proclamation, founded on the prerogative and policy of suspending the treaty with France.

Whereas a treaty was concluded on the   day of   between the United States and the French nation, through the kingly government, which was then the organ of its will: And whereas the said nation hath since exercised its right (no wise abridged by the said treaty) of changing the organ of its will, by abolishing the said kingly government, as inconsistent with the rights and happiness of the people, and establishing a republican in lieu thereof, as most favorable to the public happiness, and best suited to the genius of a people become sensible of their rights and ashamed of their chains: And whereas, by the constitution of the United States, the executive is authorised to receive ambassadors, other public ministers and consuls: And whereas a public minister, duly appointed and commissioned by the new Republic of France, hath arrived and presented himself to the executive, in order to be received in his proper character: Now be it known, that by virtue of the said right vested in the executive to receive ambassadors, other public ministers and consuls, & of the rights included therein, the executive hath refused to receive the said minister from the said republic, and hath thereby caused the activity and operation of all treaties with the French nation, *hitherto in force as supreme laws of the land*, to be suspended until the executive, by taking off the said suspension, shall revive the same; of which, all persons concerned are to take notice, at their peril.

The writer, as if beginning to feel that he was grasping at more than he could hold, endeavours, all of a sudden, to squeeze his doctrine into a smaller size, and a less vulnerable shape. The reader shall see the operation in his own words.

"And where *a treaty* antecedently exists between the United States and such nation (a nation whose government has undergone a revolution) that right (the right of judging whether the new rulers ought to be recognized or not) involves the power of giving operation or not to *such treaty. For* until the new government is acknowledged, the treaties between the nations, *as far at least* as regards *public rights*, are *of course* suspended."

This qualification of the suspending power, though reluctantly and inexplicitly made, was prudent, for two reasons; first, because it is pretty evident that *private rights*, whether of judiciary or executive cognizance, may be carried into effect without the agency of the foreign government; and therefore would not be suspended of course by a rejection of that agency. Secondly, because the judiciary, being an independent department, and acting under an oath to pursue the law of treaties as the supreme law of the land, might not readily follow the executive example, and a *right* in *one expositor* of treaties, to consider them as *not in force*, whilst it would be the *duty* of *another expositor* to consider them as *in force*, would be a phænomenon not so easy to be explained. Indeed as the doctrine stands qualified, it leaves the executive the right of suspending the law of treaties in relation to rights of one description, without exempting it from the duty of enforcing it in relation to rights of another description.

But the writer is embarked in so unsound an argument, that he does not save the rest of his inference by this sacrifice of one half of it. It is not true, that *all public rights* are of course suspended by a refusal to acknowledge the government, or even by a suspension of the government. And in the next place, the right in question does not follow from the necessary suspension of public rights, in consequence of a refusal to acknowledge the government.

Public rights are of two sorts; those which require the agency of government; those which may be carried into effect without that agency.

As public rights are the rights of the nation, not of the government, it is clear that wherever they can be made good to the nation, without the office of government, they are not suspended by the want of an acknowledged government, or even by the want of an existing government; and that there are important rights of this description, will be illustrated by the following case:

Suppose, that after the conclusion of the treaty of alliance between the United States and France, a party of the enemy had surprised and put to death every member of congress; that the occasion had been used by the people of America for changing the old confederacy into such a government as now exists, and that in the progress of this revolution, an interregnum had happened. Suppose further, that during this interval, the states of South-Carolina and Georgia, or any other parts of the United States, had been attacked and been put into evident and imminent danger of being irrecoverably lost, without the interposition of the French arms; is it not manifest, that as the Treaty is the Treaty of the United States, not of their government, the people of the United

States could not forfeit their right to the guarantee of their territory by the accidental suspension of their government; and that any attempt, on the part of France, to evade the obligations of the Treaty, by pleading the suspension of government, or by refusing to acknowledge it, would justly have been received with universal indignation, as an ignominious perfidy?

With respect to public rights that cannot take effect in favour of a nation without the agency of its government, it is admitted that they are suspended of course where there is no government in existence, and also by a refusal to acknowledge an existing government. But no inference in favour of *a right* to suspend the operation of Treaties, can be drawn from either case. Where the existence of the government is suspended, it is a case of necessity; it would be a case happening without the act of the executive, and consequently could prove nothing for or against the right.

In the other case, to wit, of a refusal by the executive to recognize an *existing government*, however certain it may be, that a suspension of some of the public rights might ensue, yet it is equally certain, that the refusal would be without right or authority; and that no right or authority could be implied or produced by the unauthorised act. If a right to do whatever might bear an analogy to the necessary consequence of what was done without right, could be inferred from the analogy, there would be no other limit to power than the limit to its ingenuity.

It is no answer to say that it may be doubtful whether a government does or does not exist; or doubtful which may be the existing and acting Government. The case stated by the writer is, that there are existing rulers; that there is an acting Government; but that they are *new* rulers; and that it is a *new* Government. The full reply, however, is to repeat what has been already observed; that questions of this sort are mere questions of fact; that as such only, they belong to the executive; that they would equally belong to the executive, if it was tied down to the reception of public ministers, without any discretion to receive or reject them; that where the fact appears to be, that no Government exists, the consequential suspension is independent of the executive; that where the fact appears to be, that the Government does exist, the executive must be governed by the fact, and can have no right or discretion, on account of the date or form of the Government, to refuse to acknowledge it, either by rejecting its public minister, or by any other step taken on that account. If it does refuse on that account, the refusal is a wrongful act, and can neither prove nor illustrate a rightful power.

I have spent more time on this part of the discussion than may appear to some, to have been requisite. But it was considered as a proper opportunity for presenting some important ideas, connected with the general subject, and it may be of use in shewing how very superficially, as well as erroneously, the writer has treated it.

In other respects so particular an investigation was less necessary. For allowing it to be, as contended, that a suspension of treaties might happen from a *consequential* operation of a right to receive public ministers, which is an *express right* vested by the constitution; it could be no proof, that the same or a *similar* effect could be produced by the *direct* operation of a *constructive power*.

Hence the embarrassments and gross contradictions of the writer in defining, and applying his ultimate inference from the operation of the executive power with regard to public ministers.

At first it exhibits an "important instance of the right of the executive to decide the obligation of the nation with regard to foreign nations."

Rising from that, it confers on the executive, a right "to put the United States in a condition to become an associate in war."

And, at its full height authorises the executive "to lay the legislature under *an obligation* of declaring war."

From this towering prerogative, it suddenly brings down the executive to the right of "*consequentially affecting* the proper or improper exercise of the power of the legislature to declare war."

And then, by a caprice as unexpected as it is sudden, it espouses the cause of the legislature; rescues it from the executive right "to lay it under an *obligation* of declaring war"; and asserts it to be "*free* to perform its *own* duties, according to its *own* sense of them," without any other controul than what it is liable to, in every other legislative act.

The point at which it finally seems to rest, is, that "the executive in the exercise of its *constitutional powers*, may establish an antecedent state of things, which ought to *weigh* in the *legislative decisions*"; a prerogative which will import a great deal, or nothing, according to the handle by which you take it; and which, at the same time, you can take by no handle that does not clash with some inference preceding.

If "by weighing in the legislative decisions" be meant having *an influence* on the *expediency* of this or that decision in the *opinion* of the legislature; this is no more than what every antecedent state of things ought to have, from whatever cause proceeding; whether from the use or abuse of constitutional powers, or from the exercise of constitutional or assumed powers. In this sense the power to establish an antecedent state of things is not constituted.[11] But then it is of no use to the writer, and is also in direct contradiction to the inference, that the executive may "lay the *legislature* under an *obligation* to decide in favor of *war*."

If the meaning be as is implied by the force of the terms "constitutional powers" that the antecedent state of things produced by the executive, ought to have a *constitutional weight* with the legislature: or, in plainer words, imposes a *constitutional obligation* on the *legislative decisions*, the writer will not only have to combat the arguments by which such a prerogative has been disproved: but to reconcile it with his last concession, that "the legislature is *free* to perform its duties according to its *own* sense of them." He must shew that the legislature is, at the same time, *constitutionally free* to pursue its *own judgment* and *constitutionally bound* by the *judgment of the executive*.

HELVIDIUS.

Printed copy (Philadelphia *Gazette of the U.S.*, 7 and 11 Sept. 1793). Reprinted in [Madison], *Letters of Helvidius*, pp. 22–33. For JM's later revisions, see "Helvidius" No. 2, 31 Aug. 1793, n. 2, and nn. 2–4, 7, and 11, below.

1. This argument in "Pacificus" No. 1 and other quotations from that essay used by JM in "Helvidius" No. 3 are found in Syrett and Cooke, *Papers of Hamilton*, 15:41–42.

2. In later edition, corrected to read "vested" (*The Federalist with Helvidius* [1818 ed.], p. 613).

3. In later edition, ", viz. the right in question," is here added (ibid.).

4. In later edition, corrected to read "*affect*" (ibid., p. 614).

5. *The Federalist* No. 69 (Syrett and Cooke, *Papers of Hamilton*, 4:596). JM cited the M'Lean 1788 edition.

6. *The Federalist* No. 24 (ibid., 4:419).

7. In later edition, "a" is here added (*The Federalist with Helvidius* [1818 ed.], p. 616).

8. Vattel, *Law of Nations*.

9. Burlamaqui, *Principes du droit politique*.

10. The text printed on 7 Sept. ends here. The *Gazette of the U.S.* misnumbered the 11 Sept. text as a continuation of "Helvidius" No. 2.

11. In later edition, corrected to read "contested" (*The Federalist with Helvidius* [1818 ed.], p. 623).

From Thomas Jefferson

Sep. 8. 93.

I have received and am charmed with No. V.[1] I thought the introduction an useful lesson to others as I found it to myself, for I had really, by constantly hearing the sound, been led into a pretty free use of it myself. I struck out the passage you desired in the last page. I struck out also the words 'and neutrality' in the following passage 'taking the proclamation *in it's proper sense* as reminding all concerned that as the US. were at peace, the laws of peace *and neutrality* were still obligatory.' Also a paragraph of 4. lines that a minister from France was hourly expected when the proclamation issued. There was one here at the time—the other did not arrive in 6. weeks. To have waited that time would have given full course to the evil.

I went through Franklin with enchantment; & what peculiarly pleased me was that there was not a sentence from which it could be conjectured whether it came from N. S. E. or West. At last a whole page of Virginia flashed on me. It was in the section on the state of parties, and was an apology for the continuance of slavery among us. However this circumstance may be justly palliated, it had nothing to do with the state of parties, with the bank, encumbered a good cause with a questionable argument; many readers who would have gone heart & hand with the author so far would have flown off in a tangent from that paragraph. I struck it out. Justify this if you please to those concerned, and if it cannot be done say so & it may still be reestablished. I mentioned to you in my last that a Fr. Consul at Boston had rescued a vessel out of the hands of a marshal by military force. Genet has at New York forbidden a marshal to arrest a vessel and given orders to the French squadron to protect her by force. Was there ever an instance before of a diplomatic man overawing & obstructing the course of the law in a country by an armed force? The yellow fever increases. The week before last about 3. a day died. This last week about 11. a day have died; consequently from known data about 33. a day are taken, and there are about 330. patients under it. They are much scattered through the town, and it is the opinion of the physicians that there is no possibility of stopping it. They agree it is a non-descript disease, and no two agree in any one part of their process of cure. The Presidt. goes off the day after tomorrow as he had always intended. Knox then takes flight. Hamilton is ill of the fever as is said. He had two physicians out at his house the night before last. His family think him in danger, & he puts himself so by his excessive alarm. He had been miserable several days before from a firm persuasion he should catch it. A man as timid as he is on the water, as timid on horseback, as timid in sickness, would be a phænomenon if the courage of which he has the reputation in military occasions were genuine. His friends, who have not seen him, suspect it is only an autumnal fever he has. I would really go away, because I think there is rational danger, but that I had before announced that I should not go till the beginning of October, & I do not like to exhibit the appearance of panic. Besides that I think there might serious ills proceed from there being not a single member of the administration in place. Poor Hutcheson dined with me on Friday was sennight, was taken that night on his return home, & died the day before yesterday. It is difficult to say whether the republican interest has suffered more by his death or Genet's extravagance. I sometimes cannot help seriously believing the latter to be a Dumourier, endeavoring to draw us into the war against France as Dumourier while a minister, drew on her the war of the empire. The Indians have refused to meet our Commissioners unless they would make the Ohio a boundary by preliminary condn. Consequently they are on their return & we may suppose Wayne in movement. Since my last which was of the 1st. your's of the 22d. Aug. & 2d. Sep. are received. Adieu.

RC (DLC); FC, partial Tr (DLC: Jefferson Papers). Unsigned. RC docketed by JM.

1. Jefferson referred to the draft of "Helvidius" No. 5.

To John Hatley Norton

DEAR SIR   ORANGE Sepr. 12. 1793

I have recd. your favor of the 15th. June, as also a preceding one on the same subject: & have delayed acknowledging them till the return of Majr. Hite, an opportunity which you seem to have had in view. As far as I recollect no claims similar to your's have yet been allowed by Congress, and some circumspection has been observed against establishing any principle that might lead to them. I can not therefore foresee much chance of success in an application for redress in your case; bu⟨t⟩ if you think proper to make the experiment, any service of mine in relation to it will be afforded with all the readiness & pleasure you have anticipated. A petition to Congress will be the proper mode of the application; and the evidence in support of the facts, ought to be collected in the usual form, & to be the best which the circumstances of the case will admit. If any of the officers belonging to the troops are alive, and can be applied to, their certificates would be proper & perhaps may be expected. I thank you for your very friendly invitation to take Winchester in my way to Philada.[1] and should be happy in such an opportunity of calling on you; but I must sacrifice the inducements to that route, to the conveniences which give a preference to the shorter & more usual one. My father & the family beg you to accept a return of their best respects for those you have so kindly presented to them. With great esteem & regard I am Dear Sir Your Obedt. friend & Servt.

Js. MADISON JR

RC (NAII). Addressed by JM to Norton at Winchester, "Hond. by Majr. Hite." Docketed by Norton: "in answer to a Letter of mine Respecting Losses of Houses in York by the Contl. Troops."

1. Norton came from Norfolk but by 1785 had moved to Winchester. His wife was Sally Nicholas, daughter of Robert Carter Nicholas (*CVSP*, 4:251; *WMQ*, 1st ser., 9 [1900–1901]: 239).

From Thomas Jefferson

Sep. 12. 1793.

The fever spreads faster. Deaths are now about 30. a day. It is in every square of the city. All flying who can. Most of the offices are shut or shutting. The banks shut up this day. All my clerks have left me but one: so that I cannot go on with business. I shall therefore set out in 3. or 4. days & perhaps see you before you get this. H had truly the fever, and is on the recovery, & pronounced out of danger.

FC (DLC: Jefferson Papers). Unsigned. Evidence that JM was the recipient of this letter is both internal and found in Jefferson's Epistolary Record (ibid.), which lists a letter to JM of this date.

"Helvidius" Number 4

[14 September 1793]

THE last papers compleated the view proposed to be taken of the arguments in support of the new and aspiring doctrine, which ascribes to the executive the prerogative of judging and deciding whether there be causes of war or not, in the obligations of treaties; notwithstanding the express provision in the constitution, by which the legislature is made the organ of the national will, on questions whether there be or be not a cause for declaring war. If the answer to these arguments has imparted the conviction which dictated it, the reader will have pronounced, that they are generally superficial, abounding in contradictions, never in the least degree conclusive to the main point, and not unfrequently conclusive against the writer himself: whilst the doctrine—that the powers of treaty and war, are in their nature executive powers—which forms the basis of those arguments, is as indefensible and as dangerous, as the particular doctrine to which they are applied.

But it is not to be forgotten that these doctrines, though ever so clearly disproved, or ever so weakly defended, remain before the public a striking monument of the principles and views which are entertained and propagated in the community.

It is also to be remembered, that however the consequences flowing from such premises, may be disavowed at this time or by this individual, we are to regard it as morally certain, that in proportion as the doctrines make their way into the creed of the government, and the acquiescence of the public, every power that can be deduced from them, will be deduced and exercised sooner or later by those who may have an interest in so doing. The character of human nature gives this salutary warning to every sober and reflecting mind. And the history of government, in all its forms and in every period of time, ratifies the danger. A people therefore, who are so happy as to possess the inestimable blessing of a free and defined constitution, cannot be too watchful against the introduction, nor too critical in tracing the consequences, of new principles and new constructions, that may remove the landmarks of power.

Should the prerogative which has been examined, be allowed in its most limited sense, to usurp the public countenance, the interval would probably be very short, before it would be heard from some quarter or other, that the prerogative either amounts to nothing, or means a right to judge and conclude that the obligations of treaty impose war, as well as that they permit peace. That it is fair reasoning, to say, that if the prerogative exists at all, an *operative* rather than an *inert* character ought to be given to it.

In support of this conclusion, there would be enough to echo, ⟨"that the prerogative in this active sense, is connected with the executive⟩ in various capacities—as the organ of intercourse between the nation and foreign nations—as the interpreter of national treaties" (a violation of which may be a cause of war) "as that power which is charged with the execution of the laws of which treaties make a part—as that power, which is charged with *the command and application of the public force.*"[1]

With additional force, it might be said, that the executive is as much the *executor* as the *interpreter* of treaties: that if by virtue of the *first* character it is to judge of the *obligations* of treaties, it is by virtue of the *second*, equally authorised to carry those obligations *into effect*. Should there occur for example, a *casus federis*, claiming a military co-operation of the United States, and a military force should happen to be under the command of the executive, it must have the same right, as *executor of public treaties* to *employ* the public force, as it has in quality of *interpreter of public treaties* to decide whether it ought to be *employed*.

The case of a treaty of peace would be an auxiliary to comments of this sort. It is a condition annexed to every treaty that an infraction even of an important article, on one side extinguishes the obligations on the other: and the immediate consequence of a dissolution of a treaty of peace is a restoration of a state of war. If the executive is "to decide on the obligation of the nation with regard to foreign nations"—"to pronounce the *existing condition* (in the sense annexed by the writer) of the nation with regard to them; and to admonish the citizens of their obligations and duties as founded upon *that condition* of things"—"to judge what are the *reciprocal rights* and obligations of the United States, and of all and each of the powers at war:"[2]—add, that if the executive moreover possesses all powers relating to war *not strictly* within the power *to declare war*, which any pupil of political casuistry, could distinguish from a mere *relapse* into a war, that *had been declared*: With this store of materials and the example given of the use to be made of them, would it be difficult to fabricate a power in the executive to plunge the nation into war, whenever a treaty of peace might happen to be infringed?

But if any difficulty should arise, there is another mode chalked out by which the end might clearly be brought about, even without the violation of the treaty of peace; especially if the other party should happen to change its government at the crisis. The executive, in that case,[3] could *suspend* the treaty of peace *by refusing to receive an ambassador* from the *new* government, and the state of war *emerges of course*.

This is a sample of the use to which the extraordinary publication we are reviewing, might be turned. Some of the inferences could not be repelled at all. And the least regular of them must go smoothly down with those, who had swallowed the gross sophistry which wrapped up the original dose.

Every just view that can be taken of this subject, admonishes the public, of the necessity of a rigid adherence to the simple, the received and the fundamental doctrine of the constitution, that the power to declare war including the power of judging of the causes of war is *fully* and *exclusively* vested in the legislature: that the executive has no right, in any case to decide the question, whether there is or is not cause for declaring war: that the right of convening and informing Congress, whenever such a question seems to call for a decision, is all the right which the constitution has deemed requisite or proper: and that for such more than for any other contingency, this right was specially given to the executive.

In no part of the constitution is more wisdom to be found than in the clause which confides the question of war or peace to the legislature, and not to the executive department. Beside the objection to such a mixture of heterogeneous powers: the trust and the temptation would be too great for any one man: not such as nature may offer as the prodigy of many centuries, but such as may be expected in the ordinary successions of magistracy. War is in fact the true nurse of executive aggrandizement. In war a physical force is to be created, and it is the executive will which is to direct it. In war the public treasures are to be unlocked, and it is the executive hand which is to dispense them. In war the honors and emoluments of office are to be multiplied; and it is the executive patronage under which they are to be enjoyed. It is in war, finally, that laurels are to be gathered, and it is the executive brow they are to encircle. The strongest passions, and most dangerous weaknesses of the human breast; ambition, avarice, vanity, the honorable or venial love of fame, are all in conspiracy against the desire and duty of peace.

Hence it has grown into an axiom that the executive is the department of power most distinguished by its propensity to war: hence it is the practice of all states, in proportion as they are free, to disarm this propensity of its influence.

As the best praise then that can be pronounced on an executive magistrate, is, that he is the friend of peace; a praise that rises in its value, as there may be a known capacity to shine in war: so it must be one of the most sacred duties of a free people, to mark the first omen in the society, of principles that may stimulate the hopes of other magistrates of another propensity, to intrude into questions on which its gratification depends. If a free people be a wise people also, they will not forget that the danger of surprise can never be so great, as when the advocates for the prerogative of war, can sheathe it in a symbol of peace.

The constitution has manifested a similar prudence in refusing to the executive the *sole* power of making peace. The trust in this instance also, would be too great for the wisdom, and the temptations too strong for the virtue, of a single citizen. The principal reasons on which the constitution proceeded in its regulation of the power of treaties, including treaties of peace, are so aptly furnished by the work already quoted more than once, that I shall borrow another comment from that source.

"However proper or safe it may be in a government where the executive magistrate is an hereditary monarch to commit to him the entire power of making treaties, it would be utterly unsafe and improper to entrust that power to an elective magistrate of four years duration. It has been remarked upon another occasion, and the remark is unquestionably just, that an hereditary monarch, though often the oppressor of his people, has personally too much at stake in the government to be in any material danger of being corrupted by foreign powers. But that a man raised from the station of a private citizen to the rank of chief magistrate, possessed of but a moderate or slender fortune, and looking forward to a period not very remote, when he may probably be obliged to return to the station from which he was taken, might sometimes be under temptations to sacrifice his duty to his interest, which it would require superlative virtue to withstand. An avaricious man might be tempted to betray the interests of the state to the acquisition of wealth. An ambitious man might make his own aggrandizement, by the aid of a foreign power, the price of his treachery to his constituents. The history of human conduct does not warrant that exalted opinion of human virtue, which would make it wise in a nation, to commit interests of so delicate and momentous a kind as *those which concern its intercourse* with the rest of the world, to the *sole* disposal of a magistrate, created and circumstanced, as would be a President of the United States."[4]

I shall conclude this paper and this branch of the subject, with two reflections, which naturally arise from this view of the Constitution.

The first is, that as the personal interest of an hereditary monarch in the government, is the *only* security against the temptation incident to a commitment of the delicate and momentous interests of the nation which concern its intercourse with the rest of the world, to the disposal of a single magistrate, it is a plain consequence, that every addition that may be made to the *sole* agency and influence of the Executive, in the intercourse of the nation with foreign nations, is an increase of the dangerous temptation to which an *elective and temporary* magistrate is exposed; and an *argument* and *advance* towards the security afforded by the personal interests of an *hereditary* magistrate.

Secondly, As the constitution has not permitted the Executive *singly* to conclude or judge that peace ought to be made, it might be inferred from that circumstance alone, that it never meant to give it authority, *singly*, to judge and conclude that war ought not to be made. The trust would be precisely similar and equivalent in the two cases. The right to say that war ought not to go on, would be no greater than the right to say that war ought[5] to begin. Every danger of error or corruption, incident to such a prerogative in one case, is incident to it in the other. If the Constitution therefore has deemed it unsafe or improper in the one case, it must be deemed equally so in the other case.

HELVIDIUS.

Printed copy (Philadelphia *Gazette of the U.S.*, 14 Sept. 1793). Reprinted in [Madison], *Letters of Helvidius*, pp. 33–39. For JM's later revisions, see "Helvidius" No. 2, 31 Aug. 1793, n. 2, and nn. 3 and 5, below.

1. Words within angle brackets were an alteration by JM of Hamilton's original sentence. "Pacificus" No. 1 read: "It appears to be connected with that [executive] department..." (Syrett and Cooke, *Papers of Hamilton*, 15:38). Thus JM's addition encouraged readers to relate his opponent's ideas with monarchism. Other variations are minor and not noted.

2. Ibid., 15:41, 37, 41.

3. In later edition, ", in that case," is omitted (*The Federalist with Helvidius* [1818 ed.], p. 626).

4. *The Federalist* No. 75 (Syrett and Cooke, *Papers of Hamilton*, 4:629–30). JM quoted from the M'Lean 1788 edition.

5. In later edition, "not" is here added (*The Federalist with Helvidius* [1818 ed.], p. 629).

To James Monroe

DEAR SIR   Sepr. 15. 93.

Since I parted from you I have had several letters from Mr. J. in which all the *facts* involving Genét are detailed. His conduct has been that of a madman. He is abandoned even by his votaries in Philada. Hutcheson declares that he has ruined the Republican interest in that place. I wish I could forward the details I have recd. but they are too confidential to be hazarded by the casual conveyance to which this is destined. They ought however to have no other effect on the steps to be pursued, than to caution agst. founding any of them on the presumed inculpability of Genét. As he has put himself on such unjustifiable ground, perhaps it is fortunate that he has done it in so flagrant a manner. It will be the more easily believed here that he has acted agst. the sense of his Constituents, and the latter will be the less likely to support him in his errors. I find that the Anglicans & Monocrats from Boston to Philada. are betrayed by the occasion into the most palpable discovery of their real views. They already lose sight of the Agent; and direct their hostilities *immediately agst. France.* This will do good, if proper use be made of it. You will see by the late papers that G. B. has made war on our commerce, by intercepting uncontraband articles bound to unblock-aded ports, and taking them to herself at her own price. This must bring on a crisis with us, unless the order be revoked on our demand, of which there is not the least probability. I understand that the malignant fever in Philada. is raging still with great violence; and all the inhabitants who can, flying from it in every direction. The mortality at first was in the ratio of 3 out of 4. It had been reduced to 1 out of 3. Mr. J. is in raptures with the performance of our friend in C–l–n–e. He means to have it appear about two weeks before the meeting of C——s. This will not coincide with the plan of the Author, who wished its publication to be in time for the meeting of the State Legislature. Think of this & let me have your ideas. On my return home I found a letter from Mr. Jones[1] wch. I inclose as the shortest way of making you acquainted with what he wishes. With all due respects to Ms. Monroe. I am Yrs. affey.

Js. MADISON JR

RC (DLC). Addressed by JM to Monroe "near Charlottesville."

1. Letter not found.

From Thomas Jefferson

SCHUYLKILL Sep. 15. [1793]

I have to acknolege yours of Aug. 27. & Sep. 2. The fever in town is become less mortal, but extends. Dupont[1] the Fr. Consul is dead of it. So is Wright[2] the painter. His wife also. Lieper[3] is said to be dead, but that is not certain. J. Barclay ill.[4] Ham. and his wife recovered. Willing[5] on the recovery. The banks are not shut up, as I had been falsely informed when I wrote you last. I have some expectation to set out tomorrow, and shall make it eight days to your house; but it is very possible I may yet be detained here two or three days. The arrangement on which I had consented to remain another quarter was that the President was to be absent three weeks, and after that I was to be absent 6. weeks. This got me rid of 9. weeks of the 13. and the remaining 4. Congress would be setting. My view in this was precisely to avoid being at any more councils as much as possible, that I might not be committed in any thing further. This fever by driving me off sooner, will bring me back sooner, & so far counteract my view. But I need not take the trouble of writing on this subject, as I shall see you as early as you will get this letter. Adieu.

RC (DLC); FC (DLC: Jefferson Papers). Unsigned.

1. François Dupont had been the French consul in Philadelphia since 25 May (Nasatir and Monell, *French Consuls*, p. 549).

2. Joseph Wright studied in London with Benjamin West and John Trumbull. Since 1792 he had been the first draftsman and diesinker of the U.S. Mint, which was then part of Jefferson's responsibility in the Department of State.

3. Thomas Leiper, a leading Philadelphia tobacco merchant, rented Jefferson the house that the Virginian vacated in the spring of 1793. Leiper corresponded with JM concerning Montpelier tobacco crops and methods of curing tobacco. He was a Republican presidential elector when JM was elected president in 1808 (Jefferson to Leiper, 11 Apr. 1793 [DLC: Jefferson Papers]; JM to Ambrose Madison, 19 May 1791, *PJM*, 14:24; Leiper to JM, 15 Dec. 1805 [DLC]).

4. John Barclay was an alderman and former mayor of Philadelphia, president of the Bank of Pennsylvania, and prominent Republican organizer (Powell, *Bring Out Your Dead*, p. 69; Walters, "Origins of the Jeffersonian Party," *Pa. Mag. Hist. and Biog.*, 66 [1942]: 449, 452).

5. Thomas Willing, a business partner of Robert Morris, was president of the Bank of the United States, 1791–1807 (Burton Alva Konkle, *Thomas Willing and the First American Financial System* [Philadelphia, 1937], pp. 28, 143, 189).

To Thomas Jefferson

[16 September 1793]

The want of oppy. has left me in debt for 3 favors those of Aug. 18. 25. & Sepr. 8th. which I now acknowledge by one which is too precarious for any thing confidential. I have long been uneasy for your health amidts [*sic*] the vapors of the Schuylkil. The new & more alarming danger has made me particularly anxious that you were out of the sphere of it. I cannot altogether condemn your unwillingness to retire from your post under the circumstances you describe; but if your stay be as unessential as I conceive it to be rendered by the absence of the P. and the fever does not abate, I pray you not to sacrifice too much to motives which others do not feel. As I intimated in my last, my time has been *totally* diverted from my object.[1] I have scarcely been able to turn it even in my thoughts. It is probable therefore tha⟨t⟩ you will not hear further from me in relation to it before you leave P. In fact the temper of the present moment & the uncertainty ⟨of m⟩any things seems to advise a postponement if nothing more. All the liberties you have taken will I am sure be approved. I have neglected hitherto to comply with your request as to a rotation farm. In the main it appears to be judicious & unobjectionable. Of this opin⟨ion⟩ are those with whom I have conferred. One or two alterations not very material occurred; but as they may be doubtful, & if proper, can be made at any time, I do not now trouble you with them. I have tried the patent plow amended by fixing the Colter in the usual way. It succeeds perfectly, and I think forms the plow best suited to its object. I am happy at the arrival of your Threshing Model. What will be about the cost of the Machine? Will it be removeabl⟨e⟩ from one to another part of an extensive farm? Adieu. Yrs. always & affy.

The other Newspapers in my next.

RC (DLC: Jefferson Papers). Unsigned. Dated 2 Dec. 1793 in the *Index to the Thomas Jefferson Papers*. Date here assigned on the basis of internal evidence and on the likelihood that this is JM's 16 Sept. 1793 letter that Jefferson received on 2 Dec., when he returned to Philadelphia (Jefferson's Epistolary Record [DLC: Jefferson Papers]).

1. JM alluded to the "Helvidius" essays.

"Helvidius" Number 5

[18 September 1793]

HAVING seen that the executive has no constitutional right to interfere in any question whether there be or be not a cause of war, and the extensive consequences flowing from the doctrines on which[1] a claim has been asserted, it remains to be enquired whether the writer is better warranted in the fact which he assumes, namely that the proclamation of the Executive has undertaken to decide the question, whether there be a cause of war or not, in the article of guaranty between the United States and France, and, in so doing has exercised the right which is claimed for that department.

Before I proceed to the examination of this point, it may not be amiss to advert to the novelty of the phraseology, as well as of the doctrines, expounded[2] by this writer. The source from which the former is evidently borrowed, may enlighten our conjectures with regard to the source of the latter. It is a just observation also that words have often a gradual influence on ideas, and when used in an improper sense, may cover fallacies which would not otherwise escape detection.

I allude particularly to his application of the term *government* to the *Executive authority alone*. The Proclamation is "a manifestation of the sense of the *government*"; "why did not the *government* wait, &c." "The policy on the part of the *government* of removing all doubt as to *its own disposition*."* "It was of great importance that our citizens should understand as early as possible the opinion entertained by the *government*, &c." If in addition to the rest, the early manifestation of *the views* of the *government*, had any effect *in fixing the public opinion*, &c.[3] The reader will probably be struck with the reflection, that if the Proclamation really possessed the character, and was to have the effects, here ascribed to it, something more than the authority of *the government*, in the writer's sense of government, would have been a necessary sanction to the act, and if the term "government" be removed, and that of "President" substituted, in the sentences quoted, the justice of the reflection will be felt with peculiar force. But I remark only, on the singularity of the stile adopted by the writer, as shewing either that the phraseology of a foreign government is more familiar to him than the phraseology proper to our own, or that he wishes to propagate a familiarity of the former in preference to the latter. I do not know what degree of disapprobation others may think due to this innovation of language, but I consider it as far above a trivial criticism, to observe that it is by no means unworthy of attention, whether viewed with an eye to its probable cause or its apparent tendency, "the government," unquestionably means in the United States the whole government, not the executive part, either exclusively, or *pre-eminently*; as it may do in a monarchy, where the splendor of prerogative eclipses, and the machinery of influence, directs, every other part of the government. In the former and proper sense, the term has hitherto been used in official proceedings, in public discussions, and in private discourse. It is as short and as easy, and less liable to misapprehension, to say, the Executive or the President, as to say the government. In a word the new dialect could not proceed either from necessity, conveniency, propriety, or perspicuity; and being in opposition to common usage, so marked a fondness for it, justifies the notice here

---

* *The writer ought not in the same paper, No. VII, to have said, "Had the President announced his* own *disposition, he would have been chargeable with egotism, if* not *presumption."*[4]

taken of it. It shall no longer detain me, however, from the more important subject of the present paper.

I proceed therefore to observe that as a "Proclamation," in its *ordinary* use, is an address to citizens or subjects only; as it is always understood to relate to the law *actually in operation*, and to be an act *purely* and *exclusively* Executive; there can be no implication in the *name* or the *form* of such an instrument, that it was meant *principally*, for the information of foreign nations; far less that it related to an *eventual stipulation* on a subject, *acknowledged* to be within the *Legislative province*.

When the writer therefore undertook to engraft his new prerogative on the Proclamation by ascribing to it so unusual, and unimplied a meaning, it was evidently incumbent on him to shew, that the *text* of the instrument could not be satisfied by any other construction than his own. Has he done this? No. What has he done? He has called the Proclamation a Proclamation of neutrality; he has put his own arbitrary meaning on that phrase, and has then proceeded in his arguments and his inferences, with as much confidence, as if no question was ever to be asked, whether the term "neutrality" be in the Proclamation; or whether, if there, it could justify the use he makes of it.

It has appeared from observations already made, that if the term "neutrality" was in the Proclamation, it could not avail the writer, in the present discussion; but the fact is no such term is to be found in it, nor any other term, of a meaning equivalent to that, in which the term neutrality is used by him.

There is the less pretext, in the present case, for hunting after any latent or extraordinary object because an obvious and legal one, is at hand, to satisfy the occasion on which the Proclamation issued. The existence of war among several nations with which the United States have an extensive intercourse; the duty of the Executive to preserve peace by enforcing its laws, whilst those laws continued in force; the danger that indiscreet citizens might be tempted or surprised by the crisis, into unlawful proceedings, tending to involve the United States in a war, which the competent authority might decide them to be at liberty to avoid, and which, if they should be judged not at liberty to avoid, the other party to the *eventual contract*, might not be willing[5] to impose on them; these surely might have been sufficient grounds for the measure pursued by the executive, and being legal and rational grounds, it would be wrong, if there be no necessity, to look beyond them.

If there be any thing in the Proclamation of which the writer could have made a handle, it is the part which declares, the *disposition*, the *duty* and the *interest* of the United States, in relation to the war existing in Europe. As the Legislature is the only competent and constitutional organ of the will of the nation; that is, of its disposition, its duty and its interest, in relation to a commencement of war, in like manner as the President and Senate *jointly*, not the President *alone*, are in relation to peace, after war has been commenced—I will not dissemble my wish that a language less exposed to criticism had been preferred; but taking the expressions, in the sense of the writer himself; as analogous to the language which might be proper, on the reception of a public Minister, or any similar occasion, it is evident, that his construction can derive no succour, even from this resource.[6]

If the Proclamation then does not *require* the construction which this writer has taken the liberty of putting on it; I leave it to be decided whether the following considerations do not forbid us to suppose, that the President could have intended, by that act, to embrace and prejudge the Legislative question whether there was, or was not, under the circumstances of the case, a cause of war in the article of guaranty.

It has been shewn that such an intention would have usurped a prerogative not vested in the Executive, and even *confessedly* vested in another department.

In exercising the Constitutional power of deciding a question of war, the Legislature ought to be as free to decide, according to its own sense of the public good, on one side as on the other side. Had the Proclamation prejudged the question on either side, and *proclaimed its decision to the world*; the Legislature, instead of being as free as it ought, might be thrown under the dilemma, of either sacrificing its judgment to that of the Executive; or by opposing the Executive judgment, of producing a relation between the two departments, extremely delicate among ourselves, and of the worst influence on the national character and interests abroad; a variance of this nature, it will readily be perceived, would be very different from a want of conformity to the *mere recommendations* of the Executive, in the measures adopted by the Legislature.

It does not appear that such a Proclamation could have even pleaded any call, from either of the parties at war with France, for an explanation of the light in which the guaranty was viewed—whilst, indeed, no positive indication whatever was given of hostile purposes, it is not conceived, that any power could have decently made such an application—or if they[7] had, that a Proclamation, would have been either a satisfactory, or an honorable answer. It could not have been satisfactory, if serious apprehensions were entertained, because it would not have proceeded from that authority which alone could definitely[8] pronounce the will of the United States on the subject. It would not have been honorable, because a private diplomatic answer only is due to a private diplomatic application; and to have done so much more, would have marked a pusilanimity and want of dignity in the Executive Magistrate.

But whether the Executive was or was not applied to, or whatever weight be allowed to that circumstance, it ought never to be presumed, that the Executive would so abruptly, so publicly, and so solemnly, proceed to disclaim a sense of the contract, which the other party might consider and wish to support by discussion as its true and reasonable import. It is asked, indeed, in a tone that sufficiently displays the spirit in which the writer construes both the Proclamation and the treaty, "Did the Executive stand in need of the logic of a foreign agent to enlighten it as to the duties or the interests of the nation; or was it bound to ask his consent to a step which appeared to itself consistent with the former, and conducive to the latter? The sense of treaties was to be learnt from the treaties themselves."[9] Had he consulted his Vattel, instead of his animosity to France, he would have discovered that however humiliating it might be to wait for a foreign logic, to assist the interpretation of an act depending on the national authority alone, yet in the case of a treaty, which is as much the treaty of a foreign nation, as it is ours; and in which foreign duties and rights are as much involved as ours, the sense of the treaty, though to be learnt from the treaty itself, is to be equally learned by both parties to it. Neither of them can have a right more than the other, to say what a particular article means; and where there is equality without a judge consultation is as consistent with dignity as it is conducive to harmony and friendship, let Vattel however be heard on the subject.

"The third general maxim, or principle, on the subject of interpretation (of Treaties) is: *'That neither the one nor the other of the interested or contracting powers has a right to interpret the act or treaty at its pleasure.* For if you are at liberty to give my promise what sense you please, you will have the power of obliging me to do whatever you have a mind, contrary to my intention, and beyond my real engagement: and reciprocally, *if I am allowed to explain my promises as I please, I may render them vain and illusive, by giving them a sense quite different from that in which they were presented to you, and in which you must have taken them in accepting them.'"* Vat. B. II. c. vii. §. 265.[10]

The writer ought to have been particularly sensible of the improbability that a precipitate and *ex parte* decision of the question arising under the guaranty, could have been intended by the proclamation. He had but just gone through his undertaking, to prove that the article of guaranty like the rest of the treaty is defensive, not offensive. He had examined his books and retailed his quotations, to shew that the criterion between the two kinds of war is the circumstance of priority in the attack. He could not therefore but know, that according to his own principles, the question whether the United States, were under an obligation or not to take part in the war, was a *question of fact* whether the first attack was made by France or her enemies. And to decide a question of fact, as well as, of principle, without waiting for such representations and proofs, as the absent and interested party might have to produce would have been a proceeding contrary to the ordinary maxims of justice, and requiring circumstances of a very peculiar nature, to warrant it, towards any nation. Towards a nation which could verify her claim to more than bare justice by our own reiterated and formal acknowledgments, and which must in her present singular and interesting situation have a peculiar sensibility to marks of our friendship or alienation, the impropriety of such a proceeding would be infinitely increased, and in the same proportion the improbability of its having taken place.

There are reasons of another sort which would have been a bar to such a proceeding. It would have been as impolitic as it would have been unfair and unkind.

If France meant not to insist on the guaranty, the measure, without giving any present advantage, would have deprived the United States of a future claim which may be of importance to their safety. It would have inspired France with jealousies of a secret bias in this country toward some of her enemies, which might have left in her breast a spirit of contempt and revenge of which the effects might be felt in various ways. It must in particular have tended to inspire her with a disinclination to feed our commerce with those important advantages which it already enjoys, and those more important ones, which it anxiously contemplates. The nation that consumes more of the fruits of our soil than any other nation in the world, and supplies the only foreign raw[11] material of extensive use in the United States would not be unnecessarily provoked by those who understand the public interest, and make it their study, as it is their interest[12] to advance it.

I am aware that the common-place remark will be interposed, that, "commercial privileges are not worth having, when not secured by mutual interest; and never worth purchasing, because they will grow of themselves out of a mutual interest."[13] Prudent men, who do not suffer their reason to be misled by their prejudices will view the subject in a juster light. They will reflect, that if commercial privileges are not worth purchasing, they are worth having without purchase; that in the commerce of a great nation, there are valuable privileges which may be granted or not granted, or granted either to this or that country, without any sensible influence on the interest of the nation itself; that the friendly or unfriendly disposition of a country, is always an article of moment in the calculations of a comprehensive interest; that some sacrifices of interest will be made to other motives; by nations as well as by individuals, though not with the same frequency, or in the same proportions, that more of a disinterested conduct or of a conduct founded on liberal views of interest, prevails in some nations than in others, that as far as can be seen of the influence of the revolution on the genius and the policy of France; particularly with regard to the United States, every thing is to be hoped by the latter on this subject, which one country can reasonably hope from another. In this point of view a greater error could not have been committed than in a step, that might have turned the present disposition of France to open her commerce to us as far as a liberal calculation of her interest would permit, and her friendship towards us, and confidence in our friendship towards her, could prompt, into a disposition to shut it as closely against us as the united motives of interest, of distrust, and of ill-will, could urge her.

On the supposition that France might intend to claim the guaranty, a hasty and harsh refusal before we were asked, on a ground that accused her of being the aggressor in the war against every power in the catalogue of her enemies, and in a crisis when all her sensibility must be alive towards the United States, would have given every possible irritation to a disappointment which every motive that one nation could feel towards another and towards itself, required to be alleviated by all the circumspection and delicacy that could be applied to the occasion.

The silence of the Executive since the accession of Spain and Portugal to the war against France throws great light on the present discussion. Had the proclamation been issued in the sense, and for the purposes ascribed to it, that is to say, as a declaration of neutrality, another would have followed, on that event. If it was the right and duty of the *Government*, that is, the *President*, to manifest to Great Britain and Holland; and to the American merchants and citizens, his *sense*, his *disposition*, and his *views* on the question, whether *the United States were under the circumstances of the case, bound or not, to execute the clause of guaranty, and not to leave it uncertain whether the Executive did or did not believe a state of neutrality*, to be consistent with our treaties, the *duty* as well as the right prescribed a similar manifestation to all the parties concerned after *Spain and Portugal had joined the other maritime enemies of France. The opinion of the Executive with respect to a consistency or inconsistency of neutrality with treaties in the *latter case* could not be *inferred* from the proclamation in the former, because the *circumstances might be*[14] *different*. Taking the proclamation in its proper sense, as reminding all concerned, that as the United States were at peace (that state not being affected by foreign wars, and only to be changed by the legislative authority of the country) the laws of peace were still obligatory and would be enforced, and the inference is so obvious and so

* *The writer is betrayed into an acknowledgment of this in his 7th No. where he applies his reasoning to Spain as well as to Great-Britain and Holland.*[15] *He had forgotten that Spain was not included in the proclamation.*

applicable to all other cases *whatever circumstances* may distinguish them, that another proclamation would be unnecessary. Here is a new aspect of the whole subject, admonishing us in the most striking manner at once of the danger of the prerogative contended for and the absurdity of the distinctions and arguments employed in its favour. It would be as impossible in practice, as it is in theory, to separate the power of judging and concluding that the obligations of a treaty do not impose war from that of judging and concluding that the obligations *do impose war*. In certain cases, silence would proclaim the latter conclusion, as intelligibly as words could do the former. The writer indeed has himself abandoned the distinction in his VIIth paper, by declaring expressly that the object of the proclamation would have been defeated "by leaving it uncertain whether the Executive did nor *did not* believe a state of neutrality to be consistent with our treaties."[16]

HELVIDIUS

Printed copy (Philadelphia *Gazette of the U.S.*, 18 Sept. 1793). Reprinted in [Madison], *Letters of Helvidius*, pp. 40–48. For JM's later revisions, see "Helvidius" No. 2, 31 Aug. 1793, n. 2, and nn. 1, 2, 5–8, 11, 12, and 15, below.

1. In later edition, "such" is here added (*The Federalist with Helvidius* [1818 ed.], p. 629).
2. In later edition, corrected to read "espoused" (ibid.).
3. "Pacificus," nos. 1 and 7, *Gazette of the U.S.*, 29 June and 27 July 1793 (Syrett and Cooke, *Papers of Hamilton*, 15:36, 130, 131, 132, 134).
4. "Pacificus" No. 7 (ibid., 15:135).
5. In later edition, corrected to read "might be willing not" (*The Federalist with Helvidius* [1818 ed.], p. 632).
6. In later edition, corrected to read "source" (ibid.).
7. In later edition, corrected to read "it" (ibid., p. 633).
8. In later edition, corrected to read "definitively" (ibid.).
9. "Pacificus" No. 7 (Syrett and Cooke, *Papers of Hamilton*, 15:132).
10. Vattel, *Law of Nations*, bk. 2, chap. 17, sect. 265. JM (or the printer) erred in citing chapter 7.
11. In later edition, an asterisk is here added and at the bottom of the page, "*Molasses" (*The Federalist with Helvidius* [1818 ed.], p. 635).
12. In later edition, corrected to read "duty" (ibid., p. 636).
13. JM paraphrased Hamilton's argument in "Pacificus" No. 7: "If the privileges which might have been conceded were not founded in a real and permanent mutual interest—of what value would be the Treaty that should concede them? . . . On the other hand may we not trust that commercial privileges, which are truly founded in mutual interest will grow out of that interest; without the necessity of giving a premium for them at the expence of our peace?" (Syrett and Cooke, *Papers of Hamilton*, 15:133).
14. In later edition, this sentence concludes "*different*: the war in the *latter case* might be *defensive* on the side of France, though offensive against her other enemies" (*The Federalist with Helvidius* [1818 ed.], p. 637).
15. "Pacificus" No. 7 (Syrett and Cooke, *Papers of Hamilton*, 15:130).
16. Ibid., 15:134.

To John Taylor

DEAR SIR   Sepr. 20th. 1793
I informed you from Albemarle of the step taken with regard to the
paper from you. Our distant friend under whose perusal it passed is
quite in raptures with it, and augurs the best consequences from it, if its
appearance be well timed. He thinks the present in every respect unpropitious, and that under any circumstances the critical moment would
be about two or three weeks before the first monday in December. He
thinks also that the effect will be the greater, if there be no indication
of the quarter of the Union producing it; and in that point of view proposes to strike out the passage relating to the slaves, which however just
in itself would be a signal for raising the cry of Virginianism agst. the
publication. If you do not object to these circumstancial alterations they
will be made. Be so good as to drop me a line on the subject as soon as
you have an opportunity. Should none offer for a more direct conveyance, the post to Fredg. will be safe, and from thence it will be forwarded
with care by Mr. J. Blair. I wish also to hear from you on the subject
of another letter written from Albemarle. Adieu

J. M. JR

RC (DLC). Addressed by JM to Taylor in Caroline County, "care of Col:
Hoomes / Bowling-Green." Docketed by Taylor.

From James Monroe

DEAR SIR   ALBEMARLE Sepr. 25. 1793.
I am still doubtful whether I shall visit Fredericksburg this term—if
I do will call on you as I go down perhaps on Monday—but I shall in
case I do not sit out on that day for Richmond, so that I shall not have
the pleasure of se[e]ing you here till the week after.
I found at Staunton impressions had been made by letters from Richmd.
Mr. M.[1] had written to Gl. Jones who was there to promote an address
correspondent with that from the metropolis. The letters however I took
with me effectually changed the current and gave it a direction against
the anti-republican faction. A meeting took place & resolutions were
passed in a tone of sentiment perfectly correct & proper. Messrs. Jay &
King were put upon the same footing with the French minister in a
resolutn. whose object was to conciliate France & express the attachment of the place to her revolution. They were enclosed to Mr. Gamble[2]
to be handed the Printer but as yet have not appeared.
I return'd home sick of the Influenza & was indisposed thro' the court
here. W. Nicholas was unwell & did not come up till the day the ct.

adjourned. Gilmer was in Rockingham—and the clerk[3] was averse & circulated resolutions of a different complexion. Finally a notice was put up for a meeting of the freeholders on the last day of the court—but few met so that the project failed, very much to the chagrin of all who did, & indeed of every one who heard of it, except a few only. It is however to be renewed at the next county court when it is intended to part the pro's & con's. A little incident has given me some pain—being sick & hearing the Clerk had shewn some improper resolutions, & that he likewise disapproved those of Staunton, I furnished Bell,[4] who called on me, with those we had approved to be copied & given to Mr. Randolph that the latter might alter the style. This was done, but unfortunately a schism took place in that family, between those drawn there and the original set—Peter Carr prefering the latter—so that both were shewn, & I am told that since those from Caroline have appeared, their correspondence with these, has been notic'd. I shall adjust this matter in the best manner possible.[5]

Mr. Jefferson I hear is arrived. I shall see him this morning. I have written a piece[6] for Richmond but doubt the propriety of its publication—as upon a review it bears the aspect of too pointed an attack upon a certain personage—& likewise treats with too much asperity G. Morris. Very affectionately I am yr. friend & servt

JAS. MONROE

RC (DLC). Addressed by Monroe to JM at Orange, "hon'd by Mr. Tazewell."

1. John Marshall.

2. Robert Gamble (1754–1810), formerly of Augusta County, was a Richmond merchant (Johnson, *Papers of John Marshall*, 2:123 n. 8).

3. John Nicholas, Jr. (ca. 1757–1836), Federalist cousin of Republicans Wilson Cary Nicholas and Congressman John Nicholas, became Albemarle County clerk in 1792 (Dauer, "The Two John Nicholases," *American Historical Review*, 45 [1939–40]: 342, 344).

4. Thomas Bell (d. 1800) of Albemarle County, a Revolutionary veteran, corresponded with Monroe and was acquainted with Thomas Mann Randolph, Jr. (J. Estelle Stewart King, *Abstracts of Wills, Inventories, and Administration Accounts of Albemarle County, Virginia, 1748–1800* [Beverly Hills, Calif., 1940], p. 47; Gwathmey, *Historical Register of Virginians*, p. 56; Monroe to Jefferson, 17 Jan. 1791, Hamilton, *Writings of Monroe*, 1:221).

5. The dispute described by Monroe was evidently resolved by the time the county court convened in Charlottesville on 10 Oct. Thomas Mann Randolph, Jr., and Peter Carr served on a committee of seventeen that unanimously approved resolutions paraphrasing those drafted by JM and Monroe (Nicholas Lewis to Washington, 24 Oct. 1793 [DLC: Washington Papers]; see also Resolutions on Franco-American Relations, ca. 27 Aug. 1793, Editorial Note).

6. Monroe wrote four essays over the pseudonym "Agricola" that the Richmond *Va. Gazette, and General Advertiser* published on 4 Sept., 9 Oct., 13 Nov., and 4 Dec. 1793 (Harry Ammon, "Agricola *versus* Aristides: James Monroe, John Marshall, and the Genet Affair in Virginia," *VMHB*, 74 [1966]: 312–20).

From John Taylor

           Bowling Green Sepr. 25. 1793

Yours of the 20th. is this instant handed to me.

Had you been present, & wielding the pencil of a Hogarth, you might have depicted a lively sensation of human nature, on having the approbation it relates, announced to it.

The approbation of the good, is only inferior to a consciousness of having served mankind, in the pleasurable emotions it excites.

The emendation of the paper, is not only permited, but highly approved of, by me.

But I observe that Freneau is publishing extracts from it.[1] This is both unwise and indelicate. Unwise, as mutilated anticipations, will weaken its effect, if it should appear in a pamphlet. Indelicate, as in that event, the performance will exhibit the ludicrous aspect, of a compilation from his news papers.

Instantly on the receipt of yours from Albermarle,[2] notifications were dispersed, and in five days; resolutions were formed by a very numerous meeting. They are in some papers, and will appear in others.[3] I hope you will approve of them. I wish they may differ enough from those of Stt.,[4] to avoid a suspicion of their being coined in the same mint. I was obliged to come forward in a speechification. But, as I thought best, the chairman fathered & conducted, the whole business. Be happy.

J. T.

RC (DLC). Addressed by Taylor to JM at Orange, "Care of Mr: J. Blair, Fredericksburg." Docketed by JM.

1. On 11 and 14 Sept. the Philadelphia *National Gazette* published anonymous extracts from Taylor's *Enquiry into the Principles* under the title "Brief Reflections on Several Subjects."
2. JM's letter to Taylor, ca. 27 Aug. 1793, has not been found.
3. On the Caroline County resolutions, see Resolutions on Franco-American Relations, ca. 27 Aug. 1793, Editorial Note.
4. On the Staunton resolutions, see ibid.

From James Maury

Dear Sir,   Liverpool 26 Septr 1793

It is long since I had this pleasure. With this you have the review of last month, in which I wish you may find Something entertaining. It is with great anxiety we Wait Intelligence from America subsequent to your being informed of the Instructions from this Government to their

Cruizers.[1] Many of our Vessells have been Captured & brought in—principally from the Suspicion of there being French property on Board: but the process in the Court of Admiralty is not ended in any case, where the captured have defended themselves.

As to the Contest on the Continent; I refer you to the News papers. Today there are some Accounts of considerable Advantages gained by the Antirevolutionists, which, in some Measure, counterbalance those lately obtained over the combined Armies before Dunkirk—where the Carnage has been dreadful. By this Days accounts vast Bodies of the Convention Troops were collecting in the Neighbourhood of Toulon in order to recover that place. This Great people united among themselves would be equal to all their Enemies at least.

The Glimmering of a Rupture with the United States aided by some other Circumstances have lately mended the Article of Tobaccoe a little. I have availed of it by disposing of some of your's which had remained on hand since last year. I am with particular Esteem & Regard dr Sir Yr most obt Servant

JAMES MAURY

3 ℔ Ct Consols 74 & a fraction
Exchange with paris 8 5/8d Sterg
            for 3 lt Tournuis
    Say 8 5/8d Sterg for 3 Livres assignats

RC (DLC). Docketed by JM. Enclosure not found.

1. On the British order in council of 8 June, see Jefferson to JM, 1 Sept. 1793, n. 3.

From Abram Trigg

SIR   MONTGOMERY COUNTY October 1st. 1793

I take the liberty to inclose you a Copy of sundry charges which have been forwarded to the President of the United States against Captain William Preston touching his conduct in an Election,[1] held for a representative in Congress each charge having a reference to such part of the deposition's with which they were accompany'd as seem to support it.

Will you Sir be so good as to favour me with your direction's how to proceed for avoiding the said Election, or if practicable to obtain my seat. It is with great diffidence I make the application; but the Occasion I hope will justify the intrusion; as I conceive essential to the existance of a republican Government that Election's of representatives of the people should be absolutely free, and that therefore this attempt by a military force to prescribe to free men who they shall choose will meet with your disapprobation. I beg leave further to observe that in Washington County, indirect measures were used in diver's respect's particularly a number of person's were poll'd that lived in the state of Kentuckey & in the Territory of the United States South of the River Ohio and the poll continued open the second day without any legal cause existing, other than its being Court day & the votes of that County mostly running in Mr. Preston's favour; when in other County's within the district the polls were closed on the first day of the Election to the exclusion of a sufficient number of votes to have given me the majority who actually appeared before sun set, and tendred their votes in my favour, All Which doing's is considered to be contrary to the Letter & Spirit of the Constitution, and flagrant breach of the rights of freemen.

Your Friendship and Friendly Offices in this business will imprint upon my mind the most lasting impressions of Gratitude & Esteem. I am Sir with the greatest Respect your Most Obedient Servant.

ABRAM TRIGG.[2]

RC (ViHi: Preston Family Papers). Enclosure not found.

1. In the congressional election on 18 Mar., Francis Preston defeated Trigg by ten votes. On 26 Dec. Trigg's petition was read in the House of Representatives and referred to the Standing Committee of Elections. William Loughton Smith reported from that committee on 17 Apr. 1794: "That Captain William Preston, brother, and agent at the election, of the sitting member, was quartered near Montgomery court-house, with about 60 or 70 Federal troops, of which he had the command." The troops intimidated the voters but in an ensuing affray fled to their barracks. Smith's report concluded "that Francis Preston is not duly elected a member of this house," but on 29 Apr. the House rejected Trigg's petition and Smith's report without a division (*Annals of Congress*, 3d Cong., 1st sess., 149, 598-99, 613).

2. Abram Trigg (b. 1750), a lieutenant colonel in the militia during the Revolution, served as a delegate with JM in the 1788 Virginia ratifying convention and as a congressman, 1797-1809 (*BDC*, p. 1830).

From Harry Toulmin

SIR,   ALEXANDRIA Octr. 11. 1793

It is with pleasure I recollect the few hours in which I was so happy as to enjoy your company though I regret that a little indisposition, which was then beginning, & which terminated in a bilious fever, prevented it me from enjoying it so much as I should otherwise have done. I had then some distant thoughts of extending my little tour to the western country—and you were so obliging as to offer to introduce me to your friends in Kentucky, should I determine upon carrying this idea into execution. I am now on my return from Carlisle and Lancaster to Winchester in this state, where it would afford me great pleasure to be favoured with a line from you to any gentleman in Kentucky, for I mean to proceed from Winchester to that country in about the space of a fortnight.

I have much reason to acknowledge with thankfulness, similar favours which you have already conferred upon me. Mr Belmain has been peculiarly obliging and friendly.

My first object in going to Kentucky is to procure some knowledge of the country for the information of friends in England: and as my partiality for America, makes me rather desire to continue here, than to return to my native country, my second object is to see if there be any prospect of my establishing myself there as an instructor of youth in classical knowledge & other branches of liberal education. At present indeed I am connected with a society in England as a minister of religion: but I believe my faith is too simple to admit of any similar connection in America.

I have great reason, however, to speak of the liberality of some worthy men with whom I have been so fortunate as to form an acquaintance, & especially Mr Belmain. With the highest esteem, I am, Sir Your obliged and most respectful Sert

H. Toulmin.

RC (DLC). Addressed by Toulmin to JM at Orange. Forwarded, probably by James Madison, Sr., to JM at Philadelphia. Docketed by JM. On the cover JM made some mathematical calculations and drew what appears to be a map.

From George Washington

Mount Vernon 14th Oct. 1793

My dear Sir,   (Private)

The calamitous situation of Philadelphia—and the little prospect from present appearances of its eligibility to receive Congress by the first Monday in Decemb'r involves a serious difficulty.

It has been intimated by some, that the President ought, by Proclamation, to convene Congress a few days before the above period, at some other place—and by others, (although in extraordinary cases he has power to convene, yet) that he has none to change the place. Mr Jefferson when here on his way home, was of the latter opinion; but the laws were not fully examined; nor was the case at that time so serious as it now is.

From the Attorney General to whom I have since written on this subject,[1] requesting an Official opinion, I have received no answer; nor is it
probable I shall do it soon, as I believe he has no communication with
the Post Office.

Time presses, and the Malady at the usual place of meeting is becoming more & more alarming. What then, do you think is the most advisable
course for me to pursue in the present exigency? Summon Congress to
meet at a certain time & place in their legislative capacity? Simply to
state facts, & say I will meet the members at the time & place just mentioned, for ulterior arrangements? or leave matters as they are, if there
is no power in the Executive to alter the place, legally?

In the first & second cases (especially the first) the delicacy of my
naming a place will readily occur to you. My wishes are, that Congress
could have been assembled at Germantown (to show I meant no partiality) leaving it to themselves if there should appear no prospect of
getting into Philadelphia soon, to decide on what sh'd be done thereafter; but acc'ts say that some people have died in Germantown also, of
the Malignant fever. Every death, however, is now ascribed to that cause,
be the disorder what it may.

Wilmington & Trenton are nearly equidistant, from Philadelphia in
opposite directions; but both are on the gr't thoroughfare and equally
exposed to danger from the Multitude of Travelers & neither may have
Chambers suffice't for the H'e of Representatives. Annapolis and Lancaster are more secure and have good accomodations; but to name either,
especially the first, would be thought to favour the Southern convenience
most, perhaps might be attributed to local views—especially as New York
is talked of for this purpose. Reading if there are proper conveniences
at it would favour neither the Southern nor Northern interest most, but
would be alike to both.

I have written to Mr Jefferson on this subject[2]—notwithstanding
which I would thank you for your opinion, & that fully, as you see my
embarrassment. I even ask more, I would thank you (not being acquainted with forms & having no one with me that is—) to sketch some
instrument for publication proper for the case you think most expedient for me to pursue in the present state of things, if the members are to
be called together as before mentioned. The difficulty of keeping Clerks
in the public Offices had, in a manner, suspended business before I left
Philad'a; and the heads of Departments having matters of private con-
cernment which required them to be absent, has prevented my return
thither longer than I had intended—but I have now called upon the
several Secretaries to meet me there or in the vicinity the first of next
month, for which I shall set out the 27th or 28th of the present.

The accounts from that City are really affecting. Two Gentlemen from New York now here (Colonels Platt & Sargent) say they were told at the Swedes ford of Schoolkil by a person who said he had it from Governor Mifflin that by the official report from the Mayor of the City upwards of 3500 had died and the disorder by all accounts was spreading, & raging more violently than ever. If cool weather accompanied with rain does not put a stop to the Malady, distressing indeed must be the condition of that City—now almost depopulated by removals & deaths. I am always, and with very sincere regards & friendship Your affectionate

GEO WASHINGTON

I would not have sent you such a scrawl, but really have no time to copy it. I came here to look a little into my own private concerns, but have no time allowed me for this purpose being followed by other matters.

Printed copy (Stan. V. Henkels Catalogue No. 694 [1892], item 67); draft (DNA: RG 59, Misc. Letters); letterbook copy (DLC: Washington Papers). The copy sold by Henkels, an autograph letter signed by Washington, was probably the RC. The draft, in Washington's hand, is greatly emended. Postscript not on draft or letterbook copy. Minor variations between the copies have not been noted.

1. Washington to Randolph, 30 Sept. 1793 (Fitzpatrick, *Writings of Washington*, 33:107–9).
2. Washington to Jefferson, 11 Oct. 1793 (ibid., 33:116–18).

From Robert R. Livingston

DR SIR   CLERMONT 20th. Octr 1793

Mr. Adair[1] the bearer of this having done me the favor to spend a few days here I found so much pleasure in his society that I am persuaded that I shall do you a mutual favor in bringing you acquainted with each other. He proposes to pass some months in Virginia. You will find him extremely well informed on most subjects & particularly so in every branch of natural history & chymistry. He will communicate to you some new discoverys & improvments which have not yet reachd us in the ordinary channels. You will not be less pleased with his politics than with his philosophy since he is a firm & decided friend to the rights of man & thinks with us on the subject of popular governments. I condole with you upon the disstress of Philadelphia. Would it not be prudent to order the offices to remove some time before the meeting of Congress so that they may perform the necessary quarantine & remove the objections which may other wise arise to their reception at such place as

Congress may think proper to adjourn to. I am extreamly anxious for their meeting which I think shd. have been long since. I am Dr. Sir with greatest esteem & regd. Your Most Obt hum: Servt

ROBT R LIVINGSTON

RC (DLC). Docketed by JM.

1. James Makittrick Adair, a Scottish physician who practiced in Antigua and England, wrote his 1766 Edinburgh M.D. thesis on the yellow fever of the West Indies. During his visit to the U.S. he corresponded with Jefferson about a model for a threshing machine (Sowerby, *Catalogue of Jefferson's Library*, 1:414; Jefferson to JM, 1 Sept. 1793, n. 8).

To George Washington

DEAR SIR   ORANGE October 24th. 1793.

Your letter of the 14th. instant did not arrive till sunday night, and being not then at home, I did not receive it till last night. I now lose not a moment in complying with its request; tho' I foresee it cannot reach you before you will have left Mount Vernon, and before you will probably have made up a final determination on some if not on all the questions proposed. These are

1. Ought the President to summon Congress at a time and place to be named by him? or,

2 If the President has no power to change the place, ought he to abstain from all interposition whatever? or

3. Ought he to notify the obstacle to a meeting at Philadelphia, state the defect of a regular provision for the exigency, and suggest his purpose of repairing to   as a place deemed most eligible for a meeting in the first instance?

4. What is the place liable to fewest objections?

From the best investigation I have been able to make in so short a time, the first expedient, tho' most adequate to the exigency, seems to require an authority that does not exist under the Constitution and laws of the U. States.[1]

The only passage in the Constitution in which such an authority could be sought is that which says "The President may, on extraordinary occasions, convene both Houses, or either of them." But the obvious import of these terms is satisfied by referring them to the time only at which the extraordinary meeting is summoned. If indeed they included a discretion as to the place as well as the time, it would be unnecessary to recur to the expedient of altering the time in order to get at an alteration of the place. The President could as well alter the place without interfering with the time, as alter the time without interfering with the place. Besides; the effect of a change as to place would not be in all respects similar to a change as to time. In the latter case, an extraordinary session running into the period of an ordinary one, would allow the ordinary one to go on under all the circumstances prescribed by law. In the former case, this would not happen. The ordinary part of the Session would be held out of the place prescribed for it—unless prevented by a positive act for returning to it.

The obvious meaning here assigned to the phrase is confirmed by other parts of the Constitution. It is well known that much jealousy has always appeared in every thing connected with the residence of the General Government. The solicitude of the Constitution to appease this jealousy is particularly marked by the 1st. paragraph of section 6th & the 3d. paragraph of section 7th. of article I. The light in which these paragraphs must be viewed cannot well be reconciled with a supposition that it was meant to entrust the Executive alone with any power on that subject.

Laying aside the Constitution and consulting the law, the expedient seems to be no less inadmissible. The Act of July 1790 "establishing the temporary & permanent seat of the Government of the U. S." cannot be understood to leave any such power in the President. And as the power, if exercised so as to interfere with the provision relating to the temporary seat, might beget an alarm lest, in the hands of a President unfriendly to the permanent seat, it should be turned on some pretext or other against that arrangement, prudential reasons unite with legal ones, for avoiding the precedent.

The 2d mode of treating the difficulty would seem to be best, if the danger at German Town were out of the way. A voluntary resort to that place might be relied on; and the members of the Legislature finding themselves together and with the President, might legalize the necessary steps, or if that should be thought wrong might deliberate and decide for themselves on the emergency. But as the danger might defeat such an expectation, it results that,

The 3d expedient is called for by the occasion; and being sufficient, is all that can be justified by it.

The 4th. point to be considered is the delicate one of naming the place.

In deciding this point, it would seem proper to attend *first* to the risk of the infection. This consideration lies, as you observe, against Trenton & Wilmington: *secondly*, to Northern and Southern jealousies. This applies to N. York and Annapolis: *thirdly*, to the disposition of Pennsylvania, which is entitled to some regard, as well by her calamity, as by the circumstance of her being in possession of the Government.

In combining these considerations we are led to look for some place within the State of Pennsylvania not materially different from Philada. in relation to North and South. Lancaster and Reading appear to have occurred. With the former I am but little acquainted. The latter I never saw. If the object of the Executive should be merely to put Congress in the most neutral situation possible for chusing a place for themselves, as would have been the case at German Town, Reading seems to have the better pretensions. If the object should be to provide a place at once marking an impartiality in the Executive, and capable of retaining Congress during the Session, Lancaster seems to claim a preference.

If the measure which my present view of the subject favors, should be deemed least objectionable, something like the following form might be given to it.

"Whereas a very dangerous and infectious malady which continues to rage in the City of Philada. renders it indispensable that the approaching Session of Congress should be held, as well as the Executive Department be for the present administered, at some other place: And whereas no regular provision exists for such an emergency; so that unless some other place be pointed out, at which the members of Congress may assemble in the first instance, great embarrasments may happen: Under these peculiar circumstances I have thought it incumbent on me to notify the obstacle to a meeting of Congress at the ordinary place of their Session; and to recommend that the several members assemble at   in the State of   at which place I shall be ready to meet them.

G. W.   P. U. S.["]

With sentiments of the highest respect and attachment I remain, Dear Sir, your affectionate humble servant

Js. Madison Jr.

RC (DLC: Washington Papers); FC, Tr (DLC). RC docketed by Washington. The Tr, in an unknown hand, was probably transcribed from the RC after JM retired from the presidency, when several of his letters to Washington, including this one, were returned for copying (JM to Bushrod Washington, 28 Aug. 1819, Bushrod Washington to JM, 23 Mar. 1820, JM to Bushrod Washington, 14 Oct. 1820 [DLC]). Minor variations between the copies have not been noted. Blank spaces in the text are JM's.

1. Jefferson wrote Washington on 17 Oct. expressing a similar view, adding that JM shared his opinion (Ford, *Writings of Jefferson*, 6:436). The entire incident is narrated in Twohig, *Journal of the Proceedings of the President*, p. 242 n. 4.

From Edmund Randolph

MY DEAR FRIEND   GERMAN TOWN October 28. 1793

I am satisfied, that there will be great manœuvring about the place of congress for the next session. New-York seemingly declines a visit from them; but steps are taken to distract preparations in this state, and produce a kind of necessity to go thither, as being the only spot, where accommodations can be found at short notice. A precedent, too is much wished by some, for violating the compact concerning the final residence, by shewing the power of congress over the temporary. I beseech you to be *here* the day before the appointed time. Yrs. afftely

EDM: RANDOLPH.

RC (DLC). Addressed by Randolph to JM, "of Orange. To the care of Mr. David Blair, merchant in Fredericksburg, who is requested to forward it immediately." Docketed by JM.

To James Monroe

DEAR SIR   OCR. 29. 1793

Inclosed are two Newspapers one of which contains the Resolutions proposed at Fredg.[1] and a letter from Bourdeaux[2] which is not uninteresting. You will find also two pieces one from Alexanda. & another answering it[3] which as connected with the present crisis may be worth reading. At Culpeper Court, the proposed meeting took effect, Genl. Stephens in the Chair.[4] The result as stated to me, is not censurable if at all on the score surmised. It has not the smallest tincture either of Anglomany or Aristocracy. I am informed that one of the Resolutions which speaks of the attempts to alienate America from France, in the *past* as well as future tense, was carried in the Come. after considerable debate, and confirmed by the people on a motion to amend. The Resolutions in Fauquier are said to be a servile eccho of those in Richmond. When you come on pray bring with you such of Davis's papers[5] as may have been recd. since I left you. I send the little balance of Tea due to Mrs. Monroe which I intended but failed to procure before my late trip. As you are becoming a worshipper of Ceres I add an Ear of Corn which is forwarder by three weeks than the ordinary sort; and if given to your overseer may supply a seasonable dish on your return next summer. Mr. Jefferson is so delighted with it that he not only requested me to forward some of it to Mr. Randolph but took an Ear with him to be brought back on his return, that there might be no possible disappointment. Should you have an oppy. after you know the day of your setting out, be so good as to drop me notice of it. My Compliments to Mrs. Monroe. Yrs. Always & Affey.

Js. Madison Jr

RC (DLC). Addressed by JM to Monroe at Charlottesville. Docketed by Monroe.

1. On the Fredericksburg resolutions, see Resolutions on Franco-American Relations, ca. 27 Aug. 1793, Editorial Note.

2. Probably an "Extract of a letter from an American gentleman at Bourdeaux to his friend in Virginia, dated August 29, 1793," which reported that the National Convention had imposed an embargo on all exports except silk and "that the Americans have sent a deputation to Paris to obtain a dispensation in their favor." The author also criticized Gouverneur Morris, the U.S. minister to France, and noted that, because of French and British trade restrictions, "the vast prospects of aggrandizement which we expect to derive from a neutrality, are vanished in air" (Philadelphia *Federal Gazette*, 23 Oct. 1793).

3. "A Virginia Farmer," first published in the *Va. Gazette and Alexandria Advertiser*, identified all American supporters of the French as being friendly toward Genet. "A Firm Republican" replied, defending the Franco-American alliance and alleging that Federalists were exploiting American antipathy toward Genet for domestic political advantage (*Va. Herald, and Fredericksburg Advertiser*, 17 and 24 Oct. 1793).

4. On the Culpeper resolutions, see Resolutions on Franco-American Relations, ca. 27 Aug. 1793, Editorial Note.

5. The Richmond *Va. Gazette, and General Advertiser*, published by Augustine Davis.

From Thomas Jefferson

Dear Sir   Germantown Nov. 2. 1793.

I overtook the President at Baltimore, & we arrived here yesterday, myself fleeced of seventy odd dollars to get from Fredericksburg here, the stages running no further than Baltimore. I mention this to put yourself & Monroe on your guard. The fever in Phila. has so much abated as to have almost disappeared. The inhabitants are about returning. It has been determined that the President shall not interfere with the meeting of Congress. R. H. & K. were of opinion he had a right to call them to any place but that the occasion did not call for it. I think the President inclined to the opinion. I proposed a proclamn. notifying that the Executive business would be done here till further notice, which I believe will be agreed. H. R. Lewis, Rawle[1] &c all concur in the necessity that Congress should meet in Phila. & vote there their own adjournment, if it shall then be necessary to change the place. The question will be between

N. York & Lancaster. The Pensylva. members are very anxious for the latter, & will attend punctually to support it as well as to support Muhlenburg & oppose the appointment of Smith (S. C.) speaker, which is intended by the Northern members. According to present appearances, this place cannot lodge a single person more. As a great favor I have got a bed in the corner of the public room of a tavern: and must so continue till some of the Philadelphians make a vacancy by removing into the city. Then we must give from 4. to 6 or 8. dollars a week for cuddies[2] without a bed, and sometimes without a chair or table. There is not a single lodging-house in the place. Ross & Willing are alive, Hancock is dead. Johnson of Maryld has *refused*. Ru. L. & Mcl. in contemplation. The last least.[3] You will have seen Genet's letters to Moultrie & to myself.[4] Of the last I know nothing but from the public papers; and he published Moultrie's letter & his answer the moment he wrote it. You will see that his inveteracy against the President leads him to meditate the embroiling him with Congress. They say he is going to be married to a daughter of Clinton's.[5] If so, he is afraid to return to France. Hamilton is ill, & suspicious he has taken the fever again by returning to his house. He of course could not attend here to-day. But the Pr. had shewed me his letter on the right of calling Congress to another place.[6] Adieu.

RC (DLC); FC (DLC: Jefferson Papers). Unsigned.

1. William Rawle was U.S. attorney for the district of Pennsylvania, 1791–1800, succeeding William Lewis (*Pa. Mag. Hist. and Biog.*, 25 [1901]: 220; *Senate Exec. Proceedings*, 1:86, 88).

2. Cuddy: a small room or closet.

3. According to the notes on his conversation with Washington that Jefferson enclosed in his second letter to JM of 11 Aug., the potential successors as secretary of state then being considered were Thomas Johnson, Edward Rutledge, Robert R. Livingston, and James McClurg.

4. The Philadelphia *Federal Gazette* published the 5 Sept. letter of Gov. William Moultrie of South Carolina—asking Genet for his response to reports that he had threatened to appeal to the people concerning the president's neutrality policy— and Genet's reply of 15 Oct., which denied the reports and asserted that Washington was "accessible to men whose schemes could only darken his glory." A week later the same newspaper printed Genet's letter to Jefferson of 27 Oct., which denied the validity of Washington's revocation of Antoine Charbonnet Duplaine's exequatur as French vice-consul for New Hampshire, Massachusetts, and Rhode Island (Philadelphia *Federal Gazette*, 24 Oct. and 1 Nov. 1793).

5. Genet married Cornelia Tappen Clinton, daughter of Gov. George Clinton of New York, on 6 Nov. 1794.

6. Hamilton to Washington, 24 Oct. 1793 (Syrett and Cooke, *Papers of Hamilton*, 15:373–76).

From Thomas Jefferson

GERMANTOWN. Nov. 9. 93.

The stages from Philadelphia to Baltimore are to be resumed tomorrow. The fever has almost disappeared. The Physicians say they have no new subjects since the rains. Some old ones are still to recover or die, & it is presumed that will close the tragedy. The inhabitants, refugees, are now flocking back generally; this will give us accomodation here. The Pr. sets out tomorrow for Reading, & perhaps Lancaster to return in a week. He will probably remain here till the meeting of Congress, should Philadelphia become ever so safe, as the members may not be satisfied of that point till they have time to inform themselves. Toulon has surrendered to Engld. & Spain. Grand Anse in St. Domingo to England. The British have recieved a check before Dunkirk, probably a great one, but the particulars cannot yet be depended on. It happened about the 10th of September. When Monroe & yourself arrive here, come to Bockeus's tavern[1] (sign the K. of Prussia) I will have engaged beds there for you for your temporary accomodation. Adieu.

RC (DLC); FC (DLC: Jefferson Papers). Unsigned.

1. Bockius's tavern was a convenient resting place on the road southward of Philadelphia (Townsend Ward, "The Germantown Road and Its Associations," *Pa. Mag. Hist. and Biog.*, 6 [1882]: 7).

From George Nicholas

DEAR SIR,   Novr. 15th. 93

I thank you for your friendly letters dated in March and August last.[1]

We have been in a great state of anxiety on account of the French, but our fears begin to subside and give way to our hopes for their success. Their cause is so good and their conduct in the general so great that we are naturally inclined to overlook their imprudencies. It is more than probable that many things which appear so to us at this distance proceed from the peculiarity of their situation. The difference of our manners may also make many things seem strange to us that are natural to them. However as I am always inclined to think well of a man tho' some of his actions will not bear a strict examination provided they in general are good, so I am willing to overlook what is improper in their conduct, and most ardently wish them success.

The situation in which America stands respecting them is delicate.

Prudence forbids her taking an active part, but I doubt honour and gratitude would speak another language. At any rate the delicacy of our situation was such as in my opinion to make it proper to say as little about it as possible. In this point of view the proclamation was certainly wrong; as far as I can judge it was unnecessary and could answer no good purpose as it gave no additional efficacy to the existing laws on the subject. But if as I conceive it was contrary to the impressions which we ought to have felt, it is a dishonourable acknowledgment that we are void of those sentiments. Supposing that the President could be justified by the duty of his office, what apology can be made for the numerous addressers who have voluntarily stept forward on this occasion. Cloak their real sentiments as they will it must be obvious to all that the profits which they expect from the neutrality are what stimulate them to this conduct; and altho' these addresses come only from the mercantile part of America yet the silence of the farmers prove that they have imbibed the same sentiment. How few of them say any thing about the French revolution, and how faint are the expressions of regard to their cause in those few, when compared with their approbation of a measure which they suppose will keep up the price of their wheat. The thinking part of the present age must despise such conduct, and posterity will regret that their ancestors should so soon tarnish the reputation they have acquired as lovers of liberty.

The game that is playing by the two parties to make French politicks answer their purposes in our internal divisions is as disgraceful to those who are concerned in it as it is insulting to the understandings of the people of America. The longer I live the more I am convinced that man will always be a dupe. The senseless multitude who are concerned in these addresses have no idea that they will be used to strengthen the hands of those who are the advocates of measures which they detest. This tho' will certainly be the case and this proclamation with the use that will be made of it, if I am not deceived will have a great effect on all the measures of the next Congress. The object of Jay and King was so apparent that I am astonished that it did not defeat them. Let Genet's conduct have been ever so improper it was highly unbecoming America as a nation to take any notice of it. There is some mystery in that business which it would have been more to the honour of the President to have cleared up.

You will probably hear something said of an attempt being made here to raise an army to go against the Spaniards.[2] The history of that business is shortly this. Genl. Clarke in February last wrote to the French minister offering his services for that purpose and stating the practicability of effecting something considerable if he had power given him to appoint the proper officers, and if he was furnished with three thousand pounds sterling. In June last he received a commission of Major General in the French service with power to appoint his officers and to draw under certain restrictions for the money. When Clarke wrote it is supposed that he was influenced by O Fallon[3] who had married his sister, before he received an answer they had parted. When the French agent got to Clarke he found him totally incapable of conducting such a business, and entirely without influence. Clarke having also lost his counsellor has become very cool in the business, expressed his own doubts of the success of it, and declared that some who had induced him to propose it had deserted him. The agent then sounded different characters in this country, but finding no disposition to engage in such an enterprise, he gave it up and has returned.

This proposition of Clarke's altho' it has ended without producing the effect which he and the French minister expected from it, will be attended with the most serious consequences. It has shewn us unquestionably that the French may be induced to join us in procuring what we are now satisfied our government wants inclination and spirit to obtain for us. The want of inclination we infer from the conduct of the former Congress and the silence of the present one. The want of spirit may be sufficiently proved from the late addresses. We can have no reason to suppose that a people who make money their god will enter into a war to procure a just right for a particular part of America when the greater part besides the expences of the war suppose that this right will be prejudicial to them. Our eyes are opened on this subject; you will hear plain truths, do not despise them. We have but one Voice on the occasion. You must determine whether America shall continue united or whether a division shall take place, which will necessarily be attended with applications to foreign powers for support. We must we will have what we are entitled to: we will no longer be amused with negociations that may be spun out for ages. When we demand a right there is no occasion for supplications either to our government or that which with holds the right from us. The Western country united can bid defiance to the rest of America and to the Spaniards too.[4]

Would our government have been quiet so long if the Delaware had been blocked up by a foreign nation! What is the difference between the two cases in point of right and duty! We retain our affection for our brethren in America and for it's government; but it is not a childish one depending on mamas: it proceeds from an opinion that that affection is reciprocal, and that mutual advantages may be derived from the government. Convince us (and that is nearly done) that this is a delusion and we would sooner be united to the savages who you court in vain than remain as a part of a government from which we derive no benefits.

It is time for our rulers to think seriously on this subject; a connection like our's if once dissolved is scarcely ever renewed. Great Britain would before the close of the war have granted twice as much to America as she refused with disdain at the beginning of it. If policy will not influence their conduct how will they reconcile it to justice to suffer a part of their fellow citizens to be oppressed and injured by a tyrant. The day for asserting the rights of nations is now come; the opportunity is favorable; our all is at stake for we can never be a flourishing people until we have what we demand and we had better lose what we possess in attempting to get what is necessary to it's free enjoyment than hold it in the terms we now do.

I have written to Col: John Taylor my ideas respecting the operations against the Indians. To him I refer you for all the information I can give on this subject.

Much is expected from, and much depends on the next session of Congress. Much national good and reputation, or much evil and discredit will result from their deliberations. It is to be lamented that when all the wisdom of America would be necessary to enable her to act properly that her councils should be distracted and divided by parties. But is not this one of the things which will always attend human governments, and a tax which all must submit to.

Wishing you health and happiness, and a sufficient number of honest members to assist in doing what is right, I am Dr. Sir, with the greatest respect and regard; yr. most obdt. servt.

G. NICHOLAS.

RC (DLC). Docketed by JM, with his notation: "interesting."

1. August letter not found.
2. For a discussion of the negotiations between George Rogers Clark, Genet, André Michaux, and Jefferson concerning the abortive French-sponsored filibuster expedition against the Spanish at New Orleans, see Thomas, *American Neutrality in 1793*, pp. 178–86.
3. James O'Fallon, an agent of the South Carolina Yazoo Company, had intrigued with James Wilkinson to separate Kentucky from the U.S. In 1791 he married Frances Eleanor Clark, sister of George Rogers Clark.
4. Nicholas alluded to the negotiations that William Carmichael and William Short were conducting for a treaty with Spain. Among other things, they hoped to gain access for American shipping to New Orleans. For Nicholas's earlier warning of the Kentuckians' alarm, see *PJM*, 13:338–40.

From Thomas Jefferson

GERMANTOWN. Nov. 17. 1793.

I have got good lodgings for Monroe & yourself, that is to say, a good room with a fire place & two beds, in a pleasant & convenient position, with a quiet family. They will breakfast you, but you must mess in a tavern; there is a good one across the street. This is the way in which all must do, and all I think will not be able to get even half beds. The President will remain here I believe till the meeting of Congress, merely to form a point of union for them before they can have acquired information & courage. For at present there does not exist a single subject in the disorder, no new infection having taken place since the great rains the 1st. of the month, & those before infected being dead or recovered. There is no doubt you will set in Philadelphia, & therefore I have not given Monroe's letter to Seckel.[1] I do not write to him, because I know not whether he is at present moving by sea or by land, & if by the latter, I presume you can communicate to him. Wayne has had a convoy of 22. waggons of provision & 70. men cut off 15 miles in his rear by the Indians. 6. of the men were found on the spot scalped, the rest supposed taken. He had nearly reached Fort Hamilton.[2] R. has given notice that he means to resign. Genet by more & more denials of powers to the President and ascribing them to Congress, is evidently endeavoring to sow tares between them, & at any event to curry favor with the latter to whom he means to turn his appeal, finding it was not likely to be well received with the people. Accept, both of you, my sincere affections.

RC (DLC); FC (DLC: Jefferson Papers). Unsigned.

1. Monroe had leased from David Seckel a house at 4 North Eighth Street for one year from June 1793. JM lived there with the Monroes during the first session, and with Dolley Madison during the second session, of the Third Congress ("Memorandum of an agreement between David Seckel & James Monroe," 18 Mar. 1793 [DLC: Jefferson Papers]; Philadelphia *Federal Gazette*, 24 Dec. 1793; JM to Monroe, 4 Dec. 1794).

2. According to an early newspaper account of the 17 Oct. skirmish that Jefferson here describes, "seventy men, are all killed and missing," but Maj. Gen. Anthony Wayne reported: "the escort lost 15 killed . . . and nine men missing." Wayne was encamped six miles north of Fort Jefferson, while the attack on his supply train took place about seven miles north of Fort St. Clair (Lexington *Ky. Gazette*, 26 Oct. and 2 Nov. 1793; *ASP, Indian Affairs*, 1:361).

To George Nicholas

DEAR SIR   ORANGE Novr. 18. 1793.

Mr. Toulmin will either hand you this, or see you in consequence of it. He is lately from England, and very warmly recommended to me by Mr. Maury our Consul at Liverpool as meriting particular attention. His primary object in visiting Kentucky is to procure a knowledge of the Country for the information of his friends in England who have an eye to America as a more eligible portion of the Earth than their native spot is at present. His next object is of a more personal nature. His partiality to our Country makes him anxious to settle in it: and as he is not likely to find a Religious Society with which he could connect himself as a Minister professing the Unitarian System taught by Priestly & others, he wishes to see if there be any prospect of his establishing himself as an instructor of youth in classical knowledge and other branches of liberal education; for which he is probably well qualified. Any friendly offices you may find it convenient to render him will be of much service to him in his plans, and will moreover be acknowledged by Dear Sir Your mo: Obedt. hble servt.

Js. Madison Jr.

RC (OFH).

To John Breckinridge

Dear Sir   Orange Novr. 19. 1793
I take the liberty of making known to you the Revd. Mr. Toulmin who visits Kentucky with a view to transmit its character to a body of his friends in England who wish to exchange their native Country for some part of ours. He has a secondary view of trying whether he can be engaged on acceptable conditions as an Instructor of youth in classical and other liberal branches of education. At present he is connected with a Religious Society in England of the principles taught by Docr. Priestly and other Dissenting Clergymen; but he supposes his faith too simple to admit of any similar connection in this Country. He has been very strongly recommended to me, and every other circumstance within my knowledge has contributed to vouch his merits. Your counsel and civilities will I am persuaded be of much use to him, and I hope you will pardon my freedom in asking them f⟨or⟩ him. With very sincere esteem & regard, I am Dr Sir your mo: obed: hble servt.

Js. Madison Jr.

RC (DLC: Breckinridge Family Papers). Addressed by JM to Breckinridge in Kentucky.

From John Beckley

Dear Sir,   Philadelphia, 20th. November 1793.
I drop a line to inform you, that I returned to this place with all my family, on Saturday last, and that there is now as perfect safety from

contagion of any kind as was ever known here; there is not known a single case of the yellow fever in the City or its suburbs; the Citizens have returned almost universally, the public Offices are all opened, as well as all the public & private seminaries, business of every kind is resumed, the Markets as fully attended & supplied as ever, and in short no vestige of the late calamity remaining, except in the mournful remembrances of those whose friends & relatives have fallen victims to it. Doctor Rush, assured me last evening that a greater degree of health had never prevailed in this City than at present. A general fumigation of houses, apparel, bedding &c. has taken place by order of the Corporation, and the lodging houses *in particular* will be as safe as ever, or perhaps the safest of any from their peculiar purifications &c. I mention these things & hope this may meet yo. at Fredericksburg, that yo. may rely on my assurance that there is not the smallest possible danger of proceeding immediately into the City, and that as far as this short notice may enable yo. to do so, it may be communicated to others of the Southern Members, as I find great pains has been taken to bring on the Eastern & pennsylva. Members to decide the choice of a speaker &c. With great regard, I am, Dear Sir, Yr: mo: obedt: Servant,

JOHN BECKLEY.

R: B. Lee, is arrived.

RC (DLC). Docketed by JM.

¶ To Henry Lee. Letter not found. *22 November 1793.* Offered for sale in Emily Driscoll Catalogue No. 8 (1949), item 58, which notes that the letter introduces James Makittrick Adair: "I ask your attentions for him . . . with an assurance that they will be both merited & repaid." Acknowledged in Lee to JM, 23 Jan. 1794.

From Maria Butler

SIR   PITTSBURGH Novb th 23–1793
I hope you will be indulgent, to the liberty I am about to take, in an address to you on a subject; that I hoped my Country would have saved me the pain of Mentioning.

Deeply interested for the present, and future wellfare, of A Little helpless charge, that has been left to my care Alone, from the fatal Fourth of Novb[1]–When I with them, was removed in a moment, from the sunshine of prosperity, and the pleasing Anticipation, of gliding down life streams in Ease and competency–To the shade of *Affliction dispair* and comparative *Want*.

Succeeding misfortunes, owing to the first great Loss, in the fall of Genl Butler, has compled me to seek the Influence of some of the Worthy Members of Congress—for A compensation to the Family, of an Old and Brave Soldier—whose best days was spent in Camps and Siges, to the satisfaction of his Countery, though finally his Blood has flowd in vain, on the plains of Miami, and the Malignancy of Fortune deny him A grave, in the land he fought for.[2] I hope with his children, to be Embraced by the liberallity of a Goverment, he spent sleepless Nights to Obtain.

It may be suggested by some, economists in Goverment, that we cannot be left unprovided for; But I answer to it, our property, being chiefly in unproductive lands, and they lieing in the paths of the savage, that they can neither be cultivated or sold at present to any advantage. And bad health, precludes any exertion, on my part, to create, a living to my Children. All the hope that remains to light the solitary Hou[r]s of repining and grief, is that my Countery will not pass me by in silence.

They [sic] Members of this state, will generaly be in favour of my Wish—and I hope it will be the case with those of yours though I am well aware; it is an unfavourab[l]e Crisis, for such Appli[c]ations Whilst so much War is to be dreaded, but I hope it will be remembered, that Common Wealths may Florish, whilst Individuals are ruined forever.

Nothing Sir but a great Anxiety to rais my Children has caused me to trouble you on this subject, which you must pardon, as being directed to you as A Man of Worth and Sensibility—From the Effervescence of a Heart full of the Bitterness of *this World* Whilst I am with respect your

MARIA BUTLER

RC (DLC). Docketed by JM.

1. Maj. Gen. Richard Butler was killed at the defeat of Maj. Gen. Arthur St. Clair by the Miami Confederacy on 4 Nov. 1791.

2. The dead from St. Clair's defeat were not buried until Maj. Gen. Anthony Wayne arrived at the site and built Fort Recovery in late December 1793 (Wildes, *Anthony Wayne*, p. 408).

¶ To James Madison, Sr. Letter not found. *Ca. 23 November 1793.* Mentioned in JM to James Madison, Sr., 25 Nov. 1793: "I wrote from Fredg. by Col: Monroe's servant & informed you that I had left with Mr. Jones £18–12–5 which would be del[i]vered to your order."

To Thomas Jefferson

DEAR SIR   FREDG. NOVR. 24. 93.

I have your 3 letters. The last of the 17th. fell into my hands here when I arrived on friday night. Col. Monroe was a day before me. Accept our thanks for your provision in our behalf at Germanto[w]n. We set off in 5 Minutes in a machine we have procured here, & which we shall keep on with till it fails us, or we can do better. I hope we shall be with you by sunday evening, or monday morning. Giles & Venable being before us, they will give you the intelligence from Richmond. The inclosed paper contains a scrap which may be of later date. If the Senate rejected as we understand, the vote relating to the procln., the answer of the Govr. *jointly* to the Come. of the two houses[1] is a curious one. Yrs. affly.

J. M. JR

RC (DLC: Jefferson Papers). Addressed by JM. Docketed by Jefferson, "recd. Dec. 2."

1. On 1 Nov. the House of Delegates passed resolutions endorsing Washington's Neutrality Proclamation and Gov. Henry Lee's actions to carry the proclamation into effect, but the Senate rejected the resolutions on 8 Nov. When a committee from both chambers on 15 Nov. notified Lee of his reelection, the House message again complimented the governor's advocacy of the Neutrality Proclamation, while the Senate remained silent on the issue. Lee nevertheless thanked both houses for "your commendation of my prompt and decided support of the President's Proclamation" (Richmond *Va. Gazette, and General Advertiser*, 6 and 20 Nov. 1793; *Journal of the Senate of the Commonwealth of Virginia*, Oct. 1793 [Richmond, 1794; Evans 28003], p. 11; see also Risjord, *Chesapeake Politics*, pp. 431–32).

To James Madison, Sr.

HOND SIR   DUMFRIES NOVR. 25. 93

Having procured at this place a substitute for Daman I shall send back Sam, after going a few miles just to try the new arrangement. He will be in Fredg. tonight and will thence make the best of his way home. A letter red. at Fredg. from Mr. Jefferson says that the fever has entirely vanished. Another of the 20th. from a gentleman in Philada confirms it in the most decided terms. And I understand here from S. Carolina gentlemen returning from their Northern Tour, that it is expected the Legislature will meet at once in Philada. Our present plan is to go to Germantown in the first instance. If we change it, it will be in consequence of the fuller information we receive as we approach the end of the journey.

I wrote from Fredg. by Col: Monroe's servant & informed you that I had left with Mr. Jones £18–12–5 which would be del[i]vered to your order. I have a letter from Mr. Maury of Liverpool of Sepr. 26, which says the carnage on the British & allied troops in the late actions at Dunkirk was dreadful & that the Republican forces were advancing to recover Toulon; but that some advantages had been gained (according to report) by the counterrevolutionalists within. I forgot to leave direction for Sawney to let M. C.¹ have the White Horse as soon as the waggon is finished: be so good as to supply the omission. Yrs. affy.

JS. MADISON JR.

Memorandm. for Majr. Lee who is requested to send J. M. jr.
    Coffee-nuts, as many & as soon as can be convenient.
    A few peccan nuts, if to be had without trouble.
    A few of the nuts or seeds of such of trees of Kentucky, as are in any
      degree peculiar to the Western Country.

RC (DLC).

1. Sawney (a slave) and Mordecai Collins were overseers at Montpelier.

From Alexander White

DEAR SIR   WOODVILLE 30th. Nov. 1793

    Though I no longer hold a seat among you I feel not the less interested in the honor and happiness of my Country, consequently every information respecting the important Scenes foreign and domestic which have opened during the recess of Congress, or which may be developed during the Session would be highly gratifying. I am sensible of the fatigue a correspondence with your numerous connections must occasion, and therefore urge no farther than to say, that whatever communications you may oblige me with, will be most thankfully received. After I was removed from Public business I felt much inclined to retire from private business likewise, but I soon discovered a vacant head and an empty Purse were very disagreeable Companions. You probably did not expect either of those to bear me company. They never have, but they approached so near that I got a slight view of their features. I found the income arising from my property would not enable me, to live in that degree of independence which is necessary to set the mind at ease, and employ it in the contemplation of pleasing subjects, "to read What Books, and see what Friends I please." I therefore concluded to return to the bar, confining my practice however to a narrow circle in which I hope for a small addition to my revenue and leisure to spend a part of my time in agreeable avocations. Upon the whole I feel a much greater degree of happiness than a Seat in Congress ever afforded me, and am inclined to believe from the present state of public affairs, that seat would not have become more pleasing. I fear the Seeds of discord are already sown, and do not consider myself qualified to take a part in the warm discussions which may probably ensue. I never could reconcile to my mind a maxim which politicians say is necessary in the conduct of public affairs, that of going into all the measures of the Party whose general object you approve. I know not how I have been led into these observations they have dropt from my pen as they probably might have done from my tongue had we been carelessly walking together to pay Card Visits—but I cannot quit the subject without mentioning my confidence in the extent of your knowledge, soundness of your judgement, coolness of your temper, Love of your Country and regard for that Constitution the formation and adoption of which has done you so much honor, that, if our political Vessel is in the danger some suppose, you will steer the middle course and be instrumental in saving her from Shipwreck. We have had a remarkably dry Season since Harvest[,] Crops of Corn light, Sold from the heap at 2 dollars, one third above a medium price at that season. Some refreshing rains lately with mild weather afford a prospect of good Crops of Winter Grain. The rains have not been sufficient to raise the Waters. Remember me to Mr. Giles and as many of my former Colleagues as opportunities offer, and believe me to be with great sincerity Dear Sir Your Obt Sert

ALEXR WHITE

P.S Letters by Mondays Mail reach Winchester on Saturday.

RC (DLC). Docketed by JM.

Madison in the Third Congress
2 December 1793–3 March 1795

EDITORIAL NOTE

During the last days of the Second Congress, JM made his longest speech of the session in support of William Branch Giles's resolutions censuring Alexander Hamilton's official conduct as secretary of the treasury (*PJM*, 14:456–68 and nn.). The result was predictable. The House of Representatives rejected those resolutions by wide margins. Republicans probably endorsed the attack on Hamilton as a delaying tactic to prevent more substantive legislation from reaching the floor until the convening of the Third Congress, in which they expected to have a House majority. They may also have seen the resolutions as a campaign issue during the Virginia congressional elections, which reapportionment and redistricting had postponed until 18 March 1793 (*PJM*, 14:141–42 n. 2).

In those elections, Republicans won eight of the ten newly created House seats. In a total delegation of nineteen, two of the three Federalist incumbents (Richard Bland Lee and Samuel Griffin) kept their seats, while Alexander White was defeated. In October 1792 the General Assembly had elected John Taylor of Caroline to Richard Henry Lee's vacant United States Senate seat and to a full term beginning in March 1793. He joined fellow Republican James Monroe, Virginia's other senator (*CVSP*, 6:103–4).

Although JM had to campaign for election to the First Congress, thereafter he was so secure that he never again was present in his constituency at election time. In 1793 that constituency—which redistricting had halved to include only Orange, Spotsylvania, Louisa, and Madison counties—reelected him without opposition. Few congressmen had the distinction of representing counties named in their honor.

Nationally, Republicans won a net gain of twenty-four House seats to the Federalists' eleven. Roughly calculated, given the lack of party discipline, the partisan alignment in the House then stood at fifty-seven Republicans and forty-eight Federalists in the Third Congress. Federalists gained a Senate seat after the February 1794 disqualification of Albert Gallatin of Pennsylvania, producing a roll call of seventeen Federalists and thirteen Republicans in the upper house.

In mid-March 1793 JM left Philadelphia and leisurely returned to Virginia with Monroe for the vacation. Politics were never far from his mind, for Jefferson kept him abreast of developments at the capital. Some of those developments spurred him to write the "Helvidius" essays of 24 August–18 September and, with Monroe's help, the resolutions on Franco-American relations of circa 27 August. "War talk" was also current as Jefferson warned JM that the Third Congress might have to convene early if the Creek Indians, incited by Spain, invaded United States territory (Jefferson to JM, 2 June 1793).

That crisis did not occur, but the yellow fever epidemic in Philadelphia led the president to consult JM on a constitutional means of convening Congress at a location other than that specified by the Residence Act of 1790. This act provided that the federal capital would be at Philadelphia until 1800 and on the banks of the Potomac thereafter. Southerners had long suspected an Eastern conspiracy to prevent the implementation of the Residence Act, and Attorney General Edmund Randolph urged JM to return to Pennsylvania to protect Southern interests before Congress convened. But the epidemic abated, thereby defusing the potential crisis, and Congress met as planned in Philadelphia (Washington to JM, 14 Oct. 1793; JM to Washington, 24 Oct. 1793; Randolph to JM, 28 Oct. 1793).

Washington asked for JM's advice less often than he had during the First

Congress. JM's leadership of the congressional opposition to Washington's administration strained relations between the two Virginians, though they remained on friendly and respectful personal terms. JM did not assist Washington with his annual address as he had done in the First Congress, though he again drafted the House's reply to the president.

The First Session, 2 December 1793–9 June 1794

Although Republicans enjoyed a majority in the House, it was not a working majority. Party discipline was only in its formative stages, thus complicating JM's opposition to administration policy. Republicans won a crucial vote when Frederick A. C. Muhlenberg of Pennsylvania defeated Federalist William Loughton Smith of South Carolina in the election for the House speakership (Jefferson to JM, 2 Nov. 1793). After that initial victory, the Republicans' legislative record rapidly deteriorated.

During the summer, news had arrived of the first of a series of British orders in council authorizing the Royal Navy to capture neutral ships trading with France or its colonies. Great Britain also arranged a twelve-month truce between Portugal and Algiers, thereby releasing Algerine corsairs to prey on American shipping. Federalists seized the initiative and called for a naval shipbuilding program. In several speeches, JM opposed the naval buildup and proposed instead that, after the truce between Portugal and Algiers expired, the United States should pay the Portuguese navy to protect American shipping in the Mediterranean and eastern Atlantic. He argued that a large navy was inappropriate for the young republic, with its cost disproportionate to the value of the shipping it would protect. Federalists won passage of the bill for a naval armament, but in a related military development Republicans successfully opposed plans for expanding the regular army (Jefferson to JM, 1 Sept. 1793, and n. 3; JM to Jefferson, 14 Mar. 1794, and n. 2, 26 Jan. and 15 Feb. 1795; JM's speeches of 6, 7, and 11 Feb., 30 May 1794, 2 and 3 Feb. 1795, and nn.).

For the past decade, JM had advocated reciprocity in foreign trade. Free trade was his goal, but the British Navigation Acts—which excluded foreigners from the lucrative carrying trade with British possessions—led him to propose commercial discrimination against Great Britain. Throughout his career, he consistently favored economic sanctions as a means of extracting trade concessions. In his congressional speeches, he often argued that a major reason for adopting the Constitution had been to vest in the federal government powers sufficient to retaliate against the British navigation system. In the First Congress he had proposed retaliatory tariffs against nations that did not have commercial treaties with the United States. This provision struck primarily at Great Britain's exclusion of American ships from West Indian ports. The House approved JM's commercial discrimination proposals for the impost and tonnage bills of 1789, but the Senate rejected them (JM's speech of 8 Apr. 1789, *PJM*, 12:66).

On 14 February 1791 Washington submitted to the House a message recounting the failure of Gouverneur Morris's negotiations for a commercial treaty with Great Britain. JM was appointed to the select committee that considered the president's message and reported a navigation bill providing for retaliatory regulations against those nations which discriminated against American ships and exports. On 23 February the House referred the committee's report to Secretary of State Jefferson and directed him to report on restrictions on American trade. With JM's assistance, Jefferson completed his report during the Second Congress but postponed its delivery while the administration negotiated further with Great Britain. The House finally received the "Report of the Secretary of State on the Privileges and Restrictions on the Commerce of the United States in Foreign Countries" on 16 December 1793, two weeks before Jefferson resigned and retired to Monticello (*Annals of Congress*, 1st Cong., 3d sess., 2015, 2022; *ASP, Foreign Relations*, 1:128, 300–304).

With Jefferson withdrawn from politics, JM had to assume additional responsibilities. As the de facto leader of the fledgling Republican party, he tried to carry into law Jefferson's reciprocity proposals. With characteristic thoroughness, JM consulted Tench Coxe, the commissioner of the revenue, for information and statistics as he prepared his speeches on commercial discrimination (JM to Coxe, ca. 13 Jan. 1794). In the Committee of the Whole on 3 January 1794, he offered seven resolutions to implement the recommendations in Jefferson's report. In speeches that day and later that month, he returned to themes he had treated throughout his career. Great Britain was dependent on the United States for imported necessities, JM argued, while America imported only expendable luxuries. Thus in his view the British were vulnerable to American economic sanctions. (Jefferson's embargo of 1807–9 ultimately put this Republican theory to the test, with unedifying results.)

Although his proposals would reduce American commercial dependence on Great Britain, congressional critics predicted that they would involve the United States in war. JM responded that reciprocity alone would not lead to war and charged that Federalist proposals for a naval and military buildup were more likely to result in armed conflict. Not least among the benefits of reciprocity, JM claimed, would be the diversion of more trade to France, America's republican ally. A draft resolution, which he deleted before presenting his proposals to the House, even called for applying the revenue generated by discriminatory tariffs toward repayment of America's debt to France.

JM's speeches on commercial discrimination in the Third Congress were marathon performances. Massachusetts Republican William Lyman described JM's 14 January reply to William Loughton Smith's speech: "On this Occasion Smith Spoke about two hours very unset and handsomely Although not with the degree of Elegance Accuracy Method and extensive Information with which Maddison Engaged our Attention for two hours and a half during which time in a full House and thronged with Spectators there was such perfect Silence that you might almost have heard a Pin Fall. In Short Eloquence which baffles every thing I had ever heard and almost description." Although JM spoke at great length, his speech was cut short when the House received a rumor of French military victories. The House adjourned early that day, with the Republicans no doubt in jubilation. Despite JM's eloquence, the Committee of the Whole passed only the first resolution; the rest were never brought to a vote (Lyman to Samuel Henshaw, 17 Jan. 1794 [PPIn]; *Philadelphia Gazette*, 16 Jan. and 3 Feb. 1794).

Resorting to a combination of maneuver and initiative against JM's resolutions, Federalists first tried to defeat them by forcing an immediate vote. New England Republicans were unsure of popular support for the resolutions and wanted to consult their constituents. On 5 February Lyman therefore urged that consideration of the resolutions be postponed until 3 March. Only three out of nineteen Virginia congressmen opposed postponement. In the congressional elections a year later, two Virginia Federalists paid dearly for their opposition to JM's resolutions. Republican agitation in their districts persuaded Samuel Griffin not to run again and led to Richard Bland Lee's defeat. In other states, Republicans similarly targeted Federalist opponents of JM's resolutions and defeated congressmen Thomas FitzSimons of Pennsylvania, Samuel Dexter, Jr., of Massachusetts, and John Watts of New York (*Annals of Congress*, 3d Cong., 1st sess., 428–32; John Dawson to JM, 25 Feb. 1794, and n. 1; JM to Jefferson, 2 Mar. 1794).

After the House postponed consideration of the resolutions, Massachusetts Republicans hoped to win public support for JM's proposals at a 13 February town meeting at Faneuil Hall in Boston. The meeting appointed a resolutions committee which on 24 February recommended "a discrimination against *Britain* and *Spain*, by imposing new duties on their vessels and goods." During a two-day debate Federalist opponents of commercial retaliation persuaded the meeting to table the resolutions (Boston *Columbian Centinel*, 12, 15, and 26 Feb. 1794).

While the committee deliberated, Federalists unlimbered their press and laid down a barrage against JM. On 19 February Benjamin Russell's *Columbian Centinel* published a letter signed "Fair Play," which tried to link JM with the discredited French minister, Citizen Genet, and argued that JM's resolutions would subordinate United States interests to those of France. On 22 February Russell's paper inquired, "Where did Mr. Maddison, any more than Mr. Ames, or Mr. Dexter [Massachusetts Federalists who opposed JM's resolutions in the House], acquire his knowledge of commerce? Not surely in the interior of *Virginia*, where no other commerce is transacted than the buying and selling of negroes?" Christopher Gore, Federalist United States attorney for the Massachusetts district, later anonymously wrote the seven-part "Manlius" series that Russell published in his paper and as a pamphlet (Evans 27062). On 10 September "Manlius" No. 3 attacked JM's resolutions, using arguments similar to those of "Fair Play." Under Russell's editorship, spanning nearly half a century, the *Columbian Centinel* continued its attack on Republican foreign policy during Jefferson's and JM's presidencies (*PJM-PS*, 1:58 n. 4, 384 n. 1).

JM's commercial discrimination proposals gained more public support in Republican strongholds than they did in Boston. On 22 February the Nineteenth Virginia Militia Regiment, meeting in Richmond to celebrate Washington's birthday, appointed a resolutions committee headed by the regimental commander. A week later the regiment unanimously approved resolutions endorsing JM's reciprocity proposals and William Branch Giles's support for them. On 27 February a New York town meeting, organized by Robert R. Livingston at Monroe's request, appointed a committee that reported resolutions including a proposal for increased taxes to support military and naval forces protecting American commerce. The Democratic Society of the City of New York endorsed the resolutions, and a copy was sent to Federalist congressman John Watts. Reconvening on 6 March at Federal Hall, the meeting attracted "on a moderate estimate, 2000 citizens," who unanimously approved the resolutions. At a Philadelphia public meeting on 8 March, Republicans thwarted Federalist plans to denounce JM's proposals. Endorsements of the proposals came from far afield; newspapers in Baltimore, Philadelphia, and Richmond printed a memorial from a committee of American captains languishing in Jamaica as a result of the British seizure of their vessels (*Va. Gazette, and Richmond and Manchester Advertiser*, 3 Mar. 1794; *Philadelphia Gazette*, 28 Feb. and 1 Mar. 1794; N.Y. *Daily Advertiser*, 5, 6, and 7 Mar. 1794; JM to Jefferson, 9 Mar. 1794, and n. 2; Joshua Barney and others to JM, 13 Mar. 1794, and n.).

Though never brought to a vote in the House, JM's resolutions served some partisan purposes. Like Giles's earlier resolutions censuring Hamilton, they could thwart Federalist-sponsored legislation and publicize an issue for which Republicans could agitate in future elections. Samuel Smith of Maryland denounced the tactics of "Maddison's party": "His resolutions which would have been Commercially wrong & politically are weak, have taken up so much time as to retard all those other useful Bills which that party delayed the passage of, without openly opposing any but the Naval Armament. So those things which ought to have been in Execution are Scarce thro' both Houses." But delay was a game that two could play, and JM himself observed of Federalist stratagems, "Delay is consequently one of the arts of opposition." Himself a merchant, Smith in his House speeches had favored acquiescing in British depredations against American shipping so long as they did not exceed the losses that would result from discriminatory tariffs. But a sudden increase of British seizures converted Smith from acquiescence to retaliation and, ultimately, from federalism to republicanism. By early March, some 250 vessels had been seized, and 150 condemned, as a result of the order in council of 6 November 1793 (Smith to Otho Holland Williams, 20 Mar. 1794 [MdHi]; JM to Jefferson, 14 Apr. 1794; Fulwar Skipwith to the secretary of state, 7 Mar. 1794, *ASP, Foreign Relations*, 1:429).

Commercial discrimination then seemed too mild a response to the increased British depredations. JM's resolutions were abandoned, and both parties proposed more drastic measures. Federalists advocated strengthening the naval and military forces, while Republicans favored economic sanctions in the form of a nonintercourse bill. Both parties agreed to joint resolutions imposing a short-lived embargo. Federalist Jonathan Dayton of New Jersey moved to sequester American debts owed to British creditors. The House never brought his proposal to a vote, probably because it would force Virginians (who owed most of those debts) to pay them to the American government. "The friends of the Measure," observed a Georgia congressman, "fearing that nothing would be done if the op[p]osition was not soften'd down by the tender of som[e]thing more conciliating in its nature agreed to suspend the resolution for sequestration that . . . [a nonintercourse bill] might be submitted for consideration." JM served on the committee that reported the nonintercourse bill, which the House passed but Vice-President John Adams's tie-breaking vote defeated in the Senate. Meanwhile Washington's administration mounted a diplomatic initiative, proposing to send Chief Justice John Jay as an envoy extraordinary to negotiate all outstanding differences with Great Britain. JM was convinced that a major motive behind Jay's mission was to frustrate the passage of congressional retaliatory measures against Great Britain (Thomas Carnes to his constituents, 2 May 1794, Noble E. Cunningham, Jr., ed., *Circular Letters of Congressmen to Their Constituents, 1789–1829* [3 vols.; Chapel Hill, N.C., 1978], 1:25; JM to Jefferson, 11 May 1794).

Another issue contributing to partisan division in the House was taxation. On 26 March 1794 the House appointed JM to the fifteen-member select committee on ways and means. The appointment of this committee was a departure from the practice in the First and Second Congresses of referring to the secretary of the treasury for reports on ways and means. Thus it represented a shift in relations between the executive and legislative branches, a qualified success for Republicans who had long opposed references to cabinet secretaries, and a defeat for Hamilton which contributed to his decision to resign as secretary of the treasury in January 1795. Not all Republicans favored appointing the committee, however, and Virginia congressman John Page predicted that it would become a tool of Hamilton's policies. JM reached the same conclusion when the committee's chairman, Hamilton's Federalist ally William Loughton Smith, reported proposals that resulted in increased impost and tonnage duties, an excise on snuff and refined sugar, and new taxes on carriages, property sold at auction, and licenses for selling wines and liquors. Republicans urged that the national debt be paid off but were reluctant to admit the necessity of taxation in some form. Among Republican critics of the excise, JM was one of the few who recognized the level of taxation required for redeeming the public debt. He began to consider a land tax as an alternative to the excise, and during the second session he proposed such a measure, but it never gained support (*Annals of Congress*, 3d Cong., 1st sess., 531–32, 597; *ASP, Finance*, 1:276–78; *U.S. Statutes at Large*, 1:390–92, 384–90, 373–76, 397–400, 376–78; JM's speeches of 1, 2, 9, and 19 May 1794, 16 Jan. 1795, and nn.; JM to Jefferson, 1 June 1794, and nn. 1, 2, 15 Feb. 1795; JM to James Madison, Sr., 4 and 19 May 1794).

As the first session ground to a close, adjournment was twice postponed. The asperity of party politics frayed tempers to the breaking point. Congressman Fisher Ames, a Massachusetts Federalist, reported with satisfaction a conversation between two senators, Republican John Taylor and Federalist Rufus King of New York: "Taylor, of Virginia, says to King—

'You are strange fellows: Formerly, you did what you chose with a small majority; now, we have a great majority, and can do nothing. You have baffled every one of our plans.' I wish he may prove a prophet. The resistance to wild projects has risen in its spirit and style, as hope declined. We have banged them as hard as we could, and they have been tamer than formerly. Taylor said, also, that, though in a minority, we had carried and were carrying all our measures, frigates, taxes, negotiation, &c." Some Northern Federalist senators even privately discussed the dissolution of the Union (Ames to Christopher Gore, 2 May 1794, S. Ames, *Works of Fisher Ames*, 1:142; memorandum from Taylor, 11 May 1794).

JM contemplated this situation with frustration. The personal attacks of the Federalist press had evidently stung him, for he later replied in an anonymous pamphlet, the *Political Observations* of 20 April 1795. During the Second Congress, he had drafted but never published a similar reply to William Loughton Smith's *The Politicks and Views of a Certain Party, Displayed* (*PJM*, 14:396–400). In his *Political Observations*, JM provided a remarkable account of the Third Congress's first session from the perspective of one of its most active participants. By the end of the session, however, he was earnestly courting Dolley Payne Todd and was distracted from politics. For political reasons he had countenanced Monroe's appointment as the United States minister to France, but the prospect of his friend's departure must have been unwelcome to JM. He accompanied the Monroes to Baltimore and saw them embark, then traveled with Joseph Jones to Virginia for the summer recess (JM to James Madison, Sr., 6 and 15 June 1794).

The Second Session, 3 November 1794–3 March 1795

In mid-October JM returned with his bride to the house at 4 North Eighth Street where he had lived with the Monroes during the previous session. Congressman Jonathan Trumbull (Federalist of Connecticut) predicted that "the present campaign of politics will be carried on with much more mildness & good humour, than the last. Mr. Madison's late connection it is said has drawn off much of his atrabilious Gall—& indeed he appears with much more complacency & sociability than I have ever yet seen in him." By the time the second session convened, JM and Jefferson clearly were providing the inspiration for the nascent Republican party. The leadership of those two Virginians resulted in the appearance of the familiar epithets "Madisonian" and "Jeffersonian" (JM to Monroe, 4 Dec. 1794; Philadelphia *Federal Gazette*, 24 Dec. 1793; Trumbull to an unspecified correspondent, undated extract, Parke-Bernet Catalogue No. 2205 [24 Sept. 1963], item 232; Philadelphia *Gazette of the U.S.*, 13 Dec. 1794; the Right Reverend James Madison to JM, 12 Nov. 1794).

The second session—the short session characteristic of all congresses until the ratification of the Twentieth Amendment—began at a slow pace as the House waited two weeks for the Senate to reach a quorum. But a political bombshell was smoldering while the stragglers took their seats in the upper house. The Whiskey Insurrection, which had broken out in western Pennsylvania in July, posed a dilemma for Republican congressmen. The whiskey rebels resisted the excise on spirits that Republicans had long opposed, but JM and his colleagues had no desire to endorse civil disobedience.

Washington considered all forms of political opposition as attacks upon himself. In his annual address to Congress, the president alleged that "certain self-created societies"—i.e., the Democratic-Republican societies—had fomented the insurrection. JM considered that address "perhaps the greatest error of his political life. . . . The game was, to connect the democratic Societies with the odium of the insurrection—to connect the Republicans in Congs. with those Societies—to put the P[resident] ostensibly at the head of the other party" (JM to Monroe, 4 Dec. 1794).

The House's replies to the president's annual addresses had previously been mere formalities. JM's 21 November draft of the reply avoided any reference to the "self-created societies," but Federalists raised the issue. The acrimonious debate on the reply lasted a week. Except in western Pennsylvania, the Democratic-Republican societies had no influence on the Whiskey Insurrection, and Republican congressmen apparently kept aloof from personal involvement with the societies. The Greenville branch of the Republican Society of South Carolina was named in honor of JM, and the Charleston branch sent him congratulations on his commercial discrimination resolutions, but no evidence of a reply has been found. In his congressional speeches, he nevertheless defended the societies' right to express their political opinions. The House finally agreed to a compromise, proposed by Virginia Republican John Nicholas, and denounced "combinations of men" (Republican Society of South Carolina to JM, 12 Mar. 1794; JM's speech of 27 Nov. 1794, and nn.).

On 15 December JM reported from committee a bill to amend the Naturalization Act of 1790. Immigration was not yet so politically divisive an issue as it became in 1798, but JM advocated strict rules for admitting foreign merchants to American citizenship (a view he still held twenty-four years later). William Branch Giles threw in a bone of contention when he sought an amendment requiring aliens to renounce titles of nobility in order to qualify for citizenship. "This last," noted JM, "raised some dust." In an attempt to expose the Federalists as favoring aristocracy, Giles asked for a rollcall vote on his amendment. Not to be outdone, Samuel Dexter, Jr., offered to vote for the amendment if it was revised to require a prospective citizen to renounce not only titles of nobility but also possession of slaves and to "declare that he holds all men *free* and equal." Dexter continued, "You want to hold us up to the public as aristocrats. I, as a retaliation, will hold you up to the same public, as dealers in slaves." After a rancorous debate, the House defeated Dexter's amendment and approved Giles's. The Naturalization Act of 1795—requiring five years' residence in the United States and three years' notice of intention before an alien could be admitted to citizenship—became the only major piece of legislation sponsored by JM that the Third Congress passed (JM's speeches of 9, 26, and 31 Dec. 1794, 1, 2, and 8 Jan. 1795, and nn.; JM to Jefferson, 11 Jan. 1795).

JM was unopposed in the election scheduled for 16 March, but rumors circulated in his constituency that he would not run again. He wrote his father, his brother William (who had represented Madison County in the House of Delegates' recent session), and Aaron Fontaine (one of JM's supporters in Louisa County), asking them to dispel those rumors and to organize the election in his district. Joseph Jones silenced similar rumors in Spotsylvania County (JM to James Madison, Sr., 23 Feb. 1795; JM to William Madison, 1 Mar. 1795; Jones to JM, 21 Mar. 1795).

With the departure of Federalists Samuel Griffin and Richard Bland Lee, the Virginia delegation in the Fourth Congress became generally antiadministration if not solidly Republican. Despite gains in Virginia, New York, and Pennsylvania that heartened Republicans, they suffered net losses (approximately calculated) of two seats in the Senate and six in the House, thereby also losing control of the House. When the Fourth Congress convened, JM faced a grim prospect: Federalist majorities of 19–11 in the Senate and 54–51 in the House.

Throughout the spring of 1795, rumors arrived of the provisions of the treaty that Jay had concluded with Great Britain the previous November. Robert R. Livingston urged a preemptive attack on the treaty, but JM demurred, fearing that opposition to the treaty would be defeated if premature. On 3 March, the day that the Third Congress adjourned, Washington summoned a special session of the Senate to consider the treaty to convene on 8 June. He and Secretary of State Randolph received the long-awaited treaty from a special courier on 7 March. They kept its contents secret, confident in the prospects of ratification by the Federalists' increased Senate majority in the Fourth Congress (Livingston to JM, 30 Jan. 1795; JM to Livingston, 8 Feb. 1795; JM to Monroe, 11 and 26 Mar. 1795; *Senate Exec. Proceedings*, 1:177).

Amid the partisan battles, some civility remained in relations between Republicans and Federalists. Samuel Dexter, Jr., vigorously opposed his Republican adversaries in congressional debates and in a protracted series of Massachusetts runoff elections which he ultimately lost. Yet he asked JM to discuss privately the differences in their political principles, and JM invited him to dinner at his home. Although JM was leading the congressional opposition, he and his bride were invited to dine with the Washingtons. Despite these outward amenities, the impending struggle over ratification of the Jay treaty in the Fourth Congress soon revealed the existence of a partisan division in American politics (Dexter to JM, 3 and 5 Feb. 1795; JM to Dexter, 5 Feb. 1795; Bartholomew Dandridge, Jr., to JM, 31 Mar. 1795).

Sources for Madison's Speeches

During the Third Congress, JM delivered sixty-one speeches of sufficient length to be printed in full in this edition. Although this number represents an increase over twenty-eight in the Second Congress, it falls short of his more than one hundred speeches in the First Congress. But since the Third

Congress met for only two sessions, compared with the First Congress's three, the number of his speeches per session approaches that of the earlier period. House speeches continued to be printed in the Philadelphia newspapers. Although JM wrote out a few of his speeches for publication, most were recorded by stenographers working for the publishers.

Toward the end of the Second Congress, the *Federal Gazette*, published by Andrew Brown, Sr., had begun to offer independent accounts of House speeches. Other newspaper publishers concluded that the readership for congressional debates was limited, but the *Federal Gazette* was prospering, and increased circulation allowed Brown to perform the public service of providing the debates in the Third Congress. He hired stenographer James Thomson Callender, who in January 1793 had fled from Edinburgh under indictment for sedition. Thus Callender began his erratic career in American journalism by transcribing the speeches in the House. The *Federal Gazette* expanded its coverage and filled the void left by other newspapers. On 1 January 1794 Brown changed its title to the *Philadelphia Gazette* and enlarged its format. Of JM's sixty-one speeches in the Third Congress, Brown's journal was the sole publisher of nineteen and the first to print thirty-one.

In his statement of intent, Brown announced, "We are ambitious to give the proceedings of the Congress at the fullest length, which is practicable." He explained his use of italics in the transcripts of speeches: "They are used where an expression is uncommonly forcible, or conveys an idea on which the argument hinges. The public may rest assured, that they always have been the exact words of the speaker, with the variation perhaps of a particle." He offered to let congressmen review the summaries of their speeches or present their own transcripts "if transmitted by six o'clock in the evening of the same day." Since other papers had abandoned the enterprise, he took pride in covering the debates throughout the Third Congress, "in defiance of a very great expence, a great degree of personal trouble, and great risk of giving personal offence." Some congressmen, he claimed, were satisfied with the result. "A member called at the office of the Philadelphia Gazette, to see the notes made on one of his speeches, before they went to press. He altered either two or three letters, but not an *entire word*, in the whole manuscript. He was reminded that it was impossible to publish his speech verbatim, or even more than a fourth part of it, but that this was *a summary of his principal ideas*. He declared himself perfectly satisfied" (*Philadelphia Gazette*, 20 Jan. and 20 Dec. 1794, 29 Jan. and 4 Mar. 1795).

Though the *Philadelphia Gazette* had already published Callender's abridgments of JM's major speeches on commercial discrimination of 14, 30, and 31 January 1794, the Virginia congressman wrote out the full texts, which Brown then printed. During the Second Congress JM had probably also provided John Carey (stenographer for the *General Advertiser* and *Dunlap's American Daily Advertiser*) with a written text of his speech on bounty payments for cod fisheries. Thus the texts of those speeches were closer to the intent of the author than those which were based on stenographers' reports. Of course, JM could also have elaborated some points more fully in his written versions than in his oral delivery of the speeches. His speeches on commercial discrimination gained added circulation when Republican Thomas Greenleaf printed them in pamphlet form in New York. These were the only speeches of JM's congressional career to be so published (JM to Jefferson, 2 Mar. 1794; JM's speech of 6 Feb. 1792, Carey to JM, 8 Feb. 1792, *PJM*, 14:220–24, 225; *Greenleaf's N.Y. Journal & Patriotic Register* first advertised the pamphlet [Evans 27258] on 31 Mar. 1794).

Several Philadelphia newspapers underwent changes of management and format in the aftermath of the 1793 yellow fever epidemic. On 9 December *Dunlap's American Daily Advertiser* became *Dunlap and Claypoole's*, when John Dunlap resumed partnership with David C. Claypoole, and on 8 November 1794 Republican Benjamin Franklin Bache added *Aurora* to the title of his *General Advertiser*. Coverage of House debates was on the wane in those two papers, which lost their stenographer when John Carey departed for London during the summer of 1793. Thereafter they usually reprinted speeches, as did the other Republican journals, Philip Freneau's *National Gazette* and Eleazer Oswald's *Independent Gazetteer*. Bache's journal was the first to print eight of JM's speeches, four of which were reprinted or otherwise reported in other papers. In one of his few independent reports, Bache described his editorial method: "His ambition is to afford his fellow citizens a sketch, and that a miniature sketch of the most important observations. It would require more time, more room and more patience in the generality of readers to justify a fuller account of Congressional debates" (*General Advertiser*, 15 Mar. 1794). Shortly thereafter, Bache drastically reduced his coverage of the speeches.

Federalist John Fenno's *Gazette of the United States*, which had provided the most complete reportage of House debates during the later sessions of the First Congress and throughout the Second Congress, was the original source for only three of JM's Third Congress speeches, two of which other papers reprinted. While it reprinted other speeches, its total coverage declined from the previous level. The *Gazette of the United States* suffered from long-standing financial troubles, but its Federalist supporters circulated a subscription which revived that newspaper in the aftermath of the yellow fever epidemic (Fenno to Hamilton, 9 Nov. 1793, Hamilton to John Kean, 29 Nov. 1793, Syrett and Cooke, *Papers of Hamilton*, 15:393–94, 418). Then on 20 February 1794 the Senate opened its doors to reporters, and for the remainder of the first session the *Gazette of the United States* printed only the upper house's proceedings. During the second session, that paper either published severely abridged versions or reprinted other accounts of debates in both houses.

Philip Freneau's antiadministration *National Gazette*, which JM and Jefferson had helped to found in 1791, was the only paper that published throughout the epidemic. Henry Lee—who had also assisted the journalistic venture of his fellow College of New Jersey graduate, Freneau—noted that "I see only scraps of Congressional debates generally so brief as to be unintelligible. I suppose the printers have not yet recovered from their share in the late Calamity" (Lee to JM, 23 Jan. 1794). Freneau's financial straits equaled Fenno's, but unlike the *Gazette of the United States*, the *National Gazette* was not rescued by its political patrons. Freneau had continued to support Citizen Genet long after Republican leaders dissociated themselves from the French minister. JM and Jefferson tacitly ceased to encourage the *National Gazette*, which published its last issue on 26 October 1793. While the polemic essays and editorials in his newspaper had added zest to journalism in the capital, Freneau never had an independent stenographer for House debates and merely reprinted speeches from other papers.

Recording the debates was no easy task. Sensitive congressmen often complained that the stenographers misrepresented them, but the legislators themselves sometimes could not agree on what their colleagues had said in the House. JM's second speech of 7 February 1794 against the naval shipbuilding program was cut short by opponents who claimed that the Virginia congressman had misquoted them. Callender expressed his frustration at trying to provide an accurate account: "We have been more particular in stating this mutual charge of mis-quotation because, we have once or twice been objected to, as not giving the exact meaning of the members. But if gentlemen do not upon some occasions understand each other, it can be no matter of surprise that other persons should sometimes fall into mistakes of the same nature." Callender, however, admired JM as an orator. After his account of the 30 May debate on the military establishment, Callender observed, "To do justice to the speeches of this gentleman, it would be requisite to print every word exactly as it is spoken; since it is impossible to abridge, without injuring it, the stile of a speaker who is, on every question alike remarkable for the most correct elegance, and the most comprehensive brevity" (*Philadelphia Gazette*, 10 Feb. and 31 May 1794).

Despite Callender's best efforts, JM was dissatisfied with the stenographer's accounts of some of his speeches. He wrote of the debate in the second session on the House's reply to Washington's annual address, "Lengthy as the debate was, I took but little part in it; and that little is very erroneously as well as defectively stated in the Newspapers." During the Second Congress, Elbridge Gerry had moved that stenographers be appointed as officers of the House, but his resolution died in committee. In the last days of the Third Congress, William Loughton Smith reported a similar proposal, which the House resolved to consider during the next session. The measure's proponents wanted to make the stenographers accountable to the House, while opponents were reluctant to endorse reports that would probably continue to be defective. Brown's willingness to print corrections reassured the majority of congressmen, who in December 1796 finally defeated resolutions to appoint an official stenographer. Thus, despite its defects, the system of private reporting seemed more attractive than any alternative at the time (JM to Jefferson, 30 Nov. 1794; *Annals of Congress*, 2d Cong., 1st sess., 563–66, 3d Cong., 2d sess., 1242, 1280–81, 4th Cong., 1st sess., 131, 271, 274–82, 286, 2d sess., 1590, 1603, 1607–11; *ASP, Miscellaneous*, 1:123, 140, 153).

(Secondary sources used for this note: Risjord, *Chesapeake Politics*, pp. 422–23, 439; Samuel Eliot Morison, *Harrison Gray Otis, 1765–1848: The Urbane Federalist* [Boston, 1969], p. 92; Ammon, *James Monroe*, p. 108; Frank A. Cassell, *Merchant Congressman in the Young Republic: Samuel*

Smith of Maryland, 1752–1839 [Madison, Wis., 1971], pp. 54–57; Jerald A. Combs, *The Jay Treaty: Political Battleground of the Founding Fathers* [Berkeley, Calif., 1970], p. 160; Madison at the First Session of the First Federal Congress, 8 Apr.–29 Sept. 1789, The Origins of Freneau's *National Gazette*, 25 July 1791, A Note on the Sources of Madison's Speeches in the Second Congress, 22 Nov. 1791–1 Mar. 1793, *PJM*, 12:53–55, 62–64, 14:56–57, 126–27; "Jefferson, Freneau, and the Founding of the *National Gazette*," Boyd, *Papers of Jefferson*, 20:747–53.)

From John Dawson

MY DEAR SIR   RICHMOND December 6. 93

Your session no doubt commencd on the last monday & the communications which you will have it in your power to make to your friends for some time will be very interesting. I feel great anxiety to learn what direction the politiks of the present congress will take & must solicit a renewal of our correspondence.

The general assembly will probably adjourn in two days. Those resolutions relative to suits commencd by citizens of one state agt. another state will be forwarded to you & to each member representing the state. They determind to appoint the general officers of the militia themselves & Generals are now to be met at every corner.[1] With much esteem Yr. friend & Sert

                                                           J DAWSON

RC (DLC).

1. "An act regulating the militia of this Commonwealth" of 22 Dec. 1792 provided that "the General Assembly shall by joint ballot of both houses" appoint the general officers of the militia. "An act supplementary to the act to amend the act for regulating the militia of this commonwealth" of 10 Dec. 1793 required the governor to commission the twenty-two generals whom the General Assembly had appointed (Hening, *Statutes*, 13:341–42; Shepherd, *Statutes*, 1:207; *Va. Herald, and Fredericksburg Advertiser*, 12 Dec. 1793).

From the Governor of Virginia

SIR,   RICHMOND December 6th. 1793.

In obedience to the direction of the General Assembly I transmit a copy of the resolutions[1] passed by that honorable body respecting the late unexpected decision of the supreme Court of the United States which asserts that Court's right of Jurisdiction in all controversies wherein a State may be a party, and I flatter myself that the request of the General Assembly will receive from you firm and zealous support. I am Sir &c.

HENRY LEE.

Letterbook copy (Vi: Executive Letterbook). Addressed "To the Representatives from this State in Congress." The resolutions that Lee enclosed may have been the printed copy: *Virginia. In the House of Delegates, Thursday, 28th November, 1793. Resolved, That a State Cannot ... Be Made a Defendant* (Richmond, 1793; Evans 26391).

1. In response to the Supreme Court decision in *Chisholm* v. *Georgia* (2 Dallas 419), the General Assembly passed joint resolutions on 3 Dec. requesting the Virginia delegation in the House, and instructing its senators, to support a constitutional amendment upholding the immunity of a state from suit. Other states submitted similar protests to Congress. On 4 Mar. 1794 JM voted with the majority when the House proposed the eleventh amendment (Shepherd, *Statutes*, 1:284; *Annals of Congress*, 3d Cong., 1st sess., 477).

Address of the House of Representatives to the President

[6 December 1793]

George Washington, President of the Ud. States

SIR,

The Representatives of the people of the United States, in meeting you for the first time since you have been again called by an unanimous suffrage to your present station, find an occasion which they embrace, with no less sincerity than promptitude, for expressing to you their congratulations on so distinguished a testimony of public approbation; and their entire confidence in the purity & patriotism of the motives which have produced this obedience to the voice of your country. It is to virtues which have commanded long and universal reverence, and services from which have flowed great and lasting benefits, that the tribute of praise may be paid, without the reproach of flattery; and it is from the same sources, that the fairest anticipations may be derived in favor of the public happiness.

The United States having taken no part in the War which had embraced in Europe the powers with whom they have the most extensive relations, the maintenance of peace was justly to be regarded as one of the most important duties of the magistrate charged with the faithful execution of the laws. We accordingly witness with approbation and pleasure the vigilance with which you have guarded against an interruption of that blessing, by your proclamation admonishing our Citizens of the consequences of illicit or hostile Acts towards the belligerent parties, and promoting by a declaration of the existing legal state of things, an easier admission of our rights to the immunities belonging to our situation.

The connexion of the United States with Europe has evidently become extremely interesting. The communications which remain to be exhibited to us, will, no doubt, assist in giving us a fuller view of the subject, and in guiding our deliberations to such results as may comport with the rights and true interests of our Country.

We learn, with deep regret, that the measures dictated by a love of Peace, for obtaining an amicable termination of the afflicting war on our frontier, have been frustrated; and that a resort to offensive measures has again become necessary. As the latter, however, must be rendered more satisfactory in proportion to the solicitude for peace manifested by the former, it is to be hoped they will be pursued under the better auspices on that account, & be finally crowned with more happy success.

In relation to the particular tribes of Indians, against whom offensive measures have been prohibited, as well as all the other important subjects which you have presented to our view, we shall bestow the attention which they claim. We cannot, however, refrain at this time, from particularly expressing our concurrence in your anxiety for the regular discharge of the public debts, as fast as circumstances and events will permit; and in the policy of removing any impediments that may be found in the way of a faithful representation of public proceedings throughout the United States, being persuaded, with you, that on no subject more than the former, can delay be more injurious, or an œconomy of time more valuable; and that with respect to the latter, no resource is so firm for the Government of the United States, as the affections of the People, guided by an enlightened policy.

Throughout our deliberations we shall endeavour to cherish every sentiment which may contribute to render them conducive to the dignity, as well as to the welfare of the United States; and we join with you, in imploring that Being on whose will the fate of Nations depends, to crown with success our mutual endeavors.

Signed by order, and in behalf of the House

FREDERICK AUGUSTUS MUHLENBURG Speaker.

Attest

JOHN BECKLEY Clerk.

Tr (DLC: Washington Papers). In the hand of Bartholomew Dandridge, Jr., Washington's private secretary. Authorship attributed to JM on the basis of his chairmanship of the committee appointed on 4 Dec. to prepare a reply to Washington's annual address to Congress. Approved by the House on 6 Dec. Tr dated 7 Dec. 1793, when the House presented its reply to the president (*Annals of Congress*, 3d Cong., 1st sess., 135, 138).

From John Dawson

DEAR SIR!   RICHMOND Der. 22. 93

Recieve my thanks for your favour of the 15.[1] which came by the last evening's stage.

You cannot expect any thing new from this quarter. We all look with g[r]eat anxiety towards Phia. for a full disclosure of the very momentous communications made by the President.[2] While G. B carri[e]d on the war only on our frontiers, the merchant, & all those in the middle secure country felt themselves very little interested. But now that she has attachd as well Algerines as well as Indians I trust that it will raise a general just indignation against that proud imperious nation, & that the Congress will as much as possible restri[c]t our commerce with her. With real regard I am dr Sir yr friend & Sert

                                                        J DAWSON

RC (DLC).

1. Letter not found.
2. On 5 Dec. Washington sent both houses of Congress his administration's correspondence on foreign relations. The documents were printed by order of the House of Representatives, and newspapers published summaries (*Annals of Congress*, 3d Cong., 1st sess., 137; Philadelphia *Federal Gazette*, 7 and 9 Dec. 1793). JM's copy of *A Message of the President of the United States to Congress Relative to France and Great Britain . . . with the Papers Therein Referred to* (Philadelphia, 1793; Evans 26334) is in the Madison Collection, Rare Book Department, University of Virginia Library.

Closed Sessions of the House

[27 December 1793]

Algerine corsairs had preyed on American shipping in the Mediterranean since the Revolution. In December 1793 reports arrived in the United States that Portugal had signed a twelve-month truce with Algiers. Britain had persuaded its Portuguese ally to halt the Algerine war—which had previously prevented the corsairs from entering the Atlantic—in order to concentrate the war effort against France. Algerine corsairs soon captured several American ships, and on 16 December the president transmitted to the House the secretary of state's report on the measures taken for "obtaining a recognition of our Treaty with Morocco, and for the ransom of our citizens and establishment of peace with Algiers." In his message, Washington asked the House to consider the report in closed sessions to protect its source of information. He asserted that publicizing the amount of tribute and ransom "might have a disadvantageous influence on future proceedings for the same objects." The Committee of the Whole considered the report in closed sessions on 24 and 26 December. The next day, a rule of the House was read which provided "that the House shall be cleared of all persons but the members and clerk" during discussion of confidential communications from the president. Boudinot spoke in favor of the rule (Craig L. Symonds, *Navalists and Antinavalists: The Naval Policy Debate in the United States, 1785–1827* [Newark, Del., 1980], pp. 27–29; "Extract of a letter from the Captain of an American vessel to his owner in America dated Gibraltar 19th. Octr: 1793" [DLC]; *Annals of Congress,* 3d Cong., 1st sess., 143, 149–50).

On the other hand, Mr. Nicholas and Mr. Madison spoke in favour of open galleries. The latter observed that the order was originally made upon a particular emergence, and never had been intended for general application. It was the business of the house at all times to favour publicity, and it ought not to be in the power of any individual to shut out the constituents of congress but for the strongest reasons. He disliked the idea of wrapping up the proceedings of the house in mystery. He had heard of nothing in yesterday's reading, after strangers were excluded that required concealment; not a single document, or a single fact. He did not wish to go into a committee till that order was reconsidered. What if after the galleries were shut, a member should make a motion, and a debate should ensue on a question foreign to the object of the communications? Were the public here also to be bolted out?[1]

Federal Gazette, 27 Dec. 1793 (also reported in *Gazette of the U.S.,* 27 Dec. 1793, *General Advertiser,* 30 Dec. 1793, and *Pa. Gazette,* 1 Jan. 1794).

1. After further debate, the galleries were cleared. When the House reconsidered its rule on closed galleries on 30 Dec., JM "said that if a whole series of papers were to be kept secret for the sake of a single letter, he saw no end to the system of concealment." The rule was amended to "leave the House at liberty to discuss confidential communications publicly, if they see proper, after they have been privately read," but the House defeated, by a one-vote margin, a motion to consider the Algerine correspondence with open galleries. In a closed session on 2 Jan. 1794, JM voted with the majority when the House passed three resolutions appropriating extra funds for tribute and ransom to the Barbary States, providing for a naval force for use against the Algerine corsairs, and appointing a committee to report on ways and means to defray the expense of that force. In a debate on the publication of those resolutions, JM on 7 Jan. "added, he hoped the publication, would be accompanied with that of every document, necessary to illucidate the subject." The House agreed to publish the resolutions (*Federal Gazette,* 31 Dec. 1793; *Annals of Congress,* 3d Cong., 1st sess., 151, 154–55; *Gazette of the U.S.,* 8 Jan. 1794).

From Alexander White

DEAR SIR   WOODVILLE 28th. Decr. 1793

The promptitude with which you answered[1] my letter is very pleasing. I shall not spend time in discussing the comparative advantages of our correspondence. Sensible of my own pleasure arising from it I shall freely express my sentiments or relate facts as they occur to my mind, and memory. The unanimity which appears to prevail in Congress in support of the great interests of our Country is to me a most pleasing circumstance. It is no more than I hoped, and indeed expected, but there were many who feared (and I am sorry to believe there were some who wished) that the influence of Genet would cause a Schism in Congress which would greatly clog the wheels of Government, and render abortive the Vigorous and decisive measures of the President in support of our rights of neutrality. I acknowledge I was not without my Apprehensions —tho' my hopes preponderated. My fears are now vanished. I believe Good, and not evil will arise from the imprudent conduct of Genet, it has not, I can venture to affirm, as far as my acquaintance extends, lessened the prevailing Attachment to the French Nation. Should he be recalled; and his conduct disavowed by their Goverment, that attachment will be encreased. From Genets conduct America has become alive to the Idea of Forreign influence, and I really believe it will be more difficult for a Forreign Minister at any future period to make an impression on our Goverment or People than it might have been had the subject never been brought to view, in the manner his imprudence has exposed it.

I am not insensible of the truly critical state in which we stand with regard to Forreign Nations, but from this too, I augur more good than evil. It will show the People of America the necessity of placing themselves in a state of defense, by establishing an effective militia, of providing for the security of our Coasts by Armed Vessels and fortifications, and perhaps of equipping a small Squadron to check the Algerines —regulations and burdens to which they would not submit until the danger became imminent. These things done I hope and believe we shall avoid a War. To whose interest is a War? The People of England complain of the War with France. Will their Goverment encrease their burdens and inflame their discontent by extending it to America? Will Spain stake the Mines of Mexico against the Wild Woods of Kentucky? I feel the degraded situation in which we are placed by the Belligerent Powers of Europe. But will a War relieve us? Let us however prepare for the worst. I have read with eagerness everything on which I can lay my hands respecting our relation to Forreign Nations—

and anxiously wait the Publication of the Presidents communications. On these subjects I flatter myself there is and will be an unanimity as to the end, a differrence of sentiments with regard to the means may therefore be adjusted without that agitation which the nature of the subjects would otherwise excite. Should this be the case my heart is at ease, tho' I confess our interior affairs are important and open a wide field for discussion, and for a differrence of sentiment both as to the means and end of particular Laws or regulations without impeaching either side of the question with the want of a due regard to the great end which ought to be equally the object of all, the General Good. A Mans own circumstances and those of his Constituents, their modes of life, and the nature of their property, make impressions not easily eradicated from the most candid heart, and naturally create a difference of opinion where their respective avocations and properties are to be affected by legal provisions. The Presidents Proclamation I ever understood as he himself explains it in his letter to me as Chairman of the Meeting at Winchester. *His words are*, "*the Proclamation* declaring the actual State of things, was thought right, and accordingly issued."[2] Adieu, and believe to be with great esteem, Your sincere Friend

ALEXR WHITE

P.S. Our Post will ride to Alexandria but once a fortnight during the three ensuing Months. The 2d & 4th. Mondays of January, & so the Mondays of every second Week thereafter during that period will be the Mails by which letters will obtain the most speedy Conveyance.

A W.

Past Nine O'Clock, I have just received the News Paper sent by last Post, whose arrival was several hours later than usual, for which I return you thanks.

RC (DLC). Docketed by JM.

1. Letter not found.
2. Washington to White, 23 Nov. 1793 (Fitzpatrick, *Writings of Washington*, 33:156).

To Tench Coxe

[29 December 1793]

Mr. Madison presents his respects to Mr. Coxe. He wishes to have a little conversation with him this forenoon or tomorrow if convenient, and will thank Mr C. to name by the bearer an hour at which Mr. M. may wait on him.[1]

RC (PHi: Tench Coxe Papers). Addressed by JM. Docketed, probably by Coxe: "recd. in the Morning of Sunday 29 Decr. 1793—appointed Mr. M. to call at his (Mr. C's) house this Evening after Tea."

1. JM probably wished to consult Coxe on questions relating to the resolutions on commercial discrimination that he presented to the House on 3 Jan. 1794.

From John Dawson

DEAR SIR   NORFOLK 29 Der 1793

I have this day written a letter to our friend Colo: Monroe relative to the arrival and continuance of a British frigate in this harbour. The contents of this letter I presume he will communicate to you, & if with myself & many in this place you are of opinion that it is a subject that demands serious & immediate attention I am persuaded that you will interest yourself in a business wh may prove very serious to our country.

On the arrival of this vessel application was made by the british councel at this place to the Executive.[1] We then learnt that she only wanted water, & a few repairs wh were absolutely necessary for her safety at sea. But we were also of opinion that we had nothing to do with the affair—that it belongd to the fœderal goverment, & to the commander in chief of the militia of State. I wish to know whether a report was made by that officer to the Secy. of State. With real esteem Yr. friend & Ser

J DAWSON

RC (DLC).

1. On 27 Nov. HMS *Dædalus* arrived in Norfolk, as British consul John Hamilton explained to Gov. Henry Lee on 6 Dec., "to have a supply of provisions and some little repair." The mayor of Norfolk reported that the frigate "has her sails unbent and appears to be repairing her rigging" and assured Lee that "every Step shall be taken to prevent any confusion from the mixture of English and French Seamen." A French fleet, moored in Hampton Roads, bottled up the *Dædalus* in port until April 1794 (*CVSP*, 6:660–61, 673, 7:76, 106).

§ List of Imports, 1789–1790. *Ca. 29 December 1793.* Summarizes information that appears to have been collected by customs officers for the Treasury Department, listing imports by country of origin totaling $15,295,638.97.

Ms (DLC). A one-page document in JM's hand, headed: "Value of *Manufactured* articles imported into the U. S. in one year ending 30 Sepr. 1790." Docketed by JM: "Signd. / Treasy. Dept. Novr. 30 1791." Conjectural date assigned on the basis of JM's 29 Dec. 1793 letter to Tench Coxe (commissioner of the revenue), in which JM requested "a little conversation with him." JM also cited figures from this Ms in his speech on commercial discrimination of 14 Jan. 1794 and alluded to "an authentic document he had examined."

¶ To John Dawson. Letter not found. *31 December 1793.* Acknowledged in Dawson to JM, 20 Jan. 1794. Discusses the proposed naval force against Algerine corsairs and probably mentions the resolutions on commercial discrimination that JM plans to present to the House of Representatives.

From Joseph Jones

Dr. Sr.   [ca. 1 January 1794]

I am to thank you for your several favors since the commencement of the session of Congress[1] and also for a present of potatoes delivered by Col. Madisons Waggoner by your desire as he informed me—they are excellent for the year and appear to be of superior quality from the common red potatoe. As yet I do not discover that any thing has taken place in your house to shew or determine the strength of parties, this however cannot long be the case as important questions must soon be discussed. In the Senate I fear from what has appeared the old leven[2] will prevail. The news respecting the Algerine vessells being in the Atlantic has excited alarm here, and will no doubt so long as it operates, affect the prices of our exports—but the number of them are not sufft. to make the risque of passing the Atlantic very dangerous, or to justify the high insurance which is said to be demanded. Our situation seems to have become serious and critical with respect to Britain whose claim to seize our Vessells with provisions appears to be a new principle—she demands the same I observe of the other neutral powers. What has become of Monroe. I have not heard from him but once since he got to Philada. Your friend & Servt

                                                    Jos: Jones

Will one of you let me know the price of wheat & Barley at Phila: also what Haynes[3] sells his strong beer at ℔ barrel if you can conveniently get information. We get no Freneau or Fenno.

RC (DLC). Addressed by Jones to JM at Philadelphia and franked. Docketed by JM, "1794." Dated ca. 1794 in the *Index to the James Madison Papers.* Conjectural date here assigned on the basis of internal evidence.

1. Letters not found.
2. "Purge out therefore the old leaven, that ye may be a new lump, as ye are unleavened. . . . Therefore let us keep the feast, not with the old leaven, neither with the leaven of malice and wickedness, but with the unleavened bread of sincerity and truth" (1 Cor. 5:7–8).
3. Haines, Twelffs and Co. were brewers at 145 High Street (James Hardie, *Philadelphia Directory and Register* [2d ed.; Philadelphia, 1794; Evans 27089], p. 62).

Commercial Discrimination

[3 January 1794]

In Committee of the Whole, JM offered seven resolutions to implement the recommendations of Jefferson's "Report of the Secretary of State on the Privileges and Restrictions on the Commerce of the United States in Foreign Countries" of 16 December 1793. For the context of those resolutions, see Madison in the Third Congress, 2 December 1793–3 March 1795.

Mr. Madison after some general observations on the report, entered into a more particular consideration of the subject.

He remarked that the commerce of the United States is not at this day on that respectable footing, to which from its nature and importance it is entitled. He recurred to its situation previous to the adoption of the constitution, when conflicting systems prevailed in the different States —the then existing state of things gave rise to that convention of delegates from the different parts of the Union, who met to deliberate on some general principles for the regulation of commerce which might be conducive in their operation to the general welfare, and that such measures should be adopted as would conciliate the friendship and good faith of those countries who were disposed to enter into the nearest commercial connections with us. But what has been the result of the system which has been pursued ever since? What is the present situation of our commerce? From the situation in which we find ourselves after four years experiment, he observed, that it appeared incumbent on the United States to see whether they could not now take measures promotive of those objects for which the government was in a great degree instituted. Measures of moderation, firmness, and decision, he was persuaded were now necessary to be adopted, in order to narrow the sphere of our commerce with those nations who see proper not to meet us on terms of reciprocity.

Mr. Madison then read the following Resolutions:

Resolved, as the opinion of this committee, that the interest of the United States would be promoted by further restrictions and higher duties, in certain cases, on the manufactures and navigation of foreign nations, employed in the commerce of the United States, than those now imposed.

1. *Resolved,* as the opinion of this committee, that an additional duty ought to be laid on the following articles, manufactured by European nations, having no commercial treaty with the United States.

    On all articles of which leather is the material of chief value, an additional duty of   per centum ad valorem.

    On all manufactured iron, steel, tin, pewter, copper, brass, or articles of which either of these metals is the material of chief value, an additional duty of   per centum ad valorem.

On all articles of which cotton is the material of chief value, an additional duty of   per centum ad valorem.

On all cloths of which wool is the material of chief value, where the estimated value on which the duty is payable is above   an additional duty of   per centum ad valorem; where such value is below   an additional duty of   per centum ad valorem.[1]

On all cloths of which hemp or flax is the material of chief value, and of which the estimated value on which the duty is payable is below   , an additional duty of   per centum ad valorem.

On all manufactures of which silk is the material of chief value, an additional duty of   per centum ad valorem.

2. *Resolved*, as the opinion of this committee, that an additional duty of   per ton, ought to be laid on the vessels belonging to the nations having no commercial treaty with the United States.

3. *Resolved*, as the opinion of this committee, that the duty on vessels belonging to the nations having commercial treaties with the United States ought to be reduced to   per ton.

4. *Resolved*, as the opinion of this committee, that where any nation may refuse to consider as vessels of the United States, any vessels not built within the United States, the foreign built vessels of such nation ought to be subjected to a like refusal, unless built within the United States.

5. *Resolved*, as the opinion of this committee, that where any nation may refuse to admit the produce or manufactures of the United States, unless in vessels belonging to the United States, or to admit them in vessels of the United States, if last imported from any place not within the United States, a like restriction ought, after the   day of   to be extended to the produce and manufactures of such nation, and that, in the mean time, a duty of   per ton extraordinary ought to be imposed on vessels so importing any such produce or manufacture.

6. *Resolved*, as the opinion of this committee, that where any nation may refuse to the vessels of the United States a carriage of the produce or manufactures thereof, whilst such produce or manufactures are admitted by it in its own vessels, it would be just to make the restriction reciprocal: but inasmuch as such a measure, if suddenly adopted, might be particularly distressing in cases which merit the benevolent attention of the United States, it is expedient, for the present, that a tonnage extraordinary only of   be imposed on the vessels so employed: and that all distilled spirits imported therein shall be subject to an additional duty of one ——— part of the existing duty.

7. *Resolved*, as the opinion of this committee, that provision ought to

be made for liquidating and ascertaining the losses sustained by citizens of the United States, from the operation of particular regulations of any country contravening the law of nations, and that such losses be reimbursed, in the first instance, out of the additional duties on the manufactures, productions and vessels of the nation establishing such unlawful regulations.[2]

Mr. Madison, took a general view of the probable effects which the adoption of something like the resolutions he had proposed, would produce. They would produce, respecting many articles imported, a competition which would enable countries who do not now supply us with those articles to do it and would encrease the encouragement on such as we can produce within ourselves. We should also obtain an equitable share in carrying our own produce; we should enter into the field of competition on equal terms, and enjoy the actual benefit of advantages which nature and the spirit of our people entitle us to.

He adverted to the advantageous situation this country is entitled to stand in, considering the nature of our exports and returns. Our exports are bulky, and therefore must employ much shipping, which might be nearly all our own; our exports are chiefly necessaries of life, or raw materials, the food for the manufacturers of other nations. On the contrary chief of what we receive from other countries we can either do without, or produce substitutes.

It is in the power of the United States he conceived, by exerting her natural rights, without violating the rights or even the equitable pretensions of other nations; by doing no more than most nations do for the protection of their interests, and much less than some, to make her interests respected; for what we receive from other nations are but luxuries to us, which if we chose to throw aside we could deprive part of the manufacturers of those luxuries of even bread, if we are forced to contest of self denial; this being the case, our country may make her enemies feel the extent of her power.

We stand with respect to the nation exporting those luxuries in the relation of an opulent individual to the labourer in producing the superfluities for his accommodation; the former can do without those luxuries, the consumption of which gives bread to the latter.

He did not propose, or wish that the United States should, at present, go so far in the line which his resolutions point to as they might go. The extent to which the principles involved in those resolutions should be carried will depend upon filling up the blanks. To go to the very extent of the principle immediately might be inconvenient: He wished only that the legislature should mark out the ground on which we think we can stand, perhaps it may produce the effect wished for, without unnecessary irritation: we need not at first go every length.

Another consideration would induce him, he said, to be moderate in filling up the blanks: not to wound public credit. He did not wish to risk any sensible diminution of the public revenue. He believed, that if the blanks were filled with judgment, the diminution of the revenue from a diminution in the quantity of imports would be counterbalanced by the increase in the duties.

The last resolution he had proposed, he said, is in a manner distinct from the rest. The nation is bound by the most sacred obligation, he conceived, to protect the rights of its citizens against a violation of them from any quarter; or, if they cannot protect, they are bound to repay the damage.

It is a fact authenticated to this house by communications from the executive, that there are regulations established by some European nations, contrary to the law of nations, by which our property is seized and disposed of in such a way that damages have accrued. We are bound either to obtain reparation for the injustice, or compensate the damage. It is only in the first instance, no doubt, that the burden is to be thrown upon the United States; the proper department of government will no doubt take proper steps to obtain redress.

The justice of foreign nations will certainly not permit them to deny reparation when the breach of the law of nations appear evidently; at any rate it is just that the individual should not suffer.

He believed the amount of the damages that would come within the meaning of this resolution, would not be very considerable.[3]

Gazette of the U.S., 4 Jan. 1794 (also reported in Philadelphia Gazette, 3 Jan. 1794, General Advertiser, 4 Jan. 1794, and Dunlap and Claypoole's Am. Daily Advertiser, 4 Jan. 1794 [which misdated the speech as 4 Jan.]); draft of the resolutions and printed copy of the resolutions (DLC: Rives Collection, Madison Papers). Draft, in JM's hand, has proposed duties ranging from 1 to 2½ percent written in the margin, other blanks filled in, and rough notes on levels of American exports to Britain gleaned from Adam Anderson, An Historical and Chronological Deduction of the Origin of Commerce . . . (6 vols.; Dublin, 1790). On the printed copy, JM added in the margin proposed duties of from 5 to 15 percent. Speech reprinted in [Henry Merttins Bird], A View of the Relative Situation of Great Britain and the United States of North America: by a Merchant (London, 1794), pp. 30–41.

1. In the draft, JM here added: "On all other articles of which wool is the material of cheif value an additional duty of   perCt. ad valorem." This provision also appears in the printed copy.

2. In the draft, JM here added another resolution which was not recorded in his speech to the committee: "Resd. as the opinion of this Come. that considering the important services rendered by the French nation to the U.S. towards the establishment of their liberties, it will be just and honorable on the part of the U.S. to make all such friendly returns as may of right be made under the law of nations; and that with this view provision ought to be made for speedily discharging

the entire debt due from the U.S. to France, in pursuance of the   article of the contract entered into on the   day of   ."

3. FitzSimons moved that the committee rise and the resolutions be printed. "After some further remarks by two or three members, Mr. Madison said he had no wish to precipitate the discussion; he was content that the committee should now rise, and that a future early day should be assigned." The committee agreed to FitzSimons's motion (*Gazette of the U.S.*, 4 Jan. 1794).

[3 January 1794]

Ames moved that JM's resolutions be taken up a week from the following Monday, to allow the members time to consider them carefully.

Mr. Madison said, he saw no necessity for a very distant day; the subject was not a new one—it existed previous to the present government, it had been repeatedly before the legislature of the United States, it had been amply dilated on in reports and public dissertations; he did not conceive there was a single proposition contained in the resolutions which had not been repeatedly revolved in the minds of every member of the house. He supposed an early discussion would be the most eligible, as the members would as it proceeded, naturally throw light upon it.

Gazette of the U.S., 4 Jan. 1794. After further debate, the House approved Ames's motion.

The Flag

[7 January 1794]

On 30 December 1793 the Senate passed "a bill making an alteration in the Flag of the United States," which proposed to add two stars and stripes to represent the new states of Vermont and Kentucky (*Annals of Congress*, 3d Cong., 1st sess., 23). In Committee of the Whole, opponents of the bill argued that the design of the flag should be permanent.

Mr. Madison was of opinion, that the symbol should answer to the state of things. If it is the wish of the two new states to be represented in the flag they ought to be gratified. The expence or trouble attending the alteration, he considered as a trifling objection indeed. He suggested the propriety of adding a clause empowering the Executive in future similar cases to order the alteration.

General Advertiser, 9 Jan. 1794 (also reported in *Gazette of the U.S.*, 8 Jan. 1794).

[7 January 1794]

The committee reported the bill to the House. Goodhue objected that "so trifling an act" should be the first passed in that session.

Mr. Madison said, that if any blame could lie on this account, it must fall on the Senate who originated the bill. The house has much important business begun, but it is saving time to dispatch this while that is maturing.

Perhaps it would have been better, that the arms and flag had been made the symbols of things not mutable; but as they had been formed emblematical of the number of States in the confederacy, they should be made true symbols.

General Advertiser, 9 Jan. 1794. On 8 Jan. JM voted with the majority when the House passed the bill. Washington signed it on 13 Jan. (*Annals of Congress*, 3d Cong., 1st sess., 166; *U.S. Statutes at Large*, 1:341).

From Joseph Jones

DR. SR.   FREDG. 8th. Janry. 1794

I am much obliged to you and Col. Monroe for your alternate attention to keeping me informed of what is passing among you and furnishing the papers of which at present I receive none but what you and he inclose me.[1] I must subscribe for one of them and suppose Dunlap and Claypole[2] the best but think the expence will be great for a newspaper if the postage is pd. by the Subscriber. As yet I do not discover that any question has been discussed & decided wch. gives evidence of the preponderance of party. Great and very important matters are before you already and these may be increased by one new matter depending on the event of European councils so as to extend your Session to considerable length—the present moment I confess appears to me very critical with respect to ourselves as with both France and G. Britain as also Spain we have some serious questions to settle. It is strange we have not for several weeks had any European intelligence of consequence and yet I think the papers announce some arrivals from that quarter. Although there may be propriety in the distance maintained betn. the Executive and Mr. Genet I am pleased to hear It did not extend altogether to the legislature for although he may be wrong as I think his conduct in some things has been so, had they pursued the example of the Executive it wod. have had the appearance of prejudging or prejudice respecting those matters wch. he professed to apply to them on. You are the best judge how far it will be prudent for the legislature to support the Executive in the extent of their proceedings respecting the French nation. If he has been wrong I wod. touch his faults with a gentle hand. I wod. not irritate the nation because he has been imprudent. E. R. I find is nominated in the room of Jefferson[3]—the Executive stream will now flow smoothly along withot. a breath to ruffle or disturb it. I wish you all well. Yr. friend & servt

JOS. JONES

RC (DLC). Docketed by JM.

1. Jones had previously subscribed to Philip Freneau's Philadelphia *National Gazette*, which ceased publication on 26 Oct. 1793.
2. *Dunlap and Claypoole's Am. Daily Advertiser.*
3. Washington nominated Edmund Randolph as secretary of state on 1 Jan., and the Senate approved his nomination the following day (*Senate Exec. Proceedings*, 1:144).

From Walter Jones

DEAR SIR.   KINSALE. WESTMORLD. COUNTY. Jany. 10th. 1794.

I am again tempted to intice you to a Correspondence, which you have so kindly Supported without a prospect of an equivalent return. I once thought that my presence where you are, would have Saved us both this Pains. However a majority of Voters, not of the Electors of the District, preferred the Services of their Sitting Member,[1] with whom you are probably not unacquainted.

As the sound suggestions of Prudence & Interest ever checked my pursuit of this object, as that Pursuit was favoured by an Excess beyond Measure, of the Property, understanding &C of the district, I had little Cause for Chagrin, as an individual: yet as a good Citizen I have to lament the Success of Arts, which disclose very indifferent Facts in the electoral character of a certain order, and confound all rational Notions of Election. In political chemistry an Election implies the unequal *division of a whole*. In the present Case there was a complete *Separation* of *Parts*.

The appearances of Oligarchical factions attached to some of our higher administrative departments, are, to me, not a little Alarming. The rise, Extent & Views of all such Combinations of exclusive Interests in the public Servants, Should be objects of constant vigilance & Scrutiny, as they are founded in the most constant & powerful Propensities in human Nature. I am well pleased that an Investigation of this nature is Commenced so early in the Session, and I hope it will be temperate, sure & unremitting. Intemperate, unsupported & hasty charges, produce Effects quite opposite, to what were intended. The Culprit avails himself of the weak parts; proclaims himself the injured Person; and the bad Practices, which at first gave some Compunction, will now be multiplied without restraint, as necessary means of Self-defence. When a man is impelled by very powerful Motives, he seldom fails to use a very winning Sophistry to justify himself, in his Competitions with his fellow-creature, but when the poor Commonwealth is a party, the Odds are beyond Comparison against her. It is for this reason, that public Servants are so often found to be supremely criminal & pernicious in their official Capacities, without being proportionably debased in their private moral Characters. Hence arises greater difficulty in the detection Conviction & punishment of their offences. Faithful Watchmen however will make difficulties a Spur to Exertion rather than a Shelter for supine[ne]ss. I devoutly pray, that you may muster Strong enough to carry thro a scrutiny with propriety & Effect: but if the oligarchy has tainted a majority of Congress, conclamatum est de Nobis![2] It has Secured Impunity, in proportion as it has extended the Means of Malversation. My Information does not authorize me to form, much less to utter a positive opinion on So delicate a subject. But I may say, that I never read or heard of more undeviating Abettors of a british Minister for the Time being, than your Mr. Ames Mr. Smith (S. C.) Mr. Wadsworth, Mr. Fitzsimmons & some others are of the *Powers that be*. This Mr. Ames manifests in his debates Such full-blown arrogance & vanity, as makes him Signally exceptionable in the Eye of republican Decorum.

You will observe that, in this long Letter, I take the Existence of oligarchy & its appendant Factions amongst us, for granted. They may be harmless Phantoms magnified & deformed by distant & indistinct Vision—if they are such I shall much rejoice, & you, who have a nearer view may smile at the deceptions, but will excuse their Causes, which I can assure you are quite disinterested.

In the hope of Stealing, now & then, an hour from the numerous occupations of your time, I remain dear Sir with sincere regard & Esteem yours

WALT: JONES

I have thought that something presented to the Public Eye, on natural Party & vitious Faction, as applicable to our united Government, both in Theory & in Fact might aid the Cause of chaste & genuine republicanism—if the subject Strikes you in the Same point of View, it would probably render my present weak motives effectual to the bestowing a Leisure day on that subject. This Letter being delayed a Post I have determined to send you a few reflexions I have written on Party &

Faction.[3] If you think their publication would serve, in the Smallest degree the Cause of chaste Government, I am very willing they Should be published a[t] Richmond or Philadelphia as you may think best. The Subject Should be followed up in a Second Paper which if this be published, I will take the trouble to prepare.

I have no Copy of the paper; & if you judge that its Publication where you are would be improper, especially as your directing the publication may be a matter of some nicety & Consideration to one in your present situation, please return it to me, as soon as you may find it Convenient to favour me with a Line.

W. J.

RC (DLC: Rives Collection, Madison Papers). Addressed by Jones to JM in Philadelphia. Docketed by JM. Enclosure not found, but see n. 3.

1. During the First and Second Congresses, John Page had represented the district composed of Essex, Richmond, Westmoreland, Northumberland, Lancaster, Gloucester, Middlesex, King and Queen, King William, and Caroline counties. On 18 Mar. 1793 he was reelected from a redistricted constituency. The Virginia redistricting act of 1792 grouped Jones's Westmoreland County with Richmond, King George, Lancaster, and Northumberland counties to form a constituency which elected John Heath (1758–1810). A William and Mary graduate, founding member of Phi Beta Kappa, and Revolutionary veteran, Heath served Northumberland County as commonwealth's attorney, 1781–84 and 1787–93, and in the House of Delegates, 1782–83. He was a congressman, 1793–97, and member of the Virginia Council of State, 1803–10. Jones succeeded to Heath's seat in the House of Representatives in 1797 (Hening, *Statutes*, 12:654, 13:332; *BDC*, pp. 1097–98).

2. Conclamatum est de nobis: "it is all over for us."

3. Jones probably enclosed a draft of "Speculator" (Philadelphia *General Advertiser*, 6 Mar. 1794).

From George Washington

DEAR SIR,   Friday 10th. Jany. 1794.

Herewith you will receive sundry Pamphlets &ca. under the patronage of Sir John Sinclair.[1] I send you his letters to me also, that the design may be better understood.

From all these, you will be able to decide, whether a plan of enquiry similar to the one set on foot in G. Britn, would be likely to meet legislative or other encouragement, and of what kind, in this Country.

These, or any other ideas which may result from the perusal of the papers, I would thank you for, as the letters remain unacknowledged, and the writer of them will expect this if nothing more.

RC (PPAmP: Feinstone Collection); letterbook copy (DLC: Washington Papers). Complimentary close and signature clipped from RC; docketed by JM.

1. The Scottish agricultural reformer Sir John Sinclair met Jefferson and John Adams during their diplomatic service in Europe. In 1793 James Makittrick Adair carried to America a letter from Sinclair to Washington announcing the formation of the Board of Agriculture in London, expressing the hope "that a similar Board will be set on foot by Congress, and, under its auspices, a statistical survey carried on" in the U.S., and enclosing his *Plan for Establishing a Board of Agriculture and Internal Improvement* (London, 1793). Washington subsequently received from Sinclair several of the board's publications and agricultural surveys. He referred these materials not only to JM but also to Jefferson and Adams, expressed great interest in the board's activities, but concluded: "It will be sometime I fear, before an Agricultural Society with Congressional aids will be established in this Country." In 1795 the London board admitted Washington to foreign honorary membership (Malone, *Jefferson and His Time*, 2:59; Sinclair to Washington, 15 June and 15 Aug. 1793, diploma of London Board of Agriculture to Washington, 25 Mar. 1795 [DLC: Washington Papers]; Washington to Adair, 4 Sept. 1793, Washington to Sinclair, 20 July 1794, Fitzpatrick, *Writings of Washington*, 33:81, 436–40).

Appropriations

[10 January 1794]

In the Committee of the Whole debate on the 1794 federal budget, Giles moved the separation of "the estimate of appropriations for the civil list, and for discharging the current expences of the government, from the articles" dealing with military appropriations. The point was to clear the way for appropriations to carry on the daily business of government.

Mr. Madison said, that members had been reduced to the most serious difficulties by delays in the payment of their salary. The civil list ought always to have a fund provided for it in the first place, because it was a mere matter of form to put it to a vote. It was otherwise with the military establishment. He trusted, THAT would never be reduced to a mere form.

Philadelphia Gazette, 14 Jan. 1794.

1. Nicholas withdrew his second to Giles's motion. The House passed resolutions that accomplished the intent of the motion—restricting "the bill making appropriations for the support of the Government" for 1794 to the civil list alone—while military appropriations were dealt with in a separate bill. In Committee of the Whole on 30 Jan., FitzSimons moved an amendment to authorize a loan to provide for the appropriations. JM "objected to connecting the two subjects. This, said he, involves a consideration of ways and means, and ought to be kept distinct from that of appropriations." Clark argued that a loan was unnecessary since the bill provided only for the civil list. JM "concurred in the idea mentioned by the gentleman last up, and observed that the objects of appropriations, and

ways and means are so distinct, that it has been thought proper, essentially to separate them in the constitution." FitzSimons responded that the anticipation of revenue was distinct from ways and means. JM "asked whether this money by loan is not to be procured by the payment of an interest of 5 per cent, and whether a tax will not be necessary to pay that interest." The House passed the bill on 24 Feb. and agreed to Senate amendments on 10 Mar. Washington signed it on 14 Mar. (*Gazette of the U.S.*, 31 Jan. 1794; *Annals of Congress*, 3d Cong., 1st sess., 462, 484; *U.S. Statutes at Large*, 1:342–45).

Santo Domingan Refugees

[10 January 1794]

On 1 January a petition was read from a committee appointed by the Maryland Assembly to distribute $13,000 in relief, raised by private subscription in Baltimore, to some three thousand French refugees from Saint-Domingue (now Haiti), "stating that their funds are nearly exhausted, and praying the relief and aid of Congress" (*Annals of Congress*, 3d Cong., 1st sess., 153). On 10 January Smith (Maryland) reported from a select committee to the House and argued that such relief was legal, citing dispatches from "our executive government to the American minister at Paris, stating that they had thought themselves authorised to advance money, for the immediate support of the fugitives. . . . He mentioned the obligations that this country, lay under to France. . . . He imagined, that in this affair, the American nation had exerted a degree of generosity unparalleled in the history of any other people."

Mr. Madison wished to relieve the sufferers, but was afraid of establishing a dangerous precedent, which might hereafter be perverted to the countenance of purposes, very different from those of charity. He acknowledged, for his own part, that he could not undertake to lay his finger on that article in the Federal constitution, which granted a right to Congress of expending, on objects of benevolence, the money of their constituents. And if once they broke the line laid down before them, for the direction of their conduct, it was impossible to say, to what lengths they might go, or to what extremities this practice might be carried. He did not agree with the member who spoke last, that nothing like the generosity of America had ever been heard of before. As one example in contradiction to this assertion, he mentioned, that when the city of Lisbon had, in 1755, been overwhelmed by an earthquake, the Parliament of England instantly voted one hundred thousand pounds, for the support of the sufferers. In doing this, they had, he believed, acted in unison with the feelings of the British nation, and such feelings did that nation the utmost honor. He likewise imagined, that the Parliament had acted agreeably to the British constitution, which allowed them an indefinite and absolute right in disposing of the money of their constituents. But as to the American Congress, the case was widely different. He was satisfied that the citizens of the United States possessed an equal degree of magnanimity, generosity and benevolence, with the people of Britain, but this house certainly did not possess an undefined authority correspondent with that of a British Parliament. He wished that some other mode could be devised for assisting the French sufferers, than by an act of Congress. He was in hopes that some other mode equally effectual, and less exceptionable, might be devised. As to what our executive government had already done, as quoted from the official dispatches, by the gentlemen who spoke last, the inference did not apply; for in that emergency, a delay would have been equivalent to a total denial. It had been said that we owed the French every sentiment of gratitude. It was true, but it was likewise true, that we owed them something else than sentiments; for we were indebted to them a very large sum of money. One of the instalments of that debt would be due in a short time, and perhaps it might be safest for Congress to advance the sums now wanted for the French refugees, in part of that debt, and leave it to the decision of the French ministry, whether they would accept of such a payment or not. He did not wish to press this expedient upon the house; but he begged leave to submit it to their consideration; and as he had not yet been able to resolve in his own mind, what line of conduct the house ought to pursue, he requested that the discussion of the question might for a short time, be deferred.

Philadelphia Gazette, 14 Jan. 1794 (also reported in *Gazette of the U.S.*, 11 Jan. 1794, and *Dunlap and Claypoole's Am. Daily Advertiser*, 14 Jan. 1794).

[10 January 1794]

Clark cautioned JM to "be careful of preserving consistency," suggesting that his seventh resolution of 3 January (which provided for reimbursing American victims of maritime seizures out of increased customs duties) was no more constitutional than the proposed relief for Santo Domingan refugees.

Mr. Madison, in explanation, replied, that the two cases were widely different. The vessels of America sailed under our flag, and were under our protection, by the law of nations, which the French sufferers unquestionably were not. As to the resolution he had proposed, it was not then before the house, and hence he could not speak to it with propriety. It was very possible that the house might find it wrong, and reject it. He wished not to be misunderstood, for he was sure, that every member in that house felt the warmest sympathy with the situation of the sufferers. He would be very glad to find a proper way for their relief.[1]

Philadelphia Gazette, 14 Jan. 1794 (also reported in *Gazette of the U.S.*, 11 Jan. 1794, and *Dunlap and Claypoole's Am. Daily Advertiser*, 14 Jan. 1794).

1. After further debate, Smith's report was referred to a Committee of the Whole on the State of the Union, which took it up on 28 Jan. Nicholas urged a private subscription among the members; Smith replied that "himself and others who had seen the scene of distress were surprised, the gentleman did not feel as they did." Nicholas protested against this personal attack and asserted that his opposition to federal relief was based on constitutional considerations. JM "professed scruples of the same kind. He thought that the gentleman from Maryland (Mr. S. Smith) would not have injured his cause, by a greater moderation of language, nor his credit for benevolence by not saying, that his sympathy arose chiefly from being an eye witness." On 4 Feb. the House passed "An act providing for the relief of such of the inhabitants of Santo Domingo, resident within the United States, as may be found in want of support." The act authorized the president to distribute from the treasury to the refugees $15,000, which was to be provisionally charged against the American debt to France. The House agreed to a Senate amendment on 10 Feb., and Washington signed the act two days later (*Annals of Congress*, 3d Cong., 1st sess., 173, 422, 442; *Philadelphia Gazette*, 31 Jan. 1794; *U.S. Statutes at Large*, 6:13).

To Tench Coxe

[ca. 13 January 1794]

. . . . 1. Of the grain & flour of late years exported to G. B. what proportion was probably consumed there. 2. Is rice or tobo. sent from Portugal or Spain at all to the French or Dutch markets, where no discrimination exists in favor of the American? 3. How far is the British discrimn. in favor of *our* woods really *operative?* 4. In estimating reexports which make a part of any manufactured article, indigo & not I[ndigo] R[oot] ashes[1] for example—How much of these articles are so re-exported? The best guide that occurs is the ratio of *exported* manufactures to the totality produced—Anderson states the latter about 50 mils. What is the amt. of the former? . . .

Printed extract (Robert F. Batchelder Catalogue No. 26 [n.d.], item 357). Listed as "1 page, 4to." Conjectural date assigned on the assumption that JM sent these queries to Coxe while preparing his responses to William Loughton Smith's speech of 13 Jan. JM's speeches of 14 and 30 Jan. treat some of the topics covered in his queries to Coxe.

1. These interpolations appear in the Batchelder catalogue and are probably misreadings for "pot and pearl ashes." See the discussion of Britain's reexportation of indigo and pot and pearl ashes in JM's speech of 30 Jan. 1794.

From Hubbard Taylor

DEAR SIR   KENTUCKY 13th. January 1794

Inclosed you will receive some papers[1] of a public nature that has very lately made their appearance; considerable exertions will be made by many to carry the design into effect. As the navigation of the Mississippi is held up as the primary object it will avail much. That we have some cause of complaint on that head is very clear to me, but wheather the present plan[2] is the most proper and secure to obtain our ends remains a doubt in my mind. A Resolution[3] will come forward from this State Legislature for that purpose, founded on petitions from the State at large. The Society from which those publications spring is held at Lexington once a month, and there is one or two others[4] in the State that keeps up a corispondence with them.

The circumstance of Genl. Clark's having reced. an appointment under the French is a matter much talked of here, and its generally thought that the French Genl. in this Country has Money to raise troops in the spring to go against the Spanish Settlements on the Mississippi which of course if it takes place will bring on some further disturbances from some quarter, how those things will be likely to terminate time must develope; but I fear not untill our little infant State wades through many difficulties that are unseen as yet.

The Assembly of this State adjourned the 21st. Decr. but little business of a general nature was done. An alteration in the Revenue for the present year[5] was made by a discrimination in the tax on Lands its divided into three Classes the first to pay 3/ the second 1/6 and the third 9d. ℔ 100 Acres—& a sale of so much of the Lands as will pay the taxs in stead of a forfeiture of the whole—also a fine on all persons who do not give in the whole of their Lands [to] the Comissr. of the district in which he resides. The time of payment for all except such as is settled stands as before untill the 4th. Feby. 95. Tax on Negroes remains @ 2/ each Horses reduced to 6d. & Cattle to 1½d ℔ head.

The Iron Works in this State has got in blast at last, the Ore is good, & plenty, they have reduced the price of Castings from 9d. to 6d. This together with the Fulling Mills of which we have a great many is very servic⟨ea⟩ble to us and is a great saving to the State. So is the paper & Oil Mills. From this mode of proceeding our State would be likely to flourish if we could get the Navigation of the Mississippi without any quarrelling or heard blows—but I fear so great an object is not to be had without one or the other of those, or perhaps both.

Salt has within these three or four weaks been from 24/ to 32/ ℔ bushell any distance from the works—which has been very alarming when 12/– has been the usual price for some time past. A Lick has been lately worked near the Ohio about 15 Miles above Limestone & found to be very good some say b[e]tter that [*sic*] the best heretofore worked; but should it be inferior it is a great thing for us.

The Groth of Cotten on the Cumberland & Green Rivers low down exceeds almost all discription from 12 to 1500 lbs. from One Acres badley tended is thought to be a moderate Crop. This article if properly incouraged wd. be a great saving to this State—if no exports was made of its Manufactories. The Merchants drains us of nearly all our Money twice a year which never more returns.

I shall wait with anxious expectation for the end of this session of Congress, or for their determinations on War opperations. The people here have generally forfieted all patience with the Secretary of the Treausery & the Secretary of War—and it appears that not a man in the whole State could be found a friend to either of them & enmity with the Eastern States daily encreases.

As I expect I have tired your patience already I shall only add my best Wishes for your health and a pleasent session & Subscribe myself Dr. Sir with great regard yrs. affe. huble set.

H. TAYLOR

RC (DLC). Docketed by JM. Enclosures not found, but see nn. 1 and 2.

1. One of Taylor's enclosures was evidently a broadside published by the Democratic Society of Kentucky: *To the President and Congress of the United States of America. The Remonstrance of the Citizens West of the Alleghany Mountains* (Lexington, Ky., 1793; Evans supp. 46731), which asserted "that Your Remonstrants are entitled by Nature and by stipulation, to the undisturbed Navigation of the river Mississippi." John Breckinridge was the society's chairman and author of the *Remonstrance* (Harrison, *John Breckinridge*, pp. 54–55).

2. Taylor probably enclosed another broadside, *Fellow-Citizens. The Democratic Society of Kentucky Have Directed Us . . .* (Lexington, Ky., 1793; Evans supp. 46729). This handbill published the society's resolution "to make an attempt in a peaceable manner, to go with an American bottom properly registered and cleared, into the sea through the channel of the Mississippi" in order to force the navigation issue on the Spanish and American governments. JM probably also received copies of this broadside and that cited in n. 1 from John Lee (Lee to James Madison, Sr., 8 Feb. 1794 [PHi]).

3. On 21 Dec. 1793 the Kentucky General Assembly passed a joint resolution asserting Mississippi navigation was "not only the natural unalienable right of the citizens of this Commonwealth, but that it has been acknowledged to be by solemn treaty" and instructing the state's U.S. senators "to assert that right to the General Government" (*Acts Passed at the First Session of the Second General Assembly* [Lexington, Ky., (1793); Evans supp. 46799], p. 54).

4. The Democratic Society of Kentucky had branches at Paris in Bourbon County and Georgetown in Scott County (E. Merton Coulter, "The Efforts of

the Democratic Societies of the West to Open the Navigation of the Mississippi," *Mississippi Valley Historical Review*, 11 [1924–25]: 378).

5. "An Act to amend an act entitled 'An Act establishing a permanent revenue' " passed on 21 Dec. 1793 (*Acts Passed at the First Session of the Second General Assembly*, p. 19).

Commercial Discrimination

[14 January 1794]

In a lengthy speech made in the Committee of the Whole, Smith (South Carolina) on 13 January opposed commercial retaliation against Britain as set forth in Jefferson's report of 16 December 1793 and JM's resolutions of 3 January 1794 (*Annals of Congress*, 3d Cong., 1st sess., 174–209). JM responded to Smith's speech on 14 January.

He began, by observing that he had expected, from what was intimated yesterday, the sequel of what was then said against the resolutions before the committee; but as there was a silence in that quarter, and no other member has risen on either side of the question, he himself would request the attention of the committee.

It had been much pressed, that in the discussion of this subject, it should be viewed in its commercial relations only. He was perfectly willing to meet every objection that could be urged on that ground: But as he conceived it impossible to do full justice to the interests of the United States without taking some collateral considerations into view; he should be obliged in the course of his remarks, to point at the political disposition and conduct of some of the nations of Europe towards this country.

The propositions immediately before the committee, turned on the question whether any thing ought to be done at this time, in the way of commercial regulations, towards vindicating and advancing our national interests. Perhaps it might be made a question with some, whether in any case, legislative regulations of commerce were consistent with its nature and prosperity.

He professed himself to be a friend to the theory which gives to industry a free course, under the impulse of individual interest, and the guidance of individual sagacity. He was persuaded that it would be happy for all nations, if the barriers erected by prejudice, by avarice, and by despotism, were broken down, and a free intercourse established among them. Yet to this, as to all other general rules, there might be exceptions: And the rule itself required, what did not exist, that it should be general.

To illustrate this observation, he referred to the navigation act of Great-Britain, which not being counterbalanced by any similar acts on the part of rival nations, had secured to Great-Britain no less than *eleven-twelfths* of the shipping and seamen employed in her trade. It is stated, that in 1660, when the British act passed, the foreign tonnage was to the British as one to four: In 1700, less than one to six: In 1725 as one to nineteen: In 1750, as one to twelve: In 1774, nearly the same. At the commencement of the period, the tonnage was but 95,266 tons: At the end of it, 1,136,162.[1]

As another illustration, he mentioned the case where two countries happened to be in such a relation to each other, that the one, by discouraging the manufactures of the other, might not only invigorate its own, but transplant the manufacturers themselves. Here the gain would be a clear one; and the effect evidently consistent with the principle of the theory.

To allow trade to regulate itself is not therefore to be admitted as a maxim *universally* found. Our own experience has taught us that in certain cases, it is the same thing with allowing one nation to regulate it for another. Were the United States in fact in commercial intercourse with one nation only, and to oppose no restrictions whatever to a system of foreign restrictions, they would of necessity be deprived of all share in the carriage, altho' their vessels might be able to do it cheapest; as well as of the only resources for defence on that side, where they must always be most exposed to attack. A small burden only in foreign ports on American vessels, and a perfect equality of foreign vessels with our own in our own ports, would gradually banish the latter altogether.

This subject, as had been remarked on a former occasion, was not a novel one. It was co-eval with our political birth; and has at all times exercised the thoughts of reflecting citizens. As early as the year succeeding the peace, the effect of the foreign policy which began to be felt in our trade and navigation, excited universal attention and inquietude. The first effort thought of, was an application of Congress to the states for a grant of power for a limited time, to regulate our foreign commerce;[2] with a view to control the influence of unfavorable regulations in some cases, and to conciliate an extension of favorable ones in others. From some circumstances then incident to our situation, and particularly from a radical vice in the then political system of the United States, the experiment did not take effect.

The states next endeavored to effect their purpose by separate but concurrent regulations. Massachusetts opened a correspondence with Virginia and other states, in order to bring about the plan. Here again the effort was abortive.

Out of this experience, grew the measures which terminated in the establishment of a government competent to the regulation of our commercial interests, and the vindication of our commercial rights.

As these were the first objects of the people in the steps taken for establishing the present government, they were universally expected to be among the first fruits of its operation. In this expectation the public were disappointed. An attempt was made in different forms and received the repeated sanction of this branch of the legislature, but they expired in the Senate:[3] Not indeed, as was alledged, from a dislike to the attempt altogether, but the modifications given to it. It has not appeared, however, that it was ever renewed in a different form in that house; & for some time it has been allowed to sleep in both.

If the reasons which originally prevailed against measures, such as those now proposed, had weight in them, they can no longer furnish a pretext for opposition.

When the subject was discussed in the first Congress at New-York, it was said, that we ought to try the effect of a generous policy towards Great-Britain; that we ought to give time for negociating a treaty of commerce; that we ought to await the close of negociations for explaining and executing the treaty of peace. We have now waited a term of more than four years. The treaty of peace remains unexecuted on her part; tho' all pretext for delay has been removed by the steps taken on ours. No treaty of commerce is either in train, or in prospect. Instead of relaxations in former articles complained of, we suffer new and aggravated violations of our rights.

In the view which he took of the subject, he called the attention of the committee particularly to the subject of navigation, of manufactures, and of the discrimination proposed in the motion, between some nations and others.

On the subject of navigation, he observed that we were prohibited by the British laws from carrying to Great-Britain the produce of other countries from their ports, or our own produce from the ports of other countries, or the produce of other countries from our own ports; or to send our own produce from our own or other ports in the vessels of other countries. This last restriction was, he observed, felt by the United States at the present moment. It was indeed the practice of Great-Britain sometimes to relax her navigation act so far in time of war, as to permit to neutral vessels a circuitous carriage; but as yet the act was in full force against the use of them for transporting the produce of the United States.

On the other hand, the laws of the United States allowed Great-Britain to bring into their ports, any thing she might please, from her own or from other ports; and in her own or in other vessels.

In the trade between the United States and the British West-Indies, the

vessels of the former were under an absolute prohibition; whilst British
vessels in that trade enjoyed all the privileges granted to other, even the
most favored nations in their trade with us. The inequality in this case
was the more striking, as it was evident that the West-Indies were dependant on the United States for the supplies essential to them, and
that the circumstances which secured to the United States this advantage, enabled their vessels to transport the supplies on far better terms
than could be done by British vessels.

To illustrate the policy requisite in our commercial intercourse with
other nations, he presented a comparative view of the American and
foreign tonnage employed in the respective branches of it, from which
it appeared that the foreign stood to the American as follows—

Spain	1 to 5
Portugal	1 to 6
The United Netherlands,	1 to 15
Denmark,	1 to 12
Russia,	— —
France,	1 to 5
Great-Britain,	5 to 1

It results from these facts that in proportion as the trade might be
diminished with Great-Britain and increased with other nations, would
be the probable increase of the American tonnage. It appeared, for example, that as the trade might pass from British channels into those of
France it would augment our tonnage at the rate of ten to one.

The above calculation, he said, had been made out on the documents
of 1790, and on the amount of the tonnage *entered* in the several ports.
A document, stating the amounts of the *actual* tonnage in the American
trade, had been just reported to that house.[4] If this, which was liable to
some remarks that might hereafter be made, was to be substituted, it
afforded another calculation, diminishing the excess in favor of Great-
Britain, but augmenting it in favor of the United States in most of the
other instances.

According to this calculation the foreign to the American tonnage
might be stated, as follows:

Spain,	1 to 16
Portugal,	1 to 17
United Netherlands,	1 to 26
Denmark,	1 to 15
Russia,	1 to 14
France,	1 to between 4 & 5
Great-Britain, nearly as	3 to 1

Such a disproportion, taking even the reduced one, in the navigation with Great-Britain, was the more mortifying, when the nature and amount of our exports are considered. Our exports are not only for the most part, either immediately necessaries of life, or ultimately as necessaries to manufactures, necessaries of employment and life to manufacturers, and must thence command a sure market wherever they are received at all: But the peculiar bulkiness of them furnishes an advantage over the exports of every other country; and particularly over those of Great-Britain. If such an advantage belonged to that nation, the policy which governs her navigation laws, would probably have given the exclusive carriage to her own bottoms. It is equally in our power, if so selfish a principle should be forced upon us, to secure to our bottoms the same monopoly; leaving to other nations with which we trade, the like exclusive carriage of their exports. The regulation would, to be sure, be mutually inconvenient; and by forcing the vessels of each party to return empty from foreign markets, be so far a tax on the intercourse. This effect, however, did not disprove the power in general which the character of our exports gave us, over the carriage of them, nor lessen the argument drawn from it. Examine it in relation to Great-Britain. The bulk of her exports to us compared with that of ours to her, is as nothing. An inconsiderable quantity of shipping would suffice for hers, whilst ours can load about 222,000 tons: Including the articles she exports from the West-Indies to this country, they bear no proportion to ours. Yet in the entire trade between the United States and the British dominions, her tonnage is to that of the United States as 156,000, employing 9,360 seamen, to 66,000, employing 3,690 seamen. Were a rigid exertion of our right to take place, it would extend our tonnage to 222,000; and leave to G. B. employment for much less than the actual share now enjoyed by the United States. It could not be wished to push matters to this extremity. It shewed, however, the very unequal and unfavorable footing, on which the carrying trade, the great resource of our safety and respectability, was placed by foreign regulations, and the reasonableness of peaceable attempts to meliorate it. We might at least, in availing ourselves of the merit of our exports, contend for such regulations as would reverse the proportion, and give the United States the 156,000 tonnage and 9,360 seamen, instead of the 66,000 tonnage and 3,690 seamen.

He here adverted to the discount of ten per cent. on the duties paid by goods imported in American bottoms;[5] remarking that it was not founded on the true policy of encouraging our shipping. It was not the *imports* but *exports* that regulated the quantity of tonnage. What was imported in American vessels, which would otherwise return empty, was no doubt, a benefit to the American merchant, but could slightly only, if at all, increase the mass of our tonnage. The way to effect this was to secure *exportations* to American bottoms.

Proceeding to the subject of manufactures, he observed that it presented no compensations for the inequalities in the principles and effects of the navigation system.

We consume British manufactures to double the amount of what Britain takes from us; and *quadruple* the amount of what she actually *consumes*.

We take everything after it has undergone all the profitable labor that can be bestowed on it: She receives in return, raw materials, the food of her industry.

We send necessaries to her: She sends superfluities to us.

We admit *every thing* she pleases to send us, whether of her own or alien production. She refuses not only our manufactures, but the articles we wish most to send her; our wheat and flour, our fish, and our salted provisions. These constitute our best staples for exportation; as her manufactures constitute hers.

It appeared by an authentic document[6] he had examined, that of the *manufactured* articles imported in 1790, amounting to 15,295,638 dollars 97 cents, we received from and *thro'* Great Britain, 13,965,464 dollars 95 cents.

During the same year, the *manufactures* imported from France, the next great commercial country, and consuming more of our produce than Great-Britain, amounted to no more than 155,136 dollars and 63 cents.

To give a fuller view of our foreign commerce, he stated the balances with the several nations of Europe and their dominions, as follow:

	Dollars.	
Spain	1,670,797	*in favor of U. S.*
Portugal	1,687,699	*do.*
U. Netherlands	791,118	*do.*
Sweden	32,965	*do.*
Denmark	126,949	*against the U. S.*
France	2,630,387	*in favor of U. S.*
G. Britain	5,922,012	*against the U. S.*[7]

This enormous balance to G. B. is on the *exports* to her. On her *consumption* the balance is still greater, amounting to nine or ten millions, to which again is to be added her profits on the re-exports in a manufactured and raw state.

It might be said that an unfavorable balance was no proof of an unfavorable trade; that the only important balance was the ultimate one on our aggregate commerce.

That there was much truth in this general doctrine was admitted; at the same time it was equally certain that there were exceptions to it, some of which were conceived to be applicable to the situation of the United States.

But whether the doctrine were just or not, as applied to the United States, it was well known that the reasoning and practice of other countries were governed by a contrary doctrine. In all of them, an unfavorable balance to be paid in specie, was considered as an evil. Great-Britain in particular had always studied to prevent it as much as she could. What then may be the effect on the policy of a nation with which we have the most friendly and beneficial relations, when it sees the balance of trade with us not only so much against her, but all the specie that pays it, flowing immediately into the lap of her greatest rival, if not her most inveterate enemy.

As to the discrimination proposed between nations having, and not having commercial treaties with us, the principle was embraced by the laws of most, if not all the states, whilst the regulation of trade was in their hands.

It had the repeated sanction of votes in the house of representatives, during the session of the present government at New-York.

It has been practised by other nations, and in a late instance against the United States.

It tends to procure beneficial treaties from those who refuse them, by making them the price of enjoying an equality with other nations in our commerce.

It tends, as a conciliatory preference, to procure better treaties from those who have not refused them.

It was a prudent consideration, in dispensing commercial advantages, to favor rather those whose friendship and support may be expected in case of necessity, than those whose disposition wore a contrary aspect. He did not wish to enter at present, nor at all, if unnecessary, into a display of the unfriendly features which marked the policy of Great-Britain towards the United States. He should be content to lay aside, at least for the present, the subject of the Indians, the Algerines, the spoliations, &c. but he could not forbear remarking generally, that if that, or any other nation were known to bear us a settled ill-will, nothing could be more impolitic than to foster resources which would be more likely to be turned against us, than exerted in our favor.

It had been admitted by the gentleman who spoke yesterday (Mr. Smith of South Carolina) to be a misfortune, that our trade should be so far engrossed by any one nation, as it is, in the hands of Great-Britain. But the gentleman added nothing to alleviate the misfortune, when he advised us to make no efforts for putting an end to it. The evils resulting from such a state of things were as serious as they were numerous. To say nothing of sudden derangements from the caprice with which sovereigns might be seized, there were casualities which might not be avoidable. A general bankruptcy, which was a possible event, in a nation with which we were so connected, would reverberate upon us with a most dreadful shock. A partial bankruptcy, had actually and lately taken place; and was severely felt in our commerce. War is a common event particularly, to G. Britain, and involves us in the embarrassments it brings on her commerce whilst ours is so disproportionately interwoven with it. Add, the influence that may be conveyed into the public councils by a nation directing the course of our trade by her capital, & holding so great a share in our pecuniary institutions; and the effect that may finally ensue on our taste, our manners, and our form of government itself.

If the question be asked, what might be the consequence of counter-efforts, and whether this attempt to vindicate our public interests would not produce them? His answer was, that he did not in the least apprehend such a consequence, as well because the measure afforded no pretext, being short of what was already done by Great-Britain in her commercial system, as because she would be the greatest sufferer from a stagnation of the trade, between the two countries if she should force on such a crisis.

Her merchants would feel it. Her navigation would feel it. Her manufacturers would feel it. Her West-Indies would be ruined by it. Her revenue would deeply feel it. And her government would feel it thro' every nerve of its operations. We too should suffer in some respects, but in a less degree, and, if the virtue and temper of our fellow citizens were not mistaken, the experiment would find in them a far greater readiness to bear it. It was clear to him, therefore, that if Great-Britain should, contrary to all the rules of probability, stop the commerce between the two countries, the issue would be a compleat triumph to the United States.

He dwelt particularly on the dependence of British manufactures on the market of the United States. He referred to a paper in Andersons history of commerce, which states the amount of British manufactures at £.51,310,000 sterling, and the number of souls employed in, and supported by them, at 5,250,000.[8] Supposing the United States to consume two and a half millions of British manufactures which is a moderate estimate, the loss of their market, would deprive of subsistence 250,000 souls. Add 50,000 who depend for employment on our raw materials. Here are 300,000 souls, who live by our custom. Let them be driven to poverty and despair by acts of their own government, and what would be the consequence? Most probably an acquisition of so many useful citizens to the United States, which form the natural asylum against the distresses of Europe. But whether they should remain in discontent and wretchedness in their own country, or seek their fortunes in another, the evil would be felt by the British government as equally great, and be avoided with equal caution.

It might be regarded, he observed, as a general rule, that where one nation consumed the necessaries of life produced by another, the consuming nation was dependent on the producing one. On the other hand, where the consumption consisted of superfluities, the producing nation was dependent on the consuming one. The United States were in the fortunate situation of enjoying both these advantages over Great-Britain. They supply a part of her dominions with the necessaries of life. They consume superfluities which give bread to her people in another part. Great Britain therefore is under a double dependence on the commerce of the United States. She depends on them for what she herself consumes: she depends on them for what they consume.

In proportion as a nation manufactures luxuries must be its disadvantage in contests of every sort with its customers. The reason is obvious. What is a luxury to the consumer is a necessary to the manufacturer. By changing a fashion, or disappointing a fancy only, bread may be taken from the mouths of thousands whose industry is devoted to the gratification of artificial wants.

He mentioned the case of a petition from a great body of buckle makers presented a few years ago to the prince of Wales, complaining of the use of strings instead of buckles in the shoes, and supplicating his royal highness as giving the law to fashions, to save them from want and misery, by discontinuing the new one.[9] It was not, he observed, the prince who petitioned the manufacturers to continue to make the buckles, but the manufacturers who petitioned their customers to buy them. The relation was similar between the American customers and the British manufacturers. And if a law were to pass for putting a stop to the use of their superfluities, or a stop were otherwise to be put to it, it would quickly be seen from which the distress and supplications would flow.

Suppose that Great Britain received from us alone the whole of the necessaries she consumes; and that our market alone took off the luxuries with which she paid for them. Here the dependence would be compleat; and we might impose whatever terms we pleased on the exchange. This to be sure is not absolutely the case; but in proportion as it is the case, her dependence is on us.

The West-Indies however are an example of compleat dependence. They cannot subsist without our food. They cannot flourish without our lumber, and our use of their rum. On the other hand we depend on them for not a single necessary, and can supply ourselves with their luxuries from other sources. Sugar is the only article about which there was ever a question, and he was authorised to say, that there was not at the most, one sixth of our consumption supplied from the British islands.

In time of war or famine the dependence of the West-Indies is felt in all its energy. It is sometimes such as to appeal to our humanity as well as our interest for relief. At this moment, the governor of Jamaica is making proclamation of their distresses. If ever therefore there was a case where one country could dictate to another the regulations of trade between them, it is the case of the United States, and the British West-Indies. And yet the gentleman from South-Carolina (Mr. Smith) had considered it as a favor that we were allowed to send our provisions in British bottoms & in these only, to the West-Indies. The favor reduced to plain language in the mouth of their planters, would run thus: We will agree to buy your provisions rather than starve, and let you have our rum, which we can sell nowhere else; but we reserve out of this indulgence a monopoly of the carriage to British vessels.

With regard to revenue, the British resources were extremely exhausted in comparison with those of the United States.

The people of Great-Britain were taxed at the rate of 40/ a head: the people of the United States at not more than 6/ a head; less than one-sixth of the British tax.

As the price of labor which pays the tax is double in the United States, to what it is in Great-Britain, the burden on American citizens is less than one-twelfth of the burden on British subjects.

It is true indeed that Britain alone does not bear the whole burden. She levies indirect taxes on her West-Indies and on her East-Indies; and derives from an acquiescence in her monopolizing regulations, an imperceptible tribute from the whole commercial world.

Still however the difference of burden in the two countries is immense.

Britain has moreover great arrears of unfunded debts. She is threatened with defects in her revenue even at this time. She is engaged in an expensive war. And she raises the supplies for it on the most expensive terms.

Add to the whole that her population is stationary if not diminishing, whilst that of the United States is in a course of increase beyond example.

Should it still be asked whether the impost might not be affected, and how a deficiency could be supplied? He thought sufficient answers might be given.

He took for granted that the articles subjected to the additional duties would continue to come according to the demand for them: And believed if the duties were prudently adjusted, the increase of the duties would balance the decrease of importation.

Our country is able to import, and probably will import, in proportion to our exports. Our exports amount, say, to twenty millions of dollars. If we import less from one country we shall import more from another. If we import less of some things we shall import more of other things; and according to our imports will be our revenue.

Suppose Great-Britain to make the rash and improbable experiment of prohibiting all commerce with the United States: She does not consume more than one-fourth of our exports; and we derive perhaps nearly half our revenue from the productions of other countries. In this point of view we should at the worst have three-fourths of our exports to pay for our reduced imports; and consequently a balance of about five millions of specie flowing into our country. The faculty which this would give to operations of revenue, together with the consideration that the labor employed on one-fourth of our ordinary exports would be employed for internal purposes, might assure us that a judicious government would easily be able to provide the means of supplying the deficiency of impost.

But it was superfluous to enter into calculations of this sort. He recurred to the utter improbability that such a contingency should happen. He was fully persuaded that the resolutions, if agreed to, would not impair the revenue.

It is objected, that Spain and Portugal who are good customers to us, and the latter particularly friendly, having no commercial treaty with us, will come within the operation of the resolutions.

Several answers may be given to this objection.

1. They do not manufacture the articles in question so as to be sensibly affected.

2. They employ but little tonnage in our trade: Spain 2,689 tons only; Portugal 2,340 tons only: They are supposed to be little anxious to increase the foreign branches of their carrying trade, being content with the internal trade carried on with their own dominions. As they have no navigation act within the purview of the resolutions, they would not be exposed to the retaliating clauses on that subject.

3. If friendly, they can be admitted to treaty on equitable conditions whenever they please.

4. They can easily be excepted, if thought expedient, either by a general proviso that the resolutions shall not extend to nations having no navigation act such as is therein described; or by providing that they shall not extend to countries south of Cape-Finisterre, a distinction familiar to the British statute-book.

It is said that Great-Britain treats the United States as well as she treats other nations, and therefore they ought to be satisfied.

If other nations were willing to bear unequal regulations, or unable to vindicate their rights, it was no example for us.

But is it true that the same degree of reciprocity subsists between the United States & Great-Britain, as between Great-Britain and other countries? He did not admit this to be the case. Where treaties existed, they stipulated in many instances, mutual and equal conditions of intercourse. He gave an example in the treaty of Methuen, in which the admission of British woolens by Portugal was balanced by the admission of Portugal wine, by Great-Britain. The treaty with France of late date, was another example, where a variety of reciprocal privileges and countervailing duties, were minutely provided for.[10] Where no treaties existed or where they were silent, there were often legal regulations reciprocating the regulations of Great-Britain. He referred to the laws of Sweden and Denmark on the subject of manufactures as instances.

It is said that Great-Britain treats us as well as other nations treat us. What nation he asked, had such a navigation act? What nation besides, excludes us from a circuitous trade? What nation excludes us from carrying our own commodities in our own bottoms, where the carriage is allowed to her bottoms?

It is said, that at least Great-Britain treats us as well as we are treated by France, who will be favored by the resolutions. This point was particularly labored yesterday, by the gentleman from South-Carolina, (Mr. Smith,) who made a comparison of those two countries the principal basis of the discussion. As they were in fact the two countries which stood in the most important relations to the United States, the subject required a pretty accurate view of their respective dispositions, regulations, and intercourse with this country.

On the subject of the dispositions of France and Great-Britain towards the United States, the gentleman, (Mr. Smith) was of a very different opinion, Mr. Madison observed, from that expressed in the message of the President. The message informed the house, that France had generally manifested a friendly disposition towards the United States, had granted advantages to their commerce, and had actually made overtures for placing it permanently on a better footing.[11] While the language of the communications, with respect to Great-Britain, sufficiently proves that there was no room for compliments of a like kind to that nation.

He meant to shew, however, from a particular review, in what light the two nations stood to us; and for that purpose should submit to the committee a comparative statement, as the gentleman had done, of their commercial policy towards us. He premised, however, that he could not follow the example of recurring to a period antecedent to the French revolution for evidence in relation to France. Mr. Smith, seemed to think that the order of things subsequent to that period, could not be regarded as a settled order. He, (Mr. Madison) on the contrary, considered it as the only settled order. He hoped and believed, that the revolution was not a fugitive thing, as some might wish, but that it was irreversibly established, and that the new republic would flourish for ever on the ruins of the ancient monarchy. He should not, however, he said, reject from his enquiry, what was done previous to the date of the republic in favor of the United States, because it could not be reasonably supposed that the disposition of the nation would be less favorable now, than it was under the former government.

He then proceeded to a view of the footing on which the commerce stood with the British and French dominions.

Wheat and Flour. In France free, that is to say, under a duty of one-eighth per cent. as a custom-house regulation, merely for ascertaining the quantity imported. This remark is to be applied to several other articles, which will be mentioned as free.

In Great-Britain, wheat and flour are prohibited, till the price is up at 6/3 sterling a bushel; which as to the United States, may be deemed a perpetual prohibition.

In the French West-Indies, these articles are also free; and as he at first stated, by a general law which had been suspended from time to time; but being told that he was mistaken, the articles being prohibited by a general law, and free only by suspensions, he said, that altho' his documents gave him other information, he should leave the fact for further examination; adding, however, that it was not essential, as the actual practice and disposition of France on this subject were chiefly to be regarded.

In the British West-Indies these articles were free, but in British bottoms only.

Rice. In France free. In Britain under a duty of 7/4 sterling the hundred. In the French islands under a duty of one per cent. In the British, free in British bottoms.

Salted Fish. In France under a duty of 8 livres the kental. In Britain prohibited. In French islands admitted under some discouragements, which did not however prevent a great consumption. In the British islands prohibited.

Salted Beef. In France under a duty of 5 livres a kental. In Britain prohibited. In French islands under a duty of 1 per cent. and 3 livres a kental. In British islands prohibited.

Salted Pork. In France, under a duty of 5 livres a kental in some ports; prohibited in others. In Britain under a prohibitory duty of 44/9 a kental. In the British and French islands prohibited.

Indigo. In France under a duty of 5 livres a kental. In Britain free. In the British and French islands prohibited.

Whale Oil. In France under a duty of 7 livres 10 sols a barrel of 520 lbs. In Britain under a duty of £.18.3. a ton. In both West-Indies prohibited.

Tar, Pitch, and Turpentine. In France under a duty of 2 per cent. In Britain, under duties, tar and pitch 11d. per barrel, turpentine 2/3 per 100 lb.

Tobacco is on a footing pretty similar in the two countries. So are wood, pot and pearl ash and flax-seed.

Indian Corn, Wood, Live Animals (except horses and mules which are free) in the French islands pay a duty of 1 per cent. In the British they are free, in British bottoms, prohibited in American bottoms.

Ships. In France, free to be naturalized. In Britain prohibited.

He proceeded to state the comparative amount of our exports and imports in the commerce with the two nations, and the balances on them as before shewn. He noticed particularly the excess of the exports to the French West-Indies which amounted to 3,284,656 dollars, over those to the British, which amounted to 2,357,583: Observing the importance of that market, and the more especially as it supplies the article of molasses, the only raw material imported into the United States, and otherwise so much valued as an article of consumption. He adverted also to the superior proportion of American tonnage in the trade with the French dominions, as had also been before shewn.

From this review, he left the committee to infer the true policy of the United States with regard to their commerce, in its two most considerable branches. He thought it clear, that in every view it was incumbent on the United States to cultivate the connection and intercourse with the French nation. As a market for our produce, their vast population, and their use of our articles of mere consumption, were peculiarly precious to our agriculture. They could do better without our trade than Great-Britain, yet they shewed more disposition to favor it. And what was by no means to be disregarded, they were the only considerable power on the face of the earth, sincerely friendly to the republican form of government established in this country.

Of all the objections which Mr. Madison had heard suggested against the resolutions, the most extravagant and chimerical was the idea of a war with Great-Britain in consequence of them. He was at a loss to say whether such an objection were a greater insult to the character of that nation or to the understanding of America. At the utmost the propositions go only to a reciprocity. They do not in fact go so far. On what imaginable pretext then can Great-Britain make war upon us. If we are no longer colonies, but independent states, we surely can do what all independent states do, regulate our trade as may suit our own interests. And Great-Britain can have the least right of any nation to complain of it, because it is her own example which we follow. If war therefore should be made on us it would only prove a fixt predetermination to make it. And in that case pretexts more plausible than any commercial regulations could easily be found or framed for the purpose.

The next ground on which he examined the subject was it's operation among the several parts of the union. It was admitted and regretted, that the immediate benefits and burdens would not be equally distributed among all the states. More than a due share of the former would flow to the northern division: More than a due share of the latter would fall on the southern. This was unavoidably produced by the unequal advances made in manufactures and navigation; and it was an inconvenience that had necessarily taken place in a variety of other instances. It would be found, however, on a fair attention to the subject, that the inequality would be less than at first appeared.

With respect to manufactures, the southern states were at least equally interested in encouraging and distributing a competition for our market, among different nations of Europe, instead of being so much in the hands of a single one.

The duty on the finer articles imported would fall on those most able to bear it; and would be pretty equally diffused through the union.

The duty on the coarser articles would be saved in proportion to the progress made in manufactures among ourselves; and he was able to say, with great pleasure, that those carried on, not in public factories, but in the household or family way, which he regarded as the most important way, were nearly, if not quite as far advanced in the southern country as in the middle and northern. Virginia was proceeding with great spirit in this branch of industry. North-Carolina he understood was doing the same; and there was no reason why the more southern states would not avail themselves of the resource, especially as they enjoyed superior advantages in the article of cotton, a primary material for the business.

The exports would not be materially affected unless Great-Britain, should contrary to all probability, renounce the benefits of the trade in them, and expose her West-India islands to the danger of famine; and in that case, the inconveniences would be not local but general.

Even in the article of tonnage the inequality at present tho' considerable, was not so great as he had imagined, before he examined the real state of it. It appeared from the official reports lately made on that subject, that the states south of Pennsylvania (which has about her due share,) have within one-third of their due quota. Georgia has more than her share. South-Carolina nearly her share. North Carolina has three eighths below her share. Virginia has about half her share. Maryland has more than her share. Delaware less than her share.

This computation is not perhaps very accurate, because it is founded on the relative population of the states. It should rather have reference to the value and volume of the produce exported from the several states. But as several of them carry on their trade thro' their neighbours, this rule of calculation would in fact be more uncertain than the other.

Whatever be the rule, Virginia, he remarked, was the state that appeared most deficient; her exports both in value and bulk, being in full proportion to her population, and her tonnage being more short of that, than could be said of any state. He had every reason, notwithstanding, to believe that the great body of the people of Virginia, would chearfully concur in any temporary sacrifices, that might be necessary to vindicate our public rights, and our commercial interests.

It was a consideration that ought to have great weight with the southern states, that a home market for their naval stores would be extended by every measure, favoring our own navigation; and that they must soon begin themselves to turn to effect their natural advantages for ship building. Having the materials on the spot, they would not be long in imitating their northern brethren, North-Carolina was singularly favored in this particular. There was not a single article used in the various component parts of a ship, which she did not possess, or could not raise within herself.

The capacity of the United States, to provide with celerity for the transportation of their produce, was strongly attested by what they had effected before the revolution. In the marine of the British empire, whilst the United States were part of it, the American built ships were to the British built as 23 to 40. New-England furnished about three fifths of the former.

In two points of view, the southern states were peculiarly interested in promoting our navigation.

First. As they are in some respects the weaker part of the Union, and have most wealth exposed on the sea, they have most need of that protection, which results from extensive marine resources. The existence of these will either prevent attack, or can readily be turned into the means of repelling it.

Secondly. As they have so much valuable and bulky produce to carry to market, it is their interest to possess a conveyance for it, that may be as little affected as possible by the contingencies and wars of other nations; and particularly of Great-Britain, a nation which is so frequently at war, and which has so disproportionate a share in our carrying trade. This subject, he said, had been placed in so striking a view, by the Secretary of State in a former report on the fisheries, that he should rely on the patience of the committee in reading the observations and calculations to which he alluded. He here read the following note at the end of that report.

"That the encouragement of our carrying business is interesting, not only to the carrying states, but in a high degree also to the others, will result from the following facts.

Dollars.

The whole exports of the United States, may be stated at   25,000,000

Great-Britain carries two-fifths of these in value, that is to say,   10,000,000

Freight and insurance on this in times of peace, are about twenty-two and one half per cent.   2,250,000

The same charges in war are very various, according to the circumstances of the war, we may say, however fifty-five per cent.   5,500,000

The difference between peace and war, freight and insurance, then is annually   3,250,000

Taxed on our agriculture by British wars, during their continuance, and our dependance on British bottoms.

Of the last one hundred years, Great-Britain has had* forty-two years of war and fifty-eight of peace, which is three of war to every four of peace, nearly.

	*Y.	M.			Y.	M.	
			1689. *May.*	⎫	8	4	*War.*
			1697. *Sept.*	⎬			
Peace.	4	8	1702. *May.*	⎫	10	3	
	6	4	1712. *August*	⎬			
			1718. *Dec.*	⎫	2	6	
	5	8	1721. *June.*	⎬			
			1727. *March*	⎫	0	2	
	12	4	1727. *May.*	⎬			
			1739. *Octo.*	⎫	8	7	
	7	0	1748. *May.*	⎬			
			1755. *June.*	⎫	7	5	
	15	7	1762. *Nov.*	⎬			
			1778. *June.*	⎫	4	9	
	6	2	1783. *March*	⎬			
			1789. *May.*				

     57   9   42

In every term of seven years then, we pay three times three million two hundred and fifty thousand dollars, or nine million seven hundred and fifty thousand, which, averaged on the years of peace & war, are annually and constantly one million three hundred & ninety-two thousand eight hundred and fifty-seven more than we should, if we could raise our own shipping to be competent to the carriage of all our productions. Besides this, many of our bulky articles, not bearing a war freight, cannot be exported, if exposed, to that, so that their total loss is to be added to that before estimated." [12]

This was a demonstration of the interest the United States had, particularly the southern states, in obtaining an independent transportation for their commodities; and the effect of the present war to which Britain as a party, in depriving them of the ordinary foreign resource, is bringing the evidence home to their feelings at the present moment.

It had been asked what ground there was for concluding, that Great-Britain would be led by the measures proposed, to change her policy towards the United States. He thought we had the best ground for relying on such an effect.

It is well known, that when she apprehended such measures would be taken, she manifested a readiness to admit a greater reciprocity into the commerce between the two countries. A bill for the purpose was brought into the house of commons by the present minister Mr. Pitt, and would probably have passed into a law, if hopes had not sprung up that they should be able to maintain their exclusive system.[13] Knox, an under secretary, appears from a collection of papers published by him, to have been the chief adviser in the cabinet, as Lord Sheffield was the great champion before the public, of this experiment. It was founded according to both these witnesses,[14] on a belief—1st. That Nova-Scotia and Canada, would soon be able to feed the West-Indies, and thereby make them independent of supplies from the United States. 2dly. That the general government was so feeble that it could not execute a plan of retaliating restrictions—and, 3dly. That local interests and prejudices predominated so much among the states, that they would never even agree in making an attempt.

It is now thoroughly understood and admitted by the most biassed judges, that the British continental colonies cannot supply the islands; that as well as the islands, they depend frequently for essential supplies on the United States. This calculation therefore has failed Great-Britain.

The next has been completely destroyed by the change of our former frail confederacy, into a government which is found to be adequate to all its national objects. This hope has therefore in like manner failed.

The only remaining hope that can induce Great-Britain to persevere in the plan of conduct she has adopted towards the United States, lies in the supposed difficulty of reconciling their different interests and local prejudices. The present occasion will decide whether this hope also shall be withdrawn from her; or whether she is to be inspired with fresh confidence in pursuing her own interests without a due respect either for our interests or for our rights.

He could not but view the present as perhaps the final chance of combining the opinions and interests of the several quarters of the Union in some proper and adequate plan. If at a moment when so many occurrences conspire to unite the public councils; when the public mind is so well disposed to second all equitable and peaceable means of doing justice to our country; and when our commerce is so critically important to the vital resources of Great-Britain, it should be found that nothing can be done, he could foresee no circumstances under which success was to be expected. To reject the propositions therefore, whilst nothing better was substituted, must convey the most unfavorable impressions of our national character, and rivet the fetters on our commerce, as well as prolong other causes which had produced such injurious consequences to our country. He would not permit himself to apprehend that such would be the event of the deliberations of the committee.

Philadelphia Gazette, 27 Feb. 1794 (also reported in *Philadelphia Gazette*, 16 Jan. 1794, *General Advertiser*, 16, 17, and 18 Jan. 1794, and *Gazette of the U.S.*, 17, 18, and 20 Jan. 1794). Reprinted in James Madison, *Speech in the House of Representatives of the Congress of the United States, Delivered January 14, 1794, by James Madison, of Virginia, in Support of His Propositions for the Promotion of the Commerce of the United States, and in Reply to William Smith, of South Carolina* (New York, 1794; Evans 27258), pp. 1–27.

1. JM gleaned these figures from Sheffield, *Observations on Commerce* (1784 ed.), pp. 136–37. For his previous use of this information, see For the *National Gazette*, 19 Nov. 1791, *PJM*, 14:119, 122 n. 3.

2. On 30 Apr. 1784 the Continental Congress passed resolutions recommending that the states grant to Congress for fifteen years the power to exclude the carrying trade of nations not having a commercial treaty with the U.S. and cargoes imported in ships not of the same country of origin (*JCC*, 26:322).

3. JM's reciprocity proposals for the impost and tonnage bills of 1789 passed the House but were defeated in the Senate (*PJM*, 12:54–55).

4. Hamilton's "Statement of the Actual Tonnage of American Vessels," 10 Jan. 1794 (*ASP, Commerce and Navigation*, 1:252).

5. This discount was provided for in section 5 of the Impost Act of 1789 (*U.S. Statutes at Large*, 1:27).

6. The figures in this and the succeeding paragraph appear in JM's List of Imports, 1789–1790, ca. 29 Dec. 1793, probably based on an "authentic document" supplied by Tench Coxe.

7. JM arrived at these figures by calculating the differences between exports and imports as stated in the "Report of the Secretary of State on the Privileges and

Restrictions on the Commerce of the United States in Foreign Countries" of 16 Dec. 1793 (*ASP, Foreign Relations*, 1:301).

8. Anderson, *Origin of Commerce* (1790 ed.), 6:699.

9. For JM's previous use of this example, see For the *National Gazette*, 20 Mar. 1792, *PJM*, 14:257–59 and n. 1.

10. Great Britain concluded the Methuen Treaty with Portugal in 1703 and the Eden Treaty with France in 1786.

11. JM paraphrased part of Washington's 5 Dec. 1793 message to Congress (*ASP, Foreign Relations*, 1:141).

12. "Report on the American Fisheries by the Secretary of State," 1 Feb. 1791, appendix no. 18 (Boyd, *Papers of Jefferson*, 19:236). JM provided this information for Jefferson in his memorandum of ca. 31 Jan. 1791 (*PJM*, 13:362–63).

13. During the last days of Lord Shelburne's government in 1783, William Pitt the younger as chancellor of the exchequer (then in his liberal period) proposed an American intercourse bill to reestablish commercial relations on the basis of reciprocity. Shelburne's ministry had already lost a vote of confidence over the terms of the peace treaty with the U.S., and the new Fox-North coalition won passage of an alternative bill that authorized the king in council to regulate trade with the U.S. (Setser, *Commercial Reciprocity Policy of the United States, 1774–1829*, p. 44; *Hansard's Parliamentary Debates*, 23:609–11, 724–25, 762; 23 Geo. 3, chap. 39, *Statutes at Large* [1786 ed.], 14:331).

14. William Knox, *Extra Official State Papers Addressed to the Right Hon. Lord Rawdon* (2 vols.; London, 1789), 2: appendix, 69–71, 75–76; Sheffield, *Observations on Commerce* (1784 ed.), pp. 168, 198–200.

Commercial Discrimination

[15 January 1794]

Ames objected to a motion to go into Committee of the Whole, since papers from the secretary of state, relating to negotiations with Britain for a commercial treaty, had not yet been printed for the House.

Mr. Madison said that it was somewhat singular, that an objection should be made to the going into a committee for the want of these papers. This want ought to have been stated upon Monday. As to the idea of a friendly disposition on the part of Britain, for entering into a treaty of commerce, he was convinced that Britain had no disposition that way. This he inferred from some passages in the speech of the President, which were, at his desire, read by the clerk. He trusted that the house would not hesitate in resolving itself into a committee of the whole immediately, in order to discuss the propositions.

Philadelphia Gazette, 18 Jan. 1794 (reprinted in *General Advertiser*, 21 Jan. 1794).

[15 January 1794]

In Committee of the Whole, FitzSimons opposed JM's first resolution of 3 January, saying it "was by far too indefinite."

Mr. Madison regarded the objection of the gentleman as entirely of a new kind. He had refused his consent to the first of the resolutions, because it was indefinite. But the propositions laid before the house a few days ago, with respect to the Algerines,[1] were fully as indefinite; and yet the gentleman who spoke last had recommended them. The order of proceedings, in the present question, were perfectly candid and regular. They were consonant to the practice of the house, and the practice of the gentleman himself.

Philadelphia Gazette, 18 Jan. 1794 (reprinted in *General Advertiser*, 21 Jan. 1794).

1. JM referred to the House resolutions of 2 Jan. providing for a naval force against the Algerine corsairs. FitzSimons was chairman of the select committee appointed to report on that naval force and the ways and means necessary to meet its cost (*Annals of Congress*, 3d Cong., 1st sess., 154-55).

¶ To John Dawson. Letter not found. *15 January 1794.* Acknowledged in Dawson to JM, 23 Jan. 1794. Mentions two causes of opposition to JM's resolutions on commercial discrimination.

From Alexander White

DEAR SIR   WOODVILLE 19th. January 1794
    I cannot dispense with making my acknowledgements for your attention, and the communications you have favd. me with[1]—in return I have little to inform you, the season has been unfavourable to the winter grain, the early fall of snow is nearly gone, and tho' we have had some moderate weather the frost has at other times been very severe.
    We are anxious to hear the event of the representation to the French Goverment on the subject of Mr Genets conduct, indeed nothing but anxious thoughts can arise from every reference to Foreign Nations. Every Nation no doubt has a right to secure peace to herself, but the manner in which that between Portugal and Algiers was brought about is truly alarming. I still however hope that by proper exertions on our part the greatest of all Calamities War, may be prevented—and that the People awakened by the sense of danger will submit to the necessary burdens. Various reports respecting men and measures circulate here, which I need not repeat, because if true, they will be authenticated

before I could possibly receive an answer to this. Sally Hite was married last Tuesday to Alexr Pitt Buchanan of Baltimore. I am with real regard Your sincere Friend

ALEXR WHITE

RC (DLC). Docketed by JM.

1. Letters not found.

From John Dawson

DEAR SIR!   RICH: Januy 20. 94.

On my return to this place on saturday evening I haves [*sic*] favourd with your letter of the 31. of the last month, with its enclosure, for which I thank you.

By the en[c]losd paper[1] you will find that the situation of the republic of France is very flattering. I was in Suffolk when the sloop arrivd, & think that the accounts which she brings may be depended on—but presume you will by this have all the particulars, as the despatches to the minister have, no doubt, gone on.

I think with you on the subject of the Algerine business, and highly approve the resolutions which you have offerd to the Committee—they will no doubt be opposd by a certain party, tho I trust without success.

I wrote Colo Monroe & yourself some time ago fully relative to the British frigate the Dædalus. I will now only observe, inter nos, that the French Consul, Oster,[2] at Norfolk, is one about whom many suspicions are entertaind at Norfolk—that he & the B. Consul, are frequently together, and in no case has he appeard to have exerted himself in behalf of his nation.

We shall be in a very disagreeable situation for some months the citizens having this day determind on a general innoculation for the small pox.[3] With real regard Yr. friend & Sert

J DAWSON

RC (DLC).

1. On 8 Jan. the Richmond *Va. Gazette, and General Advertiser* published reports that the French government had recaptured Lyons after a counterrevolutionary insurrection and had recalled Genet.

2. Martin Oster served as French vice-consul at Philadelphia, 1781–83, and Richmond and Norfolk, 1783–92. Though he took a loyalty oath, the revolutionary government recalled him. He evidently remained at Norfolk but held no diplomatic post at the time Dawson was writing. During the Napoleonic regime, he became French vice-commissary for commercial relations at Norfolk (Nasatir and Monell,

French Consuls, pp. 566–67, 550–51; Childs, "French Consul Martin Oster," *VMHB*, 76 [1968]: 39).

3. The mayor and corporation of Richmond authorized smallpox inoculations from 25 Jan. to 27 Feb. (Richmond *Va. Gazette, and General Advertiser*, 15 and 29 Jan. 1794).

Commercial Discrimination

[20 January 1794]

Smith (South Carolina) observed that supporters of JM's resolutions had argued that Britain had demonstrated no desire for a commercial treaty with the United States. Smith alleged that in the correspondence between the president and the British minister "as printed by order of the house, it appears, that there is a chasm occasioned by the omission of a letter from the secretary of state, to that minister, which letter is referred [to] in a subsequent letter."

Mr. Madison thought that there was a chasm which should be filled up, but it might do as well to defer the matter for a day or two, till enquiry should be made of the secretary of state, why it had been withheld. Upon informing the president, he would either give it up, or mention the reasons why it should not.

Philadelphia Gazette, 21 Jan. 1794. After debate, the House passed a resolution proposed by Smith requesting the president to submit "the omitted letter, or such parts as he may think proper."

§ From John Dawson. *21 January 1794, Richmond*. Introduces Francis Goode.[1]

RC (DLC). 1 p.

1. Francis Goode (1744–1795) was a justice of the peace and member of the Chesterfield County Committee of Safety in 1774. He represented his county in the House of Delegates, 1778 and 1781–82, and served in the militia as a captain, 1777, and colonel, 1787–89 (*DAR Patriot Index*, p. 274; *VMHB*, 14 [1906–7]: 90; *WMQ*, 1st ser., 5 [1896–97]: 102; Swem and Williams, *Register*, p. 379; Gwathmey, *Historical Register of Virginians*, p. 315; *CVSP*, 4:324, 5:55).

From John Dawson

DEAR SIR!   RICH: Jany 23. 94
On yesterday I recievd your letter of the 15. & on the day before wrote to you.

The opposition made to the resolutions which you presented to the house can only arise from the two causes which you mention, & from the spirit of that party, which I am persuaded is ever ready to sacrifice the interest of the country, for the advancement of individuals. I trust it will prove abortive. If it does not I shall despond.

Will you be kind enough to forward to you[1] the paper containing your answer to Mr Smith's observations, part of which I have seen. They are such as I expected. With much regard & esteem Yr. friend & Sert

J DAWSON

RC (DLC).

1. Dawson should have written "me."

From Henry Lee

Jany 23d. 94.

I had the pleasure my dear sir to receive your letter by Mr. Adair & shall pay every attention to that gentleman. He seems to be a man of letters & a man of worth. We hear nothing here but what must be known to you. A report has prevailed for some days past that Mr. Randolph is appointed Secretary of State, Lewis Attorney general[1] & Mr Genet recalled. The conduct of the latter gentleman is so different from what I had conceived from the few moments I spent with him that I am lost in my attempts to account for it. I am very happy to find Congress proceed with temper & in evident attention to our critical situation. Your late propositions I have read & approve the principle on which they are founded but do not so far understand our connexions with forgeign [sic] nations as to say to what extent the policy should be carried or whether this moment is proper to apply it. Indeed to Judge with truth on these two points a very accurate knowledge of our foreign relationships commercial & other is an indispensible prerequisite. What is the true state of the So. Carolina attempt to embody men?[2] Much is said about it but I cannot discover the situation of that matter. I see only scraps of Congressional debates generally so brief as to be unintelligible. I suppose the printers have not yet recovered from their share in the late Calamity.[3]

RC (DLC). Signature clipped.

1. Lee was misled by rumors of the appointment of Philadelphia Federalist William Lewis. Washington in fact appointed William Bradford (whom JM had known as an undergraduate at the College of New Jersey) as attorney general (*PJM*, 1:73 n. 1).

2. The Democratic societies claimed the right of citizens to expatriate themselves by serving in foreign armed forces. On 7 Dec. 1793 the South Carolina General Assembly passed a joint resolution condemning efforts by members of the Republican Society of that state to recruit U.S. citizens to serve in the armed forces of France in violation of Washington's Neutrality Proclamation (Eugene Perry Link, *The Democratic-Republican Societies, 1790–1800* [New York, 1942], pp. 136–37; *Acts and Resolutions of the General Assembly of the State of South Carolina, Passed in December, 1793* [Charleston, 1794; Evans 27718], pp. 15–16).

3. Freneau suspended the *National Gazette* on 26 Oct. 1793, promising that he would resume publication "at the opening of the next Congress." But he was unable to revive the newspaper, and some blame apparently fell on the devastating autumn yellow fever epidemic (James M. Lee, *History of American Journalism* [New York, 1917], p. 128).

Commercial Discrimination

[23 January 1794]

In Committee of the Whole, Dexter argued that British regulations had not greatly harmed American prosperity and that JM's resolutions could lead to war with Britain.

Mr. Madison next rose in reply to some remarks made by Mr. Dexter. He said that he wondered how gentlemen could suppose, that to be *war on the table*. Did they suppose Britain so unwise or so unjust as to declare a war. Every consideration of interest must prevent it. He hoped that we did not now deliberate as a colony, but as an independent people, whose measures were not to be dictated by any other powers. What could Britain gain by a contest? Would war employ her starving manufacturers? Would war furnish provisions to her West-India islands which in that case, must also starve? Would war give employment to the vessels that had formerly imported luxuries to America? Were Britain to declare war, he could give no name equal to her folly. She would plunge herself ten times deeper in the difficulties that she wanted to avoid. Every counterregulation would be a stroke against herself.

Philadelphia Gazette, 25 Jan. 1794.

[23 January 1794]

Giles defended JM's resolutions in a long speech.

Mr. Madison rose to take notice of one or two remarks, that had fallen from the gentleman from Massachusetts (Mr. Dexter). He was surprized; he owned, to hear that gentleman say, this country might be considered as enjoying perfect health, after full proof of the injustice of some regulations imposed on us, by the British, was strong in every Member's mind; whilst we are sensible that they incite the Indians on one side, and have let loose the Algerines on the other, whilst our commerce suffers by incessant spoliations; and whilst the treaty of peace, is yet unfulfilled on their part.

Mr. Dexter explained, that he agreed that in a political point of view, we are undoubtedly sufferers; but in a commercial light, the body politic is in full health.

Mr. Madison continued and observed, that before this country grows to the state of vigour intended by nature, we must remove the trammels that impede our growth. He next made some remarks on the observation that had fallen from more than one quarter, that the adoption of the resolutions would excite retaliation on the part of Great-Britain. If the paper on the table, as asserted, is war, war now exists. The resolutions only go half way towards meeting the regulations on the part of Great-Britain. On what pretence could they retaliate? The ground meant to be occupied, we have full right to possess. If, disregarding all prudence and justice, they should incline to resent it, still their interest will prevent them. Great-Britain too much depends on us, for the consumption of her manufactures, and her colonies are too dependent on us, for necessaries, to allow her to retaliate.

But the fear of what Britain might do unjustly, should not deter us from doing what we have a right to do; and notwithstanding the eloquence displayed this day, the committee must still be convinced, that they have a right to deliberate on the interests and to maintain the rights of Americans.

General Advertiser, 5 Feb. 1794.

Commercial Discrimination

[24 January 1794]

In Committee of the Whole, Dayton asserted: "If we really labor under wrongs, something more effectual than the measures proposed should be contemplated; but first it is our duty, to endeavor to obtain redress by pacific means, and before irritating measures are adopted, we should be well assured that redress has been refused."

Mr. Madison saw no ground to hope for redress from negociation, we must be satisfied that that resource has failed. He could not see, admitting we are injured, that we are bound by honor or prudence, to resent the injury, by the last appeal, to arms. It is best, he conceived, to try whether a more pacific weapon may not prove even more effectual. We can make use of none against Great-Britain, more effectual than commercial weapons, in that part, their commerce, that country is most vulnerable. He thought this the most eligible time for the exercise of those means most clearly in our power.

Gazette of the U.S., 13 Feb. 1794 (reprinted in *General Advertiser*, 13 Feb. 1794).

From Joseph Jones

Dr. Sr.   Fredg. 25th. Janry. 1794

I have yours[1] inclosing a paper of the 20th. inst. which rather weakens than strengthens the report of the good fortune of the French in vanquishing and capturing the D. York & his army, and of the retaking Toulon—events if they shall be verified that cannot fail to make a deep impression on the British nation and increase the number of opponents to the prosecution of the War. The vote agt. refering to the S. T. the ways and means for raising the necessary sum for defence[2] affords a gleam of hope that the influence of that department has not a majority in your House tho' I fear it will be found from some determinations in the Senate that the greater number still consists of the old leven. If our legislature shall not by some proper regulations counteract the British policy respecting our commerce and in an effectual manner too, we shall be contemptible in the eyes of all other nations who possess ideas of independence and national honor—these things have to me appeared so proper that I was among the number of those who in this State before general regulations could be effected was disposed to enact laws to counteract so far as we were able the policy of their navigation act.[3] It should have been among The first acts of the present general government and now when so many additional reasons concur to justify the measure it is astonishing to find any advocates for continuing the old System which is so pernicious to our prosperity and dishonorable to those who advocate and support it. Success attend your endeavours. Yr. friend & Servt

Jos. Jones

RC (DLC). Docketed by JM.

1. Letter not found.
2. On 2 Jan. JM voted with the majority when the House amended a resolution appointing a committee to report on the naval force against the Algerine corsairs. The amendment authorized the committee to report on ways and means to defray the expenses of such a force. Referring legislative proposals to congressional committees rather than to the secretary of the treasury was an issue important to Republicans, particularly Jones (*Annals of Congress*, 3d Cong., 1st sess., 154; Jones to JM, 22 Mar. 1792, *PJM*, 14:259–60 and n. 2).

3. In 1783 the General Assembly adopted a concurrent resolution, drafted by Jones, instructing the Virginia delegation in Congress "that the Legislature approve a treaty of Commerce with Great Britain upon principles of reciprocity" (Instruction to Virginia Delegates, 23-24 May 1783, Jones to JM, 25 May 1783, *PJM*, 7:69, 77).

From Charles Fierer

HOND. SIR   DUMFRIES Jany. 26th 1794

The many civilities I have received from you, Sir, on a former occasion, induces me to solicit your patronage to a petition which the Honble. Richard B. Lee will lay before the Honble. House of which you are a member. I will not take up your time with a detail of the particulars of my case, as the petition and the vouchers attending the same will explain my situation. I will only observe, that having had the misfortune lately to break a leg, which by being injured in the service of this Country during the late war, has made me a Cripple.

Should I be fortunate enough, to obtain in you, Sir, a friend to espouse my cause, my gratitude would be as lasting, as my present situation is distressing. I have the honour to be with Sentiments of perfect respect Hond. Sir, Your most Obt. & very humble Servant

CHARLES FIERER[1]

RC (NN).

1. Charles Fierer (originally Führer) (d. 1794) came to America in 1776 as a Hessian ensign. He defected, accepted a commission in the Continental line, and later served as captain of a Virginia cavalry troop. Injured in a fall from his horse in 1781, he returned to Germany to find himself declared a traitor and his estate confiscated. He published the Georgetown *Times, and Patowmack Packet* (the first newspaper in the federal district), 1789-91, and the Dumfries *Va. Gazette, and Agricultural Repository*, 1791-93. On 11 Dec. 1793 the Virginia General Assembly passed an act directing the auditor of the public accounts to issue Fierer "certificates for the balance of pay and depreciation" due for his state service. On 3 Dec. 1794 the House of Representatives passed a resolution that instructed the Standing Committee of Claims to report a bill placing Fierer on the pension list and allowing him half pay at captain's rank, but six days later he died after a long illness (Alice H. Lerch, "A Printer Soldier of Fortune," *Papers of the Bibliographical Society of America*, 30 [1936]: 92-99; *JHDV*, Oct. 1793, pp. 15-16; Shepherd, *Statutes*, 1:282; *Annals of Congress*, 3d Cong., 2d sess., 955).

¶ From James Madison, Sr. Letter not found. *27 January 1794*. Acknowledged in JM to James Madison, Sr., 21 Feb. 1794. Asks JM to collect interest on his father's U.S. treasury certificates by virtue of power of attorney. Inquires about pecan and apple trees to be planted at Montpelier. Mentions money left at Fredericksburg in November 1793 by JM for his father that has not been received.

Commercial Discrimination

[30 January 1794]

The Committee of the Whole continued its consideration of JM's resolutions.

As it appeared, he said, that most of the objections against the proposed Resolutions, had been made by those who meant to combat them, and that a question would soon be called for; it might perhaps be expected that he should review those objections, and assign the reasons which induced him to continue in the opinion he at first entertained. He wished it not to be understood, that he meant to examine every particular argument, which in the course of so extensive a discussion, had been opposed to the measure. The Committee must have perceived, that some of them had been of a nature not to merit an answer; and that others had sufficiently answered themselves. He should extend his observations to such topics only as might be thought to need explanation, and to have an influence on the question.

Previous, however, to this general survey of the ground which had been travelled over, he should so far presume on the patience of the committee, as to recur to the original opposition made by the member from South Carolina (Mr. Smith); and to take notice of some particulars in what had been urged by him, which were left unanswered at the time.

The gentleman had thought proper to introduce his discourse with a very unmerited attack on the late Secretary of State, and to mingle with it a variety of criticisms on the facts and opinions stated in his report, on the subject under consideration. The spirit and manner in which the attack had been made, and which could not have escaped the attention of the committee, would be left in that silence which may best express the sentiment they must have inspired. He should indeed have thought it less necessary to take further notice than he had already done, of the matter of the gentleman's remarks; if attempts had not been made particularly by a friend of the gentleman (Mr. Ames) to give a weight to his statements and inferences, which it would be shewn they did not merit; and if the task did not afford an opportunity of elucidating some particular points relied on, by the opponents of the resolutions.

It was made a charge against the secretary of State, that he takes no notice of the *higher* duty imposed by Great Britain on other foreign tobacco, than is imposed on American, (the former being 3/6 ster. a pound, the latter 1/3) whilst he takes care to mention the *high* duty imposed on the American; although the discrimination is in favour of the

United States, and is against Portugal, a country in particular connection with Great Britain; and although the high duty of 1/3 is immaterial to the United States, being paid by the consumer of the Tobacco in Great Britain.

It was unfortunate for the gentleman that this charge is fallacious in every member of it.

1. The discrimination is not in favour of the United States, either in its intention, or in its operation: not in its intention, because it was made in reference to this country, when it was a part of the British Empire, and not in reference to us as Independent States; not in its operation, because if the discrimination were abolished, it would bring no rival of our tobacco into the British market. This is proved by the fact, that in other markets, as that of France, where no such discrimination exists, the American tobacco is without a rival. It was well known that this and the other apparent favours to this country, were a remnant of the Old Colonial code, which having become a dead letter in the Statute book, had not yet been struck out of it.

2. If the discrimination had no effect in favor of the United States, it could not, for the same reason, be a prejudice to Portugal. If it were necessary and proper to go into the enquiry, more direct proofs could be given on this point.

3. High duties do affect the United States which produce the article, though paid by the British consumers. They have a double effect: They lessen the quantity called for; and by lessening the competition, they lessen also the price. This was a truth that could need no comment.

It was to be remarked however, that the zeal of the gentleman on this subject was such, that it had led him to extend the fallacy of his reasoning to rice, the staple article of his own State. This article pays a duty of 7/4 ster. per hundred weight, but like the duty on tobacco, being paid by the consumer, was said to be of little concern to us.

Call the price of rice 10/ sterling: the duty is 7/4. The whole class of people, then, in Great-Britain, between the class who cannot afford to eat rice at the price of 10/. and the class who are willing to eat it at 17/4 are prohibited the consumption by the duty. Was this a circumstance of no concern to the rice planters? The gentleman should have been reminded of his error by his own arguments.

As an apology for the duty imposed in Great-Britain, he tells us it was meant to prevent the use of rice as a *substitute*, for the bread-stuffs produced by Great-Britain herself. Without the preventing duty then, rice would have been *substituted* in place of wheat, in the opinion of the British Parliament, and the demand for it, in the British market, so far increased.

As a merit in the British West-India regulations over those of France, it was stated by the gentleman, that rice in the West-Indies is a common food; that in the British, the importation of it is free, in the French, subject to a duty, though an inconsiderable one. In Britain then, where there is a high duty, rice is not an article of common food: in the islands where there is no duty, it is a common food; and the advantage of the British West-India market to us over the French, is, that the duty in the latter favors *cheaper substitutes*.

Another proof of the disposition of Great-Britain to favor the United States in the West-India market, is the prohibition of all foreign rice but the American. The same remark may be repeated here, which was applied to the discrimination in favor of our tobacco. It is an old colony regulation that has no effect whatever. What other foreign rice could be brought to the West-Indies? Is it the East-India rice? That is prohibited by its distance. Is it the rice of Portugal? That is prohibited by the laws of Portugal, and probably also by the lower price of the Carolina rice.

The inference which the gentleman had drawn from the comparative regulations of Great-Britain and France on the subject of rice was so curious that it was worth a moment's attention.

The facts Mr. M. observed, stood thus. In France the duty is ⅓ per cent. In Great-Britain 7/4 sterling a hundred. In the French islands the duty is 1 per cent. In the British free with a prohibition of other foreign rice.

As the duty of 1 per cent. is scarcely sensible, and the prohibition, as shewn, is merely nominal, the inequality in the islands may be regarded as too immaterial to affect the comparison.

Passing to the two parent states, the duty in France is ⅛ per cent. The duty in Great Britain, 50 or 60 per cent.

Here then is nearly an equality in one part, and a difference of 50 or 60 per cent. in the other part of the two dominions; and yet the gentleman could say, it was not easy to pronounce, whether the article of rice stands on a better footing in the system of one, than in the system of the other.

Another charge against the secretary of state is, that his report calls the discriminating duties in Great Britain in favor of American *wood*, small, whereas they are considerable, and in several instances, high.

Mr. M. said he had not found leisure to trace this branch of our exports into all the details necessary to decide in what degree the duties were small or considerable, and in what proportion the several duties articles went to Great Britain. He observed in general that the greater part of our woods were exported to the West Indies, not to Great Britain. That in the ship-woods at least the Baltic nations were not rivals to the United States. It was known that Sweden and Denmark were so deficient in Oak that their public navies were supplied from Germany, and that the ship timbers of Russia were transported a thousand or twelve hundred miles from her interior dominions. The Fir, of which the Swedish and Danish merchant ships were built, does not last more than seven or eight years, and could not therefore be a rival to the durable woods of the United States.

He observed also that lumber, and particularly the ship woods of this country, were so precious and so sure of being in demand, that they never could fear a rival, or need a foreign bounty. This was an article very different from such as were an annual product of the earth, and as could be raised wherever the climate and soil permitted, according to the occasional demand. The forests that were to supply the ship yards were the growth of centuries, and where once destroyed, as they generally are in Europe, are rarely replaced at all, and never can become the rival to America, which enjoys them as the spontaneous gift of nature.

To enhance the merit of the British regulations, the gentleman had told us, that wood was subject to a duty of 1 per cent. in the French Islands, and in the British free, with a prohibition of other foreign wood. This was of little consequence. The duty was a trifle, and falling on a necessary article to be got no where else, probably was paid by the French islanders. And the prohibition was ideal, the American wood being the only resource for the British market.

The article of *Fish*, was admitted by the gentleman himself to be more favored by the French than the British system, tho' he admits it with reluctance and diminishes the difference as much as possible. The case however is so clear, and the facts so palpable, that they speak for themselves. Under the French regulations, this important article of our commerce, is subject to duties only, in Europe and the West Indies. Under the British, it is under prohibition in both. The amount of the whole export is 383,237 quintals of dry, and 57,424 barrels of pickled fish. Of this the French consumption, is 252,171 quintals and 45,164 barrels; that is, nearly ⅔ of the dry, and ⅘ of the pickled fish.

Here Mr. M. proceeding to the subject of whale oil, called the attention of the committee particularly to the representation and language of Mr. Smith as to the conduct of France, in inviting the fishermen of Nantucket to remove and settle at Dunkirk. Mr. Smith, he said, had not only undervalued the monopoly of the French market granted to the United States, but had, by a mutilated quotation of a report of the secretary of state on the fisheries, changed the true aspect of the attempt to draw away the Nantucket fishermen. The fact was, that although the conduct of France was very different from what was to have been wished, as well as from what was contemplated by the marquis la Fayette, who had patronized the interest of the fishermen, yet that the project of tempting them to emigrate had originated in Great-Britain, and was a *counter-project* on the part of France. How the gentleman happened to omit the antecedent attempt of Great-Britain, and thereby exaggerate that of France, Mr. M. did not undertake to explain: but it was the more extraordinary, as the whole account of the transaction was contained in the same page of the report, nay in the same paragraph, from which the gentleman had extracted his information.

Here he read the passage in that report and produced the British statute, inviting the whale-fishermen, by an offer of certain privileges to emigrate to Great-Britain.

A further charge against the secretary of state is that in his statement of the tonnage of the United States employed in the trade with the French and British dominions, he founds it, not on the *actual number of ships*, but on the number of *entries*. This charge was as singular as it was uncandid.

The report stated the fact, that the American tonnage *entering* our ports from the several nations with which the United States traded, was so and so; and, in this statement, it pursued the official returns made on the subject. What more was to be required?

In giving the fact, the Secretary imposed on no one, because he stated the tonnage to be entry tonnage, as it really was.

He followed the best guide that existed, an official return from the proper offices.

No return of the *actual* tonnage, as distinguished from the *entry* tonnage, had at the time, ever been made from any office, or called for by any act, of Congress.

The first return ever made in the latter form, was called for since the Resolutions on the table were proposed.

These considerations might have restrained the gentleman from this unwarranted attack on the accuracy of the Report.

But he ought at least to have been sure, that whilst he was charging the Secretary with following an erroneous guide, he was himself following one that was not erroneous. The examination of this point involved facts which merited the particular attention of the committee.

The statement of the *entry tonnage* of the United States in *foreign* trade for 1792, lately called for and reported, is 415,331 tons. The statement of the *actual tonnage* for the *same* year is 289,394 tons.[1]

On comparing these two quantities, it was evident that both could not be right. If the *entry* tonnage was no more than was stated, it was inconceivable that the *actual* tonnage could be as much as was stated. It would allow the vessels in the European and West India trades together, but some what more than one voyage and a third a year. It could never be supposed, that this corresponded with the fact. How then was the inconsistency in the two statements to be explained? Mr. M. said, as he did not know by what rule the actual tonnage was made up, he would form no conjecture on the subject. He hoped, and wished that some gentleman more conversant with it, would solve the phenomenon. He did not call on the gentleman from South Carolina, because he most of all, must be puzzled to account for it; having stated that our vessels in the trade to Europe make *two* voyages, and in the West India trade *four* voyages a year.

Besides the evidence contained in this comparison of the aggregate tonnage in the two different forms, in which it had been reported, the existence of error somewhere, and probably in the account of the actual tonnage resulted from a comparative view of our exports to the British dominions, for the two years of 1790 and 1792, and of the whole tonnage American and British employed in conveying them.

In the former year the exports were 9,363,416 dollars. In the latter 8,269,495 dollars: the excess for 1790, 1,093,921 dollars.

The entry tonnage, British and American for 1790, was 273,580 tons. The British *entry* tonnage for 1792 was 206,384 tons. The *actual* American tonnage for 1792, was, according to the official statement, 66,582 tons: which turned into entry tonnage, according to the proportion of the whole actual, to the whole entry tonnage for that year, makes the American entry tonnage, in the trade to Great Britain about 95,000 tons. Adding this to the British entry tonnage of 206,384 tons, the British and American together for 1792, amounts to 301,384 tons; which exceeds the tonnage of 1790 no less than 27,804 tons.

According to this calculation, which embraces the actual tonnage as stated to the house, there would be 27,804 tons more, employed in transporting 1,093,921 dollars less; making our tonnage to increase in that proportion as the employment of it decreased.

There was a possibility, Mr. M. observed, that the course of trade in the two years, might be such that more of the vessels employed in the exportations to Great Britain, might be entered in 1790 as coming from some other country, than in 1792; but as there was no known circumstance which authorized this solution, and as it seemed demonstrable in general, that error existed somewhere in the statements, and most probably in those of the actual tonnage, he concluded that it ought to be referred to that source; and consequently, that the guide followed by the secretary of state, to wit, the entry tonnage, the only one he had to follow, was not more inaccurate, than the actual tonnage would have been, which guided the member from South Carolina.

Another position of the secretary of state on which a charge is founded is, "that the *greater* part of what Great Britain receives from the United States is re-exported."[2] This position, Mr. M. reminded the committee, related to Great Britain, without comprehending the West India islands; which formed a distinct branch in the secretary's report. How far it was liable to the exceptions taken against it, would appear from an examination of facts.

To obviate criticisms, Mr. M. said he would take for the basis of his calculations, the statement given in detail by the gentleman himself, of the exports for 1790 to the French and British dominions; which though not extended to every item, approached so near to a full view of the trade, as to be adequate to the purpose.

In this statement the exports to Great Britain stand at 6,651,429 dollars: from which must be subtracted, for the comparison, the amount of the several re-exportations as far as they can be liquidated.

TOBACCO. It appears from an official document, that the tobacco exported to Great-Britain in 1791, was 67,286 hogsheads. A return for another year states the quantity to be 52,505 hogsheads.[3] It appeared from the revenue returns of Great-Britain, that the consumption of this article amounted to 9,600 hogsheads. The proportion re-exported might then be reasonably set down at four-fifths of the quantity imported.

RICE. To obtain the proportion of rice re-exported, we may take the medium quantity imported for three years immediately preceding the revolution, which, according to a table in Anderson's History of Commerce, was 486,543 cwt. By another table for the same period, the medium quantity exported was 349,653 cwt. The difference marks the consumption, and is 136,890 cwt. The quantity exported to Great Britain from the United States in 1792, was 58,978 barrels, equal to 294,890 cwt. Comparing the quantity consumed with this quantity, it appears that more than half, though less than two-thirds, is re-exported—call the re-exportation one-half only of the present importation.

INDIGO. According to a statement in Anderson, the medium importations into Great-Britain, for three years immediately preceding the revolution, were about thrice the medium quantity exported.[4] Call the proportion re-exported now, however, one-fifth only, which is probably below the fact.

From these proportions, and the data furnished by the gentleman's own statements, results the following justification of the report of the Secretary on this point.

		dollars.
Exports to Great Britain		6,651,429
Tobacco	2,754,493 dolls.		
Consumed ⅕,	550,898		
Re-exported,		2,203,495	
Rice,	773,852		
Consumed ½,	386,926		
Re-exported,		386,925	
Indigo,	473,830		
Consumed ⅘,	379,064		
Re-exported,		94,766	

Wheat and flour, perhaps the whole re-exported: and more was carried to Great-Britain in the two succeeding years, though the aggregate exports thither were less than in the year here taken: say however, that one-fourth was consumed, and let the amount stand according to the gentleman's statement, at

	1,087,840		
Consumed ¼,	271,960		
Re-exported,		815,880	
		3,501,067	

Here, then, it appears, that the re-exportations of the four articles alone, of Tobacco, Rice, Indigo and Wheat, are greater than the whole consumption in Great-Britain, of the articles imported from the United States, although the most unfavourable year has been taken, for the enquiry; and, consequently, that the position of the Secretary of State, was well founded.

If it were necessary to investigate the full amount of re-exportations, several articles might have been added to the list, such as Whale-Oil, Ginseng, Flax-Seed, &c.

Nor would it be unfair, perhaps, to include the primitive value of the articles, re-exported in the new forms given to them by art. A great proportion of what is sent from the United States to Great Britain, in a rude state, is worked into articles of merchandize, and exported in the course of trade. Take, for example, the two articles of Pot and Pearl Ashes, and Indigo.

The amount of the export of the former to Great-Britain, is stated at 747,078 dollars; of which, if no part is re-exported in its unaltered state, the whole enters into British manufactures. Supposing one-third of these particular manufactures, to be exported, which appears to be nearly the general proportion, the value of Pot and Pearl Ashes re-exported, is 249,026 dollars. The Indigo used in Great-Britain has appeared to be 379,064 dollars, one-third of which re-exported as an ingredient in manufactures, is 126,354⅔ dollars. These two items alone amount to 375,380⅔ dollars, and with many others, might be added to the mass of re-exportations. But they are stated rather to throw light on the general character of our trade with G. Britain, than to be relied on in the present case, which has been sufficiently elucidated by more direct and simple views of it.

Mr. M. proceeded to apply the calculations he had made, to the question discussed by Mr. Smith, in relation to the comparative importance of the French and British markets to the productions of the United States.

By deducting the 3,501,067 dollars, re-exported, from the 6,651,429 dollars, imported into Great Britain, he reduced her actual consumption to 3,150,362 dollars, to which adding the 1,805,744 exported to the West India market, the whole British consumption stands at no more than 4,956,106 dollars. On comparing this with the exports to the French dominions (which re-export none of any consequence) to wit, 4,424,336, the subject took a very different aspect from that which had been given to it.

But there was, Mr. M. observed, a circumstance of the utmost importance to a fair view of this question, which had been wholly overlooked by the gentleman from S. Carolina, and which cut up his calculations by the roots. The re-exportations from G. Britain were not only to be subtracted from the consumption of G. Britain, but in a great degree being made to France, were *to be added to the value of her market* to the agriculture and commerce of the United States.

The re-exportations from G. Britain to France, could not be accurately fixed by any documents to be had here. In general, they were known to be great. He would, he said, confine himself to the two articles of Tobacco and Flour, of which he estimated the amounts as follows:

The Tobacco exported from the United States, appears to be about 100,000 hhds. It is valued in the return of our exports at 4,349,567 dollars. It is known that France consumes about ¼ of the whole quantity exported, that is, 1,087,392 dollars. It appears, by the return of our exports, that the *direct* exports of this article to France, stands at 384,642 dollars. The *indirect* supplies then to France, not appearing in the returns of our exports, and to be added to them, is 702,750 dollars.

Of the Flour and Grain sent to Great-Britain, allowing, as above stated, ¼ to have been there consumed, which is probably beyond the truth, the re-exportation amounted to 815,880 dollars. It is well understood, that France was the market where these articles were finally consumed. The account may now be stated,

	dollars.
To the French Market, directly exported for consumption,	4,424,336
Tobacco indirectly exported for do.	702,705
Wheat and Flour indirectly exported for do.	815,880
Total of French consumption,	5,942,921
Total of British do.	4,956,106
Excess of French consumption,	986,815

Thus it appears, without taking into the account the other articles re-exported to France, that the market of that country for our exports, was worth to the U. States nearly a million more than the market of Great Britain—and yet the gentleman from South Carolina had represented the British market as exceeding the French in the annual amount of between three and four millions; and had pronounced, without hesitation that G. Britain in reference to our productions, was *a more important customer* than France, almost in the *ratio of two to one.*

Mr. M. returning to the Secretary's report said, he hoped after what had been shewn, it would be needless to trouble the committee, with further remarks on the subject. In dismissing it however, he could not do justice to his own impressions, without declaring his entire confidence, that the report would be regarded by all discerning and unprejudiced judges, as one of the many monuments which its Author had left behind him, of the zeal, the talents, and the patriotism with which he had discharged the duties of his station; and that he had carried with him into retirement, a purity, both in his public and private name, which nothing that could be said within or without the walls of Congress, could tarnish.

Having gone thro' the particular observations into which he had been led by the attack made on the report of the Secretary of State before the committee, he should proceed, to a more general view of what had been urged by the opponents of the resolutions he had introduced.

Among other things it had been alledged in the latter stages of the debate, that the friends of the resolutions had involved themselves in inconsistency, by shifting the ground of argument from commercial to political considerations. In answer to this charge, he remarked, that if in any instance of his public life he was free from the charge of inconsistency, it was on the subject of vindicating our national interests, against the policy of Great-Britain towards us: that in all the public stations with which he had been honored since the peace, and on every occasion which had occurred, his conduct had been marked by an adherence to this principle: that the resolutions he had last proposed were founded on this principle: that if in the first arguments supporting them, he had dwelt chiefly on commercial topics, it would be recollected that he kept the door open for political ones, if the turn of the discussions should require them: that he had forborne to enlarge on the political sides of the question, because he thought it defensible on commercial grounds, and was willing to meet it on those grounds, because he did not wish to mingle unnecessarily, irritating ideas in the discussion, and because he had supposed that every thing relating to the treaty of peace, the Indians, the Algerines, the spoliations, &c. were sufficiently imprinted on every mind, and would have all the effects they ought to have, without being particularly enforced.

Whilst he could thus repel the charge of inconsistency brought against himself; it must be evident he thought, how much room there was for retorting the charge. In the early stages of the discussion, there seemed but one sentiment as to the conduct of Great-Britain, at least in a political view; the difference turned on the question, whether we could or ought to counteract her conduct. In the latter stages of the discussion, palliations if not justifications had been multiplied & labored; not only with respect to her commercial policy, but with respect to the detention of the posts, the Indians, the Algerines, and even the spoliations of our neutral commerce; on the unlawfulness of which our executive had grounded the remonstrance and demand of indemnification lying on the table.[5]

In addition to this, he stated the inconsistency between those who maintained and those who rejected the theory of leaving commerce perfectly free; the inconsistency of rejecting this theory, and yet refusing to meet restrictions on one side, with restrictions on the other; the inconsistency of condemning a commercial discrimination between nations, as contrary to the wise example of Great-Britain, and claiming for Great-Britain the credit of making such discriminations in favor of the United States: The inconsistency of predicting that the measure would destroy the revenue, and insisting that the dutied articles would continue to be imported from the same source, through more expensive channels: The inconsistency of exclaiming against topics and remarks which may awaken the passions, and endeavoring themselves to alarm our fears; of exhorting the committee to consult its judgment alone, and substituting for argument continued addresses to the imagination.

Particular pains, he remarked, had been taken to exhibit a picture of our national prosperity, which might flatter our wishes, and forbid experiments. It was readily admitted, he said, that there were many features in the face of our affairs, which were proper themes of mutual congratulation, whether compared with the situation of other countries, or with our own, under other circumstances. And it gave him much pleasure to add, that the degree of prosperity we enjoyed, though not to be exclusively credited to the change of our federal government, or to particular measures under it, according to the exaggerations of some, was yet so far, and so evidently the fruit of that change, as to do honor to the people of America in adopting it. He mentioned two innovations making part of the constitution, which must alone, have had a powerful effect in meliorating the condition of this country, to wit: The prohibition of paper money or other violations of contracts, and the abolition of incoherent and rival regulations of trade, among the several states. But notwithstanding the flourishing state of our affairs, when viewed under certain aspects, it was equally certain that there were others, which suggested very different reflexions.

He then went into a review of the actual state of our commerce, particularly in relation to Great-Britain; and of the several injuries of another sort, which that nation had superadded to her commercial restrictions.

He repeated what he had formerly maintained, that there was more of reciprocity in the footing of commerce between Great-Britain and other countries, and between other countries and the United States, than between Great-Britain & the United States. To prove the first point he remarked that in some instances Great-Britain had treaties with other countries which defined & stipulated reciprocal privileges; in other instances, her restrictions were counter-vailed by laws imposing restrictions on her. To prove the second point, he remarked that no other nation with which the United States carried on commerce, had a navigation act similar to that of Great-Britain.

With respect to the intercourse between the United States and Great-Britain, there was, he insisted, a want of reciprocity throughout, that must strike the most superficial observer.

In the article of navigation this had been sufficiently pointed out, and being admitted on all sides, need not be repeated.

In the trade between the two countries, our best staples, wheat and flour, fish and oil, salted provisions, which amount to considerably more than one-third of our exports, were shut out of her markets; whilst all her best staples, her woolens, her cottons, her manufactures of the metals, of leather, and of silk, were admitted on moderate duties, and enjoyed in a manner a monopoly of our market.

In the articles of superfluity mutually admitted, there was nothing to compensate the inequality in other cases. Our tobacco paid a tax of four or five hundred per cent, our rice fifty or sixty per cent. and our manufactures of every sort would not be admitted if we were ever so able to send them. On the other hand, her superfluities were received under duties, which in general did not exceed from seven and an half to fifteen per cent.

In the West-India trade, besides the exclusion of our vessels, whilst her own were left free, there were a number of our productions which were not admitted into the market there, whilst our laws refused nothing that was brought to the market here.

He next turned his attention to the injuries and losses we suffered in other respects.

As he had not possessed himself of the evidence, he should, he said, leave it to those who had, to shew how far the Indians were or were not spurred on to war against us, by the agents or partisans of Great-Britain. It was a sufficient ground of complaint, that the posts were wrongfully detained; that the detention had a baneful influence on the sentiments and conduct of the Indians; and that the supplies for their warfare, were derived from a trade, authorised by the British government, and protected by the posts which of right were ours, and ought to be used for our defence. He combined this proceeding of Great-Britain, with the lawless seizure of our vessels under her instructions of the 8th of June last, observing, that whilst on one side, she violated the laws of nations, by carrying on a trade in contraband articles with those at war with us; she was on another side, violating the laws of nations, by intercepting our trade with those at war with her, in articles not contraband.

The Indian war he observed, cost us annually a sum, exceeding by one million, the sum that would probably be sufficient for the defence of our frontier, if the posts were in our hands. The fur trade depending on the posts might, he thought, be fairly valued at two hundred thousand dollars more.

The Algerine depredations appeared to have proceeded from the steps taken in pursuance of the views of the British government. If they were not immediately pointed against us, it must have been known that our trade would be the victim. The evil therefore may at least be charged to an unfriendly disregard of our interests, if not to a positive hostility to them. The pecuniary amount of this evil, cannot be rated at less than the expence of the armament proposed as a remedy. This is stated at six hundred thousand dollars for the outfit; and he did not expect that the annual expence would average much less; to which may be added, at a

very low computation, for insurance remaining after the armament, two
hundred thousand dollars.

The spoliations committed on our neutral commerce by Great-Britain,
must be of considerable, though very uncertain amount; and the consequential detriment to our trade in general from these interruptions and
dangers, of a very great, though equally uncertain amount. In order to
bring both within a safe estimate, he said he would state the former at the
limited sum of one hundred and fifty thousand dollars, and the latter
at no more than four hundred thousand dollars.

In addition to the foregoing estimates he said there was another item,
which, though of a different character, fell under a comprehensive view
of our situation; and being reducible to an amount tolerably definite,
ought to find a place here. He referred to the statement before quoted
from a report of the Secretary of State, which shewed that the loss to the
United States from a dependence on British bottoms for the carriage of
their produce was no less annually, in time of war than, three million two
hundred and fifty thousand dollars, and in war and peace averaged, no
less than one million three hundred ninety-two thousand eight hundred
fifty-seven dollars. Allowing about one third of this carriage for the reasonable share of Great-Britain (and for reasons formerly derived from
the character of our exports this was a full share) the annual loss from
the dependence might be called about one million of dollars.

These calculations he recapitulated thus:

Indian war	1,000,000 dollars
Fur trade	200,000
Algerine depredations	600,000
Insurance not reduced by the naval armament	200,000
British spoliations	150,000
Consequential detriment to our trade	400,000
Dependence on British bottoms	1,000,000
	3,550,000 dollars

From this view of things, it was impossible to deny, that however
prosperous the U. States might be in some respects, they were in others
laboring under violations of their rights and interests, which demanded
the serious attention of the legislature. Besides the unreciprocal footing
of their commerce, and the indignities offered them, it was seen that
they were burdened with an enormous extra expence, and involved in
unjust losses, amounting to more than three and a half millions of dollars a year; a tax nearly equal to the heavy one they had been obliged to
impose on themselves.

Having taken this view of our situation, he proceeded to consider how far a remedy was comprised in the resolutions before the committee, by tracing the probable operation of them, if passed into a law. (In this stage of his observations, the hour of adjournment being nearly arrived, he sat down, with an intimation that the subject would be renewed.)

Philadelphia Gazette, 28 Feb. 1794 (reprinted in *Gazette of the U.S.*, 4, 5, 6, and 7 Mar. 1794, and Madison, *Speech in the House of Representatives*, pp. 27–45; also reported in *Philadelphia Gazette*, 1 Feb. 1794).

1. JM gleaned these figures from Hamilton's "Comparative View of Tonnage, Domestic and Foreign, for the Years 1789, 1790, 1791, and 1792" of 7 and 10 Jan. 1794 (*ASP, Commerce and Navigation*, 1:251, 252).

2. JM paraphrased part of Jefferson's "Report of the Secretary of State on the Privileges and Restrictions on the Commerce of the United States in Foreign Countries" of 16 Dec. 1793 (*ASP, Foreign Relations*, 1:302).

3. JM gleaned these figures from Tench Coxe's statements of American exports for 1791 and 1792, which Hamilton submitted to the Senate on 16 Mar. 1792 and 28 Feb. 1793 respectively (*ASP, Commerce and Navigation*, 1:130, 241).

4. Anderson, *Origin of Commerce* (1790 ed.), 6:606–7.

5. Among the papers submitted to Congress with his message of 5 Dec. 1793, Washington included Jefferson's letter to Thomas Pinckney, 7 Sept. 1793. In that letter the secretary of state directed the U.S. minister to Britain to "endeavor to obtain a revocation" of the order in council of 8 June "and full indemnification to any citizens of these States, who may have suffered by it" (*ASP, Foreign Relations*, 1:239).

Commercial Discrimination

[31 January 1794]

In Committee of the Whole, JM continued his speech from the previous day.

Resuming the train of his observations, he proceeded to explain the remedial operation of his propositions.

First. They will make the British nation sensible that we can, by just and pacific means, inflict consequences which will make it her interest, to pay a just regard to our rights and interests.

To enforce this tendency, he enlarged on the ideas he had formerly expressed in relation to the dependence of Great-Britain on the commerce of the United States, and the obvious and essential dependence of the British West-Indies, on the supplies of the United States.

On the latter subject, he entered into a particular reply to the member from Massachusetts (Mr. Ames,) who had argued that the British regulation of the trade between the United States and the West-Indies, was conformable to the principles of the Colony system as established by the commercial nations of Europe, and could not therefore be reasonably complained of. 2. That the West-Indies could obtain supplies from other quarters, and did not therefore depend on the United States; nay, that there was danger, by forcing these supplies into other channels, of our losing that branch of trade altogether. 3. That the trade would hardly employ more than a dozen brigs, and was therefore not worth contending for.

In answer to the first argument of Mr. Ames, Mr. M. undertook to shew, that Great-Britain had not pursued, but violated the principle of the colony system. The true spirit of this system, he said, was to confine the trade between the parent country and the colony, to their own vessels, and to allow as little trade as possible, between the colony and foreign countries; but when a trade with a foreign country became necessary to the colony, *to allow the foreign vessels the same carrying privileges allowed to their own.* Colonies, he said, were to be considered as parts of a common empire. The trade between one part and another, as between London and Kingston in Jamaica, was to be considered, equally an internal trade with the coasting trade between London and Liverpool, or the trade between different ports of the United States: and might, if deemed expedient, be equally restrained to domestic bottoms. But when a trade was opened between a colony and a foreign country, the case was changed: the foreign country became a party, and had a reciprocal claim to the use of its bottoms, as much in the trade with the colony, as with any other part of the empire, to which the colony belonged. In support of this doctrine, Mr. M. referred to the example of every nation in Europe, except that of Great-Britain, which had American colonies. Denmark, Sweden, the United Netherlands, France, Spain and Portugal, had their colonies, as well as Great-Britain; and some of them, rigorously attached to the principles of the colony system: yet not a single one of these nations had refused, whenever a trade was permitted at all between the colonies and another country, to make the carriage common to the vessels of both the parties. Great-Britain alone had attempted a monopoly in such cases for her own vessels. Her example therefore was an innovation on the colony system, as well as an infraction of the rights of reciprocity.

In answer to the 2d position of Mr. A. he denied that permanent supplies of provisions and lumber could be derived from any other part of the world than the United States: not from the northern parts of Europe, which either did not produce, or were too remote to send them: not from the southern parts of Europe, which depended themselves on the northern parts and on America: not from Great Britain, which imported bread, for her own use, amounting one year with another according to the report of the committee of the privy council,[1] to the sum of near three hundred thousand pounds sterling, and was, certainly not an exporter of lumber: not from Ireland, which could not pretend to rival the United States in any article but that of salt provisions; and this was so much dearer that a prohibition alone of ours, could gain a market for hers. The gentleman had relied on the capacity of Ireland to extend her cultivation of wheat, so as to spare supplies of this article also. Such a revolution in her interior state was not very probable. But he ought at least to have remembered, that as the pasture lands of Ireland should be turned into wheat fields, her export of beef would decrease, in proportion as she might be enabled to export bread.

It was a waste of time, Mr. M. said, to disprove by minute enquiries, the possibility of supplying the British West Indies from the old continent, on terms that would not be worse than abandoning them altogether. The truth was, that the gentleman, (Mr. A.) had, in this particular, gone beyond the most sanguine advocates of the British policy, Mr. Knox and Lord Sheffield themselves; who limited their ultimate hopes of supporting the West-Indies without the aid of the United States, to the remaining possessions of G. Britain on this continent. He would proceed, he said, to shew what foundation there was for the opinion of these gentlemen, and the gentleman from Massachusetts, in favour of this resource. And he was able to give the most full and decisive evidence in the case, by recurring to an authentic document of our own, from which it appeared, that the continental colonies of Great Britain, instead of being able to furnish the West India colonies, were themselves dependent for the very articles wanted there, on the supplies of the United States.

In the official statement of our exports for the year as late as 1791,[2] most of the articles sent to the British continental colonies, were of a sort and an amount so directly to the point, that he hoped the committee would excuse him for repeating them in detail. He stated them as follows:

Bread-Stuffs and Roots.

Wheat,	3,125	bushels,
Rye,	2,201	
Barley	32	
Indian corn,	80,734	
Oats,	314	
Buckwheat	26	
Peas and beans,	1,418	
Rice,	84	tierces,
Flour,	27,197	barrels,
Ship-stuff,	2,515	
Rye meal,	1,774	

Indian meal,	2,396	
Buckwheat, do.	353	
Bread,	29,290	
Crackers,	364	Kegs,
Potatoes,	20	bushels,
Onions,	525	

Meats, &c.

Beef,	284	barrels
Pork,	352	
Bacon,	881	lbs.
Fresh Pork,	29,334	
—— Beef,	92,269	
Mutton,	561	carcases,
Tongues,	30	barrels,
Butter,	33	firkins,
Lard,	5,720	lbs.
Cheese,	1,826	

Live Stock.

Horned Cattle,	312	
Horses	39	
Sheep	1,517	
Hogs	178	
Poultry	361	dozen,

Wood.

Shingles,	43,000
Staves & heading	128,000
Handspikes	2
Hoops	3,000
Laths	3,000
Blocks	100
Oar-rafters	857
Trunnels	1,500
Oak Planks and Boards, }	14,267
Pine do.	270,000
Maple & beach do.	7,500

The total of the exports, including a few articles under other heads, amounted to two hundred seventy thousand two hundred fifty and nine dollars.

Here then, it is seen, that not only in the bread stuffs and meats of every sort, but in the articles of lumber and live stock, for which, by universal acknowledgment, the West Indies must depend either on the United States, or the British Continental colonies; the latter are so far from being a rival to us, or a resource to the West Indies, that they continue, at this day, to supply their own deficiencies from our market.

Mr. M. said, that he should not have employed so much of the time of the committee on this head, if the gentleman (Mr. Ames) had not attempted to revive the arguments with respect to Canada and Nova Scotia, which had misled G. Britain in her political calculations and her present views. He had heard the language of the gentleman on this subject, with astonishment. That Mr. Knox and Lord Sheffield, British subjects, viewing the prospect with British eyes, at the distance of three thousand miles, in the year 1783, when little enquiry and no experiment could assist them, should have run into the error, was perhaps not so marvellous. But, that an enlightened Citizen of America, seeing with American eyes, living in the neighbourhood as it were of the scene, in a state whose wharves afford proofs of the daily dependence of the British Continental colonies for the necessaries of life, on the market of the United States, should, in the year 1794 adopt the opinion that those colonies could supply the Islands, after a trial of nine years had probably forced the authors of the opinion, Knox and Sheffield themselves, to abandon it, could not be heard without some surprize; and must be considered at least as the fullest proof, that the gentleman had not given sufficient attention to the present subject, to claim that weight which was in general due to his observations.

Mr. M. said he was not less surprised at the 3d position of the gentleman from Massachusetts, viz. that the West-India trade could be carried on by a dozen brigs; and consequently, was not an object worth our pursuit. The plain answer to this argument was, to state the fact, that the shipping entered in one year from the British West-Indies, was not a dozen brigs, but 107,759 tons.[3]

Besides the immediate importance of this auxilliary resource for our navigation, he remarked, that there were two considerations which enhanced the value of the object: one, that as the West-India articles could be brought cheaper in American vessels, they would come cheaper to American consumers; the other, that as our supplies would at the same time be carried cheaper to the West-Indies, the people there could afford to consume the more of them.

It had been urged that the proposed restrictions on the trade with Great-Britain would produce clamors here as well as there, and that Congress might be obliged to recede, before the British government would be under the necessity of doing so. To this Mr. M. replied, that he was under no such apprehension. He thought more favorably of the good sense as well as virtue of his fellow citizens. On the side of Great-Britain it had been shewn there would be the greatest distress, and the least ability to bear it. The people there were not accustomed, like the people of the United States, to self-denying regulations. They would not have the same confidence in the justice of their cause. And it was particularly worthy of remark, that the people of Great-Britain would be disheartened, and the government alarmed, by reflecting, that their losses from the shifting of commerce into other channels, and not only of their manufactures, but manufacturers, to other places, would be permanent and irretrievable; whereas on our side, they would be temporary sacrifices for durable and valuable acquisitions.

Secondly. The resolutions would have the effect of increasing our marine, and thereby at once cheapening and securing the carriage of our productions, and providing for our safety. These advantages having been already sufficiently explained, need not, he said, be again developed.

It had been remarked by a member from Massachusetts, (Mr. Ames) that if, as stated by a report of Mr. Jefferson,[4] Great-Britain was so often at war, her wars, by depriving us of her shipping, would soon have the wished effect, of replacing it with American shipping. This reasoning Mr. M. said, supposed what was contrary to prudence and probability. What merchants would build ships, which a peace, always more or less in prospect, would throw out of employment; unless it were for special purposes, where the momentary gain might outweigh the eventual sacrifice.

It had been said that our tonnage was proved by the official returns to be increasing with an unexampled rapidity. To this Mr. M. answered: that the increase ought not to be compared with other examples, but with our own natural faculties, and reasonable expectations—that the increase of our population required an annual increase of at least five per cent; that an assumption by foreigners of American names, had probably increased the apparent quantity of our shipping; that the war or preparations for it, by withdrawing foreign shipping, had probably also had some little temporary effect; that the principal cause of the increase, was the extension of our trade with the French dominions, which some members seemed so little inclined to secure and foster, by measures which appeared to him best fitted for the purpose.

He reminded the committee of an argument, which had, on former occasions, been much pressed by several mercantile members, for encouraging our own navigation; to wit: that American vessels, from a spirit of enterprize, and a unison between private and public interests, would explore new fields of commerce, and new markets for our produce, which foreign carriers would leave unattempted. The trade to

China opened by American vessels, had been often ascribed to this cause. Mr. M. said the argument seemed to be countenanced also, by the present state of our mediterranean trade; which had, since our independence, been confined by the Barbary corsairs to foreign bottoms. Previous to the revolution, when American vessels could be the carriers, the trade was very considerable. Since the exclusion of our vessels, though the carriage of our produce is safe to British, and several other foreign vessels, yet this branch of trade had withered as much as most others have grown. In 1790, the exports cleared for the mediterranean, were but 31,726 dollars; and in the year following, the imports no more than 11,522 dollars.

Thirdly. Another effect incident to the proposed measure, would be an additional encouragement to domestic manufactures.

A gentleman from Massachusetts (Mr. Dexter) had said, he could read no such tendency in the propositions. Mr. M. thought it impossible to read the propositions with attention, and not perceive, that they must have the like tendency with the other means, by which manufactures had been promoted. If the duties already laid, were calculated to produce this effect, an increase of those duties in any instance, must have a tendency to increase the effect. In answer to the objection that, a change in the policy of G. B. might put an end to the additional duties, and ensnare those who should proceed under the influence of them, he remarked, 1. That the same might be said in some degree of the regulations now in force. A treaty with Great Britain might stipulate changes which would affect our manufacturers. But as there was a just confidence, that the interests of this class of citizens would in this case be attended to by the government; it might be expected, that equal attention would be paid to them, in any other case. 2. The progress of things in this country, and the probable accession of foreign manufacturers, might be relied on to support whatever undertakings shall have once got a footing.

4thly. The proposed resolutions would favor an advantageous competition and distribution of our trade among the manufacturing nations of Europe. At present, it may be said to be monopolized by one; so great is the disproportion of its manufactures which come to our market. That this is an evil, has been admitted, and cannot be doubted. It exposes us to the greatest and most sudden embarrassments from the caprice, the passions, the mistaken calculations of interest, the bankruptcies, and the wars of a single foreign country. Many of these embarrassments are felt at the present moment. If it were possible to liquidate them into a pecuniary statement, it would be found that, in a permanent view of our interest, there would be economy in making very considerable temporary sacrifices, for the purpose of dividing our custom among a number of competitors. It was not true, that G. Britain alone can supply the manufactures we want. France, the United Netherlands, and several other nations, are capable of supplying us with a variety of articles, as well as the nation from which they now come; and, if invited to our markets by prudent encouragements in the first instance, will soon learn to fashion their manufactures to the wants and tastes of this country. The policy of favouring particular branches of trade, even at some expence, in order to guard against the evil of depending on a single one, was exemplified by the conduct of G. Britain herself. Although he viewed her discriminations generally, respecting us, in the light he had explained; yet, he thought it possible, that in the instance of naval stores and ship-timbers, it might be her intention to foster a rivalship in a more distant quarter, in order to provide against a casual privation of the supplies of a nearer quarter. These articles are essential to the marine of G. Britain; as her marine is essential to her greatness. Were she to have no resource but in the Baltic, a war with the Baltic powers might be fatal to her. It may be wise in her, therefore, to keep open the American resource, even at the price of a tax on herself. In this case she must quarrel with both the Baltic powers and the United States at the same time, before the supplies will be cut off.

A member from Massachusetts, (Mr. Dexter) had not, Mr. M. said, been very consistent in his reasoning on this subject. He had contended against all attempts to excite a beneficial competition, on the idea that no competition could be beneficial which would not spring up of itself; and yet he had warned us against the danger, that G. Britain, by exciting a competition against the United States, in those parts of Europe, which most resemble the infant situation of our country, might establish new sources from which supplies would afterwards spontaneously flow to her, without being ever again wanted from the United States. The same remark was applicable to the reasoning of the other gentlemen who had represented the danger of exciting a permanent rivalship for the West India market, in favor of Canada and Nova Scotia.

Fifthly. The plan of the resolutions tended to conciliate nations in treaty, or disposed to be in treaty with us, into arrangements still more favourable to our commerce. This argument had peculiar weight in relation to France. It had been said that Great Britain was our best customer. The fact, he said, was that we were her best customer: but that France was our best customer. We consume more of British manufactures than any other nation in the world consumes. France consumes more of our productions, than any other nation consumes. He referred to the statements he had before offered for proof of this. Her consumption was also of the most valuable kind; and under favourable regulations would be a very growing one. It consisted of wheat and flour, salt provisions, and fish; articles which were not admitted by Great Britain; and which without the market of France, would glut every other. Of our fish she consumed five eighths of the whole exportation. Her use of our live animals was another important consideration. It amounted, in the list of our exports, to 352,795 dollars, for the year 1791. In the same year, the British demand amounted to no more than 62,415 dollars. The superior *proportion* of navigation we enjoyed in the French channels of intercourse had already been shewn. In examining the policy of cultivating and securing the French markets, he said it ought not to be forgotten, that the profits and revenue arising from the rum distilleries, depended on an article obtained almost, if not altogether, from the French dominions alone; and which was the only raw material of any consequence imported into the United States. It was paid for also, as had been much urged on other occasions by members on the opposite side, in the worst fish, which could find a vent in no other part of the world. The molasses imported into the United States in one year, amounted to upward of seven millions of gallons, more than one half of which went into the state of Massachusetts. He took notice also of the article of sugar, as rendered of great importance by our habits and our finances; and of which more than one half was supplied by the French West Indies. Out of 17,142,723 pounds imported, 9,321,829 pounds were received from that source. The residue came from the Danish, Dutch, and British dominions, in the following proportions. To wit, Danish, 2,833,016 pounds, Dutch 2,707,231 pounds, British 2,280,647 pounds. This statement was taken from the imports of 1790, the only year he had been able to examine on this point.

It had been said, Why grant privileges before a mutual grant should be secured by positive stipulation? Why throw away, by a legal regulation, what ought to be the price of treaty? He answered, that the legal regulation threw nothing away, as it was always revocable: that in the present instance, it was only meeting the legal regulations of which France had set the example: that instead of being a bar to treaty, such a course of proceeding, more than any other, would smooth the way to it, by explaining the objects, and establishing a confidence, on both sides —that it would be happy, if in all cases, where treaties are in view, this open and conciliatory process, could take the place of that reserve and mysterious negociation, with which the parties approach each other. Were Great Britain desirous of forming amicable arrangements by treaty, he asked what readier or more prudent step could she have taken for the purpose, than to have followed the example set her, by holding out in her laws, the spirit in which she was willing to meet us in negociation?

Having gone through these explanations, Mr. M. entered into a view of the principal objections to the resolutions proposed.

1. It was said they would diminish the revenue, and endanger the funds.

With respect to the public debt, his general ideas had been expressed by several who had spoken before him. He acknowledged that he had disliked and opposed the modification given to it; but after it had received the sanction of law, he had entertained no other wish on the subject, than that the debt might be honorably discharged, as fast as the circumstances of the country would permit. This he was well satisfied was the prevailing sentiment of the great body of the people. He did not believe, that there was a single state in the union, or any considerable part of a single state, that did not acquiesce (where they did not approve) in the provisions which had been made in behalf of the public creditors. At the same time, he was equally sure, that it never was either meant by congress, or understood by the public, that in mortgaging the impost for their security, it was to be an hostage to foreign countries for our unqualified acquiescence in their unequal laws, and to be worn, as long as the debt should continue, as a badge of national humiliation. The nature of the obligation could certainly import no more in favor of the creditors, than that the fund appropriated should be applied, as far as requisite, to their use; unless equivalent funds should be substituted; nor more against the public, than that all deficiencies in the fund should be made up, whether arising without, or in consequence of, a change in the laws. If it should happen, then, that in consequence of any measure, dictated by the general good, the impost should become inadequate to its object, all that could be exacted by the public creditors, would be some other provision that would supply the defalcation; and it ought not to be doubted, that the people at large, whose good was pursued, would readily support whatever other provision might become indispensible. He had made these remarks, however, with reference to an event, which he did not by any means admit to be probable. The more he had revolved the subject, the more clearly it appeared to him, that a very operative addition might be made to the duties on the enumerated articles, without endangering the aggregate product of the importations. And he entirely concurred in opinion with those, who had observed, that the greatest injury which could be done to the class of citizens holding the public paper, was to represent their interests as more to be regarded than any national considerations whatever; and to oppose to the latter, even the most imaginary contingencies to the former.

2. It was objected, that the operation of the resolutions would be more favorable, in some instances to nations in treaty than was merited; and more unfavorable, in others, to nations not in treaty, than was politic.

In answer to this objection, he observed, that Sweden and Prussia, two of the nations in commercial treaty, had but little intercourse with us;

would be in any respect but little affected; and, besides, the treaties with them were limited to a short term, the greatest part of which had elapsed.

France and the United Netherlands, the two other nations to be favored, could not reasonably be grudged the advantages they might derive from treaties, for which we had long ago received a valuable consideration in their assistance towards the establishment of our independence.

As to the nations not in treaty—

Denmark would not be affected. She had no navigation act, within the description of the resolutions; and could not feel the duties on manufactures. The whole of the imports from Denmark amounted in the year 1791 to 9,957 dollars only. Her islands also, with which the trade is carried on in our vessels, depend for their subsistence on our market.

Russia has little or no shipping in our trade, and it would not be affected if she had; as she has no such navigation act. Her *unwrought* iron may come as before. Duck and sheeting are the only two manufactures on which the resolutions would sensibly operate; and with respect to these as will presently be observed, it would be easy to make special exceptions.

The Hanse Towns, having no navigation act, would not be affected in that respect. Linens are the only articles falling within the proposed enumeration; and might, if thought requisite, be easily excepted.

Spain, has little shipping in our trade; has no navigation act, such as is to be reciprocated; and would not be sensibly touched by the duties on manufactures. She also needs our exports, and will be influenced by that consideration.

It had been asked why Spain, against whom we had complaints as well as against G. Britain, ought not to be equally an object of our regulations? He said that such a question could be best answered when the communications from the President relating to Spain,[5] should be taken up.

Portugal, like Spain, will not be affected in her navigation; nor sensibly, if at all, in the article of manufactures; and is, more than Spain, supplied with necessaries from our market. According to Zimmerman,[6] Portugal does not raise within herself, more bread than will feed her three months in the year. It is certain that she depends much on external resources, and that occasions are frequent when she can find them no where else than in the United States.

Mr. M. said he considered these explanations as a sufficient answer to the objection. He would add, however, that there were other answers some of which had been before hinted, that would afford an option of modes for the exemption of nations not in treaty.

Besides the opportunity which such nations have of removing all difficulties, by meeting us in liberal treaties they may be provided for; either by limiting every part of the measure to nations having a navigation act: Or by limiting it to nations within a geographical description; a practice familiar to the British code: Or by naming the nations to be excepted; a practice also familiar to Great-Britain: Or by naming the particular articles to be excepted; a practice no less familiar to that nation.

By some or other of these modifications the committee could be at no loss to accommodate the plan, to their own sense of propriety, and the public good.

Here Mr. M. took occasion to remark, that much of the argument against the resolutions, had proceeded from an inattention to their import, and would be answered by a simple explanation of them.

The first resolution, which was immediately the subject of debate, decided nothing with respect to a discrimination between different nations. It declared only, in general, that the situation of the United States required something to be done, in the way of commercial restrictions and duties. And yet it had been combated by many members, as if a vote in favor of it would involve all the embarrassing preferences, which their fancies could suggest.

The succeeding resolutions on the subject of additional duties on manufactures, and of a variation of the tonnage duties, were founded on a discrimination between nations in treaty, and nations not in treaty; but admitted, as he had observed, of whatever modifications or exceptions, might be judged equitable or politic. The proposed reduction of the tonnage on vessels in treaty, had been suggested by the complaint made by France of the existing tonnage on her vessels, as exceeding the burden imposed by her on ours, as well as an unkind return for the commercial benefits of which the United States were partaking under her laws. At present the tonnage imposed by us, on all foreign vessels was the same. This would not seem to be right on any principle, unless the tonnage imposed on our vessels, by all foreign nations, was the same which was not to be presumed. Whether the change he had proposed, would be an amendment of the existing law was a point to be examined. It was certainly a part of the plan which he did not regard as the most essential.

With respect to the resolutions reciprocating navigation laws, it was evident, he said, that these had no reference to the question, whether a nation were in treaty or not. They would operate equally, wherever there might be the same departure from the principle of reciprocity. If they should bear on one nation particularly, it would be because they ought to do so.

3. It had been much insisted, that trade ought to be left free to find its proper channels, under the conduct of merchants; that the mercantile opinion was the best guide, in the case now depending; and that that opinion was against the Resolutions.

In answer to this objection, he said it was obvious to remark, that in the very terms of the proposition, trade ought to be *free* before it could find its *proper* channel. It was not free at present, it could not, therefore, find the channels in which it would most advantageously flow. The dykes must be broken down before the waters could pursue their natural course. Who would pretend, that the trade with the British West Indies, or even with Great Britain herself, was carried on, under the present restrictions, as it would go on of itself, if unfettered from restrictions on her part, as it is on ours? Who would pretend, that the supplies to the West Indies for example, would not flow thither in American bottoms if they flowed freely? Who would pretend that our wheat, our flour, our fish, &c. would not find their way to the British market, if the channels to it were open for them?

It seemed to have been forgotten, that the principle of this objection struck at every regulation in favour of manufactures, as much, or even more, than at regulations on the subject of commerce. It required that every species of business ought to be left to the sagacity and interest of those carrying it on; without any interference whatever, of the public Authority. He was himself, in general, a friend to this theory: but there were a variety of exceptions to it, arising out of particular situations; as must be admitted by all who would mingle practical with theoretic views; and as has been already decided by a number of our laws.

With respect to the mercantile opinion, he was disposed to pay all due attention to it. The mercantile class of citizens was certainly an enlightened and a respectable one. Their information ought always to be received with respect, and their interests protected with care. But it did not follow that their opinion, even on questions of trade, ought to be consulted as an oracle, by those who were equally bound to watch over the interests of every class of citizens, and over the joint concerns of the whole. There were considerations of different kinds which suggested caution on this subject.

However intelligent and constant the merchant might be, in directing his operations, for commercial purposes, he might not be equally in the habit of combining with these, the various other national objects which the Legislature might be bound to consult.

The interest of the mercantile class may happen to differ from that of another class; and possibly both may differ from that of the whole community. For example, it is, generally speaking, the interest of the merchant to import and export every thing: the interest of manufacturers to lessen imports in order to raise the price of domestic fabrics, and to check exports, where they might enhance the price of raw materials. In this case it would be as improper to allow the one to judge for the other, as to allow either to judge for the whole.

It may be the interest of the merchant, under particular circumstances to confine the trade to its established channels; when the national interest would require those channels to be changed or enlarged. The best writers on political œconomy have observed, that the regulations most unfriendly to the national wealth of Great Britain, have owed their birth to mercantile counsels. It is well known, that in France, the greatest opposition to that liberal policy which was as favourable to the true interest of that country as of this, proceeded from the interest which merchants had, in keeping the trade in its former course.

If, in any country, the mercantile opinion ought not to be implicitly followed, there were the strongest reasons why it ought not, in this. The body of merchants who carry on the American commerce is well known to be composed of so great a proportion of individuals who are either British subjects, or trading on British capital, or enjoying the profits of British consignments, that the mercantile opinion here, might not be an American opinion; nay, it might be the opinion of the very country, of which, in the present instance at least, we ought not to take counsel. What the genuine American mercantile opinion would be, if it could be collected apart from the general one, Mr. M. said he did not undertake positively to decide. His belief was that it would be in favor of the resolutions.

It could scarcely be necessary, he said, to add that his remarks were not meant to be, as they were not in fact, the least reflection on any part of the mercantile order among us. They only suppose, what in political reasonings ought always to be supposed, that the prejudices of birth and personal interests will be a bias on the judgment.

4. It had been an objection to the resolutions, that they might deprive us of the aid of British capital and credit, which were necessary to the prosecution of our commerce.

Mr. M. did not admit either that the effect would happen, or that it would be ruinous to our commerce.

Unless Great Britain should, of her own choice, put a stop to the commercial intercourse with us, which for reasons before given would be so much more hurtful to herself than to this country, that it never could be presumed; the resolutions would operate only by abridging some of our importations, and by varying the channels of others. Her capital, as far as requisite here, might continue to be employed here.

On the general question concerning our dependence on British capital and credit, he observed that it could not be denied that more use was made of them at present, than was either necessary or beneficial. Credit when extended to consumers, as was the case throughout the southern states, was extremely injurious; as had been well explained by a member of Virginia (Mr. Nicholas), and as he himself had equally witnessed. When confined to merchants, it might, within certain limits, be an advantage; but it was not only his own opinion, but that of better judges, that the credit given to our merchants, was at present excessive and injurious.

In order to form a very precise judgment on this subject, it would be necessary, he said, to calculate the amount of our own capital, and its proportion to the amount of our trade. This was a thing he supposed, which could not well be done. If he had concurred in the doctrine, of which so much had been heard both within and without doors, that a funded debt and banks of discount, were equivalent to active capital, he should have a ready answer to the difficulty. The paper of the two kinds, in the United States, cannot amount to less than one hundred millions of dollars; whilst the amount of our exports or our imports, does not exceed one fourth of that capital. It is true, a part of both the public and the bank stocks, is in foreign hands; but, with the most ample deductions on that account, the residue, if operating in any considerable degree, as active capital, would be a competent resource.

As he did not however view the doctrine in the particular light in which it had been painted; it would be more to his purpose, to observe, that there was certainly in this country a real mercantile capital to a very respectable amount—that this was fast increasing with our increasing population and wealth: that if the foreign capital of one country should be withdrawn, the vacancy would probably by degrees be occupied by that of other foreign nations; that if it should happen otherwise, there was reason to believe, that a restriction of our use of foreign credit, would be rather salutary than disadvantageous; that in fine, as long as we had twenty millions of dollars worth of produce, wanted by other nations; and were willing to take for it, twenty millions worth of what they wished to part with, he was under no apprehension that the means of effectuating an exchange, would not be found. Both merchants and capital would quickly be generated by such a state of things, if they did not previously exist.

5. It had been observed by several members, in allusion to the alledged proportion of British manufactures consumed by us to the entire mass of her manufactures, that Great Britain would never part with her navigation act, in order to avoid a loss of four per cent. in the demand for her manufactures.

To this objection he answered; that the comparison ought to be our consumption, not with the entire mass of her manufactures, but with the part entering into her foreign trade; and then the loss would not be four per cent, but, at least twenty per cent; that this would not be the only loss she would sustain, if she should be unwise enough to stop the intercourse between the United States and her dominions; that it had been already shewn, that when she apprehended a restrictive system on our part, she was willing to prevent it, by relaxing her restrictive system; that in times of war, when an adherence to that system would distress her, she frequently suspends her navigation act; that at this moment it is suspended in relation to the West-Indies; that there could be little doubt, if the temporary necessity, were likely to be made permanent by firm and judicious measures on our part, that the remedy for it would be made permanent also.

6. It was objected that the present was an improper time for such resolutions.

The principal reason given for this was, that the negociation between the secretary of state and the British minister here, was still depending. To shew that this reason was unsound, Mr. M. went into an historical view of what had passed in reference to commercial arrangements. He read the message of the President to the House of Representatives, on the 14th of February, 1791,[7] acquainting them, that steps had been taken to ascertain the dispositions of the British court on the subject, and that there was no ground for favorable expectations. He stated, that in consequence of this communication, a committee was appointed, who reported that foreign vessels ought not to be allowed to bring into the United States any articles not of the produce or manufacture of the country to which they belong, and that an additional duty of twelve and an half cents ought to be laid on all distilled spirits, the production of any country or place from which vessels of the United States were not permitted to bring them; that it being very near the end of the session when this report was made, it was referred to the secretary of state, with an instruction to report to the next session an account of the foreign commercial regulations affecting the United States, with his opinion, &c. that at the next session, a letter was received from that officer, intimating that in the actual state of circumstances, the report would not be given in, unless called for by the House; that at the present session, the report now before the committee, was given in, without being called for; and was therefore a proof, that the circumstances which had caused the delay had vanished, and that at present there was nothing in train, according to the opinion of the secretary of state, which ought to restrain the Legislature from proceeding in the business.

In answer to suggestions, that the British minister had, in the correspondence with the Secretary of State, lately communicated by the President,[8] manifested a favourable disposition, which had not been improved—Mr. M. recurred to the passages which related to this point. He read from the first letter of Mr. Jefferson to Mr. Hammond, dated Nov. 29, 1791, a paragraph requesting Mr. H. "to say, whether he was authorized to conclude, or to negociate arrangements with us which may fix the commerce between the two countries, on principles of reciprocal advantage?" To this request Mr. H. on the 30th of Nov. 1791, answered, "That the king was sincerely disposed to promote and facilitate the commercial intercourse between the two countries, and that he was authorized to communicate to this government, his majesty's readiness to enter into a negociation for establishing that intercourse upon principles of reciprocal benefit." On Dec. 6, he wrote to Mr. J. in order to prevent misapprehension, that although he was not yet empowered to CONCLUDE any definitive arrangement with respect to the commercial intercourse, he still meant it to be understood, that he was fully authorized to ENTER into a negociation for that purpose, &c. The reply of Mr. J. on the 13th of Dec. informed Mr. H. that he had laid his letters before the President, and was ready to receive a communication of his full powers, for entering into the negociation, &c. This was followed on the next day by a letter from Mr. H. stating, that he had no special commission to CONCLUDE any *definitive* arrangement upon the subject of commercial intercourse—but that he conceived himself fully competent to enter into a negociation, and the discussion of principles that might be the basis of such definitive arrangement—and that this opinion of his competency was founded on the instructions which were to regulate his personal conduct, and the general *plenipotentiary* character in which he had been sent and received.

This letter, Mr. M. observed, closed the correspondence on the subject of commercial arrangements, being justly considered by the executive as a final proof, that the powers of Mr. H. were incompetent, and irrelative to the object; and that it would be improper to open a formal negociation with him, under them. His instructions might be a rule and a warrant to himself, but not being even exhibited, could be no evidence of his authority, to the executive. And his plenipotentiary commission in the ordinary form, could never be understood as relating to the special objects he proposed to discuss. According to the usage of nations, a special commission is, in such cases, always furnished and required. Mr. M. was persuaded, that no sovereign in Europe would listen for a moment to such a claim as that of Mr. H. and that the British court would have been offended at such an one from an American minister. He thought therefore that the executive had equally consulted dignity and prudence, in silently dropping the subject in the same manner they did, until Mr. H. should receive and produce adequate powers in the accustomed form; as might reasonably be expected, if his court was duly disposed to meet the United States, in an amicable arrangement of commerce, by treaty.

That the construction put by Mr. H. on his powers, was inadmissible, appeared to Mr. M. to result from the construction itself. Either the general Plenipotentiary commission was to be taken in the technical and limited sense in which it is applied to the ordinary diplomatic objects of a stationary public minister; or, in a literal sense, without regard to such limitation. In the former sense, it clearly does not extend to negociations for a treaty. In the latter sense it would extend to the *conclusion* of a treaty, and not merely to *negociation*, as Mr. H. explains and limits it.

Mr. M. adverted next to the state of the correspondence relating to the treaty of peace. It appeared, he observed, that as long ago as the 29th of May, 1792, the Secretary of State had addressed to Mr. Hammond, a full explanation of our rights and demands, under that treaty—that on the 2d June, Mr. Hammond informed the Secretary, that he should transmit it without delay for the consideration of his court; and accordingly did forward it in the course of a few days; that on the 13th Nov. 1793, previous to the present meeting of Congress, Mr. H. was desired by the Secretary, in pursuance of a charge from the President, to let him know whether an answer could yet be given to the letter of May 29, 1792. Mr. H. replied that it could not; but that he was confident the delay was to be ascribed to the continuance of the cause alluded to in a former answer to a similar request.

The cause alluded to was the interesting posture of things in Europe, which it was said, had diverted the attention of the British government to objects of a more pressing nature; and this consideration had been urged by several members, as an apology for the silence observed towards the United States. Mr. Madison thought very differently. The interval between the receipt of the letter written by the Secretary in May 1792; and the accession of Great Britain to the war against France, had been sufficient for the purpose of preparing and sending the proper instructions to Mr. H. Mr. M. added, that the prospect of being engaged in new controversies of a more serious kind instead of justifying an inattention to an existing one, ought to have quickened the efforts for a previous settlement of the latter. This is the course dictated by prudence, to nations as well as to individuals; and where a right disposition concurs, it is the natural course.

It had been mentioned as a further reason against the commercial propositions, at this time, that they might draw upon us the resentments of the Combined powers. Mr. M. could see no ground for such an apprehension. The Combined powers were pretty fully occupied with France; they could have no pretext for concerning themselves with us, in a case where we did not concern ourselves with them; and there was the less room for imagining that the combination could misconstrue the measure into an offence against them; as two of the parties, Prussia and the United Netherlands were in treaty with the United States, and are favored by the propositions.

7. It was finally contended that admitting our situation to be such as had been described, the mode proposed was an objectionable one.

Mr. M. said he had no predilections for the mode that could prevent his giving a ready preference to a better, if a better should be offered. And unless it should be said, that the Legislature ought to adjourn without doing any thing for the public relief, he thought it incumbent on those who objected to one proposition to substitute another that would be less objectionable. By this he meant a proposition not merely better in itself; but one that would probably be thought so, both within and without doors; and be more likely to coincide with the sentiments of every part of the union, as well as to conciliate a majority of voices in the public councils.

The first question, he said, was whether any thing ought to be done. If this be decided in the affirmative; as he presumed to be the sense of a majority of the committee; and if war was not in contemplation as of course was taken for granted; the next question could only lie between negociation, and commercial regulations. Negociation it had been shewn was in no train, or prospect, that could justify reliance on it. Commercial regulations alone remained. They would be pacific in their operation. They were the means best suited to the temper of our constituents. And he sincerely believed, that, if judiciously framed, they would be more likely to answer the reasonable purposes of the community, than any others that could be proposed.[9]

Philadelphia Gazette, 3, 4, 5, and 7 Mar. 1794 (reprinted in *Gazette of the U.S.*, 8, 13, 15, and 18 Mar. 1794 [incomplete; misdated 30 Jan. 1794], and Madison, *Speech in the House of Representatives*, pp. 45–69; also reported in *Philadelphia Gazette*, 1 Feb. 1794). Trade figures were given in dollars rather than pounds (errata notice in *Philadelphia Gazette*, 5 Mar. 1794) and have been silently corrected here. This speech and the one JM delivered a day earlier are printed as a single speech under the 29 Jan. entry in *Annals of Congress*, 3d Cong., 1st sess., 366–95.

1. [Charles Jenkinson, first earl of Liverpool], *Representation of the Lords of the Committee of Council, . . . for . . . Trade and Foreign Plantations, upon the Present State of the Laws for Regulating the Importation and Exportation of Corn* (London, 1790), p. 4, declared that during the years 1774–80 "this Country has upon an Average sustained a loss in this [grain] Trade of £.291,000 per Annum."

2. Tench Coxe's statement, which Hamilton submitted to the Senate on 16 Mar. 1793 (*ASP, Commerce and Navigation*, 1:104–38).

3. JM gleaned this information from a manuscript abridgment of a British Board of Trade report in Jefferson's possession (DLC: Jefferson Papers; printed as

Worthington Chauncey Ford, ed., *Report of a Committee of the Lords of the Privy Council on the Trade of Great Britain with the United States* [Washington, 1888], p. 20). Prepared under the direction of Lord Hawkesbury (then president of the Board of Trade and later first earl of Liverpool), this report was first printed in full in January 1791 for official use only. William Temple Franklin sent the abridgment to Jefferson (Boyd, *Papers of Jefferson*, 18:267–72).

4. "Report on the American Fisheries by the Secretary of State," 1 Feb. 1791, appendix no. 18 (Boyd, *Papers of Jefferson*, 19:236).

5. On 16 Dec. 1793 Washington sent to Congress his administration's correspondence relating to negotiations with Spain on commerce, Mississippi navigation, and other matters (*ASP, Foreign Relations*, 1:247).

6. Eberhard August Wilhelm von Zimmermann, *A Political Survey of the Present State of Europe* (Dublin, 1788), pp. 283–84.

7. Washington's message is printed in *ASP, Foreign Relations*, 1:121–22.

8. The letters to which JM subsequently referred were those which Washington submitted with his message to Congress of 5 Dec. 1793 (ibid., 1:189, 201–16, 237, 238).

9. In Committee of the Whole on 3 Feb., while JM was absent from the chamber, Swift moved to strike out his first resolution. His political allies, led by Nicholas, managed to postpone consideration of the motion until he arrived. To objections that the resolution had been phrased in too general terms, JM responded: "I intentionally made the first resolution as vague as it is, and not more so. I regarded this generality of expression as necessary." After further debate, the committee approved the first resolution (*Philadelphia Gazette*, 4 Feb. 1794). On 4 Feb. a proposal was made to name Great Britain in JM's first resolution as the country against which the increased customs duties were directed. JM "said, that he had at first avoided the particular mention of Britain, because he had been solicitous to expedite the business, in as civil a way as possible. It was of no concern to him whether Britain was specially mentioned or not. Her statute book had afforded many examples of that kind of stile." Smith (Maryland) and Boudinot urged that the resolution also be directed against Spain. JM "observed, that Britain had issued a proclamation respecting the stoppage of the vessels of neutral nations, of these there were but three, Denmark, Sweden, and the United States. The two former had been expressly excepted from the consequences of these restrictions. He said, that the proclamation was, in itself, a breach of the law of nations." Ames argued that the U.S. should not adopt commercial reprisals against Britain while negotiations for a treaty were pending. JM "considered the conduct of Britain as extremely atrocious. He read some extracts from the correspondence between Mr. Pinkney, and the American government. In these, the behaviour of Britain was represented, as very arbitrary and tyrannical; and it was strongly stated, that there was not the least chance of obtaining redress from the court of London, for the violences committed on the American flag" (ibid., 5 Feb. 1794).

§ From Francis Brooke. *February 1794.* Applies for the customs collectorship at Tappahannock, Virginia.[1]

RC (DLC: Washington Papers). 3 pp. Badly faded. Addressed by Brooke to JM in Philadelphia.

1. Francis Taliaferro Brooke (1763–1851) was the brother of Robert Brooke, who became governor of Virginia in December 1794. Although Francis Brooke

was married to a niece of George Washington, the president appointed Laurence Muse to the Tappahannock collectorship. A Revolutionary War veteran, Brooke represented Essex County in the House of Delegates, 1794–95. He was a state senator, 1800–1804, and later a judge in the state courts (Swem and Williams, *Register*, p. 351).

From Laurence Muse

SIR,   VIRGINIA PORT TAPPAHANNOCK Febry 1. 1794

From the inclosed, I take the liberty of soliciting your interest with the President in my favor, in the appointment of a Collector for this port, which I apprehend will take place immediately. Having been imployed in that business from the Commencement of the Collection Law under the present Government [I] flatter myself I have now acquired a Knowledge sufficient to do justice to the public, and individuals. For your friendly aid in the business I shall ever consider myself under obligations And, With much Respect I am Sir Your Obt Servt

LAURENCE MUSE[1]

RC (DLC: Washington Papers). Addressed by Muse to JM at Philadelphia. Enclosed by JM in his letter to the president, 12 Feb. 1794.

1. On 6 Mar. Laurence Muse was appointed collector and inspector of customs at Tappahannock. He succeeded his kinsman Hudson Muse, under whom he had served as a deputy (*Senate Exec. Proceedings*, 1:149; see also Muse to the president, 1 Feb. 1794, and Muse to Monroe, 22 Feb. 1794 [DLC: Washington Papers]).

From Alexander White

DEAR SIR   WOODVILLE 1st. Feb: 1794

I am favored with yours of 20th. Ulo.[1] and shall not only grant the indulgence you ask, but receive communications with gratitude in any manner you may think proper to make them. I may well do so, because in return I can only like common place conversation, speak of the weather. The latter part of December and January, until near the close, have been mild and fair beyond anything remembered at that season— a few severe days excepted, which, the ground being bare, proved very prejudicial to the small grain. On Wednesday last a dry driving snow fell, average about 10 inches. The weather since clear and cold, which we hope will repair the injury. I have seen your resolutions and introductory speech as retailed by the News Writers. The object I have much at heart I not only see but sensibly feel the measures which England has taken and continues to take to obtain & retain the Carrying Trade of the U. States, and indeed of the whole World, and by that means to secure to herself the Empire of the Sea. My only doubt is whether the present be a proper time. It appears to me of the first importance to put ourselves in a strong posture of defence—this will necessarily require new taxes. Yet to the measure I have not heard a dissenting Voice. But if the proposed commercial regulations should check our trade—our present revenues will diminish, and the prices of our produce fall. Would it not then be better to postpone this arduous enterprize till the general tranquility of Europe is restored, an event which I believe is not remote. France being now in as crippled a state as it is probable she can ever be reduced to—the Combined Powers (more particularly England) will seise that opportunity of making Peace with her. I should be well pleased to see the Goverment divorced (if you like the expression) from the Bank by a Sale of the Govermental shares—but cannot so readily reconcile to my mind the depriving a Man of the rights of Citizenship for holding a property which may be as honestly acquired and enjoyed as a Seat of Land on the Banks of the Potowmack. If the People consider it as an objection to the individual they have it in their power to exclude him. Pardon this inaccurate Scrall And believe me your affectionate Friend

ALEXR WHITE

RC (DLC). Docketed by JM.

1. Letter not found.

From Horatio Gates

DEAR SIR   NEW YORK 3d: February 1794.

Amongst the Multitude of your Friends, and Admirers, permit me to Congratulate you upon The Fame you have acquired by your Excellent, and truly Patriotic Speech, in Support of Mr: Jeffersons Report, on the Trade & Commerce of The United States: it has gaind you the General plaudit from East to West; The Murmurings of rank Tories, and Interested Factors, serve only to Increase your Popularity; Proceed, & Prosper; The Gentleman who does me the Favour to present You this Letter, is Dr: Robertson, from Bath in England, He goes to philadelphia to see his, and his Ladys Friends; & to indulge his Curiosity at the Seat of The Federal Government. Having a good property both here, and in Europe, he has given up the practice of physick and lives at his Ease; but his best recommendation is, He is a Staunch Whigg; don't you come here in

Summer? Mary, & I hope to see you again under Our Roof: believe me dear Sir Your Affectionate Humble Servant

HORATIO GATES

P. S. No late arrival from Europe.

RC (DLC). Docketed by JM.

From Pierce Butler

DEAR SIR   ⟨PHILADELPHIA Tuesday Feb: 4th 1794⟩

Puting the true Construction on this short Epistle I persuade myself You will excuse the freedom I take. It will also claim indulgence on acct. of my indisposition—the Mind and body are too closely Connected not to influence each other. I heard with satisfaction the success of Your general proposition. I congratulate You on it. The Manly manner in which You came forward, at a time when the Legislature were designedly thrown into a State of torpor, does You honor. Go on then Sir, in the same marked and distinguishd line of Conduct, and You must succeed. All honest Men; All that are Patriotick, must be with You if Your measures are decisive, as I trust they will be. The Wrongs of Britain are too manifest to need recital. Let Us Combat them with every Measure short of Hostility. The Sea Ports may Exclame—but the Landed Interest will be with You. Half way restrictions will, in my judgement, Accomplish Nothing but an Encrease of Burthen on Our Country. Such Measures must be gratifying to Paper holders, because they strengthen the security for Payment of their Interest. But at the same time they Clog Industry and burthen the Agriculture—try then, I pray You, the Nerve of the House by a Strong Measure. It is my Ardent wish to give my too feeble support to everything You bring forward—temporising will, in my opinion, Accomplish Nothing, but give time to British influence to Work. A Moderate encrease of Taxes will Ultimately fall on the Consumer. So long as the Articles are Imported there will be found Purchasors. "Lead me not into temptation" is an Excellent Caution. We have in more trying Seasons done altogether without British Goods, Why not submitt for a time to a like restraint! It can only be temporary.

I am sensible there are some difficulties to Encounter—the Eastern Gentlemen who Voted with You merit Attention. Might it not be well to Converse with them And know what woud be gratifying? that We may, if possible meet their wish. I know the importance of having them with Us. It is my Ardent wish to Cultivate their Esteem. I will Concede all I possibly can to secure their Confidence.

I am not able to write more. I must again solicit ⟨Your indulgence for the freedom I have taken, and beg You will believe me to be in truth and sincerity, Dear Sir, Your friend⟩

RC (DLC); letterbook copy (ScU). RC addressed by Butler; docketed by JM. The last part of the RC, including the signature, has been clipped. Words in angle brackets have been supplied from the letterbook copy. Minor variations between the RC and the letterbook copy have not been noted.

From Fontaine Maury

DEAR SIR   FREDG. Feby. 4. 94
    Having good reason to suppose that the Office of Collector at Tappahanock will soon be vacant, I have taken the Liberty to request you will do any thing which may be convenient to promote the Election of Mr Laurence Muse, who has long served with much reputation as a deputy in the above office, and is in all respects perfectly Qualified to do the Public every justice. Excuse the Liberty I am taking, and assure yourself it will at all times give me singular pleasure to render you acceptable returns, being with real esteem Dr Sir your mo. obt

                                    FONTAINE MAURY

RC (DLC: Washington Papers). Addressed by Maury to JM at "4 No. 8th" in Philadelphia. Enclosed by JM in his letter to the president, 12 Feb. 1794.

Commercial Discrimination

[5 February 1794]

    Lyman moved to postpone further consideration of JM's resolutions until the first Monday in March. Dexter opposed delay and urged that the resolutions be either voted on or withdrawn.

    Mr. Madison assured the gentleman from Massachusetts who wished the resolutions withdrawn, that they were brought forward upon mature reflection, and that with an intention of having the sense of the representatives of the Union upon them. Should he, he said, be finally in the minority in the business, and again hold a seat in the house by the voice of the people he again would bring them forward. Something like the resolutions offered, he believed necessary, especially at this time. Whether the subject is considered in a political or a commercial point of view, whether we endeavour to place our trade with Great Britain on a footing of reciprocity, or whether we mean to obtain redress for the injuries we suffer from that quarter, in both aspects he conceived them equally proper. Tho' of opinion that the pending questions might be decided, without the imputation of unbecoming haste, at the present time, yet he could object to comply with the wish of those gentlemen who required a short delay to consult the sense of the constituents. As the subject is of very great moment he hoped it would not be postponed, to so late a day as to endanger a fair decision on it during the present session.

General Advertiser, 7 Feb. 1794.

[5 February 1794]

Ames and Dayton opposed the motion.

Mr. Madison remarked that he was not so vain as to imagine that his propositions were absolutely perfect, neither would he allow that they were more imperfect than they could be proved to be. When the general nature of them was first explained gentlemen were so candid as to approve? If, however, he had confined himself to bringing forward the first resolution, it might, it would have been objected, that what it was meant to lead to was quite in the dark, a developement of it would have been asked; he, therefore, thought it proper to enter into the detailed view he had taken of the subject. Some parts of that detail may be exceptionable, may require amendment, he expected they would, interests must be compared, small local sacrifices must be made to obtain a great general good, he came prepared to sacrifice his own opinions in matters of lesser moment to that spirit of accommodation necessary in framing a system of regulations intended to embrace the interests of so widely extended a continent. When he spoke of the imperfections of the system he offered & of the amendments it might require he intended to be understood in this light.

General Advertiser, 7 Feb. 1794 (also reported in *Philadelphia Gazette*, 6 Feb. 1794). After further debate, JM voted with the majority when the House approved the motion (*Annals of Congress*, 3d Cong., 1st sess., 431–32).

Naval Force against Algerine Corsairs

[6 February 1794]

On 20 January the select committee on financing a naval force against the Algerine corsairs submitted its report, which proposed an appropriation of

$600,000 to support six warships. The sum was to be raised by increased impost and tonnage duties (*Annals of Congress*, 3d Cong., 1st sess., 250). On 6 February the Committee of the Whole on the State of the Union considered a resolution for building the ships.

When the resolution was read, for building four ships of 44 guns and two ships of 20 guns, Mr. Madison rose to enquire, whether there was, in the public stores of the United States, a sufficient quantity of cedar and live oak for building the six vessels? These were the kinds of timber proposed by the resolutions. He was answered, that there was not. He then observed, that it was evident this fleet could not be ready for effective service in the course of the present year. He imagined that there was another resolution, precedent as to the time of voting it, of which he did not know what had become. The resolution to which he alluded was that assigning a sum of money to buy a cessation of hostilities from the regency of Algiers.[1] He was of opinion, that the project of fitting out an armed squadron, was liable to many solid objections. There were two points of light in which this subject might be surveyed. The first of these was, whether the Algerines acted from their own impulse in this business. In that case, they were known to be in the habit of selling a peace; and if they are willing to do so, he fancied that it might be purchased for less money than the armament would cost. On the other hand, if they do not act from their own impulse, but upon the instigation of Britain, we may depend upon it, that they cannot be bought. Britain will keep them hostile. There is infinitely more danger of a British war from the fitting out of ships than from the resolutions on the report of the Secretary of State. The distance which the ships would have to sail is not less than three thousand miles: and their number is too small for a decisive advantage. The combined powers would embrace the equipment of these ships as an excellent opportunity to pick a quarrel with the United States. Mr. Madison expressed his doubts with regard to the propriety of this measure, because the expence was immense, and there was no certainty of reaping any benefit from it.

Philadelphia Gazette, 7 Feb. 1794.

1. JM alluded to the first of three resolutions that the House passed on 2 Jan. (see JM's speech of 27 Dec. 1793, n. and n. 1).

[6 February 1794]

Smith (Maryland) said that America could afford to build a navy because "our profit was twice as great at present, in commerce, as it was before the war. . . . As an evidence of this fact, he mentioned the high price of wheat at present in this market" (*Annals of Congress*, 3d Cong., 1st sess., 435).

Mr. Madison in reply to some remarks which had fallen from Mr. Smith, respecting the present high price of wheat in the American market, said that he had been informed of a place where wheat gives only four shillings and six pence per bushel, where the dollar passes for six shillings. He supposed that Britain could render very essential service to the Algerines, without embarking in a war. She has not embarked in a war to the northwest of the Ohio; but she has done the same thing in substance by supplying the Indians with arms, ammunition and perhaps with subsistence. He did not assert that Britain directed the plan of the Indian expeditions, for he had no explicit evidence that they actually did so. In the same way that they give under-hand assistance to the Indians, they would give it to the Algerines, rather than hazard an open war.

Philadelphia Gazette, 7 Feb. 1794.

Naval Force against Algerine Corsairs

[7 February 1794]

The Committee of the Whole resumed its consideration of the resolution for building a navy.

Mr. Madison thought this expedient unlikely to answer the purpose, and liable to many objections. Before the American squadron can be equipped, the truce between Algiers and Portugal must expire. When that expiration shall take place she either will not renew the truce at all, or she will stipulate that the United States shall be comprehended in it. He would save the money intended for the fleet, and hire the Portuguese ships of war, with it, as soon as the truce ends. He wished that the committee might reject the present motion, and when they did so, he would move a resolution, a copy of which he read to the committee. It was in substance, "that the sum of   dollars be provided, to be employed in such a manner as should be found most effectual for obtaining a peace with the regency of Algiers; and failing of this, that the sum should be applied to the end of obtaining protection from some of the European powers." He considered the armament at present proposed, as quite too small to answer any efficient purpose.

Philadelphia Gazette, 10 Feb. 1794 (also reported in *General Advertiser*, 10 Feb. 1794).

[7 February 1794]

FitzSimons and Goodhue, among others, favored the resolution.

Mr. Madison said that gentlemen thought so differently on this subject, and advanced arguments against his side of the question of such a different nature, that it was difficult or impossible to give them an answer. He then proceeded to quote the speech of Mr. Goodhue. That gentleman rose and said that Mr. Madison had misunderstood him. He gave an explanation of his meaning; and when Mr. Madison rose to comment upon it, Mr. Goodhue got up a second time and said that the member misunderstood his explanation. Mr. Madison then proceeded to quote the speeches of Mr. Fitzsimons and Mr. S. Smith.[1]

Philadelphia Gazette, 10 Feb. 1794.

1. The newspaper account of the debate continued: "Both these gentlemen were upon their legs more than once to contradict him as having misquoted them; a charge that he peremptorily denied. In a speech of considerable length, he was not suffered to proceed for any time together without an interruption of this nature. This produced a scene of confusion and altercation through which it was impossible to follow the members, and to prevent a charge of misrepresentation on our part it is safer to pass it over altogether. . . . In the course of this last debate some reflections were cast out against Mr. Madison which it seems better not to repeat."

From Joseph Jones

DR. SR.   FREDG. 8th. Febry. 1794

It has turned out much as I expected—there are few men who possess sufficient public spirit to relinquish or hazard individual int. for general good. British credit still maintains its influence and will continue to do so especially when aided by the monied int of this country, wch. will generally be in concert to prevent any measure that may eventually affect either. I fear the longer we continue under this influence the more powerfull it will become and we shall be tuging at the oar for the benefit and agrandisement of the British nation, in a state of debasement more dishonourable than when we laboured for them as Colonists to which humble station I would rather submit than under the character of free and independent tamely acquiesce in those measures their convenience and insolent pride shall from time to time dictate. It gives me pleasure to hear Genet may, tho' recalled, escape that censure and disgrace generally attending such event, altho' imprudent I do not wish the Executive to ob[t]ain a complete triumph. If Oswald[1] gives a genuine account of the vigor and united efforts of the French it is to be hoped they will yet vanquish the host of enemies that assail them and finally establish that form of Government the people approve. It wod. be a glorious and sweet revenge could they invade England with a strong force—the temper of the common people there seems to have in great degree changed in the course of the last year and in many places appear ripe for mischief—they deserve from the French every evil they can bring upon them for from them the French have experienced the most insidious and cruel treatme(nt). Health and happiness attend you. Yr. friend

J. JONES

RC (DLC). Docketed by JM.

1. Eleazer Oswald published the Philadelphia *Independent Gazetteer*, 1782–95 (Brigham, *History of American Newspapers*, 2:1462).

From James Monroe

DEAR SIR NEW YK. Feby 8. 1794.

I arrived yesterday too late for the post to bear the acct. of it. I found Mrs. M & the child well tho the former had been nearly lost by the sinking of the ice as she came. Mr. Kortright is living & perfectly in his senses, free from pain & perhaps not near his end. He is however on the decline & confined to his room. I find him most friendly & affectionate, but as yet I am not sufficiently acquainted with his affrs. to say any thing respecting them.[1]

I am happy to hear that yr. resolutions are postponed & by the authority you mention. I think the publick sentiment with them. I found it a subject of complaint as I passd thro Jersey that the doors of the H. of R. were not shut as those of the Senate were, because the people were already so hostile to G. B. that it wod. be difficult to keep them within bounds if encouraged in that licentious spirit by the discussions in Congress. And one officer of the latter place as I understood who came up from Phila. to Trenton, said the resolutions wod. not pass but that the Secry of T. was preparing some thing that wod. do better. But even this man said he wished France well & felt resentment towards Britn. I hope to hear regularly whilst I stay from you & Colo. Taylor. Affecy. I am yr. friend

JAS. MONROE

RC (DLC). Addressed by Monroe to JM at Philadelphia and franked.

1. Monroe had gone to New York to attend to the business interests of Lawrence Kortright, his infirm father-in-law. Kortright died on 19 Feb. (Ammon, *James Monroe*, p. 110; Philadelphia *Gazette of the U.S.*, 26 Feb. 1794).

From Hudson Muse

DEAR SIR,   VIRGINIA PORT TAPPA. Feby 8. 1794.

I have acted imprudent in granting indulgences, and by my returns from this office, made myself lyable for m[o]n[e]y in expectation of it's being ready when call'd for; by which means has lately been presented draughts for three thousand dollars, that I was not prepared to pay, and consequently were returned. And as such is conduct for which I am lyable to censure, shall esteem myself much obliged to you for doing me kindness to speake to the President, and Secretary of the Treasury, on the occasion, & apologize for me; assuring them, they may relye on the Money being ready for their order in the course of next month, and that I shall take care in future never to be in the like Situation.[1] I am dear sir, with much respect Your Obedt Sert.

HUDSON MUSE

RC (DLC). Docketed by JM.

1. Muse either resigned or was relieved of his office, but he apparently repaid the $3,000 deficit in June 1795. In a settlement of state-federal accounts, the Virginia controller reported receipt of a draft on Muse for $3,000 (*CVSP*, 8:254, 264).

From George Washington

DEAR SIR,   Saturday Morning [8 February 1794]

The Agricultural Society of Philadelphia, are preparing the "outlines of a Plan for establishing a state Society of Agriculture in Pennsylvania"[1] to be laid before the Legislature. Mr. Peters to whom sometime ago I mentioned the Pamphlets &ca. which had been sent me by Sir John Sinclair; & who is appointed to prepare the business for the Legislature —wishes to have the perusal of those Pamphlets—as at this moment— they might be particularly serviceable to him. I would, for this reason, thank you for them. They shall be returned to you, after he has availed himself of any information which is to be derived from them. I am sincerely & Affectionately Yours

GO: WASHINGTON

Photostat (DLC: Washington Papers). RC offered for sale in Thomas F. and Edith H. Madigan, eds., *The Autograph Album* (April 1934), item 231.

1. A pamphlet with this title (Evans 27512) was published later in 1794 by the Philadelphia Society for Promoting Agriculture. JM's copy is in the Madison Collection, Rare Book Department, University of Virginia Library.

To George Washington

Feby. 8th. 1794

J. Madison presents his apologies to the President for not sending the pamphlets &c. from Sir J. Sinclair, sooner for the use of Mr. Peters, as was intimated when he last had the honor of seeing the President. He had hopes of being able prior to this to have looked a little into them, and have complied with the desire of the President expressed when the papers were put into J. M's hands. It has been impossible for him to do this hitherto. To day & tomorrow he had contemplated an effort for the purpose; but it will be even more convenient for him after Mr. Peters shall have had the requisite use of them.

RC (DLC). Addressed by JM.

From George Nicholas

DEAR SIR,   Feby. 9th. 94.

I thank you for your friendly and interesting communications of the 15th of Decr.[1] The situation of America has become very critical and interesting. The part which Congress ought to act is consequently difficult and attendend [sic] with many dangers. But I apprehend that there is more danger from their not following the dictates of their judgment, than of their not being able to discern the measures which the true interests of their country would render proper.

I confess that from every thing I see and hear my opinion is fixed that party spirit and private interest influence the deliberations of that body to such a degree, that their measures are seldom dictated by public policy. The conduct of G. B. must proceed from an opinion that she has nothing to fear from the resentment of America: if she has taken up this idea either from the partiality of our rulers to her interest, or from their general weakness or fears, it is high time, that we should consider the tendency of their attachments, their real abilities, and their resolution as to supporting not the honor, but the most important privileges of the nation.

The business of the Algerines I am sorry for as it will affect the nation at large; but I am pleased with it, as it disappoints the selfish and interested views of the addressers.[2] Their friends the British too have paid them well for their servile language. I expect to find them now more clamorous than any other set of men in America for a war. They have brought dishonour on their country; they have deceived the Executive by making them believe that the language of a few interested men, was that of the body of the people. I pray that such conduct may always meet with a similar fate.

Since my last letter to you, some new attempts have been made to raise a body of men to go against the Spaniards; but they will all fail for the want of money. It is said here generally, but I cannot vouch for the truth of it, that Genl. Logan had engaged to go with the party, but that he has declined it for the present from their not being furnished with the means of procuring the necessary supplies. Report also says that a Col: Montgomery is now at the mouth of the Cumberland where he has taken several boats loaded with provisions which he supposes to be Spanish property.

The Executive appear alarmed at these things which are trifling in their nature, and seem to disregard a danger which is imminent. The inhabitants of the western country have lost all confidence in the General government. They have commenced a plan[3] for acting in concert for the purpose of obtaining their just rights; this plan will be pursued until they obtain their object or shall be satisfied that there is no chance of attaining it in their present situation. A full and satisfactory conviction that this is the case will place them in a distressing situation: but disagreeable as it will be to act in that situation they must proceed: what they demand is so clearly their right, and so indispensably necessary to their welfare, that they must and will sacrifice every thing to obtain it. Former attachments, personal affection, smaller interests, and apprehensions from dangers of different kinds, must and will give way to their determined resolution of succeeding in this business. Under these circumstances the Genl. Governmt. ought to anticipate and agree to submit to all the consequences of our being compelled to act for ourselves, or by obtaining for us what we claim prevent our being compelled to take the management of it into our own hands.

You will probably be amused by Wayne with information that he is likely to make a peace with the Northern Indians. If he holds such language the proposals he has received will not justify him in doing so: they have been made by a very small and unimportant part of the Indians. Wayne may be desirous of patching up a peace, though a partial one only, for two reasons. It will prevent the censure he merits for his injudicious conduct last fall; and it will save him from the danger of a conflict with an enemy who he is now co[n]vinced he cannot subdue. In case of a rupture with G. B. it must be of the greatest importance to keep the Indians from uniting with them. If you make peace with the Indians when their force and spirits are at their present height, the English will make them break that peace as soon as they find it to their interest to do so; and then we shall have their united forces to combat with. But if we attack the Indians in a proper manner before the English can join them in an open manner, we may subdue them as a nation, cut off a great part of their warriors and take such steps with the remainder of them as will leave them neither inclination or strength to injure us for a considerable length of time.

We have just heard that our friend Randolph has succeeded Mr. Jefferson. I fear he has placed himself on a bed of thorns. His station will make him the mark at which all who are dissatisfied with public measures, will aim their shafts. When the measures of the government must be such as will either bring the government into disgrace, or endanger it's existence from the attacks of a foreign enemy, or the effects of civil discord, set on foot by party, and inflamed by the necessary demands for the support of the war, those who conduct that government can expect neither credit or peace in the execution of their offices: but I sincerely wish he may find both in any situation in which he is placed.

Genet is a madman but do not let us quarrel with his nation. Independent of our interest in their success from the nature of their dispute and our situation; if we fix an animosity in them towards us and at the same time get to blows with G. B. I fear that France and G. B. wd. make peace, and that we without one ally would be no match for England alone, much less for her with Spain &c. as her allies. But as long as she is engaged with France we should have nothing to fear from her. The additional expence of a war with America might bring on a national bankruptcy, and even if it had not that effect would cramp all her designs. But in case of a peace with France and a war with America a part only of her present expenditures would enable her to attempt any thing against us: so that her difficulties would be decreasing and our's increasing daily.

Are men such fools that liberty can no where be enjoyed, without it's being surrounded with such dangers as if not sufficient to swallow it up, are at least equal to the making of the possessors of it unhappy. With the greatest respect and esteem I am Dear Sir, Yr. friend and servt

G: NICHOLAS

RC (DLC). Docketed by JM, with his notation: "interesting."

1. Letter not found.

2. Nicholas alluded to the Federalist public meetings that passed resolutions approving Washington's Neutrality Proclamation. He asserted the views, widely held in Republican circles, that Federalists supported neutrality in hopes of gaining profitable trade with the belligerent powers and that Great Britain had arranged the truce between Portugal and Algiers in order to unleash the Algerine corsairs against American shipping (see JM to Monroe, 29 Oct. 1793, n. 2; Nicholas to JM, 15 Nov. 1793; JM's speeches of 27 Dec. 1793, n., and 30 Jan. 1794; Political Observations, 20 Apr. 1795).

3. For a description of this "plan," see Hubbard Taylor to JM, 13 Jan. 1794, n. 2.

Naval Force against Algerine Corsairs

[11 February 1794]

In debate on the naval shipbuilding program in the Committee of the Whole, Tracy argued: "The objectors against the armament are penny-wise and pound-foolish" (*Annals of Congress*, 3d Cong., 1st sess., 449).

Mr. Madison replied to several of the arguments of the gentlemen who were in favor of the resolutions. He went into some minute details respecting trade and commerce, and particularly remarked, that there was not any security for Portugal's renewing the truce with Algiers after the present term should expire.

Philadelphia Gazette, 12 Feb. 1794. After further debate, the committee approved the ways and means committee's report of 20 Jan. by a two-vote margin. JM was in the minority when the House on 21 Feb. passed resolutions based on the report and on 10 Mar. approved "An act to provide a naval armament." Washington signed the act, as amended by the Senate, on 27 Mar. (*Annals of Congress*, 3d Cong., 1st sess., 459, 498; *U.S. Statutes at Large*, 1:351).

To George Washington

Feby. 12. 1794

Mr. Madison presents his respectful compliments to the President, and begs leave to lay before him the inclosed letters, on behalf of a candidate for a vacancy in the Custom-House Department in Virginia. Mr. M. being a perfect stranger to the candidate can add no information whatever of his own. He knows Mr. Maury well, and considers his recommendation ⟨as res⟩pectable.

RC and enclosures (DLC: Washington Papers). Enclosures were Laurence Muse to JM, 1 Feb. 1794, and Fontaine Maury to JM, 4 Feb. 1794.

From John Dawson

DEAR SIR!   RICHMOND Febry. 12. 94.

It was with much pleasure I heard by the last evenings stage that the first of your resolutions had pervaild by a majority of five in the house of representatives, & most sincerely do I wish that they may ultimately succeed, fully convincd of this important truth "that the nation which

commands our commerce, will have a weight in our public counsels.["]
The thing cannot be otherwise.

Some of our members I find are however opposd to them—& never
was I more astonishd than to find Parker among the number, as I am
assurd there are several letters from him expressive of his warmest approbation. They may not suit the meridian of the borough of Norfolk
but woud give general satisfaction in the districts.

On the 8 Inst. a frigate of the French republic, L'Charante of 44 guns,
arrivd at Norfolk in 46 days from Rochefort. Nothing particular had
transpird at the date of my information, as only one person had been
on shore. The general news was, that Toulon was not retaken—that the
French were overcoming all Catalonia & Austrian Flanders—that the
affairs of the Republic were in the most flourishing situation—immense
preparations were making throughout the Kingdom for an Anglo-
expe[di]tion—that confidence was restord, & faction destroyd. With
real esteem Yr. friend & Sert

J Dawson.

RC (DLC).

From Samuel Vaughan, Jr.

DEAR SIR   LONDON. 14 Feby. 1794
The present calamatous times afford me the opportunity of intro-
ducing to Your acquaintance Monsieur Talleyrand Perigord,[1] whom
You are by reputation well acquainted with under the Title of the
Bishop of Autun. Altho' You will lament as much as myself the cause
of his retiring to Your Continent, Yet I have no doubt You will feel a
Pleasure in showing him those civilities & attentions which his Merit &
Character entitle him to.

I beg You to rest assured of the respect I still have & always shall
have for Your distinguished Talents—& of my anxiety to hold a place
in Your Esteem. I remain Dr Sir Your faithful & obedt humble Servt

SAMUEL VAUGHAN JUNR[2]

RC (DLC). Addressed by Vaughan to JM at Philadelphia, "By favor of Monsr.
Talleyrand Perigord." Docketed by JM.

1. Charles Maurice de Talleyrand-Périgord had been in exile from France since
1792. Deported from England, he arrived in Philadelphia on 28 Apr. 1794. The
new French minister, Jean Antoine Joseph Fauchet, persuaded Washington not to
receive Talleyrand and other émigrés publicly (John L. Earl III, "Talleyrand in
Philadelphia, 1794–1796," Pa. Mag. Hist. and Biog., 91 [1967]: 282–83, 286).

2. Vaughan, a merchant formerly of Philadelphia, had been acquainted with
JM for some years (Vaughan to JM, 17 Apr. 1789, PJM, 12:84–85 and n. 3).

From Samuel Vaughan, Jr.

DEAR SIR   LONDON 14 Feby. 1794

I beg leave to introduce to Your acquaintance Monsieur Beaumé[1] lately a Member of the Constituent Assembly, & who is driven by the Dangers of the present Time to the Universal Assylum of the Oppressed & Unsuccessful Advocates in the cause of Liberty—America. The Nature of his Situation & his Merit will both interest You in his favor & ensure those civilities towards him which I am solicitous to procure him. With the greatest respect & Attention I am Dear Sir Your faithful hble Servt.

SAML VAUGHAN JUNR.

RC (DLC). Addressed by Vaughan to JM in Philadelphia, "By favor of Monsr. Beaumé." Docketed by JM.

1. Bon-Albert Briois, chevalier de Beaumetz, was a deputy in the French National Assembly who proposed reforms of the criminal law code. Fleeing into exile in 1792, he accompanied Talleyrand to America (Lalanne, *Dictionnaire historique* [1877 ed.], p. 228).

From Thomas Jefferson

DEAR SIR   MONTICELLO Feb. 15. 1794.

We are here in a state of great quiet, having no public news to agitate us. I have never seen a Philadelphia paper since I left that place, nor learnt any thing of later date except some successes of the French the account of which seemed to have come by our vessel from Havre. It was said yesterday at our court that Genet was to be recalled: however nobody could tell how the information came. We have been told that mr. Smith's speech & your's also on your propositions have got into Davis's papers, but none of them have reached us. I could not have supposed, when at Philadelphia, that so little of what was passing there could be known even at Kentuckey, as is the case here. Judging from this of the rest of the Union, it is evident to me that the people are not in a condition either to approve or disapprove of their government, nor consequently to influence it. I have been occupied closely with my own affairs, and have therefore never been from home since my arrival here. I hear nothing yet of the second person[1] whom I had engaged as an overseer from the head of Elk, and the first I fear will prove a poor acquisition. Consequently I am likely to lose a year in the reformation of my plantations. The winter has been remarkeably mild—no demand for produce of any kind, at any market of James river. Tobacco &

wheat may be bartered at low prices for goods at high. But neither can be sold for cash. This was the state of things at Richmond when business was stopped by the smallpox. Here we can get tea at 2½ Dollars, white sugar at 38 Cents, coffee @ 25. cents &c for wheat @ 66⅔. Accept for yourself, Colo. & mrs. Monroe my affectionate respects

TH: JEFFERSON

RC (DLC); FC (DLC: Jefferson Papers).

1. Eli Alexander was an overseer, 1794–95, and later a tenant at Jefferson's Shadwell estate (Betts, *Jefferson's Garden Book*, pp. 206–7; Betts, *Jefferson's Farm Book*, p. 149).

¶ To John Dawson. Letter not found. *Ca. 16 February 1794.* Acknowledged in Dawson to JM, 25 Feb. 1794. Reports that the House of Representatives on 5 Feb. postponed consideration of JM's commercial discrimination resolutions until the first Monday in March.

From Alexander White

DEAR SIR   WOODVILLE 17th. Feb: 1794

I have to acknowledge your favr. of 4th instant[1] with the enclosures, and in return as usual can say little except with respect to the weather which has been so mild as to carry of[f] the late snow and leave the grain exposed to the various changes of season which may take place, but for want of more important subjects will enter into a Family detail commencing with an event probably known to you, the marriage of Nelly Hite with Mr. Theodorick Lee last April.[2] A similar Union took place between Sally Hite and Mr Alexr Pitt Buchanan of Baltimore 14th Ulo.[3] With them Betsy Briscoe[4] is gone, and Polly Hite[5] is with her Sister Lee, so that we remain solus cum sola unless A White whose scene of Action or rather scene of thought is the Office can be considered of our company. Thus situated; the correspondence and Miscellaneous communications of absent Friends become the more engaging. Are Mr. Priestly or Mr Couper the Author of Reports The Task &c yet in Philadelphia?[6] Do they intend this way? How do they like our Country? Mr Toulman I understand has a high opinion of Kentucky as a farming Country. He spent some time with me before he went there; I was much pleased with his company, and to render the scene more agreeable Miss Madison was of the party. Has our Friend our Republican Friend Page made his appearance yet?[7] If he has give my particular Complts. and tell him he has neglected me as he was among the first I wrote to. Adieu And believe me sincerely yours

ALEXR WHITE

P. S A letter from a Gentleman in Baltimore this moment informs me, that the Court of G B. has demanded from America a categorical answer to this Question—What part will you take in the War? Is this true?

RC (DLC). Docketed by JM.

1. Letter not found.
2. Catherine (Nelly) Hite was the youngest of three daughters of John Hite of Winchester and the granddaughter of Jacob Hite (whose second wife was JM's aunt Frances Madison Beale Hite). On 20 Apr. 1793 she married Theodorick Lee (1766–1849), the younger brother of Henry, Charles, and Richard Bland Lee. The marriage was performed by the Reverend Alexander Balmain (husband of JM's cousin Lucy Taylor), who later presided at JM's wedding (Lee, *Lee of Virginia*, pp. 298, 372–73; Davis, *Frederick County Marriages*, pp. 47, 129).
3. Sarah (Sally) Hite was a sister of Catherine Hite. Alexander Balmain presided at her wedding to Alexander Pitt Buchanan. Her mother, also named Sarah, was Alexander White's second wife (Cartmell, *Shenandoah Valley Pioneers*, p. 255; Davis, *Frederick County Marriages*, pp. 22, 129).
4. In 1791 Elizabeth Briscoe was married at Winchester to JM's friend and political ally Archibald Stuart of Augusta County (*Tyler's Quarterly*, 9 [1927–28]: 284).
5. Mary (Polly) Hite was a sister of Catherine and Sarah Hite (Cartmell, *Shenandoah Valley Pioneers*, p. 255).
6. White confused the English reformer Thomas Cooper with the poet William Cowper. Joseph Priestley, Jr., and Cooper visited America in 1793, seeking a site for "an English settlement in America." Cooper returned to England and in 1794 the renowned liberal Dr. Joseph Priestley, Sr., immigrated to the U.S. He was soon joined by Cooper (Dumas Malone, *The Public Life of Thomas Cooper, 1783–1839* [New Haven, 1926], pp. 75–76, 79–80).
7. John Page took his seat in the House of Representatives on 7 Feb. (*Annals of Congress*, 3d Cong., 1st sess., 437).

¶ From James Madison, Sr. Letter not found. *17 February 1794*. Acknowledged in JM to James Madison, Sr., 10 Mar. 1794. Asks JM to make inquiries in Philadelphia about purchasing a piano for his sister Frances Taylor Madison. Requests advice on building a gristmill. Asks for information about a threshing mill (probably the model recently procured by Jefferson). Informs JM that apple trees have been purchased. Inquires about Edmond Charles Genet.

From Benjamin Stoddert and Others

Sir   George Town 18. Feby 1794

We have the honor to inclose, the proceedings of a number of the Inhabitants of the Territory of Columbia in relation to the establishment of a College in the City of Washington, or its vicinity.[1] You will perceive Sir, that the meeting have taken the Freedom to place your name in the list of those they have solicited to receive subscriptions.

If your more important avocations will permit you to pay any attention to the wishes of the persons by whom we are deputed to be thus troublesom, you would lay them under additional obligations, if you would be so good as to forward to us, by the 21st. of next month, the names of those who encourage the projected institution, by subscriptions to your paper. We have the honor to be with great respect sir Yr. most obed Servts.

BEN STODDERT
JAS M LINGAN
J MASON.

RC (DLC). Addressed by Stoddert to JM in Philadelphia and franked. Docketed by JM. Enclosure not found, but see n. 1.

1. The committee enclosed a broadside, *At a Meeting of a Number of Inhabitants of the Territory of Columbia, on the 4th of February 1794 . . .* (Georgetown, 1794; Evans 46966). Robert Peter, mayor of Georgetown, presided at the meeting where a resolution passed "that a Seminary of Learning . . . be established in the City of Washington, on the heights near Rock-Creek." JM was named on a list of forty-six "gentlemen [to] be solicited to take charge" of raising $50,000 by selling shares at $20 each. The meeting appointed Stoddert, James Maccubbin Lingan, and John Mason (three of the original proprietors of the federal district) as "a committee to cause these proceedings to be printed and copies sent to the different gentlemen named to solicit subscriptions." In a 15 Dec. 1794 letter to Edmund Randolph, Washington asked the secretary of state to consult with JM about "the measures which will be proper for me to pursue" regarding the "plan . . . for establishing a Seminary of learning upon an extensive scale in the Federal city" (Fitzpatrick, *Writings of Washington*, 34:59). The project was unsuccessful.

To James Madison, Sr.

HOND SIR   PHILADA. Feby. 21. 94.

The last I recd. from you was of the 27. Ult. I have not yet had time to examine whether I can draw your interest here by virtue of the power in my hands.[1] It does not seem necessary to decide now on the spot for the Peccan trees, if any should proceed from the Nuts left with you by Mr. Jefferson. They can be easily removed at any time. I have not fixed on any particular no. of Apple Trees. I would chuse a pretty large orchard if to be had and of the sort you think best. If a sufficient number cannot be got for Black-Meadow & Sawney's, I would be glad to have them divided; & if not worth that, to be planted rather at Sawney's. How has it happened that the Money left for you in Fredg. has not been recd.? I suppose it has never been applied for.

The British packet lately arrived has brought despatches from our Minister there which are no doubt important; but the subject of them is not yet disclosed to Congress. As the British Minister here, has also despatches, & nothing has leaked from that quarter it may be inferred that the intelligence has nothing agreeable to him in it as to the internal affairs of G. B. or agreeable to us in relation to our affairs with that Country.

The Commercial propositions moved sometime ago, were postponed till 1st. Monday in March, at the instance of some Eastern Members friendly to them, who wished to communicate with their Constituents. The proposition for a fleet to block up the Algerines was carried in its *first* stage by 47 to 45. & this small majority is going on with the ways & means. The opponents of the measure consider it as inadequate to the object—that if adequate, it wd. not be permitted by the policy which let loose the Algerines, to take effect—that if this policy did not oppose, a less sum wd. purchase peace—& that sending ships of force among the armed powers, would entangle us in the war, if any thing wd. do it.

Several French Ships of war are arrived in Chesapeak Bay, which are said to have brought a Successor to Mr. Genet, and accounts of the greatest prosperity in the affairs of France.

If Mr. Hite & my sister shd. have visited Orange—as he intended when he last wrote me, tell him that I answered his letter on that subject.[2] It is not probable that an adjournment will take place in time for me to see him before his return. What is the prospect in the Wheat fields? What account does Collins give of my Timothy? What has Louis Collins done, and what doing? &ca. My Affection to My Mother & the family. Yr Affe Son

Js. MADISON JR

RC (DLC). Franked and addressed by JM to his father in Orange County, "care of James Blair Esqe / Fredericksburg / Virginia." Docketed by James Madison, Sr. Below the signature JM's father outlined a reply (see James Madison, Sr., to JM, ca. 15 Mar. 1794).

1. Since interest on treasury notes could be drawn in Philadelphia, James Madison, Sr., gave JM power of attorney to collect interest in his name (James Madison, Sr., to JM, 11 May 1791, JM to James Madison, Sr., 3 Dec. 1791, and Power of Attorney from James Madison, Sr., 28 Feb. 1792, *PJM*, 14:20, 22 n. 2, 134, 239).

2. Letters not found.

To Horatio Gates

Your favor of the 3d. was handed me by Docr. Robertson, whose return to N. York gives me this opportunity of thanking you for his acquaintance. It has been a mortification that I could not avail myself more of it.

The Budget from Mr. Pinkney has not yet been laid before Congress. If there were any thing agreeable in the internal affairs of G. B. or in those which concern this Country, it would probably have found its way into conversation from Mr. Hammond's correspondence. I understand that great reserve has been maintained in that quarter.

You will have seen by the Newspapers that a Successor to Genet has just made his appearance.[1] I have not yet seen him; but am told his deportment, tho' a young man, promises more temperance than marked the character of his predecessor. He left France the 24 Decr. but undertakes to decide nothing with regard to Toulon, beyond the immense exertions in train for reducing it. He represents the condition of France in general as auspicious, and the Revolution as firm as a Rock.

The question so long agitated in the Senate as well as out of it, in relation to their doors, has at last been carried for opening them.[2] There being no preparation of a Gallery, the rule will not be put in practice till the ensuing Session, but is on a footing that secures it against all possible danger of being then frustrated. After it was discovered that the vote could not be defeated *19* members fell into it; some who had been most intrepid in opposing the public voice on this Subject.

The House of Reps. have been of late occupied with the project of a fleet to block up the Mediterranean. It has passed thro' several stages, but by such bare majorities that the final success of the measure is not certain. The opponents of it—among whom I include myself, think the force proposed as well as any we can afford, inadequate to the object: that if adequate the same policy that removed the portuguese fleet—would not permit ours to do what that was not allowed to do: that if a fleet would be permitted to force the Algerines into our views, they might be accomplished on better terms either by tribute to those Barbarians, or by arrangements with Portugal, who is more interested in our trade than we are ourselves.

I do not know that it will be convenient for me to visit N. York before I return to Virginia. The pleasure to which you invite me will be a motive that will have its full effect. I am sorry to hear that you sometimes complain of symtoms of infirm health. Let me recommend the best medicine in the world: a long journey, at a mild Season, thro' a pleasant

Country, in easy stages. As you best know our whole Country, you can best select the season & route that claim these merits. Present my choicest respects to Mrs. Gates, and be assured of the affectionate esteem with which I am Dear Sir Yr friend & servt

Js. MADISON JR

RC (NHi). Addressed by JM to Gates in New York, "Hon'd by Docr. Robertson." Docketed by Gates.

1. On 22 Feb. Jean Antoine Joseph Fauchet presented his credentials as French minister plenipotentiary to the U.S. (Twohig, *Journal of the Proceedings of the President*, p. 286).

2. The Senate's self-imposed secrecy rankled Virginians. Monroe carried out an instruction from the Virginia General Assembly in February 1791 when he introduced a bill aimed at opening the Senate doors. Congressman Anthony New saw the 20 Feb. 1794 resolution, which passed 19 to 8, as heralding "an event long desired, and from which the best predictions are deduced in favor of republicanism" (Ammon, *James Monroe*, pp. 83–84; *Annals of Congress*, 3d Cong., 1st sess., 46–47; Cunningham, *Circular Letters of Congressmen*, 1:19).

From John Dawson

DEAR SIR!   RICHD Feby. 25: 94.

I am favour'd with your letter. It may have been politic to pos[t]pone the resolutions offer'd by you, but realy I cannot at this distance see through it.

On the last evening a meeting of a number of Citizens was to have been held in this place to declare to their representative their opinions of his vote.[1] What the[y] did I know not but presume it will be immediately forwarded to him, & will no doubt be warmly in favour of the resolutions.

I am very anxious to hear some thing about our new French minister, & of what has become of Genet.[2] Yrs. sincerely

J DAWSON

RC (DLC).

1. Federalist Samuel Griffin, whose constituency included Richmond, was one of three Virginians who voted with the minority when the House of Representatives on 5 Feb. postponed consideration of JM's commercial discrimination resolutions. Federalists hoped to defeat the resolutions by forcing an immediate vote (*Annals of Congress*, 3d Cong., 1st sess., 431–32; JM's speeches of 5 Feb. 1794, nn.; JM to Jefferson, 2 Mar. 1794).

2. Fauchet brought orders from the French government for Genet's arrest. The former French minister sought asylum and settled in the U.S.

From Pechy Bledsoe

HONRD. SIR,   FEDRIXBURG 28th. Feby 1794.

The hapiness of having had a slight acquaintance with you, induces me to trouble you with a small piece of business, respecting The servise of a man from your own County, whose Discharge you will Receive inclos'd.

I made application to Colo. Maddison Senr. for Advice respecting the Conduction of this business. Himself, with several other Gentleman Supposed my Power of Attourney was not Sufficient to Make you a Legal power, But Rather thought it expedient for me to send on the Discharge to your Honour, who cou'd Lay in the Claim, before the Expiration of the time Limited, By Act of Congress for the purpose of Setling Claims against the United States,[1] (Which time Expires on or about the 27th March, as I have been informd) As they expected it would be sufficient to Secure it, untill a person properly authouris'd shou'd make application.

This man Serv'd Two years, which I suppose the Continental Books will Shew, as the Regiment he enlisted & serv'd in, was recruted for that Term of time.

I have the pleasure to inform you, that this state has pass a Law, in favour of the Pettion, you was so Obliging as to Draw for me respecting my own Service To Virginia.[2]

Any thing necessary, Respecting Mr. Thomasons[3] Service, I shou'd be glad to be inform'd off [sic], A Letter Directed to me Inclos'd in one to the Colo. your Father wou'd in a short time get to my hands Especially, if to the Care of my Uncle Aaron Bledsoe. I am Sir With Esteem Your Hume. Servt.

PECHY BLEDSOE[4]

RC (DLC). Addressed by Bledsoe and franked. Docketed by JM: "Peachy Bledsoe." Enclosure not found.

1. "An Act providing for the settlement of the Claims of Persons under particular circumstances barred by the limitations heretofore established" of 27 Mar. 1792 (*U.S. Statutes at Large*, 1:245).

2. On 28 Oct. 1793 Bledsoe's petition requesting "certificates for the arrears and depreciation of his pay" was presented to the Virginia House of Delegates. On 9 Dec. the General Assembly passed an act directing the auditor of the public accounts to issue Bledsoe "a certificate for the depreciation of pay due to him for his services, as a serjeant in the second state regiment," 1777–80, "together with warrants for the interest due thereon" (*JHDV*, Oct. 1793, p. 21; Shepherd, *Statutes*, 1:281).

3. Turner Thomason served in 1777 as a private in the Second Virginia Battalion. His company commander was JM's second cousin, Francis Taylor (*VMHB*, 6 [1898–99]: 125–26).

4. Little is known of Pechy (pronounced "Peachy") Bledsoe, except his military record in the Revolution and his marriage bond of July 1780 to Peggy George in Henry County (*VMHB*, 21 [1913]: 277).

From James Maury

DEAR SIR,   LIVERPOOL 1 Mar 1794

I had this pleasure the 8 November.[1]All your Sales being now closed, I lay them before you. The 3 stemed Hhds were treated in the Manner I had several Times recommended; & I am well pleased to see they have answered my Expectations.

For the News I beg to refer you to the papers wch. will be delivered to you by this opportunity. Notwithstanding the immense warlike preparations, I stil[l] flatter myself peace is not remote. I am with true Esteem dr Sir yr obliged friend & St

                                                        JAMES MAURY

℔ Venus	4 hhds	39.10—
Jessie	1. do	6.14.3
Maria	3. do	61.14.1
		107.18.4

RC and enclosures (DLC). Maury enclosed receipted accounts (4 pp.), summarized in the postscript, for sale of JM's tobacco.

1. Letter not found.

From Alexander White

DEAR SIR   WOODVILLE 1st. March 1794

I am favd. with yours of 17th Ulo.[1] with the enclosures. I have never seen a fair discussion in support of your resolutions—only desultory observations of several Members. Smith's Speach has arrived I have had a cursory reading of it only. I am not sufficiently informed to give a decided opinion with respect to equipping a Fleet to check the Algerines. I am rather inclined in favor of it—but my great object is our internal defence—Security to our Coasts and Harbours with a Militia well regulated and well armed. I am just now informed that there is in Winchester an address from General Clarke to the People encouraging them to enlist under his Banners, in the address he styles himself General of the Revolutionary Legions of Kentucky Also General St Clairs Counter Proclamation, they will be in the Winchesters paper of Monday.[2] During the Night of the 22d a heavy Snow fell. Sunday was mild—but Monday Tuesday and Wednesday were the severest days we have had this winter, the weather has since moderated and the snow wasted but yet covers the ground. Electioneering has taken deep root in this County no less than six Candidates. Our Friend Zane has been brought into trouble. Some falsehoods were propagated with regard to Mr. Pages[3] conduct in the last Assembly. Zane was mentioned as the Author. Page wrote to Zane for explanation or denial. Zane resented the insinuation, and wrote an irritating answer. Page sent a Message by General Morgan, which procured a letter from Zane disavowing his being the author of the report. Page expected some further acknowledgement, which Zane refusing to give Page published the letter above mentioned with an introduction in which he said Zane was constrained to write it[4]—to a paper war succeeded challenges, Seconds chosen times & places appointed, but at length a Quaker Alderman of Winchester (after several of the County Magestrates had refused to interfere) granted a peace Warrant. The Gentlemen were both bound to their good behaviour, and thus ended the great affair. Zane you no doubt have heard is a general.[5] If I had had anything more interesting I should not have blotted Paper with this silly Tale. Adieu, and believe me Yours sincerely

ALEXR WHITE

RC (DLC). Docketed by JM.

1. Letter not found.

2. On 3 Mar. 1794 *Bowen's Va. Centinel and Gazette; or, The Winchester Repository* summarized the 8 Feb. Lexington *Ky. Gazette* report of George Rogers Clark's 25 Jan. "proposals . . . for raising volunteers for the reduction of the Spanish Posts on the Mississippi, for opening the trade of said river" and the 7 Dec. 1793 proclamation of Arthur St. Clair, governor of the Northwest Territory, forbidding inhabitants to join or aid, and ordering civil and military officers to prevent, such French-inspired expeditions.

3. Matthew Page (b. 1762) was a cousin of Congressman John Page. He moved from Hanover County to Frederick County circa 1780 and served in the House of Delegates, 1790–94 (Page, *Genealogy of the Page Family*, pp. 140–41; Cartmell, *Shenandoah Valley Pioneers*, p. 458; Swem and Williams, *Register*, p. 414).

4. On 17 Feb. 1794 *Bowen's Va. Centinel and Gazette; or, The Winchester Repository* published Page's announcement to the "Fellow-Citizens, Freeholders of Frederick County" of 15 Feb. and Isaac Zane's letter to Page of 6 Feb. The dispute concerned allegations that Page had sponsored a bill for the relief of delinquent sheriffs.

5. Zane was appointed a brigadier general, commanding the Twelfth Virginia Militia Division (*Va. Herald, and Fredericksburg Advertiser*, 12 Dec. 1793).

To Thomas Jefferson

DEAR SIR   PHILADA. March 2d. 1794.

Your favor of the 15th. Ult: came to hand two days ago. It was not my intention that my first to you should have been procrastinated to the present date; but several causes have concurred in producing the effect. Among others I was in hopes every week to be able to furnish you with the proceedings on the subject grounded on your Commercial Report;[1] and particularly with such of them as related to yourself. It has so happened that I never could find leisure to make out for the press, the share I had in them till very lately. The earlier part of my observations were sent to the Printer several weeks ago, but never made their appearance till thursday evening last.[2] The latter part is following, as you will find, as fast as I can write it out, which from the extreme length of it, the brevity of my notes, and the time that has run since the observations were delivered, is a task equally tedious & laborious. The sequel will be forwarded to you as soon as it gets into print. As you are so little supplied with the current information it may be necessary to apprize you that after the general discussions on the measure proposed by me, had been closed, and the first general resolution agreed to by a majority of 5 or 6, several of the Eastern members friendly to the object insisted on a postponement till the first monday in March. It was necessary to gratify them, and the postponement was carried by a small majority against the efforts of the adverse party, who counted on the votes of the timid members if forced before they could learn the sense of their constituents. The Interval has produced vast exertions by the British party to mislead the people of the Eastern States. No means have been spared. The most artful & wicked calumnies have been propagated with all the zeal which malice and interest could invent. The blackest of these calumnies, as you may imagine have fallen to the lot of the mover of the Resolutions. The last Boston paper contains a string of charges[3] framed for the purpose of making the Eastern people believe that he has been the counsellor & abettor of Genèt in all his extravagances, and a corrupt tool of France ever since the embassy of Gerard. It appears however that in spite of all these diabolical manœvres, the town of Boston has been so far awakened as to have a Meeting[4] in the town house, & a pretty unanimous vote for a committee to consider the subject & report proper instructions for their members in Congress. The Committee consists of men of weight, and for the most part of men of the right sort. There are some however who will endeavor to give a wrong turn to the business. I see by a paper of last evening that even in N. York a meeting[5] of the people has taken place at the instance of the Republican party, and that a committee is appointed for the like purpose. As far as I know the names, the majority is on the right side. One motive for postponing the question so long was the chance of hearing from England, and the probability that the intelligence would strengthen the arguments for retaliation. Letters from Pinkney have accordingly arrived. As yet they are under the seal of confidence[6] but it is in universal conversation that they mark precisely and *more strongly* than ever the unjust & unfriendly features which have characterized the British policy towards the U. States. Soon after the arrival of the Packet, Mr. Randolph wrote to Hammond desiring to know whether an answer had been received to your letter of May 1792. His reply was simply that it had not.[7]

The scheme of Frigates to block up the Mediterranean has been pushed slowly, but successfully to the stage of resolutions on which a Bill is to be reported. The Majority has never exceeded two or three votes. Whether the scheme will finally take effect, is not certain. It probably will, unless accounts from Europe furnish hopes that Spain, or Portugal particularly the latter which is friendly and interested in our trade, may interpose.

Genèt has been superseded by Fauchèt, the Secretary to the Executive Council. The latter has not been here long eno' to develope his temper & character. He has the aspect of moderation. His account of things in France is very favorable on the whole. He takes particular pains to assure all who talk with him of the perseverance of France in her attachment to us, and her anxiety that nothing which may have taken place, may lessen it on our side. In his interview with the President, he held the same language; and I am told by E. R. that the P. not only declared explicitly his affectionate solicitude for the success of the Republic, but after he had done so with great emphasis, desired, in order to be as pointed as possible, that his expressions might be repeated, by E. R. who acted as Interpreter. Fauchet does not speak our language. La Forest comes over with the Minister as Consul General: And Petry, formerly Consul of S. C. as Consul for this place.[8] The political characters of these gentlemen as heretofore understood, give some uneasiness to the Republican party; and the uneasiness has been increased by the homage paid by the leaders of the other party to the new Minister. They may probably aim at practising on him, by abusing the madness of Genèt and representing the Republicans as rather his partisans, than the friends of the French cause. But if he is not an uncommon fool, or a traytor, it is impossible he can play into their hands, because the Anglicism stamped on the aristocratic faction must warn him of its hostility to his objects. Genèt has not taken any decided step in relation to his future movements. He is said to be poor; and by some to meditate a return to France with a view to join the army, by others a settlement in this Country as a farmer. If he is prudent he will not venture to France in her present temper, with all the suspicions & follies with which he is loaded. You must have seen that Brissot & his party have been cut off by the Guillotine.

I am informed by an anonymous letter[9] from N. York, that large purchases are making there, & in the Eastern States, for supplying the British armaments in the W. Indies; and that American Vessels are chartering for the conveyance of them. This is really horrible. Whilst we allow the British to stop our supplies to the French Dominions, we allow our citizens to carry supplies to hers, for the known purpose of aiding her in taking from France the Islands we have guaranteed to her; and transferring these valuable markets from friendly & to unfriendly hands. What can be done. The letter writer suggests an Embargo. Perhaps the best step wd. be to declare that so long as G. B. will not allow the French to be supplied by us, we will not allow our supplies to go to her. It is not clear however that such a measure wd. stand the clamor of the merchts. seconded by the interest of the farmers & ship owners.

RC (DLC). Unsigned. Docketed by Jefferson, "recd. Mar. 31."

1. JM referred to the proceedings in the House of Representatives on his commercial discrimination resolutions, which were intended to implement the proposals in Jefferson's "Report . . . on the Privileges and Restrictions on the Commerce of the United States" of 16 Dec. 1793.

2. On 27 Feb. Andrew Brown's *Philadelphia Gazette* began the serial publication of the full text of JM's speeches of 14, 30, and 31 Jan. 1794.

3. On the attacks by Federalist Benjamin Russell's Boston *Columbian Centinel* against JM and his commercial discrimination resolutions, see Madison in the Third Congress, 2 Dec. 1793–3 Mar. 1795.

4. On the 13 Feb. Boston town meeting, see ibid.

5. On the 27 Feb. New York town meeting, see ibid. The 1 Mar. *Philadelphia Gazette* published an article on the meeting.

6. On 24 Feb. Washington sent to Congress his administration's recent diplomatic correspondence, including extracts from Thomas Pinckney to the secretary of state, 25 Nov. 1793. This letter, which the president declared "of a confidential nature," recounted an inconclusive conversation with British foreign minister Lord Grenville concerning the western posts, Algerine pirates, and "the interruption to our commerce and neutral rights" (*ASP, Foreign Relations*, 1:327).

7. This correspondence concerned American allegations of British violations of the Treaty of Paris of 1783 (Jefferson to George Hammond, 29 May 1792, Edmund Randolph to Hammond, 21 Feb. 1794, and Hammond to Randolph, 21 Feb. 1794, ibid., 1:201–16, 328).

8. In an effort to prevent a repetition of the embarrassments caused by Genet, the French government appointed commissioners to serve with his successor, Fauchet. Besides the comte de La Forest and Jean Baptiste Petry, Georges-Pierre Le Blanc (secretary of legation and former chief of the Paris police) was also appointed a commissioner (Conway, *Edmund Randolph*, p. 237).

9. Letter not found.

From John Dawson

DEAR SIR! RICH March 2th. 94

The last evenings stage brought me your letter[1] & a paper of the 21. of the last month.

Before it was not doubted here, that M. Fauchet was appointed to succeed Genet—had arrivd with the fleet at Norfolk & immediately proceeded on to Pha. & yet by the paper of the 21. it appears that he has not arrivd, & doubts are started as to this appointment. This affair appears involvd in some obscurity, which I expect the next mail will clear up.

On yesterday all the militia companies of this city met, &, una voce, came to a number of resolutions[2] expressive of their approbation of the commercial ones before your house. They are to be pri[n]ted in the morrows paper, & a copy forwarded to the delegation. They will I think give an alarm to Mr. G[3]—if his *city* friends forsake him he may hang up his fiddle.

I rejoice to hear that the Senate has agreed to open their doors. With real esteem Yr. friend & Sert

J DAWSON

RC (DLC).

1. Letter not found.

2. On the 1 Mar. resolutions of the Nineteenth Virginia Militia Regiment, see Madison in the Third Congress, 2 Dec. 1793–3 Mar. 1795.

3. Samuel Griffin. On his opposition to JM's commercial discrimination resolutions, see Dawson to JM, 25 Feb. 1794, n. 1.

¶ To Alexander White. Letter not found. *2 March 1794.* Acknowledged in White to JM, 30 Mar. 1794. Probably reports on legislation pending in Congress, including the bill for a naval force against the Algerine corsairs.

From Joseph Jones

DR. SR. FREDG. 4th. Mar: 1794

It is with real pleasure I learn there is a probability of a favourable issue to the consultations in Boston on the commercial propositions. If, before Mr. Pinkneys communications are promulgated, the People of that City in general felt a degree of resentment to the unjust and unprecedented conduct of the British nation towards us, the knowledge that we have nothing to hope or expect from them in future but a continuation of the like treatment, cannot fail to excite in them just resent-

ment & the adoption of such measures as are calculated to counteract
the unwarrantable policy of the British nation—their present policy and
views, so far as they can be seen through, appear to me to be replete
with danger to the future freedom of commerce and navigation; for
what is it they may not attempt, if not accomplish, (stimulated by pride
and avarice) when they shall possess all the great maritime ports of
France ⟨near⟩ their coast, the French Wt India islands, and those places
in the Et. Indies belonging to France, and having as they have generally
had, untill the increased navy of France held them in check, so great a
superiority at Sea. From experience we know the British nation disposed to dictate what shall be law on the water, and to make that Trade
contraband and neutral property liable to seizure and condemnation
wch. the Law of nations does not justify—and why, because she has
Power, and having Power may enforce obedience and submission to her
will. Thus the Strong who are regardless of Law kick and buffet the
weak, and if they complain, or speak big or saucily, are kicked and
cuffed again, untill they tamely submit to the insolent and overbearing
hand of oppression. If I am to be the drudge of another let me have the
consolation to know that I have not tamely or voluntarily submitted to
that Slavish condition but am reduced to it by force, not consent. The
cordial reception of the New Minister from France and the apparent
affection manifested for his Nation so contrary to what was exhibited
through the course of Genets ministry may be well ascribed to the
readiness with which the Convention gratified the desire of the Executive here, and to the different conduct and deportment of Fauchet on
his arrival, and presenting his credentials to the Executive—but I hold
it next to impossible that he can be duped, possessing the abilities he
is said to possess, by the mere ceremony of what they call Court parade.
The inveteracy wch. at present exists between France and Britain like
oyl and water may for a moment appear to mix but will soon separate.
Our Executive indeed seeing how much the people of America in general are attached to the French revolution, and how loudly, on many
occasions, they complain of British injury and injustice, may have seriously resolved to pursue a more friendly course to France than it is
supposed they have done for some time past, especially as Mr. Pinkneys
communications will not authorise a different conduct, or an adherence
to British policy. Should Gallatine loose his seat[1] it will I think be a
public misfortune, not only as I take him to be a staunch Republican,
but a man of respectable Character and abilities. Tell Monroe and his
little woman if she is returned I wish them well. Yr. friend & Servt

Jos. Jones

RC (DLC). Docketed by JM.

1. Federalists challenged the election of Albert Gallatin as a U.S. senator from

Pennsylvania, alleging that he had not been a citizen for nine years as required by the Constitution. By a partisan 14–12 vote, the Senate declared Gallatin's election void on 28 Feb. (*Annals of Congress*, 3d Cong., 1st sess., 57).

To Thomas Jefferson

DEAR SIR   PHILADA. March 9. 1794.

I send you the continuation[1] promised in my last, which I believe makes up the whole. If there should be any chasm let me know, and I will supply it. I have some little doubt the paper of Tuesday March 4. may have been omitted, and would now add it, but can not get it conveniently in time.

The commercial propositions were postponed for one week longer, on the arrival of the appointed day. Tomorrow they will again come on, unless precluded by debates on other business, or again postponed. You will see by the inclosed in what manner the Meeting at Boston issued, and the course the subject is taking at N. York. There was a large Mercantile Meeting[2] last night in this City, for obtaining a vote of remonstrance agst. the propositions. A paper was accordingly introduced by Fitzimmons, Bingham &c. It was warmly & I am told ably attacked by Swanwick who explained & defended the propositions. He was clapped, and on the question, there were three or four nos for 1 aye to the paper. The minority had the arrogance notwithstanding to sign the paper individually, and will recruit all the names they can to day, among the Quaker's and others not present at the Meeting, in order to deliver in the paper with more effect tomorrow Morning. What the fate of the propositions will be is more uncertain than ever. Some of the friends of them, begin to say that more vigorous measures are rendered necessary by the progress of British outrages. The *additional* instruction of Novr. 6.[3] which you will find in the inclosed papers, is so severely felt by the Merchants that some of them also, without relinquishing their opposition to what is proposed, talk of measures more congenial with the crisis. An Embargo, on American vessels—on these & British also—and even on a seisure of British property, are in the mouths of some of them. The additional instruction is questioned by some as inauthentic; but it is infinitely probable that it is genuine. The doubt is founded on the earliness of its date compared with that of our last intelligence from Europe which is silent as to that matter. But it may have been decreed in the Cabinet & not put in force; or given into the hands of officers clandestinely, that the American prey might not escape. Our situation is certainly ripening to a most serious crisis. It does not appear however that in any event the commercial retaliation can be improper; but on the contrary that in every event it will be advantageous.

You will perceive that Fauchét is going on in the conciliatory plan of reversing the errors of his Predecessor.

The project of a squadron of frigates is pursued with unremitting ardor. In the course of the Bill the two 20 gun ships have been turned into 2 of 36 guns. So that the force is to consist of 6 in the whole, 4 of which will be of 40 guns. As the danger of a war has appeared to increase, every consideration rendering them at first unwise, now renders them absurd; yet the vague idea of protecting trade when it most needs it, misleads the interested who are weak, and the weak who are not interested.

I have this moment recd. a note informing me that there are letters from N. Y. containing definitive intelligence concerning Toulon.[4] The British burnt sixteen French Sail of the Line in their escaping out of the Harbour. Many of the Toulonese were drowned in attempting to get on board the British Ships. All the remaining Inhabitants were drawn up in the public Square, and underwent military execution. The information comes by a Vessel from Carthagena. Adieu. Yrs. Affy.

Js. MADISON Jr

RC (DLC). Docketed by Jefferson, "recd. Mar. 31." Enclosures not found, but see n. 1.

1. JM probably enclosed the *Philadelphia Gazette*'s continuing installments of the full texts of his speeches of 30 and 31 Jan. on commercial discrimination against Great Britain.

2. A meeting of "the Merchants and Traders of the city of Philadelphia" was called for 8 Mar. "to appoint a committee to collect information respecting the capture and detention of vessels belonging to the citizens of the United States, by the cruisers of the nations at war, to lay the same before the President of the United States, with such representation as they may find necessary." The defeat of the "remonstrance" described by JM put an end to the project (*Philadelphia Gazette*, 5 Mar. 1794; Philadelphia *General Advertiser*, 13 Mar. 1794).

3. The British order in council of 6 Nov. 1793 authorized the detention of "all ships laden with goods the produce of any colony belonging to France, or carrying provisions or other supplies for the use of any such colony" (*ASP, Foreign Relations*, 1:430).

4. JM referred to reports that the French revolutionary army had recaptured Toulon on 19 Dec. 1793 after a long siege. French royalists and British forces had occupied the city since 29 Aug. (*Philadelphia Gazette*, 10 Mar. 1794; Lefebvre, *French Revolution*, 2:15–16).

¶ To Walter Jones. Letter not found. *9 March 1794.* Acknowledged in Jones to JM, 25 Mar. 1794. Informs Jones that the success of JM's resolutions on commercial discrimination has become doubtful.

To James Madison, Sr.

HOND SIR   March 10. 1794.

Yours of Feby. 17. came to hand some days ago. I have applied to Carr,[1] and obtained the inclosed account of his Forte-Piano's. The grand ones are as large as a Harpsichord & of the same form. The small ones would not occupy more room than a common square dining table with the leaves down. The advantage of the large ones consists in the superior swell of the Notes. But on this point Fanny can get sufficient information from her friends—or from the person you have in view for her Teacher.

I can offer no advice as to the Mill.[2] You are a m⟨uch b⟩etter judge in every respect of the subject. It appears in g⟨ener⟩al that it would be better she should be leased on almost any terms than that you should be troubled with her. You know my thoughts already as to building the new one at home. I have no further acct. of the Threshing Mill.

I am glad to find that you have procured the apple Trees. My last will have shewn that the additional 20 would have my approbation.

You ask the fate of Genèt! He is superseded by Mr. Fauchét who lately arrived; and his conduct as complained of by the President disavowed. Whether he means to go to France or remain here I know not. By a little publication[3] just made in the Newspapers by Fauchét all the commissions issued by Genèt for enlisting troops are revoked; and the neutrality of the U. S. recognized.

The depredations on our commerce from G. Britain become daily more ruinous to it. A further instruction for seizing our vessels has just appeared, which will be fatal to a great part of our shipping now out. The authenticity of the document is questioned, but the prevailing opinion admits it. The demand however from the French Ships, and for the English in the W. Indies keeps up for the present the price of Wheat & flour. The former has of late been 8 or 9/. & the latter in proportion.

The Commercial Resolutions are not yet decided on, except the first one. They stand the order of today. The event of them is more uncertain than ever; some of their friends beginning to think the outrages of G. Britain require something more effacacious & even some of their enemies beginning to hold the same language. There have been meetings on the subject at Boston, N. York & in this City. In Boston the Come. reported instructions to the Representa[t]ives favorable to the Resolutions; but the arts practised to alarm the people obtained a majority for leaving the Matter to Congress. In N. York, the Come. were unanimous for something, but seem to incline towards measures of defence on the idea that war will be unavoidable. In this City a motion in a large meeting on saturday evening to remonstrate agst. the Resolutions was rejected by a large majority. The Bill for six Frigates will have its third reading to day, & will probably pass. The recapture or evacuation of Toulon is confirmed. The British destroyed the 16 sail of the line taken from the French. Many of the Inhabitants in attempting to get to the British Ships were drown'd. Those left in the Town underwent military execution.

Inclosed are the papers containing what was urged by me on the commercial question. If Majr. Hite shd. not [be] in Orange, I wish you to forward them to him. Yr. Affe son

Js. MADISON JR

RC (DLC). Franked and addressed by JM to his father in Orange County, "care of Js. Blair Esqe. / Fredericksburg / Virginia." Damaged by removal of seal. Enclosures not found. Newspaper enclosures were probably the same sent in JM to Jefferson, 9 Mar. 1794.

1. Benjamin Carr and Company's "Musical Repository" at 122 High Street advertised "A grand piano forte, with three unisons, pedals, patent desk, &c. / Portable grand, and grand square piano fortes. / Small piano fortes at different prices" (Hardie, *Philadelphia Directory* [1794 ed.], p. 23; Philadelphia *Federal Gazette*, 9 Dec. 1793).

2. On 23 Dec. 1793 the Orange County Court granted JM's brother Francis permission "to erect a water Grist Mill" on the Rapidan River in Madison County, at what was later called Madison Mills. On 29 July 1795 Francis Madison admitted JM, his father, and his brother William as partners in the mill (Orange County, Minute Book, 3:202; Madison County, Deed Book, 1:345).

3. For Fauchet's proclamation of 6 Mar., see *Philadelphia Gazette*, 7 Mar. 1794.

From Hubbard Taylor

DEAR SIR   CLARKE COUNTY KENTUCKY 10th. Mar: 1794

I wrote you in February[1] and inclosed you some publications of the Democratic Society of this State, and hope they got safe to hand. At that time I thought the remonstrance would have met with a great majority of signers, but now think differently. Altho' there are but few (if any) but most ardently wishes for the grand object the Mississippi yet many think the remonstrance couched in too harsh language.

The alarm we have had respecting the probability of a British war, together with Clarkes intended expedition has frustrated the adventurers of produce down the River, some has declined all thoughts of the scheme. This has put a Stop to the purchase of Tobo. Hemp &c. by the Merchants.

The Resolutions proposing aditional duties on importations in certain cases was pu[b]lished in our last papers they are generally applauded by all I have heard speak of them, and I hope they will succeed.

You no doubt will have heard that the Indians faild to come in at the time appointed to deliver up the prisoners[2]—their conduct has not disappointed many who are acquainted with their politicks in these matters. Wayne is still in close Winter quarters notwithstanding his many boasting threats to drink of the Lake waters in three weaks. The Cavalry after going out to Headquarters and reducing the horses much is sent back to this State to recruit there them again.

I am in great hopes you have got a good and sufficient proportion of Republicans in Congress this session the peace and happiness of the Union I suppose depends on it, but more particularly this State.

The furnace for making Iron that has so long been on hand in this Country has at length begun to produce good Castings—but no forge is yet erected; it has lessened the price of Castings at least ⅓ and are in hopes we shall soon get Iron in the same proportion.

The Small pox that made its appearance in this State this Winter has been very fatal both in the Natural way and by inoculation. Forty or upwards died in Lexington, the proportion has not been so great in the country tho but few families inoculated except near Lexington. It is thought the sickly fall Occationed its being so fatal.

None of our papers are worth inclosing or would send some forward to you. I wish you an agreable session And, I am with great regard and esteem Dr Sir yr affe. Hble. sert:

H. TAYLOR

RC (DLC). Docketed by JM.

1. Taylor probably referred to his letter to JM of 13 Jan. 1794.
2. During negotiations between a Delaware tribal delegation and Maj. Gen. Anthony Wayne at Fort Greenville on 13 Jan., one of Wayne's conditions for peace was that the Indians return sixty-one prisoners within thirty days. When the deadline passed, his suspicions were confirmed that the delegation intended only "to gain time, & to reconnoitre" (Richard C. Knopf, ed., *Anthony Wayne, a Name in Arms: . . . The Wayne-Knox-Pickering-McHenry Correspondence* [Pittsburgh, 1960], pp. 295, 299, 301, 11).

To Thomas Jefferson

DEAR SIR   Mar: 12. 1794.

The Merchants, particularly of N. England have had a terrible slam in the W. Indies. About a hundred vessels have been seized by the British for condemnation, on the pretext of enforcing the laws of the Monarchy with regard to the Colony trade. The partizans of England, considering a war as now probable are endeavoring to take the lead in defensive preparations, and to acquire merit with the people by anticipating their wishes. This new symtom of insolence & enmity in Britain, shews rather that she meditates a formal war as soon as she shall have crippled our marine resources, or that she calculates on the pusilanimity of this country & the influence of her party, in a degree that will lead her into aggressions which our love of peace can no longer bear. The commercial propositions are in this State of things, not the precise remedy to be pressed as first in order; but they are in every view & in any event proper to make part of our standing laws till the principle of reciprocity be established by mutual arrangements. Adieu

Js. MADISON JR

RC (DLC). Docketed by Jefferson, "recd. Mar. 31."

From the Republican Society of South Carolina

CHARLESTON 12th March 1794.

To Citizen James Madison, Representative from
the Commonwealth of Virginia, in Congress.

CITIZEN REPRESENTATIVE,

The patriotic principles which have distinguished your conduct in the House of Representatives of the United States in the present Session, have attracted the particular attention of your fellow Citizens: and while they with indignation reprobate the contrary conduct of some other characters, who have imposed on their Constituents by holding forth doctrines as contrary to the interest of America, as they are disgraceful; they with pleasure behold in you, Citizen, the firm Patriot & true Republican.

The Republican Society established in this City, who have for their basis, a pure love of their Country and a just respect for its Laws and Constitution, cannot withold giving a testimony of their approbation of the part you have acted in support of the Dignity of America by preserving her faith to her Allies and resenting the injuries she has received from an ungenerous and implacable Enemy. They therefore unanimously Resolved that, you should be addressed by letter conveying to you this their opinion of your Conduct; and it is with the highest pleasure and satisfaction, I do now in their name and in compliance with their Resolve, give you, Worthy Citizen, their plaudit: receive then this mark of their esteem, and continue to preserve that general approbation, by exerting your talents to save your Country from dishonour and ignominy which may be brought on her, either by the weakness or by the baseness of others. In the name of the Republican Society established in Charleston—

S. DRAYTON[1]
Citizen President

RC (DLC). Docketed by JM.

1. Stephen Drayton served in the South Carolina Commons House of Assembly, 1769–71, and was deputy quartermaster general for the southern department of the Continental army during the Revolution. In 1793 he helped to organize the Republican Society of South Carolina, received a French military commission from Genet, and recruited American forces for a projected filibuster against Florida. Before the expedition could embark, the South Carolina General Assembly ordered the arrest and investigation of Drayton and other leaders (Walter B. Edgar et al., eds., *Biographical Directory of the South Carolina House of Representatives* [3 vols. to date; Columbia, S.C., 1974–], 2:202–3; Link, *Democratic-Republican Societies*, pp. 135–37; see also Philadelphia *General Advertiser*, 7 Jan. and 3 Apr. 1794).

From Joshua Barney and Others

SIR, KINGSTON, JAMAICA March 13th. 1794

The American Masters of vessels now Forcibly detained here being occasionally Assembled for the purpose of mutual communications and comparison of Sentiments on their present Distressed situation. A Gazette from the United States was Introduced which contained the Resolutions by you proposed to the house of Representatives Jany 3d last, which were read with universal applause, and as the least token of their gratitude it was proposed that an address should be drawn up expressive of their sense of the propriety and expedience of the Resolutions, and particularly of their most sincere thanks to you who had proposed public redress that imediately affected and in fact alleviated their Grievances, this was unanimously agreed to, and the address which we now have the honor to inclose herewith prepared and signed, and we the undersigned were appointed to transmit the same to you. We with pleasure reflect that while we discharge the duty required by our confreres we have an opportunity to assure you of our Zeal and attachment to the Interests of our Country, and with how much satisfaction we would embrace any occasion to convince you of our readiness to render you any Services And are with Sentiments of the Most profound respect & Veneration Sir Your Most Obt. & Very Hble Servts.

JOSHUA BARNEY[1]
FRED FOLGER
WM. MCINTIRE

[Enclosure]

SIR,   KINGSTON JAMAICA 9th. March 1794

Seperated from our Country by the Illegal intervention of Force, detained in an unwholesome climate, by a designed procrastination of Justice, it has been through the medium of the public prints from America that we have been favored with your patriotick speech, and wise resolutions, proposed to the House of Representitives of the United States, the third of January last, when the pleasing, gratefull Accents resounded through our unfortunate little Circle, each congenial heart seemed to bound with Joy, and universal cheerfullness overspread each mind, for a moment our sufferings were forgotten, Native and Artless professions of Attachment to our Country fell from every tongue, Expressions of the most lively gratitude, and thankfulness succeeded, for the man, who was so sensible of the Dignity and Independance of his Country, and who could trace out the only true road to preserve it.

Sentiments of Honour, Justice, and public spirit so Manifestly displayed, exact our warmest thanks and merit our eternal gratitude.[2]

It is not expected that persons of our profession should be acquainted with Affairs of State, or the policy of Nations but at the same time we trust we possess sufficient decernment to know where we are well treated and where not, and our various converse with the different Nations of the World afford us peculiar advantages to learn their Temper.

The Wisdom and Seasonable propriety of the resolutions were obvious to every thinking man, and it was the opinion that sound policy and the true interest of the United States dictates the measures therein contemplated.

Permit us Sir, to think with you, that by a course of self denial, to which every good Citizen would cheerfully Submit, we could make our enemies feel the effects of our power, and to that portion of annoyance and distress we could produce by a complete interdiction on our exports, added to what we can do by the spirit and activity of our citizens, we are fully perswaded we possess the means to exact respect from any Nation.

We want words to express our unfeigned thanks for the manly, Just, and dignified manner in which you vindicate our individual rights, when invaded from any quarter, and recommending public repariation when protection could not be extended.

To some it might be cause of discouragement, to be a Member of any Government that cannot afford complete protection to every Citizen, but we shall bear our wrongs with patience and becoming fortitude, no trials, no sufferings we can experience shall ever waver our Indivisable attachment to our Country, and we hold our lives ready to sacrafice when her cause requires it, we are perswaded of her good will to protect us, but at the same time we know her incompetancy at the present moment, and we sincerely lament the cause.

In conclusion we beg leave to add our most sincere wishes that you may enjoy health and serenity of mind, & that you experience that portion of happiness to which your Virtue and Patriotism so Justly entitles you.

With a Just sense of the exalted station which you so honourably fill, with the greatest reverence for your superior abilities, and sincere veneration for your uniform attachment to the welfare of your Country, and a gratefull remembrance of your labours in public Life, we most fervently pray for your preservation, with these sentiments we subscribe ourselves, Your most Obedient Humble Servants.

JOSHUA BARNEY

[and twenty-one others]

RC and enclosure (DLC). Enclosure docketed by JM. The enclosure, in Barney's hand, was published in the *Md. Journal and Baltimore Advertiser*, 20 June 1794, and reprinted in the Philadelphia *Gazette of the U.S.*, 25 June 1794, Philadelphia *General Advertiser*, 26 June 1794, and *Va. Gazette, and Richmond and Manchester Advertiser*, 30 June 1794. The newspaper version of the enclosure was misdated 13 Mar. 1794 and signed only by Barney, Folger, and McIntire, who were identified as a "Committee of the Masters of American Vessels in Jamaica."

1. Barney distinguished himself as a naval officer during the Revolution and was known to JM as bearer of the Treaty of Paris in 1783. In July 1793 British privateers captured his merchantman the *Sampson*, but he managed to regain possession of his ship. A British warship recaptured the *Sampson* in December en route from Port-au-Prince to Baltimore and took her to Kingston. On 10 Mar. 1794 Barney was acquitted of "piratically and feloniously" recovering the *Sampson*, but in April his ship and cargo were condemned and sold. Meanwhile public agitation in Baltimore over his treatment was so intense that the British consul fled for safety to Philadelphia. Washington dispatched a ship to return Barney, who arrived in Baltimore on 16 May. The Jay treaty commissioners later fully reimbursed Barney's losses. During the War of 1812, Barney turned to privateering and served capably at the battle of Bladensburg (*PJM*, 6:328; Hulbert Footner, *Sailor of Fortune: The Life and Adventures of Commodore Barney, U.S.N.* [New York, 1940], pp. 177–90, 250, 282–84; Philadelphia *General Advertiser*, 23 May 1794; see also "List of Americain [*sic*] Vessels taken & brought into the Port of Kingston, Jamaica," 1794 [DLC]).

2. The following two paragraphs are omitted from the newspaper version.

From Horatio Gates

DEAR SIR   ROSE HILL,[1] 13th: March, 1794:

I have read with attention your Reply to Messieurs Smith, Ames, & Dexter; I am certain there is not a Sound Whigg from the River St: Croix, to the River St: Marys, that does not Honour, and applaud, the Speaker; Go on my Friend, persevere in the Glorious Cause you have uniformly supported, and there will not be a true Republican in The US. that will not with Heart, and Voice, be ready to Support, and Exalt You; I confess the Conduct of the Eastern Men astonishes me, but I know, & have long known, the Character of the Sordid Individuals that inhabit their Trading Towns; Gain is their God, and present Gain is their Polar Starr, to which they forever Steer; The Body of the people, the Agricultural and the Men that will Defend the Country, are more Public Spirited, and will when it comes to the Push, make the others Succumb. In the Circumstances of England, I trust a War will be unnecessary; there is but one reason to apprehend so serious a Calamity; & that is; The Crouned Despots may conceive, If France is not Subdued, Our Domination is at an End; and therefore Resolve, with all their Might, to try another Campaign; but it will be in Vain—And may Finally produce a Republic in England; & that, an Alliance Offensive, & Defensive, between the three great Republicks of the World, France, England, & America; This if not really the Thing Itself, will be the next thing, to the promised Milenium: In regard to The Algerines, I approve your plan, preferable to that of raising a Naval Armament; If there was no other Objection, & there are Several; The increase of patronage, should be cautiously avoided; or we shall too soon sink into the Corruptions of the Mother Country! Besides the Officering, The Jobbs, that Building, Equiping, Victualling, &c, of a Squadron of Ships of War must be taken into the Account of good things to dispose of—a word to the Wise.

I know your time is too precious to intrude upon unnecessaryly, therefore write only when you are quite at Leizure, please to Direct, and Frank the inclosed,[2] to that Great, and Good Man Mr: Jefferson; After the Congress Rises your presence will be most Wellcome to My Mary, and me, at Rose Hill, seek no other Lodging. The latter end of June, or the very begining of July, a Number of us propose first a short Vissit to the Manor of Livingston, & then to go to Balls Town Springs, near Saratoga. This Bethsida,[3] they say, cures all diseases, makes the Old Young, and the Ugly Handsome! There are good Accomodations, & excellent Living, two things, Joind to the Two others, with a good Society, & fine Girls! might Tempt even Plato, when as Young as You.

That you may Enjoy the best things this Land can Bestow, is the sincere wish, of my dear Sir Your Affectionate, & Obedt: Servt:

HORATIO GATES.

RC (DLC). Docketed by JM.

1. Rose Hill farm was a rented estate "about three miles north of New York City" (Paul D. Nelson, *General Horatio Gates: A Biography* [Baton Rouge, La., 1976], p. 288).

2. Gates to Jefferson, 14 Mar. 1794 (DLC: Jefferson Papers).

3. Gates compared the New York springs with Bethesda, the healing waters mentioned in John 5:2–4.

To Thomas Jefferson

DEAR SIR　　　　　　　　　　　　　PHILADA. March 14. 1794.

The paper of yesterday inclosed, will give you a clue to the designs of the faction which has used Sedgwick[1] for its organ.[2] His immediate prompter will be seen both in his speech and in his propositions. Whether more be seriously aimed at than to embarrass the others which have been long depending, is by some doubted. Perhaps this may be one of the objects; but you understand the game behind the Curtain too well not to perceive the old trick of turning every contingency into a resource for accumulating force in the Government. It would seem however that less subtlety has prevailed in this than in some other instances. The ostensible reason for the provisional army is not only absurd; but remote from the present sensations of the public; and at the same time disarms the projectors of the cavil & calumny used with most success against the commercial propositions, towit, that they tended to provoke war by an unnecessary alarm & irritation to G. Britain. The commercial propositions were the subject of yesterday & will probably be resumed today. We admit that the change of appearances may require something further, but we contend that they ought to make part of our code, until the end be obtained; and that they will be proper whether we are to be at peace or war. In the former case they will have their intended operation: In the latter they will put our Extive. on the right ground for negocia⟨tion.⟩

RC (DLC). Unsigned. Docketed by Jefferson, "recd. Mar. 31." Missing enclosure was probably the 13 Mar. Philadelphia *Gazette of the U.S.* (see n. 2).

1. Someone, possibly John C. Payne (an early editor), interlined "[party]" above "faction" and a long dash above "Sedgwick."

2. In the House of Representatives on 12 Mar., Federalist Theodore Sedgwick

introduced eight resolutions providing for "fifteen regiments of auxiliary troops, to consist of 1000 men rank and file each, with the proper officers," and authorizing the president at his discretion to impose an embargo during the recess of Congress. The resolutions were referred to the Committee of the Whole, which defeated them on 24 Mar. Sedgwick then moved a resolution "That measures ought to be immediately taken to render the force of the United States more efficient," which the committee approved. The House appointed a select committee to prepare "a bill to augment the military force" but defeated a bill reported by Sedgwick on 19 May and a similar Senate bill on 30 May (Philadelphia *Gazette of the U.S.*, 13 and 24 Mar. 1794; *Annals of Congress*, 3d Cong., 1st sess., 500–501, 504, 527–28, 534–35, 561, 709–10, 735, 738; see also JM's speech of 30 May 1794 and nn.).

Closed Sessions of the House

[14 March 1794]

During debate on JM's resolutions on commercial discrimination in Committee of the Whole, Parker asserted "that probably without France [i.e., French aid during the American Revolution] the legislature would not be deliberating within these walls." When "two or three persons in the gallery, upon this made a faint attempt to clap," Tracy moved that the committee rise for the purpose of clearing the galleries (*General Advertiser*, 17 Mar. 1794).

Mr. Madison believed the business was placed on its true footing. It is no doubt a hardship that the misbehaviour of one or two individuals should banish an otherwise orderly gallery, but as a line could not be drawn, clearing the galleries was the only remedy. Especially on important questions, the request of any member, who might conceive similar conduct as an attack on the independence of deliberation, would command his voice for clearing the galleries.

General Advertiser, 18 Mar. 1794. After further debate, Tracy's motion passed.

From James Madison, Sr.

[ca. 15 March 1794]

Timothy looks well; but the last sowed is much turn'd out of the
    Ground: the new Seed will be sowed as soon as the ground is dry
    enough
Wheat looks very well except the last 8 Bushels sowed
L. C[1] has got stuff enough for 8 Waggons except the Naves & some stuff

for Bar Share brakes—& is getting Shingles for a Grainary: How large will you have it

Apple Trees are all planted at Sawney's—Money is come to hand but loss in the Coin

The Dams at the Ditches are all broke: they must be done with Stone; when convenient

Ms (DLC). Notes in the hand of James Madison, Sr., for a response to JM's letter to him of 21 Feb. 1794. Written below the signature of that letter. Probably formed the basis of a letter to JM which has not been found.

1. Lewis Collins was a Montpelier overseer.

¶ To Alexander White. Letter not found. *17 March 1794.* Acknowledged in White to JM, 30 Mar. 1794. Asks for White's opinion on proposals for an embargo; reports on Theodore Sedgwick's plan for a military buildup.

From Henry Brockholst Livingston

Sir,   Rhinebeck 20th. March 1794.

Some time since I enclosed in a Letter to Mr. Bailey[1] a Member from this State a Memorial Addressed to Congress, not yet haveing heard that he has presented the Same, I have by this Conveyance written to him requesting if he has any Objections to its Appearance, that he will deliver it to you: Being persu[a]ded you will not only Introduce it for me, but also Advocate the Cause of the Agreived Soldier: In this Sir I do not so much presume upon my Acquaintance with you, as I ⟨re⟩ly upon your known Attattchment to justice and the Able support you gave the Claims of the late Army, who, will I am convinced ever retain a proper Sence of your Endeavours to Obtain redress for them, tho unattended with the desired Success. I have the Honor to be Sir, Most respectfully Yours.

                                        Henry B: Livingston

RC (DLC). Docketed by JM.

1. Theodorus Bailey of New York was serving on a House committee appointed to recommend amendments to the laws on veterans' pensions. The committee's report resulted in a joint resolution, signed by Washington on 9 June, "directing the Secretary of War to make out and return to the District Judges, certain lists in the cases of invalid pensioners" (*Annals of Congress,* 3d Cong., 1st sess., 468, 527, 780; *U.S. Statutes at Large,* 1:401). Evidence of JM's involvement on behalf of the memorial mentioned by Livingston has not been found.

¶ To Arthur Breese. Letter not found. *22 March 1794.* Acknowledged in
Breese to JM, 11 and 16 Apr. 1794. Inquires about value and prospects for
sale of JM's Mohawk Valley land.

¶ To William Walton Morris. Letter not found. *Ca. 22 March 1794.* Mentioned and enclosed in JM to Horatio Gates, 24 Mar. 1794. Also mentioned
in Gates to JM, 27 Dec. 1794. Probably concerns JM's Mohawk Valley
land and encloses a letter from JM to Arthur Breese (see Breese to JM, 16
Apr. 1794).

To Horatio Gates

DEAR SIR   PHILADA. Mar: 24. 1794

Your favor of the 13th. has lain by me unanswered till I could give
you the result of a proposition for an Embargo discussed for several
days with shut doors. The decision did not take place till friday afternoon. The measure was then negatived by 48 agst. 46 votes. Those who
took the lead in opposing it are now for transferring the power to the
Executive even during the Session of Congress.

You will find in the newspapers the havoc made on our trade in the
W. Indies. Every day adds new proofs of the ill will and contempt of
G. B. towards us. Still I do not concur with those who see in these proceedings a design to make war in form. If she can destroy the branches
of our commerce which are beneficial to her enemies, and continue to
enjoy those which are beneficial to herself, things are in the best possible arrangement for her. War would turn the arrangement agst. her
by breaking up the trade with her, and forcing that with her enemies.
I conclude therefore that she will push her aggressions just so far and
no farther, than she imagines we will tolerate. I conclude also that the
readiest expedient for stopping her career of depredation on those parts
of our trade which thwart her plans, will be to make her feel for
those which she cannot do without.

I have nothing to add to the Newspaper details with respect to events
in Europe. The campaign seems to have closed as triumphantly for the
French Republic as the fears of its enemies could have foreboded. If
that in the W. Indies should not exhibit a reverse of fortune, the public
attention may possibly be called off from the French—to "the British
Revolution." You may then renew your prophetic wishes, which have
created a Millenium under the auspices of the three great Republics.

I have forwarded your letter to Mr. Jefferson. Present my best respects to your very amiable lady, and accept the affectionate esteem with which I remain Dr. Sir Yr. Obedt. friend & servt.

Js. MADISON JR

P. S. The inclosed letter to Mr. William Morris[1] son of the General is on business somewhat interesting to me. It was to have been hand[ed] to him yesterday, but he set out for N. York sooner than was expected. Will you oblige me so far as to have him enquired for, & the letter delivered to him?

RC (MB). Docketed by Gates.

1. William Walton Morris, a younger son of Lewis Morris, served in the Revolution and in 1783 became quartermaster of the Second Continental Artillery Regiment (W. W. Morris to L. Morris, 21 Dec. 1782, "Letters to General Lewis Morris," *Collections of the New-York Historical Society*, 8 [1875]: 510-11; Heitman, *Historical Register Continental*, p. 403).

To Thomas Jefferson

DEAR SIR,   March 24th, 1794.

The past week has been spent chiefly on the question of an Embargo. It was negatived on Friday by 48 against 46, the former composed chiefly of Eastern, the latter of Southern members. The former are now for giving the power to the Executive, even during the session of Congress. In France, everything is in a state of vigor beyond what has been seen there. Fauchèt proceeds with great circumspection and prudence here.

Printed copy (Madison, *Letters* [Cong. ed.], 2:8). RC not found but calendared in John C. Payne's inventory of JM's correspondence, 2 Mar.–11 May 1794 (DLC: Rives Collection, Madison Papers).

From John Dawson

DEAR SIR!   RICH. March 24. 94.

I am much surprisd at some resolutions which I see in the papers brought forward by Sedwick. It woud appear that the fiscal party have all at once changd their ground. They seem to oppose the interest of that country, which heretofore they have advocated, & to provoke a war.

The public mind appears a good deal agitated about war—all appear to which [*sic*] to avoid it if possible—but shoud G. B. force us into it I am persuaded that a very large majority of our citizens woud sacrifice every thing, & exert every nerve to support the american character, and to chastise those proud and insolent islanders.

The comml. resolutions I find were take⟨n⟩ up on the 13 & I hope carri[e]d. Sedwicks plan is surely to defeat them, & to prevent any thing like a systematic operation on the trade of G. B.

How does M. Fauchet conduct himself? We hear that he is much courted by those who have always been much opposd to the cause of France, & that he is *particularly* attentive to them. What is become of his predecessor. With much Esteem Yr friend & Sert

J Dawson

RC (DLC).

¶ To James Madison, Sr. Letter not found. *24 March 1794, Philadelphia.* Mentioned in James Madison, Sr., to John Lee, 5 Apr. 1794 (NcD): "he says by the Accts. from France, her affairs were never in so vigorous a situation."

From Francis André

Sir   Philadelphia, March 25th. 1794.

J Read over with attention, your Speeches in Support of your Resolutions, & those of sundries against them, amongst the Chief's reasons alledged, for their voting against them, the Strongest, & most unanswerable were—

Mr. Smith of (S C) says they would affect materially those States, where manufactures had not made any great progress, & who had the more Bulky Articles of Exportations, that our Commerce yielded almost all the Revenues that flows into our public Coffers, that we must do without many Articles of necessity, we are accustomed to receive from Great Britain, expecially the Southern States, or pay a most exhorbitant price for them, that Credit obtain'd in Great Britain, could not be obtained in other Countries.

Mr. Dexter, says, they Tended only to Tax our own Citizens, to Gratify our passions.

Mr. Eames says, they would affect our Exports.

It appears to me, that if means could be devised to find out a Channel of Trade, that could be carried on without the intervention of G. B, & would supply America with Goods, it would Silance all those objections, & would be more detrimental to G. B. then the Resolutions themselves, as it would have an immediate, & directly Affect their Commerce, which your Resolutions cannot so immediately do, because in paying the Extra Duties, they would Still import from G. B, which would have a direct Tendency to Tax ourselves, but by opening a new Channel of Trade, & supplying America with Goods, without the intervention of G. B., it would be provided with them, paying no higher Duties then now, by which mean we should Reap a double advantage, to pay no dearer for our Goods, & to Suport the Revenues in the Same State they are now in, beside, this plan would not have an hostille appearance, & would not have french, Stampt on the face thereof, as Mr. Eames is pleased to say your Resolutions have. To the Knowledge of every body, many of the Articles Consumed in America, & chiefly in the Southern States, are of the Growth & Manufactures of Germany, &c—such as Glue, Gum, Window Glass, Hemp, flax, Iron, Steel, Platillas Brown Silisia Dowlases, Britanias, Stripes & Checks, Wharendorps, Bed Ticking, Plain & flowerd Lawn, Diaper, Baging, osnaburghs, Ticklenburghs, Russia Sheeting, & Duck—Ravensduck, Hessians; brown Rolls, thread & Cotton Hose, Cambricks & Laces for yr. fine Gentn. & Ladies, thread, flander Cloth, to Supply Irish Linnens, Silks, Tape Ferrets, Ribbons & many other articles too tedious to mention, Printed Callico from Holland, Gand & Antwerp, most of those Articles come here in great quantities thro'. the Channel of Great Britain, because G. B. give the Importers long Credit which the German Cannot aford, the dificulty lay then in the want of Credit, which I think might be obviated. I wish to Communicate to you (not as Legislator) but as good patriot, that wish the good of his Country, *a Plan*, which I firmly beleive would have the desired Effect, & would hurt G. B. most Sensibly.

In the first place I must give you a Short account of myself, that you may be able to form a Judgment if I am qualified to undertake what I mean to propose. I was Born in france, went to England in 1763. at the Age of 14. was Bound prentice to Silk Weaving, where I Staid 2½ years, then went to Norwich in the Woolen Manufactures of that City, & Staid 4½ years, when I had nearly finishd my prenticeship, from thence back to London, Clerk to a Grocer, & soon to Grenada, where I was Clerk for 7 or 8 years to two of the Chiefs Houses of that place, who imported all Kind of Goods from G. B. Then in 1780 I went into Business on my own account, & from 1783 to 1793 I lived in Grenada, S: Pierre W/I., & Cape françois, & dealt in Silisia Goods, thro'. the Medium of Dunkirk, so that I am pretty well acquainted both with English, German, & french Goods. If I had a Capital adequate to the undertaking of what I wish to Communicate to you, I should have Silently operated, but the Smallness of my fortune, not answering such an undertaking as to provide all America with Goods, so as to make G. B. feel we are not insensible of her Ill usage, & that we shall undertake every thing in our power to Exist without her.

If my plan had its full Effect, I would be able to import yearly for twelve Millions of Dollars, worth of Goods into America, without the Concurance of Gr. B. of the Articles which come Chiefly thro'. the Channel of G. B. tho' the dearest Market for them, by 10 or 15 ⅌C, & I am inclin'd to think, they would come to Market rather Cheaper, then 15 ⅌C then what they do now, they would Save the London Commission, freight, Insurance, Storage & profits, which for Credit are not Small, & would be the means of Cutting off a large & Beneficial Branch of their Business. I would go further, toward hurting the Britons, I would get a list of all Goods, Imported from G B. into America, & all those that could be imitated in Germany, holland & france. I would get them made on such models, that would deceive even our best American Connoisseurs & I am sure as Cheap, if not Cheaper then in England, & Introduce them to my American Customers as English Goods, for we must Confess, that the Americans are so Strongly prejudiced in favour of English Ware, as to think all others are much inferior—to Such a plan I conceive your opponents Could not object, except they Chuse, to thro' off the mark, & Stick up themselves to be Abators of Britons, it having no hostille appearance, & hope we shall have at least the option, to go to what market we please to purchase.

One thing I must Confess, that I do not see that the plan will be Generally, so favorable to Exportation, as to importation, but I am in great hopes (that as G. B. do not Consume all her Imports from America) I shall in the Course of my Travels, be able to discover in what Channels flows her overplus. I am Certain Dunkirk will take off our Hands, a vast quantity of our Tobacco, which I am almost sure to Convey there in Safety, tho' we should have a War with G. B. I Know many Articles of American produce could be Sold in many part of France, where American Ships never went, which are suply'd by Similar Articles from the North of Europe.

I should have Turnd my Thoughts to raising manufactures in this Country, but two things, without which they Cannot Succeed hinder'd me, the first is Hands, the Second Materials.

I wish to recommand to you as Legislator, to draw the attention of the Legislation to the Encouragement of raising that Indispensable Source of Wealth, Hemp & flax, if those two Materials were once a Staple Comodity in America, I would in a Short time turn my thoughts to bring over from Europe, Spinners in such a quantity, by few at a Time in the diferent Vessels, I should be obliged to Keep a going, as would soon be able to Set up a Manufactory of Linnen, Considerable enough to Suply in a great part our wants in that Article. It should be recommanded likewise to the attention of farmers, to raise as large flocks of Sheep, as they could. I see with pleasure the Gentns. in N. York State, have it into Consideration to ammeliorate their Flocks—by recommanding to Captain of Vessels to Bring over with them, the Best Sheep they can find for their fleece.

If you should have a desire to Comunicate with me after the perusal of this, write me a Line, & I will wait on you at any time—being Sincerely Sir Your most obed. Servt.

FRAS. ANDRÉ[1]

Chesnut, 4th. door, above 10th. Street

RC (DLC). Docketed by JM.

1. Hardie, *Philadelphia Directory* (1794 ed.), p. 4, described André as a "gentleman" living on Chestnut Street, between Tenth and Eleventh streets.

From Walter Jones

DEAR SIR.   March 25th. 1794.

I am obliged by the Receipt of your favours of feby. 28 & march the 9th.[1] I have waited some time for a little Leisure to persue my observations on a certain Subject; but the continued & unusual Interruption of various avocations for Some weeks past, promise such delay to the accomplishment of that purpose, that I think it improper to postpone any longer the acknowledgements justly due to your Attentions. The Printer by omissions & mistakes has made such work of the paper[2]— several Sentences are made non-sense, which I have the Comfort to think existed not in the manuscript—I clearly foresaw the delicacy of your present Situation as it respected any concern with the press, on Subjects similar to that Offered to your Consideration; I wished to have the paper reviewed by a person in whose Candour & Judgment I could Confide; and I can with truth assure you, that I know not where to make a preferable Choice. The Subject is certainly a very important one, & from the Acrimony or Servility that too generally characterises our news-paper Essayists, I think not likely to be treated with a due degree of system, temper & freedom; I therefore think, at all Events, of having a few papers prepared, against the meeting of our Assembly, & having them published in immediate succession, in one of the most popular papers at Richmond. If in the Leisure of your summer Retirement you can furnish me with any hints or observations, respecting the nature & symptoms of our actually existing Factions, they would be great aids to one so withdrawn from the principal Scene of observation as myself. Your Correspondence at all times on any subject would be very grateful to me; but at present, my dear sir, I think all the friends of the true revolutionary principles of American Independance, Should act as much as possible in Concert. The defection from them of many in this & other parts of the Country, in respect both to numbers & Character is very distressing & not a little alarming. In this part I have scarcely a *whig friend* of any note. Some of the ci-devants, whose Zeal flamed to an absurd Excess formerly in degrading the British Nation, are now as intemperate in extolling their power, their prosperity, their Virtues and their Government. They can be as merry & witty on the Sans-Culottes & Carmagnioles, from the fund of London paragraphs, as the Expectants & placemen of G. Britain, whether they Consist of Lords, Sir Thomas's, Cast Servants, low favourites, or the Fathers, Brothers Cousins or Sons of whores, who indubitably Compose a great proportion of that honourable Body. They forget that a few years ago they too had their opprobrious apellations of *Jonathans*, *Yankees* &C. from their present friends. Such men give great Shelter & Effect to the agency of the low british Inhabitants, whose exertions on the people are incessant; and the mass of the people are so unreflecting & torpid, that they are well fitted to yield to old Habits and opinions, however inconsistent with the dignity & Interest of the character they have derived from Independance on G. B. Southward of Rappahanock & upward in the State, I am told, things have a better Complexion, but I assure you, in the district of country where I live, the aspect of political Character is very disgusting to a whig of 1776.

I am the more impatient to hear the final Issue in the Congress of the Resolutions you brought in, as in your last you say their Success has become more dubious. Independent of their propriety in a Strictly Commercial point of view, in which I think they have the advantage of argument, their wholesome operation in other respects of more importance, Seems to be beyond the reach of rational Controversy, unless we make The Ledger, the Palate & the apparel of our people the only Criteria of national dignity & prosperity. No nation is really an independant one, unless their country their Laws, Government, & manners, are, taken collectively, far preferable in the View of the people to those of any other nation whatsoever. As well might we expect concord & prosperity in the married State, where either of the parties had transferred its affections to a third person. We have never posessed this necessary prejudice of an exclusive attachment to & pride in our own Country, the momen⟨t⟩ Hostilities ceased, we relapsed into our old opinions & Habits concerning Britain & her productions. It is this charm of inveterate Habits founded in former Subjection & political Nothingness, that every real american would wish to break & dissipate. The tendency of the Resolutions is evidently, pro-tanto, to break this charm; and their adoption therefore will be the wish of the real Citizens of america. It is not in the Constitution of human affairs to Command at once all the advantages that belong to any Situation. We are generally reduced to the choice of the least among Evils, and of the best among Blessings—or by a Comparison of the two avoid or persue the preponderating Side. These three Cases seem to comprehend every possible Situation of mankind; and on these Grounds the resolutions, when tried, will be impregnable. The principal Evils Seem to be, a temporary & partial Inconvenience from the Interruption in a partial degree of our Customary Channels of Supply of English Goods, with some diminution of Quantity & perhaps increase of Price: but our Inclination as well as Means will be promoted of obtaining on the best & most Direct Terms, the products of the whole world, without the prejudices of old Habits. *Public Credit*, May receive some Momentary Shock: but to me this is no objection, who ardently wish we had never heard of public Credit & the funding System; who had rather face the hazard & pretended Infamy of national Bankruptcy, than See realized the Consequences which that vile System presents in Fact or in prospect. The Diminution of Trade by the diminution of excessive Credit—may be other wise expressed—there will be fewer Stores Shops & *firms*, as they call them, but there will also [be] fewer idle fine Gentlemen at the head of them; & less fraud, dissipation of manners, & Bankruptcies. Above all we Shall begin the progress of a fixt national Character, and not remain independent de jure, & Colonists de facto. Adieu Dear Sir & beli[e]ve me with every Sentiment of affectte. regard Yours

W. JONES

RC (DLC: Rives Collection, Madison Papers). Docketed by JM.

1. Letters not found.

2. Jones probably referred to "Speculator," published in Benjamin Franklin Bache's Philadelphia *General Advertiser* on 6 Mar. 1794. In his letter to JM of 10 Jan. 1794, Jones enclosed a draft of an article "on natural Party & vitious Faction." JM may have arranged for Bache to publish Jones's piece.

To Thomas Jefferson

DEAR SIR   Mar: 26. 1794

My last informed you that an embargo had been proposed & negatived. You will see by the inclosed that on a renewal of the proposition yesterday it went thro' the H. of Reps. by a very large majority.[1] The change took place among the Eastern members whose constituents were growing so clamorous under their losses in the W. Indies, as to alarm their representatives. The Senate will have the subject before them today, and will probably concur. It is said that some further measures are to be discussed in that House. The commercial propositions have not yet recd. a vote. The progress of the evils which they were to remedy, having called for more active medicine, it has not been deemed prudent to force them on the attention of the House during more critical discussions. They will however notwithstanding a change of circumstances, cooperate with other measures as an alter[n]ative System and will be pressed to a vote at the first favorable moment. Whether they can be carried into a law at the present Session is doubtful, on acct. of the lateness of the day, and the superior urgency of other questions. The point immediately depending is the discrimination between G. B and other nations as to the proposed duties on manufactures. If this should succeed, the future parts will I think meet with little difficulty. The Enquiry into the Treasury[2] is going on, tho' not very rapidly. I understand that it begins to pinch where we most expected—the authority for drawing the money from Europe into the Bank. H. endeavored to parry the difficulty by contesting the right of the Committee to call for the authority. This failing he talks of constructive written authority from the P. but relies on parol[3] authority, which I think it impossible the P. can support him in.[4] The old question of referring the origination of Taxes[5] comes on today; and will in some degree test the present character of the House: I have written abundance of letters of late but fear they are stopped by the small pox at Richmond.

The people of Charlestown are taking a high tone. Their memorial,[6] which is signed by Ramsay—the Gadzdens Young Rutlege & a very great no. of respectable citizens marks the deliberate sense of the people. The more violent has been ex⟨pres⟩sed by hanging & burning the effigies of Smith, Ames[,] Arnold, Dumourier & the Devil en groupe.[7]

RC (DLC). Unsigned. Docketed by Jefferson, "recd. Apr. 16."

1. On 25 Mar. the House of Representatives unanimously passed a resolution imposing a thirty-day embargo "on all ships and vessels in the ports of the United States bound to any foreign port or place." Washington signed the joint resolution, as amended by the Senate, on 26 Mar. (*Philadelphia Gazette*, 26 and 28 Mar. 1794; *U.S. Statutes at Large*, 1:400).

2. On 16 Dec. 1793 Hamilton requested that the House conduct an investigation into his administration of the Treasury Department. He wanted to silence suggestions that the previous investigation, authorized as a result of William Branch Giles's resolutions late in the final session of the Second Congress, had been too brief. On the same day, the House tabled Giles's resolution to revive the investigation. The Senate on 20 Jan. 1794 passed similar resolutions moved by Albert Gal-

latin, but they were never implemented after Gallatin was disqualified from his Senate seat. On 24 Feb. the House appointed a select committee as proposed by Giles's resolution. It had "power to send for persons, papers, and records" and met regularly with Hamilton and other treasury officers. The House tabled the committee's report on 22 May (Syrett and Cooke, *Papers of Hamilton*, 15:460–65). The committee's report is printed in *ASP, Finance*, 1:281–301. JM's copy of *Report of the Committee Appointed to Examine into the State of the Treasury Department . . .* (Philadelphia, 1794; Evans 27909) is in the Madison Collection, Rare Book Department, University of Virginia Library.

3. Parol: word of mouth.

4. The House select committee appointed to examine the Treasury Department investigated, among other things, what portion of loans raised in the Netherlands for discharging the Revolutionary debt owed to France "has been drawn to the United States, at what dates and by what authority." JM, Giles, and other Republicans suspected Hamilton of diverting to the Bank of the United States funds appropriated for repayment of the debt to France. On 24 Mar. Hamilton argued, as he had done in the earlier investigation during the last session of the Second Congress, that Washington had authorized all foreign debt transactions and that they were all "conformable with the laws." Hamilton reminded Washington of a letter, written during the president's 1791 southern tour, approving the secretary of the treasury's arrangements for the Dutch loans. Washington at first did not recall the letter but soon acknowledged it privately. The secretary of the treasury cited but never divulged the letter during the House investigation of his conduct. JM later concluded that Hamilton "forbore to avail himself of the document he possessed, or to involve the President in the responsibility he was willing to take on himself" (introductory note to Hamilton to Frederick A. C. Muhlenberg, 16 Dec. 1793, Hamilton to the select committee, 24 Mar. 1794, Hamilton to Washington, 24 Mar. 1794, Washington to Hamilton, 7 May 1791, Syrett and Cooke, *Papers of Hamilton*, 15:462–63, 16:194, 195 n. 3, 196, 8:330; Fleet, "Madison's 'Detatched Memoranda,'" *WMQ*, 3d ser., 3 [1946]: 545–48; see also JM to Jefferson, 14 Apr. 1794, n. 3).

5. On the appointment of the House select committee on ways and means on 26 Mar., see Madison in the Third Congress, 2 Dec. 1793–3 Mar. 1795.

6. On 24 Mar. Congressman Andrew Pickens presented to the House a 1 Mar. South Carolina petition denouncing the British order in council of 6 Nov. 1793 and the resultant losses to American shipping. The petitioners viewed "the present degrading neutrality, as more injurious to the interests . . . of the republic, than an actual state of war" and pledged to support their representatives "if your wisdom should think it necessary to suspend all commercial intercourse between Great Britain and the United States" (*Philadelphia Gazette*, 26 and 31 Mar. 1794).

7. On 14 Mar. the Republican Society of South Carolina at Charleston passed resolutions denouncing British policies toward the U.S. and approving JM's proposals for commercial discrimination. On the following day, "the statue of Wm. Pitt was removed from his old place of residence. . . . In his place two effigys were hung up; and before the Exchange four others, said to represent some of the Delegates in Congress, whose political principles did not coincide in opinion with the freemen of Charleston" (Philip S. Foner, ed., *The Democratic-Republican Societies, 1790–1800: A Documentary Sourcebook of Constitutions, Declarations, Addresses, Resolutions, and Toasts* [Westport, Conn., 1976], pp. 387–89; *Columbia Gazette*, 28 Mar. 1794; see also *Boston Gazette*, 14 Apr. 1794).

From John Dawson

DEAR SIR! RICH March 27. 94

By this mail I enclose to Colo Monroe a paper containing an extract of a letter which I receivd from Norfolk, and which gives an account of the success of our brave & generous allies on the Rhine,[1] which I hope may prove true.

That the object of the fiscal gentry is to defeat any thing like a systematic operation of the trade of G. B. & to quiet the public mind I am fully persuaded, & therefore do hope that Sedwicks plan of an army will not succeed.

Shoud it, I take this early opportunity of mentioning to you, that Capn Alexander Quarrier,[2] who commands a company of artillery in this place is willing to accept of an appointment, not below a majority.

I feel a particular anxiety that he shoud be gratified. His services during the war entitle him to it. What recommends him most to me is a knowledge of his political princ[i]ples. Altho a Caledonian he is the most zealous republican I know. His activity on every occasion to demonstrate this has renderd him obnoxious to his countrymen in general, & to all those who are in sentiment different from himself. I am fully persuaded that he will make an active & faithful officer, & for these reasons do earnestly solicit any aid you may have it in your power to give him. With Esteem Yr. friend

J DAWSON

RC (DLC).

1. Dawson referred to a report that French armies had forced the allies to retreat across the Rhine in December 1793 (*Va. Gazette, and Richmond and Manchester Advertiser*, 27 Mar. 1794).

2. Alexander Quarrier (1746–1827) migrated from Scotland to Philadelphia in 1775 and served as a captain of Pennsylvania troops during the Revolution. Circa 1787 he moved to Richmond, where he was a coachmaker and land speculator. By 1792 he commanded the artillery battery of the city militia. His battery participated in public celebrations of French military victories and probably supported the city militia's resolutions of 1 Mar. 1794 endorsing JM's commercial discrimination proposals. He was later in charge of the Public Guard in Richmond (Johnson, *Papers of John Marshall*, 2:266 n. 2; *DAR Patriot Index*, p. 553; *CVSP*, 5:555; Philadelphia *Dunlap and Claypoole's Am. Daily Advertiser*, 22 Apr. 1795).

From Alexander White

DEAR SIR WOODVILLE 30th. March 1794.

Your favors of 2d. & 17th. instant came to hand together on the 22d. the mail carrying the former not having reached Alexandria when the Winchester Post in course left it.

I have had little time to consider the questions you propose, but will hazard an opinion. The laying Embargos is connected with War as well as with commerce, and indeed is more frequently an instrument of the former than the latter, Congress having the sole power in both these cases, their right to lay an Embargo will hardly be disputed—and having the right unrestrained by any Provision in the constitution, they may exercise that right in the most efficacious manner. If an Embargo could only be laid by a particular Act of Congress the necessary delays attending that mode of proceeding more especially in the recess would render the measure abortive whether the object were hostile or commercial. I therefore see no objection to vesting that power in the President under proper regulations—such as that an Embargo laid by the President during the recess should not continue in force more than a certain number of days after the Meeting of Congress, and if laid during the Session that the President should give immediate notice of the measure with his reasons for adopting it, and that the Embargo should be void if not confirmed by Congress within a limited time. The right of Congress I conceive to be the same they may cause that authority to be exercised during the Session as well as during the Recess, it is matter of expedience only—though there is undoubtedly much greater reason for granting it during the recess of Congress than during their Session. General Clarke most certainly enlisted men and was preparing to attack the Spaniards, I think he is not gone—but cannot speak positively. We have pleasing accounts from another quarter, if true, and you must know the certainty—that the British have released all our Vessels and paid damages for detention. Should this be the case, the old Lion has lain down to lick his paws at our feet. It has been my decided opinion that we ought to put ourselves in the strongest posture of defence possible. Whether Sedgwicks Plan of 15,000 Troops is a proper mode of doing it, I am not prepared to determine. In general I am for rendering our Militia effective (perhaps more regular Troops may be necessary) fortifying our Harbours—and building proper Vessels for the defence of our Bays and Harbours. I have been and remain doubtful as to the propriety of equipping a Squadron to act against the Algerines—but to attempt to meet G. B. on the Ocean would be highly imprudent, as the experience of last war evinced. Adieu and believe me Yours sincerely

ALEXR WHITE

RC (DLC). Addressed by White to JM at Philadelphia and franked. Docketed by JM.

To Thomas Jefferson

DEAR SIR   PHILADA. Mar. 31. 1794.

I have written of late by almost every mail, that is, three times a week. From your letter to Monroe I fear the small pox has stopped them at Richmond.[1] I shall continue however to inclose you the newspapers as often as they are worth it. It is impossible to say what will be the issue of the proposition discussed in those of today.[2] I forgot to mention in my last that the question whether the ways & means should be referred to the Secy. of T. as heretofore, or to a Come. lately came on & decided the sense of the House to be degenerated on that point.[3] The fiscal party, perceiving their danger, offered a sort of compromise which took in Mercer & with him sundry others in principle agst. them. Notwithstanding the success of the strategem, the point was carried by 49 agst. 46. If the question had divided the House fairly there would have been a majority of ten or a dozen at least.

RC (DLC). Unsigned. Docketed by Jefferson, "recd. Apr. 16."

1. Jefferson observed that "the small pox at Richmond has cut off the communication by post to or through that place. . . . I have never received a letter from Philadelphia since I left it except a line or two once from E. R." (Jefferson to Monroe, 11 Mar. 1794, Ford, *Writings of Jefferson*, 6:500).

2. JM probably referred to Jonathan Dayton's 27 Mar. motion in the House of Representatives. Dayton, a New Jersey Federalist, proposed that debts owed by American citizens to British creditors be sequestered and paid into the federal treasury, "there to be held as a pledge for the indemnification" of citizens for losses inflicted by "persons acting under the commission or authority of the British King." His resolutions were referred to the Committee of the Whole, where after two days of debate they were abandoned (Philadelphia *Dunlap and Claypoole's Am. Daily Advertiser*, 31 Mar. 1794; *Annals of Congress*, 3d Cong., 1st sess., 535–56; see also Madison in the Third Congress, 2 Dec. 1793–3 Mar. 1795).

3. On the appointment of the House select committee on ways and means on 26 Mar., see Madison in the Third Congress, 2 Dec. 1793–3 Mar. 1795.

To Robert R. Livingston

DEAR SIR   PHILADA. April 3d. 1794

This will be handed you by the Revd. Mr. Toulmin of the Unitarian Sect from England, whose attachment to liberty has led him to this land of it. You will find him intelligent, and modest, and in every respect deserving the attention I solicit for him.

I was lately called on by a French gentleman who said he was your neighbour, and afforded me an opportunity of dropping you a few lines which I meant to have availed myself of, but was disappointed. I should however only have told you what you quickly see in all the newspapers. The embargo would have been the principal article of information. That measure was embraced with considerable unanimity, after much hesitation & some opposition from the Eastern quarter. A sequestration of British debts has since been proposed, and yesterday another mode of warring on the unfriendly system of G. B. was proposed by Mr. Clarke.[1] You will find it in the paper of this evening which I inclose. Measures of this cast are a little checked by the revocation of the Edict of Novr. 6.[2] which is urged here as more conciliatory than it deserves.

The Executive have recd. letters today from Mr. Pinkny of the 9th.[3] & Mr. Short of the 19th.[4] of Jany. The former contain little more I understand than an account of the new instruction of Jany. 8th. The latter are written from Madrid and suggest that Spain is by no means in good humour with G. B. and is retained in the connection with her more by a fear of France than any other cause. Mr. S. speaks of the Affairs of France as in a state of the most compleat triumph. With the greatest esteem I am Dear Sir Yr. Most Obed. servt.

Js. MADISON JR

RC (NHi: Livingston Papers). Addressed by JM to Livingston in New York. JM's direction, "Mr. Toulmin," is followed by "3 Broadway" in an unknown hand. Postmarked "N YORK. Ap 13." Docketed by Livingston.

1. In the House of Representatives on 2 Apr. Abraham Clark of New Jersey proposed nonintercourse in "articles of the growth or manufacture of Great Britain or Ireland" until the British vacated the U.S. western posts and compensated Americans for losses in shipping as a result of the orders in council (*Philadelphia Gazette*, 3 Apr. 1794; see also JM's speech of 18 Apr. 1794 and nn.; Madison in the Third Congress, 2 Dec. 1793–3 Mar. 1795).

2. The British order in council of 8 Jan. 1794 revoked that of 6 Nov. 1793, which had interdicted all trade with the French West Indies. The new order continued to prohibit direct trade between the islands and Europe but in effect allowed the American carrying trade of noncontraband goods with unblockaded French West Indian ports (*ASP, Foreign Relations*, 1:430, 431).

3. In his 9 Jan. letter to the secretary of state, Thomas Pinckney described a conversation with British foreign minister Grenville concerning the orders in council (ibid., 1:430).

4. JM should have written "9th" (William Short to the secretary of state, 9 Jan. 1794, ibid., 1:442–44).

From Thomas Jefferson

Dear Sir   Monticello Apr. 3. 1794.

Our post having ceased to ride ever since the inoculation began in Richmond till now, I received three days ago, & all together your friendly favors of Mar. 2. 9. 12. 14. and Colo. Monroe's of Mar. 3. & 16. I have been particularly gratified by the receipt of the papers containing your's & Smith's discussion of your regulating propositions. These debates had not been seen here but in a very short & mutilated form. I am at no loss to ascribe Smith's speech to it's true father. Every tittle of it is Hamilton's except the introduction.[1] There is scarcely any thing there which I have not heard from him in our various private tho' official discussions. The very turn of the arguments is the same, and others will see as well as myself that the style is Hamilton's. The sophistry is too fine, too ingenious even to have been comprehended by Smith, much less devised by him. His reply shews he did not understand his first speech: as it's general inferiority proves it's legitimacy as evidently as it does the bastardy of the original. You know we had understood that Hamilton had prepared a Counter-report, & that some of his humble servants in the Senate were to move a reference to him in order to produce it. But I suppose they thought it would have a better effect if fired off in the H. of Representatives. I find the Report however so fully justified that the anxieties with which I left it are perfectly quieted. In this quarter all espouse your propositions with ardour, & without a dissenting voice. The rumor of a declaration of war has given an opportunity of seeing that the people here, tho' attentive to the loss of value of their produce, in such an event, yet find in it a gratification of some other passions, & particularly of their antient hatred to Gr. Britain. Still I hope it will not come to that: but that the propositions will be carried, and justice be done ourselves in a peaceable way. As to the guarantee of the French islands, whatever doubts may be entertained of the moment at which we ought to interpose yet I have no doubt but that we ought to interpose at a proper time and declare both to England & France that these islands are to rest with France, and that we will make common cause with the latter for that object. As to the naval armament, the land armament, & the Marine fortifications which are in question with you, I have no doubt they will all be carried. Not that the Monocrats & Papermen in Congress want war; but they want armies & debts: and tho' we may hope that the sound part of Congress is now so augmented as to ensure a majority in cases of general interest merely, yet I have always observed that in questions of expence, where members may hope either for offices or jobs for themselves or their friends, some few will be debauched, & that is sufficient to turn the decision where a majority is at most but small. I have never seen a Philadelphia paper since I left it, till those you inclosed me; and I feel myself so thoroughly weened from the interest I took in the proceedings there, while there, that I have never had a wish to see one, and believe that I never shall take another newspaper of any sort. I find my mind totally absorbed in my rural occupations. We are suffering much for want of rain. Tho' now at the 3d. of April, you cannot distinguish the wheat feilds of the neighborhood yet from hence. Fruit is hitherto safe. We have at this time some prospect of rain. Asparagus is just come to table. The Lilac in blossom, & the first Whip-poor-will heard last night. No Martin's yet. I have some hopes Short has sent Cortez's letters[2] for me by Blake.[3] Pray ask E. R. if he has. My best affections to Colo. & mrs. Monroe. The correspondence with Hammond has never yet come into this quarter. Accept sincere assurances of affection.

TH: JEFFERSON

RC (DLC: Rives Collection, Madison Papers); FC (DLC: Jefferson Papers).

1. Some material for William Loughton Smith's 13 Jan. speech, opposing JM's commercial discrimination resolutions, came from Hamilton's "View of the Commercial Regulations of France and Great Britain in Reference to the United States" of 1792–93 (see Syrett and Cooke, *Papers of Hamilton*, 13:407, for a discussion of the authorship of Smith's speech).

2. Hernando Cortés, *Historia de Nueva-España*, ed. Francisco Antonio Lorenzana y Butron (Mexico, 1770). This work contained three letters from Cortés to Emperor Charles V. For a discussion of Jefferson's efforts to obtain a copy, see Sowerby, *Catalogue of Jefferson's Library*, 4:266–69.

3. James Blake was a courier who carried diplomatic dispatches between the U.S. government and its commissioners in Madrid, William Short and William Carmichael, who were attempting to negotiate a treaty with Spain (Jefferson to Blake, 12 July 1793 [DLC: Jefferson Papers]).

To James Madison, Sr.

HOND SIR   PHILA. April 7. 1794.

Being reminded by your late letters[1] of your certificates and the power of attorney to draw the interest, I have searched thro' all my papers without being able to find either of them. I shall make another search, but it occurs to me that I may have carried these papers to Virga. & omitted to bring them back, and I have a faint impression of this sort on my memory. Be so good as to look among your papers, where they will be found if the impression be right; and to write without delay on the subject. It will be proper to inclose the papers to me if you meet with them.

No question has yet been taken on the sequestration of British debts. This motion was made by a member from N. Jersey. Another member from that State has moved that all trade with G. B. be stopped till the Treaty be executed, and the late depredations paid for. On this there has been neither question, nor debate. You will find in the inclosed paper the letter just recd. from Mr. Pinkney, the American Minister at London.[2] My affecte. regards to my mother.

RC (DLC). Unsigned.

1. Letters not found.
2. On 5 Apr. the *Philadelphia Gazette* published Thomas Pinckney's 9 Jan. letter to the secretary of state (see JM to Robert R. Livingston, 3 Apr. 1794, n. 3).

From John Dawson

DEAR SIR! RICHMOND April 7. 94.

The last mail brought us no letters from Philadelphia, which is matter of much surprise as the news-papers came, & of much regret as most people are exceedingly anxious to know the determination of congress on the several very important subjects now before them.

The January packet which I find has arriv'd, brings the instructions of the B. King to the commanders of armd vessels of the 8th. These in the opinion of many are *materially* different from those given on the 6th. of november. In my judgment the difference is immeterial. For altho they may in some instances bear less hard on individuals, still they go to a violation of our rights as a neutral nation, & therefore ought not to be acquiescd in. Whatever steps it may be necessary to take on the spur of the occasion, I am fully convincd that the resolutions offerd sometime since by you, are the only things which can give us permanent security, & prevent that influence which the nation possessing our commerce must ever have on our public councils.

We have for some time had much talk of war. Whether we shall have it or not depends I think on the complexion of the proceedings of the B. Part. which I believe met on the 4 Jany. That the ministry of that country may wish for a war with this, is not improbable—but that the people shoud appears highly so, as their interests are immediately & materially effected by it.

Before this I presume the sequestration bill has pass'd. Several of the most open, & violent B. subjects in this place have in the course of the last week taken the oaths of fidelity to the state. This is clearly done to shelter their property, & doubt not but the same has happend in other places.

The elections of members to the general assembly have just commencd. From the temper of the public mind I have reason to think they will *in general* be republican—all of which I have yet heard, are so.

The French fleet I learn was to have saild from Hampton road on yesterday. They had cleard out, & passd the line of entry, & clearance, before the account of the embargo arrivd.

The military plan, as at first proposd has I find been lost, at which I rejoice. It may be, that something in that line may offer, & I cannot help again mentioning to you Quarrier, whom I before took the liberty of recommen[d]ing, as a person who I am persuaded woud make a most valuable officer, Especially in the artillery. With real Esteem Your friend & Sert.

J DAWSON.

RC (DLC).

From Alexander White

DEAR SIR   WOODVILLE 7th April 1794
When I consider the momentous struggle in which you are acting—I feel a reluctance to intrude, and yet cannot avoid expressing my regret that I had no intelligence from you by last Post. Public Prints however informed me of two important facts which had not before been fully authenticated the resolution of Congress for laying an Embargo, and the British Kings instructions rescinding those of 6h. Novr. 1793. What effect will the latter have on the minds and measures of Congress—they bear the appearance of relaxation, but if all the French West India Ports should be declared blockaded (and I think this not improbable) what real advantage will accrue to America from the change of System?

You will have the pleasure of hearing from General Scott[1] that the Genêtites of Kentucky have not been able to raise a man Officers excepted; if we can escape a European War, we shall yet go on well. Is the piece published as Lord Dorchesters Speech to the Indians[2] believed to be genuine? The last few weeks have been generally dry. For some days past it has been cold with frost, but the fruit has yet escaped. Grain in strong fresh ground looks well, but that in old or thin land is much injured by the winter. Our election took place on Tuesday. The Poll stood for Mat: Page 384. Archd Magill 285 Jas. Singleton 211—Wm.

McGuire 164–Robt Page 162–Thomas Bush 153–Number of Voters 679. Our Post now goes weekly, I am Sir Yours sincerely

ALEXR WHITE

RC (DLC). Docketed by JM.

1. In the week before White wrote this letter, Maj. Gen. Charles Scott, commander of Kentucky mounted militia, passed through Winchester on his way to Philadelphia for consultations with the secretary of war (Philadelphia *General Advertiser*, 15 Apr. 1794; Knopf, *Anthony Wayne*, p. 328). For a discussion of the steps taken by Kentucky and federal authorities to stop George Rogers Clark's filibuster, see Thomas, *American Neutrality in 1793*, pp. 185–86.

2. In the "Reply of His Excellency Lord Dorchester, to the Indians of the Seven Villages of Lower Canada . . ." of 10 Feb. 1794, the governor of Canada claimed that the U.S. had violated the Treaty of Paris of 1783, "and as they kept it not on their part, it doth not bind on ours." Since American settlers had encroached on the territory disputed between Canada and the U.S., Dorchester stated that "I shall not be surprised if we are at war with them in the course of the present year" (*Philadelphia Gazette*, 26 Mar. 1794).

¶ To John Dawson. Letter not found. 7 *April 1794*. Acknowledged in Dawson to JM, 14 Apr. 1794; mentioned in JM to Jefferson, 14 Apr. 1794. Encloses newspapers with accounts of the diplomatic correspondence that Washington submitted to Congress on 4 Apr. Asks Dawson to have JM's letters to Jefferson taken out of the Richmond post office and forwarded privately to Monticello, since the mail has ceased to move during the Richmond smallpox epidemic. Acknowledges Dawson's recommendation of Alexander Quarrier.

From Arthur Breese

SIR.   WHITESTOWN Ap. 11th. 94.

Your letter of the 22d. Ultimo. I Recd. a few days since. I live on the Sadaqueda Patent, three Miles from Lot No. 2.[1] and am perfectly well acquainted with its general, situation, quality &ca. It is situated on the Mohawk river, near the confluence of two large Creeks, The Oriskany, & The Nine Mile Creeks–at the Distance of Nine Miles from Fort Stanwix, at which place a Canal, will be cut, so that the waters of Wood Creek, & the Mohawk, can communicate.[2] There will then be an uninterupted Navigation for small Boats, to the Lake Ontario, excepting a trifling obstruction at the Falls of Oswego. The Country in every direction from the Lot is rapidly settling–the quality of the soil is unexceptionable. The rear as good as the Front. Prices of Land in its Neighborhood, in an unimproved State, is four Dollars Per acre–and the average worth of your Lot, is at least, that. Since I have been here, land has rose, Fifty Per Cent. which is nearly two years. And you may reasonably calculate a proportionable rise, for several years to come, Provided we are not engaged in a war, with some of the Belligerent Powers; such an event would check the settlement of this Country, and of course the price of Land must fall. People in this Place are generally Poor, few that would be able to advance you the Money, for the whole of the Lot, 'tho they might for part. So that you must calculate upon selling on a short credit. Town Lots in this Village are selling for £50. the acre, few can be obtained for that.

Your Lot being principally feasible Land, I suggest the Propriety of laying it out in 100. acre Lots, & selling it to Settlers at five Dollars an acre, upon a short credit, with Interest.

If I can contribute to'ads the consummation of your wishes—it shall be with Much Chearfulness. I have the Honor to be Sir, with Much Respect Yr. Most Obet. Humbe. Servt.

ARTHUR BREESE[3]

RC (DLC). Addressed by Breese to JM at Philadelphia and franked. Docketed by JM.

1. JM and Monroe had purchased a 900-acre Mohawk Valley tract, Lot 2 of the Sedachqueda Patent, as a speculation in 1786. JM took over Monroe's interest in 1792 and finally sold the land in 1796 (Brant, *Madison*, 2:339–42).

2. In 1792 the New York legislature passed an act incorporating the Western Inland Lock Navigation Company, which planned improvements on the Mohawk River. The company's early efforts, directed by Philip Schuyler, were unsuccessful (Nathan Miller, "Private Enterprise in Inland Navigation: The Mohawk Route prior to the Erie Canal," *N.Y. History*, 31 [1950]: 398–99).

3. Arthur Breese moved in 1793 to Whitestown (now Whitesboro), New York, near the headwaters of the Mohawk River. He later became clerk of the Supreme Court of Western New York.

To Thomas Jefferson

DEAR SIR   PHILADA. Apl. 14. 1794.

Having recd. one letter only from you, and that of very old date, I conclude that mine which have been numerous do not pass thro' the obstructions thrown in the way of the Mail by the small pox. I continue however to write, hoping that the channel will have been reopened by the time each letter may get to Richmond. I have also written a request to Mr. Dawson to have my letters to you taken out of the post office and forwarded from Richmond by private hands if necessary.

Three propositions levelled at G. B. have latterly occupied the H. of Reps. 1. to sequester British debts. 2. to establish a lien on British merchandize or the value of it, as it arrives. 3. to suspend imports from G. B. & Ireland till the spoliations be redressed & the Treaty of peace be executed. The last has taken the pas[1] in discussion. A majority are apparently in favor. Delay is consequently one of the arts of opposition. It is uncertain therefore when a vote will be obtained. It is probable also that much will depend on the state of foreign intelligence which is hourly changing in some of its circumstances. The Executive is said to meditate an envoy Extraordy. to G. B.[2] as preferring further negociation to any legislative operation of a coercive nature. Hamilton is talked of, is much pressed by those attached to his politics, and will probably be appointed unless overruled by an apprehension from the disgust to Republicanism and to France. His trial is not yet concluded. You will see the issue it will have in the inclosed papers. The letter from the P. is inexpressibly mortifying to his friends,[3] and marks his situation to be precisely what you always described it to be. The committee on ways & means was unfortunately composed of a majority infected by the fiscal errors which threaten so ignominious and vexatious a system to our country. A land tax will be reported, but along with it excises on articles imported, and manufactured at home, a stamp tax pervading almost all the transactions of life, and a tax on carriages as an *indirect* tax. The embargo will soon be a subject of deliberation again, as its continuance if proper ought to be decided some time before its expiration. Whether this will be the case cannot now be foretold. The French continue to triumph over their Enemies on the Rhine. We learn nothing from the W. Inds. except that Martinique had not surrendered on the 25th. Ult.

I put into the hands of your Cabinet workman here the Editn: of Milton sent you from France. He was packing up things for you which afforded a commodious berth for it. Yrs. always & Affy

Js. MADISON JR.

Fauchet has informally intimated the distaste to Gour. M.[4] whose recall will follow of course.

RC (DLC). Docketed by Jefferson, "recd. Apr. 23."

1. Pas: right of precedence.

2. By early April Washington and his cabinet began to consider sending an envoy extraordinary to resolve outstanding differences with Great Britain. Federalist leaders wanted Hamilton to be appointed. Virginia Republicans John Nicholas and Monroe, in letters to the president, remonstrated against sending any envoy and were explicitly against appointing Hamilton. On 14 Apr. the secretary of the treasury withdrew himself from consideration, but Washington had already ruled out Hamilton and on 16 Apr. nominated John Jay. The envoy's powers and in-

structions were not divulged to the Senate, which nevertheless confirmed Jay's appointment on 19 Apr. after much partisan maneuvering (Syrett and Cooke, *Papers of Hamilton*, 16:261–65; *Senate Exec. Proceedings*, 1:150–52).

3. The House select committee appointed to examine the Treasury Department asked Hamilton to present to Washington the treasury secretary's account of presidential verbal and written authorization of foreign loan transactions and to "obtain from him, such declaration concerning the same, as the President may think proper to make." Washington declared to Hamilton that approval of those transactions was "upon the condition, that what was to be done by you, should be agreeable to the Laws." The treasury secretary was dissatisfied with this qualified testimonial (Abraham Baldwin to Hamilton, 5 Apr. 1794, Washington to Hamilton, 8 Apr. 1794 [second letter], Hamilton to Washington, 8 Apr. 1794, Syrett and Cooke, *Papers of Hamilton*, 16:241, 249, 250–53; see also JM to Jefferson, 26 Mar. 1794, n. 4).

4. At a later time someone here added the remaining letters of "Morris."

To Alexander White

DEAR SIR   PHILADA. Apl. 14. 1794
I have recd. your two favors of Mar. 31.[1] & Apl. 7. The motion of Clarke to suspend the imports from G. B. & Ireland till redress be obtained on the spoliations & the treaty has been the subject of much debate and is not yet decided. It is generally supposed that a considerable majority of the House are in favor of it. It is a subject however on which opinions may be much influenced by contingent events. The revocation of the act of Novr. 6. has not been without a mollifying effect: but it is so generally ascribed to other motives than goodwill to us, and so evidently susceptible of the abuse you mention that it is considered by none as a decisive change of policy towards this Country. The other propositions of different sorts have all slept on the table since this of Clarke has been in agitation. It is said that the idea of a Minister extraordinary is under the favorable deliberations of the Executive Cabinet, as a measure preferable to any Legislative operation in the first instance. Lord Dorch⟨es⟩ter's Speech is believed to be genuine: tho' questioned at first, and still ⟨so⟩ by a few. The French continue to triumph over Wurmser & Brunswick. Yrs

J MADISON JR

RC (NjP). Addressed and franked by JM. Docketed by White.

1. JM probably meant White's letter of 30 Mar. 1794.

From John Dawson

I thank you, my dear Sir, for your favour of the 7th & the papers enclosd.

On searching into the post office I found that there were a number of letters from you as well as Colo Monroe, for Mr. Jefferson. They have stopt here for some time owing to the communication being cut off. The post however set out yesterday morning for Charlottesville with them, & I believe there will be no farther interruption.

The language of Lord Greenville does not appear to me to be markd with the openness and candour of friendship.[1] Disappointed in their expectation of success against the French the B. Court will probably pursue a different line of conduct towards this country that [*sic*] they woud have done, had the events in Europe favourd their wishes.

I thank you for your attention to Quarriers wishes, & am fully persuaded that he merits confidence.

We have receivd very few returns of the Elections. A very close one is expected here this day, of the result of which I will inform you in the Evening. With real esteem Yr friend & Sert

J DAWSON

RC (DLC).

1. For Thomas Pinckney's 9 Jan. report of a conversation with British foreign minister Grenville, see *ASP, Foreign Relations*, 1:430.

From James Madison

DEAR UNCLE.   FALMO// 14th April 1794

I have had it in contemplation to write You, some time past, but thought it most prudent to defer it as long as possible, knowing that yr attention was taken up wth business of much more importance, than answering my letters. I am now advancd in years, and think I am nearly master of the business now pursueing, think it needless to continue longer with Mr Dunbar.

I have a desire to commence business on my own acct. and in doing which, am under the disagreeable necessaty, of beging yr assistance, this request is I know a very ungreatfull one, and I assure you Uncle it hurts my feelings much, when I make it, but what can I do. Tho it gives me some satisfaction to think I may at a future period have it in my power, to make full compensation, both to you and others. Am anxious to hear from you. From Yr much dependant Nephew

Jas Madison[1]

I write this in great haste.

Currt. Prices of produce.

Wheat	3/9 & 11/.	
Corn	13/	
Rye	3/4	} best prices
Tobacco	12/.	
Flour	24/.. 26/.	

RC (NN).

1. The son of JM's brother Francis, James Madison had attended Hampden-Sydney Academy, where his tuition was two years in arrears in 1788 (*PJM*, 11: 121 n. 2). At the time he wrote this letter, he was an assistant to the Falmouth, Virginia, merchant Robert Dunbar, who marketed the Montpelier wheat crop.

Draft of a Resolution on the Nonintercourse Bill

[ca. 14 April 1794]

Resold. that if from the operation of the foregoing suspension of commercial intercourse with G. B. the public revenue arising from imports shd. become inadequate to the punctual discharge of the interest on the public debt, it will be the duty of the Legislature to make up such deficiency by other resources, and to discharge the accruing arrears with as little delay as possible; and that for so doing the public faith ought to be particularly & solemnly pledged.

Ms (DLC: Rives Collection, Madison Papers). In JM's hand; headed by him at a later time, "Philada. 179–." Dated March 1794 in the *Index to the James Madison Papers*. Probably written while the House of Representatives in Committee of the Whole considered resolutions for the nonintercourse bill. This draft resolution appears to answer objections raised on 14 Apr. by Federalists Zephaniah Swift and Samuel Dexter, Jr., who argued that the bill, by reducing imports, would jeopardize revenue necessary for paying the public debt and its interest (*Annals of Congress*, 3d Cong., 1st sess., 581, 590; see also JM's speech of 18 Apr. 1794 and nn.). No evidence has been found that the resolution was introduced in the House.

¶ From James Madison, Sr. Letter not found. *15 April 1794.* Acknowledged in JM's letter to his father of 25 Apr. 1794. Informs JM that his corn crop is deficient. Inquires about breeding two of JM's mares. Describes a granary to be built at Montpelier. Comments on a piano to be bought in Philadelphia.

From Arthur Breese

SIR.   WHITESTOWN Ap. 16th. 94.

Some time since by the Mail I recd. a letter from you respecting Lot
No. 2.* I forwarded my answer immediately. By the last Mail I Recd.
a letter from Mr. Wm. Morris, inclosing one from you to me.[1] For fear
that my first letter should get lost, I now inform you that I am perfectly
well acquainted, with the general situation, & Quality of your Lot; and
that it is worth four Dollars the acre, cash, & five upon a Credit. No
Land in the Neighborhood of it, can be obtained for Less. My first Letter
informs you with prescision, the quality of the soil &ca. If we are not
engaged in a war with Europe, Land will appreciate much in Value.
Any further Information, or assistance, that I can give you, shall be
done with Chearfulness. I am Sir with much respect Yr. obedient Servant.

                                                ARTHUR BREESE

* Sadaqueda Patent

RC (DLC).

1. The letters to Breese have not been found.

From Walter Jones

DEAR SIR.   NORTHUMD. CTHOUSE Apl. 16th. 1794

I this day received yours of the 31st. March,[1] and was truly Surprised
at being informed you had never heard from me, since your former
favours were sent on. I wrote to you pretty much at large about the 18th.
of March,[2] and informed you that my reason for having, at that time,
deferred writing so long, was the hope that I might find Leisure to send
you an Inclosure, successive to the former, which however, to this day,
I have never found. I think the Subject persued with System & Temper,
would be a very useful one, & I have thoughts for preparing it against
the meeting of our assembly. It would give me great pleasure to Communicate with you on this Subject or any other, but have little expectation of it, but thro the Epistolary Medium. If on your return, I could be
informed thro what channel in Fredericsburg Letters would most directly pass to you, you would find me perhaps a troublesome Correspondent. Business will call me to that place as well as Richmond before
Midsummer—I should derive singular Satisfaction, if either Trip Should
produce a personal Interview.

We are much alarmed here at the prospect of war; and deprecate it as an Event, in which we have every thing to hazard, & nothing to gain. The merciless internal auxiliaries, which any nation, that could send a Small hostile fleet & army to our Coasts, might acquire, makes the view singularly distressing to us of the South—we have once escaped a Servile War, almost by Miracle: but it cannot rationally be hoped that we Shall again avoid it, in a like Conjuncture, especially since our Libertines in Philosophy & our Fanatics, have so vitiously meddled with the question of Emancipation. We have just heard that Captn. Knowles of the british Frigate dædalus, is taken into Custody at norfolk, as a hostage for the Treatment of Some american in the B. west Indies. It is at present a Confused report, and we are anxious to know the Truth of the fact & its probable Consequences. Adieu Dear Sir & believe me yours with my affectionate Esteem

WALT: JONES

RC (DLC: Rives Collection, Madison Papers). Docketed by JM.

1. Letter not found.
2. Jones evidently meant his letter to JM of 25 Mar. 1794.

From George Washington

DEAR SIR　　　　　　　　　　　　　　　　　　April 16th. 1794.

Not 'till yesterday did I receive the Agricultural Pamphlets from Mr: Peters. Knowing that you had not finished the perusal you intended to give them, I return them to you for that purp⟨ose⟩. After you have examined them at your leizure I wd. thank you for such remarks as shall have occurred to you on the occasion for I have yet to acknowledge Sir Jno. Sinclairs politeness in sending them to Your Affecte. Servt

GO: WASHINGTON

RC (MeHi). Addressed by Washington. Docketed by JM.

Nonintercourse with Great Britain

[18 April 1794]

On 2 April Clark moved a resolution calling for nonintercourse with Great Britain, and on 14 April the Committee of the Whole reported the resolution to the House (*Philadelphia Gazette*, 3 Apr. 1794; *Annals of Congress*, 3d Cong., 1st sess., 594). JM offered the following amendment on 18 April.

"Whereas the injuries suffered and likely to be suffered by the United States, from a violation of our neutral rights and commercial interests on the part of Great Britain, and also from a failure in the execution of the 7th article of the treaty of peace make it expedient that our commercial intercourse with that nation should not remain as extensive as it now is, therefore resolved, that from the   day of   next our commercial intercourse with that nation be suspended."[1]

Philadelphia Gazette, 19 Apr. 1794 (reprinted in *Gazette of the U.S.*, 19 Apr. 1794, *General Advertiser*, 19 Apr. 1794, and *Dunlap and Claypoole's Am. Daily Advertiser*, 21 Apr. 1794).

1. The newspaper account of the proceedings continued: "The chief difference, our readers will observe, between this proposition and the original resolution is, that in this it is not specified on what conditions the intercourse shall be restored; leaving, therefore, to a future legislature, when they are satisfied with the reparation which negociation may procure from Great-Britain, to renew our commercial relations with that country." On 21 Apr. the House agreed to JM's amendment, filled up the blanks with the date 1 Nov., and passed the resolution. JM was appointed to the committee to prepare a bill pursuant to the resolution. On 23 Apr. Clark reported "a bill to suspend the importation of certain goods, wares, and merchandise," which was passed by the House on 25 Apr. but defeated by Vice-President Adams's tie-breaking vote in the Senate on 28 Apr. (*Annals of Congress*, 3d Cong., 1st sess., 602–3, 605, 90).

To James Madison, Sr.

HON'D SIR   PHILADA. Apl. 21. 1794

I have at last found your Certificates, but have not yet applied for the Interest. The power of Attorney is probably lying in the office where it was left at the last draught of Interest.

You will see that *Jay* has been appointed to try the effect of a Minister Exty. to G. B. The proposition for enforcing our demand of redress by making our market a condition of it, is not yet come to a final question. A majority are clearly in favor of it; but the Eastern members are violently opposed to any other step than mere negociation, and spin out the discussion by unwearied resistance.

Martinique has surrendered to the British.[1] In Europe France is overwhelming the armies combined agst. her. A vessel is just arrived from England and is said to bring letters from Mr. Pinkney. I have had no opportunity of learning more than what you will collect from the newspapers.

The embargo is continued till the 25th. of May.[2] The adjournment of

Congs. is still unfixed, and depends so much on foreign intelligence as well as the business before them that I can not hazard a guess as to the time.

RC (DLC). Unsigned.

1. The British seizure of Martinique on 23 Mar. revived the issue of whether or not the U.S. was obligated to defend the French West Indies under the terms of the Franco-American alliance treaty of 1778.

2. The joint resolution of 26 Mar. provided for an embargo lasting only thirty days. By a joint resolution of 18 Apr., Congress extended the embargo for another thirty days (*U.S. Statutes at Large*, 1:400, 401).

¶ To Alexander White. Letter not found. *21 April 1794.* Acknowledged in White to JM, 26 Apr. and 5 May 1794. Discusses constitutional objections to Chief Justice John Jay's appointment as envoy extraordinary to Great Britain. Reports that public opinion in England continues to support the war against France.

To James Madison, Sr.

HOND. SIR   PHILADA. Apl. 25. 1794

Yours of the 15th. came to hand yesterday. I am sorry to learn that my crop of Corn proves so deficient. I must get the favor of you to have as much engaged as will do. If my directions for sowing oats have been followed, the less will be wanted. M. C.[1] may fence in part of the meadow as he proposes for a pasture. I leave to your own judgment to decide whether the two mares shall be put to Majr. M.s or Bishops Horse. If the Colts when dropped shd. be fine, it may [be] well to prefer the former, if not the latter may be tried. My brother William's advice may be taken. I approve the size of the Granary you have prescribed to L. C.[2] As soon as that jobb is over, he can be making provision for the Stable according to directions formerly given, unless something more urgent interfere. You have never mentioned to me whether Mr. C's mill pond has affected my meadow. I will attend to your wishes as to a Forte Piano &c. Unless the girls have extraordinary talents for music I doubt the advantage of bestowing much time on an accomplishment, which will be but imperfectly attained, and as experience shews, but for a few years exercised. You may let Mr. W. Webb know that Nothing is yet done in his affair; & Mr. A. Webb,[3] that his claim is not allowed.

The non-importation law was on a second reading yesterday agreed to 57. to 34. Its passage thro' the Senate is doubtful, or rather improbable. My last informed you that the Embargo is continued till May 25.

RC (DLC). Unsigned. Addressed by JM. On the cover, James Madison, Sr., outlined his reply of 5 May 1794.

1. Mordecai Collins.
2. Lewis Collins.
3. Augustine Webb (1763–1827), the son of William Crittenden Webb of Orange County, served as a private in the Revolution and married Lucy Crittenden in 1788 (*WMQ*, 2d ser., 5 [1925]: 172; *DAR Patriot Index*, p. 723).

From Alexander White

DEAR SIR   WOODVILLE 26h. April 1794

Your favr. of 21st instant is come to hand. Your kind attention amidst the multiplicity of business has my most grateful acknowledgements. I am really sorry the appointment of Mr Jay is disapproved of. From what I have observed and heard of his character I confess I was pleased with it. The constitutionality never occurred to me, and I do not recollect any clause in the Constitution, which could extend to the case, and having received an unexpected Call from home I have not time to look into it.

The Spring has been rather dry and cold though upon the whole it may be considered as not unfavourable. I am with real regard Dear Sir Your Obliged Friend

ALEXR WHITE

RC (DLC). Docketed by JM.

To Thomas Jefferson

DEAR SIR   PHILA. Apl. 28. 1794.

I have recd. yours of the 3d. instant. I have already informed you of my having forwarded you the French Edition of Milton red. from E. R. Cortez's letters are not come to hand. It seems that Blake by whom you expected them is not the person thro' whom the Milton came, and that he is not yet arrived. The correspondence with Hammond has been forwarded in detachments by Col. Monroe.

The non-importation bill has passed the H. of Reps. by 59. agst. 34. It will probably miscarry in the Senate. It prohibits all articles of British or Irish production after the 1st. Novr. until the claims of the U. S. be adjusted and satisfied. The appointment of H. as envoy Extry was likely to produce such a sensation that to his great mortification he was laid aside, & Jay named in his place. The appointment of the latter would have been difficult in the Senate, but for some adventitious causes. There were 10 votes agst. him in one form of the opposition[1] and 8 on the direct question. As a resignation of his Judiciary character might, for any thing known to the Senate, have been intended to follow his acceptance of the Ex. trust, the ground of incompatibility could not support the objections, which, since it has appeared that such a resignation was no part of the arrangement, are beginning to be pressed in the Newspapers. If animadversions are undertaken by skilful hands, there is no measure of the Ex. administration perhaps that will be found more severely vulnerable.

The English prints breathe an unabated zeal for the war agst. France. The Minister carries every thing as usual in Parlt. notwithstanding the miscarriages at Toulon &c., and his force will be much increased by the taking of Martinique and the colouring it will give to the W. India prospects. Nothing further appears as to the views prevailing in relation to us. The latter accts. from the W. Inds. since the new Instruction of Jany. 8 are rather favorable to the Merchants & alleviate their resentments: so that G. B. seems to have derived from the excess of her aggressions a title to commit them in a less degree with impunity. The French arms continue to prosper, tho' no very capital event is brought by the latest arrivals.

RC (DLC). Unsigned. Docketed by Jefferson, "recd. May 6."

1. On 19 Apr. the Senate defeated the motion:
"*Resolved*, That any communications to be made to the Court of Great Britain may be made through our Minister now at that Court, with equal facility and effect, and at much less expense, than by an Envoy Extraordinary; and that such an appointment is at present inexpedient and unnecessary.

"That to permit Judges of the Supreme Court to hold at the same time any other office or employment, emanating from and holden at the pleasure of the Executive, is contrary to the spirit of the Constitution, and, as tending to expose them to the influence of the Executive, is mischievous and impolitic" (*Senate Exec. Proceedings*, 1:152).

To Joshua Barney and Others

GENTLEMEN   PHILADELPHIA May 1. 1794

I have been favored with your letter of Mar: 13. from Jamaica with its inclosure, in which the American Masters of Vessels detained in that Island have been pleased to express their sentiments on the Resolutions proposed by me in the House of Representatives on the 3d. of January last. Having long regarded the principles on which those Resolutions were founded, as the basis of a policy most friendly to the just interests of our country, and most honorable to its public councils, I cannot be insensible to the approbation they may obtain from my fellow Citizens, and particularly from those more immediately attached to the prosperity of our commerce and navigation. Under this impression I have received the communication transmitted by you in such polite and friendly terms; and I hope it will be believed that I mingle with it all the sympathy which is due to the distresses of those who have been the victims of depredation. With the sincerest wishes that their unfortunate situation may speedily be exchanged for one which will correspond with their rights and their merits, I remain Gentlemen, with great respect and regard Your Obed: & Hble Servt.

Js. Madison Jr

Draft (DLC). Addressed to "Joshua Barney, Fredk Folger and Wm. McIntire Esqrs."

From George Joy

Dear Sir   London 1st. May 1794

I have yet to thank you for your favor of the 17th. May 1792[1] wch. Mr: Pinckney was so good to deliver me on his arrival and for wch. I should have made my acknowledgements before but for the constant Expectation of the pleasure of seeing you in America.

In perusing some detached parts of the diplomatic Correspondence in wch. Mr Jefferson has displayed statistical Abilities so much superior to the European Ministers it has occurred to me that he could not be in possession of certain Documents wch. have heretofore fallen in my way. I find that in Corroboration of many Arguments founded in reason (the proper foundation of the Law of Nations) he has quoted the written opinions of those respectable Authors, who had made that Law their study, wch. were not written for the purpose; and has not been sparing of his labor in referring to Authorities in point; and very much in point his Authorities are, God knows. I conclude therefore that he would have referred to Authorities in other Cases if they had been at hand—for instance that he would not have said on the subject of free ships making free Goods, in his letter to Genet of the 24th. July last[2] "that England had adhered to the rigourous principle except, as far as he remember'd, *the single Instance* of her *treaty* with *France*"; if by reference to her treaties he could have seen that not only in the single Instance of her

Treaty with France (meaning I suppose the Treaty of 1786) *and* in the Commercial Treaty of 1713 with the same Nation (Art: 17) *but* in the Treaties with Holland of July 1667 (Art: 3 referring provisionally to Art: 35 of the Treaty between France and the States General) and that of Febry. 1668 (Art: 10) and the Treaty Marine of 1674 (Art: 8) she has made stipulations contravening the rigourous principle—in her treaty with Spain too it is expressly provided (1667 Art: 26) that Enemy Ships shall make Enemy Goods and by implication of this Article combined with Art: 23 of the same Treaty Free Ships make Free Goods. With Prussia the general law of Nations is not expressly amended tho' some Ambiguity hangs on the 10th & 11th Articles of the Treaty of 1766. With Denmark & Sweden it is less equivocal, the rigorous principal being *expressly* recognised[a]—with the Piratical States again not only do free Ships make free Goods but the Property and Persons of the Confederates are protected in Enemy Ships—with the Porte Free Ships make free Goods.

I notice also in Mr Jefferson's letter to Mr: Pinckney of the 7th Septr: 1793[3] he says "*possibly* Great Britain may be bound by Treaty to admit the Exception (therein mentioned) in favor of Denmark and Sweden" —an Expression conveying a Doubt wch. would not have existed if he had had the Treaties before him—*possibly* also Mr Jefferson might have availed himself of the Explanation with Denmark (4th July 1780) to set forth to Mr Hammond the acknowledged Ideas wch. are entertained of the *Term* contraband wch. if I understand it right partakes of the nature of the *ex Ore tuo* Argument to confirm the right of neutral ships to carry such Goods to France, unmolested by British Cruizers, as are there declared not to be comprehended in this term—be this as it may, having met with a Collection of Treaties in a convenient form (published by Chalmers)[4] I have thought it might not be unacceptable to Mr Jefferson; but as I have not the honor to be known to him at all I have presumed on your friendship to transmit the Books to him. I have taken the liberty to add another Copy wch. I hope you will find a convenient addition to your own Library and have had the Treaties of 1793[5] bound in with the 2nd Volume of each. I order'd the same to be done with the Treaty of the 19th Ult: between this Country Prussia and Holland but being printed in a 4to: form only it could not be effected; I therefore send it seperate. By this you will see that in the Auction for the Hirelings of Prussia this Country has outbid France for the year at least and notwithstanding the Provision for renewal of this Bargain on similar terms

[a] Denmark 1670 Art: 20 and Passports subjoined.
     Sweden Apl: 1654 Art: 12 Do: 1656 Art: 4 & Passports subjoined.
     Ditto 1661 Art: 12 & Passports subjoined.

at the End of this period a Pretext may probably be found for increasing the demand according to the state of the Market.

Great scenes are acting at this Moment upon the Continent. Enthusiasm and Numbers are on the side of the French. Discipline, I apprehend, on the side of the Allies; and these last contrary to expectation were first in the field—they have taken the Ground wch. was most vulnerable but that wch. the french might reasonably wish them to take provided they feel themselves secure against internal Commotions and particularly if they are, as I understand, in sufficient force to issue a considerable body of Troops from the Neighbourhood of Lisle & Dunkirk on the one hand and Maubeuge on the other—how the Campaign will finish must of course be very doubtful—I am inclined to think favorably to the French —the greatest hope of the Allies must rest upon an internal diversion in their favor—without this they cannot be ignorant of the impossibility of subjugating France—this hope is founded on two Circumstances wch. if not equally plausible may be equally fallacious—'tis encouraged by the Reports of the Emigrants, desperate in their Circumstances and having even greater reason to try all hazards than those wch. prompted the American Refugees to similar representations; and the intemperate and sanguinary Measures of France, where without doubt the greatest Despotism reigns at this Moment, furnish another Cause for them to hope that Civil Dissentions will favor the return of Monarchy—the first of these tho' feeble is strengthened by the difficulty wch. Ministers meet with to obtain better information, wch. has been so great as to induce them to apply to some American Gentlemen from France on the subject; who have prudently and properly declined to have any intercourse with them—the second tho' much to be regretted and a real injury to the republican Cause in point of reputation, is not likely to destroy it *in France* if I may Credit the uniform testimony of a number of my Friends arrived lately from Paris and different parts of that Country—by these it appears that those who are most opposed to some of the Measures of the existing Government, and who have the Courage to declare it, are yet determined to suffer everything rather than receive the Law from foreigners; God forbid that this should be the Lot of any People; and succour the Polanders in their spirited and almost desperate Efforts to relieve themselves from it!

I cover this letter to my Friends Messrs. J. Wd. & Wm. Gibbs of Philadelphia[6] to whose Care I send the Books also, that you may have no trouble with them and in the Event of your absence from that City they will be governed in sending them to you or retaining them for your return by the information they may receive at Mrs. House's of the time when you are expected.

Mrs. Joy and my Brother desire to be remember'd to you with much Esteem and I am very respectfully, Dr sir, Your most obedt: servt:

GEO: JOY.

N 56 Hatton Garden.

RC (DLC). Addressed by Joy to JM, "North 8th Street, two Doors from the / Corner of Market Street / ☜ Theresa / care of Messrs. Gibbs." Cover also marked, "Receiv'd & forwarded by / Yr. obedt. Servts / J W & W Gibbs / Philada. 18 Novr. 1794." Docketed by JM.

1. Letter not found.
2. Printed in *ASP, Foreign Relations*, 1:166–67.
3. Printed ibid., 1:239–40.
4. George Chalmers, ed., *A Collection of Treaties between Great Britain and Other Powers* (2 vols.; London, 1790).
5. *Authentic Copies of Treaties* (London, 1793).
6. Josiah W. and William Gibbs were merchants with premises at 92 North Second Street (Hardie, *Philadelphia Directory* [1794 ed.], p. 56).

Excise

[1 May 1794]

On 23 April the Committee of the Whole took up the report of the select committee on ways and means (*Annals of Congress*, 3d Cong., 1st sess., 604; on the context of that report, see Madison in the Third Congress, 2 Dec. 1793–3 Mar. 1795). On 1 May a resolution for an excise on manufactured snuff and tobacco was read.

Mr. Madison had always opposed every tax of this nature, and he should, upon all occasions, persist in opposing them. If we look into the state of those nations, who are harnessed in taxes, we shall universally find, that, in a moral, political and commercial point of view, excise is the most destructive of all resources. He did not say this, because excise had been a frequent topic of popular declamation. He was not guided by that, but he knew, and was sensible, that it produced almost in every case the most disagreeable consequences. Yet he admitted, that the Excise upon ardent Spirits, was a very natural expedient, in the American government, who saw such immense quantities of foreign spirits imported. Much of the collection of this tax on tobacco, would depend on the oath of the manufacturer, and this was but another term for the multiplication of perjuries. The tax would therefore injure the morals of the people. He liked much better some other taxes in the list before the house; and recourse might be had to them. He should oppose this tobacco duty, with every vote that he gave on the question.

Philadelphia Gazette, 2 May 1794.

Excise

[2 May 1794]

In Committee of the Whole, Dexter (a Federalist) countered arguments that an excise was antirepublican by pointing out that his constituents in Massachusetts were good republicans but supported the excise.

Mr. Madison professed an aversion to all comparisons; but if they must be made, it was proper to draw them with the strictest regard to truth. He agreed with the gentleman from Massachusetts lately up, that the citizens of that state were good republicans, but so were the citizens of other states. Laws were fast equalizing the manners of Americans, all over the continent; and no where with more rapidity than in Virginia. The people there were not less truly republican than others. There had not been a single insurrection, in that state, since the first declaration of independence; nor any resistance to the laws. Excise had indeed been very unpopular in the Southern states, compared with what it was in the Eastern; but for this there was a very good reason. The tax was not only one, to which they had not been accustomed, but it fell much more heavy upon the Southern than upon the Eastern states, where it was likewise familiar. The people of Virginia had never been discontented, even when paying heavy taxes, before the institution of the federal government, at the amount of the taxes themselves. Their dissatisfaction arose from the knowledge that, at that time, but a small part of these taxes went into the public treasury. The collectors, in raising the revenue, speculated upon a bad paper medium, and by certain maneuvres, (which the member did not explain, but which are notoriously known) they turned the greater part of what they received into their own pockets. This was the only reason why the Virginians had formerly discovered discontent. As to the subject before the house, it was proper to chuse taxes the *least unequal*. Tobacco excise was a burden the *most unequal*. It fell upon the poor, upon sailors, day-labourers, and other people of these classes, while the rich will often escape it. Much had been said about the taxing of luxury. The pleasures of life consisted in a series of innocent gratifications, and he felt no satisfaction in the prospect of their being squeezed. Sumptuary laws had never, he believed, answered any good purpose. Something had been said about the difference between direct personal taxes, and those raised by indirect means, such as excise and customs. He quoted an author of respectable character, in England, who estimated the expence of uplifting *direct* taxes, in that country, such as the land tax, at three per cent. and that of uplifting *indirect* taxes, such as those of excise and customs, upon the

321

whole, at *thirty* per cent.* This last was perhaps an exaggeration, and must be in part, a conjecture. But such a conjecture proved that the proportion upon *indirect* taxes was at least very considerable. Excise had at first been resorted to upon a few manufactures. The dealers indemnify themselves at the expence of their customers. At the same time, they endeavoured to evade the duties, and thus there commences a struggle, which has many bad effects, both upon industry and public morals. In Europe, when tobacco is excised, the government forbids it from being planted. (Some years ago, the British farmers were obliged, by an act of parliament, to pull up and burn their tobacco, before it was full grown.) No such measure he hoped would be adopted here, but it was hard to say where the business might one day end. Statesmen, in general, did not study the liberty, the virtue, or the comforts of the people, but merely to collect as much revenue, as they were able. Taxes were not, for the most part, the work of patriotism. An excise established in America would discourage the emigrations from Europe, that might, at this time, be so much expected. He was determined to vote against the resolution.

* Some years ago, the expence of collecting the revenues of Britain was about Two millions and two or three hundred thousand pounds of Pennsylvania currency. The expence hath since increased. Some taxes do not, in many parts of the country, defray more than half the charge of collecting them.

Philadelphia Gazette, 3 May 1794. After further debate, the committee approved the resolution for a tax on manufactured snuff and tobacco.

To James Madison, Sr.

HON'D SIR   PHILADA. May 4. 1794.

By a vessel which sails for Fredg. today, I have sent a small box containing the following articles 6 ps. very coarse muslins, 1 ps. of finer. 2 lb. Tea, 3 Books on Medicine, a few pamphlets & a Sett of marking instruments. The muslins were bought as being extremely cheap, and useful for various purposes. If my mother or sister wants any part of them they will make free with them. If the finer piece should not be applicable to any better purpose, I allotted it for shirts, in which it is said to wear as well as linnen. The coarser ps. I supposed might be dealt out in part to my negro women if thought proper, as far as would give them each some kind of garment. The cost would be a trifle, and they wd. probably be better pleased than with some thing in the ordinary way of equal value. I wish however that free use may be made of these as already hinted. The coarse ps. cost about 4 dolrs. each. The fine one abt. 4/. Va. Curry. a yard. The two books by Hamilton[1] are for Dr. Taylor[2] whom you will ask to accept of them. The other by Wallis[3] I send for yourself. It is said to be an able performance. If Dr. Taylor on perusal of it shd. wish a copy, I will forward one for him. You will find that I have recovered the pamphlet by the French Chymist on the mine[r]al waters of Virga.[4] The Squash seed is of the same kind with that inclosed lately in a letter.

As I retain the conviction I brought from home in favr. of the Mill at my brothers, I have been endeavoring to dispose of the piece of land on the Mohawk river. But the acct. I have of it embarrasses me. I perceive that by selling it now, I shall get 40 or 50 perCt. less than it will probably fetch in a year or two. I am assured by *correct & authentic* information, that it is of the best quality, that the country is rapidly settling all around it, that the navigation of the river will soon be opened, and that at a very few miles distance land of the same quality sells for 8 or 10 dollars an acre. Within three miles, lotts in a town lately laid out, sell for £50 an acre and are with difficulty got for that. I can not at present get more than between 4 or 5 dollrs. an acre. The gentleman[5] who gives me my information is a respectable lawyer residing within three miles of the land, and intimately acquainted with it, as well as with that part of the Country. He writes me that within 2 years past Similar lands have risen at least 50 perCt. & that the prospect of future rise is at least as great. Notwithstanding these circumstances I am so much disposed to forward the plan of the Mill which I view as particularly favorable to the interest of my brothers as well as myself, that I [*sic*] if a pursuit of it depends essentially on my contribution, I shall not hesitate to make the sacrifice. Whether this be the case you can best decide & I will thank you for a line on the subject immediately on the receipt of this. Perhaps your funds ⟨ma⟩y be competent to the demand of the present year. I am persuaded also that notwithstanding the low rate of the pu⟨bl⟩ic paper, there would be less loss in your sale of that, than I should suffer from the present sale of the land.

The bill for suspending importations from G. B. & Ireland which passed the H. of Reps. by 59 agst 34 was rejected in the Senate, who are determined to rely on the extraordinary mission of Jay to sue for satisfaction. The H. of Reps. are occupied with new taxes to defray the expence of the naval armament, the fortifications &c. An increase of the impost, a stampt tax, further excises, and a land tax, are all proposed. I much fear that the aversion to the last will soon involve this Country in the pernicious revenue systems of Europe; and without ultimately avoiding the thing dreaded, as a land tax will be sure to be added on the first great occasion, that may arise. It is not certain how much longer the session will be spun out. I hope it will end at farthest within the present month. If I should determine to make the sale above mentioned,

I shall probably be obliged to make a trip to New York before I return to Virginia.

RC (DLC). Signature clipped. Franked and addressed by JM to his father in Orange County, "care of Js. Blair Esqe. / Fredericksburg / Virginia."

1. Several medical books by Dr. Alexander Hamilton (1739-1802) had been published by the time JM wrote this letter: *The Family Female Physician* (Worcester, Mass., 1793; Evans 25580), *Outlines of the Theory and Practice of Midwifery* (Philadelphia, 1790; Evans 22551; and Worcester, Mass., 1794; Evans 27084), and *A Treatise on the Management of Female Complaints . . .* (New York, 1792; Evans 24376).

2. Dr. Charles Taylor (1755–1821), JM's second cousin and Francis Taylor's brother, married Sarah Conway. He received a military land bounty for his services as a surgeon during the Revolution. In 1793, with other Orange County investors, he became a bonded agent of the Loyal Company, which had claimed lands in western Virginia since 1749 (*DAR Patriot Index*, p. 667; Blanton, *Medicine in Virginia in the Eighteenth Century*, pp. 389-90, 407; *Tyler's Quarterly*, 4 [1922–23]: 86–92).

3. George Wallis, *The Art of Preventing Diseases* (New York, 1794; Evans 28021).

4. John Rouelle, *A Complete Treatise on the Mineral Waters of Virginia* (Philadelphia, 1792; Evans 24757).

5. Arthur Breese.

From James Madison, Sr.

[5 May 1794]

X Where shall the Laths, & plank be procured
X for the granary—
X Send the memorials—
X Forte Piano—no books. ⟨per brass?⟩ Wire
   pay Mr Blair when you come home 18/
X C——s Mill does no damage
X Excuse [*sic*] Law
X Bill of exchange

Ms (DLC). Notes in the hand of James Madison, Sr., for a response to JM's letter to him of 25 Apr. 1794. Written on the cover of that letter. Probably formed the basis of a letter (not found) of 5 May 1794 (acknowledged in JM to James Madison, Sr., 19 May 1794). Edge of Ms damaged.

From Alexander White

I have to thank you for your favr of 21st. Ulo. I deem it peculiarly unfortunate that any appointment by the President should at this time be considered as exceptionable. With regard to Mr Jay I confess I cannot discover any constitutional ground of objection. Whatever impropriety there may be in his holding two offices at the same time and receiving compensations for each, the constitution seems not to have provided a remedy, though the subject of incapacitation was considered, and provided for by the latter clause of the 6 section of that instrument. I am extremely sorry the spirit for carrying on the war against France still prevails in England. We shall never have perfect peace while the war rages in Europe, and if it should be of long continuance I fear we shall not be able to avoid taking a part in it. Should England succeed in subduing the French Islands I do not believe she will be permitted to retain them—after the conclusion of Peace—for however desirous the Emperor and others may be to place a Monarch on the thrown of France, when they find that impracticable, they will I conceive be still desirous to restore to France such a degree of power as to enable her to form a counterpoise to England in the scale of European Politics—this she cannot do without a Navy—and a Navy she cannot maintain without a forreign Trade. A young man of some credit has just arrived from Kentucky and says, that General Clarke has actually fallen down to the Mouth of the Ohio with 600 Men, where he now lies, and stops every boat on the River. I have not seen the young man, but from what I know of him, and the channel through which the account came from him to me, I fear it is true. The Weather has been uncommonly warm for several days, the Mercury at 9 O'clock Saturday Morning in Sunshine was at 94. Adieu and believe me sincerely Yours

              Alexr White

RC (DLC). Docketed by JM.

¶ From William Madison. Letter not found. *5 May 1794.* Stan. V. Henkels, Jr., Catalogue No. 1478 (1933), item 106, described this letter as consisting of two pages, "telling about recent elections and the dislike of Mr. Jay."

From John Dawson

Dear Sir!   Rich: May 6. 94

On my return to this place on the last evening I receivd your letter[1] with the enclosure for which I thank you.

The rejection of the resolution of your house for prohibiting the commercial intercourse with great Britain, by the senate gives much discontent, as far as I have heard observation on it. The nomination of a envoy exty. at the time it was mad⟨e⟩ appears to me singular, & no doubt had its influence on the fate of the resolution. But the person appointed I think in almost every point of view one of the most improper that coud have taken place.

We have nothing worthy communicating. With real esteem Yr. friend & Sert

J Dawson

RC (DLC).

1. Letter not found.

¶ To Gustavus B. Wallace. Letter not found. 7 *May 1794.* Acknowledged in Wallace to JM, 13 May 1794. Discusses JM's recommendation of Wallace to the War Department for a military appointment.

Excise

[9 May 1794]

On 7 May the Committee of the Whole reported eight resolutions on ways and means of raising revenue. JM voted with the minority when the House upheld provisions for a carriage tax, a stamp duty, and an excise on tobacco (*Annals of Congress*, 3d Cong., 1st sess., 653–56, 666–67). On 9 May the House considered the first resolution, which increased the impost. Clark moved that an additional duty of 10 percent be placed on British goods; FitzSimons claimed "that there was a progressive diminution of trade with Britain compared to increase of American commerce with other nations."

Mr. Madison thereupon read a paper containing a state of trade with Britain.

In 1791, the exports from that country to America were to the value of

		Dollars.
		19,502,070
Imports from America to Britain in the same time.		5,511,843
		13,990,226
1792, Exports		19,711,369
		4,798,848
		14,913,527[1]

Philadelphia Gazette, 10 May 1794.

1. Clark withdrew his motion. JM was in the majority when the House de-

feated an increase in duties on domestic tonnage but in the minority when additional foreign tonnage duties were also defeated. He again voted with the minority on 10 May when the House defeated increased tonnage duties on British ships and upheld a tax on deeds. The House then passed the eight resolutions and ordered the select committee on ways and means to report bills pursuant to the resolutions (*Annals of Congress*, 3d Cong., 1st sess., 670–73; see also JM's speech of 19 May 1794 and nn., and JM to Jefferson, 1 June 1794, and nn. 1 and 2).

To Thomas Jefferson

DEAR SIR   PHILADA. May 11. 1794

Col. Monroe wrote you last week, and I refer to his letter[1] for the state of things up to that date. The H. of Reps. has been since employed chiefly on the new taxes. The Report of the Committee which was the work of a subcommittee in understanding with the Fiscal Department, was filled with a variety of items copied as usual from the British Revenue laws. It particularly included, besides stamp duties, excises on tobacco & sugar manufactured in the U. S. and a tax on carriages as an *indirect* tax. The aversion to direct taxes which appeared by a vote of seventy odd for rejecting them will saddle us with all those pernicious innovations, without ultimately avoiding direct taxes in addition to them. All opposition to the new excises, tho' enforced by memorials from the manufacturers was vain. And the tax on carriages succeeded in spite of the Constitution by a majority of twenty, the advocates for the principle being reinforced by the adversaries to luxury. Six of the *N. Carolina* members were in the majority. This is another proof of the facility with which usurpation triumphs where there is a standing corps always on the watch for favorable conjunctures, and directed by the policy of dividing their honest but undiscerning adversaries. It is very possible however that the authors of these precedents may not be the last to lament them. Some of the motives which they decoyed to their support ought to premonish them of the danger. By breaking down the barriers of the constitution and giving sanction to the idea of sumptuary regulations, wealth may find a precarious defence in the sheild of justice. If luxury, *as such*, is to be taxed, the greatest of all luxuries, says Payne, is a great estate. Even on the present occasion, it has been found prudent to yield to a tax on transfers of stock in the funds, and in the Banks.

The appointment of Jay continues to undergo the animad[v]ersions of the Press. You will see that the Democratic Societies are beginning to open their batteries upon it. The measure however has had the effect of impeding all legislative measures for extorting redress from G. B. The non-importation bill which passed the H. of Reps. by a great majority, was so instantly & peremptorily rejected in the Senate as an interference with the proposed Mission, that no further efforts of the same type have been seriously contemplated. Clarke did indeed move to insert among the new ways & means an additional duty of 10 perCt. on *British* manufactures, but the symptoms of desertion soon induced him to withdraw it. A member from N. Carolina afterwards was incautious eno' to try a discriminating duty on British tonnage and by pushing it to a question with the yeas & nays, placed us in a very feeble minority. Notwithstanding this effect of the Executive measure, there is little serious confidence in its efficacy; and, as involving the appointment of Jay, is the most powerful blow ever suffered by the popularity of the President.

The embargo is Still in force. A member from Connecticut moved a few days ago to abridge its term a few days, as a notification that it would not be continued. A large majority was against taking up the proposition;[2] but how far with a view to adhere to the embargo, I know not. Yesterday a motion was laid on the table by Smith (of S. C) for continuing the embargo to June 25.[3] The motion from that quarter excited surprize: and must be either a fetch at popularity, an insidious thing, or suggested by an idea that the balance of the effects of the embargo is in favor of G. Britain.

There are no late accounts of moment from Europe. Those from the W. Indies, as well with respect to the treatment of our vessels as the effects of the embargo, are so various & contradictory that it is impossible to make any thing of them. Yrs. Affecy.

Js. MADISON JR

RC (DLC). Docketed by Jefferson, "recd. May. 21."

1. Monroe to Jefferson, 4 May 1794 (Hamilton, *Writings of Monroe*, 1:292–96).
2. On 8 May the House of Representatives voted to defer consideration of Zephaniah Swift's resolution to terminate the embargo (*Annals of Congress*, 3d Cong., 1st sess., 657–58).
3. On 12 May JM was with the majority when the House voted 13–73 to defeat William Loughton Smith's resolution to continue the embargo (ibid., 675, 683).

Memorandum from John Taylor

PHIA. May 11. 1794

On the 8th. or 9th. instant T.[1] asked leave of absence of the Senate, and expressed seriously his intention to resign. K.[2] soon after invited T. into one of the committee rooms, and informed him, that he wished to converse with him seriously & candidly upon a very important subject. He stated that it was utterly impossible for the union to continue. That

the southern and eastern people thought quite differently. That the former cloged and counteracted every operation of government. That when
I & S[3] of S. C.[4] were out, the southern interest would prevail. That the
eastern would never submit to their politicks. And that under these circumstances, a dissolution of the union by mutual consent, was preferable
to a certainty of the same thing, in a less desirable mode. About this time
E.[5] joined K & T, as if by accident, tho' T. thought from concert. K then,
protesting that he had never mentioned the subject to E. before, ran
over the same ideas, in which E. concured. K was throughout the chief
spokesman, tho' E. occasionally joined him, & appeared intirely to concur with him. It was pressed upon T. in this dilemma, that a friendly
intercourse among the members, for fixing the outlines of a seperation
was desirable. K. declared that he was very indifferent as to the line of
division, from the potowmack to the Hudson. T. expressed his approbation of a friendly & cool discussion of great political subjects in conversation, but approved highly of supporting the union if possible,
thought that no material contrariety of interests opposed it, but if he was
mistaken, agreed that an amicable seperation was certainly preferable.
Previously to coming to this extremity, T. said that an effort ought
to be made to unite the two parties which distracted the government;
that he considered the debt as the great cause of these parties. Because
if we might judge from their mutual accusations, one party suspected
that the other was determined to use this debt as a political machine, &
to counteract its payment, whilst the other suspected the first of an intention to destroy it. Suppose therefore said T. the two parties were to
act in such a manner as to remove these mutual suspicions, might it not
give new vigor to the union? If it was proposed for instance, to disband
the indian army—to employ one third of its present expence in sudden
excursions upon the heels of each other into the indian country—instead
of lessening the taxes, to devote by the strongest sanction the two thirds
saved to the payment of the principal of the debt—to impose a new tax,
founded upon the principle of equality, for the same object—to open a
land office, particularly as to a great extent of country in the fork between the ohio—& Illinois, upon which there are no Indians, and to devote its product to the same object. Would not these measures prove
that one party was willing to pay the debt—that the other, had annexed
no political designs to its continuance—& would not a union of parties
result from a removal of their mutual suspicions? Besides the western
people would be better pleased, & more essentially benefited—the general belief now existing, that the lands are held up, tho' devoted by law
to this object, to give great land jobbers an opportunity to sell, and to
enable them by legislative intrigues and corruption, to push their speculations beyond the Ohio, would be gratified—and the frauds in the im-

position of taxes, dictated by local interests, would be rendered unnecessary. But K. would not agree to any thing of this kind—he said that there were other essential subjects of difference between the extremities of the union, besides the debt. That they never had and never would think alike. That M.[6] whose conduct he had narrowly watched, particularly on the committee of ways & means, had some deep & mischievous design—that tho' he should be of opinion to disband the army after this year if something very material did not happen, yet he would allow no money for carrying on the indian war, but leave it to support itself—that he would not consent to open the land office—and that in short he saw no remedy but a dissolution of the union. T. pressed K to state his suspicions of the designs of M.—to declare what points he wished to be conceded by his opponents—to state the supposed objects of the two parties, which disunited them, independant of the debt—and to say whether some alternative preferable to a dissolution of the union, could not be hit upon. But K declined any explanations of these kinds, contending that the only remedy for the political dissentions, was a dissolution of the union. And nothing being concluded upon, the conversation ended.

Remarks.

T. upon reflection, considers the above as worthy of being communicated to M. He is thoroughly convinced that the design to break the union is contemplated. The assurances—the manner—the earnestness —and the countenances—with which the idea was uttered, all disclosed the most serious intention. It is also probable that K & E, having heard that T. was against the constitution, have thence imbibed a mistaken opinion, that he was secretly an enemy to the union, and conceived that he was a fit instrument (as he was about retiring) to infuse notions into the supposed antifederal temper of Virginia, consonant to their views. T. cannot help believing that these views go far beyond what even this proposition discloses. A British interest is what he fears lurks at bottom. The southern temper greatly obstructs a close political connexion with Britain. Those who would get the power to the eastward, would easily effect it as to that moiety—and then Britain & the east united, could operate powerfully in various ways, to bring the south to their terms.

M. will see clearly, that this communication, tho' proper to be made to him, ought not to be disclosed to others.[7]

Ms (CSmH). In Taylor's hand. Docketed by JM, whose interlinear additions were probably made at a later time. A facsimile is printed with an introduction in Gaillard Hunt, ed., *Disunion Sentiment in Congress in 1794* (Washington, 1905).

1. JM here interlined "Taylor." On the same day that he wrote this memorandum, Taylor resigned from the U.S. Senate (*BDC*, p. 1794).

2. JM here interlined "King." A week earlier, Taylor had had another encounter with Senator Rufus King of New York. See Madison in the Third Congress, 2 Dec. 1793–3 Mar. 1795.

3. JM here interlined "Izard & Smith."

4. JM here interlined "Carolina."

5. JM here interlined "Elsworth."

6. JM here interlined "Madison."

7. JM added below Taylor's concluding sentence, "The language of K & E.
probably in terrorem."

From William Cooper

SIR   [12 May 1794]
    The inclosed Resolutions of this Town, passed at a very large Meet-
ing of the Inhabitants, being conceived of importance to the United
States, are dispatch'd by Express.

                              WILLIAM COOPER. Town Clerk

[Enclosure]

At a legal and very numerous Meeting of the Freeholders, & other
Inhabitants of the Town of Boston at Faneuil Hall on Monday the 12th
day of May 1794
    Resolved, As the sense of the Inhabitants of this Town, that the Gen-
eral Embargo, imposed by the Legislature of the United States on the
Navigation & Commerce within the same, is a measure, founded in the
highest policy & Wisdom—passed by a very great Majority.
    Resolved, that the Inhabitants of Boston will cordially acquiesce in
the continuance of the Embargo, untill in the opinion of Congress, the
objects contemplated by that measure shall be fully accomplished—
passed unanimously.

                              Att. WILLIAM COOPER Town Clerk

RC and enclosure (DLC). Both in a clerk's hand, except for Cooper's signatures. Addressed to JM "or Col Parker, or Mr Giles, Members / of Congress /
Philadelphia." Directed, "To be delivered / Thursday 2 oClock." Docketed by JM.

From Alexander White

DEAR SIR   [ca. 12 May 1794]
    I have the pleasure to contradict the report from Kentucky mentioned
in my last of General Clarkes having fallen down the Ohio with 600
Men, I have seen the young man alluded to, and others who came with

him. A report prevailed that a Mr Montgomery who has a Colonels commission under Clarke had taken Post at the mouth of the Ohio, and stopped all boats going down the river, but of this there was only a report not credited by the more intelligent. We have had great changes of weather from the excessive heat mentioned in my last—to severe frosts on the 7th. & 8th. instant, it is again moderate. I am Dear Sir Yours sincerely

ALEXR WHITE

RC (DLC). Docketed by JM, "May 1794." Dated ca. 5 May 1794 in the *Index to the James Madison Papers.*

¶ To Alexander White. Letter not found. *12 May 1794.* Acknowledged in White to JM, 19 May 1794. Discusses tax legislation pending in Congress.

From Gustavus B. Wallace

DR. SIR   FREDBG May 13h. 1794

Yours of the 7th. Inst. I reciv'd by Saturdays Mail, and have to thank you for puting in my Name at the War office. Old point Comfort was the place I wished to Command or Norfolk, if point Comfort was not fortified. I am much obliged to you, for the paper your Letter inclosed. The Command Task I think I am eaqual to—tho not able to campain it in my old age a garrison will have no Riding or Marching.

We have nothing new here but much rejoicing on the Successes of the French. I am Sir Your Most obt. & Very Humble st

GUS B WALLACE

RC (DLC). Docketed by JM.

From Thomas Jefferson

DEAR SIR   MONTICELLO May 15. 1794.

I wrote you on the 3d. of April, and since that have received yours of Mar. 24. 26. 31. Apr. 14. & 28. and yesterday I received Colo. Monroe's of the 4th. inst. informing me of the failure of the non-importation bill in the Senate. This body was intended as a check on the will of the Representatives when too hasty. They are not only that but completely so on the will of the people also: and in my opinion are heaping coals of fire not only on their persons, but on their body as a branch of legislature. I have never known a measure more universally desired by the people than the passage of that bill. It is not from my own observation of the wishes of the people that I decide what they are, but from that of the gentlemen of the bar who mix much with them, & by their intercommunications with each other, have under their view a greater portion of the country than any other description of men. It seems that the opinion is fairly launched into public, that they should be placed under the controul of a more frequent recurrence to the will of their constituents. This seems requisite to compleat the experiment whether they do more harm or good? I wrote lately to mr. Taylor for the pamphlet on the bank.[1] Since that I have seen the 'Definition of parties,'[2] and must pray you to bring it for me. It is one of those things which merits to be preserved. The safe arrival of my books at Richmond, & some of them at home, has relieved me from anxiety, & will not be indifferent to you. It turns out that our fruit has not been as entirely killed as was at first apprehended. Some latter blossoms have yeilded a small supply of this precious refreshment. I was so improvident as never to have examined at Philadelphia whether negro cotton & oznabrigs can be had there. If you do not already possess the information, pray obtain it before you come away. Our spring has on the whole been seasonable, & the wheat as much recovered as it's thinness would permit. But the crop must still be a miserable one. There would not have been seed made but for the extraordinary rains of the last month. Our highest heat as yet has been 83. This was on the 4th. inst. That Blake should not have been arrived at the date of your letter, surprizes me. Pray enquire into the fact before you leave Philadelphia. According to Colo. Monroe's letter this will find you on the point of departure. I hope we shall see you here soon after your return. Remember me affectionately to Colo. & mrs. Monroe, and accept the sincere esteem of Dear Sir your sincere friend & servt

TH: JEFFERSON

RC (DLC: Rives Collection, Madison Papers); FC (DLC: Jefferson Papers). RC addressed by Jefferson and franked.

1. [Taylor], *Enquiry into the Principles.* In his 1 June 1794 letter to Jefferson (DLC: Jefferson Papers), Taylor enclosed copies of this pamphlet and probably that noted below.

2. [John Taylor], *A Definition of Parties; or, The Political Effects of the Paper System Considered* (Philadelphia, 1794; Evans 27781).

From James Madison

DEAR UNCLE   FALMO// the 15th May 1794
I wrote you some time past, and my not receivg an answer, conclude, it did not reach Phila. The purpose of it was, that I had it in contemplation, to commence business on my own a/c, and was under the disagreeable necessity of begg. yr assistance. You will please write me immediately on the business.

Please direct the letter to the care of Robt Patton Fredbg. From Yr Dependant Nephew

JAS. MADISON

RC (NN).

Protection of the Frontier

[16 May 1794]

The Committee of the Whole took up the report of a select committee to which had been referred a memorial from the House of Representatives of the Territory South of the River Ohio (which later became Tennessee), requesting a more effective defense against the Indians.

Mr. Madison objected to some part of the report. It had been stated by the committee, that the governor of that country should be authorised, in case of any irruption by the Indians, to attack them with an armed force, and compel them to an *observance* of the treaties made with the United States. Mr. Madison considered this language as irregular, because by the laws, and universal sense of nations, when hostilities are once commenced between two different states, existing treaties are *at an end;* and therefore an armed force cannot compel the observance of old treaties, but the formation of new ones. He stated several objections to the method pointed out in the report of the select committee for giving military aid to the back settlers.

Philadelphia Gazette, 17 May 1794. After debate in the Committee of the Whole, the House passed a "bill for the more effectual protection of the Southwestern Frontier settlers" on 29 May (*Annals of Congress*, 3d Cong., 1st sess., 730; see also JM's speech of 6 June 1794 and nn.).

To James Madison, Sr.

HOND. SIR   PHILADA. May 19. 1794
Your favor of the 5th. came to hand a few days ago. I hope you will have secured me the corn & a plenty of it. I am at a loss to give directions

concerning the laths & plank. If M. C.[1] can conveniently spare the Horses to bring it from my brothers, it will no doubt be best to get it from him. Otherwise it will cost less in the end to take it of Mr. C. I will attend to the Forte Piano & the Dictionary for my sister. As I have not yet sold my land & probably shall not at present, it will be convenient to receive a bill for about 200 dollars, or more if you can spare it. No time shd. be lost in remitting it. Mr. Dunbar will probably be able to accomodate you. I am offered 3600 Dollars for the land, but am advised by good judges not to listen to any thing like that price. The discontent as to the excise has probably been stirred up for some electioneerg. purpose, and will subside of course; unless fostered by other excises now in agitation here, to wit, on manufactured Tobo. & refined Sugar. I oppose these, & wish it were possible to get rid of the principle altogether without a worse alternative. A land tax tho' far preferable to excises in my judgment, & as appears, in that also of my Constituents, is yet viewed in a very unfavorable light generally. It was lately proposed by a Committee of ways & means, & rejected in the House by a vast majority. You will have seen by the papers that the Embargo is not to be continued. The price of flour is in consequence at 50/. Pa. Cy. There are no late accts. of importance from abroad. The adjournment of Congs. will probably tho' not certainly take place in 15 or 20 days. I hope M. C. & Sawney will make ready for Harvest without waiting for my presence, as I can not be sure of being there in time. My dutiful regards to my mother & yourself

Js. Madison Jr

RC (DLC).

1. Mordecai Collins.

From Alexander White

Dear Sir   Woodville 19h May 1794

I am favd with yours of 12th. instant—since which a Gentleman has arrived from Philadelphia who left it on Wednesday, and says the Embargo is not to be continued.

I should myself prefer a direct tax to an extension of the Excise, or to the introduction of any new indirect tax which has yet occurred to my mind. Whether a tax on Carriages (except as an article of manufacture in the hands of the Maker or Vendor) can come under the latter description is at least equivocal. By a direct tax I understand a tax in which no one participates except the man who pays it. With this understanding of the Constitution I cannot distinguish between a tax on my Carriage, and a tax on any other part of my property real or personal. Adieu and believe me Yours &c

ALEXR WHITE

RC (DLC). Docketed by JM.

Excise

[19 May 1794]

On 17 May Smith (South Carolina) reported from the select committee on ways and means "a bill laying certain duties upon manufactured tobacco and refined sugar" (*Annals of Congress*, 3d Cong., 1st sess., 700). Debate on 19 May focused on the issue of whether or not the revenue raised by the new duties was needed.

Mr. Madison thought that the arguments on each side of this question might be reduced to a narrow compass. If peace continues, he supposed it likely, that the revenue would not fall so far short, as the committee had apprehended. But if there was a war, the expence would much exceed any thing yet thought of. He was for laying aside the business at present, and if a rupture with England should ensue, he would then recommend, once for all, a *direct* tax, and that these excise acts should be entirely thrown aside. If there was no war, he believed that no new taxes were required; let the matter therefore die, as to the present. He disapproved the principle of the tax, and should, on that account, think himself justified in voting against it.

Philadelphia Gazette, 20 May 1794. JM voted with the minority when the House defeated a motion to reject the bill. On 24 May the House passed the bill, which Washington signed into law on 5 June (*Annals of Congress*, 3d Cong., 1st sess., 707, 720; *U.S. Statutes at Large*, 1:390).

Repayment of Loan to France

[24 May 1794]

On 18 March Washington transmitted to the House a request from French minister Fauchet for an advance of loan payments due to France. The House referred the president's message to a select committee chaired by Smith (South Carolina), whose report the House tabled on 17 April (*Annals of Congress*, 3d Cong., 1st sess., 524, 600).

Mr. Madison moved, that a late message from the President, which had been referred to a select committee, should come before a committee of the whole house. The message was relative to an advancement of money to the ambassador of the republic of France. Some time ago, it had been found that there was no money in the treasury, but what had been appropriated. There was now money unappropriated.[1]

Philadelphia Gazette, 26 May 1794.

1. The House made the message the order of the day for 26 May, when the Committee of the Whole considered it. At the House's request, Hamilton submitted his "Report on Loans Negotiated in Europe Not Already Laid before the Legislature" on 27 May. Two days later JM reported from committee "a bill providing for the payment of a certain sum of money to the French Republic," which was passed by the House on 30 May but defeated in the Senate on 7 June (*Annals of Congress*, 3d Cong., 1st sess., 722–23, 731, 739, 130; Syrett and Cooke, *Papers of Hamilton*, 16:431–32 and nn.).

To Thomas Jefferson

DEAR SIR   PHILADA. May 25. 1794.

Your favr. of the 15th. Inst: came to hand yesterday. I will procure you the "Definition of parties," and one or two other things from the press which merit a place in your archives. Osnabrigs can be had here. Negro Cotton I am told can also be had; but of this I am not sure. I learn nothing yet of Blake. The inclosed paper will give you the correspondence of E. R. & Hammond on an occurrence particularly interresting.[1] You will be as able to judge as we are of the calculations to be founded on it. The embargo expires today. A proposition some days ago for continuing it was negatived by a vast majority; all parties in the main concurring. The Republican was assured that the Embargo if continued would be considered by France as hostility: The other had probably an opposite motive. It now appears that throug⟨h⟩out the Continent the people were anxious for its continuance, & it is probable that its expiration will save the W. Inds. from famine, without affording any sensible aid to France. A motion was put on the table yesterday for re-enacting it.[2] Measures of this sort are not the fashion. To supplicate for peace, and under the uncertainty of success, to prepare for war by taxes & troops is the policy which now triumphs under the patronage of the Executive. Every attack on G. B. thro' her commerce is at once discomfited; & all the taxes, that is to say excises, stamps, &c. are carried by decided majorities. The plan for a large army has failed several times in the H. of Reps. It is now to be sent from the Senate, and being recomended by the Message of the P. accompanying the intelligence from the Miami,[3] will probab[l]y succeed. The influence of the Ex. on events, the use made of them, and the public confidence in the P. are an overmatch for all the efforts Republicanism can make. The party of that sentiment in the Senate is compleatly wrecked; and in the H. of Reps. in a much worse condition than at an earlier period of the Session.

RC (DLC). Unsigned. Docketed by Jefferson, "recd. June 10."

1. JM probably enclosed the *Philadelphia Gazette* of 24 May, which published the correspondence between Edmund Randolph and British minister Hammond concerning Lord Dorchester's speech to a delegation of Indians in Canada, which predicted war with the U.S. Washington had recently submitted this correspondence to Congress (*ASP, Foreign Relations*, 1:461–63; see also Alexander White to JM, 7 Apr. 1794, n. 2). JM's copy of *Congress of the United States. In Senate, May the 23d, 1794. Ordered, That the Message from the President . . . of This Day, with the Communications Referred to Therein, Together with Communications Referred to in Message of the President . . . of the 21st Instant, Be Printed . . .* (Philadelphia, 1794; Evans 27893) is in the Madison Collection, Rare Book Department, University of Virginia Library.

2. On 24 May Congressman Alexander Gillon of South Carolina introduced, and after debate withdrew, a motion to renew the embargo (*Annals of Congress*, 3d Cong., 1st sess., 722).

3. On 21 May Washington sent to Congress documents relating to "the state of affairs between us and the Six Nations" and reports of British provocation of Indian attacks on the U.S. frontier (*ASP, Indian Affairs*, 1:477–82).

From James Monroe

DEAR SIR   PHILA. May 26. 1794.

I have been with Mr. R. & have given him no final answer.[1] The fact appears to be that the message to me was directly from the President, so that a decision settles it. He has also had an interview with Mr. Dayton.

May I request of you to go to Mr. Randolph, & settle the matter with him. I promised him you wod. in the course of ½ an hour. If it has not the approbation of my few friends & yourself in particular &[2] certainly will decline it. Weigh therefore all circumstances, & paying as little regard to private considerations as shod. be, tell him for me what answer to give. I write in haste in the Senate, being engaged on the balance bill. Yr. friend & servt

JAS. MONROE

An answer must be given the President immediately.

RC (DLC). Addressed by Monroe.

1. Edmund Randolph conveyed to Monroe Washington's offer of appointment

as U.S. minister to France, to replace Gouverneur Morris. After complying with the U.S. request for Genet's recall, the French government asked for the recall of Morris, who was hostile to the revolutionary regime. The president wanted to nominate a prominent Republican, but Robert R. Livingston and JM had already declined the post. On 27 May Washington nominated Monroe, whom the Senate confirmed the following day (Ammon, *James Monroe*, pp. 112–14; *Senate Exec. Proceedings*, 1:157).

2. Monroe obviously meant "I."

¶ From James Madison, Sr. Letter not found. *26 May 1794*. Acknowledged in JM to James Madison, Sr., 6 June 1794. Concerns a bill of exchange for JM from William Triplett for $200 on a Philadelphia mercantile house.

¶ To John Sitman and Others. Letter not found. *28 May 1794*. Acknowledged in Sitman and others to JM, 22 Jan. 1795. Concerns an address that Sitman has sent to JM (possibly a "petition of sundry inhabitants of the towns of Salem, Beverly, and Danvers, in the State of Massachusetts," which was read in the House of Representatives on 7 Apr. 1794 [*Annals of Congress*, 3d Cong., 1st sess., 561]).

Military Establishment

[30 May 1794]

On 1 April the House approved a resolution to raise an additional military force of 25,000 men "during a war which may break out between the United States and any foreign European Power" but on 19 May rejected a "bill to augment the military force of the United States." On 30 May the House took up a Senate bill—"An act to increase the Military Force of the United States, and to encourage the recruiting service"—which authorized the president to raise an additional 10,000 troops for three years. Debate pitted Federalist advocates of military preparedness against Republican opponents of standing armies (*Annals of Congress*, 3d Cong., 1st sess., 558, 709–10, 735).

Mr. Madison did not accede to the principle of the bill. He did not see any such immediate prospect of a war, as could induce the house to violate the constitution. He thought that it was a wise principle in the constitution, to make one branch of government raise an army, and another conduct it. If the Legislature had the power to conduct, an army, they might embody it for that end. On the other hand, if the President was empowered to raise an army, as he is, to direct its motions when raised, he might wish to assemble it for the sake of the influence to be acquired by the command. The Constitution had wisely guarded against the danger on either side. He could not, in the present case consent to the breaking down of this barrier of public Safety. He saw no necessity for it; nor any violent probability, that this country will be speedily invaded by any force, to which the present military establishment cannot make an adequate resistance. Let us hear from the Minister whom we have just sent to Britain, before we take such abrupt and expensive measures. We shall certainly hear from him, at least, before we are invaded. Now if we enter into a calculation of the time requisite for his arrival in Britain, for commencing his business, and for sending back an account of what kind of reception he has met with, we shall find that by this period, Congress will have sat down again; or at least the interval will be so small, as to make it not worth while to embrace any measure of this kind. Upon the whole, he could not venture to give his consent for violating so salutary a principle of the constitution, as that upon which this bill incroached.

Philadelphia Gazette, 31 May 1794. Speech misdated "Friday, May 29" (the fourth Friday of May 1794 was the thirtieth). After further debate, JM voted with the majority when the bill was defeated (*Annals of Congress*, 3d Cong., 1st sess., 738).

To Thomas Jefferson

DEAR SIR   PHILADA. June 1. 1794

The Stamp Act was poisoned by the ingredient of the tax on transfers.[1] The centinels of Stock uniting with the adversaries of the general plan formed a large majority. The carriage tax which only struck at the Constitution, has passed the H. of Reps. and will be a delicious morsel to the Senate.[2] The attempt of this Branch to give the P. power to raise an army of 10,000, if he should please, was strangled more easily in the H. of R. than I had expected. This is the 3d or 4th. effort made in the course of the Session to get a powerful military establishment, under the pretext of public danger and under the auspices of the P.'s popularity. The bill for punishing certain crimes &c. including that of selling prizes has been unexpectedly called up at the last moment of the Session.[3] It is pretended that our Citizens will arm under French Colors if not restrained. You will be at no loss for the real motive, especially as explained by the circumstances of the present crisis. The bill for complying with Fauchet's application for a million of dollars, passed the H. of R. by a large majority. The Senate will certainly reject it. Col. M.[4] is busy in preparing for his embarkation. He is puzzled as to the mode of getting to France. He leans towards an American vessel which is to sail from Baltimore for Amsterdam. A direct passage to F is scarcely to be had, and is incumbered with the risk of being captured & carried into England. It is not certain that Negro Cotton can be had here. German linnens of all sorts can. Nothing of Blake. Tomorrow is the day of adjournment as fixt by the vote of the two Houses; but it will probably not take place till the last of the week.[5] We have had 8 or 10 days of wet weather from the N. E., which seems at length to be breaking up. Yrs. Affy.

Js. MADISON JR

RC (DLC). Docketed by Jefferson, "recd. June 10."

1. The third of eight House ways and means resolutions of 10 May called for a stamp tax including duties on transfers of government and bank stock. This tax was rejected on 27 May, when JM voted with the majority (*Annals of Congress*, 3d Cong., 1st sess., 658–59, 673, 725–26).

2. The bill for a carriage tax was a result of the second resolution of 10 May on ways and means. Although on 29 May JM "objected to this tax on carriages as an unconstitutional tax; and, as an unconstitutional measure, he would vote against it," the bill passed and Washington signed it on 5 June (ibid., 654–55, 672, 730; *U.S. Statutes at Large*, 1:373–75).

3. On the Neutrality Act, see JM's speech of 2 June 1794 and nn.

4. James Monroe.

5. Concurrent resolutions set the adjournment of the Third Congress's first session for 3 June, then postponed it. The session ended 9 June (*Annals of Congress*, 3d Cong., 1st sess., 713–14, 758, 760, 768–69, 784).

Madison's Courtship and Marriage
ca. 1 June–15 September 1794

EDITORIAL NOTE

In eighteenth-century American society the relationship between husband and wife was a private, almost secret, matter. History and biography have been poorer for this fact, as witness Martha Washington's destruction of her husband's letters after his death. Thus the affectionate exchanges between John and Abigail Adams have long stood out and been cited as unusual survivals of that era of intense privacy. William T. Hutchinson and the other early editors of this project understood the relationship of JM and his beloved Dolley and accordingly announced at the outset (*PJM*, 1:xxxv) that letters to and from Dolley Madison "which throw light upon her husband's career" would be printed. In short, there is more to a statesman's life than politics and tobacco prices. For example, Catharine Coles's 1 June 1794 letter to Dolley Payne Todd, disclosing that "he hopes that your Heart will be calous to every other swain but himself," reveals an aspect of JM's life that would be obscured if we consider only the Virginia congressman's political correspondence in this period. The narrative of JM's courtship has been well told in Ketcham, *James Madison*, pp. 376–82, Brant, *Madison*, 3:401–14, and Virginia Moore, *The Madisons: A Biography* (New York, 1979), pp. 10–17.

Catharine Coles to Dolley Payne Todd

PHILIDELPHIA 1 June 1794

I told you my Dear Cosen that I should not stay very Long here after you was gone we propose Leaveing this next Wednesday for New york.

Now for some News all the good Folks in this House are well only Cosen Sally[1] is sikish, Capn Preston[2] is gone, Sukey & Mrs Grenup[3] are all so. Mr Grove[4] is in the Pouts about you, tell Anny[5] I have not seen Mr Porter[6] so I cant tell how he Looks, the General is pretty so so, J——— B——— Round the Corner is melancholy, Lawrance[7] has made me his Confidant Poor Fellow I fear he will not meet with Suckcess, now for Mad———[8] he told me I might say what I pleas'd to you about him to begin, he thinks so much of you in the day that he has Lost his Tongue, at Night he Dreames of you & Starts in his Sleep a Calling on you to relieve his Flame for he Burns to such an excess that he will be shortly consumed & he hopes that your Heart will be calous to every other swain but himself he has Consented to every thing that I have wrote about him with Sparkling Eyes, Monroe goes to France as Minister Plenipo. M——— has taken his House do you like it. Poor Coln Bur has Lost his Wife he is gone to New York. Dont you think that I have wrote enough for this time adieu. Mr Coles Joins m⟨e⟩ in affectionate Love to you your Mother[9] & Sisters & remember us to all frien⟨ds.⟩ Your Sincere friend

CATHARINE COLES[10]

RC (ViU: Dolley Madison Papers). Addressed by Catharine Coles to Dolley Payne Todd in Virginia. Docketed by Dolley Payne Todd. On the cover is written, in unknown hands, "Wm. W. Wilkins Esqr." and "Mrs. Coles Letters must be directed to the care of Mr. James Thompson of New York."

1. Sarah (Sallie) Coles (1789–1848) was the daughter of John Coles II of Enniscorthy in Albemarle County, Virginia, and a cousin of Dolley Payne Todd's. During JM's presidency she was often a guest at the executive mansion. In 1816 she married Andrew Stevenson, who later served as Speaker of the House of Representatives and U.S. minister to Great Britain (Edward Boykin, ed., *Victoria, Albert, and Mrs. Stevenson* [New York, 1957], pp. 3–12).

2. William Preston, a captain in the Fourth Sublegion, was Congressman Francis Preston's brother (Heitman, *Historical Register U.S. Army*, 1:806; Abram Trigg to JM, 1 Oct. 1793, and n. 1).

3. Mary Catherine Pope Greenup, daughter of Nathaniel Pope of Virginia, was the wife of Kentucky congressman Christopher Greenup.

4. Probably William Groves, a schoolmaster who lived at 14 North Sixth Street (Hardie, *Philadelphia Directory* [1794 ed.], p. 61).

5. Anna Payne (1780–1832), Dolley Payne Todd's sister, married Massachusetts congressman Richard Cutts in 1804 (Moore, *The Madisons*, p. 10; Hunt-Jones, *Dolley and the "Great Little Madison,"* p. 21).

6. Probably John Porter, a physician who lived at 191 South Front Street (Hardie, *Philadelphia Directory* [1794 ed.], p. 122).

7. Probably John Lawrence, a gentleman who lived at 197 Chestnut Street (ibid., p. 88).

8. Twice in this paragraph someone (probably Dolley Payne Todd) later filled in the remaining letters of "Madison."

9. Mary Coles Payne (1745–1807) was Dolley Payne Todd's Quaker mother. In 1761 she married John Payne (1741–1792), who soon converted to Quakerism, manumitted his slaves, and in 1783 moved the family from Hanover County, Virginia, to Philadelphia. When her husband went bankrupt in the starchmaking business, she took boarders (including Aaron Burr) into her house at 231 New Street. After John Payne's death, she lived at Harewood, the Jefferson County estate of her son-in-law George Steptoe Washington (Ketcham, *James Madison*, pp. 377–78; Moore, *The Madisons*, pp. 3–6, 210–11).

10. Catharine Thompson Coles (1769–1848) married Dolley Payne Todd's cousin, Congressman Isaac Coles of Halifax County, in 1790 (*VMHB*, 21 [1913]: 203).

Neutrality

[2 June 1794]

On 13 March Vice-President Adams broke a tie in the Senate to pass the Neutrality Act, which prohibited citizens from enlisting or accepting commissions in foreign military forces, fitting out foreign privateers and warships, or participating in filibuster expeditions. On 31 May JM was in the minority when the House voted to consider the act immediately (*Annals of Congress*, 3d Cong., 1st sess., 68, 743–44). In Committee of the Whole on 2 June a motion was made to strike out the act's sixth section, which forbade the sale within the United States of prizes captured by foreign warships or privateers. Smith (South Carolina) opposed the motion, citing Jefferson's printed diplomatic correspondence to buttress his arguments against permitting the sale of French prizes in American ports.

Mr. Madison replied to Mr. Smith, in substance, as follows.

He should not follow Mr. S. in the long argument which he had extracted chiefly from the correspondence of Mr. Jefferson; because, were it admitted to be well founded, it did not reach the true point to be decided. It was not merely a question, whether we were bound by treaty to permit the sale of French prizes. There was another question, whether we were bound, by the law of nations and of neutrality, to refuse that permission. It had not been shewn, that we were bound to such refusal. A neutral nation might treat belligerent nations unequally, where it was in consequence of a stipulation prior to the war, and having no particular reference to it. It was laid down expressly, by all the best writers, that to furnish a military force to one of the parties, in pursuance of such a stipulation, without a like aid to the other, was no breach of neutrality; and it amounted to the same thing whether the equilibrium were destroyed by putting an advantage in one scale, or taking a privilege from the other. The executive had expounded the law of nations, and our treaties, in this sense, by leaving the sale of French prizes free, and forbidding the sale of British prizes. For the legislature to decide, that we were bound by the laws of neutrality to forbid the sale of French prizes also, would be to make themselves the expositor of the law of nations, to condemn the exposition of the executive—to arm Britain with a charge against the United States, of having violated their neutrality, and, what ought particularly to be avoided, to arm her with claims of indemnification for injuries done her by the sale of prizes. Such a proceeding would be the more impolitic and extraordinary, as it could not fail *to give extreme disgust to the French Republic*, by withdrawing a privilege which it had been determined could be rightfully allowed her; and, as the British minister, lord Grenville, had admitted in his conversations, with Mr. Pinkney, that Britain had reason to be satisfied, on the whole, with the conduct of the United States, as a neutral nation.

Philadelphia Gazette, 7 June (also reported ibid., 3 June 1794). After further debate, the committee struck out the section, and JM voted with the majority when the House upheld the committee's action. The House then passed the amended act, which the president signed on 5 June (*Annals of Congress*, 3d Cong., 1st sess., 756–57; *U.S. Statutes at Large*, 1:384).

To James Madison, Sr.

Hon'd Sir   Phila. June 6. 1794.

I recd. yours of the 26 Ult: on the subject of the bill of exchange, and at the same time a draught from Mr. Triplet[1] for 200 dollars on a house here which has accepted it. I have not yet fixt on a Forte Piano but have several in my eye; and will make a choice as soon as I can satisfy myself, and will have it forwarded it [*sic*] as soon as an opportunity offers. The adjournment is put off till monday next. I shall set out in a few days thereafter, in company with Col: Monroe who is to embark at Baltimore for France. If I could fix the time, I should be glad to have a conveyance provided for me from Fredg; but that cannot yet be done. I wish however you could keep horses ready to be sent down in case previous notice should get to your hand. If the little chair is not unfit for use I would prefer that mode. I shall have a servant with me. I refer to the inclosed papers for several articles of foreign information. Yr. Affe. Son

Js. MADISON JR

RC (DLC). Addressed by JM.

1. Probably the Fredericksburg merchant William Triplett (Rutland, *Papers of George Mason*, 1:ciii; Crozier, *Virginia County Records: Spotsylvania County*, p. 381).

Protection of the Frontier

[6 June 1794]

On 5 June the Senate amended "An act for the more effectual protection of the Southwestern frontier settlers," providing for raising a regular infantry regiment of 1,140 men instead of relying on militia. The amendments revived the debate in the House over the perceived threat of a standing army (*Annals of Congress*, 3d Cong., 1st sess., 123–24, 774–77).

Mr. Madison said that he would not enter at large into this subject, but there was one circumstance in the business, which struck him as very strange. It was proposed to raise a new corps, at a bounty of twenty dollars. The present army wanted more than the whole number of this corps to fill up its deficiencies; and yet the proposal for completing them *had been refused*. Thus are we to be at the expence of supporting the skeleton of an army. Was it not better to fill up the old corps, than to put ourselves to the inconvenience of raising a new one?

Philadelphia Gazette, 9 June 1794. After further debate, JM voted with the majority when the House rejected the Senate amendments, thus killing the bill (*Annals of Congress*, 3d Cong., 1st sess., 799, 781).

From Joseph Mussi

SIR   Monday Eveng 9. June 94.

My Brother Stephen Mussi partner in the houses under the firm of Bolongaro Simonetta in frankfurt, & Bolongaro Simonetta, & Co. in Amsterdam having allready procured Sevl. Loans, will be disposed to Lend any Sum to the united States at four, & a half ⅌ Ct. interest, Commission, & all Charges encluded, if requested. Whenever you understand that the Executive Should wish it, I Shall immediately write to my Brother, & as a Citizen of united states I'ill be happy of any opporty. to be of Service.

We Spoke of it few weeks ago after dinner at the house of major Butler, who told me to mention it to you. I wish you good voyage to virginia, & remain with Sentiments of true esteem—Sir your most obt. Servt.

Jos. Mussi[1]

I beg to present the enclosed with my best Compliments to Mr. Jefferson.

RC (DLC). Docketed by JM.

1. Mussi was a Philadelphia merchant with premises at 230 High Street, where Jefferson lived at the end of his term as secretary of state. He supplied Italian marble to Jefferson and the commissioners of the federal district (Hardie, *Philadelphia Directory* [1794 ed.], p. 111; Mussi to James Hoban, 12 Dec. 1793, Mussi to the commissioners, 7 Apr. 1794 [DNA: RG 42, Letters Received]; Jefferson to Mussi, 17 Sept. 1794 [DLC: Jefferson Papers]).

To James Madison, Sr.

Hond Sir   Baltimore June 15. 1794

I got here the evening before last, and shall leave this the day after tomorrow in company with Mr. Jones who met Col. Monroe here. I shall probably be three days on the road to Fredg. and must there provide a conveyance home; unless you should have been able to save me from that necessity. If Mr. Blair shd. send this by an immediate opportunity, there may possibly be time after the receipt of it to forward horses to meet me at Fredg. where I shall halt a day if no more. I mentioned in my last that I wd prefer travelling from Fredg. in a chair if that arrangement be practicable. Yr Affe. son

Js. Madison Jr

RC (ViU). Addressed by JM to his father in Orange County, "care of Js. Blair Esqe / Fredericksburg / Virginia." James Madison, Sr., made many notes on the cover concerning financial and legal transactions.

Power of Attorney from James Monroe

Baltimore June 17. 1794.

Mr. Madison will be pleased to receive from Genl. Wilkinson, or draw on him for the sum of three hundred dolrs. or thereabouts (due me by him) according as the Genl. shall direct. He will likewise receive whatever is obtained from Genl. Bradley[1] from the sale of our Vermont property, or otherwise from the sale or upon acct. of it. He will likewise be pleased, in case he is applied to, give advice as to the course to be taken for obtaining justice agnst J. Kortright and others under the will L. Kortright (father of Mrs. M.) of New York[2]—and whatever he does in the above will be satisfactory & binding on me.

JAS. MONROE

Ms (DLC). In Monroe's hand.

1. Stephen Row Bradley, a Revolutionary veteran, was a U.S. senator from Vermont, 1791–94.
2. Monroe was one of his father-in-law's executors. Lawrence Kortright bequeathed to his son, Capt. John Kortright, "a full suit of mourning, having provided for him amply more than his patrimony"; the bulk of his estate went to three of his four daughters. Thomas Knox, another of Lawrence Kortright's executors and sons-in-law, later asked JM to send him some of Monroe's letters "which may be useful to the Suit in Chancery with J. Kortright. Old Mr. Kortright not long before he died . . . wrote to Mr. Monroe to settle for him his concern in lands at Smiths Clove with Judge Morris. John Kortright claims this tract under purchase from his Father of some years standing. These letters if they can be come at, will at least prove that the old Gentn. did not mean it as a bona fide sale" (will of Lawrence Kortright, *Collections of the New-York Historical Society*, 38 [1905]: 270; Knox to JM, 12 Dec. 1795 [DLC]).

From Walter Jones

DEAR SIR.   June 18th. 1794.

I remain your Debtor for two Letters,[1] which obligation would have been Sooner discharged, but that the accounts we heard of the adjournment of Congress rendered it improbable that my Letters would find you in Philadelphia.

I write this by a transient & hasty opportunity, which allows not time for any reflexions or questions on public affairs. I just take time to mention that many weeks ago an Intimation Came to me from a distant part, that one of our Senators meant to resign,[2] & a proposition, that I should take measures, to become his Successor. I cannot finally resolve yet, upon the Course I shall take; and indeed it would depend much upon the probable prospect of not being repulsed, if I attempted it. I hear that Colo. Hopkins is looked upon generally as one who will Succeed, and I do not hear of any other person particularly named. Our part of the Country is So out of the Line of general Intelligence that we Collect with difficulty the general opinion of the State.

Should you think proper to mention my Name, to the Delegates you

347

may meet with, & to write me Some time hence on the prospect you take of the probable Success of my declaration, it would contribute much to Shape my resolution. I am dear Sir with affectionate and sincere Esteem

WALT: JONES

RC (DLC: Rives Collection, Madison Papers). Docketed by JM.

1. Letters not found.
2. Both U.S. senators from Virginia resigned: John Taylor of Caroline on 11 May and Monroe on 27 May. On 18 Nov. the General Assembly elected Henry Tazewell to succeed Taylor and Stevens Thomson Mason to succeed Monroe, thus preserving the Republican complexion of Virginia's senatorial delegation. Tazewell took his seat on 29 Dec., but Mason did not appear in Philadelphia until a special session of the Senate convened on 8 June 1795 to consider the Jay treaty (*BDC*, p. 56 and nn. 22–25; *JHDV*, Nov. 1794 [Evans 29799], pp. 19–20; see also Risjord, *Chesapeake Politics*, pp. 448–49).

¶ To Joseph Jones. Letter not found. *Ca. 1 July 1794.* Alluded to in Jones to JM, 6 July 1794. Reports the poor condition of wheat crops between Fredericksburg and the mountains of Virginia.

¶ To John Lee. Letter not found. *Ca. 1 July 1794.* Mentioned in JM to Lee, 15 Nov. 1794. Requests information on Ambrose Madison's and JM's Kentucky lands.

¶ To Hubbard Taylor. Letter not found. *Ca. 1 July 1794.* Mentioned in JM to John Lee, 15 Nov. 1794. Requests information on Ambrose Madison's and JM's Kentucky lands.

From Joseph Jones

DR. SR.   FREDG. 6th. July 94

Your accot. of the crops of wheat from this place to the little mountains is confirmed by almost every person I have seen and conversed with on the subject except Fountaine Maury who seems to entertain an opinion that the Crops below the mountain as well as in the upper country are much better than reported and greatly preferable to the crops of last year. My information respecting the crops of wheat from this dow[n]ward represent them as ruined in many places and in others reduced at least to a half and a third at best. Upon the whole it cannot be questioned but the crop will be very short of the usual quantity. Col. Carter and myself were to have gone for Loudon[1] in a few days after you left us but a proposition coming forward for a grand field day on the 4th. July suspended our seting out untill the 5th. the time agreed on —that day the Col. seemed disposed to devote to rest in consequence of the hard service of the day preceeding and on this day we have been delayed by the rain but from present appearances I have no doubt shall commence our Journey Tomorrow. It will be seven or eight days before we get back and then after resting three or four days it is my intention to move your way. Perhaps I may go through Culpeper. Nothing has yet arrived from Philadelphia. Mr. Williams was to have sailed about a week past by whom the parcels you expect may probably arrive and before I return. I had a letter from Monroe dated the 22d. ulto. off new pt. Comfort in the Bay where they had been detained two or three days for want of a fair wind to go to sea—they sailed the morning after we left Baltimore and altho' the next day there was a brisk wind and as he said the ship had much motion they escaped sickness except that Joe[2] complained a little but did not decline his dinner. The driver on his return with the Horses & chair met with an accident. The Horse fell and broke one of the Shafts for which a demand was made by Rect of fifteen shillings wch. I refused to pay as extravagent and withall a questionable charge. At length however as he fell to 7/6 I gave it him rather than have a dispute or any thing said further abt. it. Adieu. Yr. friend & Servt

Jos: Jones

There has already been some severe actions in Flanders wch. at length seems to have terminated in favor of the Republicans.

RC (DLC). Addressed by Jones to JM at Orange. Docketed by JM.

1. Jones subsequently purchased land in Loudoun County from Col. Charles Carter, Jr., of Ludlow in Stafford County. Monroe became a joint owner with Jones of that land. At the death of Jones's son, Joseph Jones, Jr. (1779–1808), Monroe inherited the balance of the estate with its six-room frame cottage called Oak Hill. In 1819 Monroe began construction of a larger house on the site (JM to Monroe, 4 Dec. 1794; Edmund Pendleton to Carter, 24 Dec. 1794, Mays, *Papers of Edmund Pendleton*, 2:629–30; Ammon, *James Monroe*, pp. 291, 408).

2. Jones's fifteen-year-old son, Joseph Jones, Jr., accompanied Monroe to France aboard the *Cincinnatus* commanded by Joshua Barney (Ammon, *James Monroe*, p. 116).

From Joseph Jones

Dr: Sr   FREDG 22d. July 1794

I expected to have been with you before now but have been unwell a few days past wch. has delayed me. Anty. goes up with a few things to

Monroes wch. I suppose will be wanting there while I am up.[1] He brings all the Coffee that came here in the Matt package—package and Coffee weighed 38 lb whe. it was the whole that should have come I am uninformd. I have sent you a pine apple cheese which I hope will prove good those in general that have been used here were approved of as good. I shall go through Culpeper and if nothing unforeseen prevents will set off Tomorow. You have several packages at Andersin's or Blairs. Yr. friend & Servt

Jos: Jones

RC (DLC). Docketed by JM.

1. Monroe had authorized his uncle Joseph Jones to look after his house west of Charlottesville and another recently purchased Albemarle County estate. In 1799 Monroe completed Highland (later called Ash Lawn) on that estate (Ammon, *James Monroe*, pp. 115–16, 163).

¶ To Joseph Jones. Letter not found. *Ca. 12 August 1794.* Alluded to in Jones to JM, 14 Aug. 1794. Explains that JM cannot meet Jones in Charlottesville as planned owing to Antoine's illness. Asks Jones to inform Jefferson of the delay.

From Joseph Jones

Dr. Sr.   CHARLOTTE[s]VILLE 14th. Augt. 1794

We have long expected you and was apprehensive something disastrous had happened to prevent your coming up. I am sorry for poor Antoine's situation wch. certainly demands your attention and is a satisfactory apology for your declining to leave home untill he is apparently free from danger. I delivered the pamphlets to Mr. Jefferson who was a few days past very well and to whom I shall communicate what you desire respecting the delay of your visit. It is my intention to set out on Monday or Tuesday and will endeavour to take a view of Merrys land. I have yet come to no determination but am to have some conversation with Mr. Charles Carter respecting some land in this neighbourhood to day as he wrote me he should be at Court. Had it been convenient for you to have made your visit when proposed it wod. have been a gratification to me who have been rather lonesome and obliged to have recourse to the reviews and some other pamphlets for amusement and passing away leisure hours. My health has been much restored. Yr. friend & Servt

Jos: Jones

RC (DLC). Docketed by JM.

To Dolley Payne Todd

ORANGE Aug: 18. 94. I recd. some days ago your ⟨p⟩recious favor from Fredg.[1] I can not express, but hope you will conceive the joy it gave me: The delay in hearing of your leaving Ha⟨n⟩over which I regarded as the only ⟨s⟩atisfactory proof of your recove⟨r⟩y, had filled me with extreme ⟨. . . dis⟩quietude, and the co⟨mmun⟩ication of the welcome event was ⟨e⟩ndeared to me by the *stile* in which it was conveyed. I hope you will never have another de⟨li⟩*beration*, on that subject. If the sentiments of my heart can gua⟨r⟩antee those of yours, they assure me there can never be a caus⟨e⟩ for it. Is it not cruel that I should be obliged to mingle w⟨ith⟩ the deliciou⟨s . . .⟩ your letter the pain . . .

. . . I cannot ⟨di⟩smiss my fears that his illness may at least be prolonged. ⟨O⟩n the most favorable supposition, I can not venture to expect that he will be able to travel in less than 10 or 12 days. I should not hesitate to set out without him, tho' in several respects inconvenient were it not forbidden by his utter ignorance of our language, and my being the only ⟨pe⟩rson here who knows a word of his; ⟨so⟩ that in case his ⟨il⟩lness should continue his distress as well as that of those around him would be inexpressible; to say noth⟨in⟩g of the difficulty of followi⟨n⟩g me in the event of his getting wel⟨l.⟩ This adverse incident is t⟨he⟩ more mortifying as I had spared ⟨n⟩o efforts and made some sacrifices, to meet you at ⟨. . .⟩ than I hoped when we ⟨par⟩ted. I limited . . .

. . . set out. If he so far recovers that I can leave him, without being a⟨ble⟩ in a few days, according to appearances, to travel, I shall then endeavo⟨r⟩ to proceed without him, and let him make his way after me as well as he can: In the mean time, allow me to hope that this unavoidable delay, will not extend its influence to the epoch most ⟨. . . an⟩d to repeat the claim ⟨wh⟩ich I apprised . . .

RC (DLC). Damaged by folds, the RC consists of three portions of pages.

1. Letter not found.

William W. Wilkins to Dolley Payne Todd

PHILADELPHIA August 22nd. 1794.

I will not delay a Moment my ever dear and valued friend to reply to your last interresting Epistle.[1] Flattered as I am by your Condecension in consulting me on this important Occasion and truly and disinterestedly solicitous for your Welfare—the Task I undertake is far from being a painful one. As your friend I feel not the least Hesitation in forming my Opinion—ought I then to feel any reluctance in communicating it?

Mr. M——n is a Man whom I admire. I knew his Attachment to you and did not ther⟨efor⟩e content myself with taking his Character from the Breath of popular Applause—but ⟨consul⟩ted those who knew him intimately in private Life. His p⟨ersonal⟩ Character therefore I have every reason to believe is good and amiable. He unites to the great Talents which have secured him public Approbation those engaging Qualities that contribute so highly to domestic Felicity. To such a Man therefore I do most freely consent that my beloved Sister be united and happy.[2]

Yes my dear and amiable Julia you have my fullest and freest Approbation of the Step you are about to take. No Wish is dearer to my Heart than your Happiness & Heaven is my Witness that nothing is less selfish than my Attachment to you. That I have not been insensible to your Charms ought not I think to be regarded as a Fault—few persons in similar Situations would not have felt their irresistible Influence; but none I will venture to say could have mingled in their Emotions more true Respect and more fraternal Affection than I have.

With respect to the Settlement on your Son[3]—I will give ⟨yo⟩u my Sentiments frankly. You are placed in a critical Situation in this Affair—the Eyes of the World are upon you and your Enemies have already opened their Mouths to censure and Condemn you. I hope you will disappoint them—I believe you will now be just—for you have hitherto always been generous. I must confess I conceive it to be your duty to make some Settlement upon him and I know you too well to doubt your Inclination to do it. The only Question can be to what Amount and in what Manner shall this Settlement be made.

Mr. M——n is as I am informed a Man of genteel tho not of large property. He has a right to expect some part but does not want the whole of your Estate. I would suggest therefore that your House and Stables situate in Fourth Street be previously to your Marriage conveyed to Trustees in Trust to receive the Rents Issues and profits during the Minority of your Son and apply the same first to discharge the Sum of ⏧350 with the Interest (being the remaining Sum due of the purchase Money & which ought to be regarded as an Incumbrance on the premises) & in the second place to the support & Education of your Son (stipulating if you please that for this purpose the payments of the proceeds be made to your future Husband and yourself as it is to be presumed your Son will always remain under your joint Care and Protection) and in trust farther to convey the premises to your Son in fee Simple upon his arriving to the Age of twenty one Years—but if he should die before he attains that Age to convey to yourself and your Heirs.

Your Son as a residuary Legatee of his Grand Father will be intitled to something—but the Amount of the Legacy is wholly uncertain. The provision which I have mentioned will in your Circumstances be a generous one—I only fear it will be thought unreasonably great. But those who know Julia as well as ⟨I do⟩ will look for Conduct at once maternally affectionate and exaltedly bountiful.

If I have given my Opinion with too much freedom—I earnestly solicit your pardon. I am sensible that neither Age or Wisdom or Relationship authorize me to advise—but your own Command has opened my Lips and Friendship bids me be sincere. With the truest—warmest Wishes for your Happiness I am my dear Julia ever & affectionately yours

WM. W. WILKINS[4]

My respects to Mrs. payne. Hallowell[5] informs me that he considered himself *obliged* to pay the Money to Isaac[6] & has paid it to his Order. Compliments to Miss Anna. I must beg her pardon for detaining these Letters so long in my possession as I expected daily to hear from you & wished to dispatch in one packet. I shall attend as usual to your Affairs till my power is revoked.

RC (DLC: Dolley Madison Papers). Addressed by Wilkins to Dolley Payne Todd, "Martinsburg / Virginia / Particular Care of / Geo. [Steptoe] Washington Jun Esque."

1. Letter not found.
2. The remainder of this sentence, heavily crossed through but faintly legible, reads: "⟨and am Satisfied?⟩ that an honorable asylum is offered to my gentle friend who has been so undeservedly and so vindictively persecuted and over whose Safety I have long anxiously watched!" Wilkins referred to Quaker opposition to Dolley Payne Todd's intention to marry a non-Quaker. In December the Pine Street Meeting of Philadelphia excommunicated her (Ketcham, *James Madison*, p. 381).
3. John Payne Todd (1792–1851) was Dolley Payne Todd's son by her first marriage (ibid., pp. 377, 615–16).
4. Wilkins was a Quaker lawyer with offices at 119 South Second Street (Hardie, *Philadelphia Directory* [1794 ed.], p. 167). In an undated fragment of a letter to Dolley Payne Todd, probably ante August 1794 (ViU), Wilkins conceded the futility of his romantic interest but explained why he addressed her as "sister" and by the private name of Julia: "The harmonious name of Julia calls up a thousand pleasing and tender Images before me—permit me, my lovely friend, to indulge this dilation of Heart and scribble to thee with the frankness of a Brother."
5. John Hallowell was a lawyer with offices at 73 South Second Street (Hardie, *Philadelphia Directory* [1794 ed.], p. 63).
6. Isaac Payne, Dolley Payne Todd's brother, died in Norfolk, Virginia, later in 1794 (Moore, *The Madisons*, pp. 6, 50; Brant, *Madison*, 3:412).

¶ From Hubbard Taylor. Letter not found. *22 August 1794.* Acknowledged in JM to Taylor, 15 Nov. 1794. Provides information on Ambrose Madison's and JM's Kentucky lands and promises to make further inquiries about them.

¶ To Thomas Jefferson. Letter not found. *1 September 1794, Orange.* Mentioned in JM to Jefferson, 5 Oct. 1794. Discusses deer for stocking Jefferson's park at Monticello. Received by Jefferson 18 Sept. (Jefferson's Epistolary Record [DLC: Jefferson Papers]).

From James Monroe

DEAR SIR   PARIS Sepr. 2 ⟨1794⟩

To morrow will make one month since our arrival here, and such have been my ingagments that altho' I resolved that I wod. begin a letter to you every succeeding day yet when the day arrived it was not in power heretofore. You will readily conceive the variety of the objects to which I have been forced to attend, many of which requiring the utmost effort of my judgment, all delicate and interesting, and you will readily admit my embarrassment when you know that I have not had a single person (Mr. S.[1] excepted and who is new in this line) with whom I could confidentially confer. I wished not to write you a superficial letter, but whether I shall be forced to hurry this is what I cannot at present determine. Between Bal:[2] & Paris, we were 45. days. The passage was free from storms & between the soundings of each coast short, being only 29. days. We enjoyed our health; none were sea sick except Joseph[3] a few days & myself an hour or two. Mrs. M & the child escaped it altogether. We landed at Havre & left it for this the day after, whither we arrived in three days, being the 3. of Augt. We are yet at lodgings, but expect to be fixed in Mr. M.'s house which I took, in less than a week. I found Mr. Morris from town but he came in, in two or three days after my arrival.

About a week before my arrival Robertspiere had been executed with St. Just Couthon & others so that the scene upon which I had to commence was a troubled one. The publick councils were yet somewhat agitated but tranquility and joy upon acct. of that event reigned every where else. The whole community seemed to be liberated from the most pestilent scourge that ever harrassed a country; I found I had better look on for some days, merely to inform myself of the course to be taken to obtain my recognition.

I found myself under difficulties from the commenc'ment. The fall of Roberspiere had thrown a cloud over all whom it was supposed he had any connection with, or in whose appointment he had been any-wise instrumental. This included my fellow passenger,[4] so that it was not prudent to avail myself of his aid in presenting me, or even making known my arrival to the Committee of publick safety. And I was averse to taking the introduction of my predecessor for as good a reason. I did not know the ground upon which the Americans stood here, but suspected as the acquisition of wealth had been their object in coming, they must have attached themselves to some preceding party & worn out their reputations. Upon mature reflection, therefore I resolved to wait the arrival of my predecessor & present myself as a thing of course with him. I concluded it could do me no detriment as it was the official mode, and more especially as he would have to file off at the moment I took my ground. This was done. He accompanied me to the office of foreign affrs., notified his recall & my succession. I left with the com-missary a copy of my credentials, & requested my recognition from the competent department as soon as possible & which was promised.

But my difficulties did not end here. Eight or ten days elapsed and I was not accepted, nor had I heard a syllable from the Committee or seen a member. And upon enquiry I was informed that a minister from Geneva had been here 6. weeks before me and was not yet recd. Still further to increase my embarrassment I likewise heard that the com-missary to whom I was presented being of Robertspiere's party was out of favor, and that probably his letter covering my credentials had not been read by the Committee. I could not longer bear with this delay: I foresaw that the impression to be expected from the arrival of a new minister might be lost, and that by the trammel of forms and collision of parties I might while away my time here for ever without effect. I was therefore resolved to place myself if possible above these difficulties, by addressing myself immediately to the convention. I knew this would attract the publick attention and if my country had any weight here, produce a proportional effect not only upon that body, but upon every subordinate department. The result was as I had expected; my letter being read in the Convention was well recd., taken immediately to the committee of publick safety, reported on in two hours afterwards by that body & a decree passed the same day for my admission on the next, at two in the afternoon. It was at the same time intimated by a special messenger from the President that he shod. be glad to have a copy of what I shod. say an hour or two before I was presented. I had of course but little time to prepare my address. I thought it expedient to make the occasion as useful as possible, in drawing the two republicks more closely together, by the ties of affection by shewing them the interest which every department of our government took in their success & prosperity. With this view I laid before the Convention, with suitable solemnity the declarations of the Senate & H. of R., and added a similar one for the President.[5] The effect surpassed my expectation. My reception occupied an hour and an half, of not merely interesting but distressing sensibility, for all who beheld it. It was with difficulty that I extricated myself from the House and committee of p: safety and indeed the crowd which surrounded it, after the business was over. The cordial declaration of America in favor of France and of the French revolution (for altho' I have not mentioned the word revolutn. after the example of both houses, yet after the example of both and especially the H. of R. I have strongly implied it) in the view of all Europe, and at a time when they were torn in sunder by parties, was a gratification which overpowerd them.

I doubt not this measure will be scanned with unfriendly eyes by many in America. They will say it was intended that those things should have been smuggled in secretly and as secretly deposited afterwards. But they are deceived if they suppose me capable of being the instrument of such purposes. On the contrary I have endeavoured to take the opposit ground, with a view of producing the best effect here as well as there. And I am well satisfied that it has produc'd here a good effect. It is certain that we had lost in a great measure the confidence of the nation. Representations from all parties had agreed, (and men of different characters . . .[6]

RC (DLC). Incomplete.

1. Fulwar Skipwith, a relative of Jefferson's, served as U.S. consul at Martinique, 1790–94. After the British seized that island in March, he returned to the U.S. and accompanied Monroe to France as secretary of the legation. He became consul general at Paris in 1795 and commercial agent there in 1801 (Ammon, *James Monroe*, p. 116; *Senate Exec. Proceedings*, 1:48, 49, 189, 403, 405).

2. Baltimore.

3. Joseph Jones, Jr.

4. Georges-Pierre Le Blanc, former police chief of Paris, had recently been secretary of the French legation to the U.S. (Conway, *Edmund Randolph*, p. 237; Ammon, *James Monroe*, p. 116).

5. Edmund Randolph had submitted to Congress a translation of the Committee of Public Safety's 10 Feb. letter reporting recent military successes and expressing a desire for closer relations between France and the U.S. On 24 Apr. the Senate passed a resolution requesting the president to reply to the letter "in such manner as shall manifest their sincere friendship and good will for the French Republic." A resolution passed by the Republican-controlled House on 25 Apr. was more effusive, mentioning the "friendly and affectionate manner" of the committee's address and asking the president to convey "an unequivocal assurance that the Representatives of the people of the United States have much interest in the happiness and prosperity of the French Republic." Washington delegated this duty to Randolph, who wrote cordial replies on 10 June (*ASP, Foreign Relations*, 1:447–48, 673–74; *Annals of Congress*, 3d Cong., 1st sess., 86–87, 606).

6. The remainder of the letter is missing, but in his reply of 4 Dec. 1794, JM mentioned Monroe's "conjecture both as to the facility given to the Envoy Extry: [John Jay] by the triumphs of France, and the artifice of referring it to other causes."

Dolley Payne Todd to Eliza Collins Lee

HAIR-WOOD[1]—September the 16th.[2] [1794]

I receav'd your precious favour from Bath[3] & should have indulged myself in writing an answer but for the excessive weakness In my Eyes. And as a proof my dearest Eliza[4] of that confidence & friendship which has never been interrupted betwe[e]n us I have stolen from the family to commune with you—to tell you in short, that in the cource of this day I give my Hand to the Man who of all other's I most admire. You will not be at a loss to know who this is as I have been long ago gratify'd In haveing your approbation. In this Union I have every thing that is soothing and greatful in prospect—& my little Payne will have a generous & tender protector.

A Settlement of all my real property with a considerable Adition of Money is made upon him with Mr. M———s full approbation. This I know you feel an Interrest in or I should not have troubled you with it—you also are acquainted with the unmerited sensure of my Enimys on the subject.

Mr. & Mrs L. Lee[5] have left the neighbourhood to our great regret as we wished much their presence to day, they being the only Family Invited except *his* sister & Brother Washington—but how shall I express the anxiety I feel to see you? That friend whose goodness, at many interresting periods I have greatfully experienced would now rejoice us by a sight of her—tell your dear Lee that he must not suplant D P T in your Affections but suffer her whilst she deserves it to share with him your ever valuable Esteem. Adeiu! Adeiu.

It is yet uncertain whether we shall see you before the meeting in Phila. Mama, Madison, Lucy,[6] Gorge,[7] Anna[8] and Hariot[9] joine in best love to ⟨you⟩ & yours.

DOLLEY PAYNE TODD

Evening.
Dolley Madison! Alass!

RC (DLC: Dolley Madison Papers). Addressed by Dolley Payne Todd to Eliza Lee in Loudoun County, "favour'd by Mr. J. Armistead." Last page damaged, probably removing part of postscript.

1. Harewood was George Steptoe Washington's estate near Charles Town, in what is now Jefferson County, West Virginia.

2. Dolley Payne Todd first wrote "15th," then altered the date to read "16th."
3. Letter not found.
4. Eliza Collins Lee, a close friend of Dolley Payne Todd's in Philadelphia, married Congressman Richard Bland Lee on 19 June (Lee, *Lee of Virginia*, p. 370).
5. Ludwell Lee, son of Richard Henry Lee, was married to Flora Lee, a descendant of the Steptoe family (ibid., pp. 323, 326).
6. Lucy Payne Washington (1777–1848), a sister of Dolley Payne Todd, married George Steptoe Washington in 1793 (Hunt-Jones, *Dolley and the "Great Little Madison,"* p. 23; Jackson and Twohig, *Diaries of George Washington*, 6:352).
7. George Steptoe Washington (ca. 1773–1808) was George Washington's nephew (Jackson and Twohig, *Diaries of George Washington*, 4:93).
8. Anna Payne.
9. Harriot Washington (1776–1822) was the sister of George Steptoe Washington (ibid., 5:19).

From James Monroe

DEAR SIR   PARIS Sepr. 20. 1794.

Mr. Swan[1] of Boston who has resided for some years past in this city in the character of a Merchant & in which line he has been extensively engaged will present you this. He leaves this for the purpose of purchasing & shipping to this country the productions of ours & relies much on the advances to be made by our govt. for the means. He will I understand be sole agent in that line of this republick in America. He well knows yr. disposition on this head & will confer with you in regard to it. I beg you to be attentive to him as he has been very obliging to us here. I have written you very fully by the way of Bordeaux, and as Mr. S. proposes landing at Chs.town, shall have more early opportunities of apprizing you of those events of the present day which may escape him. We are well. Very sincerely I am yr. friend & servt

JAS. MONROE

RC (DLC).

1. James Swan emigrated from Scotland to Boston in 1765 and served in the Revolution. He went to France in 1787 and with the aid of Lafayette became a contractor in naval stores. In 1795 he bought a controlling share of the U.S. government securities constituting the outstanding debt owed to France since the Revolution. As an agent of the French government and a broker, he profitably exchanged foreign for domestic securities. In a letter of 30 June 1795, Monroe confided to JM that "Swan who is a corrupt unprincipled rascal had by virtue of being the Agent of France and as we had no minister & he being (tho' of the latter description) the only or most creditable resident American here, had a monopoly of the trade of both countries. Indeed it is believed that he was connected with the agents on one side and the Minister on the other. . . . But good may come from it, and especially if the allurement here will draw them off from the other side of the channel" (Hamilton, *Writings of Monroe*, 2:313–14). His later speculative ventures failed, and Swan died in debtors' prison in Paris.

From Henry Lee

My dear sir   Alexa. sepr. 23d. 94.

I hear with real joy that you have joined the happy circle & that too in the happiest manner. To your lady present my most respectful congratulations. She will soften I hope some of your political asperitys. The day which blessed you cursed me. I left my family to join the troops destined to restore order in Pensylvania.[1] What a cursed event, who could have supposed such a disaster possible in this day of reason, among a people of reason. Surely these things must influence our political leaders to harmonize more than they have lately done & to regard as a solemn truth that tolerable happiness to a nation had better be preserved than risked in pursuit of greater felicity. We are more than tolerably happy & we ought to be content. Whatever may be my difficultys or whatever my fate I sincerely wish you & your better half every good which mortality permits. Farewel

                                                                HENRY LEE

Present me to my friend & relation Mr W & ask him if he received a long letter written by me from Norfolk.

RC (DLC). Docketed by JM.

1. The Whiskey Insurrection broke out in July. As governor of Virginia, Lee led the militia of his state, as did the governors of Pennsylvania, New Jersey, and Maryland, against the excise resisters in western Pennsylvania. On 20 Oct. Washington appointed Lee commander of the combined military force. A Federalist who had temporarily cooperated with Republicans in opposing Hamilton's financial policies, Lee had already broken with his erstwhile colleagues by supporting Washington's Neutrality Proclamation. His role in the Whiskey Insurrection completed his rapprochement with the Federalists. During his absence the Virginia House of Delegates declared the governorship vacant, and the General Assembly elected Republican Robert Brooke to succeed him (Charles Royster, *Light-Horse Harry Lee and the Legacy of the American Revolution* [New York, 1981], pp. 130–37, 140–41; Leland D. Baldwin, *Whiskey Rebels: The Story of a Frontier Uprising* [rev. ed.; Pittsburgh, 1968], p. 229; JM to Jefferson, 24 Nov. 1793, and n. 1; Risjord, *Chesapeake Politics*, pp. 447–48).

To Thomas Jefferson

Dear Sir   Harewood Ocr. 5. 1794.

On my return to Orange I dropped you a few lines on the subject of the deer. On my way into this part of the Country I passed Col. John Thornton of Culpeper,[1] who has a Park, and will spare you with pleasure two or three, if you can not be otherwise supplied. He thinks he could by advertizing a premium of 10 or 12 dollars a head procure from his neighbors as many fawns to be delivered at Monticello as you would want.[2] If you chuse to make use of his assistance, a line to the care of Mr. Fontaine Maury at Fredg. would soon get to hand.

This will be handed to you by Mr. Bond who is to build a large House[3] for Mr. Hite my brother in law. On my suggestion He is to visit Monticello not only to profit of examples before his eyes, but to ask the favor of your advice on the plan of the House. Mr. Hite particularly wishes it in what relates to the Bow-room[4] & the Portico, as Mr. B. will explain to you. In general, any hints which may occur to you for improving the plan will be thankfully accepted. I beg pardon for being the occasion of this trouble to you, but your goodness has always so readily answered such draughts on it, that I have been tempted to make this additional one.

I write at present from the seat of Mr. G. Washington of Berkeley, where, with a deduction of some visits, I have remained since the 15th. Ult: the epoch at which I had the happiness to accomplish the alliance which I intimated to you I had been sometime soliciting. We propose to set out in 8 or 10 days for Philada. where I shall always receive your commands with pleasure, and shall continue to drop you a line as occasions turn up. In the mean time I remain Yrs. Mo: affecy

Js. Madison Jr

RC (DLC). Docketed by Jefferson, "recd. Dec. 31."

1. John Thornton (ca. 1749–1822) of Thornton Hill, now in Madison County, rose to the rank of lieutenant colonel in the Continental line in 1778 and as a militia colonel commanded a regiment at Yorktown. He married Jane Augusta Washington, a niece of George Washington (*DAR Patriot Index*, p. 677; Stanard, "The Thornton Family," *WMQ*, 1st ser., 5 [1896–97]: 197).

2. As part of his 1771 landscaping plans for Monticello, Jefferson planned a deer park, which he began to stock in 1776. During his visit to England in 1786, he took notes on several deer parks (Betts, *Jefferson's Garden Book*, pp. 69, 96, 113–14).

3. Isaac Hite was planning the construction of Belle Grove near Middletown in Frederick County. JM and his bride had recently visited Old Hall (the house that antedated Belle Grove on the site) for two weeks. Their stay was extended while Dolley recovered from an ailment (George M. Smith, "Belle Grove's Olmstead Papers," *Historic Preservation*, 24 [1972]: 26).

4. Jefferson's plan for the first floor of Monticello, circa 1771, included a "North Bow-room," which created an exterior projection in the shape of a half-octagon. No similar room was built at Belle Grove (Fiske Kimball, ed., *Thomas Jefferson, Architect* [1916; New York, 1968 reprint], pp. 25, 29–30 and n. 1, drawings 24, 150; Frederick D. Nichols, "Belle Grove in the Developing Civilization of the Valley of Virginia," *Historic Preservation*, 20, nos. 3–4 [1968]: 18 n. 3).

To James Madison, Sr.

DEAR & HOND SIR   HAREWOOD October 5. 1794.

I have detained Sam by whom I send this so much longer than I intended & you expected that many apologies are due for the liberty. I hope it will be a sufficient one that I found him indispensable for a variety of little services, which I did not particularly take into view before I left Orange. These he can himself explain, and I therefore leave the task to him; proceeding to the history of what relates to myself. On my arrival here I was able to urge so many conveniences in hastening the event which I solicited that it took place on the 15th. Ult. On the friday following we set out accompanied by Miss A. Payne, and Miss Harriot Washington, on a visit to my sister Hite, where we arrived the next day, having stopped a night in Winchester with Mr. Balmain. We had been a day or two only at Mr. Hite's, before a slight indisposition which my wife had felt for several days ended in a regular Ague & fever. The fits tho' succeeded by compleat intermissions were so severe that I thought it prudent to call in a Physician from Winchester. Docr. Mackay not being in the way Docr. Baldwin attended, and by a decisive administration of the Bark soon expelled the complaint. She has since recovered very fast & I hope notwithstanding a slight indisposition this morning which may be the effect of fatigue & change of weather, that no return is in the least to be apprehended. We left Mr. Hites the day before yesterday. Our time was passed there with great pleasure on our side, and I hope with not less on the other. Our departure however was embittered by the loss sustained the night preceeding by my sister, which you will have an account of from Mr. H. by this opportunity. In about 8 or 10 days we expect to set out for Philada. Your daughter in law begs you and my mother to accept her best and most respectful affections, which She means to express herself by an early opportunity. She wishes Fanny also be sensible of the pleasure with which a correspondence with her would be carried on.

I saw Fraily at Mr. Hite's. He promises stedfastly to be with you in about a fortnight at farthest; and to do every thing on his part requisite for a vigorous prosecution of the undertaking at Bernard's Ford.[1]

I must ask the favor of my mother to make out a memorandum of the Cloathing &c. to be obtained at Mr. Dunbars for the negroes; & of yourself to have it transmitted along with a list of other articles such as Salt Iron &c—which may [be] wanted for the winter's use. I heard with great satisfaction by Mr. Howard that her complaint which appeared in so doubtful a character when I left her, had taken a turn that promised an early & I hope entire recovery. With my sincerest prayers that perfect health & every other good may attend you both, I remain Yr. Affete son

Js. MADISON JR

I called soon after I came into the neighbourhood on Mrs. F. Hite, & found her & family well. I intend to repeat my visit if possible & to introduce her new relation to her.

RC (PHi).

1. Adam Frailey was a millwright who built a mill for Isaac Hite "upon the principles of reaction, in which are to be two machines." The Madison family consulted him about the gristmill that they planned to build at Barnett's Ford (also called Bernard's Ford) on the Rapidan River in Madison County (Joseph Barnes to Charles Morrow, 29 Jan. 1792, *WMQ*, 1st ser., 25 [1916–17]: 33; JM to James Madison, Sr., 17 Nov. 1794; Orange County, Minute Book, 3:182; Frailey to James Madison, Sr., 8 Feb. 1796 [PPPrHi]).

From Richard Taylor

DEAR SIR   JEFFERSON KENTUCKY 11th. Ocr. 1794

When your Brother the late Mr. Ambrose Madison[1] was in Kentucky I purchased a Tract of Eight hundred Acres of Land of him the remainder of Hancock Eustaces Survey after he had sold Majr Croghan One hundred & six acres[2] & Mr. Hancock Lee[3] had got his claim satisfied. I have payed for the Land all but one Thousand Acres of Land on Green river oposit the mouth of Rough creek which I am ready to convey at any time. Your Brother beeing on his Journey & in a Hurry he cou'd not make me a Deed nor did I ask him for any obligation for his makeing one for he gave Mr. Hubard Taylor a Genl. Power to do all his Business in Kentucky Directing him to make me a Deed to the afore-mentioned Land, but from his remote Situation from me & the Land it has been Neglected. Now I shou'd bee obliged to you to Inform me How I can gett a Title to the Land as I expect Mr. Taylors Power ceases on the Death of your Brother. This sir is a mater of present concern to me as I have parted with some of the Land. As for News we have very little here, only Major Whitley[4] went against the Chicka-mogas with Five hundred Kentucky & Cumberland Volunteers Kill'd & Took upwards of Fifty & did not loose one man. As for Politticks as you corrispond with Mr. Hubard Taylor and Mr. Nicholas one of whom is a Violent Democrat the other for supporting Government so long as he thinks it a good one of which last I believe there is a large Majorraty in our State. As for Famaly News we have Six sons & one

Daughter all well. Have nothing more to add but that I remain with great regard your most Obt. Servt

RICHD: TAYLOR

RC (DLC). Docketed by JM.

1. Ambrose Madison died on 3 Oct. 1793. For details of Kentucky lands purchased by him, his father, and JM, see Ambrose Madison to Hubbard Taylor, 1 Sept. 1792 (KyU: Hubbard Taylor Papers); James Madison, Sr., to John Lee, 5 Apr. 1794, 30 Oct. 1794, and 1 May 1795 (NcD); Brant, *Madison*, 3:357–58.

2. William Croghan purchased this "land lying on the Ohio River about 5 miles above the falls" on 12 Mar. 1792. Taylor later received Croghan's payment of £94 for Ambrose Madison (Richard Taylor, undated receipt [DLC]).

3. Hancock Lee (1740–1819) was a brother of Maj. John Lee and Mary Willis Lee Madison (the widow of Ambrose Madison). A native of Fauquier County, he explored Kentucky with his cousin (and JM's second cousin) Hancock Taylor, who was killed by Indians. The Indians held Lee in captivity, circa 1771–74. He had settled permanently in Kentucky by 1776 (Rutland, *Papers of George Mason*, 1:lxix; Lee, *Lee of Virginia*, p. 537).

4. William Whitley (1749–1813) moved from Augusta County to Kentucky in 1775. He led the expedition that on 13 Sept. 1794 burned Nickajack, a Chickamauga town on the south bank of the Tennessee River. A member for Lincoln County in the Kentucky House of Representatives in 1797, he died at the battle of the Thames (Collins, *Collins' Historical Sketches of Kentucky* [1878 ed.], 2:760–61, 776; *Philadelphia Gazette*, 1 and 8 Nov. 1794).

¶ To Joseph Jones. Letter not found. *Ca. 18 October 1794, Philadelphia.* Acknowledged in Jones to JM, ca. 28 Oct. 1794. Informs Jones of JM's marriage and safe arrival in Philadelphia. Inquires about a china tea set.

From Isaac Story

RESPECTED SIR,   MARBLEHEAD Oct. 27. 1794

I take the liberty to request an interest in your attention to a certain matter, which nearly affects me, as it is the concern of my Parent.[1] He was appointed Clerk to the Navy-board in Boston[2] with a salary of fifty five dollars per month; after this he was instituted by the Commissioners, as their Cashier, but without having any stipend affixed for this service.

And accordingly six millions of dollars passed through his hands in this capacity; & when a dissolution of the board took place, he received a certificate from them of what was due to him for wages. When Mr. Imlay[3] was appointed Commissioner for this State, my father applied for a settlement, but he declined, supposing that it did not fall within the line of his department. In the year 1792 my Father forwarded a petition to Congress, which was committed to the Secretary of the Treasury, & it lay by him for some time. He repeatedly wrote to him, & at last the Secretary assured him, before the commencement of the last session of Congress, that it should have his most early attention. But unexpected business so crouded upon him that he declared he could do nothing about it, & should deliver that, with other petitions, back to Congress. However Congress did not receive them, & they are still in his hands.

What, my dear Sir, I have to request is, that you would use your influence that the Secretary may make a speedy report, before business presses upon him. It is exactly in the same predicament with Mr. Carnes's matter,[4] which was finished by the Secretary. The voucher was a certificate of what was due from under the hands of the Commissioners.

I have applied to the Honble. Messrs. Cabot, Elsworth, Goodhue Holten, Niles, & Boudinot on this interesting Subject, & if you will confer together, & unite your influence, I am persuaded, that there will be a speedy & happy termination of the business.

And my father will receive not only the fifteen hundred dollars which are due to him as Clerk; but an equitable allowance for officiating as Cashier of that Board.

I would not only plead it as an act of justice, which claims your attention; but as an act of humanity & tenderness to an aged gentleman, who stands in need of this debt for his support & comfort in this last stage of his existence.

And I shall esteem it as an act of kindness done to me, once your fellow-student, who am with respect your most obedt. & most hum. Sert

Isaac Story[5]

RC (DLC). Docketed by JM.

1. William Story was registrar of the Court of Admiralty in Boston before the Revolution. Though he opposed the Stamp Act, a mob attacked his office in 1765. In his old age he lived with his son Isaac in Marblehead; another son, William, was a clerk in the Treasury Department (Perley Derby and Frank A. Gardner, "Elisha Story of Boston and Some of His Descendants," *Essex Institute Historical Collections,* 50 [1914]: 299–302, 312).

2. Naval boards at Boston and Philadelphia had assisted the Marine Committee of the Continental Congress, 1777–81 (Syrett and Cooke, *Papers of Hamilton,* 11: 55 n. 3, 56).

3. William Imlay served as a federal commissioner to settle the accounts of Massachusetts and as U.S. commissioner of loans for Connecticut (ibid., 11:57 n. 10; *Senate Exec. Proceedings,* 1:57).

4. See "Report on the Petition of the Executors of Edward Carnes," 28 Feb. 1792 (Syrett and Cooke, *Papers of Hamilton,* 11:55–57).

5. The Reverend Isaac Story graduated from the College of New Jersey in 1768.

A Federalist, he was pastor of the Second Congregational Church of Marblehead, 1771–1802 (James McLachlan, *Princetonians, 1748–1768: A Biographical Dictionary* [Princeton, N.J., 1976], pp. 655–57).

From Joseph Jones

DR. SR.   FREDG. [ca. 28 October 1794]
I have your favor from Philadelphia and very sincerely rejoice with you on your late change of condition and safe arrival in the City. Present my congratulations to your Lady. The tea china you mention is here and shall be packed up carefully and sent by Capt. Lambert who informs me he shall leave this place Tomorow evening or next day for Philadelphia. Monroe must certainly be safe in France from all accounts tho' we have no letters from him. He got there at a moment of great agitation but which like a sudden gust or squal has soon blown over. When I parted from Monroe he intimated to me that if any balances from him shod. be pressed for or I shod. enter into any engagement wherein he should be concerned and wch. was then contemplated and has since taken place and I shod. want his aid before I should hear from him that probably I could thro' Mr. Edmd. Randolph obtain money on his accot. Presuming this might be done I lately mentioned it to him that I wished to obtain 1000 dols. on accot. as agent for Monroe of which he might retain abt. £120 due by Walker Carter[1] in Philadelphia and the balance I shod. draw for if to be had. Mr. Randolph informed me he wod. have W. Carters settled and expected I might in a few days be accommodated with the balance but did not speak certainly. An immediate and pressing demand on Col. Carter has induced me to take the liberty to draw a bill of £50 this money on Mr. Randolph on Monroes accot. and to request he will have it paid, this I shod. not have done but from necessity having already advanced all I had or could raise on ⟨acct.⟩ the land purchased from Col. Carter in wch. Monroe is in part concerned. Will you speak with Randolph on it and inform me what is the prospect of its Being paid that if it shod. not be honored I may try some way of providing for it in time. I do not choose to draw on Monroe before I hear from him and am informed th[r]o' what channel to make the drafts. Yr. friend & Servt

JOS: JONES

Lambert goes to Lloyd & Sparks.[2]

RC (DLC). Docketed by JM, at a later time, "Decr. 1794." Conjectural date assigned on the basis of internal evidence and by comparison with Jones to JM, 4 Nov. 1794, which mentions this letter.

1. Walker Randolph Carter was a son of Col. Charles Carter, Jr., of Ludlow in

Stafford County (Hening, *Statutes*, 9:574–76). Jones had recently concluded a joint purchase with Monroe of Loudoun County land from Charles Carter, Jr.

2. Lloyd and Sparks were merchants with premises at 41 South Wharves (Hardie, *Philadelphia Directory* [1794 ed.], p. 92).

From Thomas Jefferson

TH: J. TO J. M. MONTICELLO Oct. 30. 94.

In the moment of the departure of the post it occurs to me that you can, by the return of it, note to me the amount of Mazzei's claim against Dohrman,[1] for the information of the Van Staphorsts.[2] I will put off my answer to them for that purpose. The day you left me I had a violent attack of the Rheumatism which has confined me ever since. Within these few days I have crept out a little on horseback, but am yet far from being well, or likely to be so soon. I wish much to see the speech, & to know how such an armament against people at their ploughs, will be represented, and an appeal to arms justified before that to the law had been tried & *proved* ineffectual, by the *fact*, not by the certified *opinion* of a magistrate paving the way to an embassy.[3] Adieu, a thousand respects to mrs. Madison & joys perpetual to both.

RC (DLC).

1. For a discussion of JM's and Jefferson's assistance to Arnold Henry Dohrman, and Dohrman's debt to Philip Mazzei, see *PJM*, 2:34 n. 4.

2. Mazzei was indebted to the Amsterdam bankers Nicholas and Jacob Van Staphorst (Mazzei to JM, 22 June 1787, *PJM*, 10:71).

3. Washington's 19 Nov. annual address to Congress recounted the federal government's response to the Whiskey Insurrection, citing the 4 Aug. certificate of James Wilson, an associate justice of the Supreme Court: " 'In the counties of Washington and Allegeny, in Pennsylvania, laws of the United States were opposed, and the execution thereof obstructed by combinations, too powerful to be suppressed by the ordinary course of judicial proceedings, or by the powers vested in the marshal of that district.' " The necessity of federal intervention was disputed between Republicans and Federalists and between federal and state authorities. Pennsylvania governor Thomas Mifflin and secretary Alexander James Dallas opposed the use of military force and asserted that action by civilian state officials would suffice to deal with the insurrection (Fitzpatrick, *Writings of Washington*, 34:30; Baldwin, *Whiskey Rebels*, pp. 184–85).

From Alexander Spotswood

DR SR. Octr. 30. 1794

A numerous family, has determined me to sell of my estate, and remove to the State of Kentucky. Being Told that some person has been viewing Situations, on the potowmack, to Establish a publick foundry for cannon, & Manufactory for Small arms—and not knowing who to apply to, Take the liberty of offering through you for the Above purpose—The best Situation in the world.

My Iron mine tract of 22,000 Acres 10, Miles above fredericksburg; fronting many Miles on the river, where there Are Situations for every kind of water Works—exclusive of the river, fine Inland never failing Streams, with An Inexhaustable fund of Iron ore the best in America for casting; In war it always Sold 30/s 10d. pr. Ton & in peice 10/s. 5d. more than any Iron exported from America for casting cannon, shot &c. When the furnace existed it used to run from 600—to 750 Ton of iron annually.[1] This valluable Work was obliged to be put down, by the depravity of a Gaurdian, who spent & wasted all the fund for Supporting the Same. If mr. Maury has any of the advertisemts. left of this land, I will on going to Town Inclose one. Should my information be Wrong be so kind as to shew the Advertisement, should one come, to Mr Morris —or a Mr Greenleaf.[2] This place is in a healthy & plentiful Country; which ought to be a great object in chuseing a place for publick works, where large Numbers, of Workmen is to be employed—and in Establishing a work of this kind, it must be a great Saveing to make the Mettle. Many want this land, but wish to get it for nothing. Yr. goodness will excuse this trouble from dr sr yr obliged He st

ALEXR SPOTSWOOD

This land of mine contains the only Iron ore below the ridge.

RC (DLC). Docketed by JM.

1. Spotswood's iron furnace was erected by his grandfather early in the eighteenth century. Known as the Germanna Furnace in its operative heyday, the ironworks and mines were part of a 45,000-acre estate (Louis B. Wright, *The Prose Works of William Byrd of Westover* [Cambridge, Mass., 1966], pp. 357-58).

2. James Greenleaf began speculating in federal district property in 1793 and with Robert Morris and John Nicholson founded the North American Land Company in 1795 (Allen C. Clark, *Greenleaf and Law in the Federal City* [Washington, 1901], pp. 67, 27).

From Philip Freneau

DEAR SIR,   MONMOUTH, EAST JERSEY, November 2d. 1794

As I hear there is a probability of a new printer being wanted for the House of Representatives, I take the liberty to Solicit Your interest in favour of Mr. Francis Bailey,[1] by whom, You may rest assured, the work of every kind will be executed to perfect Satisfaction. If Mr. Childs and

Mr. Swaine[2] should resign the business; I make no doubt but Your influence with Mr. Beckley will be exerted for this purpose. Mr. Bailey is an old, tried Republican; and, perhaps I scarcely need tell You, has stood forth in the worst of times, both as a printer and Soldier, a friend to the rights, liberties, and interests of this country. Such characters Merit consideration; and permit me to tell You, that in my opinion, it would be preferable that the *whole* of the work were entrusted to his care; dividing the business, I never could persuade myself, answered any good purpose: and if one such person as Mr. Bailey were made responsible for the whole, considering his attention and abilities, and the *capital* printing apparatus he is furnished with, I am convinced the House would find their account in having the work done by him. I am, Sir, with perfect esteem—Your sincere friend

PHILIP FRENEAU

RC (DLC). Docketed by JM.

1. Bailey, a Revolutionary veteran, had been the official printer for the Continental Congress and the state of Pennsylvania. He published the Philadelphia *Freeman's Journal*, 1781–92, and some of Freneau's works.

2. Francis Childs was printer of the N.Y. *Daily Advertiser*, 1785–96, and Freneau's Philadelphia *National Gazette*, 1791–93. An official printer for the state of New York and Congress, he published most U.S. government imprints, 1789–96. John Swaine was his partner, 1789–94 (Brigham, *History of American Newspapers*, 2:1391, 1490; Evans, *American Bibliography*, 7:419, 8:428, 430, 9:486, 488, 10:443, 447, 11:395).

From Alexander White

DEAR SIR　　　　　　　　　　　　　WOODVILLE 2d Novr. 1794.

Your passing through this Country without giving me the pleasure of seeing you was no small disappointment, and having some acquaintance with the amiable Lady to whom you are now united, my disappointment was not lessened from that circumstance. I requested Mr. Balmain not only to make known our wishes, but to let us know when you came to Town, that Mrs. White and myself might have waited on you and Mrs. Madison, but he says the shortness of your stay there, did not permit him to comply with my request.

You are again entering upon the political Field. I hope it will be less turbulent than the last Scenes you have gone through. As we did not aid France—when there was danger of impending ruin, it will be unnecessary to engage the War on her account now, when the World seems to sink before her. Great Britain certainly will not provoke a war. But I will cease observations which can be attended with no utility—

to express my grateful sense of your attention during last Session. Is it fair to ask a continuance when you enjoy the means of spending your leisure moments so much more delightfully? A news paper by next Post containing the Presidents Speech will be thankfully received. Mrs. White joins in Complts. to Mrs. Madison and yourself, and in hopes that having more leisure during the next recess of Congress we may have the pleasure of seeing you. I am with real regard Dear Sir Your most Ob Servt.

ALEXR WHITE

RC (DLC). Docketed by JM.

From Joseph Jones

DR. SR.   FREDG. 4th. ⟨November 179⟩4

I last week informed you I had packed up the china and sent it on board a vessell commanded by Capt. Lambert (his name is Lambeth) who expected to sail the next day. He goes to the house of Lloyd and Sparks of Philadelphia. A spell of rainy weather that commenced while he was loading has detained him untill to day, so that you may expect him soon after the receipt of this letter. I inclose the receipt.

That you may understand the reason of my drawing a Bill for £50 on Mr. Randolph and also requesting him to settle a demand agt. Walker Carter of about £125. on accot. of Col. Monroe proceeded from my having contracted with Col. Carter for his Loudon land, in which purchase Monroe was if I made it to be concerned. The Colonels first proposition was to have six hundred pounds paid down but afterwards from growing and pressing demands upon him he found it necessary to demand a prompt payment of £1500. Finding the offer I made him the best that upon his terms came forward, he closed with me. Having no communication from Monroe through what channel to make draughts for such part of the first payment as I shod. have occasion to call upon him for, I informed Mr. Randolph That Monroe had intimated to me, before we parted, that if my engagements for him were of such nature as to make it necessary, I might probably on application to him be assisted on his accot.—and requested to know from him if I could get on Monroes accot. 1000 dols. If so he might retain a sum he stood answerable for accot. of Walker Carter, and furnish me the balance. Mr. Randolph informed me he wod. in consequence of my application settle Walker Carters debt, and wished me to wait awhile for the balance expecting daily to hear from Monroe. Hearing nothing from Monroe or any further communication from Mr. Randolph, and being pressed by Col. Carter to assist him with £50 to settle an unavoidable demand, I at length ventured to make the draught on Mr. Randolph as Agent for Monroe, assuring him none other shod. be made untill we heard from him. I will thank you therefore to speak with Mr. Randolph on the matter and prevail on him if it can be done to honor the bill, for which and the other sum if it be necessary a bill on Monroe may be furnished by me, so soon as I am informed in what manner to make the draughts. If there is no prospect of the bill being paid, I beg you to inform me of it withot. delay, that I may make provision here. The first payment I can accomplish with the remnant of the 1000 dols., if I am not much disappointed here—I mean the £1500 down, besides exonerating the land of 1100t. to Col. Pendleton due by Judts. and elegits served on the land for which he has agreed To accept good bonds in payment, these I can furnish. Also 1000 to the ⟨Ets.⟩ of Wm. Carr of Dumfries. For the balance I have two annual payments. Upon the whole I think the bargain good @ 3 dols. ℔ acre the sum agreed on for about 5000 acres even altho' it is incumbered as I have mentioned, and with many Leases at low rent. The money incumbrances are to be deducted from the price. I mention these circumstances between ourselves, not wishing them to be spoken of. When you commence operations let me hear from you as usual. I take Baches paper furnish me any others you can spare. You have with your Lady my best wishes. Yr. friend & ⟨Servt.⟩

JOS: ⟨JONES⟩

RC (DLC). Addressed by Jones to JM in Philadelphia and franked. Docketed by JM. Damaged by removal of seal.

From James Innes

MY DEAR SIR   Wednesday one oClock Nov 5th. [1794]

Since I saw you this morning it has been communicated to me as the wish of the president that I should spend this afternoon with him[1]— as he is more at leisure than he probably may be hereafter to communicate to me the objects of my Western mission. I take the liberty therefore of sending you my apology for not waiting upon you on to day which I hope may be considerd in its proper light—and not viewed as a mark of Inattention from one, who will never fail to be with the most sincere respect & Esteem yr friend & Sert

JAS: INNES.

RC (DLC). Dated 5 Nov. 1791 in the *Index to the James Madison Papers*. Date here assigned on the basis of circumstances described in n. 1.

1. Edmund Randolph had asked Innes, attorney general of Virginia, to explain to Kentucky officials the administration's plans for Thomas Pinckney's mission to negotiate with Spain for navigation rights on the Mississippi River. Innes met with Washington on 5 Nov. 1794 to discuss his impending journey to Kentucky. He carried to that state JM's letters of 15 Nov. to John Lee and Hubbard Taylor (Reardon, *Edmund Randolph*, pp. 278–79, 451 nn. 62, 66, 67; Syrett and Cooke, *Papers of Hamilton*, 17:283–84 n. 2; for correspondence between Innes and Gov. Isaac Shelby of Kentucky, see Philadelphia *Gazette of the U.S.*, 21–23 Apr. 1795).

From Thomas Jefferson

TH: J. TO J. MADISON.   MONTICELLO Nov. 6. 94.

A merchant neighbor of mine, sets out to-day for Philadelphia for his fall goods, and will return with them by water himself. This furnishes me a favorable opportunity of gleaning & getting the books I left in Philadelphia. But I must ask your friendly aid. Judge Wilson has Mably sur l'histoire de la France 4. v. 12mo.[1] & Houard's Britton, Fleta, Glanville &c 4. v. 4to.[2] which he promised to deliver you. Pray press for them in my name. E. R. has several, partly lent here during my absence, partly in Philadelphia. I write to him[3] by this post to ask his lodging them with you. He will probably need being sent to for them. After a very long drought which threatened to be fatal to our small grain, we have had two most abundant rains at an interval of a week, both followed by warm weather. The thermometer in the middle of the day from 55. to 69. It has been once only at the freezing point. Smart white frosts in the neighborhood, but none has extended yet to this place. Fine beef 2d. Corn from the tub 8/, both cash. Wheat 5/ in goods @ 61⅓ per cent on the Philadelphia price, which brings the wheat down to half a dollar at Philadelphia. The Sheriffs, who are now going down with their money, declare that there never was so miserable a collection; men, hitherto the most punctual, having been obliged to ask indulgence, from the scarcity of cash. My best respects to mrs. Madison. Adieu.

RC (DLC); FC (DLC: Jefferson Papers).

1. Gabriel Bonnot de Mably, *Observations sur l'histoire de France* (new ed.; 4 vols.; Kehl, 1788).

2. David Houard, *Traités sur les coutumes anglo-normandes* . . . (4 vols.; Paris, 1776). This work includes editions of the twelfth- and thirteenth-century English legal treatises *Britton*, *Fleta*, and the *Tractatus de legibus et consuetudinibus regni Angliæ* commissioned by Ranulf de Glanville.

3. Jefferson to Edmund Randolph, 6 Nov. 1794 (DLC: Jefferson Papers).

¶ To Joseph Jones. Letter not found. 7 *November 1794*. Acknowledged in Jones to JM, 16 Nov. 1794. Apparently concerns china being shipped to JM in Philadelphia, a bill on Monroe's account that has been presented to Secretary of State Edmund Randolph for payment, and a request that ham and bacon be shipped from Fredericksburg to JM.

To James Madison, Sr.

HON'D SIR   PHILADA. Novr. 10. 1794

My last was as far back as the return of Sam from Harewood. I have postponed writing untill the Session should commence for two reasons. One you will readily conjecture: The other that I might inclose the introductory proceedings. From the want of a Quorum of Senators, these have not yet taken place.[1] It was expected that the defect would be supplied to day. Whether it will be or not I cannot yet say. We have no late information from England. The first communication with Jay which has been published in our gazettes, was dry & equivocal on the part of Ld. Grenville.[2] It is thought however that his mission will not be without effect; especially if the French successes continue to alarm the British Govt. Another favorable circumstance is the naval equipment by Denmark & Sweeden. The former has 30 sail of the line in service. You will have seen Monroe's reception by the Natl. Convention.[3] This is all the acct. recd. with respect to him; no letters public or private having yet come to hand. The Western insurgents appear to have been brought either by reflection or fear to a perfect submission to the laws. By a vessel which sailed yesterday for Fredg. I have sent you a barrl. of Sugar containg 112 lb. The price £5.12. Pa. Curry. It is very high, but the quality very good. It was not to be got cheaper, & as I knew of your disappt. thro' Mr. Hite, I thought it best to secure a supply limited to that quantity. The same vessel carries another Barrl. with 1½ bushls. of Red Clover seed, which I wish you to make Sawney sow in Feby. on the old mountain field. There will be eno' for the whole field whether in Wheat or Rye, and he will so distribute it as to make it hold out. It is to be sown on the top of the Wheat or Rye, taking advantage of a snow if there be one particularly just before it melts. But this circumstance is by no means essential, and ought not to retard the sowing beyond the last of that Month. The price of wheat here has been up at 12/. P. C. & flour £3. It is not so high at present but is not much below it; and the purchase is pretty spirited. I expected to have inclosed the letter from Dolley promised in my last but must wait till the next post. She has written it; but an interruption at the moment of sending this to the Office; prevents her letting me have it in time, and the delay of a moment may lose the oppy. altogether. We have both been well since our arrival here. She joins all her affections to mine, for my mother & yourself. Yr. dutiful son

Js. MADISON JR.

RC (DLC).

1. The second session of the Third Congress convened on 3 Nov. JM took his seat, and the House achieved a quorum, on 4 Nov. A quorum was not present in the Senate until 18 Nov. (*Annals of Congress*, 3d Cong., 2d sess., 869, 890).

2. John Jay to William Lord Grenville, 30 July 1794, and Grenville to Jay, 1 Aug. 1794 (*Philadelphia Gazette*, 20 Oct. 1794; reprinted in *ASP, Foreign Relations*, 1:481–82).

3. JM referred to reports of the National Convention's tumultuous reception of Monroe as U.S. minister to France on 15 Aug. (*Philadelphia Gazette*, 29 and 31 Oct. 1794; see also *ASP, Foreign Relations*, 1:672–74; Ammon, *James Monroe*, pp. 119–21; Monroe to JM, 2 Sept. 1794).

Admission of a New Congressman

[11 November 1794]

On 13 April John Francis Mercer of Maryland resigned his House seat, and during the recess Gabriel Duvall was elected to the vacancy. On 7 November the House referred Duvall's credentials to the Standing Committee of Elections. On 11 November Murray objected to reading the committee's report before admitting Duvall.

Mr. Madison was for the report being read. It would only delay the admission of the gentleman for a few minutes. It was therefore better to receive it, and then take him in. There was a question, if Mr. Mercer was now to appear before the house, could he take his seat? Mr. Madison would not undertake to answer the question. It was a delicate one. He would have the report read. If it was favourable, act as concurring with it. If not so, lay it aside, and admit the member from Maryland to qualify without taking any notice of it.

Philadelphia Gazette, 12 Nov. 1794 (also reported in *Gazette of the U.S.*, 11 Nov. 1794, and *Dunlap and Claypoole's Am. Daily Advertiser*, 12 Nov. 1794).

[11 November 1794]

Parker spoke in favor of Murray's objection.

Mr. Madison was still for reading the report of the committee. His object was to accelerate the reception of the Gentleman, which would *inevitably* and *properly* take place. If the House were to admit him to qualify, without first reading the report, it might hereafter be asked,

Why was a report made at all, when the House refuse to read it? It might, on a future occasion, be said, "Perhaps that report has been unfavourable, and the House have contradicted the report of their own committee."

Philadelphia Gazette, 12 Nov. 1794 (also reported in *Gazette of the U.S.*, 11 Nov. 1794). Murray waived his objection, the report was read, and the House admitted Duvall to his seat.

From the Right Reverend James Madison

MY DEAR SIR,   WILLIAMSBURG Novr. 12h 1794

I cannot refrain sending you my sincere Congratulations, upon an Event, which promises you so much Happiness. It was my Intention to have paid you a short Visit, in September, upon my Return from the Mountains, but heard, when in your Neighbourhood, that you were from Home, & engaged in the Pursuit, which terminated so agreably to yourself, & I trust also, to the amiable Partner whom you have selected. Present her too, if you please, with my Congratulations & ardent Wishes for your mutual Happiness.

About two Years past, Mr. Jefferson proposed to me the Scheme of establishing an University for this State, in some central Position, Upon a liberal & extensive Plan.[1] He observed, that he should probably be in the succeeding Assembly, & that his primary Object wd. be to procure such an Establishment. But, when at his House, in Sepr. last, the Subject was revived, he said, that he had adjured public Business of any Kind; & of Course, never expected to be again in the Virga. Legislature; but wd. most readily cooperate with others in digesting the Plan for an University, which he had still much at Heart. He observed, that you also had Thoughts of retiring from Congress, & might probably become a Member of our Legislature; that, in such a Case, the Plan wd. be as likely to succeed under your Patronage as his own. Two Questions then I shall take the Liberty to state, upon the Supposition, that you may retire from Congress.

Will you give your Aid in perfecting the Plan? Will you, when it is perfected, become it's Patron & Advocate in the Virga Legislature?

I have mentioned the above, not only as an Object of great Importance to the Community in general, but also, because my own Movements may be affected by the opinion wh. you may entertain upon the Subject. I have Thought of retiring to some comfortable little Farm in a healthy Part of the Country.

Opinions here, are very various as to Mr. Jay's Letter to the Bh. Ct. It seems to want not a little of that manly republican Firmness, which demands, but never petitions for Justice: it does not evince that dignified Sense of unprovoked Injuries, which the Magnanimous Monarch has heaped upon us, & for which his Justice will never compensate. There is, in short, nothing Jeffersonian in it. Our Friend Monro's Speech shews a good republican Heart, but I wish it had been a little more luminous. With the most sincere Esteem, I am D Sir Yr. Friend

J MADISON

RC (DLC). Addressed by Bishop Madison to JM in Philadelphia and franked. Docketed by JM.

1. For a discussion of Jefferson's early efforts on behalf of higher education in Virginia, see Malone, *Jefferson and His Time*, 1:283–85.

From Killian K. Van Rensselaer

DR SIR   ALBANY Novr. 14th. 1794.

The Bearer Robert S. Van Rensselaer[1] (son of Coll. Philip Van Rensselaer)[2] has it in contemplation to make a tour through some part of Europe, he is a young Gentleman of respectability and Character and Recommend him to you as such. His father will evince his Gr⟨at⟩itude to you & I will consider myself under obligations also, if you will furnish him with letters to Mr. Munro[3] & Mr. Pinckney in Europe, with whom I have no acquaintance.

Chancellor Livingston & Coll. Burr have both interested themselves in obtaining letters, and I must beg the favour of your attention to this request also. I am Dr. Sir with Sentiments of Esteem Yours

K. K. VAN RENSSELAER[4]

RC (DLC). Docketed by JM.

1. For a selection of Robert S. Van Rensselaer's letters, 1795–96, during his tour of Europe, see Catherina V. R. Bonney, *A Legacy of Historical Gleanings* (2 vols.; Albany, 1875), 1:113–19, 126–28.

2. Philip Van Rensselaer, brother of Killian K. Van Rensselaer, served as deputy quartermaster general and a member of the Committee of Safety at Albany during the Revolution (ibid., 1:69, 77, 79).

3. See JM to Monroe, 14 Dec. 1794.

4. Killian Killian Van Rensselaer attended Yale College and became a private secretary to Philip Schuyler. He was a Republican congressman from New York, 1801–11 (*BDC*, p. 1853).

To John Lee

DEAR SIR   PHILADA. Novr. 15. 1794.

My last requested the favor of you to give me such information as you might be able on the subject of my brother's & my joint interest in Kentuckey. I wrote at the same time and made the same request to our friend Mr. H. Taylor. I write again to him as well as to you by the present opportunity and hope thro' your mutual and friendly assistance, to be able to understand and arrange every thing necessary to do justice to my brother's estate, as well as to myself. It will give me pleasure at all times to hear from you, and on this particular subject as early as may be convenient.

I have not yet recd. any draught for the last payment due for the land: nor do I know whether you wish me to wait for one, or to make the remittance to you. Whatever your choice may be, you will please to let me know. In case a draught on me be preferred, I must request the favor of you to make it payable at 20 or 30 days sight if it be not inconvenient, as it might possibly find me in a place or at a moment not suited to discharge it.

This will be forwarded by Col. James Innes who is charged I understand with explanations for your Country on the measures & prospects relating to the Missi[ssi]ppi. It appears from the last accts. from Europe that G. B. is beginning to relax in her injurious policy towards this Country, and that some favorable issue may be expected to the mission of Mr. Jay. As far as this change may be the effect of misfortunes to the combined arms, the cause is increasing every moment. The French have signalized themselves more of late than at any period of the war. They have penetrated considerably into Spain, as well as regained their lost towns and overrun much of the territorey of their enemies in the Netherlands. It is not improbable that they are before this in Amsterdam. In Poland also events are taking place which increase the alarm of all the sovereigns of Europe: & of the K. of Prussia in particular who finds himself not only embarrassed there, but threatened with serious commotions in his own Dominions. I refer to the quicker and fuller accts. you will have from Fort Pitt, of what has past in that quarter.[1] With very sincere esteem & regard I am Dr. Sir Yr. friend & servt

Js. Madison Jr

RC (owned by John Howell—Books, San Francisco, 1982).

1. JM referred to the legal proceedings conducted by Judge Richard Peters against the whiskey rebels in western Pennsylvania (Baldwin, *Whiskey Rebels*, pp. 240–41).

To Hubbard Taylor

Dear Sir   Philada. Novr. 15. 1794.

I recd. your obliging favor of the 22d. Augst. a few days before I left Virginia, and postponed acknowledging it till my return here. I now make use of the opportunity by Col. Innis, who is engaged in a Mission to Kentuckey for the purpose of explaining the public measures & present prospects relating to the Navigation of the Mississippi.

I thank you for the information you give as to the state of my deceased brother's & my interest in your country; & particularly for your promise to make more accurate enquiries on that subject. Having left every thing in which we were jointly concerned to his management, I am more ignorant of it than you can well imagine, and must rely on your goodness & that of Majr. Lee, to supply the information for a proper settlement. All that I know & can recollect, is that one half the land on Panther Creek is mine, tho' the Patents stand in his name only.[1] This is well known to a number of our friends, and can produce no other difficulty than that of a friendly suit to establish the fact in the minority of my neice.[2] The land sold to Col: Taylor[3] was also a partnership property, and of course the payments in other land must be the same. The land yet to be surveyed on Sandy[4] was wholly mine, but I promised my brother, in case he would get it surveyed & patented, he should have half of it. If you should be able to have the land secured as I hope will be the case, I shall do whatever equity & liberality can require on that head. I must ask the favor of your continued attention to this matter until Mr. Green[5] shall have fulfilled his undertaking. I do not know who the person is acquainted with the beginning. If it should be Mr. Henpenstall,[6] I am sure he will render any service he conveniently can. The expence requisite for this or any other business you may be so kind as to charge yourself with in my behalf, will always be punctually defrayed. My only concern is that I can not, as I would wish, in every instance, previously supply you with the means. Whereever you can anticipate the amount however, and an opportunity offers, I hope you will make free to draw on me. It will be most convenient, where the case will admit, to make the bills payable at 10, 20, or 30 days sight according to circumstances. I shall write to Majr. Lee by this opportunity, and let him know that I have written to you. When you write again, which I hope will be soon, you will oblige me by being as particular on all these subjects as you can. I will thank you also to let me know the probable value of the several parcels of land I have mentioned, that is, the land on Panther Creek—the 1000 Acres got of Col. R. Taylor, & whether it was conveyed, or if so to my brother alone or to us jointly—and the land on Sandy.

This is the 12th. day from that appointed for the meeting of Congs. and the Session is not yet opened in form, owing to the want of a quorum in the Senate. I cannot therefore send you even the speech of the President. The last despatches from Mr. Jay are said to promise a favorable result to his mission. It is probable that not a little will depend on the state of things on the Continent. This according to all accts. is turning more & more agst. the combined powers. The French have for sometime past been pushing their victories with more rapidity than ever. They have regained all their lost towns, and taken a variety of others; and the public is prepared to expect the news of further advances into the Netherland⟨s⟩ (perhaps even to Amsterdam) as well as into Spain where they have already forced their way with astonishing success. No letters public or private have been yet recd. from Col. Monro⟨e.⟩ It appears from foreign gazettes that his first inter⟨view with⟩ the Natl. Convention was marked with peculiar cord⟨iality &⟩ affection on both sides. As to the state of matters in the Western district of this State, you will have fuller as well as quicker information from the Spot. The result of the insurrection ought to be a lesson to every part of the Union against disobedience to the laws. Examples of this kind are as favorable to the enemies of Republican Government, as the experiment proves them to be dangerous to the Authors. Offer my regards to all friends & be assured of the esteem with which I am Dear Sir Yrs. affectly.

Js. MADISON JR.

RC (KyU: Hubbard Taylor Papers). Addressed by JM to Taylor in Kentucky, "Hond. by Col. Innes." Docketed by Taylor. Damaged by removal of seal.

1. On 16 Aug. 1780 Ambrose Madison patented two 1,000-acre tracts on Panther Creek that were not surveyed until 1797 (Jillson, *Old Kentucky Entries and Deeds*, p. 244; Jillson, *Kentucky Land Grants*, p. 205; "A List of the Lands belonging to James Madison of Orange County in Virginia, lying in the State of Kentucky," 1793? [DLC: John J. Crittenden Papers]).

2. Nelly Conway Madison, daughter of Ambrose and Mary Willis Lee Madison, married Dr. John Willis (1774–1812) of Whitehall, Gloucester County. By 1805 the Willises were living in Orange County (Lee, *Lee of Virginia*, p. 537; *WMQ*, 1st ser., 6 [1897–98]: 27; John Willis to JM, 19 Aug. 1805 [DLC: Dolley Madison Papers]).

3. See Richard Taylor to JM, 11 Oct. 1794, and n. 1.

4. On 12 Nov. 1783 Ambrose Madison patented 6,029 acres on Sandy Creek (surveyed in 1796) (Jillson, *Old Kentucky Entries and Deeds*, p. 123; Jillson, *Kentucky Land Grants*, p. 205).

5. Willis Green (1752–1813) served as a second lieutenant in William Grayson's regiment during the Revolution. He resigned his commission in 1778 and went to Kentucky "as a surveyor, to locate land warrants for various persons." He represented Jefferson County in the Virginia House of Delegates, 1781–82, and attended the Kentucky conventions of 1785 and 1788. He served as deputy registrar of the

Virginia land office for Kentucky, 1783–92, and Lincoln County clerk, 1783–1813
(*DAR Patriot Index*, p. 284; *WMQ*, 1st ser., 6 [1897–98]: 211; Collins, *Collins' Historical Sketches of Kentucky* [1878 ed.], 2:87–88; Swem and Williams, *Register*, p. 381). On 1 Sept. 1792 Ambrose Madison urged Taylor "to hurry W. Green abt. the survey on sandy. I think the time given for surveying there expires in Decr. unless you[r] governmt should prolong the time" (KyU: Hubbard Taylor Papers).

6. Abraham Haptonstall accompanied Hancock Taylor (JM's second cousin), Willis Lee (Taylor's cousin and Ambrose Madison's brother-in-law), and Isaac Hite (cousin of JM's brother-in-law of the same name) on a surveying expedition to Kentucky, 1773–74. He patented land on Panther Creek in 1780 and on the South Fork of the Elkhorn River in 1783 (Collins, *Collins' Historical Sketches of Kentucky* [1878 ed.], 2:367, 549, 764; Lee, *Lee of Virginia*, pp. 536–37; Cartmell, *Shenandoah Valley Pioneers*, pp. 257, 260; Jillson, *Kentucky Land Grants*, p. 61; Jillson, *Old Kentucky Entries and Deeds*, p. 106).

To Thomas Jefferson

DEAR SIR   PHILADA. NOVR. 16. 1794.

I have recd. your two favors of Ocr. 30 & Novr. 6, the former not in time to be answered on Monday last. Mazzei's claim on Dorhman is £2000 N. Y. Currency, with interest at 7 per Ct. from Novr. 1788. It is secured by a Deed of Trust empowering me to sell a tract of land granted to Mr. D. by an Act of Congress of Octr. 1. 1787. (see Journals of that date). Mr. Randolph thinks that a Court of Equity would not interfere with a summary execution of the trust. I hear nothing from Dorhman; nor can even say whether he is still in N. York. I have mentioned to Mr. R. the books and he has promised to let me have them. Judge Wilson is on the Southn. Circuit, and I suppose the volumes in his hands can not be got till he returns. I will however make the trial. The gentleman by whom they are to be sent to you has not yet made his appearance.

The Senate having not yet a Quorum I cannot send you the P.'s Speech. You will have seen by the papers that the Western Scene is closed. H. is still with the army. You will perceive his colouring on all the documents which have been published during his Mentorship to the commander in cheif.[1] When I first arrived here the conversation ran high for a standing army to enforce the laws. It is said the Militia will all return with the same doctrine in their mouths. I have no doubt that such an innovation will be attempted in earnest during the session, if circumstances should be favorable. It is probable however that the P. will not embark in the measure; and that the fear of alarming N. England will be another obstacle.

The elections for the next Congs.[2] are generally over except in Virginia & N. Carola. & N. York. In N. Hampshire the choice is much the same. In Masshts. there has been a violent contest in most of the districts. All that will probably be gained is a spirit of enquiry & competition in that quarter. Ames is re-elected after the most unparall[el]ed exertions & calumnies in his favor, and according to report by the addl. aid of bad votes.[3] Dexter is to run a second heat but will probably succeed.[4] Sedgwick's fate is not known. The chance is said to be in his favor; but it is agreed that he will be well sweated. As he has not yet appeared, he is probably nursing his declining popularity during the crisis. From N. Y. we are promised at least half of the new representatives for the republican scale.[5] N. Jersey has lost old Clarke who will no doubt be replaced by a successor of other sentiments. In this State, the election, notwithstanding its inauspicious circumstances, is more republican than the last. Nine at least out of thirteen are counted on the right side; among them Swanwick in the room of Fitzimmons, a stunning change for the aristocracy.[6] Maryland pretty much as heretofore.[7] I shd. have first noted that in Delaware Patten the Republican ex-member, is chosen by a large Majority.[8] The representation of Maryland will vary little from the present. In S. C. Smith has been carryed by the British merchants in Charleston & their d[e]btors in the Country, in spite of the Rutledges & Pinkney's who set up agst. him Jno. Rutlege jur. Tucker was also a candidate. Smith had a majority of all the votes. In general the changes also in that State will be for the worse. The death of Gillon has made way for Barnwell if he chuses to step in. Hunter also is out; but it is said his successor (a Mr. Harper) will be a valuable acquisition, being sound able & eloquent.[9] The prospects for the Senate are—the reelection of Langdon for N. H. The election of Payne, an incognitum, in place of Bradley for Vermont who appears to have been out of favor with both parties—the reelection of King in N. Y. owing to the death of 2 Repubn. members of the State Legislature—the chance of a Republican successor to R Morris, said to be a good one; a like chance in Delaware. In Maryland the Chance is bad, but nothing worse than the present delegation is to [be] apprehended. Potts has resigned, & Henry it is supposed will either withdraw or be rejected.[10] The event in Virga. you will know. The information from N. C. is not decisive, but favorable; the same as to S. C. Izard has relinquished his pretensions. In Georgia the question lies between Gun & Telfair. The former it is thought will be rechosen.

I must refer to Newspapers which I suppose you occasionally see from Richd. for the posture of things in Europe. In general they are extremely favorable to F. and alarming to all the Sovereigns of Europe. England seems still bent notwithstanding, on the war. She is now to subsidize the Emperor as well as the K. of Prussia. Accordg. to the intelligence handed to the public it would seem that the humiliating memorial of Jay inspires less contempt, than the French victories do terror, and that the tone towards this Country will be much changed. It is even intimated that satisfactory arrangements will be made on most, if not all the points in question. Not a line official or private from Monroe. His enthusiastic reception you will have seen.

Prices here are very different from those you mention. Wheat at 12/- Corn 6/6. Beef at 8d. & other things in proportion. House Rent 50 PerCt. higher than last Winter. Mrs. M. offers her best returns to you. Always & affecy. Yours

Js. MADISON

RC (DLC). Franked and addressed by JM to Jefferson at Monticello. Docketed by Jefferson, "recd. Dec. 2."

1. Hamilton accompanied Washington when the president left Philadelphia on 30 Sept. to meet the army in western Pennsylvania. Washington stayed with the army until 19 Oct., but the secretary of the treasury remained another month. Hamilton transmitted the president's instructions and his own advice to the army's commander, Henry Lee. Lee's general orders and communications with local officials were published in the Philadelphia newspapers, and in editorials Benjamin Franklin Bache denounced Hamilton's presence with the army (Jackson and Twohig, *Diaries of George Washington*, 6:178, 195; Hamilton to Lee, 20 Oct. and 13 Nov. 1794, Hamilton to Washington, 19 Nov. 1794, Syrett and Cooke, *Papers of Hamilton*, 17:331–36, 367–69, 391; Philadelphia *General Advertiser*, 29 Oct., 3, 5, and 6 Nov. 1794; *Philadelphia Gazette*, 14 Nov. 1794; *Supplement to the Philadelphia Gazette*, 15 Nov. 1794).

2. On the national results of the 1794–95 congressional elections, see Madison in the Third Congress, 2 Dec. 1793–3 Mar. 1795.

3. In the Boston congressional election on 3 Nov., Federalist incumbent Fisher Ames defeated Dr. Charles Jarvis. Republicans and Federalists accused each other of securing the support of ineligible voters (Bernhard, *Fisher Ames*, pp. 237–41).

4. Republican Elbridge Gerry had represented the Middlesex district in the First and Second Congresses. Federalist Samuel Dexter, Jr., represented the third western district in the Third Congress, but the 1794 redistricting of Massachusetts placed him in the second middle district—roughly equivalent to the old Middlesex district—where Republican Joseph Bradley Varnum won more votes than Gerry and Dexter. Though Gerry withdrew from the race, three runoff elections were held before Varnum gained a majority over Dexter (Stanley B. Parsons, William W. Beach, and Dan Hermann, *United States Congressional Districts, 1788–1841* [Westport, Conn., 1978], pp. 10, 46, 79; Philadelphia *Aurora General Advertiser*, 14 Nov. 1794, 3 Feb. 1795; see also Dexter to JM, 3 Feb. 1795, and n. 1).

5. The party balance in the New York delegation to the House of Representatives shifted from three Republicans and seven Federalists in the Third Congress to six Republicans and four Federalists in the Fourth Congress (JM to Jefferson, 15 Feb. 1795; John Beckley to JM, 20 Apr. 1795).

6. As a result of the 1794 congressional election, Republican representatives in the Pennsylvania delegation increased their majority from 7–5 (plus one member of undetermined partisanship) in the Third Congress to 9–4 in the Fourth Congress. In Philadelphia, Republican John Swanwick defeated the Federalist incum-

bent Thomas FitzSimons (Parsons et al., *United States Congressional Districts*, pp. 58–61).

7. During the course of the Third Congress, Maryland Republicans had increased their numbers as a result of several resignations and defections. As JM predicted, their 5–3 majority in the House delegation remained unchanged in the Fourth Congress (Risjord, *Chesapeake Politics*, p. 656 n. 61).

8. John Patten opposed administration policies in the Third Congress until the pro-administration Henry Latimer contested his election and took his seat on 14 Feb. 1794. Patten then won reelection to the Fourth Congress. The Delaware General Assembly elected Latimer to the U.S. Senate, and he resigned his House seat on 7 Feb. 1795 (*BDC*, pp. 1268, 1515).

9. Alexander Gillon, an opponent of administration policies, represented the Beaufort-Orangeburg district of South Carolina in the Third Congress until his death on 6 Oct. 1794. In the elections to the Fourth Congress on 13–14 Oct., Federalist John Barnwell won in that district, and in the Ninety-Six district Robert Goodloe Harper defeated the Federalist incumbent, John Hunter. When Barnwell declined to serve, the Beaufort-Orangeburg district elected Republican Wade Hampton on 19–20 Jan. 1795. Harper also won the by-election on 10–11 Nov. 1794 to fill out Gillon's term, took his seat on 9 Feb. 1795, and represented the Beaufort-Orangeburg district for the remainder of the Third Congress. He then served as the Ninety-Six district's congressman until 1801. Though Harper was elected as a Republican, Pierce Butler warned JM that "he will be liable to impressions, and apt to be hurri[e]d away by the feelings of the moment." Soon after his arrival in Philadelphia, Harper became a Federalist (Edgar et al., *Biographical Directory of the South Carolina House of Representatives*, 2:55, 3:270–71, 309–10, 362; Charleston, S.C., *Columbian Herald*, 13 and 29 Oct., 19 Nov. 1794, 30 Jan. and 4 Mar. 1795; Philadelphia *Gazette of the U.S.*, 4 Nov. 1794; Butler to JM, 23 Jan. 1795).

10. Neither of Maryland's U.S. senators was up for reelection in 1794. Federalist Richard Potts finally resigned on 24 Oct. 1796, Republican John Henry on 10 Dec. 1797 (*BDC*, pp. 1561–62, 1107).

From Joseph Jones

Dr. Sr.   Fredg. 16th. Novr. 1794.

Your favor of the 7th. I received on Friday evening on my return from Richmond. I am in hopes the China has got safe and sound to hand. I have not heard from Mr. Randolph but take for granted what you mention that the bill will be paid as he had accepted it. I promised no further application should be made untill we heard from Monroe although my engagements for him and some small balances due from him when he went away will not well admit of delay. Certainly we shall hear from him by the French Corvette lately arrived at Baltimore with it is said despatches for the Minister. Mr. Jay's representation was not in the stile of firm demand for compensation for injuries done to our citizens but rather supplicating the benevolence of his Britannic Majesty for relief. What his Powers or instructions were I know not but if they were such as to justify the language of his representation they merit contempt rather than applause. Grenville's answer is a palpable evasion of justice or rather a dishonourable denial of it. The injuries have been done under the authority of the nation. The nation therefore shod. redress them. Can Americans expect justice from the Courts while the acts of the King in Council are the rule of decision? After the Courts have decided shod. there be Occasion for the interference of the governmt. Then it may be proper to appt. Comrs. who in concert with American Comr. are to discuss the measures and principles on which the business is to be finally settled, very civil and satisfactory indeed. Who is to supply the Chief Justices place in the Courts in the mean time for I think it will require some years to get through the work or is Mr. Jay to continue our Envoy with the emoluments of that Office superadded to those of Chief justice in which Character he does nothing to intitle him to payment. I hope the Republican interest in the legislature will be strengthened from the North, as it is in danger of loosing support from the South by a late election, or at least of gaining nothing from that quarter. Wise is chosen Speaker. Harvie got only 19 votes for the chair. Who will be the Senator or Senators (for they say Taylor will certainly resign) is very uncertain—there are many spoken of Tazewell, C Lee Corbin, Harvie, Dawson W. Nicholas—also yourself and Giles. Some say Henry is willing to serve as Govr. Shod. the fact be ascertained he will be elected, otherwise the contest will I expect rest bet. Brooke & Wood. The first will probably succeed. I have tried all over the Town for Hams, there are none. Some midlings & a few shoulders alone can be got. Mrs. Willis sometimes has bacon to sell I have requested her Brother who dines with her to day to inquire, and let me know—if any they shall be secured. I am Yr. friend & Servt.

Jos: Jones.

P. S. Mrs. Willis has no bacon to spare. I shall make further inquiry for bacon.

RC (DLC).

To James Madison, Sr.

Dear & Hond Sir   Philada. Novr. 17. 1794

 I now inclose the letter omitted in my last. We have not had the pleasure of a single line from Orange since yours[1] recd. just before leaving Berkeley. I hope it will not be long before our expectation is gratified on this point; and that you will be able to tell us all that we wish in favor of the re-establishment of my mothers health and the continuation of your own. I shall be glad also to have a word added with respect to matters at my two Farms. In my last I informed you of my having sent 1½ bushls. of Clover seed for the field at Sawney's where Wheat was sowed among Corn. The barrel containing it, with another containing 112 lb. Sugar for you were consigned to Mr. Anderson. I hope both will have arrived safe.

The Senate have not yet a Quorum, and of Course the business of the Session can hardly be said to be commenced, nothing being done, but some small matters in the H. of Reps. which made a Quorum the 2d. day. The army sent agst. the Insurgents is announced to be on the return, the object of their destination being accomplished. The accounts from Europe shew more & more the irres[is]tible force of the French armies & the distresses of their combined Enemies. From England the information tho' not decisive is favorable to the views of this Country. Not a word official or private is yet come to hand from Col. Monroe. The enthusiastic reception given him by the Natl. Convention was communicated thro' the foreign Newspapers. Wheat has been as high as 12/6. It is now about 12/. where the weight & quality are good. Did Fraily attend according to promise and what has been done towards the Mill? I hope at least that a legal commencement[2] of the work has not failed. Yr. Affee. son

Js. MADISON JR

RC (DLC).

1. Letter not found.

2. The gristmill that Francis Madison was planning to build on the Rapidan River involved several legal proceedings. On 22 July 1793 the Orange County Court granted a writ for the condemnation of an acre of John Baylor's land which would be flooded by the milldam. On 23 Dec. the court confirmed the condemnation and granted Francis Madison permission to build the mill. On 29 July 1795 he admitted JM, his father, and his brother William as partners in the mill (Orange County, Minute Book, 3:182, 202; Madison County, Deed Book, 1:345).

Admission of a Territorial Delegate

[18 November 1794]

On 11 November Speaker Muhlenberg presented to the House a letter from James White, enclosing his credentials as a delegate from the Territory South of the River Ohio (which later became Tennessee), in accordance with the terms of the Northwest Ordinance and other relevant legislation. The House referred the letter to a select committee which reported a resolution that White be admitted to his seat "with a right of debating, but not of voting." On 17 November in Committee of the Whole, Wingate moved to amend the resolution to allow the delegate to debate in the Senate as well as the House (*Annals of Congress*, 3d Cong., 2d sess., 873, 883–89). JM "said that the resolution, as passed by the select committee, was so properly expressed, that he did not believe it could admit of any amendment or alteration whatever" (*Philadelphia Gazette*, 18 Nov. 1794). The Committee of the Whole rejected Wingate's amendment and passed the resolution, which the House approved on 18 November.

Mr. Madison said, that in new cases, there often arose a difficulty by applying old names to new things. The proper definition of Mr. White is to be found in the laws and rules of the constitution. He is not a member of Congress, therefore, and so cannot be directed to take an oath, unless he chooses to do it voluntarily.

Philadelphia Gazette, 19 Nov. 1794. Murray moved to require White to take the oath. After debate, the House rejected the motion.

From Joseph Jones

Dr. Sr.   Fredg. 19th. Novr. 1794.

I have your favors of the 12th. and 14th. of the month[1] with the Papers inclosed. It is somewhat strange we have no letters public or private from Monroe when so many opportunities have offered since his arrival and in particular the Corvette arrived at Baltimore with despatches for the Minister of France. The Republic appears to pursue her victories in all quarters and to bid fair to vanquish the violence of party at home—the removal from the Com: of public safety of those Members who appeared to be contending for controul may establish unanimity and moderation in their councils. If it shall not abate the enthusiasm of the people for Liberty, and cool the ardor of the Armies the policy which they profess to adopt in the interior cannot fail to produce happy effects. The head *important* in Baches paper does not open to my view any well founded hope or prospect of a speedy or successfull issue of Mr. Jays negociation.[2] The Pensylvania or at least the Philadelphia election seems to have Run in favor of the Republican party. I lament that Ames has outvoted Ja[r]vis. Wheat here is 6/ & 6/3. The Merchants say they have lately suffered mu⟨c⟩h by some shipments to Baltimore in consequence of the wheats heating in the vessell, the quality of wheat is generally bad and slovenly managed. The promptitud⟨e⟩ of the militia in turning out to support the laws will I hope be a stumbling block to the advocates for a standing Army.

Not being able to procure you any bacon I send you half my remaining stock. They are small and may serve as a relish. Yr. friend & Servt

Jos: Jones.

There is a vessell now loading for Philaa. on board of which I will send the package and will by next post inform you her name & the Commander wch. at present I do not know.

RC (DLC). Docketed by JM.

1. Letters not found.

2. Jay's negotiations in Britain reportedly "have made a considerable advance towards a settlement . . . and there is reason to expect that definitive arrangements will be received before the rising of Congress" ("Important," Philadelphia *Aurora General Advertiser*, 13 Nov. 1794).

From Joseph Jones

Dr. Sr.   Fredg. 21t. Novr. 1794.

The inclosed paper will inform you on board what vessell and to whom consigned the small cask I send you goes—it contains Anthony informs me four gammon and one shoulder. I wish I could have sent you more and larger peices but you must be content with what and such as they are. I set out in the morning for Loudoun and Albemarle and shall not return in less than 8 or 10 days. Your letters to me in Fredericksg. I shall receive on my return. Health and happiness attend you. Tazewell and S. T. Mason I hear are the Senators to Congress. Yr. friend & Servt.

Jos: Jones.

RC (DLC). Docketed by JM. Enclosure not found.

Address of the House of Representatives to the President

[21 November 1794]

The House of Representatives calling to mind the blessings enjoyed by the people of the United States, and especially the happiness of living under Constitutions and laws which rest on their Authority alone, could not learn with other emotions than those you have expressed, that any part of our fellow Citizens should have shewn themselves capable of an insurrection.[1]

We feel with you the deepest regret at so painful an occurrence in the annals of our country. As men regardful of the tender interests of humanity, we look with grief, at scenes which might have stained our land with civil blood. As lovers of public order, we lament that it has suffered so flagrant a violation: as zealous friends of republican government, we deplore every occasion, which in the hands of its enemies, may be turned into a calumny against it.

This aspect of the crisis, however, is happily not the only one, which it presents. There is another which yields all the consolations which you have drawn from it. It has demonstrated to the candid world, as well as to the American people themselves, that the great body of them, every where, are equally attached to the luminous and vital principle of our constitution, which enjoins that the will of the majority shall prevail: that they understand the indissoluble union between true liberty and regular government; that they feel their duties no less than they are watchful over their rights; that they will [be]² as ready, at all times, to crush licentiousness, as they have been to defeat usurpation: in a word, that they are capable of carrying into execution, that noble plan of self government, which they have chosen as the guarantee of their own happiness, and the asylum for that, of all from every clime, who may wish to unite their destiny with ours.

These are the just inferences from the promp[t]itude with which the summons to the standard of the laws has been obeyed; and from sentiments which have been witnessed in every description of citizens, in every quarter of the Union. The spectacle therefore when viewed in its true light may well be affirmed to display in equal lustre, the virtues of the American character, and the value of Republican government. All must particularly acknowledge and applaud the patriotism of that portion of citizens who have freely sacrificed every thing less dear than the love of their country, to the meritorious task of defending its happiness.

In the part which you have yourself borne through this delicate and distressing period, we trace the additional proofs it has afforded of your solicitude for the public good. Your laudable and successful endeavors to render lenity in executing the laws conducive to their real energy, and to convert tumult into order without the effusion of blood, form a particular title to the confidence and praise of your constituents. In all that may be found necessary, on our part to complete this benevolent purpose, and to secure ministers and friends of the laws against the remains of danger, our due co-operation will be afforded.

The other subjects which you have recommended, or communicated, and of which several are peculiarly interesting, will all receive the attention which they demand.³ We shall on this, as on all occasions, be disposed to adopt every measure which may advance the safety and prosperity of our Country. In nothing can we more cordially unite with you, than in imploring the supreme Ruler of Nations to multiply his blessings on these United States: to guard our free and happy Constitution against every machination and danger; and to make it the best source of public happiness, by verifying its character of being the best safeguard of human rights.[4]

FC (DNA: RG 233, Journals); Tr (DLC: Washington Papers). FC in a clerk's hand; Tr in the hand of Bartholomew Dandridge, Jr., Washington's private secretary. Authorship attributed to JM on the basis of his chairmanship of the committee appointed on 20 Nov. to prepare a reply to Washington's annual address to Congress. FC dated 21 Nov. 1794, when JM reported the reply from committee. The House approved the amended reply on 28 Nov. Tr dated 29 Nov. 1794, when the reply was presented to the president (*Annals of Congress*, 3d Cong., 2d sess., 892, 947, 950). Tr headed: "George Washington, President of the United States. / Sir." Minor variations between the FC and the Tr have not been noted. For amendments, see nn. 1 and 3. For House proceedings on the reply, see JM's speeches of 24 and 27 Nov. 1794 and nn., JM to Jefferson, 30 Nov. 1794, and JM to Monroe, 4 Dec. 1794.

1. In the Tr (which was the version the House finally approved) is here added: "And we learn, with the greatest concern, that any misrepresentations whatever, of the Government and its proceedings, either by individuals or combinations of men, should have been made and so far credited, as to foment the flagrant outrage, which has been committed on the laws." This was a response to the allegation, in Washington's 19 Nov. annual address to Congress, that "certain self-created societies" had incited the Whiskey Insurrection (Fitzpatrick, *Writings of Washington*, 34:29). For a discussion of the political impact of the attack on the Democratic societies in the president's address, see Baldwin, *Whiskey Rebels*, pp. 260–62.

2. Word in brackets supplied from Tr.

3. In the Tr is here added: "We are deeply impressed with the importance of an effectual organization of the militia. We rejoice at the intelligence of the advance & success of the army under the command of General Wayne; whether we regard it as a proof of the perseverance, prowess & superiority of our troops, or as a happy presage to our military operations against the hostile Indians, and as a probable prelude to the establishment of a lasting peace, upon terms of candor, equity and good neighbourhood. We receive it with the greater pleasure, as it increases the probability of sooner restoring a part of the public resources to the desirable object of reducing the public debt." This was a response to the section in Washington's address concerning Maj. Gen. Anthony Wayne's 20 Aug. victory over the Indians at Fallen Timbers in northwestern Ohio (Fitzpatrick, *Writings of Washington*, 34:35–36).

4. The Tr concludes: "Signed by order, and in behalf of the House, Frederick Augustus Muhlenberg, / Speaker. / Attest / John Beckley, Clerk."

¶ To Alexander Balmain. Letter not found. *23 November 1794.* Acknowledged in Balmain to JM, 8 Dec. 1794. Encloses a copy of Washington's 19 Nov. annual address to Congress denouncing "certain self-created societies."

House Address to the President

[24 November 1794]

The Committee of the Whole took up the House's reply to the president that JM had reported. Dayton moved an amendment concerning Indian and military policy (see Address of the House of Representatives to the President, 21 Nov. 1794, n. 3).

Mr. Madison observed, that it had been the wish of the committee who framed the address to avoid entering into the minutiæ of the speech, lest their answer should exceed the usual limits. However as it seemed a wish to amplify in some particular parts, perhaps it would not be amiss to glance at the policy observed towards foreign nations. He therefore wished to add, to the motion made, if the original mover had no objection that it should be tacked to it, a clause to the following purport: "Solicitous also as we are for the preservation of peace with all nations we cannot otherwise than warmly approve of *a* policy in our foreign transactions, which never loses sight of that blessing."[1]

Aurora General Advertiser, 25 Nov. 1794 (reprinted in *Dunlap and Claypoole's Am. Daily Advertiser*, 26 Nov. 1794; also reported in *Gazette of the U.S.*, 25 Nov. 1794, *Philadelphia Gazette*, 25 Nov. 1794, and *Independent Gazetteer*, 26 and 29 Nov. 1794).

1. This amendment responded to the following section of Washington's annual address to Congress: "My policy in our foreign transactions has been, to cultivate peace with all the world; to observe treaties with pure and absolute faith; to check every deviation from the line of impartiality; to explain what may have been misapprehended, and correct what may have been injurious to any nation; and having thus acquired the right, to lose no time in acquiring the ability, to insist upon justice being done to ourselves" (Fitzpatrick, *Writings of Washington*, 34:37).

[24 November 1794]

Smith (New Hampshire) and Hillhouse proposed further amendments. The committee approved Dayton's amendment after separating it from JM's. JM "proposed an alteration in the latter part of the amendment he had offered, and to make it read '—which keeps in view as well the maintenance of our national rights as the continuance of that blessing'" (*Aurora General Advertiser*, 25 Nov. 1794). In debate Republicans supported JM's amendment because it approved the stated objectives of Washington's foreign policy without endorsing specific aspects such as Jay's mission. Federalists criticized it because it avoided a general approval of the president's policy.

Mr. Madison conceived the clause as he offered it perfectly explicit and unequivocal. The President says, that peace has been his object, it is proposed that the house shall say in answer that that is the policy they wish pursued also, and the amendment he proposed, he was of opinion, did this unequivocally.[1]

Aurora General Advertiser, 26 Nov. 1794 (reprinted in *Dunlap and Claypoole's Am. Daily Advertiser*, 27 Nov. 1794; also reported in *Gazette of the U.S.*, 25 Nov. 1794, *Philadelphia Gazette*, 25 Nov. 1794, and *Independent Gazetteer*, 29 Nov. 1794).

1. Debate became extremely divisive. Tracy urged JM "rather to withdraw his motion of amendment altogether than bring it forward at such an expence of the good temper of the house. The present session had commenced with good auspices, and much cordiality, and he would be extremely sorry to disturb this tranquility." JM "said that he felt sensibly the force of the remarks made by the gentleman who was last up" and therefore withdrew his amendment (*Philadelphia Gazette*, 25 Nov. 1794).

House Address to the President

[27 November 1794]

After JM withdrew his amendment concerning foreign policy, FitzSimons proposed an amendment that denounced the "self-created societies." This provoked an extended and heated debate in the Committee of the Whole, which approved Giles's motion to strike out the words "self-created societies" (*Annals of Congress*, 3d Cong., 2d sess., 898–99, 907–8, 914). On 26 and 27 November the House considered reinstating those words.

Mr. Madison—said he entirely agreed with those gentlemen who had observed that the house should not have advanced into this discussion, if it could have been avoided—but having proceeded thus far it was indispensably necessary to finish it.

Much delicacy had been thrown into the discussion, in consequence of the chief magistrate; he always regretted the circumstance, when this was the case.

This he observed, was not the first instance of difference in opinion between the President and this house. It may be recollected that the President dissented both from the Senate and this House on a particular law (he referred to that apportioning the representatives)[1]—on that occasion he thought the President right. On the present question, supposing the President really to entertain the opinion ascribed to him, it affords no conclusive reason for the House to sacrifice its own judgment.

It appeared to him, as it did to the gentleman from Georgia, that there was an innovation in the mode of procedure adopted, on this occasion.[2] The house are on different ground from that usually taken—members seem to think that in cases not cognizable by law, there is room for the interposition of the House. He conceived it to be a sound principle that an action innocent in the eye of the law, could not be the object of censure to a legislative body. When the people have formed a constitution, they retain those rights which they have not expressly delegated. It is a question whether what is thus retained can be legislated upon. Opinions are not the objects of legislation. You animadvert on the *abuse* of reserved rights—how far will this go? It may extend to the liberty of speech and of the press.

It is in vain to say that this indiscriminate censure is no punishment. If it falls on classes or individuals it will be a severe punishment. He wished it to be considered how extremely guarded the constitution was in respect to cases not within its limits. Murder or treason cannot be noticed by the legislature. Is not this proposition, if voted, a vote of attainder? To consider a principle, we must try its nature, and see how far it will go; in the present case he considered the effects of the principle contended for, would be pernicious. If we advert to the nature of republican government, we shall find that the censorial power is in the people over the government, and not in the government over the people.

As he had confidence in the good sense and patriotism of the people, he did not anticipate any lasting evil to result from the publications of these societies; they will stand or fall by the public opinion; no line can be drawn in this case. The law is the only rule of right; what is consistent with that is not punishable; what is not contrary to that, is innocent, or at least not censurable by the legislative body.

With respect to the body of the people, (whether the outrages have proceeded from weakness or wickedness) what has been done, and will be done by the Legislature will have a due effect. If the *proceedings* of the government should not have an effect, will this declaration produce it? The people at large are possessed of proper sentiments on the subject of the insurrection—the whole continent reprobates the conduct of the insurgents, it is not therefore necessary to take the extra step. The press he believed would not be able to shake the confidence of the people in the government. In a republic, light will prevail over darkness, truth over error—he had undoubted confidence in this principle. If it be admitted that the law cannot animadvert on a particular case, neither can we do it. Governments are administered by men—the same degree of purity does not always exist. Honesty of motives may at present prevail—but this affords no assurance that it will always be the case—at a future period a Legislature may exist of a very different complexion from the present; in this view, we ought not by any vote of ours to give support to measures which now we do not hesitate to reprobate. The gentleman from Georgia had anticipated him in several remarks—no such inference can fairly be drawn as that we abandon the President, should we pass over the whole business.[3] The vote passed this morning[4] for raising a force to compleat the good work of peace order and tranquility begun by the executive, speaks quite a different language from that which has been used to induce an adoption of the principle contended for.

Mr. Madison adverted to precedents—none parallel to the subject before us existed. The inquiry into the failure of the expedition under St. Clair[5] was not in point. In that case the house appointed a Committee of enquiry into the conduct of an individual in the public service —the democratic societies are not. He knew of nothing in the proceedings of the Legislature which warrants the house in saying that institutions, confessedly not illegal, were subjects of legislative censure.[6]

Gazette of the U.S., 2 Dec. 1794 (also reported in *Supplement to the Philadelphia Gazette*, 29 Nov. 1794, and *Independent Gazetteer*, 20 Dec. 1794).

1. On Washington's first exercise of the presidential veto, on the apportionment bill of 1792, see *PJM*, 14:261 n. 1.

2. Baldwin spoke just before JM. "Adverting to the usual process in conducting transactions of this nature, he observed, that the present appeared to be a deviation, if not an entire innovation, on the usual mode. During the recess, the PRESIDENT collected and arranged the information which he deemed proper to lay before the House; it cannot, therefore, be expected, that the House should at once, at the threshold of the session, enter into a minute answer to the communications of the PRESIDENT, containing facts and opinions the result of five or six months experience and reflection, before they have had time to examine those opinions, and investigate those facts" (*Annals of Congress*, 3d Cong., 2d sess., 933).

3. In his speech, Baldwin concluded: "He was fully of opinion, that, rather than spin out the debate to any further length, it would be much more eligible to leave the subject altogether, and take up the other business of the nation. He was sure that the PRESIDENT, for whom he professed the highest respect, could not be pleased with this mode of conducting that before them" (ibid., 934).

4. On the morning of 27 Nov., the House passed the "bill to authorize the President to call out and station a corps of militia in the four Western counties of Pennsylvania, for a limited time." Washington signed the bill on 29 Nov. (ibid., 932; *U.S. Statutes at Large*, 1:403).

5. In Committee of the Whole on 24 Nov., Dayton had argued "that these societies had produced the Western insurrection, and, therefore, the Committee were just as well entitled to institute an inquiry in this case, as formerly, regarding the failure of the expedition of General St. Clair" (*Annals of Congress*, 3d Cong., 2d sess., 905). On JM's role in the first exercise of legislative oversight of the executive branch, by the 1792 House select committee inquiry into Maj. Gen. Arthur St. Clair's military defeat, see *PJM*, 14:268–69 and nn., 270–71 and n. 1.

6. After further debate, JM was in the minority when the House voted 47–45 to reinstate the words "self-created societies" in FitzSimons's amendment. The House, however, then defeated the amendment, which only nineteen members supported.

On 28 Nov. Nicholas offered a compromise amendment denouncing "combinations of men," which the House approved (*Annals of Congress*, 3d Cong., 2d sess., 944-47; for the text of Nicholas's amendment, see Address of the House of Representatives to the President, 21 Nov. 1794, n. 1).

From George Nicholas

DEAR SIR,   Novr. 29th. 94.

I am indebted to you for your two last agreeable and friendly favors;[1] the acknowledgment of that debt would not have been so long postponed, if [it] had not been from an expectation of collecting some thing worthy your attention. But after waiting some months I find the present moment as barren of important intelligence as any preceeding one.

Our campaign has ended, and altho no calamity has befallen our army, it is certain that they have gained no great or signal advantage. The official account which represented the engagement[2] as an important and brilliant victory obtained over the united force of the indians and Canadians with the loss of hundreds to the enemy, has gradually diminished until it is said that the enemy had not more than 700 combatants in the field, and that they did not lose more than 30 or 40 of them. It will remain for you to calculate and determine whether such a victory is a sufficient compensation for the expence incurred: and others ought to reflect whether the additional experience of this year will not be sufficient to prove beyond all doubt that the present mode of conducting the war is an improper one.

But the expences and consequences of our little movements will be so inconsiderable when compared with those of the army nearer to you, that I suppose little will be said or thought of them. The army has exhibited a spectacle which I never expected to have lived to see; 20,000 american citizens drawn into the field to act against their fellow citizens: and what is still more strange a great part of them volunteers. Men must be far advanced into that state which will make them proper objects for slavery, when they place such a blind reliance on any man's judgment or representations, as to be induced to offer their services to be the butchers of their countrymen. And that is a strange and inconsistent law which will not put it in the power of the President to call out the militia to enforce the laws when he shall judge it proper, but authorizes him to do it, when one of his servants, shall suppose it to be necessary upon ex parte information laid before him by order of the President: and by this means put it in the power of the President to do it when he pleases without being responsible for it's being improperly done. If he

393

is to be responsible for the late movement it is impossible that he can justify the levying and marching such an army upon such an occasion. If it was proper for government to have resorted to an armed force before the other powers had been sufficiently used, two hundred men would have been as adequate to the task as the 20,000. But it may be said that the information which was received by the executive of the situation of that country caused him to entertain a different opinion. If the event has proved that information to be false, he was in fault not to have obtained better: there cannot be a greater defect in the executive of any government, than to place it's confidence on improper persons in the first instance and afterwards to act from an implicit confidence in their false uncandid and partial representations.

I feel the truth of these observations the more forcibly because I have good reason to believe that the public opinion in your part of America, respecting the intentions of the inhabitants of this country, has been formed upon information of the kind above mentioned. Is it not generally believed with you that it is our wish and intention to seperate from the Union, and that our navigation is only made use of as a pretext to enable us to execute our real designs? If this idea is taken up to the eastward it must have proceeded either from conjectures formed there without any thing to justify them; or upon opinions formed upon false information from this quarter. I can with great truth assure you that as far as I know or believe no such wish or intention does prevail here; and I am satisfied that such an attempt would be opposed by 99 out of 100 of the people. All that we want is to be put upon an equal footing with our fellow citizens in the enjoyment and protection of our most undoubted and invaluable rights: the only means which we mean to use for their attainment are proper and constitutional representations to those whose duty it is to obtain them for us. The rights are sufficiently important to engross our whole attention; and these not having been properly attended to heretofore will justify the warmest representations that we can now make on this subject. No secret purpose ought to be supposed to influence our conduct when the ostensible one is alone sufficient to justify it. If it should still be thought that there is a secret purpose covered by this ostensible object, remove the cause of complaint, and then if the complaint itself is not at an end I will agree that the opinion is well founded. Put us upon the same footing with the other free men in America and I pledge myself that time will show that we are at least as much attached to the American government as any part of it's citizens. This must necessarily be the case if we consider only our own local interests. For we are more exposed than any other part of the government and therefore in greater want of the aid of a powerful government. But if we are to be subject to all the inconveniences which attend the being a member of that government, and enjoy none of the advantages which ought to follow that connexion, we then pay the price without receiving the considerations: how long we may continue to be satisfied in that situation is more than I can undertake to determine. As our attachment to the american government is founded on a conviction that it is to the interest of every part of that government to continue united, and that it is peculiarly the interest of this part of it, as long as the government is conducted on those general principles on which it is founded, it will only be necessary for the government to act up to those principles to insure a continuance of that attachment. My political creed on this subject is short and I believe is similar to that of most people in this country.

I believe that we have an undoubted right to the navigation of the western waters;

that we cannot exist as a people without the uninterrupted enjoyment of that right;

that the Spaniards will never permit us to enjoy that right without compulsion;

that it is not the wish or the interest of the greater part of America that we should enjoy this right;

that it is the duty of the genl. government to obtain for us this right at every hazard;

that they have power sufficient to effect it;

and that if they do not obtain it for us, that we shall be at full liberty to use our own strength to obtain it, *as soon* as we shall be convinced that that strength is adequate to the purpose.

As a citizen of America I felt myself much interested in the success of the commercial resolutions which you introduced at the last session of Congress; and as much disappointed at their not being finally adopted. The question involved on them was unconnected with the temporary measures which were necessary for the existing moment. Indeed that very crisis proved the propriety of the principle you advocated as nothing else could prevent our being thrown into a similar situation at the pleasure of any government stronger than we are at sea. The art of the opposite party in advocating the temporary measures in exclusion of your's is obvious. Persevere; the true public interest must finally be seen and will prevail: besides the importance of this question of itself; the urging of it will have a greater tendency to open the eyes of the people of the eastern states to the conduct and policy of their representatives in Congress than every other question put together which ever will be agitated in Congress. As long as they can persuade their people that the southern members are inimical to the general government; that their conduct proceeds from that disposition; and that the opposition of the eastern members to their measures proceeds from a proper degree of attachment to that government, they will be safe. But once satisfy the people that their representatives have opposed a measure which is not only essentially necessary to the prosperity of America as a nation, but peculiarly so to *their* part of America, and they will see immediately the pernicous tendency of their measures, and change them for men of different principles.

I shall be happy in hearing from you as often as your leisure will permit; and am with the greatest respect and esteem, Dr. Sir, yr. most obdt. servt.

G: NICHOLAS.

RC (DLC). Docketed by JM.

1. Letters not found.
2. Nicholas referred to Maj. Gen. Anthony Wayne's 20 Aug. victory over the Indians at Fallen Timbers in northwestern Ohio.

To Thomas Jefferson

DEAR SIR   PHILADA. Novr. 30. 94

Mr. Fleming has been here & set out on his return yesterday. I did not however know of his arrival till a very short time before his departure. Contrary to your expectation he returns by land, not with his goods. On this acct. added to the lateness of the Season, and my not being able to get all your books, I concluded it would be best to put off sending what I could get, till the Spring, when they can all be sent together, and perhaps be less exposed to accidents. The books in the hands of Wilson could not be obtained in his absence. And Mr. R. has not been able yet to find the Book on Mineralogy left with him.[1] You will see by the inclosed[2] that you are to receive a sett of Chalmer's Treaties. I send you the letter to me accompanying it, for the sake of the references which if correct may deserve notice; tho' they come from a Quarter not very learned one would suppose on such subjects. You will be so good as to return the letter, as I am yet to answer it.

The attack on the most sacred principle of our Constitution and of Republicanism, thro' the Democratic Societies, has given rise to much discussion in the H. of Reps. and has left us in a critical situation. You will have seen the P.'s Speech. The answer of the Senate was hurried thro', with the most full and emphatic eccho of the denunciation of these Societies.[3] In the mean time the answer of the H. of Reps.[4] tho' prepared & reported without any loss of time, was, contrary to usage, printed for consideration, and put off from Friday, till monday. On the intervening saturday, the Senate presented them, which with the P.'s reply was immediately out in the Newspapers. I refer for both to the Richd. Newspapers which you will probably have seen. The answer of the H. of Reps. both as reported & as agreed to are inclosed. The Come. consisted of Sedgwick Scott & myself. The draught was made as strong as possible on all proper points, in order the better to get it thro', without the improper one. This succeeded in the Come.; Scott concurring in the *expediency* of silence on that; tho' in the House he changed his ground. When the report was taken up on Monday Fitzimmons moved "to *reprobate* the self-created Societies &c. which tho' in strictness not *illegal*, contributed by their proceedings to mislead the weak & ignorant." This opened the debate which you will no doubt have an oppy. of reading in the Virga. papers if you chuse. It so happens that I can not send them by the mail. The argts. in favor of the motion fell with equal weight on the press & every mode of animadverting on public men & measures. After some time the proposition was new modelled, and in a less pointed shape underwent discussion for several days. On the first question wch. tried the sense of the House, the division was 47 agst. 45. for the usurped power. This was in a Committee of the whole. On a renewal of the same question in the House the decision was reversed by 47 in the affirmative & 45 in the negative. A motion was then made to limit the censure to the Societies within the scene of insurrection, which was carried by the casting vote of the Speaker. In this form the whole proposition was abandoned. This was on thursday. On friday, it being foreseen that some evil accomodation would come from the other side & succeed, It was proposed by Mr. Nicholas to insert the sentence which distinguishes the first ¶ of the Answer agreed to, from the Report. An attempt was made to add "& self created Societies," after "combinations," but it had so little prospect of success that it was withdrawn. The Answer was presented on saturday, and rec'd the reply[5] in the inclosed paper, which you will be at no loss to understand. The Republicans were considered by their opponents as rather victorious by the result in the House. The reply of the P. is claimed by the latter as a final triumph on their side; and it is probable that so it will prove. You will easily conceive my situation thro' this whole business. It was obvious that a most dangerous game was playing agst. Republicanism. The insurrection was universally & deservedly odious. The Democratic Societies were presented as in league with it. The Republican part of Congs. were to be drawn into an *ostensible*, patronage of those Societies, and into an ostensible opposition to the President. And by this artifice the delusion of N. Engld. was to be confirmed, and a chance afforded of some new turn in Virga. before the elections in the Spring. What the success of this game will really be, time must decide. If the people of America are so far degenerated already as not to see or to see with indifference, that the Citadel of their liberties is menaced by the precedent before their eyes, they require abler advocates than they now have, to save them from the consequences. Lengthy as the debate was, I took but little part in it; and that little is very erroneously as well as defectively stated in the Newspapers. No private letters from Monroe. An official one of Sepr. 15[6]—speaks of the utmost prosperity at home—of the irresistable discipline & enthusiasm of their armies, and of the most unalterable affection to this Country. All that is given out from Jay's negociation is in favr. of some advantageous result. How is your Rheumatism—& Mr. Randolph's complaint?

RC (DLC). Unsigned. Docketed by Jefferson, "recd. Dec. 16." For surviving enclosure, see n. 2. Other enclosures not found.

1. Emanuel Mendes da Costa, *A Natural History of Fossils* (London, 1757). Edmund Randolph never returned this volume to Jefferson (Sowerby, *Catalogue of Jefferson's Library*, 1:497).

2. George Joy to JM, 1 May 1794.

3. Federalist Rufus King reported from committee the reply of the Senate to Washington's 19 Nov. annual address to Congress. The reply asserted that "the proceedings of certain self-created societies . . . have been influential in misleading our fellow-citizens in the scene of insurrection." Washington responded that he was satisfied to learn "that the Senate discountenance those proceedings, which would arrogate the direction of our affairs, without any degree of authority derived from the people" (*Annals of Congress*, 3d Cong., 2d sess., 793–94, 796).

4. See Address of the House of Representatives to the President, 21 Nov. 1794, and n. 1.

5. In his 29 Nov. reply to the House, Washington stated in part that "it is far better that the artful approaches to such a situation of things should be checked by the vigilant and duly admonished patriotism of our fellow-citizens, than that the evil should increase until it becomes necessary to crush it by the strength of their arms" (*Annals of Congress*, 3d Cong., 2d sess., 950).

6. Monroe to the secretary of state, 15 Sept. 1794 (*ASP, Foreign Relations*, 1:675–76).

From James Monroe

DEAR SIR   PARIS Novr. 30th. 1794.

By not hearing from you before this I conclude I shall not untill after you shall have commenc'd the session in Phila. Indeed I calculate upon hearing at the same time from Mr. Jefferson and Mr. Jones, for surely they will not decline writing by you to be forwarded thence with your communications. I therefore wait the lapse of sufficient time to bring yr. letters here with that kind of patience which arises from a conviction I shall not get them sooner. You will I presume be able at the same time

to give me a good idea of the prospect before you, and which I conclude
has become more decisively settled, in regard to the European powers,
than when I left you: for surely the publick mind has before this expressed itself, in this respect, with such a degree of force, as to have left
no alternative to the representative.

I gave you in my last, wh. contained several sheets, a detail of the
incidents up to that date, with respect to the general state of affrs. here
as well as of those which more particularly regarded myself. The interval between that & the present time, presents to view a series of events
favorable to France, both in her internal & external operations. The fall
of Robertspiere bequeathed to the convention the remnant of a controversy, whose fortune seemed to be marked by that event. The issue
at stake with him was, whether the party of the mountain and which was
in truth always the minority in the convention, or in other words the
Jacobins whose principal members consisted of that party, connected
with the military force & commune of the city (who were likewise all
of that society) shod. by means of terror, for as they had the force of
the city in their hands they could at pleasure & legally put it in motion,
or the majority in the convention shod. govern France. His fate settled
the point: in that respect, but yet it did not give entire repose to the
country. As only the principal members of the party were cut off it
was natural that those who were left shod. still be disquieted; it was
likewise natural that many of those in the preponderating party, should
be well disposed in gratification of private revenge, to pursue the advantage they had gained and endeavor to exterpate all their enemies.
I am happy however to assure you, that no event has taken place which
in any respect discredits the councils of the country: on the contrary I
infer from what has passed the happiest result for the future. The
mountain party in convention & more especially in the Jacobin society
have done much to provoke the indignation of the convention, but the
indignation of the publick mind has constantly preceded that of that
body, if indeed it can be said to have shewn any. It has in no instance
taken any step which was not previously marked out & called for by
the publick voice. In the extremities of this society, which was exciting
by all kind of practices, commotions thro' the country, it at length
yeilded to solicitations from many quarters to shut its door in Paris;
and to similar solicitations & denunciations from every quarter, it has
likewise yeilded, after solemn discussion, & in the most formal manner,
one of its members, to trial before the revolutionary tribunal; one
Carrere a man infamous for every possible vice & enormity and which
were perpetrated in his mission to Nantes.

There was a strong disposition in the preponderating party not to
proceed to this extremity agnst the Jacobins of Paris, from the appre-

hension it might be deemed an incroachment upon the essential rights of men, establishing in that respect a dangerous precedent, but as it was in truth in a state of rebellion agnst the convention, and it was manifest that if it prevailed the representative body would be annihilated, and complete disorder insue, there seemed to be a necessity for that body to adopt a remedy commensurate with the evil. None would be so but that of shutting up their door and which was accordingly done, and since which things have remained in a state of tranquility.

Whether any other members of the late dominant party will be executed for I take it for granted Carrere will be is in my opinion doubtful. If any have committed enormities in their missions thro' the country like him they certainly ought to be. There was obviously a belief existing generally upon my arrival, that some of the old committee of p: safety merited the fate of Robertspiere, but it was equally obvious that a majority were of opinion it were best to cultivate the esteem of the world, by sheathing the sword of justice & suffering even villains to escape. I was therefore persuaded it would be practicable to suspend the guillotin at that point, yeilding to it only such men as Carrere, and whose punishment would tend to retrieve the injurd fame of France, and form a bright ornament in the character of the present party; and subsequent events have convinc'd me that this was then practicable: perhaps it is still so: but the members of the late dominant party have lately committed several capital blunders, and put in hazard their own safety when it might otherwise have been avoided. It was certain that the safety of these members depended upon the magnanimity, the benevolence and the patriotism of the majority of the present reigning party. To these virtues therefore shod. the appl. have been made, nor shod. any step have been taken to diminish the effect. The contrary however has been the case in many respects, for it is well known that some of these members & particularly Billaud Varrennes were active in stirring up the Jacobins agnst the Convention, this member having in pointed terms denounc'd the reigning party not many days before the hall was shut up, to the society. Barrere likewise presented himself forward a few days after that event, in a manner to excite the disgust of that party by seconding a motion for breaking up the Convention & putting the constitution into motion, a measure he was formerly opposed to, and perhaps would not now have thought of had the Jacobins retained the ascendancy. At this too I was the more surprised because he was noted for dexterity upon all previous occasions, in the vicisitudes of the several preceeding parties, and had likewise observed his usual circumspection in other respects since the fall of Robertspiere. These members have likewise erred in the countenance they have given to Carrere, for instead of drawing a line between themselves and him & yeilding him to the justice of their country, they appeared for sometime to consider his as a common cause, and acted accordingly. It is true in the close of the business, and when the appeal nominal, as yeas & naes were taken, of 500 members present 498 voted there was cause of accusation, & that he shod. be sent to the tribunal revolutionary & the other two were for his trial but hesitated on some collateral point.

Upon the whole however I am of opinion that as it respects the publick councils every thing bears the happiest aspect. There may yet be some irregularities, but not of the kind heretofore experienc'd. And with respect to the state of the war the prospect is still more brilliant. Mæstricht & Nimeughen have lately surrendered and opened the road directly for Holland, upon wh. the French troops are now pressing with an energy not to be resisted. The probability is they will take possession of it unless prevented by inundation, a resource not to be relied on in case the winter shod. be severe, and which will in any event ruin the country for many years to come. This must strike terror into Engld. & probably shake that govt. In Spn. their success has been equally great. The Sph. forces have been routed in several actions, many prisoners & posts taken, & in fact the prospect of atchieving in that quarter what they please. The present is certainly the moment for our govt. to act with energy. They shod. in my judgment put the British beyond the lakes & open the Missisippi & by so doing we shod. be courted into peace by those powers rather than threatened with war; and merely by negotiation we know we can do nothing, on the contrary we play the game that those powers wish us to play, for we give them time to try their fortune with France reserving to themselves the right of pressing us after that contest shall be over, let the issue be as it may, even in case they ⟨shod⟩ be, as they certainly will be defeated. If we took this step at this moment France would in my opinion not make peace without us, in case they considered it as war, but as they find that we stand well with France they wod. probably not consider it in that light. One other great advantage resulting from this measure is that it wod. be supported by the wishes of all America & take with it in particular the suffrage of the western people. This wod. terminate at once the discontents in that quarter: how much more wise & benevolent is that policy which points the force of the country against the invaders of the publick rights than that which turns it against the members of the society itself. I do not by this mean to intimate that the effort to crush the mov'ment at Fort Pitt was unwise—I think otherwise for the law must be supported, but I likewise think that if the one above suggested would produce the same effect in that respect, and a very salutary one in many others it ought to be adopted. Indeed I am persuaded it has been adopted, for many reports authorize a belief that Genl. Wayne has had a rencounter with the British & taken from them the post at the rapids of the Miamis.[1]

You will readily conceive that the mission of Mr. Jay & his continuance in Engld. have greatly embarrass'd my movments here. It has been intimated in such manner as to inspire doubts that a mere reparation for injuries cod. not be the sole motive; and in proportion as those doubts have existed have they produc'd a repellant disposition towards me not from any real distrust in me, but from a distrust of the Ex: admn. I have done all in my power to remove it and hope I have now succeeded. But I trust he will not stay there the winter for by so doing he only gives the British time, which they want, & keeps alive the ill founded suspicion here.

You will hear with surprise that I have been favd. with a letter from Mr. Gardoqui and that the object was to get within the republick upon pretence of ill-health but in my judgment to begin a negotiation for peace. I laid his letters for I recd. two, before the committee intimating what I believed to be the object & avail'd myself of the opportunity to state our situation with Spn.; so that instead of bringing his wishes forward in a manner to create a belief we assisted Spn. in her efforts for peace, as was I presume intended by writing me on the subject, I took the opportunity of urging France to make no peace with her untill the Missisippi be opened, since in case we were involv'd in a war with her France wod. be forc'd to join, so that it were better compromise the whole at once. I am certain the incident has produc'd a good effect.

Soon after this it was intimated to me by the Committee of P. S. that they wanted to borrow some money of us. I then took occasion to state our situation with Engld. in like manner pressing them to make our dispute theirs—and whether we embarked in the war or not to aid our negotiation for the posts so as to have theirs & our dispute settled at the same time. I am convinc'd the communication has been useful.

I think it probable they will ask our aid in money—& I most sincerely wish we may give it. I shod. suppose we might lend 40. or 50. millions of livres, by the genl., the State govts. & individuals. If a loan of the latter kind was opened guarantied by the congress the whole wod. be loaned by foreigners if necessary and I am sure it wod. be paid by this govt. as they have great resources in national property.[2]

I have nominated Mr. Skipwith as Consul for Paris. If appointed I shall want some one to supply his place. I leave this to yr.self in concert with Mr. R. to send the suitable person. First however I wish you to communicate to Colo. Burr that if Mr. Prevost[3] will come it shall be for him. Mr. Purvyance[4] is here in trade & declines the offer in case Mr. P. will not accept as in that case it wod. be offered. How wod. Mr. Dawson do if Prevost wod. not come. I fear he is distressed and as an old acquaintance having some claim on me[5] & which I never wish to disappoint, I confess if he wod. be benefited by it which I doubt under any other alternative, I shod. be glad to serve him. But this is only for yr. consideration for I leave it to you as mentioned above in concert with Mr. R.

I feel extremely anxious to hear from you. My conduct here is by this time before you & the subject of criticism—and yr. measures are greatly interesting to me. I hope therefore soon to hear on these topics as well as whatever else you deem necessary to be notic'd.

We had in idea a loan here to be vested in America. I am satisfied it may be procured if desirable. Provided I established the fund in Hamburg for instance to the amt. of 5. or 10.000 £ sterg. to be securd by landed security such as the property purchased could you draw for it so as to answer the purpose? Where wod. you vest it? Answer me upon these points & in the interim I will endeavor in reply to assure you where the fund will be plac'd & to what amount. I really think it may be counted on. And in the interim if a most elegible contract offers itself you may draw on me to be paid in Hamburg at three months sight for three thousand pounds Sterg. in one two or three bills. I am sure I can borrow the money there of Van Stophort of the house of V. S. of Amsterdam; this gentn. lives here but cod. place the money there for me & I think wod. at a word.

I wrote you not long since by a Mr. Swan—his character is better known to me now than it then was. Be cautious of him & give the same hint to Mr. R. Majr. B.[6] & other freds. to whom I wrote. This you may do without compromitting me except where perfectly safe.

There are many things here which I think wod. suit you. I beg you to give me a list of what you want, such as clocks carpets glas⟨s⟩ furniture table linnen &ca—they are cheaper infinitely than with you considering I have advantage of the exchge & you might pay the amt. to Mr. Jones. Tell Mr. R. I shall also be glad to serve him. I beg you to command me freely for I need not tell how happy it will make me to serve you. Ask Taylor if I shall send him a good watch.

Will you be so kind as obtain from Colo. Orr or if he has them not get him to bring them hereaft⟨er⟩ my patents for my western land consisting of 20.000 acres on Rock Castle & 5 or 6.000 beyond the Ohio & give to Mr. Jones. Captn. Fower acts for me. My other items you will recollect of Vermont & New Yk. Remember me affectionately to all friends of both houses, to Mr. Beckley—to Mr. Yard[7] & Dr. Stevens[8] &

families. Tell them Mrs. M. & child are well & desire to be remembered. Very affecy. I am Dear Sir Yr. friend & servant

JAS. MONROE

Mr. Paine who is of my family[9] desires to be remembered to you. He will be with you in the spring. Not being able to present Mr. Fauchets draft here for 3000 dolrs. on acct. of the depreciatn I shall return it to Mr. Randolph & subject it to Mr. Jones's order. Will you attend to this.

RC (DLC). Docketed by JM, with his notation: "Opened at Halifax & thence forwarded in that state." On the opening of this captured letter and Monroe's diplomatic correspondence by British officials, see Edmund Randolph to George Hammond, 21 May, 22 May, and 23 June 1795 (DNA: RG 59, Domestic Letters); Hammond to Randolph, 21 May 1795, two letters (DNA: RG 59, Notes from the British Legation).

1. John Graves Simcoe, lieutenant-governor of Upper Canada, had built Fort Miami at the foot of the Maumee Rapids in April. The battle of Fallen Timbers was fought within sight of the fort on 20 Aug. Maj. Gen. Anthony Wayne burned a trading post and crops in the vicinity, but British forces retained possession of Fort Miami until the Jay treaty was ratified. Newspapers printed an exchange of diplomatic correspondence between Edmund Randolph, British minister George Hammond, and Simcoe concerning the British occupation of Fort Miami (Knopf, *Anthony Wayne*, pp. 335, 351–54; Philadelphia *Gazette of the U.S.*, 5 Dec. 1794).

2. For a discussion of the issues confronting Monroe as U.S. minister to France, see Ammon, *James Monroe*, pp. 118–30.

3. John Bartow Prevost was Aaron Burr's stepson. In 1778 Monroe had met Prevost's mother, Theodosia Bartow Prevost, and in May 1794 Burr urged Monroe to appoint Prevost as his secretary. Monroe eventually passed over Prevost, "for I consider Burr as a man to be shunned . . . an unprincipled adventurer and whom it is better to get rid of at once." Jefferson appointed Prevost a judge of the superior court for the territory of Orleans in 1804 (ibid., p. 25; Burr to Monroe, 30 May 1794 [DLC: Monroe Papers]; Monroe to JM, 5 Aug. 1795 [partly in code] [DLC: Rives Collection, Madison Papers]; *Senate Exec. Proceedings*, 1:476, 477, 2:8, 10).

4. John Henry Purviance, a native of Baltimore, succeeded Fulwar Skipwith as Monroe's private secretary. He later served in the same capacity when Monroe was minister to England, 1803–4 (Ammon, *James Monroe*, pp. 143, 233, 620 n. 28).

5. John Dawson had been a political colleague of Monroe's since the Virginia ratifying convention of 1788. In a House of Delegates debate on proposed constitutional amendments, Federalist Francis Corbin on 7 Dec. 1793 had denounced Monroe's support for further amendments. Dawson confronted Corbin and threatened to inform Monroe of the incident; the House declared Dawson guilty of a breach of its privileges (Risjord, *Chesapeake Politics*, pp. 432–33).

6. Probably Pierce Butler.

7. James Yard was U.S. consul at Saint Croix, Danish West Indies, 1791–92. He was a merchant with premises on the Walnut Street Wharf and at 139 Chestnut Street in Philadelphia (*Senate Exec. Proceedings*, 1:76; Yard to Jefferson, 30 Oct. 1792 [DNA: RG 59, Consular Despatches, Saint Croix]; Hardie, *Philadelphia Directory* [1794 ed.], p. 172).

8. Edward Stevens was James Yard's brother-in-law and had known Alexander Hamilton from childhood in the West Indies. Trained in medicine at Edinburgh,

in 1793 he treated the treasury secretary and his wife for yellow fever in Philadelphia. His cold bath treatment for the disease was publicized as the "Federalist" cure, as opposed to the "Republican" purging treatment of Benjamin Rush (Syrett and Cooke, *Papers of Hamilton*, 15:325 n. 1, 332 n. 2).

9. Thomas Paine was released from prison through Monroe's efforts and lived at the U.S. minister's residence from November 1794 to the spring of 1796 (Ammon, *James Monroe*, pp. 135–37).

¶ From James Madison, Sr. Letter not found. *3 December 1794.* Acknowledged in JM's 14 Dec. 1794 letter to his father. Asks if JM can contribute financially toward the gristmill that JM's family planned to build. Inquires about milling JM's wheat crop.

To James Monroe

DEAR SIR   PHILADA. DECR. 4. 1794

I did not receive your favor of Sepr. 2d. the only one yet come to hand, till yesterday. The account of your arrival and reception had some time ago found its way to us thro' the English Gazettes. The language of your address to the Convention was certainly very grating to the ears of many here; and would no doubt have employed the tongues and the pens too of some of them, if external as well as internal circumstances had not checked them; but more particularly, the appearance about the same time of the Presidents letter and those of the Secretary of State.[1] Malicious criticisms if now made at all are confined to the little circles which relish that kind of food. The sentiments of the P. will be best communicated by Mr. R. You are right in your conjecture both as to the facility given to the Envoy Extry: by the triumphs of France, and the artifice of referring it to other causes. The prevailing idea here is that the mission will be successful, tho' it is scarcely probable that it will prove so in any degree commensurate to our rights, or even to the expectations which have been raised: Whilst no industry is spared to prepare the public mind to eccho the praises which will be rung to the address of the Negociator, and the policy of defeating the commercial retaliations proposed at the last session. It will not be easy however to hide from the view of the judicious & well disposed part of the Community, that every thing that may be obtained from G. B. will have been yielded by the fears inspired by those retaliating measures, and by the state of affairs in Europe.

You will learn from the Newspapers and official communications the unfortunate scene in the Western parts of Penna. which unfolded itself during the recess. The history of its remote & immediate causes, the measures produced by it, and the manner in which it has been closed, does not fall within the compass of a letter. It is probable also that many explanatory circumstances are yet but imperfectly known. I can only refer to the printed accounts which you will receive from the Department of State, and the comments which your memory will assist you in making on them. The event was in several respects a critical one for the cause of liberty, and the real authors of it, if not in the service, were in the most effectual manner, doing the business of Despotism. You well know the general tendency of insurrections to increase the momentum of power. You will recollect the particular effect, of what happened some years ago in Massachts. Precisely the same calamity was to be dreaded on a larger scale in this Case. There were eno' as you may well suppose ready to give the same turn to the crisis, and to propagate the same impressions from it. It happened most auspiciously however that with a spirit truly republican, the people every where and of every description condemned the resistance to the will of the Majority, and obeyed with alacrity the call to vindicate the authority of the laws. You will see in the answer of the House of Reps. to the P's speech, that the most was made of this circumstance as an antidote to the poisonous influence to which Republicanism was exposed. If the insurrection had not been crushed in the manner it was I have no doubt that a formidable attempt would have been made to establish the principle that a standing army was necessary for *enforcing the laws.* When I first came to this City about the middle of October, this was the fashionable language. Nor am I sure that the attempt would not have been made, if the P. could have been embarked in it, and particularly if the temper of N. England had not been dreaded on this point. I hope we are over that danger for the present. You will readily understand the business detailed in the Newspapers, relating to the denunciation of the "Self created Societies." The introduction of it by the President was perhaps the greatest error of his political life. For his sake, as well as for a variety of obvious reasons, I wish'd it might be passed over in silence by the H. of Reps. The answer was penned with that view; and so reported. This moderate course would not satisfy those who hoped to draw a party-advantage out [of] the P.'s popularity. The game was, to connect the democratic Societies with the odium of the insurrection—to connect the Republicans in Congs. with those Societies—to put the P. ostensibly at the head of the other party, in opposition to both, and by these means prolong the illusions in the North—& try a new experiment on the South. To favor the project, the answer of the Senate was accelerated & so framed as to draw the P. into the most pointed reply on the subject of the Societies. At the same time, The answer of the H. of R. was procrastinated till the example of the Senate, & the commitment of the P. could have their full operation. You will see how nicely the House was divided, and how the matter went off. As yet the discussion has not been revived by the newspaper combatants. If it Should and equal talents be opposed, the result can not fail to wound the P's popularity more than any thing that has yet happened. It must be seen that no two principles can be either more indefensible in reason, or more dangerous in practice—than that 1. arbitrary denunciations may punish, what the law permits, & what the Legislature has no right, by law, to prohibit—and that 2. the Govt. may stifle all censures whatever on its misdoings; for if it be itself the Judge it will never allow any censures to be just, and if it can suppress censures flowing from one lawful source it may those flowing from any other—from the press and from individuals as well as from Societies, &c.

The elections for the H. of Reps. are over in N. Engd. & Pa. In Massts. they have been contested so generally as to rouse the people compleatly from their lethargy, tho not sufficiently to eradicate the errors which have prevailed there. The principal members have been all severely pushed; several changes have taken place, rather for the better; and *not one* for the worse. In Pena. Republicanism claims 9 out of 13, notwithstanding the very disadvantageous circumstances under which the election was made. In N. Y. it is expected the proportion of sound men will be increased. In Maryland the choice has been much as heretofore. Virga. & N. C. will probably make no changes for the worse. In the former Mr. Griffin resigns his pretensions. Mr. Lee will probably either do so or be dropped by his constituents.[2] In S. Carolina the death of Gillon will probably let in Mr. Barnwell. In Delaware Patten is elected in lieu of Latimer. On the whole the prospect is rather improved than otherwise. The election of Swanwick as a Republican, by the commercial & political Metropolis of the U. S. in preference to Fitzimmons, is of itself of material consequence, and is so felt by the party to which the latter belongs. For what relates to the Senate, I trust to the letters which you will receive from Brown & Langdon, whom I have apprized of this opportunity of answering yours. I shall observe only that Tazewell & S. Tho: Mason were elected by the most decided majorities, to fill your vacancy and that of Col. Taylor who gave in his resignation. Not a single anti-republican was started. Mr. Dawson was a candidate and got 40 votes agst. 122. Brooke[3] is also Govr. by a pretty decided vote. We had 90 odd agst. 60 odd given to Wood his only competitor.

I had a letter lately from Mr. Jefferson; He has been confined by the Rhematism since August, and is far from being entirely recovered. Mr. T. M. Randolph has also been in a ticklish situation. What it is at present I can not say. Mr. Jones was well a few days ago. He was then setting out to Loudon where he has made a great purchase of land from Col.

Chs. Carter. I infer from his letters to me that you are included in it. He will no doubt write you fully on that subject, or more probably has written already.

I have not recd. any thing from Wilkinson—nor from Vermont: nor heard any thing relating to your interests in N. York. I have given notice to Mr. Yard & Docr. Stephens of this conveyance and expect both will write. Mrs. Heilager is also here on her way to St. Croix and will no doubt write to Mrs. Monroe. She tells me all friends are well in N. York. I hope her letter will give all the particulars which may be interesting.

When in Albemarle last fall I visited your farm along with Mr. Jefferson; and viewed the scites out of which a choice is to be made for your House. The one preferred by us is that which we favored originally on the East side of the road, near the field not long since opened. All that could be suggested by way of preparation was, that Trees be planted promiscuously & pretty thickly ⟨in⟩ the field adjoining the wood. In general your farm appeared to be as well as was to be expected. Your upper farm I did not see, being limited in my stay in that quarter.

I have just seen Mr. Ross, who tells me he has recd. your letter. He would write by this opportunity, but wishes to be more full than the time will permit. We expect another will offer in a few weeks when we shall all continue our communications. I should say more to you now, if I could say it in cypher.

Present my best respects to Mrs. Monroe and Eliza, and tell them I shall be able on their return to present them with a new acquaintance who is prepared by my representations to receive them with all the affection which they merit, & who I flatter myself will be entitled to theirs. The event which put this in my power took place on the 15th. of Sepr. We are at present inhabitants of the House which you occupied last winter & shall continue in it during the Session. With my sincerest wishes for your happiness and that of your amiable family, I remain affectionately

J///////////

Hamilton has given notice that he means to resign. Knox means to do the same.[4] It is conjectured that the former will contend for the Govr. of N. York. Burr will be the competitor.

RC (DLC). Addressed by JM to Monroe in Paris. Docketed by Monroe. JM obscured his signature, perhaps from a concern that the letter might be intercepted.

1. Philadelphia newspapers printed Washington's 28 May letter of credence for Monroe to the French Committee of Public Safety (DLC: Washington Papers)

and Edmund Randolph's two letters of 10 June to that committee (see Monroe to JM, 2 Sept. 1794, n. 5) (*Aurora General Advertiser*, 15 and 18 Nov. 1794; *Philadelphia Gazette*, 15 and 19 Nov. 1794).

2. Federalist Richard Bland Lee, who represented the district composed of Fairfax, Loudoun, and Prince William counties, had opposed JM's commercial discrimination proposals. On 7 June 1794 the Democratic-Republican Society of Dumfries adopted a resolution declaring him "altogether unworthy of the future confidence of Good Republicans." Republican Richard Brent defeated Lee in the congressional election on 16 Mar. 1795 (Parsons et al., *United States Congressional Districts*, p. 74; Foner, *Democratic-Republican Societies*, p. 350; *BDC*, pp. 633, 1277; Hening, *Statutes*, 13:332).

3. Robert Brooke (ca. 1761–1800) studied at the University of Edinburgh and served in the Revolution. He represented Spotsylvania County in the House of Delegates, 1791–94. A Republican, he served as governor, 1794–96, and attorney general, 1796–1800, of Virginia (St. George Tucker Brooke, "The Brooke Family," *VMHB*, 19 [1911]: 100–101; Swem and Williams, *Register*, pp. ix, 352).

4. Hamilton's resignation as secretary of the treasury took effect on 31 Jan. 1795; Knox resigned as secretary of war effective 31 Dec. 1794 (Hamilton to Washington, 1 Dec. 1794, Syrett and Cooke, *Papers of Hamilton*, 17:413; Knox to Washington, 28 Dec. 1794 [DLC: Washington Papers]).

From Joseph Jones

[ca. 5 December 1794]

... We are here much at a loss to account for Hamilton's letter giving notice of his intention to resign. . . . It will make an opening which, if filled by a proper person, of staunch republican principles, will prove an important acquisition. . . . Is there any reason to expect Mr. Jay's mission will produce compensation for the plundered merchants and the execution of the treaty of peace? ...

Printed extract (*The Collector*, 7 [1894–95]: 83). Listed as "2 pp, 4to, 1794."

From Alexander Balmain

DEAR SIR   WINCHESTER 8th. Decr. 1794

I wrote you, as I said I would, by Mr. Adam Douglass one of our Merchants, but, to my great Mortification, he did not deliver the letter, & brought it back to me. I waited on Doctor Baldwin with the money you left in my hands as a compensation for his Professional Services. The Doctor said it was perfectly satisfactory, & that he had made no charge against you upon his books.

I am now to thank you for your favor of the 23d Ult. enclosing the

Presidents Speech. If in expressing what has occurr'd to me on this very delicate subject, & that too before I saw any of those debates it has unhappily occasioned in your house I should appear to differ from one whose character I respect & whose abilities & virtues are so greatly superior to my own I trust you will make every allowance, & ascribe it not to a love of contradiction, but to what I conceive to be a regard to the freedom of opinion, & of truth, as far as it is understood by me. In general, I would observe, The Knowledge & Morals of the people are the only foundations on which their liberties can securely rest. Of Morals humility appears to be a very principal ingredient. The Self created Societies disclaim it, deeming themselves competent to decide on every subject & every question. As to knowledge not having made Politics a regular study, a few Members only excepted, it seems impossible they should know much about them. I candidly confess myself adverse to these Societies, in their Origin, their principles, their object & their end, & cannot persuade myself that they are necessary in a government like our's—Or that they contribute ought to the illumination of the Understanding or the improvement of the heart. If the President thought that an opposition to the laws was fomented by these societies, in tracing the progress of that opposition, it would have appeared to be his duty to have said so. If it was a fact, & deem'd so by the Senate, they could do no less than Second his denunciation. Perhaps it would have been as well not to have taken any Notice at all of these combinations— Passing them over in silent contempt. This conjecture which rose within me, previous to my reading the debates, has been strengthen'd since. I sincerely regrett the heat & ferment with which this subject has agitated the house of R——s. Pity it is that so much time should be thus wasted. One thing appears certain to Me, that these Societies have contributed greatly to much distress, embarrassment, public & private calamity. They therefore, in my judgment, merited so much notice, as to be held up to the people whose Friends they had poisoned, as the Objects of reprehension & reprobation. To this let me add, that if the Majority of the people in the U. S. be averse to such societies as I believe they are, why should not their Representatives censure them. After all it is possible, that human weakness may have had its share in dictating the Denunciation. The P——t is unquestionably a great & a good man. How far his feelings have been hurt by the arrogant censures of uninformed presumptuous individuals, it is not for Me to say. Acting as I believe he did from the purest principles of Patriotism conscious to himself of no sinister Motives, he must have been More than Man not to have felt some degree of resentment, and a hypocrite if he had dissembled it. To feel as a Man, & to express those feelings with candor is in My Judgment true policy.

Thus Sir, I have given you a long letter on a subject, (politics) which I have not studied much, & must again beg pardon for the crudeness & inaccuracy of the sentiments & expression. The Post is about setting out. I must therefore conclude by offering my best respects, in which, I am joined by Mrs. Bn. to Mrs. Madison, yourself & Miss Payne. I am, with the truest esteem & respect, Dr. Sir, Your Most obedt servant

ALEXR. BALMAIN

RC (DLC). Docketed by JM.

From Thomas Jefferson

TH: J. TO MR. MADISON.   Dec. 9. 94.

I write this merely as a way bill. The Orange post arrives at Charlottesville on Tuesday morning about 10. oclock & returns in half an hour. The Richmond post arrives in Charlottesville on Tuesday evening & returns on Friday morning. I wish to know the difference this makes in the conveyance of a letter to Philadelphia. I therefore write this by the Orange post, and will write such another by that of Richmond, & pray you to note to me the days on which you recieve both. Your favor of Nov. 16. came to hand the 2d. inst. Our militia are returning it is said, without having been to Detroit. Where then have they been?[1] The explanation of this phænomenon is ardently wished here. Adieu. Yours affectionately.

FC (DLC: Jefferson Papers).

1. Jefferson's rhetorical question raised the issue—of current concern to Republicans—that the military forces were suppressing domestic resistance (the Whiskey Insurrection) rather than attacking the British, who continued to occupy Detroit and other U.S. western posts. In his 20 Nov. 1794 letter to William Branch Giles (DLC: Jefferson Papers), Jefferson wrote, "We are here big with expectations of hearing that Detroit is attacked by Govr. Lee, as the declared purpose of that armament is hardly sufficient to be used as the ostensible one. It is presumed that the Executive must have serious information from mr. Jay."

Military Establishment

[9 December 1794]

Nicholas called for a committee "to enquire how far the act of Congress for the defence of the frontier had been complied with, and what number of the men ordered to be raised are yet to be enlisted." JM had reported that act from committee in 1792 (*PJM*, 14:199 and n. 1).

Mr. Madison observed that a gentleman from New-Jersey (Mr. Dayton) had stated three different ways, in which the act was explained. He said that nothing required greater precision than a law which authorised the levying of troops. He suggested the propriety of an enquiry into the defects of the law in question, that there might be no room for mistake in applying it.

Philadelphia Gazette, 9 Dec. 1794 (reprinted in *Aurora General Advertiser*, 16 Dec. 1794, *Dunlap and Claypoole's Am. Daily Advertiser*, 17 Dec. 1794, and *Independent Gazetteer*, 17 Dec. 1794). Nicholas amended his motion as suggested by JM. The House appointed a committee to conduct the inquiry, chaired by Nicholas who reported on 15 Dec. (*Annals of Congress*, 3d Cong., 2d sess., 976).

Naturalization

[9 December 1794]

On 8 December the House appointed JM chairman of a select committee to report a bill to amend the Naturalization Act of 1790.

Mr. Madison gave notice that to-morrow, he should move for leave to bring in a bill, to amend an act for establishing a uniform system of naturalization in the United States. He did not wish to discourage foreigners who desired to incorporate themselves with the body political of America. At the same time, he thought the present law did not fully answer the purpose for which it was designed.

Philadelphia Gazette, 9 Dec. 1794 (reprinted in *Aurora General Advertiser*, 16 Dec. 1794, *Dunlap and Claypoole's Am. Daily Advertiser*, 17 Dec. 1794, and *Independent Gazetteer*, 17 Dec. 1794).

From Joseph Jones

Dr Sr.   Fredg. 11th. Decr. 1794.

Since my last to you I have recd. a letter from Monroe dated the 4th & 6th Septr.[1] It came by the last post and cost me 5/9—from whence or how it came I cannot discover by the marks on the letter. He informs me they were all well, and that he expected to write to Yourself and Mr. Jefferson by the same opportunity—that he had before written to the Secretary of State. The news it contains we have long since had. With respect to money matters he says he had requested Mr. Randolph to furnish me on his accot. with 1000 Dols.—this I expected wod. have been done as I informed Mr. Randolph on my application to him Col.

Monroe having spoken to that effect when we parted—this was meant to enable me to satisfy any balances due from him here that called for present payment as well as to aid in the purchase from Carter shod. I make it. The inclosed abstrac⟨t⟩ from his letter will shew you what he has written respecting these matters. I shall inclose one also to Mr. Randolph. Presuming the balance of the 1000 dols. not already advanced will be furnished to my draught (which I conjecture will be about £125. this money[)]] could a bill Be negociated on Monroe for about £200 payable in Paris Amsterdam or Rotterdam it wod. enable me to compleat the first payment to Carter wch. is to be the last day of this month and also to satisfy some balances from him that require present payment—subsequent arrangements can be made in time for the remainder of what he may owe or have to pay on accot. of the land purchased from Carter. You will be so kind as to converse with Mr. Randolph and give me information on these matters as the time of payment is at hand and a deed for the Land taken. I am Yr. friend & Servt

Jos: Jones.

RC (DLC). Docketed by JM. Enclosure not found.

1. Monroe's 4 Sept. letter to Jones has a postscript of 6 Sept. (photocopy [DLC: Monroe Papers]).

From Thomas Jefferson

Th: J. to J. Madison   Friday morning. Dec. 12. 1794.

I wrote you a kind of way-bill by the Orange post, which arrived at, & left Charlottesville on Tuesday forenoon. I write this by the Richmond post which leaves Charlottesville on Friday Morning. The object is to know what difference there will be in the arrival of the two letters at Philadelphia.

We have nothing new for you; for it is not new that we have fine weather. It is, & has been delicious, with only two short intervals of cold. In one of them (about the 22d of Nov.) it was extraordinarily cold, the mercury being at 19°. But it was only three mornings below freezing. In the other (Dec. 4.) it was one morning below the freezing point. But it has never once continued so thro the day. We have had fine rains at proper intervals, which is the only interruption our ploughs have had. Corn has sold at 6/6 per barrel, half goods, half cash. It is now at 8/. Purchasers talk of that, sellers of 10/. Wheat 5/ in goods. Adieu. Yours affectionately.

FC (DLC: Jefferson Papers).

To James Madison, Sr.

Your favor of the 24th. Ulto: was answered last week.[1] I have since recd. that of the 3d. inst: the cheif object of which is to learn whether I shall be able to contribute an effective proportion to the advances which will be wanted for the Mill. To this enquiry I can only say in general that, tho' it is possible I may not be able to co-operate as much as might be desireable, I have several resources from each of which I have a prospect that is promising. I can in any event resort to a sale of my land in N. York which I am well informed continues to rise in value, and will always be vendible. The monies which I have recd. and expect to receive here in the course of the winter, would of themselves answer all my purposes, were it not for the enormous expense of living, and the necessity of adding some expensive articles to our stock of accomodations. Among these will be a carriage to remove us to Virga. in the Spring. The one we have, tho' a very neat & costly one, was so infamously executed, and suffered so much from the roads, above the mountains & on the way here, that it is a perfect wreck. No workman will undertake to refit it for much less than the price of a new one, nor allow me more than a hundred dollars for it, tho' it cost near four times that sum; and will, from the universal rise of prices, require more than four times that sum to replace it. Of the general expense of living here I can scarcely give you an idea. Prices of all kinds are 50 PerCt. higher than the last year, when they were thought to have attained their ultimate point of extravagance. The allowance from the public, tho' sufficient for those who have no families, is far short where there is one. Notwithstanding all these drawbacks, I shall, however, if my receipts be not unnecessarily delayed, be able to bear my part in pushing on the Mill. I have several times suggested to you the sale of your certificates in my hands. I still think it an eligible measure, and the present moment is a favorable one. Stock is now at 22/6 in the pound, and it is very possible the state of things in Europe may force it up a little higher. If you will forward me a power to sell I can have it disposed of; and if you do not need the money yourself will allow you six perCt. till repaid, and engage to repay it within one year or two years at farthest; within which time I shall probably have it amply & easily in my power. I know not what to say as to the manufacturing of my wheat: but am willing to follow your judgment as it may decide in regard to your own crop. Flour is here at ten dollars a barrel. I suppose Mr. Dunbar will be as ready to take my crop in that state as in wheat, and allow me the market price. I wish the proceeds to pass into his hands, as I rely on his aid for the last payment to Majr. Lee, whenever I am drawn on for it. We have nothing new since my last. If you wish to have any thing procured here and sent round in the Spring, the sooner you apprise me of it the better, as favorable oppys. of getting what you want may occur in the course of the winter. As the post now goes by Orange Court House, you can write when you please, and I hope you will write often. Be so good as to let me know in your next how much wheat I have for market at each of the two places, as well as what the present aspect of the fields is. I am sorry to hear of the continued ill health of Mr. & Mrs. Macon. I hope it will press on him the expedien⟨cy⟩ of withdrawing himself from the waters of Chickahominy. ⟨We⟩ are well and offer our joint affections to you all. Yr. affe. son

Js. Madison Jr

RC (DLC). Franked and addressed by JM to his father at Orange Court House, "via Fredericksburg." Docketed by James Madison, Sr. Damaged by removal of seal.

1. Neither the letter from James Madison, Sr., nor JM's reply has been found.

¶ To the Right Reverend James Madison. Letter not found. *Ca. 14 December 1794.* Acknowledged in Bishop Madison's letter to JM of 24 Dec. 1794. Probably informs the bishop that JM does not plan to retire from Congress and so cannot sponsor in the Virginia General Assembly a state-supported university. Encloses John Penington's *Chemical and Economical Essays.*

¶ To James Monroe. Letter not found. *14 December 1794, Philadelphia.* Introduces Robert S. Van Rensselaer. RC offered for sale by Leonard & Co., Auctioneers, *Catalogue of a Valuable Private Library, Including . . . Rare Autograph Letters* (Boston, 9 May 1866), p. 15, item 7.

¶ To Hubbard Taylor. Letter not found. *Ca. 14 December 1794.* Acknowledged in Taylor to JM, 16 Jan. 1795. Agrees with Taylor's proposed settlement with Maj. William Moore of Orange County. Probably inquires about Kentucky lands belonging to JM's mother-in-law, Mary Coles Payne.

Compensation to Victims of the Whiskey Insurrection

[17 December 1794]

In his annual message to Congress, Washington urged that Congress provide compensation to victims of the Whiskey Insurrection. On 17 December the House began consideration of resolutions giving effect to his suggestion (*Annals of Congress*, 3d Cong., 2d sess., 790, 954, 967, 973, 987, 989).

Mr. Madison remarked that great respect was due to this proposition, both on account of the interesting occasion that produced it, and of *the quarter from whence it came*. But the more he revolved the subject in his mind, the more he was convinced that great circumspection was requisite, and that the House, for many reasons, ought to take as much time in deliberating upon what they were to do, as the nature of the subject will admit. He recommended the proposal of some gentlemen to let the affair lie over to next session.

It is no doubt proper to encourage a spirit for suppressing insurrections, and this measure is certainly calculated to promote that spirit. But, in his own judgment, Mr. Madison feared that it would likewise *encourage* insurrections. A great body of people were commonly engaged in such disturbances, who were not worth hanging, and to whom an established government usually held out an amnesty. By this means, great multitudes came in, and received pardon before the operations of chastisement began. The mob therefore, would in this case reason thus. As a croud we have a good chance to escape the gallows. Let us then plunder as fast as possible, because government will disburse the loss, and we shall not be forced to disgorge our booty. Mr. Madison thought that speculations of this kind might be entertained by future insurgents, if the house were instantly to vote a complete indemnification to the sufferers. Mr. Madison held the highest respect for the arguments and feelings of gentlemen who espoused the other side of the question. What he himself had just now suggested, he did not regard as *decisive* considerations, but yet as considerations of weight. His own impression was to *let the matter lie over till next session*, and then, those who had done their best in prosecuting, would come forward to that House, to claim compensation, under the most auspicious circumstances, and all which they can have recovered, will be saved to the state.

Philadelphia Gazette, 18 Dec. 1794 (reprinted in *Dunlap and Claypoole's Am. Daily Advertiser*, 20 Dec. 1794, and *Independent Gazetteer*, 24 Dec. 1794). Some words obscured by the damaged margin of the *Philadelphia Gazette* are here restored from *Dunlap and Claypoole's Am. Daily Advertiser*.

From James Monroe

DEAR SIR   PARIS Decr. 18. 1794.

I enclose you three letters one for Mr. R.[1] and the other two for whom ever you may think it best to direct them. You will in case they are delivered take a copy of one for yr.self, for I have not had time to write you nor indeed is it necessary on that subject as I send them open to yr. inspection. You will know whether there is any thing in the report & act accordingly either by presenting or suppressing all. I really wish mine to Mr. R. to be seen by the Pr: if expedient to be delivered. As to the persons to whom to be addressed I leave it entirely to you (advising that you consult with no one on that point lest it be known they were not addressed by me) but am inclined to think that one shod. be addressed to Langdon, & the other either to Burr, Butler or Ross.[2] As you will take a copy, you will be able to shew it to our Virga. friends and others as by my request & which will apologize for my not writing them. After all there is but one kind of policy which is safe, which is the *honest policy*. If it was intended to cultivate France by sending me here Jay shod. not have been sent to Engld.: but if indeed it was intended to cultivate Engld. it was wise to send some such person as myself here, for it was obvious that in proportion as we stood well with France shod. we be respected by Engld. I have not time to write you further at present than to assure you that the affrs. of the republick are in every respect in the most flourishing condition: wise, humane, & just in its councils, & eminently successful in its armies, & also that we are well. Affecy. I am yr. friend & servt

JAS. MONROE

As the letters are closed in great hurry, see that there are no inaccuracies. If Mr. Skipwith is confirmed, pray send Prevost off immediately. I repeat again that I put this business entirely under yr. care. You will readily conclude, if the report is entirely without foundation & wh. I most earnestly hope it is, that it will be best to suppress the whole.

RC and enclosures (DLC). RC docketed by JM. Sent via Le Havre (JM to Monroe, 6 Apr. 1795, which acknowledges receipt). Monroe stated that he was enclosing three copies of his 18 Dec. 1794 private letter to Edmund Randolph. One copy, in a clerk's hand except for Monroe's signature, is docketed by JM. Another copy, printed in Hamilton, *Writings of Monroe*, 2:154–61, is in a clerk's hand except for date, emendations, and signature in Monroe's hand. The third copy has not been found.

1. In the enclosure, Monroe informed the secretary of state that British newspaper accounts of the Jay treaty had arrived in France. The accounts "stated that Canada is to be ceded with the posts, that priviledges are to be given in the west Indias and other stipulations which imply an alliance offensive & defensive as likewise a commercial treaty." Monroe argued against any rapprochement with Britain, which in his view would jeopardize U.S. relations with France.

2. The Pennsylvania General Assembly elected Federalist James Ross as a U.S. senator after Albert Gallatin's disqualification. He took his seat on 24 Apr. 1794 and served until 1803. Washington appointed him a commissioner to deal with the Whiskey Insurrection, in which capacity he mollified the resistance leaders in western Pennsylvania.

From James Monroe

DEAR SIR.   PARIS Decr. 18. 1794.

I have addressed to your care a letter for Mr. R. & two others, to be addressed by you according to circumstances either to Langdon, Burr, Butler, Ross or any other person in case you shod. deem it proper to be presented at all & sent them in a packet by Havre. This which covers one for Mr. R. is to go by Bordeaux. I submit it entirely to you either to present or suppress it as the state of things in relation to the object may advise. In case it is presented you will excuse its being address'd to you, on acct. of its being a private letter & the necessity of preventing in case he shod. be absent its getting into the hands of another. Believe me sincerely yr. friend & servant

JAS. MONROE

RC (DLC). Docketed by JM, with the notation: "viâ Bourdeaux / accompanying letter of —— to Mr. R." Receipt acknowledged in JM to Monroe, 26 Mar. 1795. Monroe enclosed a copy (not found) of his 18 Dec. 1794 private letter to Edmund Randolph, which JM forwarded to Randolph (JM to Monroe, 27 Mar. 1795; acknowledged in Randolph to Monroe, 7 Apr. 1795, *ASP, Foreign Relations*, 1:701; see also Monroe's first letter to JM, 18 Dec. 1794, n. and n. 1).

Compensation to Victims of the Whiskey Insurrection

[19 December 1794]

The House continued its consideration of a resolution requesting the president "to cause an ascertainment to be made of the losses sustained by the officers of Government and other citizens, in their property, (in consequence of their exertions in support of the laws,) by the insurgents in the Western counties of Pennsylvania" (*Annals of Congress*, 3d Cong., 2d sess., 995). Hillhouse "moved to strike out the word *in* from the first resolution, and put into its place, *by the actual destruction of*—their property."

Mr. Madison apprehended that this amendment left the resolution as bad as it was before, if not worse. A person in the western counties had his horse stolen by the insurgents. But this did not imply the *absolute destruction* or *annihilation* of the horse. The amendment meant either too much or too little. It certainly could be no improvement on the resolution.

Philadelphia Gazette, 20 Dec. 1794. The House approved the resolution as amended by Hillhouse and on 6 Jan. 1795 passed a bill pursuant to the resolution, which Washington signed into law on 27 Feb. (*Annals of Congress*, 3d Cong., 2d sess., 1020, 1060; *U.S. Statutes at Large*, 1:423).

¶ To Joseph Jones. Letter not found. *Ca. 20 December 1794*. Referred to in Jones to JM, 23 and 26 Dec. 1794 and 13 Jan. 1795. Mentions that Secretary of State Edmund Randolph plans to write Jones about his request to draw a sum of money on Monroe's account.

To Thomas Jefferson

DEAR SIR   .   PHILADA. Decr. 21. 1794.

Your favor of the 9th. by the Orange post arrived here on the 18th. that of the 12 by the Richmond post, on the 20st. so that it appears the latter was one day less on the way. It is to be remarked however that as the Orange post leaves Charlottesville on tuesday, he might easily be in Fredericksburg on thursday, in time for the mail which passes thro' it on that day to Dumfries. If this despatch is not required of him it ought to be. It would make a difference of two days in the journey. Or at least the post might wait a day in Charlottesville and be in time for the saturday's mail at Fredericksburg.

Our weather here has been as fine as you describe yours. Yesterday there was a change. It was cold, cloudy, and inclined to snow. To day we have a bright day, and not very cold. Prices here are very different from yours. Wheat is at 13 or 14/. & flour in proportion. In general things are 50 PerCt. beyond the prices of last Winter. The phenomenon you wish to have explained is as little understood here as with you; but it would be here quite unfashionable to suppose it needed explanation. It is impossible to give you an idea of the force with which the tide has set in a particular direction. It has been too violent not to be soon followed by a change. In fact I think a change has begun already. The danger will then be of as violent a reflux to the opposite extreme.

The attack made on the essential & constitutional right of the Citizen, in the blow levelled at the "self-created Societies" does not appear to have had the effect intended. It is and must be felt by every man who values liberty, whatever opinion he may have of the use or abuse of it by those institutions. You will see that the appeal is begun to the public sentiment, by the injured parties. The Republican Society of Baltimore set the example.[1] That of Newark has advertised a meeting of its members.[2] It is said that if Edwd. Livingston, as is generally believed, has outvoted Watts, for the H. of Reps. he is indebted for it to the invigorated exertions of the Democratic Society of that place, of which he is himself a member.[3] In Boston the subject is well understood, and handled in the Newspaper on the republican side, with industry & address.[4]

The Elections in Massts. have turned out rather better than was of late expected. The two republican members have stood their ground; in spite of the most unexampled operations agst. them. Ames is said to owe his success to the votes of negroes & British sailors smuggled under a very lax mode of conducting the election there. Sedgwick & Goodhue have *bare* majorities. Dexter is to run another heat, but will succeed; Gerry, his only considerable compet[it]or & who would outvote him, refusing to be elected. There are several changes in the remainder of the Delegation, and some of them greatly for the better.[5] In New York there will be at least half republicans; perhaps more. It has unluckily happened that in 2 districts two *republicans* set up agst. *one* Anti: The consequence is that a man is re-elected who would not otherwise have taken the field: and there is some danger of a similar consequence in the other district. In N. Jersey, it is said that not more than one of the old members will be returned. The people all over the State are signing with avidity a remonstrance agst. the high salaries of the Govt.[6]

Hamilton is to resign, according to his own notification the last of Feby.[7] His object is not yet unfolded. Knox, as the shadow, follows the substance. Their successors are not yet designated by any circumstance that has escaped.

What think you of a project to disfranchise the insurgent Counties by a bill of exclusion agst. their Reps. in the State Legislature? The object is to pave the way for Bingham or Fitzimmons—as Senator—& to give an example for rejecting Galatine in the H. of Reps. at the next Congress—of which he is a member. The proposition has been laid on the table, and the event is uncertain.[8] There is some probabil[it]y the violence of the measure may defeat it; nor is it certain I am told that if carried thro', it would answer the purpose of its authors.

RC (DLC). Unsigned. Docketed by Jefferson, "recd. Dec. 31."

1. On 9 Dec. the Republican Society of Baltimore issued an announcement "To the Government and People of the United States" denying the allegation in Washington's annual address to Congress that the Democratic societies had fomented the Whiskey Insurrection (Philadelphia *Aurora General Advertiser*, 17 Dec. 1794; reprinted in Foner, *Democratic-Republican Societies*, pp. 339–43).

2. The Republican Society of Newark, New Jersey, advertised a 17 Dec. meeting at which "a question of considerable importance relative to the right of opinion, is to be the subject of discussion" (Philadelphia *Aurora General Advertiser*, 20 Dec. 1794). Resolutions passed at the meeting are reprinted in Foner, *Democratic-Republican Societies*, pp. 148–49.

3. In the congressional election in New York City on 9–11 Dec., Republican Edward Livingston defeated the Federalist incumbent, John Watts.

4. On 8, 11, and 13 Dec. Thomas Adams's Boston *Independent Chronicle* published several letters countering Washington's attack on "self-created societies."

"A Friend to Constitutional Rights" and "An Old Soldier" inquired whether the Society of the Cincinnati might be considered a "self-created society." In 1798 Adams was indicted under the Sedition Law (James Morton Smith, *Freedom's Fetters: The Alien and Sedition Laws and American Civil Liberties* [Ithaca, N.Y., 1956], pp. 247–57).

5. The 1794 congressional elections produced no change in the 11–3 Federalist majority in the Massachusetts delegation (Parsons et al., *United States Congressional Districts*, pp. 44-46, 76–80).

6. On 20 Dec. the Philadelphia *Aurora General Advertiser* printed the text of the New Jersey petition. On 1 Jan. 1795 Thomas Claiborne of Virginia moved a resolution for reduction of federal salaries, which the House rejected on 27 Jan. "by a very great majority" (*Annals of Congress*, 3d Cong., 2d sess., 1032–33, 1135–46).

7. Hamilton's resignation took effect 31 Jan. 1795 (see JM to Monroe, 4 Dec. 1794, n. 4).

8. A joint resolution, introduced in the Pennsylvania House of Representatives on 16 Dec. 1794 and passed by the General Assembly on 9 Jan. 1795, disqualified legislators representing the western counties that were, "at the time of the election, in a state of insurrection." One member declined to stand for reelection, but three others were returned to their seats by mid-February (Philadelphia *Aurora General Advertiser*, 20 Dec. 1794; Baldwin, *Whiskey Rebels*, p. 262).

§ Committee Report. *22 December 1794.* Recommends amending "the Amendments proposed by the Senate to the Bill intituled 'An Act to regulate the pay of the non-commissioned Officers, musicians and privates of the militia of the United States, when called into actual service, and for other purposes.'" Increases enlistment and reenlistment bounties, death benefits to widows and orphans, and rations.[1]

Ms (DNA: RG 233). 2 pp. In a clerk's hand.

1. On 19 Dec. the House appointed JM chairman of a select committee to consider the Senate's amendments to the bill. On 23 Dec. the House agreed to the Senate's amendments and added an amendment of its own based on JM's report. The Senate disagreed with the House amendment and requested a conference. JM led the House delegation to the conference committee, which dropped the provision for death benefits to widows and orphans. On 30 Dec. the House passed the amended bill, which Washington signed on 5 Jan. 1795 (*Annals of Congress*, 3d Cong., 2d sess., 995, 1003, 1009–10, 1020–21, 1024, 1027–28; *U.S. Statutes at Large*, 1:408–9).

From Joseph Jones

DR SR.   FREDG. 23d. Decr. 1794

In expectation of hearing from Mr. Randolph respecting Monroes affairs, I have postponed writing to him, which I shod: have done soon after the receipt of his letter. By your letter I find Mr. Randolph meditated writing to me what he wod. do but I have not heard from him and the moment is at hand that requires my compleating the first payment. Perhaps my writing to him and inclosing an abstract of Monroes letter will remind him of it and bring forth an answer. The sum you mentioned may answer if I shall be so fortunate as to receive some money I expect to get otherwise I shall fall about £100 short and I had rather raise that same by the Sale of negros than draw the bill for £200 I had proposed to you but if the 1000 dols. cannot be procured and very speedily I must request you to inform me of it and whr. a bill on Amsterdam or Hamburg will sell. In a few days I shall trouble you with a letter for Monroe whr. I hear from Randolph or not. Yr. friend

Jos: JONES

RC (DLC). Docketed by JM.

From the Right Reverend James Madison

MY DEAR SIR   Decr. 24h. 1794

I confess your Answer, respecting the proposed University, was in a great Measure anticipated. But as Mr Jefferson originated the Idea, or Proposition, & referred me to your Aid, I wished to have your own Declaration upon the Subject. Should any fortunate Circumstances place either yourself or Mr J. in the Legislature, this great & important Object might be, I am persuaded, readily effected; otherwise, I am equally persuaded it is utterly unattainable. The Proposition then must sleep, till one or other of you, shall think proper to awake it.[1] As to myself, I was anxious to see the good Work begun, not only on Acct. of its Importance as it must strike the mind of every one; but in this Age of Revolutions, I wished to see my Country distinguished for a Revolution, which might liberate the human Mind from Shackles more shameful, more injurious & more oppressive than any others which Ignorance or Ambition may have imposed. I want to see adopted a Mode of Education, which shall tend to strengthen & not depress the mental Faculties, which shall substitute Things for Words, which shall habituate the infant Mind to think, to reason at as early a Period as its Powers will permit, & thus conduct it gradually to real Science.

I have transcribed the Statute of this Coll. respecting the Presidt. as perhaps the most satisfactory Mode of communicating the Information desired.

The Debates respecting "the self created Societies" were very unfortunate; & surely tended to belittle the House exceedingly. The best Answer, on every Occasion, I think might be contained in half a Doz.

Words—"Sir, we have recd. your Speech, & shall pay due Attention to the Subjects recommended to our Consideration." How much Time & Money & Dignity might have been thus saved!

You were so obliging as to send me Dr. Pennington's Essays.[2] Should you be acquainted with the Dr it wd. give him some Satisfaction to be informed, that his Ideas respecting Fermentation receive no small Confirmation from Expts. on the Sweet Springs. This Fall, I made several Expts. upon the Air wh. they discharge; it has all the Properties ascribed to fixed Air; and "the Water alone will raise Dough, quicker than Yeast." Yrs most sincerely & Affy.

J MADISON

May all the Compts of the Season attend Mrs. M. & yrself.

RC (DLC). Addressed by Bishop Madison to JM in Philadelphia and franked. Docketed by JM. Enclosure not found.

1. After a long "sleep," the idea of a state university awoke in the General Assembly when the combined efforts of Joseph C. Cabell and Thomas Jefferson produced legislation that became law in 1819 (Malone, *Jefferson and His Time*, 6:274–82).

2. John Penington, *Chemical and Economical Essays* (Philadelphia, 1790; Evans 22757). Penington, a Philadelphia Quaker physician and member of the American Philosophical Society, died in the yellow fever epidemic of 1793 (Sowerby, *Catalogue of Jefferson's Library*, 1:387–88).

From Joseph Jones

DR. SR.   FREDG. 26th. Decr. 1794

I have delayed my writing to Monroe in daily expectation of hearing from Mr. Randolph on the subject of the money you mentioned in your letter to me that I might be able to communicate to Monroe what has been or will be done here; so soon as I hear from Randolph I shall inclose you a letter to put into such channel of conveyance as you may think best. The attempt to stigmatise and to draw from the two houses a censure on the societies has been very generally condemned, and justly —for surely nothing could be more unworthy the respective branches of the legislature than to blindly pass a censure on individuals or societies. If they had transgressed the laws in any manner they should have been accused and legally punished. The Bal[t]imore society has taken the matter up with temper and firmness, and it will I think be difficult for those who have been so forward to censure to justify their conduct to the people at large. I had requested information wher. it was expected Mr. Hamilton wod. retire and wher. it was known what was the cause of his disgust. It is reported, that Pinkney is to go to Madrid if so I suspect H. looks to London. I am this moment by a Gent. just come in informed, that H. told H. Lee, in the Western counties while they were lately there on the expedition that he meant to retire and go to the Bar where he could make his 2000 ⅌ ann. whereas since in office he had spent what he had before—abt. 3000*l*, except a Lott and house and that if he was now to die his family must depend on the G. Father for support—this account differs widely from common report. I understand there are speculations made on the pay of subalterns and Soldiers —that these thoughtless, extravagant people, sell to some annexed to, and of the Army, their monthly pay for a small sum advanced in the commencmt. of the month. It is hardly possible I believe to prevent such practices. I see meetings called, in several places, of the R. Societies. The result will no doubt be a publication of something in justification of their general conduct and in reprobation of the attempt to censure them. These cannot fail to be sensibly felt by the P., who has certainly very improperly introduced the subject to the legislature. For Gods sake get Mr. Randolph to let me know what sum I can depend on from Philada. The bal. of the 1500 becomes due 1st. Janry. and if I am to sell Negros to make it up the sooner I know it the better as now is the time to place them on a Plantation or hire them out. Yr. friend

J. JONES

In my absence a servant of Genl. Spotswoods called and left the inclosed. I supposed it contained a medal and opened it but found the contents a dollar—you will I expect understand the matter.

RC (DLC). Addressed by Jones to JM in Philadelphia and franked. Docketed by JM.

Naturalization

[26 December 1794]

On 15 December JM reported the bill to amend the Naturalization Act of 1790, which the Committee of the Whole took up on 22 December. Dexter objected to "the facility with which foreign agents may become citizens, and thereby save the tonnage on their vessels." He moved to amend the bill "with a proviso that those who will renounce all foreign allegiance forever, and those who declare on oath their intentions of becoming citizens of the United States, shall pay no more tonnage for the time until they become citizens than persons naturalized." JM, "instead of making exceptions in favour of the owners of ships, thought, that if any power at all was to be exerted by the Legislature of the Union, it ought rather to influence commerce, and prevent injury being done in that channel. The present clause did not belong, in his opinion, to the present subject, but to commercial regulations" (*Philadelphia Gazette*, 23 Dec. 1794). Dexter withdrew his motion. On 26 December Giles moved an amendment requiring that a prospective citizen's character witnesses be "attached to a *Republican* form of government." After debate Giles altered his amendment to read "attached to the principles of the government of the United States."

Mr. Madison was of opinion that the word was well enough understood to signify a free Representative Government, deriving its authority from the people, and calculated for their benefit; and thus far the amendment of his colleague was sufficiently proper. Mr. Madison doubted whether he himself should however vote for the clause thus amended. It would perhaps be very difficult for many citizens to find two reputable witnesses, who could swear to the purity of their principles for three years back. Many useful and virtuous members of the community may be thrown into the greatest difficulties by such a procedure. In three years time a person may have shifted his residence from one end of the continent to the other. How then was he to find evidence of his behaviour during such a length of time? But he objected to both amendments on a different ground. It was hard to make a man swear that he *preferred* the Constitution of the United States, or to give any general opinion, because he may, in his own private judgment think monarchy or aristocracy better, and yet be honestly determined to support this government as he finds it.

Philadelphia Gazette, 27 Dec. 1794 (reprinted in *Dunlap and Claypoole's Am. Daily Advertiser*, 31 Dec. 1794). After further debate, the committee revised and approved Giles's amendment.

From Horatio Gates

MY DEAR SIR   NEW YORK 27th: December. 1794:
    Permit me thus late to present you, & Mrs: Maddison, mine, & my Marys Compliments of Congratulation; and to Wish ye both every Earthly Felicity; make us also happy by saying you will both pay a Vissit to Rose Hill next Summer; When your Letter came inclosed last Spring for Mr: William Morris,[1] He was supposed to be Dying of a putrid Fever; His Brother the Lawyer took charge of it, & promised you should have an Answer, as soon as His Brother was Capable to send one; I hope you received it. I have this morning received the inclosed Letter from Dr: Murray at Annapolis;[2] He is concerned with me in a

Tract of Land on the Scioto; & is with me alarmed, at the Danger of our Losing Our property; by not paying a Tax laid by the Legislature of Kentucky, which we neither knew, nor heard of, until it was Impossible within the Time prescribed to Comply with the Law; You will please to Observe Doctor Murray, Says, "The only Act of that Assembly in this Country, is, I am informed, in the Hands of Mr: Randolph Secretary of State": please to request a Sight of it, and have the kindness to give me your Opinion, what may yet be done to save Our property! I hope you left our Mutual Friend, Mr: Jefferson, well in Virginia; & that, there is hopes we may see him to the Eastward next Summer. When you have Leizure to favour me with an Answer, be so obliging as to return me the Inclosed. I should acquaint you that I had paid a Draught of Col: Andersons of one hundred, & Twenty Dollars; & Dr: Murray wrote him, he was ready to pay the rest of his Demand, immediately upon receiving the patents: with Marys, and my most respectfull Compliments to Mrs: Maddison, I am, My dear Sir Your faithfull Humble Servant,

HORATIO GATES

Poscript

I clearly see Holland is lost to the Allies, & if the Duke of York, is not a better Gen:, than I suppose Him; His Army will be Captured!

RC (DLC); draft (NHi: Pintard Papers). RC docketed by JM.

1. JM to Morris, ca. 22 Mar. 1794 (not found).
2. James Murray to Gates, 23 Dec. 1794 (NHi: Gates Papers).

From Thomas Jefferson

DEAR SIR   MONTICELLO Dec. 28. 94.

I have kept mr. Joy's letter[1] a post or two, with an intention of considering attentively the observations it contains: but I have really now so little stomach for any thing of that kind that I have not resolution enough even to endeavor to understand the observations. I therefore return the letter, not to delay your answer to it, and beg you in answering for yourself, to assure him of my respects and thankful acceptance of Chalmer's treaties, which I do not possess: and if you possess yourself of the scope of his reasoning, make any answer to it you please for me. If it had been on the rotation of my crops, I would have answered myself, lengthily perhaps, but certainly *con gusto*.

The denunciation of the democratic societies is one of the extraordinary acts of boldness of which we have seen so many from the faction of Monocrats. It is wonderful indeed that the President should have permitted himself to be the organ of such an attack on the freedom of discussion, the freedom of writing, printing & publishing. It must be a matter of rare curiosity to get at the modifications of these rights proposed by them, and to see what line their ingenuity would draw between democratical societies, whose avowed object is the nourishment of the republican principles of our constitution, and the society of the Cincinnati, a *self-created* one, carving out for itself hereditary distinctions, lowering over our constitution eternally, meeting together in all parts of the Union periodically, with closed doors, accumulating a capital in their separate treasury, corresponding secretly & regularly, & of which society the very persons denouncing the democrats are themselves the fathers, founders or high officers. Their sight must be perfectly dazzled by the glittering of crowns & coronets, not to see the extravagance of the proposition to suppress the friends of general freedom, while those who wish to confine that freedom to the few, are permitted to go on in their principles & practices. I have put out of sight the persons whose misbehavior has been taken advantage of to slander the friends of popular rights; and I am happy to observe that as far as the circle of my observation & information extends, every body has lost sight of them, and viewed the abstract attempt on their natural & constitutional rights in all it's nakedness. I have never heard, or heard of a single expression or opinion which did not condemn it as an inexcusable aggression. And with respect to the transactions against the excise-law, it appears to me that you are all swept away in the torrent of governmental opinions, or that we do not know what these transactions have been. We know of none which according to the definitions of the law, have been any thing more than riotous. There was indeed a meeting to consult about a separation. But to consult on a question does not amount to a determination of that question in the affirmative, still less to the acting on such a determination: but we shall see I suppose what the court lawyers, & courtly judges & would-be Ambassadors will make of it. The excise-law is an infernal one. The first error was to admit it by the constitution. The 2d. to act on that admission. The 3d. & last will be to make it the instrument of dismembering the Union, & setting us all afloat to chuse which part of it we will adhere to. The information of our militia returned from the Westward is uniform, that tho the people there let them pass quietly, they were objects of their laughter, not of their fear, that 1000 men could have cut off their whole force in a thousand places of the Alleganey, that their detestation of the excise law is universal, and has now associated to it a detestation of the government, & that separation which perhaps was a very distant & problematical event, is now near, & certain & determined in the mind of every man. I expected to have seen some justification of arming one part of the society against another, of declaring a civil war the moment before the meeting of that body which has the sole right of declaring war, of being so patient of the kicks & scoffs of our enemies, & rising at a feather against our friends, of adding a million to the public debt & deriding us with recommendations to pay it if we can, &c &c. But the part of the speech which was to be taken as a justification of the armament reminded me of parson Saunders's demonstration why minus into minus makes plus.[2] After a parcel of shreds of stuff from Aesop's fables & Tom Thumb, he jumps all at once into his Ergo, minus multiplied into minus makes plus. Just so the 15,000 men enter after the fables in the speech. However the time is coming when we shall fetch up the lee-way of our vessel. The changes in your house I see are going on for the better, and even the Augean herd over your heads are slowly purging off their impurities. Hold on then, my dear friend, that we may not ship-wreck in the mean while. I do not see in the minds of those with whom I converse a greater affliction than the fear of your retirement; but this must not be, unless to a more splendid & a more efficacious post. There I should rejoice to see you: I hope I may say I shall rejoice to see you. I have long had much in my mind to say to you on that subject. But double delicacies have kept me silent. I ought perhaps to say, while I would not give up my own retirement for the empire of the Universe, how I can justify wishing one, whose happiness I have as much at heart as yours, to take the front of the battle which is fighting for my security. This would be easy enough to be done, but not at the heel of a lengthy epistle. Let us quit this, & turn to the fine weather we are basking in. We have had one of our tropical winters. Once only a snow of 3. inches deep, which went off the next day, & never as much ice as would have cooled a bottle of wine. And we have now but a month to go through of winter weather. For February always gives us good samples of the spring of which it is the harbinger. I recollect no small news interesting to you. You will have heard I suppose that Wilson Nicholas has bought Carr's lowground's and Harvey's barracks.[3] I rejoice in the prosperity of a virtuous man, & hope his prosperity will not taint his virtue. Present me respectfully to mrs. Madison, and pray her to keep you where you are for her own satisfaction & the public good, and accept the cordial affections of us all. Adieu.

RC (DLC); FC (DLC: Jefferson Papers). Unsigned.

1. George Joy to JM, 1 May 1794.

2. Nicholas Saunderson, *The Elements of Algebra* (2 vols.; London, 1740–41), 1:56–57.

3. Carr's lowgrounds formed one-third of about 1,500 acres that Jefferson's nephews, Peter and Dabney Carr, had recently inherited. Peter Carr was Wilson Cary Nicholas's brother-in-law. Col. John Harvie owned the Albemarle County

barracks where British and German prisoners of war lived, 1779–80 (Jefferson to Thomas Mann Randolph, Jr., 26 Dec. 1794 [postscript of 27 Dec.] [DLC: Jefferson Papers]; John Hammond Moore, *Albemarle: Jefferson's County, 1727–1976* [Charlottesville, Va., 1976], pp. 57–64).

§ Memorandum from Thomas Leiper. *Ca. 29 December 1794.* Opposes the provisions of the 1794 statute that imposed duties on snuff. "The Excise is excessively high." Philadelphia tobacconists "are of the opinion it will introduce Smuggling from Great Britain," where drawbacks encourage reexport of snuff manufactured there from American tobacco. Urges that the tax be "laid direct upon our Mills"—instead of on the product—"which of the two is the fairest way and will prevent us from defrauding the revenue and the Honest Man." Discusses the failure of British excise laws to prevent smuggling. In Glasgow there is an excise officer to inspect every two snuff manufacturers. The oaths required of the snuff makers are unavailing, even though "Glasgow is the first Church going Town in Europe and I take it the most religious. . . . And they also require a standing Army to Dragoon the People into a compliance to the Laws frequent Bloodshed between the Military and the Smuglers is the consequence. The excise system will most certainly create dependants on the Executive and a Standing Army to Assist them to enforce the Law when all this is done what will follow? as certain as I now write an Aristocracy." The American excise on distilled spirits is based on the British law "made by Willm. Pitt & Co. . . . How it Came into Congress we cannot tell but the Bill as reported is in the Hand writing of a Clerk of The Treasury. . . . All the evils of this Country have proceeded from our leading characters haveing an over fondness for British Laws and Customs." Charges that William Duer, before his bankruptcy, had attempted "to engross the whole business" of snuff manufacture "on the continent." The whiskey rebels resisted "an Excise which they were taught and did beleive to be the Horror of all free States." Urges that the excise be replaced by a tax on real estate, which during the present prosperity could, with the impost, quickly pay off the national debt. "The time will come when the People of this country will say to the People of Europe you must take our Tobacco Manufactured and they will be obliged to comply for . . . they can procure it no where else, and the Manufacturers here can give it to them cheaper than their own manufacturers because the Tobacco can go at one third less freight and the Snuff at one half it will add to the vallue of our Exports on Tobacco 100 ℔Ct. & 300 ℔Ct. on Snuff the Tobacco Manufactory may be carried on by any Planter. . . . We could wish Congress to consider these things and have the Tobacco trade made free the writer of this is so thoroughly convinced of this truth that he would give One Half of his Estate towards the payment of the National Debt to have the Word Excise out of the Constitution. . . . All the People in Europe are becomeing more free every Day & why may not America?"

Ms (DLC). 16 pp. In an unidentified hand. Headed: "Observations on the Law for Exciseing Snuff." Docketed by JM: "From Ths. Leiper." Dated 1790 in the *Index to the James Madison Papers.* On 29 Dec. 1794 Pennsylvania Federalist Thomas

Hartley presented to the House of Representatives a petition from Leiper "and others tobacconists and citizens of Philadelphia" (*Philadelphia Gazette*, 30 Dec. 1794, 27 Feb. 1795). This memorandum contains arguments similar to those in the petition. On 5 Jan. 1795 the House appointed a select committee to consider alterations to the act imposing duties on domestic snuff and referred the petition to that committee. On 6 Jan. JM was appointed to the committee. Leiper had also petitioned the Senate when the bill taxing snuff was first proposed (*Annals of Congress*, 3d Cong., 2d sess., 1023, 1058, 1060, 1081; ibid., 1st sess., 110; see also JM to Jefferson, 11 Jan. 1795, and n. 3). This memorandum was clearly influenced, if not written, by James Thomson Callender (see his anonymous pamphlet, *A Short History of the Nature and Consequences of Excise Laws; . . . the Horror of All Free States* [Philadelphia, 1795; Evans 28384], pp. 48–49, 55; JM's copy is in the Madison Collection, Rare Book Department, University of Virginia Library). Leiper later provided financial support for Callender's children.

¶ From Edmund Pendleton. Letter not found. *30 December 1794.* Acknowledged in JM to Pendleton, 8 Jan. 1795. Congratulates JM and his wife on their marriage.

Naturalization

[31 December 1794]

On 29 December the Committee of the Whole considered the provision in the naturalization bill that required that an American citizen who had expatriated himself "should not be allowed to enter into the list of citizens again without a special act of Congress, and of the state from which he had gone." (On the Democratic societies' advocacy of the right of expatriation of American citizens who had accepted French military commissions from Genet, see Henry Lee to JM, 23 Jan. 1794, n. 2, and Republican Society of South Carolina to JM, 12 Mar. 1794, n. 1.) JM "did not think that Congress by the Constitution had any authority to *readmit* American citizens at all. It was only granted to them to admit aliens" (*Philadelphia Gazette*, 30 Dec. 1794). On 31 December Giles moved that aliens be required to renounce titles of nobility in order to qualify for American citizenship.

Mr. Madison approved of the motion. He regarded it as exactly to the business in hand, to exclude all persons from citizenship, who would not renounce forever their connection with titles of nobility. The propriety of the thing would be illustrated by this reflection, that if any titled orders had existed in America before the revolution, they would infallibly have been abolished by it.

Philadelphia Gazette, 1 Jan. 1795 (reprinted in *Independent Gazetteer*, 3 Jan. 1795). Giles withdrew his motion, and the Committee of the Whole reported the amended bill to the House.

From Edmund Randolph

E. R. to J. M.   Thursday Evening [January–April 1795?]

Consul Bond has just notified me, that he has a draft upon me for 660 dollars, due to-day.[1] I have 400, and am anxious to be precise in time with him. Be so good, as to lend me the remainder of that sum, which I can replace at any moment after tomorrow.

RC (DLC). Dated 30 Oct. 1794 in the *Index to the James Madison Papers*, but conclusive evidence for affixing a proper date is lacking. Presumably the note was written sometime before JM left Philadelphia ca. 6 Apr. 1795. Randolph resigned as secretary of state on 19 Aug.

1. In August 1793, when Jefferson was preparing to resign as secretary of state, he discussed with Washington possible successors. According to his "Anas," Jefferson answered the president's inquiry about Randolph: "I knew that the embarrassments in his private affairs had obliged him to use expedts which had injured him with the merchts & shop-keepers & affected his character of independance; that these embarrassments were serious, & not likely to cease soon" (Ford, *Writings of Jefferson*, 1:258).

From Edmund Randolph

E. R. to J. M.   Saturday morning. [January–April 1795?]

My mind has been occupied with the subject, upon which we conversed. It is immense, critical, and may form an important epoch. Think precisely & extensively upon it, and let me hear from you.

I find, that what I expected to have been done was not. My note in Bond's hands was paid; but the money was not delivered by the person, who ought to have done it, and consequently the money was advanced for me by a man, whom I hardly know. Would it be convenient to you to procure the check this morning? Do not say so, if it be otherwise.

RC (DLC). Addressed by Randolph. Randolph wrote on the cover, "Letter from Vienna 2d. octr. / Emperor intended to go to Pays bas—p⟨. . .⟩." Undated in the *Index to the James Madison Papers*. Conjectural date here assigned by comparison with Randolph's other note to JM concerning his debt to Phineas Bond.

From Edmund Randolph

[January–April 1795?]

It shall be done. Put your name upon the check; it is not payable to bearer.

RC (DLC). Addressed by Randolph. Conjectural date here assigned by comparison with Randolph's notes to JM concerning his debt to Phineas Bond.

Naturalization

[1 January 1795]

The House took up the naturalization bill.

As to the granting of privileges to aliens, Mr. Madison remarked, that there was no class of emigrants from whom so much was to be apprehended as those who should obtain property in shipping. Much greater mischief was to be feared from them than from any influence in votes, at an election. If he were disposed to make any distinction of one class of emigrants more than another, as to the length of time before they would be admitted citizens, it would be as to the mercantile people. We understood the meaning of the member to be that these persons may, by possessing themselves of American shipping and seamen, be enabled clandestinely to favour such particular nations in the way of trade, as they may think proper.

> *Philadelphia Gazette*, 2 Jan. 1795. The House approved the amendments reported by the Committee of the Whole. For a similar statement advocating strict rules for admitting foreign merchants to American citizenship, see JM to Richard Peters, 22 Feb. 1819, Madison, *Writings* (Hunt ed.), 8:424–25.

[1 January 1795]

Giles revived his amendment requiring prospective citizens to renounce titles of nobility. Dexter opposed the amendment. "He imagined that, by the same mode of reasoning, we might hinder his holiness the Pope from coming into this country. He entered at some length into the ridicule of certain tenets in the Roman Catholic religion. . . . Mr. Dexter thought that priestcraft had done more mischief than aristocracy."

Mr. Madison said that the question was not perhaps so important as some gentlemen think it, nor of so little consequence as others seem to think it. It is very probable that the spirit of republicanism will pervade a great part of Europe. It is hard to guess what numbers of titled characters may, by such an event, be thrown out of that part of the world. What can be more reasonable than that when crouds of them come here, they should be forced to renounce every thing contrary to the spirit of the constitution. He did not approve the ridicule attempted to be thrown out on the Roman Catholics. In their religion, there was nothing inconsistent with the purest republicanism. In Switzerland, about one half of the Cantons were of the Roman Catholic persuasion. Some of the most democratical Cantons were so; Cantons, where every man gave his vote for a Representative. Americans had no right to ridicule Catholics. They had, many of them, proved good citizens, during the revolution. As to hereditary titles, they were proscribed by the constitution. He would not wish to have a citizen who refused such an oath.

Philadelphia Gazette, 2 Jan. 1795.

[1 January 1795]

Giles called for a roll-call vote on his amendment. Dexter offered to vote for the amendment if it was revised to require a prospective citizen to renounce not only titles of nobility but also possession of slaves, "and declare that he holds all men *free* and equal."

Mr. Madison mentioned regulations adopted in Virginia for gradually reducing the number of slaves. None were allowed to be imported into the state.

The operation of reducing the number of slaves was going on as quickly as possible. The mention of such a thing in the house had in the mean time a very bad effect on that species of property, otherwise, he did not know but what he should have voted for the amendment of Mr. Dexter. It had a dangerous tendency on the minds of these unfortunate people.

Philadelphia Gazette, 2 Jan. 1795.

Naturalization

[2 January 1795]

A heated debate ensued on Giles's and Dexter's amendments. Dexter explained that he had introduced his amendment because Giles had called for a roll-call vote. "You want to hold us up to the public as aristocrats. I, as a retaliation, will hold you up to the same public, as dealers in slaves."

Mr. Madison, when the amendment was first suggested, had considered it as highly proper, and naturally connected with the subject. No man can say how far the Republican revolution that is now proceeding in Europe will go. If a revolution was to take place in Britain, which for his part he expected and believed would be the case the peerage of that country would be thronging to the United States. He should be ready to receive them with all that hospitality, respect and tenderness to which misfortune is entitled. He should sympathize with them, and be as ready to afford them whatever friendly offices lay in his power, as any man. But this was entirely distinct from admitting them as citizens of America, before they were constitutionally qualified to become so. In reply to the remark of Mr. Boudinot that a renunciation of their titles might injure their families, Mr. Madison observed that if a British revolution took place, these fugitives would, as aliens, be incapacitated from holding real estates. In discussing this question, we had been reminded of the Marquis de la Fayette. He had the greatest respect for that character, but if he were to come to this country, this very gentleman would be the first to recommend and acquiesce in the amendment on the table. He had urged the necessity of utterly abolishing nobility in France, even at a time when he thought it necessary for the safety of the State that the king should possess a considerable portion of power; and Mr. Madison believed that if he were now at freedom, he was as completely stript of every thing relative to nobility, as it was possible that he could be. It had been said that it was needless to make emigrants renounce their rank, and that oaths were no security. He was ready to allow, that oaths were in any case but a very poor security, but they had been adopted in other parts of the bill, and the same reason which recommended them on former occasions might recommend them now.

Philadelphia Gazette, 3 Jan. 1795 (reprinted in *Gazette of the U.S.*, 9 Jan. 1795).

[2 January 1795]

Sedgwick denounced Giles's amendment as "frivolous" and said of the proposal for a roll-call vote, "The motives for pushing this call could be nothing else but to stigmatize members of that House, as wanting to introduce a nobility, whereas they opposed the amendment on no such account, but merely *because it was not worth their taking it up.*"

Mr. Madison denied the assertion of Mr. Sedgwick, that the amendment was trifling; and the member himself seemed to betray, by his behaviour, a consciousness that HE *had not promoted conciliation.* An abolition of titles was essential to a republican revolution, and therefore such an abolition had been highly proper in France. The sons of the Cincinnati could not have inherited their honours, and yet the minds of the Americans were universally disgusted with the institution, and in particular, in South Carolina; yet a member from that state (Mr. W. Smith) has told the house, that his constituents were under no fears of aristocracy, and that they could hear titles without emotion.[1] . . . Even the chief magistrate of South-Carolina had told the cincinnati that these distinctions ought to be laid aside.

Philadelphia Gazette, 3 Jan. 1795. After further debate, JM voted with the majority when the House defeated Dexter's amendment and passed Giles's. The House again referred the bill to JM's select committee.

1. The *Philadelphia Gazette* here inserted a clarification of Smith's previous remarks.

From Walter Jones

DEAR SIR.   Jany. 4th. 1795.

I acknowledge your obliging & Speedy answer[1] to my last, as well on my part, as on the part of those at whose Instance, I gave you Some trouble.

I much rejoice, that your house warded off the blow, that, under the recent Impressions of the Insurrection, was so well aimed to exalt executive power on the depression of popular Spirit.

The Subject of Government is thought to be better understood in america, than elsewhere, and yet I am persuaded that we are much in Error, by Supposing that any form of Government can be very good. They are all much more nearly allied, than most people think, especially the Executive Branch, which however clogged & checked, differs only in degree, but not in kind or tendency from the most unqualified Despotism. If I can find time to give my thoughts on this matter a tolerable form for public view, you shall hear of it.

You have lately had a very interesting Subject under debate, of which I have not heard the Issue. I allude to the naturalization Bill. I earnestly pray the result may be, a total exclusion of the naturalized from all functions of Government. The Contrary would be unwise were we accustomed to receive men of property Talents and character from abroad, but as far the greater part, who affect Such functions, are needy & unknown adventurers, swept from every Corner of the british empire, it is a more than Common prostitution of our Safety & Dignity, to admit them into Governmen⟨t.⟩ Population would Surely be enough consulted, by giving foriegners an easy access to Marriage, to the acquisition & Security of all Species of property, to the participation of Social ties & Enjoyments, but The functions of government I would never concede to them. A number of Speculative Notions respecting Liberty & Liberality were hurried into act, during the fervour & Spirit of our revolution; which More deliberate reflexion, or a greater Knowledge of practical Life, than we then posessed, would have Condemned as Mischievous or ridiculous. This easy admission of Strangers to Government, has ever appeared to me participant of both Qualities. A memorable Instance this State can furnish.

The increasing & warm Sentiments towards you, which have grown up with me, without much direct personal Intercourse, will Serve to justify the Sincerity of the good wishes & respects I tender to your Lady; and am Dear Sir with affectionate Esteem yours

WALT: JONES.

RC (DLC: Rives Collection, Madison Papers). Docketed by JM.

1. Letter not found.

From Samuel Stanhope Smith

EDITORIAL NOTE

JM's friend of long standing, the Reverend Samuel Stanhope Smith, was serving as vice-president of the College of New Jersey. On 5 May 1795 he succeeded his father-in-law and JM's former tutor, John Witherspoon, as president of the college. He had corresponded sporadically with JM since the Virginian's college days. Two sermons that Smith preached early in 1795 were not, however, calculated to sustain warm relations with JM. The Presbyterian Synod of New York and New Jersey had called for a general fast on 6 January. In his Princeton sermon on that date, Smith advocated fasting and—among other concerns—denounced the whiskey rebels, "who, for the wretched purposes of party, or for the shameful license of intoxication, are willing to throw the whole nation into the wildest tumult and confusion." On 1 January Washington had issued a proclamation (drafted by Hamilton) appointing 19 February "as a day of public thanksgiving and prayer . . . for the seasonable check which has been given to a spirit of disorder in the suppression of the late Insurrection." On the day of thanksgiving Smith again censured the Whiskey Insurrection in a Philadelphia sermon. JM later objected that such proclamations were liable "to a subserviency to political views; to the scandal of religion, as well as the increase of party animosities." After those political sermons, JM confined his correspondence with Smith to official college matters and as president made no effort to help when Smith's son was dismissed from a territorial post in New Orleans (*PJM*, 1:46 n. 4; Richard A. Harrison, *Princetonians, 1769–1775: A Biographical Dictionary* [Princeton, N.J., 1980], p. 45; Syrett and Cooke, *Papers of Hamilton*, 18:2–3; Smith, *A Discourse on the Nature and Reasonableness of Fasting* . . . [Philadelphia, 1795; Evans 29531], p. 24; Smith, *The Divine Goodness to the United States of America* [Philadelphia, 1795; Evans 29532], pp. 26–29 [JM's copy is in the Madison Collection, Rare Book Department, University of Virginia Library]; Fleet, "Madison's 'Detatched Memoranda,'" *WMQ*, 3d ser., 3 [1946]: 561–62; Smith to JM, 3 Sept. 1799 [DLC]; Smith to JM, 14 Apr. 1809, *PJM–PS*, 1:115–16, 116 n. 1; Dolley Madison to Smith, 10 Jan. 1810 [NjP]).

Dr. Sir, PRINCETON Janry. 4th. 1795

The purpose of this letter is to inquire whether you have preserved any notes of your discourses on the federal constitution, or the constitution of Virginia—or of any reflections you have made on these subjects either in favour, or in correction of any of their articles. And, if you have such notes, in what manner I might be permitted to take a copy.

I have it in view to introduce into the philosophical course of this college some general observations on the federal constitution, & on the constitutions of the respective states. And in the execution of this design I wish, if it be possible, to avail myself of the accuracy of your ideas on a subject which you have so thoroughly studied, & which no man understands better than you.

With my compliments to Mrs. Madison whom I have once had the pleasure to see, I am, Dr Sir, Yr. Mo. obdt. hble. servt.

SAML S SMITH

RC (DLC). Docketed by JM.

¶ From James Madison, Sr. Letter not found. *5 January 1795*. Acknowledged in JM's letter to his father of 26 Jan. 1795. Inquires about marketing JM's wheat crop. Mentions need for timothy seed. Requests items to be shipped from Philadelphia: mill stones and bolting (sifting) cloths (for the gristmill that JM's family planned to build), and tea for JM's sister, Sarah Catlett Madison Macon. Asks what horses should be used for spring plowing. Requests that JM make inquiries about the claim of Mr. Laundrum and selling his father's U.S. treasury certificates. Asks what has happened to James Madison (son of JM's brother Francis).

To Edmund Pendleton

My dear Sir PHILADA. Jany. 8. 1795.

I have recd. your favor of the 30 Ult: and am joined by my partner in the sincerest returns for your kind congratulations and friendly wishes. I hope this will find you in more confirmed health, and enjoying the commencement of a new year with every prospect that can make it a happy one.

One of the papers inclosed gives you the latest news from Europe. It is to be hoped that the dawn of peace may not be overcast. We have nothing of late date either from Jay or Monroe. No communications whatever as to the negociations of the former have yet been laid before Congress. The accounts which circulate thro' private channels have flattered in general the wishes entertained by all for his success. In the other paper you will see the opinion of this gentleman when an advocate for the constitution, on the nature of the tax on carriages. If it remains the same, when he is to decide as Cheif Justice, we may yet hope to see this breach in the Constitution repaired.[1] The H. of Reps. have been engaged in revising the Naturalization law, which has been found not duly guarded agst. intrusions and evasions. The new bill, as passed the House, requires of the candidates for Citizenship residence for five years, an oath of abjuration as well as of allegiance, satisfaction to the Court of good character, attachment to the *principles* of the Constitution, and of being well disposed to the good order & happiness of the U. S. On the motion of Mr. Giles a clause was added requiring of all who may have belonged to the order of Nobility, or borne any hereditary title, to make an express renunciation on these points in Court and upon record. You will think it strange perhaps that this should have met with opposition, and yet it became a question of some heat, tho' opposed rather as unimportant than improper. Several of the conditions have reference to the present state of Europe, and the danger of an influx to this Country both of aristocracy & licentiousness. It seems not amiss that we should be on our guard agst. both extremes. There will be a serious effort made to begin an effectual operation for paying off the public debt. The increase of the impost presents a fund that will of itself, if not diverted, answer the purpose. The Legislature of this State has just past an exclusion vote in each House agst. the Representa[t]ives & Senators from the Counties lately in insurrection. I am not able to say on what principle. I wish it may not have been too much a work of party. If they proceed to any business not urgent, before the vacant seats can be refilled, it will wear so much of that appearance as to threaten a revival of discontents which ought to be buried as much as possible. How is Col. Taylor—& how employed? Offer him if you please my best and sincerest wishes for his health & happiness. With the truest esteem & affection I am Dr. Sir, Yrs.

Js. Madison Jr.

Tazewell has been here a short time only & Mason has not been heard of.

RC (DLC). Franked and addressed by JM to Pendleton, "care of Col. Hoomes / Bolling Green / Virginia." Docketed by Pendleton.

1. In 1796 (after John Jay resigned as chief justice) the U.S. Supreme Court upheld the constitutionality of the carriage tax in *Hylton* v. *U.S.* (3 Dallas 171). "An Act laying duties upon Carriages" of 5 June 1794 was part of the series of tax bills passed during the first session of the Third Congress. JM had argued that the burden of the carriage tax unconstitutionally fell on a particular section, the South (JM to Jefferson, 1 June 1794, and n. 2). He probably referred to [John Jay], *An Address to the People of New-York, on the Subject of the Constitution* (New

York, 1788; Evans 21175), pp. 16–17, which warned of the consequences of tax inequities between the states (reprinted in P. L. Ford, *Pamphlets on the Constitution*, p. 84). On 8 June 1788 Washington had sent a copy of this pamphlet to JM (*PJM*, 11:101 and n. 1).

From Edmund Randolph

E. R. to J. M.   Thursday[1] [8 January 1795]

Mr. Fauchet's communication about weights and measures goes to congress to-day.[2] I inclose to you, as *a private* man, Rittenhouse's opinion upon them;[3] not thinking it proper to add that opinion to what is said to the house.

RC and enclosure (DLC). RC docketed by JM, with the date "1794." Dated 30 Oct. 1794 in the *Index to the James Madison Papers*. Date here assigned on the basis of circumstances described in n. 2. For enclosure, see n. 3.

1. Randolph first wrote, then crossed out, "Wednesday."
2. In his 8 Jan. 1795 message to Congress, Washington submitted several documents, including a translation of French minister Fauchet's 2 Aug. 1794 letter to Randolph concerning plans for the metric system. Fauchet professed to "see in the adoption of the new measures by America a mean of cementing the political and commercial connexions of the two nations" and enclosed the 11 Dec. 1793 decree of the Committee of Public Safety ordering "a measure in copper, and a weight divided in the form decreed for the standards" sent to the U.S. government (*ASP, Miscellaneous*, 1:115–16).
3. Randolph enclosed a copy of David Rittenhouse's 24 Oct. 1794 letter to him. In that letter, the director of the Mint praised the French proposals and copper model measures for the metric system: "They are well executed, and the simplicity of their subdivisions must strongly recommend them."

Naturalization

[8 January 1795]

JM reported the revised naturalization bill on 5 January. In debate on 8 January, the House considered filling up the blank in the section of the bill that set the number of years, after an alien declared his intent to become a citizen, before he could be naturalized.

Mr. Madison said that he feared the house would never see an end of the discussion, if they went on at this rate, for by descending to discriminate all the qualifications of a citizen, they run the hazard of losing the bill altogether, from the mere waste of time. *Ten* years were named by Mr. Murray to fill up the first blank, and seven years by Mr. Hartley. These terms he thought by much too long. This would oblige the friends of the bill to vote against it.

Philadelphia Gazette, 9 Jan. 1795. After further debate, the House filled up the blank in question with the word "three" and passed the bill, which Washington signed on 29 Jan. (*U.S. Statutes at Large*, 1:414–15).

To Thomas Jefferson

DEAR SIR　　　　　　　　　　　　　PHILA. Jany. 11. 1794[1] [1795]

The last subject before the H. of Reps. was a Bill revising the Naturalization law, which from its defects & the progress of things in Europe was exposing us to very serious inconveniences. The Bill requires 1. A probationary residence of 5 instead of 2 years, with a formal declaration on oath of the intention 3 years at least prior to the admission. 2. an oath of *abjuration*, as well as of allegiance. 3. proof of good character, attachment to the principles of our Government, and of being well disposed to the good order & happiness of the U. S. 4. Where the candidate has borne any title or been of any order of Nobility, he is to renounce both on record. This last raised some dust. The Eastern members were weak eno' to oppose it; and Dexter as a setoff moved a correspondent clog on emigrants attached to slave holding. Whether they will [be] able to throw the dust they have raised into the eyes of their Constituents I know not. It will not be easy I think to repair the blunder they have committed if it reaches the people. On the yeas & nays there [were] more thn. 60 for & little more than 30 agst. the clause. The Bill is gone to the Senate. Our revenue from trade is so increased as to supply a fund for commencing the discharge of the public debt. The excises laid at the last Session will probably be left as they stand. The treasury bench have attempted to make them perpetual, and brought about a Report of a Come. to prolong them till the year 1801.[2] Another Come. after conferring with the Sugar Bakers & Snuff Makers have agreed on a Counter Report which will probably defeat the project.[3] The French gain victories faster than we can relate them. In Spain, Sardinia & Holland they are equally sweeping every thing before them. They were not in Amsterdam but expected in a few days. The patriotic party was openly revived, and it was not doubted that the Stadholder would move off to England for his personal safety. The D. of York has been well drubbed again at Nimeguen. It was said to be agitated in the British Cabinet whether he should not with all his troops be withdrawn from the Continent. It is surmised that Prussia has actually treated with France, and that the Emperor is taking the same Course. It is indeed agreed that France can dictate peace to all her enemies, except England; and that she will probably do so in order to have a fair campaign with Engld. alone. Nothing final yet from Jay. It is expected here that he will accomplish much if not all he aims at. It will be scandalous, if we do not under present circumstances, get all that we have a right to demand. Not a word from Monroe. Knox is succeded by Pickering. The successor to H. not fixt, but likely to be Wolcot. H will probably go to N. Y. with the word *poverty* for his label. The Legislature of Pennsylva. have voted out the Western Members. It is said they will suspend important business till the seats can be refilled—but this will make little difference as the City party will still be a majority. Bingham will be the Senator—Unless the Germans can be prevailed on to vote for Tench Coxe. They like neither the one nor the other; not Bingham because an Aristocrat—not Coxe on the old score of his being a Tory in the War.

RC (DLC). Unsigned. Docketed by Jefferson, "recd Jan. 20."

1. Jefferson here added "for 95."
2. On 15 Dec. 1794 William Loughton Smith reported this recommendation from the House select committee appointed to prepare a plan for redemption of the public debt (*ASP, Finance*, 1:317).
3. JM had opposed "An Act laying certain duties upon Snuff and Refined Sugar" of 5 June 1794 during the Third Congress's first session. On 5 Jan. 1795 the House appointed a committee chaired by William Loughton Smith "to inquire and report whether any, and what, alterations ought to be made to the act." JM was appointed to the committee the following day. On 10 Feb. Smith reported a bill with a clause which—as urged by the Philadelphia snuff makers—replaced the duty on snuff with one on the manufacturing mills. In debate on 27 Feb., JM "was clearly in favor of the clause, as much better than the original idea." Contrary to JM's prediction, the new act—signed by Washington on 3 Mar.—extended the duty to 1801. Nevertheless on the day after the bill became law, a meeting of Philadelphia tobacconists drank a toast to JM: "May he find a majority who will adopt his ways and means for payment of the national debt, without having recourse to partial taxation" (JM's speech of 19 May 1794 and nn.; *U.S. Statutes at Large*, 1:384–90, 426–30; *Annals of Congress*, 3d Cong., 2d sess., 1058, 1060, 1208, 1258; Memorandum from Thomas Leiper, ca. 29 Dec. 1794, and n.; Philadelphia *Aurora General Advertiser*, 7 Mar. 1795).

Cabinet Secretaries' Reports

[12 January 1795]

On 30 December 1794 Washington sent to Congress a message submitting a report from the secretary of war. Written shortly before Knox left office, the report recommended, among other things, " 'That all persons who shall be assembled or embodied in arms, . . . for the purpose of warring against the Indians, . . . shall thereby become liable and subject to the rules and articles of war, which are, or shall be established for the government of the troops of the United States.' This was a section of a bill which the Senate passed the last session, entitled 'An act for the more effectual protection of the Southwestern frontiers;' but it was disagreed to by the House" (*ASP, Indian Affairs*, 1:543–44). In debate, House Republicans opposed consideration of unsolicited reports from cabinet secretaries as an infringement on legislative independence. Murray moved to refer the message and report to the Committee of the Whole. Nicholas moved to amend Murray's motion by striking out the mention of Knox's report and referring only the message from the president to the Committee of the Whole.

Mr. Madison [spoke against] [1] the clause copied from that proposed by the Senate, and rejected by the House of Representatives, and which considered a number of men unlawfully embodied against the Indians, as if called out according to law, in order by such a fiction to bring them under martial law. This he thought the most forced construction, at the expence of the Constitution, that had ever occurred; as well as a thing absolutely wrong in itself. But altho' he viewed the clause as so extremely exceptionable, he was not disposed to criticise it with rigour. He thought the truest as well as the most candid supposition was, that the Secretary in making a report immediately to the President, had not adverted to the appearance it might wear to the House of Representatives—and it might be natural for him to support his opinion to the President, with that of one branch of the legislature. If the report had been addressed to the House of Representatives, it was not to be doubted the Secretary's delicacy would have guarded him against the insertion of such a clause. In like manner it was pretty certain that the President, in a message entirely from himself would never have used the words in the paper transmitted. In this view the error might fairly be ascribed to inadvertence. Mr. M. was also not against, but for, referring the report along with the message, as inseparable from it.[2]

Philadelphia Gazette, 14 Jan. 1795. This account corrected a version printed ibid., 13 Jan. 1795.

1. The newspaper account began: "Mr. Madison was misunderstood in the account of his remarks in the Philadelphia Gazette of Tuesday evening."
2. The House defeated Nicholas's amendment and approved Murray's motion.

§ From Gustavus B. Wallace. *12 January 1795, Charleston, South Carolina.* Introduces [Robert Goodloe] Harper and asks JM to introduce him to [John] Nicholas and [William Branch] Giles of the Virginia delegation in the House of Representatives.

RC (DLC). 1 p. Addressed by Wallace to JM at Philadelphia, "by favr. of Mr. Harper." Docketed by JM.

¶ From Pierce Butler. Letter not found. *Ca. 12 January 1795.* Mentioned in Butler to JM, 23 Jan. 1795. Introduces Robert Goodloe Harper.

From Joseph Jones

Dr. Sr. Fredg. 13th. Janry. 1795.

I have a letter from Mr. Randolph authorising me to draw on him for £200 on Monroes account which I presume is all he can admit of but is short of the sum I had proposed and he from your communication intended to advance—whatever sum Monroe has requested him to furnish me, I wish him to supply, if he thinks he can with propriety do it, otherwise not by any means. I do not wish any direct application to him on the subject as I have already both to yourself and Mr. Randolph been rather troublesome—shod. however an occasion or opportunity offer when with propriety you could introduce the conversation I hope you will not omit it as from the present state of things in Europe I do not expect to avail myself of any assistance by bills either payable in Amsterdam or Hamburg. By your letter[1] he spoke of an order of 2000 dols. to be applied here and that I might draw for 1000 in 90 days— if the 2000 dols. was to be at my call, I had drawn only for £125 & 50*l.* so that of the 2000 there wod. remain £425. Of this sum if I have not mistaken the matter Mr. Randolph has wrote to me I might draw for £200 only. Some circumstance unknown to me may have occasioned this departure. These details are mentioned that you may understand if you already do not, the transactions between Mr. Randolph and myself and if at any time you have an opportunity of conversing on the business can explain to me his motives—the duties of his office will not allow him much time to attend to these matters and therefore I am unwilling to write, further than I have to him. What has been the issue of the proposition for vacating the seats of the members from the western Counties of Penna. Inform me what course is taken to contrive the public despatches to Monroe as I shod. think that the most likely and sure way I could send to Monroe wod. be through the Secre⟨y.'s⟩ office. Winter is come at last—the river is closing up. Yr. friend & Sert

Jos: Jones

RC (DLC). Docketed by JM.

1. Letter not found.

Excise

[15 January 1795]

In his 19 November 1794 annual address to Congress, Washington urged "a definitive plan for the redemption of the Public Debt." On 15 December Smith (South Carolina) reported from committee such a plan (*Annals of Congress*, 3d Cong., 2d sess., 791, 894, 979, 1010). On 15 January the Committee of the Whole considered the second resolution in Smith's report, which proposed that previous time limits on excises be repealed and "the said several acts be continued in force until the year 1801." Tracy argued that "a great deal of the value of a tax consisted in its permanency."

Mr. Madison said that the argument in favour of *permanency*, advanced by the gentleman from Connecticut, had force as well as plausibility. But his reasoning would operate against all experimental taxation whatever. It had been said that voting for or against the snuff and sugar excise, would be a criterion of the disposition to pay off the public debt. That criterion will not be assumed by those who are to judge the point. The whole dispute is about a branch of the revenue, said to be worth eighty or ninety thousand dollars per annum, an object not of very much importance. The select committee, however, had doubted extremely whether the revenue would be efficient at all. He begged that it might be understood that the question is not, shall the tax be now repealed, but only is it proper that it should be continued beyond the time originally intended, before it has been tried? In answer to what the gentleman from Connecticut had said of *permanency*, he thought it would argue greater stability for the government not to prolong the tax any farther, till the end of the period at first stipulated. Experience would, by that time, have assisted in forming a final opinion on the subject.

Philadelphia Gazette, 16 Jan. 1795 (reprinted in *Gazette of the U.S.*, 20 Jan. 1795).

¶ From Stephen Moylan. Letter not found. *15 January 1795, Philadelphia.* Described as a two-page letter in the lists probably made by Peter Force (DLC, series 7, container 2); also mentioned in Stan. V. Henkels Catalogue No. 694 (1892), item 128.

From Hubbard Taylor

DEAR SIR   CLARKE COUNTY 16th. Jay 95

I Recd. yours soon after my arrival in Kentucky, informing me that you had acceeded to my proposition in settling with Majr Moore.

Your Land on Sandy was surveyed by direction of Majr Lee previous to my return, it Joins as I am told a tract of John Greens. If so, it may be of more value than was apprehended, as there is a valuable Salt lick on the Land claimed by Green. It is also said that there is a valuable mind [*sic*] in the neighbourhood, of lead at least—some say silver. I only mention this that in case of any application to purchase you may be on your gard. Majr Lee is acquainted with this circumstan[c]e, and altho. he, no more than myself mean to excite your attention too much yet I thought it right to mention it.

That such a mind is found I have no doubt.

I have seen Mr. Bullock[1] but not long enough with him to get much satisfaction, one tract of Mrs. Paynes Lands[2] will be got in a part of the Country that is very valuable, lying near the upper blue hills. It is a doubt with Mr. Bullock wheather the entry on (Green River) (Petmans Creek) belongs to Mrs. Payne or not. As I shall have occation to write you again shortly shall only add that I am with Compts. to Mrs. Madison Dr Sir with much esteem Yr: Affe: Hbl: Set

H. TAYLOR

RC (DLC). Addressed by Taylor to JM at Philadelphia. Docketed by JM.

1. Edmund Bullock succeeded Taylor as a member for Fayette County in the Kentucky House of Representatives, 1793–98. A state senator for that county, 1805–17, he was Speaker of the House, 1796–98, and of the Senate, 1816. He also served with Taylor as a trustee of Transylvania University (Collins, *Collins' Historical Sketches of Kentucky* [1878 ed.], 2:170–71; Robert and Johanna Peter, *Transylvania University* . . . [Louisville, Ky., 1896], p. 114 n.).

2. Mary Coles Payne, Dolley Madison's mother, later gave her Kentucky lands to her son, John Coles Payne (Dolley Madison to Anna Payne Cutts, 8 May 1804 [owned by Mrs. George B. Cutts, Wellesley, Mass., 1982]).

Excise

[16 January 1795]

In Committee of the Whole, Smith (Maryland) opposed excises but asked rhetorically, "Why not lay excises on the following, who have excluded the importing of similar articles, and who equally may be said to have obtained a monopoly of the supply of their respective goods? viz: Rope-makers, saddlers, boot-makers, shoe-makers, tanners, curriers, ship-builders, carvers, cabinet-makers, coach-makers, and a variety of others" (*Annals of Congress*, 3d Cong., 2d sess., 1116).

Mr. Madison did not think that the turn which the debate had taken was at all a proper one. The question before the House was only this, whether it was at present proper to prolong the taxes comprehended in the resolution. The house can, for this time, go on without deciding the point. The proper statement of the question hereafter would perhaps be, whether it was better to proceed with excising all those articles of manufacture mentioned by the gentleman from Maryland, or to lay one general and efficient tax on property. The present taxes consisted of two sorts, viz. permanent, as the impost, &c. and temporary, as the excises in question. The permanent taxes could therefore be applied to the permanent object of reducing the public debt; and the temporary taxes to the temporary object, as the military establishment, &c. Instead of the question asked whether the public debt could be discharged by taxes for two years, it would be as proper to ask whether a military establishment, to which no appropriations could be constitutionally made for more than two years, ought to be provided for by taxes of indefinite continuance. He did not deny that there might be a reversionary appropriation of such taxes to the public debt, after the temporary purpose should have expired. But the practicability of such an arrangement was not a sufficient answer to the objections against making permanent new taxes uncertain in their product, contested in their principles, and which had been adopted under other circumstances, for other purposes.

The present subject, he said, in relation to the discharge of the public debt, had in every view been extremely magnified. Its importance lay, he thought, chiefly in its leading the attention of the committee to a comparison of the two general resources for paying off the public debt, namely, excises, and taxes apportioned on the several states according to the constitutional rule, and collected from individuals according to their property. If nothing more was intended than merely to pay the annual two per cent. which the funding law permitted Congress to pay, it was probable the impost alone might yield a competent surplus, without resorting either to excises, or apportioned taxes. But if, as was professed, and as, he hoped, was intended, a great and effective plan was to be sought after, for the purpose of freeing the public from the evil of the debt, with as much dispatch as possible, we must then face the alternative of a system of excises, or of a general tax on property. Between these different modes of revenue, a choice was to be made. He pressed it on the attention of the committee, that if excises were to be preferred, it was in vain to hope they could be limited to a few trifling subjects, such as manufactured snuff and sugar. They must be extended to all the manufactures mentioned by the gentleman from Maryland (Mr. S. Smith). The whole country would be covered in fact with excises. Every manufactory must be made to contribute, and even then it would not be possible to draw forth as much revenue as would be paid in the other mode. He was aware that objections and prejudices existed against a tax laid on property. He regretted that such a difference of opinion prevailed not only in Congress, but in different parts of the union on this subject. He was persuaded nevertheless that a tax on property was not only a more economical, and in every respect a more eligible resource, than a general system of excises, yielding the same amount of revenue, but that on the whole a majority of the people of America would be found less averse to it. He could speak with confidence on this point, as far as his own communications extended. Much he thought, of the dislike to a tax on property might be removed by taking different objects in different states, as might be most convenient or acceptable to them. This was perfectly consistent with the constitution, which did not require uniformity in this instance. In some states a tax on land, in others a tax on other articles of property; or partly on land and partly on other articles, might be most satisfactory; and the tax laws of the states would always assist in digesting the regulations for the purpose. He supposed that if this course should be taken, a million, or even two millions of dollars or more, could be raised in a year, and that the people would be willing to make such an exertion, rather than be saddled with a permanent debt; whereas he did not believe, that an excise system, if extended to every article manufactured in the country, could be made to produce any thing like such a sum. If, however, he was deceived in this point, and a general system of excises adequate to the purpose should be proposed, and it should be apparent that the general disposition was more favourable to such a system, than to a tax apportioned in the manner prescribed in the constitution, he was ready to give up his objections. Much as he disliked excises, he thought a perpetual public debt a still greater evil. But he should much prefer another system, and he repeated the caution, that the alternative was not between a tax on property, and the petty excises in question, which could not be felt in the work of sinking the debt; but between such a tax and excises spread over a sufficient number of manufactures to produce an equal sum of revenue. He again also suggested to the attention of the committee that the question was not whether the laws should be repealed, but whether they should remain as they stood, till their merit could be better known, and the whole subject be more fully taken up; and that all that was at this time aimed at with respect to the debt, would be attained by allotting the temporary part of the revenue to temporary purposes.[1]

Philadelphia Gazette, 17 Jan. 1795 (reprinted in *Gazette of the U.S.*, 23 Jan. 1795).

1. The newspaper account continued: "This is the substance of what Mr. M. said. He made several other observations which have escaped." JM voted with the minority when the House on 21 Feb. defeated an amendment specifying the laws that

authorized the commissioners of the sinking fund to repay the public debt. "An Act making further provision for the support of Public Credit, and for the redemption of the Public Debt," signed by Washington on 3 Mar., extended the existing excises until the public debt was redeemed (*Annals of Congress*, 3d Cong., 2d sess., 1243; *U.S. Statutes at Large*, 1:433–38).

From Alexander White

DEAR SIR   17th. January 1795

Your favr. of 28 Ulo.[1] would have been sooner acknowledged, had not the winter arrangement of the Post, by which the mail goes only once a fortnight taken place. I flatter myself the result of Jays mission will be favourable, and that the horrible carnage which has so long desolated and disgraced Europe will cease. England cannot wish to encrease her Enemies—and France has it now certainly in her power to establish a free and independent Republic—the object of the War on her part is then obtained. Will she risk all her glory, and more particularly the opportunity of establ[ish]ing her freedom which in the present state of things seems certain, for the chemerical project of reducing all Goverments to her own standard? The Prospect of paying off our national debt is to me a pleasing circumstance—the more so as it will not require additional taxes. I never entertained a doubt of the unconstitutionality of the tax on Carriages.

If the policy which has heretofore prevailed, still continues—of encouraging emigrations from Europe, I doubt the proposed amendment to the system of naturalisation will not accord with it. Many an honest European will swear to be faithful to these states, and would in fact be so, who would feel a reluctance to abjure allegiance to the Country which gave him birth. I was once enthusiastic in the cause of emigration—but I confess some recent transactions have cooled me a little.

We have had a remarkably mild winter, scarcely a snow to cover the ground till last thursday. Amazing prices for produce, and every circumstance concurring to render the People content and happy. Adieu and believe me Yours sincerely

ALEXR WHITE

RC (DLC). Docketed by JM.

1. Letter not found.

From John Dawson

DEAR SIR! RICHMOND Januay. 18, 95
We have an account here that France has made peace with Prussia,
which seems to gain belief—the enclosd hand bill I receivd from a friend
at Norfolk & is taken from a letter to Mr. Pennock of that place.

We also hear that the duke of York has met with another severe defeat
—that he lost great part of his army, & that the rest savd themselves by
flight. At what time do you expect to adjourn? With much esteem
Your friend & Sert

J DAWSON

RC (DLC). Enclosure not found.

¶ To Joseph Jones. Letter not found. *Ca. 21 January 1795*. Acknowledged in
Jones to JM, 29 Jan. 1795. Concerns the personal financial arrangements that
Monroe as U.S. minister to France has made with Secretary of State Ran-
dolph. Encloses a pamphlet.

From John Sitman and Others

DEAR SIR, MARBLEHEAD Jany. 22. 1795
Wee are now to acknowledege Your favours Wee have recived by
your Kind Letter of may 28 1794, Constrainned with hart felt Sincerity,
for your friendly attention, to those papers commited to Your Care,
with our address,[1] and trust, from upright princibles wee where em-
bolden, to look up to a Gentlemen, whose Character Stoop so fare in
Vindication of the rights of mankind.

Wee are made acquainted by your Goodness Sir, that our petitions,
was further prolonged to the next Sesions of Congress, for more fully
debating the princibles, and where made to understand, in the mean
while, if wee had any thing further to Offer, wee had time thus to due.

Wee would Observe that Marblehead being perticular in its Situwa-
tion, its Customs and Manners being riveted in the breast, of all the
Natives both Young & old, being attached to it by habit respeting the
fishing buisness, which Nature seemes to have situwated her for, not
having any advantage agricultere, seeme to be Competed to this Mode of
liveing, which leaves more then common Numbers of Widows & Off-
rans, the laws of Congress, binding those concrned in this Branch of
buisness, to certain rules prescribed for the Benifit of receiving the
Bounty.

This finaly Oversits the former Customs of this place, for the Industrys man brought up in a hard Labourous way, from 12 Years of age acquiring this Buisness, is somewhat Simelar, to the old Solider, which is continuwed in Service, being enured to the Same, for where there is a breach to be made against an Enemey, he must be foremost in the front.

So in this Oucupation, Must the persons, be early brought up in the Buisness, be at every beck & call, where this Buisness Laboures, (Wee would Venture, to applie this Matter to convince the Mind[)], a Widow has two Sons, one shee puts out as an app[r]entice to a Master, for the purpose of learning a trade, shee cannot expect any advantage by this child, for the time is the Masters,[2] the other Son, shee sends a fishing on board one of those Vesell on Cuttails in the fishing buisness at 12 Years of age, for the purpose of lear[n]ing the Oucupation, he has is half fish clear from the Scale, at the Years of 17, or 18 he has acquired this buisness, and now is fit to be asked to go on shares, wee ask, what rong has been don to this child, he now recive, what he gave away in his Younger Years to acquire this buisness, & not only so, but 9 Years income is recived by the Widow, his Mother, for the benifit of this family, when her Other Son, time is intirly lost as to any advantage they can reape.

But to explaine our selves more fully, (this mode of tell fish being Establish in marblehead[)], what is to become of the Younger part of the male inhabitance, they are now fit to be taking on board of our Vesells on Cuttails, our Skippers will refuse them, because the proffits of their oucupation is lost, they will endeavour to obtaine men Equall to themselves, to Share the hardships in all its parts, as Well as reap the advantages that Arises from the buisness, (Wee Would Sijest then, where is the Nursery for the fishing buisness[)], for if the Youth is not taken, as they will not be, on this plan, what is to be don, the buisness will dwindle away in this place and come to nothing.

But will the Honl. Lejeslature, put the raw Cuntryman, on Equality, with the man that is been brought up in this buisness from is Early days, must theise men, due the duty of Others, without the least compensation, they mite acquire the Catching in a few Years, but what is to be don with the dresing and Other duites on board the Vesell on princibles of Equality, can it be expected that the first men on board the Vesell, will leave their lines, for the purpose of Saveing there fish from Destruction, when at the same time his liveing & that of their familys depends on their former experince, (haveing endeavoured to explaine oursleves to the Honl Lejeslature[)], Wee Never had an Idea, that the Cuttails, should have only one half of the bounty of the fish, that they caught, (wee ever suppose they had a right to all the bounty on all the fish

450

they caught, which was agreeable to us, and talied with the Wise Adminstration of the Lejeslature[)].

But on the Other side of the Question, Wee Never Supposed the raw unxperince man, should reap the same Advantage in the fishing buisness, (as the man which is been brought up to it from his Early days, untill he is fully able to due all its dutys[)]. This Sir, Wee Venture this as our last, to the Wisdom of the Honl Lejasture of theise United States, and if they Deney us the priveledge of going in our Own way with bounty annexed, (Wee trust they will adhere to the prayer of the last petitions, and Grant us the bounty[)], to Such of us Now are Defishent for the Year 1793, as the Goverment has had the benifit of the duty of the Salt which Wee expended on our Fish, (in order to Convince Congress[)], Wee have inclosed two Voyages made up on the same fair, with the same expences, which will shew, how the best men which go in our Vesells are deprived of their former advantages, and the proffits Shifts, and finally fall into the hands of the owners of fishing Vesell, and the inferior persons, going in them.

Thus Sir, wee have endeavoured, to give You all the Light, on this Buisness, which lay in our power, and risk the fate of it in your hands, and remain With the Greatest Personall respect, Your Most Obed Hume Servants,

JOHN SITMAN
BURRILL DEVEREUX
RICHD PEDRICK

PS. One of those Voyages is made up in the tell Fish mode, (the other on Shares, & cuttails[)].

RC (DLC). Docketed by JM. Enclosures not found.

1. The Fisheries Act of 1792 replaced a drawback (refund) of the import duty on salt to American exporters of salted fish with an allowance based on tonnage to owners of fishing vessels. JM consistently opposed bounties for developing industries and persuaded the House of Representatives to adopt the term "allowance" in the bill. On 7 Apr. 1794 the House referred to a committee chaired by William Lyman a Massachusetts petition requesting an increase in the allowance. On 23 May the House passed a resolution supporting the increase and ordered Lyman's committee to prepare implementing legislation, but no evidence has been found that such a bill was introduced (*U.S. Statutes at Large*, 1:229–32; *PJM*, 14: 220 n., 220–224, 224 n. 3; *Annals of Congress*, 3d Cong., 1st sess., 561, 714).

2. The Fisheries Act excepted apprentices from the benefits accruing to fishermen from the allowances. The act required shipowners, in order to qualify for the allowance, to "make an agreement . . . with every fisherman employed therein, excepting only any apprentice . . . that the fish or the proceeds of such fishing voyage . . . shall be divided among them in proportion to the quantities or number of said fish they may respectively have caught" (*U.S. Statutes at Large*, 1:231).

From John Adams

DEAR SIR   PHILADELPHIA January 23. 1795
Will you be so good as to read the inclosed Letter from Dr Belknap and tell me, from your Recollection of what passed in Congress in 1779. 1780 & 1781, whether there is any Colour for the Imputation cast on our Country by Dr Kippis.[1] I cannot say as Dr Belknap has been informed that Dr Kippis is my Correspondent. I never wrote a Letter to him or received a Letter from him that I recollect. I visited him and he visited me. I often heard him in his Pulpit, and frequently met him in society in London, and ever conceived and entertained a good opinion of his Candour, and a great Idea of his Information. I doubt not he wrote what he believed: but he has certainly been misinformed.

I doubt not he will readily correct his Error, as soon as he shall be convinced of it. And if you will be so obliging as to recollect what passed within your Knowledge relative to Dr Franklin's Recommendation, and write it to me, I will convey it to Dr Belknap and perhaps take some other Measures to shew that Dr Franklins Liberality of sentiment was never censured, but on the Contrary was Admired by his Fellow Citizens. With great Esteem I have the Honour to be, sir your most obedient

JOHN ADAMS

RC (MHi). JM evidently returned the RC and its enclosure in his 3 Feb. 1795 reply to Adams, for the RC was printed with the correspondence described in n. 1 below. See also Adams to Jeremy Belknap, 4 Feb. 1795 (MHi: Belknap Papers).

1. The Reverend Andrew Kippis was pastor of the London Presbyterian congregation in Princes Street, 1753–95. In his article on Capt. James Cook in *Biographica Britannica* (2d ed.; 5 vols.; London, 1778–93), 4:235, Kippis recounted that in 1779 Benjamin Franklin, as U.S. minister to France, had recommended that American warships not attack Cook, who was then expected to return to Europe from his last voyage of exploration. Kippis erroneously claimed that Congress had countermanded Franklin's order. The issue was somewhat moot, for the Hawaiians killed Cook before his ships reached Europe. Jeremy Belknap, corresponding secretary of the Massachusetts Historical Society, nevertheless brought Kippis's error to the attention of Adams and other American political leaders. Belknap published their testimonials denying Kippis's allegation, including JM's 3 Feb. 1795 reply to Adams, in the *Collections of the Massachusetts Historical Society*, 4 (1795; Evans 29049): 79–85.

From Pierce Butler

DEAR SIR   CHARLESTON Jany. the 23d. 1795
Mr. Harper, a Delligate from this State, desirous of the honor of Your acquaintance, so very earnestly entreated me to give Him a letter to

You that I coud not parry it. You will receive at his hand a few lines from me. If it is the means of keeping Him right, it may, in a degree, Apologise for the liberty I took. It is necessary however, that I shoud frankly give to You my opinion of Him. My acquaintance with Him is slender. I think He has abilities, & some information. He is fired with Ambition; And has nothing of the Mauvais haunt[1] about Him. He is polite and generous in His feelings—Yet He is not a Man that, from my slender acquaintance, I woud unbosom to. He may be made Useful if He takes a right bias. He will be liable to impressions, and apt to be hurri[e]d away by the feelings of the moment.

I yesterday Conversed with a Man from Paris. He told me that He often Conversed with our friend Mr. Monroe. He was well, but in his opinion neither Mrs. or Mr. Monroe are pleased with their Situation. He says they have no society. I regrett it on their Acct. I conclude there will be little done the present session unless to draw tighter the Cord. I remain with great respect & Esteem Dear Sir Yr. friend & Obedt. Servant

P Butler

RC (DLC). Docketed by JM.

1. *Mauvaise honte:* bashfulness.

From Joseph Jones

Dr. Sr.   Fredg. 23d. Janry. 1795

On my return from Loudoun the evening before last I received yours of the 14th.[1] Nothing final has I presume been yet effected by Mr. Jay or it wod. be laid before the legislature and if any thing beneficial to this country is ultimately obtained from G. Britain we may ascribe it altogether to her distressed situation in consequence of the successes of the French republic. Altho' it is reasonable to conclude that all parties at war wish for peace or at le[a]st that peace in their present situation would suit them best, yet do I conceive it will not easily be effected. For altho' France may adhere to her declared sentiment of not seeking conquest for herself yet she may and I suppose will contend that if left to herself to settle her own government so shall Flanders and other conquered countrys at the time of the treaty be allowed to do the same —here they will split especially as England is opposed to accommodation. The crowned heads appear to be so humbled that I expect they will not strenuously contend for a renunciation of those republican principles wch. they asserted tended to unhinge justice and subvert all order and good government. I almost wish before the squable is wholely settled that the republicans could amus⟨e⟩ the Islanders with a sight of the Sans culotes and entertain them a little with the Carmagnole step and the bayonet. I cannot help thinking they wod. stare and run off as fast in as out of the Island. Monroe left with me a survey of 20.000. acres of land on Rock castle in Kentuckey to dispose of. I understand it lies in the Wilderness where the lands are general⟨ly⟩ of inferior quality —report says that such surveys or almost any others may be disposed of in Philadelphia. If something could be got for this I wod. sell it—will you be at the trouble to obtain information. I see a proposal for publishing Guthries geography improved.[2] If you think the work will be worth having please to subscribe for me and inform me the sum to be paid and I will send a bank note. I shall trouble you with a short letter to Monroe by the next or following Post—have those sent heretofore found a passage. Yr. friend & Servt

Jos: Jones

RC (DLC). Docketed by JM.

1. Letter not found.
2. William Guthrie, *A New System of Modern Geography* (2 vols.; Philadelphia, 1794–95; Evans 27077, 28782).

To Thomas Jefferson

Dear Sir   Philada. Jany. 26. 95.

I have recd. your favor of Decr. 28. but [not] till three weeks after the date of it. It was my purpose to have answered it particularly, but I have been robbed of the time reserved for the purpose. I must of consequence limit myself to a few lines and to my promise given to the Fresco Painter to forward you the inclosed letter.[1] Nothing since my last from Jay or Monroe. The Newspapers as usual teem with French victories and rumors of peace. There seem to be very probable indications of a progress made to this event, except in relation to G. B. with whom a Duet Campaign is the cry of France. The Naturalization has not yet got back from the Senate. I understand however it will suffer no material change. They have the prudence not to touch the Nobility clause. The House of Reps. are on the Military estabt. & the public debt. The difficulty & difference of opinion as to the former, produced a motion to request the P. to cause an estimate of the proper defence &c.[2] It was in its real meaning, saying we do not know how many troops ought to be provided by our legislative duty, and ask your direction.

It was opposed as opening the way for dragging in the weight of the Ex. for one scale, on all party questions—as extorting his opinion where he shd. reserve for his negative, and as exposing his unpopular opinions to be extorted at any time by an unfriendly majority. The prerogative men chose to take the subject by the wrong handle, and being joined by the weak men, the resolution passed. I fancied[3] the Cabinet are embarrassed on the subject. On the subject of the Debt, the Treasury faction is spouting on the policy of paying it off as a great evil; and laying hold of two or three little excises passed last session under the pretext of war, are claiming more merit for their zeal that [sic] they allow to the opponents of these puny resources. Hamilton has made a long Valedictory Rept. on the subject.[4] It is not yet printed, & I have not read it. It is said to contain a number of improper things. He got it in, by informing the Speaker, he had one ready, predicated on the *actual* revenues, for the House whenever they shd. please to receive. Budinot the ready agent for all sycophantic jobbs, had a motion cut & dry just at the moment of the adjournment, for informing him in the language applied to the P. on such occasions, that the House was ready to receive the Rept. when he pleased, which passed without opposition & almost without notice. H. gives out that he is going to N. Y. and does not mean to return into public life at all. N. Jersey has changed all her members except Dayton whose zeal agst. G. B. saved him. There are not more than 2 or 3 who are really on all points Repubns. Dexter is under another sweat in his district, and it is said to be perfectly uncertain whether he or his Repub: competitor will succeed. Adieu Yrs.

Js. M. Jr.

RC (DLC). Docketed by Jefferson, "recd. Feb. 11. 95."

1. Ignatius Shnydore (or Schneider) to Jefferson, 20 Jan. 1795 (not found, but listed in Jefferson's Epistolary Record [DLC: Jefferson Papers]). For the past three years, Jefferson had been trying to persuade Shnydore, a New York "drawing-master and sign-painter," to execute frescoes at Monticello. Since Jefferson and Shnydore could not agree on a price, the plans for frescoes were never carried out (Betts, *Jefferson's Farm Book*, pp. 500–503; William Duncan, *The New-York Directory, and Register, for the Year 1794* [New York, 1794; Evans 26919], p. 168).

2. For the House proceedings on the military establishment bill, see JM's speeches of 2 and 3 Feb. 1795 and nn.

3. At a later time someone altered this word to read "fancy."

4. "Report on a Plan for the Further Support of Public Credit," 16 Jan. 1795 (Syrett and Cooke, *Papers of Hamilton*, 18:56–148; see also introductory note, ibid., pp. 46–56).

To James Madison, Sr.

Your favr. of the 5th. came to hand a few days ago only. I must leave it to your judgment to dispose of my wheat at Sawney's. If there be any doubt about the fate of the flour to be made from it, I had rather it shd. go to Mr. Dunbar without that risk, or to Mr. Triplet if the conveyance cannot be procured. If it can, I had rather Mr. D. should have it, as my business is with him. I am sorry I did not know what you mention about the Timothy sooner. I would have sent seed along with the Clover seed, to resow the meadow ground. If resowing can be yet done in tolerable time Mr. Collins ought to get the Seed at Fredg. or Elsewhere without a moment's delay. In the former case Mr. Dunbar will supply the money. In the latter you can let him have the money left to pay for the seed Mr. Taylor had engaged. You may take the fallow either from Sawney's or Black-Meadow as you think most proper, for the Mill business. I do not wish Tamerlane to be plowed if it can be avoided, as I must use him for the saddle on my return. If both the Mares be not with foal one of them if really wanted may be used. Do you mean that I am immediately to provide Mill stones & Bolting Cloths? I wish you to write me immediately & particularly on the subject. I shall attend to Laundrums affair & the tea for Mrs. Macon. Also to your money & certificates; but I can tell you before I enquire that if I am *to sell, a new* power will be essential for that purpose. I have heard nothing of Js. Madison, except that he was at Fanny Hites after I left that neighbourhood, and talked of coming to Philada. I suppose he must have gone to Baltimore.

The newspapers continue to talk of peace in Europe except as to England whom the French are unwilling to let off without a campaign with her alone. The information is credited, tho' not yet authenticated. Nothing from Mr. Jay. The expectations & private accts. are in favor of some valuable result to his demands. Congress are engaged on the subject of the Military establishment, & providing a fund for paying off the pub. debt. Nothing final is yet done on either. We are well and offer our love to my mother & your self. Yr. Affe. son

Js. MADISON JR

Fanny has answered[1] & very handsomely the letter referred to her.

RC (DLC). Franked and addressed by JM to his father at Orange Court House. James Madison, Sr., wrote on the cover: "Mrs. Webb's Business / Types. Small Money / David & Nathan Sellers / Wrote on Feb. 18." These notes probably formed the basis of a reply (not found).

1. Letter not found.

To James Todd

SIR   PHILADA. Jany. 27. 1795

Mr. Wilkins who had been requested and had undertaken to settle
with you the business in which I have become interested by my marriage with the widow of your brother,[1] being under an indisposition
which prevents his attending to it, it is necessary for me to enter on the
task myself. For this purpose I shall be glad of an interview with you,
without delay, either at my house or yours as may be most convenient
to you. From the last information given me by Mr. Wilkins I conclude
you have disposed of the property which was to be sold, and are otherwise prepared to favor me with an immediate settlement. You will excuse, Sir, the earnestness of my request, as the time approaches for our
leaving this city; and it is indispensible to my arrangements, as well
as required by the duty which the Parent and Guardian owes to the
interests of your infant nephew, that a full adjustment ⟨should be pre-
vio⟩usly closed.[2] I am Sir, with respect, Your Obedt. hble. servt.

JS. MADISON JR.

RC (owned by W. Parsons Todd, Morristown, N.J., 1966; deposited at PPIn).
Addressed by JM to Todd, "Front-Street." Docketed by Todd.

1. John Todd, Jr. (1764–1793), a Quaker lawyer, married Dolley Payne in 1790.
He died in the Philadelphia yellow fever epidemic (Moore, *The Madisons*, pp.
8–10).

2. James Todd was the brother of John Todd, Jr. On 7 Feb. 1794 Dolley Madison
had written him: "As I have already suffered the most serious Inconvenience from
the unnecessary Detention of my Part of my Mother in Law's property and of the
Receipt Book and papers of my late Husband—I am constrained once more to request—and if a request is not sufficient, to *demand* that they may be delivered this
day—As I cannot wait thy return from the proposed Excursion without material
Injury to my Affairs. The bearer waits for thy answer." The parents of James and
John Todd, Jr.—John Todd, Sr. (a teacher), and Mary Todd—died in the yellow
fever epidemic (Paul G. Sifton, " 'What a Dread Prospect . . .': Dolley Madison's
Plague Year," *Pa. Mag. Hist. and Biog.*, 87 [1963]: 186–87, 184; Mathew Carey,
A Short Account of the Malignant Fever, Lately Prevalent in Philadelphia [Phila-
delphia, 1794; Evans 26736], p. 159). On 6 Mar. 1795 James Todd wrote seven
promissory notes to JM, payable on thirty days' sight, totaling $1,969.13 (owned by
W. Parsons Todd, Morristown, N.J., 1966; deposited at PPIn). Each note is endorsed by JM and others. One of JM's endorsements is dated 17 Mar. 1795.

From Arthur Breese

DEAR SIR.   WHITESTOWN Jany. 28. 94. [1795]

You must pardon me, for not answering your letter,[1] before this time.
My opinion is that if you could sell one half of your Lot in the rear,

457

for something near its Value, It would be advisable for you so to do. Since the receipt of your letter, I have used every exertion to sell the rear part of the Lot, or rather 200 acres of the same. But the term for payment expiring so soon was unable to procure a Purchaser.

Land in this Neighborhood of late seems to have taken a stand, neither rises or falls. The Speculations that are at present made, being further West.

Your tract of Land is very good but being situated upon the North side of the Mohawk, where the Settlemts. are but few—land tho' equally as good, with that on the South side, will not command so great a Price. Four Dollars & a half is the full worth of the rear part of your Lot ℈. accre, and that cannot be procured in Cash. Indeed the people here cannot give Cash for Land. They are from the Eastern States, and all that a man brings in the Country with him is his wife & Six or Eight children. *Credit* then is what they ask for, and if they can obtain that, little do they care for the price.

If you consider it prudent to sell upon a few years Credit, suggest to me the price that you can afford to do it at, and with great Chearfulness I will endeavor, to make for you an advantageous sale. I am Sir, With much respect Yr. very Obt. & faithful Servt.

ARTHUR BREESE

RC (DLC).

1. Letter not found.

From Joseph Jones

DR. SR.   FREDG. 29th. Janry. 1795

I thank you for the papers and your late favor explaining the business of Monroe with Mr. Randolph. Be pleased to attend to transmitting the inclosed.[1] Mr. Brent[2] is not I presume the Author of the Pamphlet you sent,[3] from him it was expected something would appear in answer to Lees address to the people of the district[4] which savored not a little of selfimportance and exaltation of himself above his Colleagues. This pamphlet was I suppose written before his vote agt. Giles's motion respecting the renunciation of Titles. There is a flying story here that Mercer is gone to Philadelphia in consequence of an invitation from H—l—n. Yr. friend

JOS: JONES

RC (DLC). Docketed by JM.

1. In his 23 Jan. 1795 letter to JM, Jones wrote that he would "trouble you with a short letter to Monroe by the next or following Post." This letter has not been found.

2. Richard Brent (1757–1814), Daniel Carroll's nephew, represented Stafford County, 1788, and Prince William County, 1793–94, in the Virginia House of Delegates. During the campaign in the congressional district composed of Fairfax, Loudoun, and Prince William counties, he anonymously attacked the Federalist incumbent, Richard Bland Lee, in a pamphlet that helped him to win the election on 16 Mar. 1795. He served as a Republican in the House of Representatives, 1795–99 and 1801–3, House of Delegates, 1800–1801, state Senate, 1808–9, and U.S. Senate, 1809–14 (BDC, p. 633; Jones to JM, 10 Feb. 1795, and n. 1; Leonard, General Assembly of Virginia, p. 259 and n. 4).

3. JM had probably sent Jones a copy of [Richard Bland Lee], Marcellus; Published in the Virginia Gazette, November and December, 1794 ([Richmond, 1794]; Evans 27263). For Lee's authorship of this pamphlet, which denied that the Federalists favored aristocracy, see Charles Lee to Richard Bland Lee, 31 Dec. 1794 (ViU).

4. In his 8 Dec. 1794 circular letter to his constituents, Lee tried to justify his voting record, which had usually differed from that of the rest of the Virginia delegation in Congress. He gave his reasons for opposing JM's commercial discrimination resolutions and for supporting the assumption of state debts, a Potomac site for the federal capital, Washington's Neutrality Proclamation, and Jay's mission to Great Britain (Philadelphia Dunlap and Claypoole's Am. Daily Advertiser, 12 Feb. 1795).

¶ From James Madison, Sr. Letter not found. 29 January 1795. Acknowledged in JM's 8 Feb. 1795 letter to his father. Requests that JM obtain at Philadelphia wire for sifters (for the gristmill that JM's family planned to build). Mentions a loss incurred by JM's brother William. Discusses a land transaction being considered with Prettyman Merry.

From Robert R. Livingston

DEAR SIR   NEW YORK 30th. Jany 1795.

You will probably think when you have read this that I avail myself of slight circumstances to open a correspondence with you And perhaps it will be candid to own thus, that desire has had no little influence upon my pen. I do not find that you have at Philadelphia any direct intelligence from Mr Jay it may therefore be useful to you to know the intelligence we have recd a little more particularly than you can learn it from our papers. There are two letters here from well informed merchants (one of whom has been consulted by Lord Greenville) stating that the Posts were to be evacuated the 30th. of June 1796 with a provisoe that if circumstances shd then render the evacuation inconvenient they may be retained six months Longer. That a free intercourse of traders with the import & export of goods shall be admitted in & thro' those posts to the territory of either Nation by the traders of both. That comms. shall be appointed to adjust matters relative to the paymt.

of debts due to Britain. With respect to the injuries our trade has sustained nothing is said, this I suppose is considered as settled by the accounts we have recd. of the opening the court of appeals.

You will at once see that if this is realy the treaty (of which I have no doubt) that Mr. Jay has sacraficed the essential interests of this country by not attending to a circumstance well known here to wit that the navigation of the lakes must necessarily be on our side that our posts are the only possible entrepo's for the indian trade and that the grand portage being exclusively ours no goods can be carried into the western country by the way of Canada but thro' our territories. By the treaty of Paris therefore the whole fur trade an object of 800,000 dols. a year was s[e]cur[e]d¹ to the United States & it is this circumstance alone which has hitherto prevented their evacuation since without them Canada would be perfectly useless. Supposing then that at the end of two years (which is very uncertain) these posts shd be evacuated the indian trade will still remain in the hands of the British because having the advantage of a free transportation of goods & supplies thro' our territories they may esstablish strong posts & trading houses in their own territory from whence the best furs come & thus continue to curb the indians & govern their trade, add to this that the knowledge the Canadians have of, & their close connection with the indians will if they are admitted on equal terms prevent our sustaining a rivalship with them. Whereas had the posts been surrendered upon the footing of the former treaty the united States would have carried on this commerce *exclusively* merely by refusing the import or export of goods or furs to & from Canada. The Indians in the british territory could not in that case have avoided taking their supplies, & selling their furs to us. As for the evacuation, I think we might either have relyed on our own force to command it at an earlier period than Mr. Jay has fixed, or obtained it on a general peace thro' the intervention of France. On this last subject I proposed a plan to Mr Munroe & Mr. Fauchette last sepr. who immediatly pressed the thing in France and were it [not]² for Mr. Jays concession I shd. have had good hopes of seeing our business done thro' that channel. They seem so sensible in England of the important advantages they have gained that several private Letters express an anxiety least we should not ratify the treaty. To prevent this is certainly the duty of every man that wishes well to the country, yet such is the violence of party that I fear no public consideration will have that effect. Permit me Sir to suggest one idea on this head. You have yet no official account of the treaty you may therefore fairly suppose that the posts may be yielded before the next meeting of Congress.

Would it not be proper to bring in a law predicated upon that Idea, whereby you prohibited the exportation or importation of Articles to or from Canada into our western territories. The preamble to this Law & the debates upon it will open the eyes of the public more than any thing that can be done after the treaty is officialy announced when every possible exertion will be made to support it. I am Dear Sir with much esteem & respect Your Most Obt hum: Servt

Robt R Livingston

RC (DLC); draft (NHi: Livingston Papers). Draft misdated 30 Jan. 1796. Minor variations between RC and draft have not been noted.

1. Letters in brackets are here supplied from the draft.
2. Word in brackets is here supplied from the draft.

Military Establishment

[2 February 1795]

On 20 January FitzSimons moved that the House request the president to submit a plan for the defense of the frontiers. After JM "doubted if it was agreeable to the Constitution," FitzSimons withdrew his motion. On 21 January the Committee of the Whole took up Nicholas's report, which recommended that the military establishment be authorized to continue in service until 1 June 1798 (*Annals of Congress*, 3d Cong., 2d sess., 1120, 1121, 1122, 1163). On 2 February Dayton proposed instead a resolution that the military establishment be continued by enlistments for a maximum term of three years at the president's discretion.

Mr. Madison . . . seemed rather favourable to lowering than augmenting the number of troops in the service of the United States. He alluded to the report of the treaty said to be entered into between this country and Britain, from which it might be inferred that the Indian hostilities on the north west of the Ohio would slacken.

Philadelphia Gazette, 4 Feb. 1795.

¶ To Alexander White. Letter not found. *2 February 1795.* Acknowledged in White to JM, 14 Feb. 1795. Apparently discusses news reports of Jay's negotiations with Great Britain, the prospects for peace in Europe, and legislation pending in Congress.

To John Adams

DEAR SIR   PHILADA. Feby. 3. 1795

I have been induced to this delay in acknowledging your letter of the 23d, inclosing one to you from Mr. Belknap of the 2d. Ulto. by a desire to obtain from my memory all the information it might have ever possessed in relation to the error in Docr. Kippis' life of Capt: Cook.

I was not a member of Congress till March 1780. It is probable therefore that, if his directions to American Commanders, in favor of Capt: Cook issued, as is stated, in March 1779, they must have been transmitted to that Body, and undergone its consideration, before I could have been present. After I became a member, nothing was ever done on the subject, as far as my memory can inform me. I do not even recollect that the subject ever fell incidentally, under any public discussion. I have however a pretty strong impression, that it occasionally entered into the conversation of the members, as it often did into that of intelligent Citizens out of doors, and that I never heard a sentiment uttered which did not applaud the magnanimity of the idea which considered Capt: Cook's expedition as consecrated to the general good of all Mankind, and consequently not included in the hostilities between particular nations.

I beg leave to suggest to you, Sir, if it has not already occurred, that Mr. Charles Thomson, will be more likely than any other individual to answer the wishes of Mr. Belknap. Besides the general accuracy to be expected from him, he must a[s] Secretary to Congress be particularly intimate with every thing that passed in that Assembly. With the highest respect and esteem, I have the honour to be, Sir, Your most Obedient humble servan⟨t⟩

Js. MADISON JR

P. S. I have shewn the above to Mr. Muhlenbourg the Speaker, and Mr. Boudinot, a member of the House of Representatives. The former was a Member of Congress during the years 1779, 80, & 81; The latter from July 1780 to the peace in 1783. Both of them concur in what I have stated, and recollect nothing more particular on the subject.

RC (MHi).

From Samuel Dexter, Jr.

SIR,   PHILAD. 3d. Feby. 1795

The subject of this is confidential. I have lately been told by a Gent. well acquainted with you, that he believed you were of opinion that a part of America is systematically struggling for a Government incompatible with equal rights, & that your political conduct is governed by this apprehension. This has induced me strongly to wish for a conversation with you on the subject, if perfectly agreable to you, confidential or not as you may chuse. Before I was concerned in administering the Government, I have had a similar suspicion; but since I have been here every thing has tended to form a very different opinion. I have found myself compelled steadily to oppose measures, which appear to me to lead to abuse of equal rights, & of course to Anarchy, & ultimately to tyranny. My respect, & that of the public, for your talents & Integrity have ever induced me to wish exceedingly for knowledge of the Motives for your present line of politics, when compared with your former Measures. A confidence that the motives are proper prevents me from feeling it indelicate to ask an explanation; & an expectation that neither my Constituents nor myself—shall consent to my being here another Session[1] makes this the only time to receive it. If the proposed Interview be perfectly agreable to you, I will thank you for the information & for the time, which will be convenient. If on any account it is otherwise, I am content to know it without assigning any reason, or even by silence. I am Sir with great respect Your Ob. servt.

SAML. DEXTER JUR

RC (DLC: Rives Collection, Madison Papers). Addressed by Dexter. Docketed by JM. On the cover, JM wrote a copy of his 5 Feb. 1795 reply to Dexter.

1. In the runoff congressional election for the second middle district of Massachusetts on 1 Feb., Dexter placed a close second behind Republican Joseph Bradley Varnum, but neither candidate had a majority. Dexter was finally defeated after two more runoff elections (Philadelphia *Aurora General Advertiser*, 3 and 21 Mar., 3 and 29 Apr. 1795; see also JM to Jefferson, 16 Nov. 1794, and n. 4). He later served as a U.S. senator, 1799–1800, secretary of war, 1800, and secretary of the treasury, 1801. Though a Federalist, he remained on friendly terms with JM and stayed on at the Treasury Department in Jefferson's administration until Gallatin assumed office in May 1801. He declined JM's offer of appointment as U.S. minister to Spain in 1815.

From Hubbard Taylor

DEAR SIR   SPRING HILL CLARK COUNTY 3d. Feby. 95

Inclosed you will receive some papers respecting a late decision of our Court of appeals, which has given rise to great deal of argumentation respecting the Claims of Settlements & pre-emptions granted by the Commissione[r]s in the years 79 & 80. The Memorial[1] is said [to] be drawn by Mr. Jno. Brackengridge, signed chiefly by the holders of

Settlts. & preemptts. That great indavidual disstress will be the consequence seems to be agreed on all hands—as those kind of titles were conceived to be finally settled—emigrants purchased more freely of them than of any others (the Military excepted) and made no scruple to warrant them, admiting that the decisions of the commissioners was final where no fraud had been practised. The matter was taken up by the assembly and the two Judges, Muter & Sabastion was cited to appear, and an application was made to have a vote passed by two thirds of the Legislature to have them removed from Office, it faild; there was then a resolution brought in passing a censure on the Judges declaring them to have been actuated from impure & currupt motives, the want of Judgement & that the decree Kenton vs. McConnell was contrary to the plain meaning of the Strict letter & spirit of the law. This also faild in the lower house. It was however revived in the Senate and then agreed to in the House of Reps. What will be the consequence no one knows—the Judges has not resigned as yet. Procrastinations in decisions are more particularly prejudicial here than in most states, as it cramp[s] industry & deters emigrants from venturing among us.

As to the news of the Western Army you will see gentlemen by one of whom I shall send this letter who will be better abble to give you the latest accts than I can. I propose to send this by Docr. Ridgely[2] a Gentleman of the highest Carracter and in no degree attatched to any of the parties which has run so high in this state. I have had frequent conversations with the Dcr. with whoom I am intimate and the utmost confidence may be placed in any thing he shall communicate.

The perport of Mr. Innis Mission is not yet known. I am sorry to say there appeard to be a coolness subsisting (on his arrival) in the appearance of Many who ought to be the foremost to set all difficult Matters in a fair point of view, in preference to holding out doubts & suspicions. If it should be the wish of Mr. Innis that the Assembly be called expect it will be done.

As to the Lands you & your brother held in this Country proper cure shall be taken that they shall not be forfieted or sold for the payment of the Tax's. And it will always give me pleasure to serve you in any thing that is in my power that I am capable of doing. Be pleased to present my Compliments to my unknown connection Mrs. Madison & beleave me to be, with much esteem Dr Sir Yr Affe: Hble: Sert:

H. TAYLOR

The vindictive spirit with wh. some of the assembly acted, is generally thought, to have proceeded from personal dislike to the Judges.

RC (DLC). Docketed by JM. For surviving enclosure, see n. 1.

1. Taylor's enclosures included the Lexington *Ky. Gazette* of 6 Dec. 1794, which is in JM's portfolio of newspaper clippings (DLC, series 7, container 3). That issue published a memorial to the Kentucky General Assembly protesting the state Court of Appeals decision in *Kenton* v. *McConnell*. For a discussion of this case and its political impact, see Coward, *Kentucky in the New Republic*, pp. 81–83.

2. Frederick Ridgely served as a surgeon's mate during the Revolution and practiced as a physician in Lexington from 1792. He was surgeon-general in Maj. Gen. Anthony Wayne's western army in 1794 and professor of medicine at Transylvania University from 1799 (Heitman, *Historical Register Continental*, p. 467; Hopkins, *Papers of Henry Clay*, 1:127 n.; Robert Peter, *The History of the Medical Department of Transylvania University* [Louisville, Ky., 1905], pp. 10–11).

Military Establishment

[3 February 1795]

The Committee of the Whole rejected Nicholas's report on the military establishment and took up Dayton's resolution.

Mr. Madison, after all that had been said, was still of opinion that there had been a change in our situation, and so there might be a possibility that a reduction was proper. By the arrangements made in this session, it might be practicable to reduce the numbers *nominally* and yet have a real augmentation, because the new regulations would actually bring more men into the field.[1]

Philadelphia Gazette, 6 Feb. 1795 (reprinted in *Gazette of the U.S.*, 10 Feb. 1795 [speech misdated 30 Jan. 1794]).

1. After further debate, the House passed the resolution and appointed Dayton chairman of a select committee that on 11 Feb. reported "a bill for continuing and regulating the Military Establishment of the United States." In Committee of the Whole on 13 Feb., JM moved an amendment "that the troops should only be employed for the protection of the frontier." The committee defeated his amendment and reported the bill to the House. JM voted with the minority when the House defeated an amendment to reduce the military establishment to 2,500 men "whenever there shall be peace with the Indian tribes." He "renewed his amendment proposed in the committee in other words. The substance was, that regulars ought not to be used against citizens, for enforcing the laws of the United States, but only for protection against foreign invasion, and the Indian tribes." JM was again in the minority when the House defeated his amendment. On 14 Feb. the House passed the bill, which (as amended by the Senate) Washington signed on 3 Mar. (*Annals of Congress*, 3d Cong., 2d sess., 1212, 1221–23, 1275; *Philadelphia Gazette*, 14 Feb. 1795; *U.S. Statutes at Large*, 1:430–32).

To Samuel Dexter, Jr.

(Copy of answer)

SIR   Feby 5. 1795

Your letter of the 3d. inst: did not fall into my hands till late last evening. As the conversation you propose can on no acct. be objectionable to me, I shall concur in it with the pleasure I ought to feel in complying with your wishes. Perhaps I ought myself to wish for an oppy. of removing one at least of the impressions you are under, which may not do justice to the consistency between my present & former line of politics. As you refer the time of our being together, to me, I will take the liberty of asking your Company at dinner on Sunday, en famille, if you are unengaged for that day, and after dinner we can be conveniently alone & free from interruption. I shd. have proposed an earlier day, but that is the first that I can command.

FC (DLC: Rives Collection, Madison Papers). Written on the cover of Dexter to JM, 3 Feb. 1795.

From Samuel Dexter, Jr.

SIR,   Thursday 5th. Feby. [1795]

I received your favour of this Morning, & will with pleasure take a family dinner with you on Sunday. You mention an impression on my mind respecting difference in former & present political Conduct, if this be wrong, I shall be particularly happy in its removal. I really have believed, perhaps from misrepresentation, that the fact was unquestionable, & that the only question was as to the Motive. Yours with esteem

S DEXTER JUR

RC (DLC: Rives Collection, Madison Papers). Undated in the *Index to the James Madison Papers*. Date here assigned by comparison with JM to Dexter, 5 Feb. 1795.

From Thomas Jefferson

TH: J. TO J. MADISON.   MONTICELLO Feb. 5. 95.

Congress drawing to a close, I must trouble you with a bundle of little commissions

1. to procure for me a copy of the correspondence between Genet, Hammond & myself at large.
2. a pamphlet entitled 'Sketches on rotations of crops,'[1] to be had I believe at Dobson's. The author in a note pa. 43. mentions some for-

mer publication of his, which I should be glad to have also; as I am sure it must be good. Who is the author? Is it Peters? I do not think it is Logan.

3. to procure for me from some of the seedsmen some of the seed of the Winter vetch[2] (it is the Vicia sativa, semine albo of Millar[3]) as it is cheap, you may be governed in the quantity by the convenience of bringing. I think it must be valuable for our fall-fallows.

4. to commission your barber to find for me such a seal as he let you have.

5. to enquire of J. Bringhurst whether Donath[4] is returned from Hamburg, who was to bring me some glass? I know nobody who can give the information but Bringhurst, and I would not trouble you with it could I have got a word from him otherwise. But I have written twice to him, & got no answer, and I have sent twice to Philadelphia by a neighbor of mine, whom he has put off by saying he would write to me. If I could only find out whether Donath is returned, & what is his address in Philadelphia, I could then enquire about my glass of himself by letter.

We have now had about 4. weeks of winter weather, rather hard for our climate—many little snows which did not lay 24. hours, & one 9. I. deep which remained several days. We have had few thawing days during the time. It is generally feared here that your collegue F. Walker will be in great danger of losing his election. His competitor is indefatigable attending courts &c. and wherever he is, there is a general drunkenness observed, tho' we do not know that it proceeds from his purse.[5] Wilson Nicholas is attacked also in his election. The ground on which the attack is made is that he is a speculator. The explanations which this has produced, prove it a serious crime in the eyes of the people. But as far as I hear he is only investing the fruits of a first & only speculation. Almost every carriage-owner has been taken in for a double tax: information through the newspapers not being actual, tho legal, in a country where they are little read. This circumstance has made almost every man, so taken in, a personal enemy to the tax. I escaped the penalty only by sending an express over the county to search out the officer the day before the forfeiture would have been incurred. We presume you will return to Orange after the close of the session, and hope the pleasure of seeing mrs. Madison & yourself here. I have past my winter almost alone, mr. & mrs. Randolph being at Varina. Present my best respects to mrs. Madison, & accept them affectionately yourself. Adieu.

RC (DLC); FC (DLC: Jefferson Papers).

1. [John Beale Bordley], *Sketches on Rotations of Crops* (Philadelphia, 1792; Evans 24129).

2. For discussion and excerpts from correspondence concerning Jefferson's use of vetch in crop rotation, see Betts, *Jefferson's Farm Book*, pp. 189, 310–19.

3. Philip Miller, *The Gardener's Dictionary* (London, 1768).

4. John Bringhurst was a "fancy goods merchant" with premises at 12 South Third Street; Josiah Donath was a merchant with a shop at 28 South Front Street (Hardie, *Philadelphia Directory* [1794 ed.], pp. 17, 40).

5. In the congressional elections on 16 Mar., Samuel Jordan Cabell (1756–1818) defeated his fellow Republican Francis Walker in the district composed of Albemarle, Amherst, Fluvanna, and Goochland counties. A Revolutionary veteran and member of the Society of the Cincinnati, Cabell represented Amherst County in the House of Delegates, 1785–92. An Antifederalist at the Virginia ratifying convention of 1788, he later cooperated with French Strother of Culpeper County in opposing JM's proposal for discriminating between original and subsequent holders of government securities. JM imputed the opposition of Cabell and Strother to "personal animosity." Cabell served in the House of Representatives, 1795–1803 (Hening, *Statutes*, 13:332; Swem and Williams, *Register*, p. 354; JM to Edmund Randolph, 21 Mar. 1790, *PJM*, 13:110).

To Robert R. Livingston

DEAR SIR   PHILADA. Feby. 8. 1795

I am much obliged by your favor of the 30th. Ult. The information it gives on the subject of the Treaty is more exact on some points than any I had before received, particularly in relation to the footing on which the Posts are to be left. If Mr. Jay has really turned our exclusive right into a thoroughfare, which will in its operation be almost an exclusive right to G. Britain, it will certainly form an objection to the Treaty which ought neither to be concealed nor mitigated to the public; and that such is the tenor of his stipulated arrangement, is but too probable from the accounts to which you refer. It is a question however of some nicety whether the mode of *forcing* a discussion in Congress which might bring the subject into public view, would not risk as much as it would promise. As it would be impossible to avoid the appearance of an *anticipated attack*, on the Treaty, it could be said with so much plausibility that the treaty ought to be seen and understood in the whole, before it be prejudged in any of its parts, and that regulations of a distrustful aspect were particularly improper in the very moment of friendly adjustment, that the view in urging the discussion might be successfully perverted into a prejudice against the general object pursued, and the effect of future disquisitions at a more proper season, be thereby diminished. I shall however reflect attentively on the idea you have suggested, and sound some of my most judicious friends on it also. It will be some consolation in this case, that if the Treaty should be in an inadmissible shape, it will be in the power of less than a majority of the Senate, to defend the U. S. against it. And this may the more be expected, as the extracts and comments in the Newspapers are already summoning the public mind to an enquiry into the terms and merits of the Treaty.

The House of Reps. are engaged as you will see by the Newspapers, on a provision for sinking the public debt. The friends to excises take advantage of the popularity of the object to enforce those as the means, and the general dislike of direct taxes in the majority of the House, if not out of doors, favor the same policy. It is pretty clear however that a debt which will require more than 30 years (the term calculated) to pay it off, will never be paid. Emergences may be fairly presumed to add to the debt faster than such an operation will substract [*sic*] from it. We must therefore reconcile ourselves either to a perpetual public debt —or to some considerable exertion in the way of direct taxes apportioned on the States, or of excises extended to objects which will yield an equivalent revenue. With very great esteem I am Dear Sir Your most Obedt. hble servt.

Js. Madison Jr.

RC (NHi: Livingston Papers); Tr (NN: Livingston Papers, Bancroft Transcripts). RC franked and addressed by JM to Livingston at New York. Docketed by Livingston.

To James Madison, Sr.

Hond. Sir   Feby. 8. 1795.

Your favor of Jany. 28. came to hand two days ago. I have not had time yet to look out for the wire for Sifters, but shall attend to it. I wait to hear from you further on the subject of Bolting cloths &c. before I execute the commissions in your former letter, as my last will have informed you. I am very sorry for the loss of my brother William; but there is no remedy for such cases, but patience, and redoubled industry. I can not give any precise answer to Mr. Merry without knowing more precisely his terms, as well as the proportion of his land which is arable. It would seem that his price is too high considering the loss of his house, and the great quantity of land that can never be put to use. Deducting this, the price would amount probably to 8 or 10 dollrs. an acre, which exceed any thing known in that quarter.

We are yet in the dark as to the Treaty concluded by Mr. Jay; no copy being arrived. The scraps from private letters afford too imperfect as well as too inauthentic an account of it to justify an opinion on its merits. We are in hourly expectation of the official despatches.

Congress are employed on a plan for paying off the debt. It is proposed to prolong the taxes laid last year and appropriate them with other surpluses to the purpose. But without new taxes, 30 years at least will be required for the operation, a period which may be expected to generate as much new debt as will be discharged of Old. If we are ever therefore to be out of debt, additional taxes direct or indirect will be necessary. We are well and offer our affections to my mother & yourself.

Js. Madison Jr

RC (DLC). Franked and addressed by JM to his father at Orange Court House.

From Joseph Jones

Dr. Sr.   10th. Febry. 1795

Mr. Brent has lately published a small Pamphlet in answer to Mr. Lees address to the people of the District.[1] This as well as the one you sent me are ample expositions of Lees conduct in Congress and will prove satisfactory to those who will be at the trouble to read and are capable of judging of them—the bulk of the people are not so and will not examine them. Had Mr. Brent in his letter to the people confined himself to some striking objections to his Antagonists conduct and which from their nature were most likely to reach their feelings, and have avoided so lengthy a discussion, it wod. have been more generally read by them and better understood, in that respect and that only Lee's will have the most influence among the people, at le[a]st I fear so, as it is comparatively short and soon read over. I am willing to suppose, tho' I lament the event, that Monroe had written his friends by the advise boat that was taken, as an apology for the tradiness [sic] of his communications of which I think we have some reason to complain. The period of the Session approaching I presume you have decided your course for the interval and where you mean to spend your Summer. Wolcott I see succeeds Hamilton. The trading part in particular and others in general appear muc⟨h⟩ pleased to hear Jay has concluded his embassy so favour-⟨ably⟩ as represented by private communications. You no doubt have or soon will have the official information. There appears little hope of peace from the last accounts which seem to contradict our preceeding intelligence. Yr friend & Servt

Jos: Jones

RC (DLC). Docketed by JM.

1. [Richard Brent], *To the Freeholders of the District of Fairfax, Loudoun, and Prince-William* ([Richmond?, 1794]; Evans 27808). This pamphlet attacked Richard Bland Lee and the circular letter to his constituents that attempted to justify his voting record as a congressman (see Jones to JM, 29 Jan. 1795, n. 4).

From John Francis Mercer

DEAR SIR   MARLBROUGH, Feby. 11th. 1795.

Mr. John Fenton Mercer[1] the bearer of this is the eldest Son of my late Brother. By a clause in his fathers Will his Estate cannot be divided for three years to come, & that time he proposes to pass in some of the Armies of france probably the Northern Army. I know no situation more improving for a young Man than the family of an old experienc'd General Officer, & from my knowledge of this young Gentleman's talents & disposition I have great expectation of the benefits he woud derive from such an opportunity. He only wants prudence to make a most valuable man & that can only come from experience. Your forwarding him in this view if in your power will be an additional obligation to many which I acknowledge.

I have had no opportunity of congratulating you before on your becoming a free Mason[2]—a very ancient & honorable fraternity. I am sure you are now much wiser & I do not doubt you are much happier altho' you were very wise & happy before, at least in my opinion. I hold a lodge on your road pray let me take you some time by the hand in it & let Mrs. Mercer welcome, the fair prophetess who has converted you to the true faith. A Man who has got his head somewhat clear of a large load of leaden politics[3]—feels of course a little light headed to that you must attribute the levity of this style which is only intended to assure you of my respect & friendship for you & yours.

                                                JOHN F MERCER.

RC (DLC). Docketed by JM.

1. John Fenton Mercer (1773–1812) was the son of James Mercer of Marlborough in Stafford County, who had died in 1793 (*WMQ*, 1st ser., 17 [1908–9]: 209).

2. JM is not known ever to have become a Freemason. Mercer figuratively compared the bond of JM's recent marriage with that of Masonry.

3. Mercer had resigned his seat in the House of Representatives on 13 Apr. 1794 (*BDC*, pp. 1399–1400).

From John Sevier

SIR   GREENVILLE. 13th February 1795

This will be handed you by the revd. Mr. Balsh[1] president of the Greenville college lately established by law in our territory. The board of Trustees flatter themselves that the legislature of the United States will encourage And patronize this laudable institution, And from the Knowledge I have of your Great regard for literature, take the liberty to Recommend Mr. Balsh to your favourable Notice And Attention. I have the honor to be sir With regard And Much respect Your Obedt. Hbl Servt.

JOHN: SEVIER

RC (DLC). Addressed by Sevier to JM, by "Mr. Balsh." Docketed by JM.

1. The Reverend Hezekiah Balch graduated from the College of New Jersey in 1766. He taught school in Fauquier County, Virginia, and served as a Presbyterian minister in Pennsylvania, North Carolina, and the transmontane region that is now Tennessee. He participated with Sevier in the attempt to establish the state of Franklin and from 1795 until his death in 1810 served as president of Greeneville College (later merged with Tusculum College). Sevier was a member of the college's Board of Trustees, which authorized Balch to solicit funds for the college from Washington and members of Congress. Washington donated $100 (McLachlan, *Princetonians, 1748–1768*, pp. 545–48; Allen E. Ragan, *A History of Tusculum College, 1794–1944* [Greeneville, Tenn., 1945], pp. 1–6; trustees of Greeneville College to Washington, March 1795 [DNA: RG 59, Misc. Letters]; Balch to Washington, 18 Dec. 1795 [DLC: Washington Papers]).

From Alexander White

DEAR SIR   WOODVILLE 14th. February 1795

Your favr. of 2d instant came to hand in course of Post. What a man wishes he will readily believe, I feel a confidence that the accounts of Jay's successful negotiation are well founded, and that a general Peace in Europe is an event not remote. These circumstances I consider as ensuring the prosperity of our own Country, and I flatter myself that the proceedings of the present Session will go far towards promoting internal peace, content and security. Sixty Millions of debt is a burden we should wish to be rid of—although the honest Farmer, the Militia Man and the veteran Soldier or their Widows and Children dispersed throughout the Union, were quarterly receiving the interest of their well earned Services at the hands of a grateful Country, but situated as the debt is, there are other sensations which induce a wish for a speedy discharge of it. I therefore hope a difference of opinion with respect to the mode of taxation will not prevent the business from being put in a fair train before the rising of Congress. The perfecting the militia Law I consider as another important object.

The beginning of winter was rather unfavourable, but we have lately had fine Snows, and I hope the grain will yet be good. Adieu—and believe me Yours &c

ALEXR WHITE

P. S. A Gentleman from Baltimore informs me Jays dispatches are arrived, with the Treaty with England—but that there is little prospect of Peace in Europe, the Belligerent Powers making immense preparations for another Campaign.

RC (DLC). Docketed by JM.

To Thomas Jefferson

DEAR SIR   PHILADA. Feby. 15 1795

Your favor of the 5th. came to hand yesterday. I will attend to your several commissions. Mr. Hawkins tells me, that the seed of the Winter Vetch is not to be got here.

Altho' nearly three months have passed since the signing of the Treaty by Jay, the official account of it has not been received, and the public have no other knowledge of its articles than are to be gleaned from the imperfect scraps of private letters. From these it is inferred that the bargain is much less in our favor than might be expected from the circumstances which co-operated with the justice of our demands. It is even conjectured that on some points, particularly the Western posts, the arrangements will be inadmissible. I find that in N. Y. there are accounts which are credited,[1] that the posts, after the surrender, are to be *thoroughfares*, for the traders and merchandizes of both parties. The operation of this will strike you at once, and the sacrifice is the greater, if it be true as is stated, that the former regulation on this subject, secured to the U. S. the monopoly of the fur trade, it being impossible for the Canadian Traders to get to & from the markets, without using our portages, and our parts of the lakes. It is wrong however to prejudge, but I suspect that Jay has been betrayed by his anxiety to couple us with England, and to avoid returning with his finger in his mouth. It is apparent that those most likely to be in the secret of the affair, do not assume an air of triumph.

The elections in N. York give *six* republicans instead of the former *three*. E. Livingston had in the City 205 votes more than Watts the present member. In Massachts. the elections are in several instances, still to be repeated. Dexter is to run a *third* heat. In the last his rival outvoted him, but was disappointed by a few scattering votes, which prevented his having a majority of the whole. It is said that if nothing new turns up, Varnum will be sure to succeed on the next trial. The choice of Senators continues to run on the wrong side. In Delaware, where we were promised of late, a republican, it was contrived by a certain disposition of offices as some tell us, or according to others, occasioned by particular sickneses, that Latimer of the H. of Reps.

473

lately dropped by the people, has been appointed by the Legislature. N. Carolina has appointed Bloodworth whom you may recollect. His country ment [*sic*] here do not augur favorably of his political course. Clinton has declined a re-election to the Govt. of N. Y. His party set up Yates & Floyd agst. Jay and Van-Ranslaer. Hamilton does not interfere with Jay. It is pompously announced in the Newspapers, that poverty drives him back to the Bar for a livelihood.

The Session has produced as yet, but few acts of Consequence. Several important ones are depending on the subjects of the Militia, of the military Establishment, and the discharge of the public debt. On the first little more will probably be done than to digest some regulations which will be left for public consideration till the next session. On the second, the present military Establishment will be continued and compleated; notwithstanding the late treaty with the Six Nations, the success of Wayne agst. the other tribes, and the disappearance of ominous symtoms in the aspect of G. Britain. I am extremely sorry to remark a growing apathy to the evil and danger of standing armies. And a vote passed two days ago, which is not only an evidence of that, but if not the effect of unpardonable inattention, indicates a temper still more alarming. In the Military Acts now in force, there are words, limiting the use of the army to the protection of the Frontiers. The Bill lately brought in revised the whole subject, and omitted this limitation. It was proposed to re-instate the words. This was rejected by a large majority. It was then proposed to substitute another phrase free from the little criticisms urged agst. the first proposition. The debate brought out an avowal that the Executive ought to be free to use the regular troops, as well as the Militia in support of the laws against our own Citizens. Notwithstanding this the amendment was lost by 8 votes. The House was very thin, & it is supposed, that the majority would have been in favor of the amendment, if all the members had been present. The mischeif however is irremediable, as the Senate will greedily swallow the Bill in its present form. This proceeding is the more extraordinary when the President's speech and the answer of the House of Reps. are recollected and compared with it. The third subject is the reduction of the public debt. Hamilton has in an arrogant valedictory Report presented a plan for the purpose. It will require about *30 years* of uninterrupted operation. The fund is to consist of the surpluses of impost & Excise, and the temporary taxes of the last Session which are to be prolonged till 1781.[2] You will judge of the chance of our ever being out of debt, if no other means are to be use⟨d.⟩ It is to be lamented that the public are not yet better reconciled to direct taxes which alone can work down the debt faster than new emergences will probably add to it. Of this dislike the partizans of the Debt take advantage not only to perpetuate it, but

to make a merit of the application of inadequate means to the discharge
of it. The plan of Hamilton contained a number of new irredeemabili-
ties, among the remodifications proposed by him. All these have been
struck out.

Mr. Christie of the House of Reps. intends to visit England in the
interval between the present & next session. He is ambitious of a line
from you introducing him to Mr. Pinkney, and has made me his solicitor
for it. He is a man of good sense, and second to none in a decided &
systematic devotion to Republicanism. Will you oblige us both by inclosing me such a letter. You need not fear its reaching me, as I shall be
detained here some time after the adjournment. Adieu

RC (DLC). Unsigned. Franked and addressed by JM to Jefferson at Charlottesville. Docketed by Jefferson, "recd. Mar. 3."

1. For a report on the contents of the Jay treaty, see Livingston to JM, 30 Jan.
1795.
2. At a later time someone, possibly John C. Payne, here interlined "1817."
Hamilton's "Report on a Plan for the Further Support of Public Credit" of 16 Jan.
proposed to extend until 1801 the revenue measures passed during the first session
of the Third Congress (Syrett and Cooke, *Papers of Hamilton*, 18:91).

From James Monroe

DEAR SIR   PARIS Feby. 18. 1795.

I was yesterday favored with yours of the 4th. of Decr. the only one
yet recd. I had perfectly an[ti]cipated the secret causes & motives of
the western business, and was extremely happy to find that the patriotism of the people in every quarter, left to its own voluntary impulse and
without any information that was calculated to stimulate it, was sufficient to triumph over the schemes of wicked and designing men. I
have been always convinced that this was a resource to be counted on
with certainty upon any emergency, & that the more frequent these
were, the sooner wod. the possibility of success in such schemes be destroyed, & our govt. assume a secure and solid form. I likewise perfectly
comprehended the motive and tendency of the discussion upon the subject of the societies, but was persuaded that the conduct of the societies
themselves upon that occasion, together with the knowledge diffused
every where of the principle upon which they were formed, would
give that business likewise a happy termination. This was the case in
one house and will I doubt not likewise be so in the publick mind if
the discussion shod. be provoked. The fact is, such societies cannot
exist in an enlightened country, unless there is some cause for them:

their continuance depends upon that cause. For whenever you test them by the exigence and it is found inadequate they will fall: and if there is one an attack upon them will encrease it, for they are not even to be put down by law. I was fearful the conduct of the Jacobin society here would injure the cause of republicanism every where, by discrediting popular complaints and inclining men on the side of government however great its oppressions might be. But that society was different from those that ever existed before; it was in fact the government of France, and the principal means of retarding the revolution itself; by it all those atrocities which now stain & always will stain certain stages of the revolution were committed: and it had obviously become the last pivot upon which the hopes of the coalisd powers depended. This society was therefore the greatest enemy of the revolution, and so clear was this that all France called for its overthrow by some act of violence. It is easy for designing men to turn the vices of one society somewhat similar in its origin, and which became such only in the course of events by degenerating and losing sight of the object which gave birth to them, agnst. all others, altho' the parellel may go no farther than that stage in which they all had merit. As the conduct of the Jacobin society made such an impression upon affrs. here it became my duty to notice it in my official dispatches: I accordingly did so by giving an historic view of its origin progress & decline, truely & of course under the above impression, & which I think will be found marked upon the statment to an observant reader: for in one stage viz from the deposition of the king I say that the danger was from confusion alone, since the old government was overset & the new one entirely in the hands & exerted virtuously for the sole benefit of the people, and it is intimated in the close that however enormous the vices may be provided treasonable practices be not discovered, that its overthrow must be left to publick opinion only. It became my duty to notice this subject & I think I have done it with propriety; however examine it & write me what you think of it.[1]

I recd. some days past a letter from Mr. Randolph[2] containing a severe criticism upon my address to the Convention & the publication of the papers committed to my care, and which justified that address & makes its defense agnst the attacks of that party with you. I was hurt at the criticism & equally surprised, for I did not expect it would be avowed that it was wished I shod. make a *secret* use of them, giving them weight by any opinion which might be entertained of my own political principles, or in other words that I would become the instrument of that party here thereby putting in its hands my own reputation, to be impeached hereafter in the course of events. They were deceived if they supposed I was such a person. On the contrary I was happy in the

opportunity furnish'd not only on acct. of the good effects I knew it
would produce in other respects, but likewise as it furnishd me with
one of presenting to the eyes of the world the covenant which subsisted
between them and me: by the publication they are bound to the
French nation & to me to observe a particular line of conduct. If they
deviate from it they are censurable, and the judicious part of our countrymen as well as posterity will reward them accordingly. The fact is
I would not upon my own authority make those declarations of their
sentiments, & therefore I was glad to embrace the opportunity to let
them speak for themselves. I felt some concern for Mr. Randolph because I feared it would expose him to some attacks, but I concluded he
would despise them: for in truth I do not apply to him the above comments. I have answered[3] those criticisms with suitable respect but as
becomes a free and independant citizen whose pride is to do his duty
but who will not yeild when he is undeservedly attacked. I have reviewed the state of things upon my arrival & shewed the necessity of
some bold measure to retrieve it. What I have stated in my reply is true;
I have many documents to prove it in each particular. Tis possible this
business may end here, for I have since recd. a letter[4] in answer to my
2. first & which were not then recd. by Mr. Randolph, in a different
style; and to which latter I shall likewise write a suitable answer:[5] but
it is also possible it may not. I have therefore thot. proper to transmit
to you a copy of it, that you may perfectly comprehend the state of
this business with the ground upon which I rest. Perhaps it may be
proper for you to shew it in confidence to others but this is entirely
submitted to you. I wish it seen by Mr. Jefferson & Mr. Jones.

The state of parties in America is as well known by the Committee of
publick safety & other leading members as it is there. It was mentioned
by some person to Merlin Doui that Hamilton & Knox were going out
of office, & he instantly replied he would have it inserted in the Bulletin
& communicated to the departments, as an event auspicious to France
as well as America. This however was prevented, because the commn.
had been recd. by one person only.

Fortunately the successes of this republick have been great even beyond the expectation of every one. The entire conquest of the 7. U.
provinces closed in the midst of winter for a few months the last campaign: indeed so great has the success been that they have scarcely an
enemy before them, and I believe they may march whither they please
in the course of the next. Their conduct in Holland too in other respects
has done as much service to the cause of liberty, almost as their arms.
A revolution which was immediately commenc'd has made a rapid
progress there & will no doubt be soon completed. I think if our sage
negotiator in London had waited a little longer till the victories of

France were more complete (& it was certain they would be so), he might have gained terms satisfactory to all of his countrymen: but perhaps being a *conciliating* negotiator, he could not take advantage of that argument—perhaps he wished for the honor of Engld. to deprive the republican party in America of the opportunity of saying *his success* was owing in any degree to *that cause.*

I think upon the whole yr. prospects independant of foreign causes are much better than heretofore; the elections have been favorable: but with the aid of foreign causes they are infinitely so.

We are well—our child is at school in a French family, & already speaks the language tolerably well. Joe is also at school & rather in a line of improv'ment. I have little leasure & of course am but little improved in the language. We desire to be affecy. remembered to yr. lady whose esteem we shall certainly cultivate by all the means in our power. If a loan is obtained can it be laid out to advantage? Inform on this head. Remember me to Mr. Beckley, to Tazewell, Mason & all my friends & believe me sincerely yrs.

Jas Monroe

PS. Pinckney is abt. sitting out for Spn.—suppose the peace with France is made before his arrival what success will he have?

RC (DLC); enclosure (DLC: Rives Collection, Madison Papers). RC and enclosure docketed by JM. Sent under the care of Pierre Auguste Adet, the recently appointed French minister to the U.S. (see Monroe to JM, 25 Feb. 1795). Monroe enclosed a clerk's copy of his 12 Feb. 1795 letter to Randolph (printed in *ASP, Foreign Relations,* 1:694–95).

1. On 23 Feb. the *Philadelphia Gazette* published "Extracts from three letters, written by a Gentleman in Paris to his friend in this City; the AUTHENTICITY of which may be depended on." In fact the letters extracted were Monroe to Edmund Randolph, 16 Oct., 7 Nov., and 20 Nov. 1794 (*ASP, Foreign Relations,* 1:680–81, 683, 686), in which the minister criticized the role of the Jacobin clubs in the Reign of Terror and described their proscription after the fall of Robespierre. Monroe's comments provided grist for the mill of the American debate then raging over the "self-created societies." The extracts were reprinted in the N.Y. *Herald,* which identified Monroe as the author, on 28 Feb., and in [Edmund Randolph], *Germanicus* ([Philadelphia, 1795]; Evans 27597), pp. 73–77. First published between 19 Jan. and 1 Apr. in *Dunlap and Claypoole's Am. Daily Advertiser,* Randolph's thirteen anonymous "Germanicus" letters attacked the Democratic societies. In his letter of 11 Mar. 1795, JM warned Monroe about "this use of your observations" and urged "that your own judgment may be the better exercised as to the latitude or reserve of your communications."

2. Edmund Randolph to Monroe, 2 Dec. 1794 (*ASP, Foreign Relations,* 1:689–90).

3. Monroe to Randolph, 12 Feb. 1795 (ibid., 1:694–95).

4. Randolph to Monroe, 5 Dec. 1794 (ibid., 1:690–91).

5. Monroe to Randolph, 18 Feb. 1795 (ibid., 1:696).

To James Madison, Sr.

HOND. SIR   Feby. 23. 1795

Inclosed is the explanation from the offices concerning Mr. L's claim. The Treaty made by Mr. Jay is not yet come to hand & we know nothing more of its articles than what has been conjectured from the hints in the Newspapers. I have already let you know that if you mean that I shd. sell your paper, you must forward the proper powers. The period is becoming favorable. It can now be sold at par. As I shall not be able to get off for some time after the adjournment, you may venture to write & communicate with me till I give you notice that your letters will be too late. If you, my mother or Fanny want any particular articles to be got let me know it. I understand it is reported in some parts of my District that I decline being a candidate in March. Perhaps I ought on many considerations to do so—but I have said nothing from which the Report could spring, and find myself constrained again to sacrifice both my inclination and interest. If you have an opportunity of seeing or dropping a few lines to any particular friend in Louisa (say Mr. A. Fontaine)[1] I should therefore be glad you would contradict the Report, as well as let it be known, that it is not in my power to be in the district before the election as I would wish. I rely on you & my brother W. to give the proper explanations in Orange & Madison Counties. Congs. will adjourn on the 3d. of March. Yr. Affe. son

Js. MADISON JR

RC (DLC). Enclosure not found.

1. Aaron Fontaine (1753–1823) was appointed an ensign in the Louisa County militia in 1779. He moved to Louisville, Kentucky, by 1802. His son, Maury Fontaine, was a naval midshipman, 1809–11 (*DAR Patriot Index*, p. 243; Gwathmey, *Historical Register of Virginians*, p. 280; *WMQ*, 1st ser., 4 [1895–96]: 183 n. 9; Callahan, *List of Officers of the Navy*, p. 199; Aaron Fontaine to JM, 19 Aug. 1811 [NN]).

From Thomas Jefferson

TH: J. TO J. M.   Feb. 23. 95.

I inclose two letters to the President[1] & Secretary of state[2] open for your perusal & consideration. I pray you to bestow thought on the subject, & if you disapprove it, return me my letters, undelivered, by next post. If you approve of them, stick a wafer in them & have them delivered. I also put under your cover a letter to the Fresco painter[3] from whom you inclosed me one. His not having furnished me with his address obliges me to give you this trouble. Nothing new. Adieu affectionately.

RC (DLC); FC (DLC: Jefferson Papers). Enclosed in Jefferson to David Rittenhouse, 24 Feb. 1795 (FC, DLC: Jefferson Papers).

1. Jefferson to Washington, 23 Feb. 1795 (DLC: Washington Papers). In this letter, Jefferson recommended the proposal of Sir Francis d'Ivernois to reestablish the University of Geneva, recently "demolished" by revolution, in Virginia. For excerpts from other correspondence relating to d'Ivernois's proposal, see Sowerby, *Catalogue of Jefferson's Library*, 1:127.

2. Jefferson to Edmund Randolph, 23 Feb. 1795 (DLC: Jefferson Papers).

3. Jefferson to Ignatius Shnydore (or Schneider), 21 Feb. 1795 (not found, but listed in Jefferson's Epistolary Record [DLC: Jefferson Papers]).

Survey of the Southern Coast

[24 February 1795]

The Committee of the Whole took up the report of a select committee recommending that the federal government grant a loan to a project to survey the coast of Georgia.

Mr. Madison would not hastily undertake to say that the grant of money was improper to be made to this affair, as a public good. He did not at present wish to enter into that. He considered a loan, however, as the worst of all possible shapes, in which the request could come before the house, for it was impossible to say where the practice of lending might stop. If assistance was to be granted in this case, he did not see why the survey should not be extended to other parts of the Union, where it was equally necessary. Every private undertaker might, in this way, solicit a loan, when the object of his scheme was not public advantage but private emolument.

Philadelphia Gazette, 25 Feb. 1795. After further debate, JM "doubted whether the state of Georgia was not at present more able than the United States to subscribe." The Committee of the Whole rejected the report of the select committee.

From James Monroe

DEAR SIR   PARIS Feby. 25. 1795.

Being under the necessity of explaining the motives of my conduct upon my arrival, to the Executive, & in consequence of presenting a statmt. of the circumstances under which I acted, I have thought I could not better convey my ideas to you on that head than by enclosing a copy of the paper. This will of course be kept from Mr. R. because of his official station, & all others from whom it ought to be kept. I have sent a copy under the care of the minister Mr. Edet[1] who was to depart some days since: but as he did not & probably will not in some days I have deemed it expedient to send a duplicate to the executive & likewise to yrself by Bordeaux to be forwarded by some American vessel. Three days after the letter above referred to was written, a second was likewise, & in a different tone: But being on the Executive journal, my vindication ought to be there too. It is proper to observe that my first & second letters were intermediately recd. by Mr. Randolph.

The revolution in Holland progresses with great rapidity & will most probably comprize the 7. provinces under a single govt. founded of course on the sovereignty of the people. Here great tranquility continues to reign. Indeed it has never been otherwise since my arrival, than during the same space I presume it was in Phila. Bread is scarce in some quarters but the people are beyond example patient under it. I do not think a real distress is to be apprehended, but if such were to happen, I am convinc'd the yeomanry wod. emulate by their fortitude, the bravery of their compatriots in the army.

Nothing is yet done with Prussia. The death of Goltz in Switzerland interrupted a negotiation which was depending. Tis reported that France demanded of that power the abandonment of Poland, & for which she proposed to give Hanover.

With Spn. a negotiation is said to be depending. I am persuaded if Jay's treaty is rejected provided it contains any thing improper that we can not only get a decision of this govt. to suppt. our claims there but with Spn. Tis possible this latter point may be aided from this quarter independt. of the contents of that project, provided they are not very exceptionable—but the thing wod. be certain in the opposit view of the case.

I trust he has gaind all that we claimed, for that nothing could be refused in the present state of things, or indeed when the treaty was formed, must be certain, provided he did not convince the admn., that as he had adopted the conciliatory plan he would in no possible event change it.

We had some idea of procuring a loan in Holland to a moderate amt. to be vested in land, is this still yr. wish? I am persuaded it may be done; inform me therefore whether it is desirable, to what amt., and whether it would suit you to draw for it on such persons as I shod. designate. What I intimated sometime since is not meant to be derogated from here: for I can by loans, answer yr. drafts upon three months sight for one two & even three thousand pounds strg. payable in Hamburg or Holld. I have recd. but one letter from you to the present time. I wish the paper enclosed to be shewn Mr. Jones & Mr. Jefferson. We are happy to hear you have added a particular associate to the circle of our friends & to whom you will make our best respects. Sincerely I am yr. friend & servant

JAS. MONROE

Colo. Orr promised to procure my patent for a tract of land on Rock Castle, Kentuckey, of Captn. Fowler for me. Will you be so kind as remind him of this & endeavor to get it to be deposited with Mr. Jones, or sent here, as I mean to sell it after I shall have quitted this station—the latter is prefered.

I have written by Edet to Burr, Langdon, Brown & some others.

The liberation of our country from the councils of H. & K. had like to have been announc'd in the Bulletin. Be assured characters are well understood here.

RC and enclosure (DLC). RC and enclosure docketed by JM. Monroe enclosed a clerk's copy of his 12 Feb. 1795 letter to Edmund Randolph (printed in *ASP, Foreign Relations*, 1:694–95). Bottom of last page of enclosure, probably containing Monroe's signature, has been torn off.

1. Pierre Auguste Adet was French minister to the U.S., 1795–97.

¶ To Joseph Jones. Letter not found. *25 February 1795*. Acknowledged in Jones to JM, ca. 3 Mar. 1795 and 22 Mar. 1795. Mentions Monroe's land on the Rockcastle River in Kentucky and the price for which Congressman Alexander Dalrymple Orr estimated that it could be sold.

New Hampshire Memorial

[27 February 1795]

On 25 February the House received "A memorial and remonstrance of the Legislature of the State of New Hampshire . . . praying the interference and support of Congress, in favor of the judicial power of the State Court, against an encroachment of the Judiciary of the United States, in reversing a decree of the Supreme Judicial Court of the State of New Hampshire, which was rendered in a case decided before the adoption of the present Constitution." The House appointed JM chairman of a select committee to consider the memorial (*Annals of Congress*, 3d Cong., 2d sess., 1252). The case in question was *Penhallow* v. *Doane's Administrators* (3 Dallas 54); the New Hampshire memorial is printed in *ASP, Miscellaneous*, 1:124. On 27 February JM submitted the following written report.

That, the subject of the said memorial being of a nature wholly judicial, and having undergone a course of judicial investigation, and of final decision by the Supreme-Court of the United States, the Committee have conceived themselves precluded from all enquiry into the particular merits of the case: nor can perceive any ground, on which legislative interference could be proper.

Ms (DNA: RG 233). In a clerk's hand. Headed: "Made on the 27th. February, 1795. and ordered to lie on the table / Report, on the memorial of the Legislature of New Hampshire referred on the 26th. instant."

¶ To Aaron Fontaine. Letter not found. *Ca. 27 February 1795.* Mentioned and enclosed in JM to William Madison, 1 Mar. 1795. Asks Fontaine to explain to voters in Louisa County that JM is standing for reelection but cannot be present at the congressional election on 16 Mar. Mentions the illness of his wife and sister-in-law.

Indian Lands

[28 February 1795]

On 17 February Washington forwarded to Congress the laws passed by the Georgia General Assembly authorizing the Yazoo land sales (on those sales, see JM to Monroe, 27 Mar. 1795, and n. 4). The House appointed JM to a select committee chaired by Sedgwick, who on 26 February reported resolutions authorizing "the military force of the United States to apprehend . . . all persons who, unauthorized by law, may be found in arms on any lands westward of the lines established by treaties with the Indian tribes." The resolutions also authorized the civil authority to try, fine, and imprison such persons (*Annals of Congress*, 3d Cong., 2d sess., 1231, 1254, 1256, 1259). On 28 February the House considered the resolutions and Venable's amendment, "Unless it shall be in immediate pursuit of the Indians who have recently committed hostilities."

Mr. Madison did not think the expression explicit; he therefore proposed another which was to prevent the pursuers from coming within a certain number of miles of an Indian town. He was extremely doubtful whether his amendment or any other would effectually answer the end proposed. He was convinced that no law of any kind would be able to hinder people from crossing the line in pursuit of Indians, who might have carried off their families.[1]

Philadelphia Gazette, 3 Mar. 1795.

1. JM voted with the majority when the House rejected Venable's amendment. The House appointed JM to the committee that reported an act pursuant to the

resolutions. The Senate rejected the provision for the apprehension of armed citizens in the Indian lands, and Washington signed "An Act making provision for the purposes of Trade with the Indians" on 3 Mar. (*Annals of Congress*, 3d Cong., 2d sess., 850; *U.S. Statutes at Large*, 1:443).

To Thomas Jefferson

[ca. 1 March 1795]

Bringhurst says he has written to you and will write again. Donath is in Philada. He was disappointed in the importation of his Glass, by the Protest of Bills occasioned by the Yellow fever in Philada. If you still want the Glass, it will be proper to renew your orders to Donath. Letters addressed to him to the care of Jno' Bringhurst, or without that precaution will be pretty sure to get to him.

RC (MHi). Unsigned fragment. Conjectural date and recipient assigned by comparison with Jefferson to JM, 5 Feb. 1795. In his 15 Feb. reply, JM wrote, "I will attend to your several commissions."

To William Madison

DEAR BROTHER   PHILADA. March 1. 1795.

In my last to my father I desired him to let Mr. A. Fontaine or some other friend in Louisa know that I could not be in the district before the election &c. I now inclose a letter to him, which I wish you to seal & forward. If no certain conveyance offers in time, it will [be] requisite to send it to Louisa Court House on the day of the Election; and by Morda. Collins if necessary. Since the date of it my wife has grown better, the pleurisy being slight, and medical aid being immediately applied. Her sister is also better but not out of danger. She has been at the point of death, with a pleu[r]isy combined with bilious symtoms. The pleurisy rages a good deal in the City at present. It is ascribed to the great & sudden changes of weather, particularly to the intense cold of late after some very mild weather. The letter to Mr. Fontaine will give you the few remarks to be made on public subjects. We shall set out for home as soon as some business I have to do and the roads will admit. It will probably be the first of April before we get to the end of the journey. As there will be time for you to write after you receive this, let me know more particularly what kind of chairs you want, and whether there be any other articles you wish to be added. I shall be glad also to know what the amount of my *market* crop of Wheat has been, & what the present prospects are. Wheat is here near about 2 dollrs. a bushel, flour 10 dollrs. a barrel. I must leave it to you & my father to explain my absence to your two Counties. Yrs. affy.

Js. MADISON JR

RC (DLC). Docketed by William Madison.

Exportation of Arms

[2 March 1795]

The House approved a proviso to a Senate resolution "authorizing the exportation of arms, cannon, and military stores in certain cases." The Senate disagreed to the proviso, "that there should be none sent to the dominions or territories of any of the European powers now at war." In the House debate, Federalists favored the proviso while Republicans (who wanted to aid France) opposed it.

Mr. Madison was of opinion with his colleague from Virginia, (Mr. Giles) that the proviso would *narrow our national rights*. Besides even the passing of the proviso is worth nothing, for we may send military stores to Hamburg, and from thence they may be transported to any of the nations at war.

Philadelphia Gazette, 3 Mar. 1795 (reprinted in *Gazette of the U.S.*, 5 Mar. 1795). The House struck out the proviso and converted the resolution into an act, which Washington signed on 3 Mar. (*U.S. Statutes at Large*, 1:444).

¶ To Joseph Jones. Letter not found. *2 March 1795*. In his letters to JM of 21 and 22 Mar. 1795, Jones acknowledged this letter and another from JM of 4 Mar. (also not found). In the letters JM encloses a letter to John Whitaker Willis (not found), mentions false rumors that he declines to stand for reelection to Congress, and reports the illness of his wife and sister-in-law.

From Joseph Jones

DR. SR.   [ca. 3 March 1795]

I have your favor of the 25th. ult. and in consequence of the information given respecting Monroes land on Rock castle I inclose the Survey and a memdum. of his respecting it.[1] The patent may be taken out for any thing I know as Mr. Fowler (who owed Monroe money) was to do it and contrive it to you, but it is probable that Monroe being absent Fowler may have neglected to perform his promise in paying the fees and taking out the patent. You will observe what Fowler says about

485

the land. I think it had better be sold for the price you mention or even one fourth of a dollar rather than keep it and if you can make sale of it I request you will do so and any thing to be done on my part as his Attorney shall be complied with. If any credit is to be given you will of course attend to the paymt. being safe in event. Money is wanting and if it can be obtained for the land it will stop all demands. You will let me hear from you as soon anything is concluded in this business. The extracts from M——es letters being published confirms me in the opinion I had entertained who is the author of Germanicus.[2] It is strange Monroe did not favor one of his friends with a letter by either of the opportunities that conveyed the public despatches. I go to Loudoun on Thursday the 5th. and shall not return untill about the 16th or 17. provided we survey the land wch. is intended to commence on Monday the 9th. Yr friend & Servt.

Jos: Jones

RC and enclosures (DLC). RC dated 1794–96 in the *Index to the James Madison Papers*. Conjectural date assigned on the basis of internal evidence and by comparison with Jones to JM, 21 and 22 Mar. 1795, which mention this letter. Enclosures filed separately by date in the Madison Papers (DLC). For enclosures, see n. 1.

1. Jones enclosed a 16 Mar. 1786 survey by Hugh Ross of Monroe's lands on the Rockcastle River in Kentucky and a 31 Dec. 1792 memorandum by Monroe attesting: "The twenty thousand acres on the waters were located for me by William Buckner, a respectable inhabitant of Kentucky and deputy surveyor for the county within which it lies. . . . The fees of every kind are paid on it, and tis expected the patent will soon issue. For this I will be responsible." The memorandum includes an extract from John Fowler's 11 Dec. 1792 letter to Monroe, affirming that "the within plat of land is a very excellent survey."

2. On Edmund Randolph's "Germanicus" letters and his role in publishing Monroe's official correspondence, see Monroe to JM, 18 Feb. 1795, n. 1.

From Thomas Jefferson

Th: J. to Mr. Madison.   Monticello Mar. 5. 95.

Your favor of Feb. 15 is duly recieved & I now inclose the letter for mr. Christie,[1] which you will be so kind as to deliver to him open or sealed as you think best, & apologize to him for my availing myself of the opportunity of getting the vetch from England which you say is not to be had in Philadelphia. The universal culture of this plant in Europe establishes it's value in a farm, & I find two intervals in my rotation where I can have crops of it without it's costing me a single ploughing. My main object is to turn it in as a green dressing in the spring of the year, having sowed it on the fall fallow. In the mean time, should a short crop of fodder or hard winter call for it as fodder, it is a most abundant & valuable green fodder through the whole winter. We are in despair here for F. Walker. The low practices of his competitor though seen with indignation by every thinking man, are but too succesful with the unthinking who merchandize their votes for grog. He is said to be a good republican: but I am told this is the only favorable trait in his character. Adieu affectionately.

RC (DLC); FC (DLC: Jefferson Papers). RC addressed by Jefferson to JM at Philadelphia and franked.

1. Jefferson to Thomas Pinckney, 5 Mar. 1795 (DLC: Jefferson Papers). This was a letter of introduction for Maryland congressman Gabriel Christie, who Jefferson attested "is entirely orthodox in his republicanism." Jefferson also asked Pinckney to send him some winter vetch seeds from England.

To James Monroe

DEAR SIR   PHILADA. March 11. 1795.

Along with this I forward a large packet which Mr. Beckley has been so kind as to make up for you. It will give you such information as is not contained in the newspapers, and which forms a proper supplement to them.

I have not yet recd. a single line from you except yours of Sepr. 2d. long since acknowledged. Your last letters of the official kind were duplicates of Ocr. 16. Novr. 7. & 20. You will perceive in the Newspapers that the parts of them relating to the Jacobin Societies have been extracted & printed. In New York they have been republished with your name prefixed.[1] The question agitated in consequence of the President's denunciation of the Democratic Societies, will account for this use of your observations. In N. York where party contests are running high in the choice of a Successor to Clinton who declines, I perceive the use of them is extended by adroit comments, to that subject also. It is proper you should be apprized of these circumstances, that your own judgment may be the better exercised as to the latitude or reserve of your communications.

The Treaty concluded with G. Britain did not arrive before the adjour[n]ment and dispersion of Congress. The Senators received a summons to reassemble on the 8th. of June, on the calculation that the Treaty could not fail to be recd. by that time. It arrived a few days after.[2] It is a circumstance very singular that the first knowledge of its contents as finally settled, should not have come to the Executive till more than three months after the date of it. What its contents are, the Executive alone as yet know the most impenetrable secresy being observed. You will easily guess the curiosity and disappointment of the public. Complaints however are repressed by the confidence that some adequate reasons exist for the precaution. The arrival of this Treaty and the delicate relations in which we stand to France, are beginning to turn the public attention to the prospect of meliorating the Treaty with her, and the arrangements that may have been taken on either side for the purpose. It is certainly much to be desired that the crisis should not be suffered to elapse without *securing* to this Country the precious advantages in commerce which we now enjoy from the indulgence or temporary embarrassments of that Nation, and still more that the possibility should be precluded of any collisions that may endanger the general friendship already stipulated between them.

You will receive by this conveyance a letter from Mr. Jones which will inform you among other things that young Jno. Mercer, son of the late Judge is about to visit you with letters from his uncle &c. I am desired by his uncle to co-operate in his introduction to France, and shall of course give him a letter to you. As you know him much better than I do, and will hear from Mr. Jones who now must know him better than either, my letter will be more of form than any thing else. Mr. Jones will also probably inform you that he has commissioned me to try Whether your property in Kentucky could be turned at this place into the means of executing in Virga. some arrangements in which you are interested. I have not as yet succeeded, and much question whether I shall be able to do so. I have heard not a word from Genl. Wilki[n]son, nor can I give you any better acct. from Vermont, or N. York.

I have been detained here since the adjournment by indisposition in my family, and shall now wait till the roads get better which I hope will be the case in 8 or 10 days. Before I leave the City, I will write again. I deplore the want of a Cypher—and the cramp it puts on our Correspondence. My sincerest regards to you all. Adieu.

RC (DLC). Unsigned. Addressed by JM to Monroe at Paris. Marked in another hand: "Rue de Clichy No 6" (Monroe's residence, La Folie de la Bouexière). Docketed by Monroe. Enclosure not found.

1. On the publication of Monroe's official correspondence, see Monroe to JM, 18 Feb. 1795, n. 1.

2. On the arrival in Philadelphia of the Jay treaty on 7 Mar., see Madison in the Third Congress, 2 Dec. 1793–3 Mar. 1795.

To John Lee

DEAR SIR   PHILADA. Mar. 14. 1795.

My last reminded you of the debt for which I am responsible at your call, and requested to make your draught on me either here, or in Virginia, giving me a few days for preparation. As I am now about leaving this It is proper I should apprize you of it, that you may address to me in Virginia only. I shall probably be obliged to recur again to the aid of Mr. Dunbar, and shall be glad if your accomodation should again in any manner happen to co-incide with his. I take the liberty also of repeating my request of any information you may be able to give relating to my little interests in your State, and particularly to those connected with the Estate of my late brother.

I postponed this which will follow Mr. Greenup by the mail to be taken up by him at Pittsburg, in hope of being able to give you some acct. of the Treaty with G. B. which had not arrived at his departure. It has since come to the Executive, but is kept a profound secret; and will probably be so kept, till the meeting of the Senate, according to Summons on the 8th. of June. The French had not got to Amsterdam at the date of the last accts. but were so near it that the event could only be defeated by some very improbable occurrence. G. B. is Still madly devoted to the War. With my best respects to Mrs Lee & all other particular friends I am Dr. Sir Yrs.

JAMES MADISON JR

RC (DLC: John J. Crittenden Papers). Addressed by JM to Lee in Kentucky, "Hond. by Mr. Greenup."

¶ To Arnold Henry Dohrman. Letter not found. *20 March 1795*. Acknowledged in Dohrman to JM, 24 Mar. 1795. Concerns Dohrman's debt to Philip Mazzei.

From Giuseppe Ceracchi

DEAR SIR   HOME the 21 March 1795

Been wondered at the daley of the National Monumt suscription coming out,[1] i called this morning upon the Gentilmen of the departements. Mesr. Randolph kindedly assured me that he would signe the papers as soon as they were send to him. Fifty of them signed only by Mr Wolcott are not gon farther till now, than to the Secretary of War office, by this may be consived that it would require a month more before the signature would been don. But much more wondered i have in hear Mr Bradford and Mr Boudinot spoke aiganst the projet, and representing it as the most redicelous and improper, and emploing all the documents of a lawior or a friar in expressing the narrow compas of there soll, i thought to hear the imploration of holy Ignorance descending from heven upon the people of America, as it was implored in Room last Year in contradiction of comun sense; Then i could not holpe to remarke that there resoning was contrary to the sanction they give to my Plan with there signatures, to which Mr Boudinot ansered that he did it as well as other Gentilmen, that did the same act, merely to encoreg my feling, and to give me some credit, fulisch and indiferent carrecter expressed in this sentiment of M: Boudinot make me belive that a plot of not uncomun Kind are agent the plan of National Monument for some other objet that i cant discover.

I am redy to decline of any farther attempt if you think it prudente, upon which i desire your oppinion. I am Sir with full respect Your Most Obt servt

Jos CERRACHI

RC (PHi). Addressee not indicated. For circumstantial evidence that JM may have been the recipient, see n. 1 and documents there cited, and Cerracchi to JM, 8 May 1795 (PHi) and ca. 11 May 1795 (PHC).

1. In 1783 the Continental Congress had authorized a monument to commemorate the American Revolution, but no work had begun when Cerracchi, an Italian sculptor, submitted a proposal to Congress in 1791. After the House rejected his plan, Cerracchi attempted to raise funds by private subscription. His prospectus for the monument contained a letter from sixty-one subscribers, including JM and Washington. JM recollected that "I knew him well, having been a lodger in the same house with him, and much teased by his eager hopes, on which I constantly threw cold water, of obtaining the aid of Congress for his grand project. . . . But just as the circular address was about to be despatched, it was put into his head that the scheme was merely to get rid of his importunities, and being of the *genus irritabile*, he suddenly went off in anger and disgust" (Cerracchi to JM, 28 July 1792, *PJM*, 14:344–45 and nn.; Syrett and Cooke, *Papers of Hamilton*, 11:111–12 nn. 2 and 3; [Cerracchi], *A Description of the Monument Consecrated to Liberty* [Philadelphia, 1795; Evans 28403]; JM to George Tucker, 30 Apr. 1830, Madison, *Letters* [Cong. ed.], 4:71).

From Joseph Jones

DR. SR.   FREDG. 21t. Mar: 1795.

I returned last evening from Loudoun where I had been two weeks geting the land surveyed and fixing some hands on a small part of it or your favors of the 2d. & 4th. should have been sooner noticed. My absence prevented my attending to your letter to J. Willis but no inconvenience has resulted from it. The story you mention had been circulated and some had asked me if I thought it true or had received any intimation of the sort from you and generally I answered I had no doubt of your willingness to serve as I was satisfied if you meditated retirement and had decided on it, you wod. have communicated your intention to me as well as others. In Fredk. & Berkeley—Rutherford outvoted Morgan about 450. In Loudoun Fairfax and Prince William—Brent has ousted Lee by a large majority. It is somewhat extraordinary that Monroes letters shod. be published to serve electioneering purposes which I shod. suppose could not be done but by the permission or connivance of the P———t or S———y of State. With respect to him it is an uncandid and ungenerous perversion of his intention and sentiments. I am in hopes Mrs. Madison and her Sister are restored to health I sincerely wish you all the enjoyment of that greatest of blessings. I inclosed a survey of Monroes Rock fish land. Did you receive it and what may be expected from it. I set out on this day or Tomorow week for Richmond where the circuit commences on the 1t. of Apr:—the letter for Miss Washington shall be sent to Mr. Lewis's[1] where the young Lady I understand resides. Yr. friend & Servt.

Jos: Jones

RC (DLC). Mistakenly docketed by JM, "Mar. 1. 1795."

1. George Lewis (1757–1821), a son of Fielding and Betty Washington Lewis, was named after his uncle, George Washington. A Revolutionary veteran, he served as a major with Virginia troops during the Whiskey Insurrection. His wife, Catherine Daingerfield Lewis (1764–1820), was JM's grandniece. At the time Jones was writing, the Lewises lived in Fredericksburg (*WMQ*, 1st ser., 8 [1899–1900]: 98; Jackson and Twohig, *Diaries of George Washington*, 4:112, 6:192, 194).

From Joseph Jones

Dr. Sr.   Fredg. 22d. March 1795

I wrote to you by the last post acknowledging the receiit [*sic*] of yours of the 2d. & 4th. of this month which I found here on my return from Loudoun. I then mentioned to you my having inclosed to you before I left home in consequence of your letter to me on the subject Monroes survey of 20000 acres of Land on Rock Castle I also sent with it an abstract from Fowlers letter respecting its quality and mentd. that Fowler being indebted to Monroe had undertaken to get out the Patent and contrive it to you in Philadelphia. Since my last I have been applied to for the Terms on wch. I wod. sell the survey but not knowing the issue of the matter in Philadelphia I could only answer that it had been sent there for Sale but if not disposed of I wod. when informed make the necessary communication. This application is from a Mr. Lacey in Loudoun and is I expect a matter of speculation whereby to gain some profit by resale as I understand he lately did gain £250 in a purchase and resale of Land Wats. in a few days. I suspect he will not give the price you said Orr thought could be got. If the Survey can be sold on pretty good terms in Phila. let it be done—if not I wod. then offer it to Lacey and in that case the survey or a copy of it will be wanting. This Tract is in the Wilderness and I am told of mean quality and had I think better be sold during the present rage for back lands and to avoid future Expence which it will not bear. Your letter for me will find me at Richmond after the 30th. of this month where and at Petersburg I shall be untill towards the last of April. When are the Senate to meet to consider the treaty? I shod. suppose they would be called sooner than June. It is in a state of perspiration or when it transpires will it be free from a sweat? Has no part of it yet leaked out.

A bead to be added to that in the Aurora of the 3d. inst.[1]

> In Loudoun district—Virginians bent
>   the Ship of State to free
> from dangerous steerage, took in *Brent*
>   and turned out Pilot *Lee*

It was said Lee was so much mortified—he either was or feigned to be unwell and went to his bed sooner than usual—seriously I think the change independent of political principles or sentiments of the Men favourable to the public welfare for of most young Men you will meet with few possess equal abilities or a better heart. The other Gentns. Moral Character was I think good. I may perhaps trouble you to bring me some imperial and Guinea Hyson—of this you shall hear further. Yr. friend & Servt

JOS: JONES

RC (DLC). Docketed by JM.

1. On 3 Mar. 1795 the Philadelphia *Aurora General Advertiser* published "Samuel Sweetbriar's Chaplet. / Another Bead.":

> Virginians! long we've weathered out
>   The storm, on faction's sea,
>   We hope you ne'er will veer about
>   Nor clap the helm a *Lee*.

On 3 Apr. that newspaper published Jones's parody with an article on the Virginia congressional election.

To Thomas Jefferson

Your two last favors contained, one of them the letter for Mr. Christie, which has been sent to him; the other accompanied the letters to the President & Mr. Randolph. The two latter were duly delivered also. The President touched on the subject the other day in conversation with me, and has no doubt written to you on it.[1] There are difficulties I perceive in the way of your suggestion, besides the general one arising from the composition of the scientific body, *wholly* out of foreign materials. Notwithstanding the advantages which might weigh in the present case, agst. this objection, I own that I feel its importance. It was not sufficient however to induce me to withold your remarks from the P. as your letter would have authorised me to do. Whilst[2] I am acknowledging your favors, I am reminded of a passage in a former one,[3] which I had proposed to have answered at some length. Perhaps it will be best, at least for the present to say in breif, that reasons of *every* kind, and some of them, of the most *insuperable* as well as *obvious* kind, shut my mind against the admission of any idea such as you seem to glance at. I forbear to say more, because I can have no more to say with respect to myself; and because the great deal that may & ought to be said beyond that restriction will be best reserved for some other occasion, perhaps for the latitude of a free conversation. You ought to be preparing yourself however to hear truths, which no inflexibility will be able to withstand.

I have already told you of my failure to get from E. R. one of your books which has slipped out of his memory as well as his hands. I have since after repeated applications got from Wilson Houdon's Fleta Bracton &c.[4] Mably, he says, he lent to Gallatine with your permission. This was not mentioned however till very lately; and Gallatine is at present in N. Y. As soon as he returns I will renew my efforts. I have procured for you "the Sketches on rotations,["] which I find to be truly a good thing. It was written by Mr. Boardley. The other publications referred to in p. 43. are not to be had of the Booksellers. I propose, if an oppy. offers, to get them thro' some friend who can carry the enquiry to the author himself. I have also procured you the correspondences with Hammond &c. All these with some other things deemed worth your possessing, I shall pack up for a conveyance by water to Richmd. addressing them to the Mercht. there from Staunton, whose name I cannot at this moment recollect.

The Treaty with England arrived soon after the adjournment. It is kept an inpenetrable secret by the Executive. The Senate are Summoned to meet it the 8th. of June. I wish it may not be of a nature to bring us into some delicacies with France, without obtaining fully our objects from G. B. The French it is said are latterly much less respectful than heretofore to our rights on the seas. We have no late private letters from Monroe. His last public ones were no later than Novr. 20. They contained a History of the Jacobin clubs, in the form of an apology for the Convention. Extracts on that subject were immediately put into the Newspapers, and are applied to party purposes generally, particularly in N. Y. where the election of Govr. is on the anvil. Yates & Jay are the candidates. The last accts. from Amsterdam foretell in the next the capture of that place by the French. The inclosed speeches of Pitt & Fox will give you the English politics, and a general view of the crisis in Europe.

I have been detained here by a sick family; & am so at present, by the state of the roads, which are kept bad by the rains and the frosts. I am extremely anxious to be on the journey and shall set out as soon as I can prudently venture. Yrs. always & mo: affectly.

Js. Madison Jr

RC (DLC); partial Tr (DLC: Nicholas P. Trist Papers). RC docketed by Jefferson, "recd. Apr. 7." Partial Tr in Trist's hand; filed with JM to Trist, 4 Feb. 1828 (see n. 2 below).

1. Washington to Jefferson, 15 Mar. 1795 (Fitzpatrick, *Writings of Washington*, 34:146–49).
2. Trist's extract begins with this sentence and continues to the end of the paragraph.
3. Jefferson to JM, 28 Dec. 1794.
4. JM referred to David Houard's *Traités sur les coutumes anglo-normandes*, which includes editions of *Fleta* and *Britton*. These works were condensations of Henry de Bracton's thirteenth-century treatise *De legibus et consuetudinibus Angliæ* (Sowerby, *Catalogue of Jefferson's Library*, 2:214; see also Jefferson to JM, 6 Nov. 1794, and n. 2).

From Arnold Henry Dohrman

Sir   New York 24 March 1795.

In reply to the Letter of 20 March, with which you honrd. me, I am oblidged to say, that unavoidable misfortunes & embarrassments had till now impeded me from complying with the Final settlement of the Debt due Mr. Mazzei, that I was just now beginning to acquire the means to fullfill the payment & had contemplated to advise you thereof, but from a delay in a material event which will enable me to do it, & which in a few days will be decided I had postponed it, & therefore take the Liberty to request you to grant me a few days longer, to enable me to make provision for the payment without sacrifying my township, & if convenient (I hope to be excused) to inform me when you expect to leave Philadelphia, that I may have every indulgence which your generous feelings, wishes to allow me, in order to raise the money on more easy terms; it being impossival for me at present to leave this city, prevents me from thanking you personnally for the humanity with which you have managed this infortunate affair, if while I hope for your Answer my affair is decided, information shall be given immediately, else on the return of your Letter, I confidently shall be prepared for a consideraval part of the payment, perhaps for the whole. With perfect Estem I have the honour to remain Sir Your most Obedt. humble Servant

ARND. HENRY DOHRMAN

RC (NN). Addressed by Dohrman to JM at Philadelphia. Docketed by JM.

To James Monroe

DEAR SIR   PHILADA. March 26. 1795.

My last was written about ten days ago for a conveyance intimated to be in the view of the office of State. I have since that recd. yours committed to Mr. Swan[1] and two hours ago that of Decr. 18. covering the private one for Mr. Randolph. The other referred to as sent by the way of Havre is not yet come to hand.

Mr. Swan is much embarrassed in his operations by the enormous price of Wheat and flour. The latter has been above ten dollars a barrel, and is now at that price. The former has been as high as 15/3, and is now very little below that. Mr. S. is apprehensive that he will be compelled to direct his attention to some other quarter of the world. It is matter of double regret that such a necessity should happen. The causes of this extraordinary rate of produce are differently explained. The deficiency of the last harvest is certainly a material one. The influence of Bank Credits on mercantile enterprize and competition may be another; tho' this cause cannot at this moment operate, as the Banks are in another paroxism of distress and have for some time discontinued their discounts. The idea of *great* demands from Europe, particularly from France has no doubt contributed to the effect; tho' this can not particularly refer to the object of Mr. Swan, because the high prices preceded his operation, and in fact are not peculiar to the articles he wants, or limited to articles having any relation to them. In general prices are exorbitantly high, and in this place incredibly so. The markets have been nearly 100 PerCt. advanced in some, and fifty in most, instances, beyond the state of them prior to your departure. House Rents have kept the same course. These circumstances denote some general and deeply rooted cause.

From as near a view as I have yet been able to take of your letter to Mr. R. I see no reason why I should hesitate to deliver it. I cannot forbear believing that the Report of stipulations offensive and defensive is quite without foundation; but your view of things on the contrary supposition involves a variety of interesting ideas; and your communications and reflections in general with regard to the Treaty, as proceeding from one in your position and of your sentiments, merit too much attention in the Executive Department, to be witheld altogether from it. I mentioned in my last that the Treaty was come, but kept a profound secret. In that state it remains. Its contents have produced conjectural comments without number. As I am as much out of the secret as others, I can say nothing that goes beyond that character. I should hope it to be impossible that any stipulation, if any should be attempted, inconsistent with the Treaties with France, can ever be pursued into effect. I cannot even believe that any such stipulation would be hazarded. The President, to say nothing of the people, would so certainly revolt at it, that more than wickedness would be requisite in the authors. At the same time it is possible that articles may be included that will be ominous to the confidence and cordiality of France towards the U. S: not to mention that any arrangements with G. B. (beyond the simple objects you mention) made at the present juncture and extorted by the known causes, must naturally appear in the light you represent. How the instructions to Jay may square with what he may have done; or both or either with the language you were authorised to hold, must await future lights. As I do not know how far official communications may or may not put you in possession of the Contents of the Treaty before this arrives, and as it appears you had no previous or contemporary knowledge of the particulars, I ought not to decline the task of giving you what appears to me to be the most probable account of them; premising that I speak without the least clue or hint from the official quarter, & what is truly to be taken for conjecture, or at most for inferences from circumstances mostly of newspaper publicity. 1. It is generally agreed that the posts are to be surrendered; but not before June 1796; and it is among the reports, that they are afterwards to be a sort of thoroughfare for both parties. This wd. be a very disagreeable and a very unpopular ingredient. 2. The compensations for losses are supposed to be in a train primarily judicial, eventually diplomatic. The sufferers I believe are very little sanguine, but they are in general silent from causes which you will readily imagine. 3. I should have mentioned the other stipulations in the treaty of peace, besides the delivery of the posts. On this little is said except in general that they are to be executed on both sides. Perhaps the question of interest during the war, & complaints on the British side from State laws affecting their debts, may be referred along with some of the American losses from privateers & admiralty Courts, to Commissioners. This however is purely conjectu[r]al. 4. A footing of reciprocity with respect to the trade directly with G. B: so far as to put British & American vessels on the same footing in American ports—& American & British footing in the British ports. As this wd. take from our vessels the advantage they now enjoy, particularly with respect to the difference of ten perCt. in the duties, it would be injurious, and if not countervailed, unpopular. 5. An admission of American vessels to the British W. Inds. if under 100 or perhaps 75 tons. Whether the right be renounced of reducing British vessels to the same size is a question of some consequence in relation to this point. 6 The Treaty in relation to the commerce with G. B. to continue for 12 years; to that with *the W. Indies for 4 years.* I should be led from some particular circumstances not to doubt the latter limitation, if the aspect & effect of it were not so strikingly revolting. Having had but a few moments notice of this oppy I am obliged to conclude a very hasty letter with abrupt assurances of the affectionate ⟨esteem⟩ with which I am Dr. Sir Your friend & servt.

Js. Madison Jr.

I hope to be able to write again before I leave this which will be in 7 or 8 days.

RC (DLC). Addressed by JM to Monroe at Paris. Docketed by Monroe. Damaged by removal of seal.

1. Monroe to JM, 20 Sept. 1794.

Memorandum to James Monroe

Philada. Mar. 26. 95

Memorandum

The wants incident to my new situation seduce me into an unwilling tax on your goodness. As it is probable that many articles of furniture at second hand, may be had in Paris, which cannot be had here of equal quality, but at a forbidding price, it has occurred to me, to ask the favor of you to have the following procured & forwarded.

1. Suit of Bed Curtains of Damask, Chints, or Dimity as the price may be
3. Corresponding Window Curtains
3 do. for a Parlour
2 Carpets of different sizes
1 Tea Sett of China
1 Service of do

I make this request on the idea that you can have it executed witht. personal trouble, and can conveniently make the temporary advances. I leave the particular directions entirely to your own judgment, to which I wd. pray the addition of a hint from Mrs. Monroes better one if I were not afraid of intruding on her goodness. You will be able to judge of the stile suitable to my faculties & fashions, by the rule you mean to pursue in providing for your own future accomodation. Were I sure that you could easily have effect given to this application, and that in every respect it would be consistent with your conveniency, I would ask the favor of you to go beyond the enumerated articles into others which you may know to be acceptable to a young House-Keeper.[1] Those which are enumerated wd. be particularly so, if they could to [sic] got in time to arrive here for next Winter's use; but whether or not, they are desirable.

Ms (DLC). In JM's hand. Addressed by JM to Monroe at Paris. Docketed by Monroe.

1. For a discussion of the household furnishings that Monroe purchased for JM in Paris, see Hunt-Jones, *Dolley and "The Great Little Madison,"* pp. 18–20.

To James Monroe

DEAR SIR   PHILADA. March 27. 1795

I wrote to you yesterday acknowledging yours by Mr. Swan and answering that of the 18th. Decr. which covered your very interesting remarks in a confidential letter to Mr. Randolph. The latter was sent to Mr. R today, there being no good reason for witholding it as you authorised me to do. I write this cheifly on acct. of the Bearer Mr. John Mercer son of our friend the judge, who means to visit France in order to enter the school of experience under the auspices of some military character of eminence. As he carries letters to you from his uncle Jno.

Mercer, and is personally better known to you than to myself, I can only rely on your paying him a proper friendly attention, and express my sincere wishes that he may reap all the beneficial fruits which can be afforded by the present scenes of Europe.

You will learn from Mr. Mercer that the elections in Virginia are over and in part known. The only two districts in which the question turned on *political* rather than *personal* considerations, were those in which Alexandria & Winchester stand. In the former Mr. Lee & Mr. Brent; in the latter Mr. Rutherford, and Genl. Morgan were the candidates. Mr. Brent was elected by a considerable, and Mr. Rutherford by a greater majority. In Mr. Griffin's district it is probable that Mr. Clopton is the successful candidate; tho' it is possible that he may be outvoted by Mr. Basset who is also well spoken of.[1] Mr. Barnwell who was elected as successor to Gillon, has resigned; and Col. Hampton of very different politics has taken his place. In Massachussetts several elections remain unfinished; Among which is that lately represented by Mr. Dexter. There have been two trials without an effective vote. In the last Mr. Varnum had more votes than Mr. Dexter, and it is expected will finally prevail. Mr. Ames election I am told will be contested, on account of bribery & bad votes. For the Senate, your old friend Jacob Read Esqr. succeeds Mr. Izzard. His success is represented as one of those casualties which are incident to elections. Your friend Bloodworth succeeds Mr. Hawkins from a like cause. Bingham is successor to Morris. The contest in N. York for Govr. lies between Yates & Jay. Of the issue it is difficult to judge. Something will depend on the return or absence of the latter, and also on the colouring which may most sucessfully be given to the Treaty with G. B.

I inclose several papers containing the publications of Lee & Brent, and a small pamphlet mentioned in a former letter, written by our friend N.[2] The 'cautionary hints' are from the pen of S. G. Tucker.[3] You will see from the proceedings in Georgia what a scene is opened there by a landjobbing Legislature. Wilson & Pendleton the fedl. Judges, tho' not named in the law are known adventurers. The former is reprobated here by all parties. The two Senators Gun & Jackson are now pitted agst. each other, and the whole State is in convulsions. It is not improbable that attempts may be made to set aside the law, either as having some flaw, or by the paramount authority of a Convention wch. is to meet in the course of the summer.[4] These dangers with the frowns of the federal Govt. seem to have benumbed the speculations which were likely to follow on that subject, & which have attained a scrip mania on others of the territorial kind.

In my letter of yesterday I took the liberty of asking the favor of you to have procured for me a few articles of furniture, on the supposition that they can be had at second hand, cheap; and that it will not be inconvenient to make the requisite advances; referring the stile & the price to your own knowledge of my situation, & authorising you to go beyond the enumerated articles into any others you may judge to be desirable to me from the fashion & the price. The articles I mentioned particularly were a suit of handsome bed curtains—3 corresponding window do. 3 parlour do. 2 Carpets of different sizes—1 Tea Sett of China—1 Service of do. I rely on your goodness to excuse the trouble, which I impose on you. I take the liberty, you are to understand, on the belief & the condition that you can have the thing done without much personal attention. If I were not afraid of intruding too much on Mrs. Monroe's goodness, I wd. ask the aid of her counsel in the directions you may give towards the supply of my household. My best respects wait on her. With sentiments of perfect esteem & attachment I remain Dr. Sir Yr. friend & servt.

Js MADISON Jr

RC (DLC). Addressed by JM to Monroe at Paris, "Hond. by Jno. Mercer Esqe." Docketed by Monroe.

1. Federalist Samuel Griffin, who represented the district that included Richmond, 1789–95, declined to stand for reelection. In the congressional election in that district on 16 Mar., Republican John Clopton defeated Federalist Burwell Bassett, Jr., by 10 votes. When Bassett contested, the House Committee of Elections disqualified 70 out of 854 votes but ruled that Clopton had won by 6 valid votes. Bassett (1764–1841), a nephew of Martha Washington, attended the College of William and Mary. He represented New Kent County, 1787–89, and James City County, 1819–21, in the Virginia House of Delegates. He succeeded his father as a state senator, 1793–1805. He became a Republican by 1799 and served as a congressman from the district that included Williamsburg, 1805–13, 1815–19, and 1821–29. Clopton (1756–1816) graduated from the College of Philadelphia (now the University of Pennsylvania) in 1776. He was a veteran of the Revolution and represented New Kent County in the House of Delegates, 1789–91. He was a congressman from 1795 until his death except for one term, 1799–1801, when John Marshall defeated him. During that term he served on the Virginia Council of State (Parsons et al., *United States Congressional Districts*, pp. 31, 73, 131, 133, 205, 207, 282; JM to Monroe, 4 Dec. 1794; Risjord, *Chesapeake Politics*, p. 665 n. 24; *Annals of Congress*, 4th Cong., 1st sess., 265–66; BDC, pp. 562, 755; Jackson and Twohig, *Diaries of George Washington*, 1:218, 4:155; Swem and Williams, *Register*, pp. 346, 360).

2. The pamphlet to which JM referred has not been found.

3. Columbus [St. George Tucker], *Cautionary Hints to Congress, Respecting the Sale of Western Lands* (Philadelphia, 1795; Evans 28459).

4. The Yazoo land fraud began in 1789 when the Georgia General Assembly sold sixteen million acres of western lands (for about three cents an acre) to a group of speculating companies. After that venture collapsed, the General Assembly on

7 Jan. 1795 made another grant of thirty-five million acres to four companies in which many legislators themselves held shares. Prominent shareholders included Patrick Henry, U.S. Supreme Court justice James Wilson, Georgia federal district court judge Nathaniel Pendleton, Jr., and South Carolina congressman Robert Goodloe Harper. A rumor falsely linked even JM with the frauds. The land grants divided Georgia politics, and the state's two U.S. senators, James Gunn and James Jackson, led the opposing factions. Gunn, a director of the Georgia Company, defended the sales. The Yazoo grants remained an issue in national politics through the presidencies of Jefferson and JM. In 1810 the U.S. Supreme Court upheld the grants in *Fletcher* v. *Peck* (C. Peter Magrath, *Yazoo: Law and Politics in the New Republic: The Case of* Fletcher v. Peck [New York, 1967], pp. 1–12; James Madison, Sr., to JM, 11 May 1791, *PJM*, 14:21, 22 n. 5).

From Robert Rutherford

MY DEAR SIR   BERKELEY COUNTY March 30th. 1795.

The 16th. Secured my reelection, against every artifice & misrepresentation, that could be engendered in the lowest walks of Society, together with inflaming weak fantastical minds to a pitch of real ferosity, as all these were to mount the war Horse and ride triumphant to Military honours, under the banners of this mighty son of Mars.[1] But I have reason to be ever thankful & to Congratulate our common Country, that Such a Draggooning insolence of temper was Compleatly defeated by a great & well Judging Majority. No fraud was left untryed—one Sharper it is said Voted Eight times under feigned names, & out of about 500. Votes listed to this champion I am well assured, there is not 200 legal. Mine were a Thousand lacking one Single Vote, and were mostly legal. So that my predictions to you were about realized, and would have been much more compleat, if the Snow on the morning of Election had not prevented great numbers of my aged friends, & others at a distance & just then Suffering under a kind of influenza, from attending. I Can dilate my mind to you, who I well know to be a patriot in the fullest acceptation of that noble character—so that I rejoyce with you and every other generous friend to our Country, in the change adjoining my district. For tho' I have charity to hope there was an honesty of heart in the former representative,[2] yet his mind was so entangled by the party—who are Very artful—and he naturally rather torpid, & a little Mulish, that enlargement of Sentiment was done away. While I consider his successor[3] as a real acquisition to the Cause of the people and to that Goverment of equality & brotherly love which we intend[e]d in granting the few powers to the union. But it is a pitiable Case, after all that the people have done & Suffered that there is a party, which would make these few powers an Hydra, before which the generous free people must fall prostrate. These high toned goverment men have from the first exerted every effort to melt down, the sovereign, seperate independance of the several states, to mould the business into a State of Consolidation, & to disfigure the Federal Goverment, by the wretched features of the Corrupt, British goverment. But I rejoyce with my Country that the Patriots preponderate, and the people are more & more enlightened, by their own observations, and the Zeal & Care of their faithful representatives. It is really laughable to observe, the monyed interest, Certificate mongers and Stock Jobbers ⟨a⟩larmed when ever the people Speak out about abuses, How they pretend, to raise the Cry of the constitution being in danger, & endeavour to make the honest Patriot President their rallying point, when in reallity if some of them Could fill their Coffers, the Constitution the President, and the people, might go headlong to perdition, without a Sigh, and the Wicked goverment from which we have emancipated ourselves—might again ride triumphant in all the insolence of arbitrary power. That haughty, Stubborn aristocratic insolence of heart, which never felt an emotion Save what has been produced by pride and the most sordid Self interest, is astonished at the Sentiments of Patriotism, to Such altogether inconceivable, while the generous Patriot and friend to the people & their goverment is by them Considered as Courting popularity. But happily the people are pregnant with Just observation & determined not to be Cast into tumult anarchy or disorder, while they are as determined to watch their own goverment and if amendments are necessary, that Such shall take place in a peacable & legal manner, without Violence or disorder, I have Very often revolved in my mind the Select Militia Bill, proposed, and am more and more Convinced that it would be extremely improper—because it would Cast an imense weight into the Scale of the Federal Goverment as all Military men Croud round the Center of power. Besides it would be Very expensive & near akin to a Large Standing army. It would cheerish a Licentious, immoral disposition & an unnecessary, high toned martial temper, dangerous to the Civil authority. Let the Patriot Labour to make the people happy, let the Hives be full & the bees will defend them. These Consequences will naturally follow. No people was ever less prepared to resist a mighty power, than the Americans were but Concurring in opinion they prevailed, under every disadvantage. If the people Continue to be happy, they will defend themselves, their rights and their property's. I shall ever Contend that the Federal goverment, has nothing to do with our sons, till they, by the exigency's of the Case, may be called into Service. Training is teaching in the planest acceptation of the term. If any want arms, that are not able to purchase them, the united people must buy them no doubt, which is organizing. This is all that is necessary. Except that a few states revise their Militia Laws. Virginia & many other States can do little more than what is already done & indeed it is quite Sufficient. I am happy to hear that you have no opposition, & that our mutual friend Mr J. N[4] was nearly in the same way. May this letter find you & Mrs. Madison in the fullest injoyment of health & Miss Payn perfectly recoverd. To these I beg you make my complyments agreable, as well as to your good Parents & family. Mrs. Rutherford presents her kind respects. I am with unfeigned Esteem Dear Sir your Most Hble sert

R RUTHERFORD[5]

RC (DLC). Docketed by JM.

1. Brig. Gen. Daniel Morgan, hero of the battle of Cowpens, was Rutherford's Federalist opponent in the congressional district composed of Frederick and Berkeley counties on 16 Mar. He had recently commanded the Virginia militia suppressing the Whiskey Insurrection. In public letters to the voters of the district, Morgan made much of his military record and denied that he favored a standing army, while Rutherford also denounced the whiskey rebels and praised the conduct of Washington and the Virginia militia (Philadelphia *Gazette of the U.S.*, 5 and 12 Jan. 1795; Philadelphia *Aurora General Advertiser*, 12 Mar. 1795).

2. Richard Bland Lee.

3. Richard Brent.

4. John Nicholas.

5. Rutherford served as a congressman with JM, 1793–97. Though elected with Federalist support, he voted consistently with the Republicans. His daughter Deborah married JM's cousin George Hite (Risjord, *Chesapeake Politics*, pp. 423, 659 n. 18; Cartmell, *Shenandoah Valley Pioneers*, p. 255; *PJM*, 1:137 n. 1).

From John Carey

SIR,   LONDON, March 31, 1795.

Permit me to request your acceptance of a copy of as much of the President's official correspondence as I have yet printed.[1] And, as you were so good to interest yourself heretofore in the publication, and to honor me with your opinion on the subject, allow me, Sir, to add my regret that I have not the series complete, and am for the present prevented from publishing two or three volumes more, by a chasm of seven months and a half immediately succeeding the conclusion of the second volume, and the want of several of the inclosures referred to in the letters now in print. It was my intention to have copied all these, and to have made diligent inquiries in order to enable me to supply the necessary notes and illustrations, if I could have made it convenient to stay a little longer in America: and in the spring of 1793, (a short time before that dreadful visitation which I so happily escaped by being absent) I was desirous—Mr. Beckley knows I was—to have remained in Philadelphia till the fall of the year, to complete my collection, had my finances admitted of it. If, however, by your good offices, which I have already experienced and retain in grateful remembrance, the obstacles, which at present oppose a complete and satisfactory publication, can in any wise be removed, permit me, Sir, to request your interposition. If a proper person could be found, to copy out the parts I want,* and send them to me to London, I would immediately proceed to print the succeeding volumes, and would send him such number of copies as might be deemed a reasonable compensation for his trouble. Or if there were a vacancy for any employment that I might be deemed qualified to fill, and which would defray my ordinary expenses during my stay, I would myself re-cross the Atlantic, and devote a year or two, if necessary, to the completion of the task.

Excuse me, Sir, for presuming thus to address you, or indeed for presuming to address you at all, though encouraged to it by my knowledge of your public spirit, and the desire I have heard you express that these documents should be made public.

With perfect respect, and with sincere wishes, that, in the uninterrupted enjoyment of health, you may long continue to serve your country, already so much indebted to your patriotic exertions, I have the honor to be, Sir, your most obedient humble servant.

JOHN CAREY.

* They are all noted in the margin of a copy that I send to the President.

Should you condescend to honor me with a line, or verbal message, in answer to this request, it may be directed to *Mr. Hamilton's, Falcon Court, Fleet Street.*

PS. As small parcels are exposed to risk on shipboard, I have not made a separate package of the volumes intended for you, but desired Mr. Rice of Market Street to send you one of the best-bound sets from a number that I have shipped off to him. Should he, through hurry of business, forget the circumstance, I request you will be kind enough to order your servant to call for the book. A second set will accompany yours, which is intended for Mr. Jefferson, and which I beg you will have the goodness to forward to him.

RC (DLC); FC (NN). RC docketed by JM.

1. George Washington, *Official Letters to the Honorable American Congress, Written, during the War between the United Colonies and Great Britain, by his Excellency, George Washington . . .* , ed. John Carey (2 vols.; London, 1795). JM had known Carey when he was a bookseller and stenographer of congressional proceedings for Philadelphia newspapers (Carey to JM, 8 Feb. 1792, *PJM*, 14:225 and n. 1). Beginning in July 1792, with Jefferson's permission, Carey searched the State Department records for Washington's letters to the Continental Congress, his edition of which was published three years later. For excerpts from correspondence relating to Carey's project, see Sowerby, *Catalogue of Jefferson's Library*, 1:236–39.

From Bartholomew Dandridge, Jr.

Tuesday 31. March—1795

Bw. Dandridge[1] presents his compliments to Mr. Madison, & by direction of The President, asks the pleasure of Mr. & Mrs. Madisons company to dine in *a family way* tomorrow at 3 o'Clock.

an answer if you please.

P.S. Will Mr. Madison be good enough to give the enclosed letter a conveyance to G S Washington?

RC (MdAN). Addressed by Dandridge.

1. Bartholomew Dandridge, Jr. (d. 1802), a nephew of Martha Washington, had succeeded Tobias Lear as the president's private secretary in 1793 (Jackson and Twohig, *Diaries of George Washington*, 6:93, 179).

To William Branch Giles

[PHILADELPHIA, 3 April 1795]

. . . I have not forgotten my promise to drop you a few lines on the arrival of the Treaty in case it sh'd happen during my stay here, but have hitherto omitted to write because the arrival of the Treaty has not added a particle to the public knowledge of its contents. You will have known that the Senate are to meet for the purpose of receiving the communication on the 8th of June. I am chiefly induced to take up my pen at present by the pleasure of mentioning the acct's first rec'd from Holland. Amsterdam with all that country have bowed to the standard of Liberty. The Stadtholder has resigned and fled. A Revolutionary system is commenced in form, and nothing remains in the way of a quiet and compleat establishment of a third Republic on the rights of man. . . .

It appears also that steps are taken by the present authority of Holland that will immediately reduce G. B. to dilemma of combating the revolutionary powers there, or giving up the war on those of France. None ought to wish so much as herself that the latter may be embraced as the only safe and prudent course. . . .

Typescript (John Clark to Franklin F. Hopper, 7 Aug. 1916 [NN]). RC offered for sale in Stan. V. Henkels Catalogue No. 1078 (1913), item 894. Listed as "1½ pp., folio. . . . Autograph address and wax seal on reverse." In this letter JM evidently congratulated Giles on his reelection to Congress (see Giles to JM, 12 Apr. 1795).

¶ To Arnold Henry Dohrman. Letter not found. *3 April 1795.* On this day JM wrote letters to Dohrman and Joseph Jones but sent each to the incorrect recipient. These letters were respectively acknowledged in Dohrman to JM, 6 Apr. 1795, and Jones to JM, 7 Apr. 1795. The letter intended for Dohrman but received by Jones concerned Dohrman's debt to Philip Mazzei.

¶ To Joseph Jones. Letter not found. *3 April 1795.* On this day JM wrote letters to Jones and Arnold Henry Dohrman but in error sent them to the incorrect recipients. These letters were respectively acknowledged in Dohrman to JM, 6 Apr. 1795, and Jones to JM, 7 Apr. 1795.

¶ To George Joy. Letter not found. *3 April 1795.* Acknowledged in Joy to JM, 10 Aug. 1795 (DLC). Encloses some books, including one by Tench Coxe (probably *A View of the United States of America* [Philadelphia, 1794; Evans 26829]). Apparently discusses the suppression of the Whiskey Insurrection and the secrecy of the Jay treaty.

To Philip Freneau

DEAR SIR   PHILADA. April 6. 1795

I delayed acknowledging your favor long ago recd. until I could inform you of the prospects of Mr. Bailey in whose favor it was written. I have now the pleasure to tell you that altho' his wishes are not to be immediately fulfilled, he is likely to obtain under the auspices of Mr. Beckley & Mr. Randolph a share of employment hereafter which may be very valuable to him. I congratulate you on the public intelligence just recd. from Holland which gives joy to all true Republicans, and wish you all the private happiness, which an exchange of your former troubled scenes, for the shade & tranquility of your present life, can afford. Remember however that as you have not chosen any longer to labour in the field of politics, it will be expected by your friends, that you cultivate with the more industry your inheritance on Parnassus. With my best respects to Mrs. Freneau, I remain Dear Sir, Your friend & servt.

Js. MADISON JR

RC (NjR). On the verso, Freneau wrote the following lines of verse:

> And are You here (the turnkey said)
> I rather would have seen You dead—?
> Yes—I am here, the wight replyd
> And rather so than to have died.

To James Monroe

DEAR SIR   PHILADA. April 6. 1795

I have written several letters of late in which I have been pretty full in my details and remarks. In one of them I acknowledged your letter to Mr. R of Decr. 18. and stated my reasons for not witholding it. I have since recd. the original of that letter sent by the way of Havre, together with the copies of it submitted to my discretion; which I have thought it most consistent with your intentions, not to forward at all. I have however rather come to that decision as the safer one, than under any particular impression that a contrary course would have been improper. This will go by Docr. Edwards,[1] who furnishes a good opportunity for the Cypher inclosed, of the rect. of which I wish to be apprised as soon as possible. As the Docr. will not embark for some time, and more particularly as he will be possessed of every information I could give, I shall not enlarge at present. I am on the point of setting out for Virginia with my family, whence I shall write as occasions invite. You will recollect that the Post now passes by my door, and consequently your let⟨ters⟩ wherever they may arrive, will get quickly & safely to hand. With my best respects & regards to you both I am Dr. Sir Yr. friend & servt.

Js. MADISON JR

RC (DLC). JM enclosed a cipher key to the code that Jefferson had sent him on 11 May 1785 (DLC: Monroe Papers).

1. Dr. Enoch Edwards of Philadelphia was one of several Americans "whose enthusiasm for the revolutionary cause had drawn them to France." Monroe "talked rather too freely with him, for Edwards was inclined to be indiscreet" (Ammon, *James Monroe*, p. 134).

From Arnold Henry Dohrman

SIR,   NEWYORK 6 April 1795.

I recd. your Letter dated 3 April, but to my great surprise, commencing to peruse it, I find you have made a mistake by addressing the Letter intended for me to some other person, I have therefore without investigating the contents returned you the Letter inclosed.

The Ship which I expected would enable me to make a final settlement of Mr. Mazzeis concern, is finally arrived, & has brought me the means, it will only take one or two days more to make arrangements, I request to inform me wether this money is to be remitted to Europa, in such a Case unexeptionable Bills on London might answer the same purposes as Cash, I request you will favour me with yr. commands of which I have been deprived by this unforeseen accident. Where is Mr. Mazzei now. With due Respect I have the honr. to remain Sir Your very Obedt. humb Servant

                                                    ARND. HENRY DOHRMAN

RC (NN).

From Joseph Jones

DR. SR.   RICHMOND 7th. Apr: 1795.

As soon as I returned from Loudoun I wrote you a letter which I supposed wod. be in time for you to answer about the time I shod. leave Fredericksburg for this place, that is that I might receive the answer by that time—yours of the 3d. inst. I have this moment recd. and can only inform you that I had requested information respecting the Rock Castle land as well as other things—and informed a proposition respecting them had been made to me by a Mr. Lacey of Loudoun but conceived the best course wod. be to effect the sale if practicable in Philadelphia. I do not know what is alluded to with respect to Mr. Mazzia or wod. give you my answer. If it respects Monroes affairs I know your respect for him wod. induce you to do what you thot. for the best and I am satisfied any thing you may think proper to do will be agreeable to him as well as to Dr Sr. yr friend & Servt.

                                                    JOS: JONES.

If you return by Fredg pray use my house. I have had no letter from you since early in March, but the above.

RC (DLC). Docketed by JM.

From William Branch Giles

DEAR SIR   RICHMOND April 12th. 1795

Your very friendly favor of the 3d. Instant, I received upon my arrival at this place two days ago. The extention of government upon its only solid and durable foundation, 'the rights of man,' is a circumstance peculiarly interresting to the whole human race, and in this great revolution in the condition of man, my sympathy has been particularly excited from an attachment to the nation which has been the means of effecting it. I speak of the revolution now, as effected, for at this period, a counterrevolution would afford a more wonderful occurrance in the human history than the commencement and progress of the late revolution have done. I thank you for the pleasure you express upon my reelection, but the paper has misinformed you as to the unanimity of votes.

There were found 8 or 10 Dissenting voices in the district; the result of the most extraordinary and illiberal calumny, which can be conceived. Richmond seems to have been the focus, and these votes a few diverging rays. This pittyful effort has terminated in so much disappointment and disgrace, that I believe the assertion of the paper will remain uncontradicted, as the authors can promise themselves no credit or advantage from the real state of facts.

I have been fortunate in having twice fallen in with your friend General Lee—since my return to Virginia—political hostility immediately ensued, and I discover that his feelings are hurt beyond description, from the late political occurrences in this country.[1] In the course of wine after dinner two days ago, Mr. Lee introduced you as a toast—but proceeded to remark (I thought with concern) that he had been informed from good authority, that you had made frequent remarks reflecting upon his reputation as an Individual. I took the liberty of observing that it was probable the information he had received had been exagerated—that some of his official acts had been the subjects of animadvertions from many gentlemen; but that I was possitively certain you had said nothing respecting Mr. L. which could not be justifyed. I further informed him that I had taken the liberty of makeing critisims upon parts of his official conduct, which I was ready to repeat and explain—but in the course of explanation Business drew Mr. L. from the table. I have intruded upon a table conversation without forgetting its

509

sacredness, from the confidence that you will make a proper use of it.

Be pleased to make my best respects to the ladies of your family and accept my best wishes for your personal happiness & prosperity &c

Wm. B. Giles

RC (DLC: Rives Collection, Madison Papers). Docketed by JM.

1. On Henry Lee's political misfortunes, see Lee to JM, 23 Sept. 1794, n. 1.

From John Beckley

Dear Sir,   New York, 20th: April 1795.

I was detained by bad weather & other causes, so that I did not reach this until friday evening. The next day I saw Mr: Dorhman, who promises fairly, altho' at the same time he talks of the scarcity of Money, his distresses &c. I expect to see him again to day, and you may be assured nothing in my power shall be omitted to obtain of him a full and satisfactory settlement.

I have not seen General Lamb,[1] long enough to know any thing of the issue of the letters committed to his care.

There has been no late arrival and is therefore no foreign News. The Election of Governor & Lt: Governor comes on to day, and the great probability is that Yates and Floyd will succeed.

In Massachusetts Varnum is 50 votes a head of Dexter, and within three of gaining his Election. Another trial must now be had, in which it is thought his success is certain. In this State, Havens, Livingston, Van Cortlandt, Bailey, Hawthorn, & Williams are on the republican side, and since the issue of the Virginia Elections is known, no doubt can be entertained of a decided Majority of the same Character in the next H: Rs. By the bye, they talk of a republican from Connecticut, whose name I have forgotten, in room of Trumbull.[2]

I hope you reached home in safety & without accident or injury. Be pleased to present my best regards to the ladies & accept them yourself, from, Dear Sir, Your friend & Servt.

John Beckley.

RC (DLC). Docketed by JM.

1. John Lamb was collector for the port of New York, 1784–97.

2. Federalist Jonathan Trumbull, a member of the House of Representatives, 1789–95, had been Speaker, 1791–93. In October 1794 the Connecticut General Assembly elected him to the U.S. Senate. That state's House delegation (elected at large) remained solidly Federalist in the Fourth Congress (Parsons et al., *United States Congressional Districts*, p. 34).

Political Observations

April 20, 1795.

A VARIETY of publications, in pamphlets and other forms, have appeared in different parts of the union, since the session of Congress which ended in June, 1794; endeavoring, by discoloured representations of our public affairs, and particularly of certain occurrences of that session, to turn the tide of public opinion into a party channel. The immediate object of the writers, was either avowedly or evidently to operate on the approaching elections of Federal Representatives. As that crisis will have entirely elapsed, before the following observations will appear; they will, at least, be free from a charge of the same views; and will, consequently, have the stronger claim to that deliberate attention and reflection to which they are submitted.

The publications alluded to, have passed slightly over the transactions of the First and Second Congress; and so far, their example will here be followed.

Whether, indeed, the funding system was modelled, either on the principles of substantial justice, or on the demands of public faith? Whether it did not contain ingredients friendly to the duration of the public debt, and implying that it was regarded as a public good? Whether the assumption of the state debts was not enforced by over-charged representations; and Whether, if the burdens had been equalized only, instead of being assumed in the gross, the states could not have discharged their respective proportions, by their local resources, sooner and more conveniently, than the general government will be able to discharge the whole debts, by general resources? Whether the excise system, be congenial with the spirit, and conducive to the happiness of our country; or can even justify itself as a productive source of Revenue? Whether again the bank was not established without authority from the constitution? Whether it did not throw unnecessary and unreasonable advantages into the hands of men; previously enriched beyond reason or necessity?* And whether it can be allowed the praise

---

* According to the plan of the bank, originally recommended, in the report of the Secretary of the Treasury, the charter was to continue until the final redemption of that part of its stock, consisting of public debt; that is until the whole of the six percent stock should be redeemed; for the part held by the bank could not be finally redeemed until the final redemption of the entire mass. In the progress of the bill through Congress, the term, not without difficulty (as it appears) was fixed at about twenty years. Notwithstanding this reduction, the market value of bank stock, has given an average profit to the subscribers of thirty or forty per cent on their capitals; or an aggregate profit of three, on the aggregate capital of eight millions; and it could not otherwise happen, than that this immense gain, would fall into the hands of those, who had gained most by purchases of

of a salutary operation, until its effects shall have been more accurately traced, and its hidden transactions shall be fully unveiled to the public eye: These and others are questions, which, though of great importance, it is not intended here to examine. Most of them have been finally decided by the competent authority; and the rest have, no doubt, already impressed themselves on the public attention.

Passing on then to the session of Congress preceding the last, we are met in the first place, by the most serious charges against the southern members of Congress in general, and particularly against the representatives of Virginia. They are charged with having supported a policy which would inevitably have involved the United States in the war of Europe, have reduced us from the rank of a free people, to that of French colonies, and possibly have landed us in disunion, anarchy, and misery; and the policy, from which these tremendous calamities was to flow, is referred to certain commercial resolutions moved by a member from Virginia, in the house of Representatives.[1]

To place in its true light, the fallacy which infers such consequences from such a cause, it will be proper to review the circumstances which preceded and attended the resoluti⟨ons⟩.[2]

It is well known, that at the peace between the United States and

---

certificates, because the great purchasers being most on the watch, having the best intelligence, and in general actually attending in person, or by agents, on the operations of the government, would of course, be the first to seize the proffered advantage, in exclusion of the primitive, the distant, and the uninformed, if not misinformed, holders of the subscribable paper.

It has actually happened, that the first provision for redeeming the debt, at the stipulated rate, has been postponed for five years: and the provision now made, if no interruption whatever should take place, will not effect the object within less than twenty-five or thirty years.[3] It will not be difficult to compute the additional profit, which would have accrued to the stockholders, had the original plan been adopted. But there is another, and perhaps a more important view of the tendency of a plan making the duration of the charter, to depend on the duration of the public debt. It would have stimulated, by the strongest motive of interest, that important and influential corporation, to impede the final discharge of the public debt, in order to prolong its charter and its emoluments. At present indeed it has but too obvious a temptation to favor the continuance and increase of public debts; since new debts call for anticipations by loans of its paper; and produce new taxes, by which the circulation of its paper is extended.

Those who attend to this subject, with minds clouded, neither by prejudice nor by interest, will rightly decide on the union which has subsisted between a seat in Congress and a seat at the bank. The indecorum as well as evil tendency of the alliance, has, by provoking the censorial notice of the public, produced a temporary dissolution of it. Query, whether there be not a remnant of the abuse, in the case of such as are at the same time stockholders of the bank and members of Congress? In the latter character, they vote for borrowing money on public account, which in their former character they are to lend on their own account.

Great Britain, it became a question with the latter, whether she should endeavor to regain the lost commerce of America, by liberal and reciprocal arrangements; or trust to a relapse of it, into its former channels, without the price of such arrangements on her part. Whilst she was fearful that our commerce would be conducted into new and rival channels, she leaned to the first side of the alternative, and a bill was actually carried in the House of Commons, by the present Prime Minister corresponding with that sentiment.[4] She soon, however, began to discover (or to hope) that the weakness of our Federal Government, and the want of concurrence among the state governments, would secure her against the danger at first apprehended. From that moment all ideas of conciliation and concession vanished. She determined to enjoy at once the full benefit of the freedom allowed by our regulations, and of the monopolies, established by her own.

In this state of things, the pride, as well as the interest of America were every where aroused. The mercantile world in particular, was all on fire; complaints flew from one end of the continent to the other; projects of retaliation and redress, engrossed the public attention. At one time, the states endeavored by separate efforts, to counteract the unequal laws of Great Britain. At another, correspondencies were opened for uniting their efforts. An attempt was also made, to vest in the former Congress, a limited power for a limited time, in order to give effect to the general will.[5]

All these experiments, instead of answering the purpose in view, served only to confirm Great Britain in her first belief, that her restrictive plans, were in no danger of retaliation.

It was at length determined by the Legislature of Virginia to go to work in a new way. It was proposed, and most of the states agreed, to send commissioners to digest some change in our general system, that might prove an effectual remedy. The Commissioners met; but finding their powers too circumscribed for the great object, which expanded itself before them, they proposed a convention on a more enlarged plan, for a general revision of the Federal Government.

From this convention proceeded the present Federal Constitution, which gives to the general will, the means of providing in the several necessary cases, for the general welfare; and particularly in the case of regulating our commerce in such manner as may be required by the regulations of other countries.

It was natural to expect, that one of the first objects of deliberation under the new constitution, would be that which had been first, and most contemplated in forming it. Accordingly it was, at the first session, proposed that something should be done analagous to the wishes of the several states, and expressive of the efficiency of the new government.

A discrimination between nations in treaty, and those not in treaty, the mode most generally embraced by the states, was agreed to in several forms, and adhered to in repeated votes, by a very great majority of the house of Representatives. The Senate, however, did not concur with the house of representatives, and our commercial arrangements were made up without any provision on the subject.[6]

From that date to the session of Congress ending in June, 1794, the interval passed without any effective appeal to the interest of Great Britain. A silent reliance was placed on her voluntary justice, or her enlightened interest.

The long and patient reliance being ascribed (as was foretold) to other causes, than a generous forbearance on the part of the United States, had, at the commencement of the third Congress, left us with respect to a reciprocity of commercial regulations between the two countries, precisely where the commencement of the first Congress had found us. This was not all; the western posts, which entailed an expensive Indian war on us, continued to be withheld; although all pretext for it had been removed on our part. Depredations, as derogatory to our rights, as grievous to our interests, had been licenced[7] by the British Government against our lawful commerce on the high seas. And it was believed, on the most probable grounds, that the measure by which the Algerine Pirates were let loose on the Atlantic, had not taken place without the participation of the same unfriendly counsels.[8] In a word, to say nothing of the American victims to savages and barbarians, it was estimated that our annual damages from Great Britain, were not less than three or four millions of dollars.

This distressing situation spoke the more loudly to the patriotism of the Representatives of the people, as the nature and manner of the communications from the President, seemed to make a formal and affecting appeal on the subject, to their co-operation. The necessity of some effort was palpable. The only room for different opinions seemed to lie in the different modes of redress proposed. On one side nothing was proposed, beyond the eventual measures of defence, in which all concurred, except the building of six frigates, for the purpose of enforcing our rights against Algiers. The other side considering this measure, as pointed at one only of our evils, and as inadequate even to that, thought it best to seek for some safe, but powerful remedy, that might be applied to the root of them; and with this view the Commercial Propositions were introduced.

They were at first opposed on the ground, that Great-Britain was amicably disposed towards the United States; and that we ought to await the event of the depending negociation. To this it was replied, that more than four years of appeal to that disposition, had been tried in vain, by the new government; that the negociation had been abortive, and was no longer depending; that the late letters* from Mr. Pinckney, the minister at London, had not only cut off all remaining hope from that source, but had expressly pointed Commercial Regulations as the most eligible redress to be pursued.

Another ground of opposition, was, that the United States were more dependant on the trade of Great Britain, than Great Britain was on the trade of the United States. This will appear scarcely credible to those who understand the commerce between the two countries, who recollect, that it supplies us chiefly with superfluities; whilst in return it employs the industry of one part of her people, sends to another part the very bread which keeps them from starving, and remits moreover, an annual balance in specie of ten or twelve millions of dollars.† It is true, nevertheless, as the debate shews, that this was the language, however strange, of some who combated the propositions.

Nay, what is still more extraordinary, it was maintained that the United States, had, on the whole, little or no reason to complain of the footing of their commerce with Great Britain; although such complaints had prevailed in every state, among every class of citizens, ever since the year 1783; and although the Federal Constitution had originated in those complaints, and had been established with the known view of redressing them.

As such objections could have little effect in convincing the judgement of the House of Representatives, and still less that of the public at large; a new mode of assailing the propositions has been substituted. The American People love peace; and the cry of war might alarm when no hope remained of convincing them. The cry of war has accordingly been echoed through the continent, with a loudness proportioned to the

* See his letter of 15th August, 1793, to the Secretary of State, in the printed communications from the President to the Congress.[9]

† This balance is not precise, but may be deemed within the amount. It appears from a late, and apparently an office statement from *Great Britain* of exports and imports between Great Britain and the United States, that the actual balance in the year 1791, was *three millions, thirty one thousand two hundred and fifteen pounds, fourteen and nine pence sterl.* and in the year 1792, *three millions, two hundred and thirty one thousand, and ninety pounds, seven shillings and four pence sterl.* equal to *fourteen millions, three hundred and sixty thousand, four hundred and one dollar.* As this relates to the trade with Great Britain only, the balance in our favor in the West India trade is to be deducted. There is reason however to believe, that it would not reduce the general balance so low, as is above stated; besides, that the balance against us, in the trade with Ireland, is not taken into the account.

emptiness of the pretext; and to this cry has been added, another still[10] more absurd, that the propositions would in the end, enslave the United States to their allies, and plunge them into anarchy and misery.

It is truly mortifying to be obliged to tax the patience of the reader, with an examination of such gross absurdities; but it may be of use to expose, where there may be no necessity to refute them.

What were the Commercial Propositions? They discriminated between nations in treaty, and nations not in treaty, by an additional duty on the manufactures and trade of the latter; and they reciprocated the navigation laws of all nations, who excluded the vessels of the United States, from a common right of being used in the trade between the United States, and such nations.

Is there any thing here that could afford a cause, or a pretext for war, to Great Britain or any other nation? If we hold at present the rank of a free people; if we are no longer colonies of Great Britain; if we have not already relapsed into some dependence on that nation, we have the self-evident right, to regulate our trade according to our own will, and our own interest, not according to her will or her interest. This right can be denied to no independent nation. It has not been, and will not be denied to ourselves, by any opponent of the propositions.

If the propositions could give no right to Great Britain to make war, would they have given any color to her for such an outrage on us? No American Citizen will affirm it. No British subject, who is a man of candor, will pretend it; because he must know, that the commercial regulations of Great Britain herself have discriminated among foreign nations, whenever it was thought convenient. They have discriminated against particular nations by name; they have discriminated, with respect to particular articles by name, by the nations producing them, and by the places exporting them. And as to the navigation articles proposed, they were not only common to the other countries along with Great Britain; but reciprocal between Great Britain and the United States: Nay, it is notorious, that they fell short of an immediate and exact reciprocity of her own Navigation Laws.

Would any nation be so barefaced as to quarrel with another, for doing the same thing which she herself has done; for doing less than she herself has done, towards that particular nation? It is impossible that Great Britain would ever expose herself by so absurd, as well as arrogant a proceeding. If she really meant to quarrel with this country, common prudence, and common decency, would prescribe some other less odious pretext for her hostility.

It is the more astonishing that such a charge against the propositions should have been hazarded, when the opinion, and the proceedings, of America, on the subject of our commercial policy is reviewed.

Whilst the power over trade, remained with the several States, there were few of them that did not exercise it, on the principle, if not in the mode, of the commercial propositions. The eastern States generally passed laws, either discriminating between some foreign nations and others, or levelled against Great Britain by name. Maryland and Virginia did the same, so did two, if not the three, of the more southern States. Was it ever, during that period, pretended at home or abroad, that a cause or pretext for quarrel, was given to Great Britain or any other nation? or were our rights better understood at that time, than at this, or more likely then, than now, to command the respect due to them.

Let it not be said, Great Britain was then at peace, she is now at war. If she would not wantonly attempt to controul the exercise of our sovereign rights, when she had no other enemy on her hands, will she be mad enough to make the attempt, when her hands are fully employed with the war already on them? Would not those who say now, postpone the measures until Great Britain shall be at peace, be more ready, and have more reason to say in time of peace, postpone them until she shall be at war; there will then be no danger of her throwing new enemies into the scale against her.

Nor let it be said, that the combined powers, would aid and stimulate Great Britain, to wage an unjust war on the United States. They also are too fully occupied with their present enemy, to wish for another on their hands; not to add, that two of those powers, being in treaty with the United States, are favored by the propositions; and that all of them are well known to entertain an habitual jealousy of the monopolizing character and maritime ascendency of that nation.

One thing ought to be regarded as certain and conclusive on this head; whilst the war against France remains unsuccessful, the United States are in no danger, from any of the powers engaged in it. In the event of a complete overthrow of that Republic, it is impossible to say, what might follow. But if the hostile views of the combination, should be turned towards this continent, it would clearly not be, to vindicate the commercial interests of Great Britain against the commercial rights of the United States. The object would be, to root out Liberty from the face of the earth. No pretext would be wanted, or a better would be contrived than anything to be found in the commercial propositions.

On whatever other side we view the clamor against these propositions as inevitably productive of war, it presents neither evidence to justify it nor argument to colour it.

The allegation necessarily supposes either that the friends of the plan could discover no probability, where its opponents could see a certainty, or that the former were less averse to war than the latter.

The first supposition will not be discussed. A few observations on the other may throw new lights on the whole subject.

The members, in general, who espoused these propositions have been constantly in that part of the Congress who have professed with most zeal, and pursued with most scruple, the characteristics of republican government. They have adhered to these characteristics in defining the meaning of the Constitution, in adjusting the ceremonial of public proceedings, and in marking[11] out the course of the Administration. They have manifested, particularly, a deep conviction of the danger to liberty and the Constitution, from a gradual assumption or extension of discretionary powers in the executive departments; from successive augmentations of a standing army; and from the perpetuity and progression of public debts and taxes. They have been sometimes reprehended in debate for an excess of caution and jealousy on these points. And the newspapers of a certain stamp, by distorting and discolouring this part of their conduct, have painted it in all the deformity which the most industrious calumny could devise.

Those best acquainted with the individuals who more particularly supported the propositions will be foremost to testify, that such are the principles which not only govern them in public life, but which are invariably maintained by them in every other situation. And it cannot be believed nor suspected, that with such principles they could view war as less an evil than it appeared to their opponents.

Of all the enemies to public liberty war is, perhaps, the most to be dreaded, because it comprises and develops the germ[12] of every other. War is the parent of armies; from these proceed debts and taxes; and armies, and debts, and taxes are the known instruments for bringing the many under the domination[13] of the few. In war, too, the discretionary power of the Executive is extended; its influence in dealing out offices, honors, and emoluments is multiplied; and all the means of seducing the minds, are added to those of subduing the force, of the people. The same malignant aspect in republicanism may be traced in the inequality of fortunes, and the opportunities of fraud, growing out of a state of war, and in the degeneracy of manners and of morals, engendered by both. No nation could preserve its freedom in the midst of continual warfare.

Those truths are well established. They are read in every page which records the progression from a less arbitrary to a more arbitrary government, or the transition from a popular government to an aristocracy or a monarchy.

It must be evident, then, that in the same degree as the friends of the propositions were jealous of armies, and debts, and prerogative, as dangerous to a republican Constitution, they must have been averse to war, as favourable to armies and debts, and prerogative.

The fact accordingly appears to be, that they were particularly averse to war. They not only considered the propositions as having no tendency to war, but preferred them, as the most likely means of obtaining our objects without war. They thought, and thought truly, that Great Britain was more vulnerable in her commerce than in her fleets and armies; that she valued our necessaries for her markets, and our markets for her superfluities, more than she feared our frigates or our militia; and that she would, consequently, be more ready to make proper concessions under the influence of the former, than of the latter motive.

Great Britain is a commercial nation. Her power, as well as her wealth, is derived from commerce. The American commerce is the most valuable branch she enjoys. It is the more valuable, not only as being of vital importance to her in some respects, but of growing importance beyond estimate in its general character. She will not easily part with such a resource. She will not rashly hazard it. She would be particularly aware of forcing a perpetuity of regulations, which not merely diminish her share; but may favour the rivalship of other nations. If anything, therefore, in the power of the United States could overcome her pride, her avidity, and her repugnancy to this country, it was justly concluded to be, not the fear of our arms, which, though invincible in defence, are little formidable in a war of offence, but the fear of suffering in the most fruitful branch of her trade, and of seeing it distributed among her rivals.

If any doubt on this subject could exist, it would vanish on a recollection of the conduct of the British ministry at the close of the war in 1783. It is a fact which has been already touched, and it is as notorious as it is instructive, that during the apprehension of finding her commerce with the United States abridged or endangered by the consequences of the revolution, Great-Britain was ready to purchase it, even at the expence of her West-Indies monopoly. It was not until after she began to perceive the weakness of the federal government, the discord in the counteracting plans of the state governments, and the interest she would be able to establish here, that she ventured on that system to which she has since inflexibly adhered. Had the present federal government, on its first establishment, done what it ought to have done, what it was instituted and expected to do, and what was actually proposed and intended it should do; had it revived and confirmed the belief in Great-Britain, that our trade and navigation would not be free to her, without an equal and reciprocal freedom to us, in her trade and navigation, we have her own authority for saying, that she would long since have met us on proper ground; because the same motives which produced the bill brought into the British parliament by Mr. Pitt, in order to prevent the evil apprehended, would have produced the same concession at least, in order to obtain a recall of the evil, after it had taken place.

The aversion to war in the friends of the propositions, may be traced through the whole proceedings and debates of the session. After the depredations in the West-Indies, which seemed to fill up the measure of British aggressions, they adhered to their original policy of pursuing redress, rather by commercial, than by hostile operations; and with this view unanimously concurred in the bill for suspending importations from British ports;[14] a bill that was carried through the house by a vote of fifty-eight against thirty-four. The friends of the propositions appeared, indeed, never to have admitted, that Great-Britain could seriously mean to force a war with the United States, unless in the event of prostrating the French Republic; and they did not believe that such an event was to be apprehended.

Confiding in this opinion, to which Time has given its full sanction, they could not accede to those extraordinary measures, which nothing short of the most obvious and imperious necessity could plead for. They were as ready as any, to fortify our harbours, and fill our magazines and arsenals; these were safe and requisite provisions for our permanent defence. They were ready and anxious for arming and preparing our militia; that was the true republican bulwark of our security. They joined also in the addition of a regiment of artillery to the military establishment, in order to complete the defensive arrangement on our eastern frontier. These facts are on record, and are the proper answer to those shameless calumnies which have asserted, that the friends of the commercial propositions were enemies to every proposition for the national security.

But it was their opponents, not they, who continually maintained, that on a failure of negociation, it would be more eligible to seek redress by war, than by commercial regulations; who talked of raising armies, that might threaten the neighbouring possessions of foreign powers; who contended for delegating to the executive the prerogatives of deciding whether the country was at war or not, and of levying, organizing, and calling into the field, a regular army of ten, fifteen, nay, of TWENTY-FIVE THOUSAND men.[15]

It is of some importance that this part of the history of the session, which has found no place in the late reviews of it, should be well understood. They who are curious to learn the particulars, must examine the debates and the votes. A full narrative would exceed the limits which are here prescribed. It must suffice to remark, that the efforts were varied and repeated until the last moment of the session, even after the departure of a number of members; forbade new propositions, much more a renewal of rejected ones; and that the powers proposed to be surrendered to the executive, were those which the constitution has most jealously appropriated to the legislature.

The reader shall judge on this subject for himself.

The constitution expressly and exclusively vests in the legislature the power of declaring a state of war: it was proposed, that the executive might, in the recess of the legislature, declare the United States to be in a state of war.

The constitution expressly and exclusively vests in the legislature the power of raising armies: it was proposed, that in the recess of the legislature, the executive might, at its pleasure, raise or not raise an army of ten, fifteen, or twenty-five thousand men.

The constitution expressly and exclusively vests in the legislature the power of creating offices: it was proposed, that the executive, in the recess of the legislature, might create offices, as well as appoint officers for an army of ten, fifteen, or twenty-five thousand men.

A delegation of such powers would have struck, not only at the fabric of our constitution, but at the foundation of all well organized and well checked governments.

The separation of the power of declaring war, from that of conducting it, is wisely contrived, to exclude the danger of its being declared for the sake of its being conducted.

The separation of the power of raising armies, from the power of commanding them, is intended to prevent the raising of armies for the sake of commanding them.

The separation of the power of creating offices, from that of filling them, is an essential guard against the temptation to create offices, for the sake of gratifying favorites, or multiplying dependants.

Where would be the difference between the blending of these incompatible powers, by surrendering the legislative part of them into the hands of the executive, and by assuming the executive part of them into the hands of the legislature? In either case the principle would be equally destroyed, and the consequences equally dangerous.

An attempt to answer these observations, by appealing to the virtues of the present chief magistrate, and to the confidence justly placed in them, will be little calculated, either for his genuine patriotism, or for the sound judgment of the American public.

The people of the United States would not merit the praise universally allowed to their intelligence, if they did not distinguish between the respect due to the man, and the functions belonging to the office. In expressing the former, there is no limit or guide, but the feelings of their grateful hearts. In deciding the latter, they will consult the constitution; they will consider human nature, and, looking beyond the character of the existing magistrate, fix their eyes on the precedent which must descend to his successors.

Will it be more than truth to say, that this great and venerable name is too often assumed for what cannot recommend itself, and for what there is neither proof nor probability, that its sanction can be claimed? Do arguments fail? Is the public mind to be encountered? There are not a few ever ready to invoke the name of Washington; to garnish their heretical doctrines with his virtues, and season their unpallatable measures with his populari⟨ty⟩.[16] Those who take this liberty, will not, however, be mistaken; his truest friends will be the last to sport with his influence, above all, for electioneering purposes. And it is but a fair suspicion, that they who draw most largely on that fund, are hastening fastest to bankruptcy in their own.

As vain would be the attempt to explain away such alarming attacks on the constitution, by pleading the difficulty, in some cases, of drawing a line between the different departments of power; or by recurring to the little precedents which may have crept in, at urgent or unguarded moments.

It cannot be denied, that there may, in certain cases, be a difficulty in distinguishing the exact boundary between legislative and executive powers; but the real friend of the constitution, and of liberty, by his endeavors to lessen or avoid the difficulty, will easily be known from him who labours to encrease the obscurity, in order to remove the constitutional land-marks without notice.

Nor will it be denied, that precedents may be found, where the line of separation between these powers has not been sufficiently regarded; where an improper latitude of discretion, particularly, has been given, or allowed, to the executive departments. But what does this prove? That the line ought to be considered as imaginary; that constitutional organizations of power ought to lose their effect? No—It proves with how much deliberation precedents ought to be established, and with how much caution arguments from them should be admitted. It may furnish another criterion, also, between the real and ostensible friend of constitutional liberty. The first will be as vigilant in resisting, as the last will be in promoting, the growth of inconsiderate or insidious precedents, into established encroachments.

The next charge to be examined, is the tendency of the propositions to degrade the United States into French colonies.

As it is difficult to argue against suppositions made and multiplied at will, so it is happily impossible to impose on the good sense of this country, by arguments which rest on suppositions only. In the present question it is first supposed, that the exercise of the self-evident and sovereign right of regulating trade, after the example of all independent nations, and that of the example of Great-Britain towards the United States, would inevitably involve the United States in a war with Great Britain. It is then supposed, that the other combined powers, though some of them be favored by the regulations proposed, and all of them be jealous of the maritime predominance of Great Britain, would support the wrongs of Great Britain against the rights of the United States. It is lastly supposed, that our allies (the French) in the event of success in establishing their own liberties, which they owe to our example, would be willing, as well as able, to rob us of ours, which they assisted us in obtaining; and that so malignant is their disposition on this head, that we should not be spared, even if embarked in a war against her own enemy. To finish the picture, it is intimated, that in the character of allies, we are the more exposed to this danger, from the secret and hostile ambition of France.

It will not be expected, that any formal refutation should be wasted on absurdities which answer themselves. None but those who have surrendered their reasoning faculties to the violence[17] of their prejudices, will listen to suggestions implying, that the freest nation in Europe is the basest people on the face of the earth; that instead of the friendly and festive sympathy indulged by the people of the United States, they ought to go into mourning at every triumph of the French arms; that instead of regarding the French revolution as a blessing to mankind, and a bulwark to their own, they ought to anticipate its success as of all events the most formidable to their liberty and sovereignty; and that, calculating on the political connection with that nation, as the source of additional danger from its enmity and its usurpation, the first favorable moment ought to be seized for putting an end to it.

It is not easy to dismiss this subject, however, without reflecting, with grief and surprize, on the readiness with which many launch into speculations unfriendly to the struggles of France, and regardless of the interesting relations in which that country stands to this. They seem to be more struck with every circumstance that can be made a topic of reproach, or of chimerical apprehensions, than with all the splendid objects which are visible through the gloom of a revolution. But if there be an American who can see, without benevolent joy, the progress[18] of that liberty to which he owes his own happiness, interest, at least, ought to find a place in his calculations: And if he cannot enlarge his views to the influence of the successes and friendship of France, or our safety as a nation, and particularly as a republic, how can he be insensible to the benefits presented to the United States in her commerce? The French markets consume more of our best productions, than are consumed by any other nation. If a balance in specie be as favorable as is usually supposed, the sum which supplies the immense drains of our specie, is derived also from the same source, more than from any other. And in the great and precious article of navigation, the share of American tonnage employed in the trade with the French dominions, gives to that trade a distinguished value; as well to that part of the union which most depends on ships and seamen for its prosperity, as to that which most requires them for its protection.

Whenever these considerations shall have that full weight, which a calm review will not fail to allow them, none will wonder more than the mercantile class of citizens themselves, that whilst they so anxiously wait stipulations from Great Britain, which are always within our command, so much indifference should be felt to those more important privileges in the trade of France, which, if not secured by a seasonable improvement of the commercial treaty with her, may possibly be forever lost to us.

Among the aspersions propagated against the friends, and the merits arrogated by the opponents, of the commercial propositions, much use has been made of the envoy-ship extraordinary to Great Britain.[19] It has been affirmed, that the former was averse to the measure, on account of its pacific tendency; and that it was embraced by the latter, as the proper substitute for all commercial operations on the policy of Great Britain. It is to be remembered, however,

1. That this measure originated wholly with the executive.

2. That the opposition to it in the senate (as far as the public have any knowledge of it) was made, not to the measure of appointing an envoy extraordinary, but to the appointment of the chief justice of the United States for that service.

3. That the house of representatives never gave any opinion on the occasion, and that no opinion appears to have been expressed in debate by any individual of that house, which can be tortured into a disapprobation of the measure, on account of its pacific tendency.

4. That the measure did not take place until the commercial propositions had received all the opposition that could be given to them.

5. That there is no spark of evidence, that if the envoy-ship had never taken place, or been thought of, the opponents of the propositions would have concurred in any commercial measures whatever, even after the West-India spoliations had laid in their full claim to the public attention.

But it may be fairly asked of those who opposed first the Commercial Propositions, and then the Non-Importation bill, and who rest their justification on the appointment of an envoy extraordinary; wherein lay the inconsistency between these Legislative and Executive plans?

Was it thought best to appeal to the Voluntary Justice, or liberal policy of Great Britain, and to these only? This was not certainly the

case with those, who opposed the Commercial Appeals to the interest
and the apprehension of Great Britain; Because they were the most
zealous for appealing to her fears, by military preparations and menaces.
If these had any meaning, they avowed that Great Britain was not to be
brought to reason, otherwise than by the danger of injury to herself.
And such being her disposition, she would, of course, be most influenced by measures, of which the comparative operation would be most
against her. Whether that would be apprehended from measures of the
one, or the other kind will easily be decided. But in every view, if *fear*
was a proper auxiliary to negociation, the appeal to it in the Commercial
Measures proposed, could not be inconsistent with the Envoyship. The
inconsistency belongs to the reasoning of those who would pronounce
it proper and effectual to say to Great-Britain, do us justice, or we will
seize on Canada, though the loss will be trifling to you, whilst the cost
will be immense to us; and who[20] pronounce it improper and ineffectual
to say to Great-Britain, do us justice, or you will suffer a wound, where
you will most of all feel it, in a branch of your commerce, which feeds
one part of your dominions, and sends annually to the other, a balance
in specie of more than ten millions of dollars.

The opponents of the commercial measures may be asked, in the next
place, to what cause the issue of the envoy-ship, if successful, ought to
be ascribed?

Will it have been[21] the pure effect of a benevolent and conciliatory
disposition in Great Britain towards the United States? This will hardly
be pretended by her warmest admirers and advocates. It is disproved by
the whole tenor of her conduct ever since we were an independent and
republican nation. Had this cordial disposition, or even a disposition to
do us justice, been really felt; the delay would not have been spun out
to so late a day. The moment would rather have been chosen, when we
were least in condition, to vindicate our interest, by united councils and
persevering efforts. The motives then would have been strongest, and
the merit most conspicuous. Instead of this honorable and prudent
course, it has been the vigilant study of Great Britain, to take all possible
advantage of our embarrassments; nor has the least inclination been
shewn to relax her system, except at the crisis in 1783, already mentioned, when, not foreseeing these embarrassments, she was alarmed for
her commerce with the United States.

Will the success be ascribeable to the respect paid to that country by
the measure, or to the talents and address of the envoy.

Such an explanation of the fact, is absolutely precluded by a series of
other facts.

Soon after the peace, Mr. Adams, the present Vice President of the
United States, was appointed Minister Plenipotentiary to the British

Court. The measure was the more respectful as no mutual arrangement had been premised between the two countries, nor any intimation received from Great Britain, that the civility should be returned; nor was the civility returned during the whole period of his residence. The manner in which he was treated, and the United States, through him, his protracted exertions, and the mortifying inefficacy of them, are too much in the public remembrance to need a rehearsal.

This first essay on the temper of Great Britain, towards the United States, was prior to the establishment of the Federal Constitution. The important change produced in our situation by this event, led to another essay, which is not unknown to the public. Although in strictness, it might not unreasonably have been expected, after what had been done in the instance of Mr. Adams, that the advance towards a diplomatic accommodation should then have come from Great Britain, Mr. G. Morris was made an agent for feeling her pulse, and soothing her pride, a second time. The history of his operations is not particularly known. It is certain, however, that this repetition of the advance, produced no sensible change on her disposition towards us, much less any actual compliance with our just expectations and demands. The most that can be said is, that it was, after a considerable interval, followed by the mission of Mr. Hammond to the United States, who, as it is said, however, refused, notwithstanding the long residence of Mr. Adams at the court of London, without a return of the civility, to commit the dignity of his master, until the most explicit assurances were given, that Mr. Pinckney should immediately counterplace him.

The mission of this last respectable citizen, forms a third appeal to the justice and good will of the British Government, on the subjects between the two countries. His negociations on that side the Atlantic, as well as those through Mr. Hammond on this, having been laid before the Congress, and printed for general information, will speak for themselves. It will only be remarked, that they terminated here in the disclosure, that Mr. Hammond had no authority, either to adjust the differences connected with the Treaty of Peace, or to concur in any solid arrangements, for reciprocity in Commerce and Navigation; and that in Great Britain, they terminated in the conviction of Mr. Pinckney, that nothing was to be expected from the voluntary justice or policy of that country, and in his advice, before quoted, of *Commercial Regulations*, as the best means for obtaining a compliance with our just claims.

All who weigh these facts with candor, will join in concluding, that the success of the envoyship must be otherwise explained, than by the operation of diplomatic compliments, or of personal talents.

To what causes then will the United States be truly indebted, for any favorable result to the envoyship?

Every well-informed and unprejudiced mind, will answer, to the following:

1. The spirit of America, expressed by the vote of the House of Representatives, on the subject of the Commercial Propositions, by the large majority of that house (overruled by the casting voice in the Senate) in favor of the non-importation bill, and by the act laying an embargo. Although these proceedings would, doubtless, have been more efficacious,[22] if the two former had obtained the sanction of laws, and if the last had not been so soon repealed;* yet they must have had no little effect, as warnings to the British government; that if her obstinacy should take away the last pretext from the opponents of such measures, it might be impossible to divide or mislead our public councils with respect to them in future.

There is no room to pretend, that her relaxation in this case, if she should relax, will be the effect, not of those proceedings, but of the ultimate defeat[23] of them. Former defeats of a like policy, had repeatedly taken place, and are known to have produced, instead of relaxation, a more confirmed perseverance on the part of Great-Britain. Under the old confederation, the United States had not the power over commerce: of that situation she took advantage. The new government which contained the power, did not evince the will to exert it; of that situation she still took the advantage. Should she yield then at the present juncture? The problem ought not to be solved, without presuming her to be satisfied by what has lately passed—that the United States have now, not only the power, but the will to exert it.

The reasoning is short and conclusive; in the year 1783, when Great Britain apprehended Commercial Restrictions from the United States, she was disposed to concede and to accommodate. From the year 1783 to the year 1794, when she apprehended no Commercial Restrictions, she shewed no disposition to concede or to accommodate. In the year 1794, when alarming evidence was given of the danger of Commercial Restrictions, she did concede and accommodate.

If any thing can have weakened the operation of the proceedings above referred to on the British government, it must be the laboured and vehement attempts of their opponents to show, that the United States had little to demand, and every thing to dread, from Great Britain; that the commerce between the two countries was more essential to us, than to her; that our citizens would be less willing than her subjects to bear, and our government less able than hers to enforce,

* That this is particularly true of the embargo, is certain, as well from the known effect[24] of that measure in the West Indies as from the admission of the West India planters in their late petition to the King and Council of Great Britain.[25]

restrictions or interruptions of it. In a word, that we were more dependent on her, than she was on us; and, therefore, ought to court her not[26] to withdraw from us her supplies, though chiefly luxuries, instead of threatening to withdraw from her our supplies, though mostly necessaries.

It is difficult to say, whether the indiscretion or the fallacy of such arguments be the more remarkable feature in them. All that can be hoped is, that an antidote to their mischievous tendency in Great Britain may be found in the consciousness there, of the errors on which they are founded, and the contempt which they will be known to have excited in this country.

2. The other cause will be, the posture into which Europe has been thrown, by the war with France, and particularly by the campaign of 1794. The combined armies have every where felt the superior valour, discipline, and resources of their republican enemies. Prussia, after heavy and perfidious draughts on the British treasury, has retired from the common standard, to contend with new dangers peculiar to herself. Austria, worn out in unavailing resistance, her arms disgraced, her treasure exhausted, and her vassals discontented, seeks her last consolation in the same source of British subsidy. The Dutch, instead of continuing their proportion of aids for the war, have their whole faculties turned over to France. Spain, with all her wealth and all her pride, is palsied in every nerve, and forced to the last resorts of royalty, to a reduction of salaries and pensions, and to the hoards of superstition. Great Britain herself has seen her military glory eclipsed, her projects confounded, her hopes blasted, her marine threatened, her resources overcharged, and her government in danger of losing its energy, by the despotic excesses[27] into which it has been overstrained.

If, under such circumstances, she does not abandon herself to apathy and despair, it is because she finds her credit still alive, and in that credit sees some possibility of making terms with misfortune. But what is the basis of that credit? Her commerce. And what is the most valuable remnant of that resource? The commerce with the U. States. Will she risk this best part of her last resource, by persevering in her selfish and unjust treatment of the United States?

Time will give a final answer to this question. All that can be now pronounced is, that if, on the awful precipice to which G. Britain is driven,[28] she will open neither her eyes to her danger, nor her heart to her duty, her character must be a greater contrast to the picture of it drawn by the opponents of the commercial measures, than could have easily been imagined. If, on the other hand, she should relent, and consult her reason, the change will be accounted for by her prospects on the other side of the atlantic, and the countenance exhibited on this; without supposing her character to vary, in a single feature, from the view of it entertained by the friends of such measures.

That the rising spirit of America, and the successes of France, will have been the real causes of any favorable terms obtained by the mission of Mr. Jay, cannot be controverted. Had the same forbearance, which was tried for ten years on the part of the United States, been continued; and had the combined powers proceeded in the victorious career which has signalized the French arms; under this reverse of circumstances, the most bigotted Englishman will be ashamed to say, that any relaxing change in the policy of his government, was to be hoped for by the United States.

Such are the reflections which occur on the supposition of a successful issue to the envoy-ship. Should it unhappily turn out, that neither the new countenance presented by America, nor the adverse fortunes of Great Britain, can bend the latter to a reasonable accommodation, it may be worth while to enquire, what will probably be the evidence furnished by the friends and adversaries of commercial measures, with respect to their comparative attachments to peace?*

If any regard be paid to consistency, those who opposed all such measures must be for an instant resort to arms. With them there was no alternative, but negociation or war. Their language was, let us try the former, but be prepared for the latter; if the olive branch fail, let the sword vindicate our rights, as it has vindicated the rights of other nations. A real war is both more honorable and more eligible than commercial regulations. In these G. B. is an overmatch for us.

On the other side, the friends of commercial measures, if consistent, will prefer these measures, as an intermediate experiment between negociation and war. They will persist in their language, that Great-Britain is more dependent on us, than we are on her; that this has ever been the American sentiment, and is the true basis of American policy; that war should not be resorted to, till every thing short of war has been tried; that if Great-Britain be invulnerable to our attacks, it is in her fleets and armies; that if the United States can bring her to reason at all, the surest as well as the cheapest means, will be a judicious system of commercial operations; that here the United States are unquestionably an overmatch for Great-Britain.

It must be the ardent prayer of all, that the occasion may not happen for such a test of the consistency and the disposition of those whose counsels were so materially different on the subject of a commercial vindication of our rights. Should it be otherwise ordained, the public judgment[29] will pronounce on which side, the politics were most averse to war, and most anxious for every pacific effort, that might at the same

* *When this was written, the result of Mr. Jay's mission was wholly unknown.*

time be an efficient one, in preference to that last and dreadful resort of injured nations.

There remain two subjects belonging to the session of Congress under review, on each of which some comments are made proper by the misrepresentations which have been propagated.

The first is, The naval armament.

The second, The new taxes then established.

As to the first, it appears from the debates and other accounts, to have been urged in favor of the measure, that six frigates of one hundred and eighty four guns, to be stationed at the mouth of the Mediterranean, would be sufficient to protect the American trade against the Algerine pirates;[30] that such a force would not cost more than six hundred thousand dollars, including an out-fit[31] of stores and provisions for six months, and might be built in time to take their station by July or August last; that the expence of this armament would be fully justified by the importance of our trade to the south of Europe; that without such a protection, the whole trade of the Atlantic would be exposed to depredation; nay, that the American coast might not escape the enterprising avarice of these roving Barbarians; that such an effort on the part of the United States, was particularly due to the unfortunate citizens already groaning in chains and pining in despair, as well as to those who might otherwise be involved in the same fate. Other considerations of less influence may have entered into the decision on the same side.

On the other side, it was said, that the force was insufficient for the object; that the expence would be greater than was estimated; that there was a limit to the expence, which could be afforded for the protection of any branch of trade; that the aggregate value of the annual trade, export and import to Spain and Portugal, appeared from authentic documents[32] not to exceed three and an half millions of dollars;* that the profit only, on this amount, was to be compared with the expence of the frigates; that if the American vessels engaged in those channels, should give place to vessels at peace with Algiers, they would repair to the channels quitted by the latter vessels; so that it would be rather a change than a loss of employment; that the other distant branches of our trade, would be little affected and our own coast not at all; that the frigates, at so great a distance on a turbulent sea, would be exposed to dangers, as well as attended with expences, not to be calculated; and if stationed where intended, would leave our trade up the Mediterranean

---

* It appears by a late official document,[33] that the amount of the trade since that period has considerably increased in value; but it may be remarked, that in the same ratio, the motives to renew the protection, have been strengthened in Portugal and Spain.

as unprotected as it is at present. That in addition to these considerations, the frigates would not be ready by the time stated, nor probably until the war, and the occasion would be over; that if the removal of the Portuguese squadron from the blockade really proceeded, as was alledged from Great-Britain, she would, under some pretext or other, contrive to defeat the object of the frigates; that if Great-Britain was not at the bottom of the measure, the interest which Portugal had in our trade, which supplies her with the necessaries of life, would soon restore the protection she had withdrawn; that it would be more effectual as well as cheaper, to concert arrangements with Portugal, by which the United States would be subjected to an equitable share only, instead of taking on themselves the whole of the burden; that as to our unfortunate citizens in captivity, the frigates could neither be in time nor of force, to relieve them; that money alone could do this, and that a sufficient sum ought to be provided for the purpose: that it was moreover to be considered, that if there were any disposition in Great-Britain, to be irritated[34] into a war with us, or to seek an occasion for it; those, who on other questions had taken that ground of argument, ought to be particularly aware of danger, from the collision of naval armaments, within the sphere of British jealousy, and in the way perhaps of a favorite object.

No undue blame is meant to be thrown on those, who did not yield to this reasoning, however conclusive it may now appear. The vote in favor of the measure was indeed so checquered, that it cannot even be attributed to the influence of party. It is but justice, at the same time, to those who opposed the measure, to remark, that instead of the frigates being at their destined station in July or August last, the keel of one only was laid in December; the timber for the rest being then in the forest, and the whole of the present year stated to be necessary for their completion; that consequently it is nearly certain now, they will not be in service, before the war in Europe will be over,* and that in the mean time it has turned out as was foretold, that Portugal has felt sufficient motives to renew the blockade; so that if the frigates had been adapted to the original object, they would not be required for it; more especially, as it has likewise turned out according to another anticipation, that money would alone be the agent for restoring the captive exiles to their freedom and their country.

---

* It may be added, that the original estimate and appropriation for the annual support of the frigates, was two hundred and forty-seven thousand, nine hundred dollars[35] only; whereas the sum required at the last session, by the Secretary of War, for six months support, in the year 1795, is two hundred twenty-four thousand seven hundred and fifty-four dollars;[36] making the annual support four hundred forty-nine thousand, five hundred and eight dollars.

It may possibly be said, that the frigates, though not necessary or proper for the service first contemplated, may usefully be applied to the security of our coasts, against Pirates, Privateers, and Smugglers. This is a distinct question. The sole and avowed object of the naval armament was the protection of our trade against the Algerines. To that object the force is appropriated by the law itself. The President can apply it to no other. If any other now presents itself, it may fairly be now discussed, but as it was not the object then, the measure cannot be tested by it now. If there be sufficient reasons of any sort for such a naval establishment, those who disapproved it for an impracticable and impolitic object, may with perfect consistency allow these reasons their full weight. It is much to be questioned, however, whether any good reason could be found for going on with the whole undertaking; besides, that in general the commencement of political measures under one pretext, and the prosecution of them under another, has always an aspect, that justifies circumspection if not suspicion.

With respect to the new taxes, the second remaining subject, a very brief explanation will be sufficient.

From a general view of the proceedings of Congress on this subject, it appears, that the advocates for the new taxes urged them. 1st. On the probability of a diminution of the import for 1794, as an effect of some of the questions agitated in Congress on the amount of exports from Great Britain to the United States. 2dly. On the probability of war with Great Britain, which would still further destroy the revenue, at the same time that it would beget an immense addition to the public expenditures. On the first of these points, those who did not concur in the new taxes, at least in all of them, denied the probability of any material diminution of the import without a war: On the other point, they denied any such probability of a war, as to require what was proposed; and in both these opinions, they have been justified by subsequent experience. War has not taken place, nor does it appear ever to have been meditated, unless in the event of[37] subverting the French Republic, which was never probable; whilst the revenue from the import, instead of being diminished, has very considerably exceeded any former amount.

It will not be improper to remark, as a further elucidation of this subject. 1st. That most, if not all, who refused to concur in some of the new taxes as not justified by the occasion, actually concurred in others which were least objectionable, as an accommodating precaution against contingencies. 2d. That the objection to one of the taxes[38] was its breach of the constitution; an objection insuperable in its nature, and which there is reason to believe, will be established by the judicial authority, if ever brought to that test; and that the objections to others were such as had always had weight with the most enlightened patriots of America.

3. That in the opinions of the most zealous patrons of new Ways and Means, the occasion, critical as they pressed it, did not ultimately justify all the taxes proposed. It appears in particular, that a bill imposing a variety of duties, mostly in the nature of stamp duties, into which, a duty on transfers of stock, had been inserted as an amendment, was in the last stage defeated, by those who had in general, urged the new taxes, and this very bill itself in the earlier stage of it.

These, with the preceding observations, on a very interesting period of Congressional history, will be left to the candid judgement of the public. Such as may not before have viewed the transactions of that period, through any other medium than the misrepresentations which have been circulated, will have an opportunity of doing justice to themselves, as well as to others. And no doubt can be entertained, that in this as in all other cases, it will be found, that truth, however, stifled or perverted for a time, will finally triumph in the detection of calumny, and in the contempt which awaits its authors.

Printed copy owned by Jefferson (DLC: Rare Book Division). Jefferson's copy contains many corrections in an unknown hand. Pages 9 and 10 in that copy are missing and in their place have been inserted proof pages from Madison, *Letters* (Cong. ed.), 4:491–92, which incorporate some corrections. The present edition incorporates all corrections in Jefferson's copy; significant changes are noted below. Pages 1–8 of the pamphlet (Evans 29017) are printed in larger type than pages 9–24. JM implied that he was the author of "a fugitive publication answering the misrepre[sen]tations of the Session prior to the last." He wrote this anonymous pamphlet before the date that it bears—"It was extorted by the entreaties of some friends, just at the close of the Session," i.e., 3 Mar.—and probably gave a copy to Jefferson soon after its publication (JM to Jefferson, 14 June 1795 [DLC]). He left Philadelphia circa 6 Apr. (JM to Monroe, 6 Apr. 1795). In his coded 26 Jan. 1796 letter to Monroe, JM admitted authorship and noted: "It is full of press blunders." He sent a copy to Jefferson in his letter of 27 June 1823 (Madison, *Letters* [Cong. ed.], 2:74, 3:327–28). Jefferson wrote on the title page of his copy: "by James Madison."

1. Federalist Benjamin Russell's Boston *Columbian Centinel* published some of the most virulent attacks on JM's commercial discrimination resolutions. See Madison in the Third Congress, 2 Dec. 1793–3 Mar. 1795.

2. In uncorrected copies of the pamphlet, this word is "reason."

3. On the public debt provisions passed during the second session of the Third Congress, see JM's speeches of 15 and 16 Jan. 1795 and nn.

4. On William Pitt the younger's American intercourse bill of 1783, see JM's speech of 14 Jan. 1794 and n. 13.

5. On the commercial reciprocity proposals of the Continental Congress, see ibid., n. 2.

6. For a discussion of JM's reciprocity proposals for the impost and tonnage bills of 1789, see *PJM*, 12:54–55.

7. Corrected from "evinced."

8. For the contention that Britain had arranged the peace between Portugal and

Algiers in order to unleash the Algerine corsairs against American shipping, see JM's speeches of 27 Dec. 1793, n., and 30 Jan. 1794.

9. Reprinted in *ASP, Foreign Relations,* 1:241.

10. Corrected from "stile."

11. Corrected in proof pages from "making."

12. Corrected in proof pages from "genius."

13. Corrected in proof pages from "denomination."

14. On the nonintercourse bill, see JM's speech of 18 Apr. 1794 and nn.

15. On the Federalist-sponsored military establishment bill, see JM to Jefferson, 14 Mar. 1794, n. 2, and JM's speech of 30 May 1794, nn.

16. Corrected from "hospitality."

17. Corrected from "evidences."

18. Corrected from "prospects."

19. JM referred to the appointment of Chief Justice John Jay as envoy extraordinary to Great Britain in April 1794.

20. Corrected from "so."

21. This word omitted in uncorrected copies.

22. Corrected from "officious."

23. Corrected from "defect."

24. Corrected from "affidavit."

25. On 17 Jan. 1795 the Philadelphia *Aurora General Advertiser* reprinted from the *West India Royal Gazette* of 7 Oct. 1794 "To the Right Hon. Henry Dundas, his Majesty's Secretary of State for the Home Department. The Memorial of the West-India Planters and Merchants," which urged that the British Navigation Acts be relaxed and that the West Indies be opened to American shipping.

26. Corrected from "act."

27. Corrected from "excuses."

28. Corrected from "drawn."

29. Corrected from "justice."

30. On the naval armament bill, see JM's speeches of 27 Dec. 1793, nn., and 6, 7, and 11 Feb. 1794 and nn.

31. Corrected from "out-set."

32. Tench Coxe's 20 Mar. 1794 report, "A Summary of the Value and Destination of the Exports of the United States," which covered the year ending 30 Sept. 1793, estimated exports to Spain and its dominions as $2,237,950; to Portugal and its dominions, $997,590 (*ASP, Commerce and Navigation,* 1:297).

33. Coxe's 26 Feb. 1795 report, "A Summary of the Value and Destination of the Exports of the United States," covering the year ending 30 Sept. 1794, estimated exports to Spain and its dominions as $3,749,978; to Portugal and its dominions, $992,561 (ibid., 1:312).

34. Corrected from "initiated."

35. The committee report that Thomas FitzSimons submitted to the House of Representatives on 20 Jan. 1794 estimated the "annual expense of the said armament" at $247,960 (*ASP, Naval Affairs,* 1:1).

36. On 18 Nov. 1794 the secretary of war estimated "the Pay and Subsistence of the Navy of the United States, calculated upon a scale of six months" at $220,754.40. Knox's estimate was enclosed in the report that Oliver Wolcott, Jr., comptroller of the treasury, submitted on Hamilton's behalf to the House of Representatives on 25 Nov. 1794 (*Sundry Estimates and Statements Relative to Appropriations for the Service of the Year 1795* [Philadelphia, 1794; Evans 27953], pp. 2, 27–29).

37. "Event of" omitted in uncorrected copies.

38. On the carriage tax, see JM to Jefferson, 1 June 1794, and n. 2.

Index

NOTE: Persons are identified on pages cited below in boldface type. Identifications in earlier volumes are noted within parentheses. Page numbers followed only by n. (e.g., 129 n.) refer to the provenance portion of the annotation.